SOVEREIGNTY IN TRANSITION

This new work brings together a group of leading scholars from law and cognate disciplines to assess contemporary developments in the framework of ideas and the variety of institutional forms associated with the concept of sovereignty. Sovereignty has been described as the main organising concept of the international society of states—one which is traditionally central to the discipline and practice of both constitutional law and of international law. The volume asks to what extent, and with what implications, this centrality is challenged by contemporary developments that shift authority away from the state to new sub-state, supra-state and non-state forms. A particular focus of attention is the European Union, and the relationship between the sovereignty traditions of various Member States on the one hand and the new claims to authority made on behalf of the European Union itself on the other are examined. The collection also includes contributions from international law, legal philosophy, legal history, political theory, political science, international relations and theology that seek to examine the state of the sovereignty debate in these disciplines in ways that throw light on the focal constitutional debate in the European Union.

Sovereignty in Transition

Edited by
NEIL WALKER
Professor of Law at the European University Institute

·HART·
PUBLISHING

OXFORD – PORTLAND OREGON
2003

Hart Publishing
Oxford and Portland, Oregon

Published in North America (US and Canada) by
Hart Publishing c/o
International Specialized Book Services
5804 NE Hassalo Street
Portland, Oregon
97213-3644
USA

Hart Publishing is a specialist legal publisher based in Oxford, England.
To order further copies of this book or to request a list of other
publications please write to:

Hart Publishing, Salter's Boatyard, Folly Bridge,
Abingdon Road, Oxford OX1 4LB
Telephone: +44 (0)1865 245533 or Fax: +44 (0)1865 794882
e-mail: mail@hartpub.co.uk
WEBSITE: http//www.hartpub.co.uk

British Library Cataloguing in Publication Data
Data Available
ISBN 1–84113–337–X (hardback)

Typeset in Minion by Excel Infoteck Services, Chandigarh, India.
Printed and bound in Great Britain on acid-free paper by
Biddles Ltd, www.biddles.co.uk

Contents

Preface	vii
About the Contributors	xi

Part A—Disciplinary Perspectives

1. Late Sovereignty in the European Union *Neil Walker*	3
2. Sovereignty: Unpopular and Popular *Bert Van Roermund*	33
3. Ten Tenets of Sovereignty *Martin Loughlin*	55
4. Sovereignty and Representation in the European Union *Hans Lindahl*	87
5. Sovereignty and Constitutionalism in International Law *Bardo Fassbender*	115
6. From State Sovereignty to the 'Sovereignty of Citizens' in the International Relations Law of the EU? *Ernst-Ulrich Petersmann*	145
7. Sovereignty, Post-Sovereignty and Pre-Sovereignty: Three Models of the State, Democracy and Rights within the EU *Richard Bellamy*	167
8. Sovereignty and Plurinational Democracy: Problems in Political Science *Michael Keating*	191
9. Discussing Sovereignty and Transnational Politics *Jef Huysmans*	209
10. 'Que les Latins appellent maiestatem': An Exploration into the Theological Background of the Concept of Sovereignty *Govert Buijs*	229

Part B—Constitutional Perspectives I: The View from the States

11. Sovereignty in France: Getting Rid of the Mal de Bodin.   261
    Jacques Ziller

12. Sovereignty Über Alles: (Re)Configuring the German Legal Order   279
    Miriam Aziz

13. The Legacy of Sovereignty in the Italian Constitutional Debate   305
    Marta Cartabia

14. United Kingdom—Divided on Sovereignty?   327
    Kenneth Armstrong

15. Do Not Mention the Word: Sovereignty in Two Europhile Countries:
    Belgium and The Netherlands   351
    Bruno de Witte

16. State Sovereignty and European Integration: Public International Law,
    EU Law and Constitutional Law in the Polish Context   367
    Cezary Mik

17. Postmodern Versus Retrospective Sovereignty: Two Different
    Discourses in the EU and the Candidate Countries?   401
    Anneli Albi

18. The Debate About Sovereignty in the United States: A Historical and
    Comparative Perspective   423
    Jeffrey Goldsworthy

Part C—Constitutional Perspectives II: The View from Europe

19. Sovereignty and the Supremacy Doctrine of the European
    Court of Justice   449
    Gráinne de Búrca

20. Sovereignty at the Boundaries of the Polity   461
    Jo Shaw

21. Contrapunctual Law: Europe's Constitutional Pluralism in Action   501
    Miguel Poiares Maduro

Index   539

Preface

TODAY IN THE European Union and beyond, the concept of sovereignty is a much-contested one. In many academic and political circles, the 'golden age' of state sovereignty is treated as at best a distant memory and at worst a malign myth – an ideological construct which serviced earlier power structures of dubious legitimacy and which provides an increasingly inappropriate framework of explanation and justification for the contemporary history of political authority. In this critical vein, the idea of sovereignty is subject to growing challenge as outmoded, as fragmented, as incoherent, and not least as normatively unattractive or inadequate as a way of making sense of emergent patterns of legal and political authority and imagining their future. At the same time, in other academic circles, and, perhaps more tellingly, in legal and political practice, sovereignty retains an important currency and remains a key operating premise of systems of constitutional, international and supranational law.

According to its critics, sovereignty is a superannuated concept insofar as the Westphalian system of states organised around the axes of internal state sovereignty (as conceived within constitutional law) and external sovereignty (as conceived within international law) is challenged by the growth of transnational patterns of commerce, culture and communications and by the development of non-state or post-state sites of legal and political authority to regulate these new patterns—paradigmatically but by no means exclusively in the form of the European Union. As the disparity between purely legal conceptions and sources of authority and actually existing articulations and locations of political authority in the globalizing era becomes more pronounced, the increasingly diverse efforts of theorists to find a continuing or renewed role for sovereignty which acknowledges and accounts for this gap provokes the additional charge of fragmentation. To the extent, moreover, that this rapidly transforming world order is one in which not only are many old claims to sovereignty being challenged but many new or emergent claims to sovereignty are also being made, the difficulties of reconciling the age-old tension between 'ruler sovereignty' and 'rule sovereignty'—between the will to power as the source of normative order and normative order as the source of power—is more vividly highlighted and the accusation of conceptual incoherence becomes more insistent. To cap it all, sovereignty is ever more exposed to normative criticism as a notion which is deeply sedimented within our conception of modern statehood and, in consequence, closely associated with some of the less palatable incidents of the system of states, including the themes of legitimate violence, of monolithic and exclusionary order, and of irreconcilable conflict and competition between sites of authority.

Yet the idea of sovereignty cannot just be wished away. Neither is it obvious that it will simply wither away, nor that its secular decline should be approved or encouraged. It is precisely because the Westphalian system, though challenged, is by no means yet fully transcended in our contemporary politics, that claims even to old-fashioned state sovereignty are defended or asserted more diversely, more frequently, more visibly and often with greater urgency than ever before. Equally, the self-referential claims to legal and political authority of new or putative post-state polities such as the EU, but also of sub-state nationalist movements, are themselves affected and informed by the strong symbolic and epistemic legacy of the classical state sovereigntist perspective. In normative terms, too, sovereignty, for all its negative associations, continues to offer an organising frame for the constitution and regulation of old and new—state and nonstate—political communities, and so arguably also supplies a necessary precondition for the continuation of the virtues associated with political community—in particular the ideas of effective, citizen-engaging and representative governance.

Paradoxically, then, it seems that it is the very challenge to the old order that demands such urgent re-examination of the building blocks of that order. If the Westphalian order is under structural pressure, are its indispensable conceptual foundations such as sovereignty simply rendered redundant? Or are they capable of reinforcement in the cause of modified renewal of the old order? Or are they, perhaps, ripe for transformation and reassembly within a radically new configuration? Through the posing of this series of alternatives we can perhaps begin to identify a shared framework of inquiry—an organising theme for the project of this book. The key notion in terms of which we can discover some common ground—even if it is only a foothold from which we can better understand our differences—would seem to be that of transition. Regardless of what the longer term may be hoped or expected to bring, the Westphalian system is palpably in a process of contested, fluctuating and indeterminate transition, and as the conceptual key to that system, sovereignty can only be expected to reflect these unsteady trends. And nowhere is the new series of questions over sovereignty more urgently, vigorously and significantly joined than in the context of the European Union and its relationship with its constituent states.

The aim of the present volume is to bring together discussion of the practical and the theoretical and of the regional and the global, around this theme of sovereignty in transition. To that end, it seeks to examine the new debate over sovereignty within the EU not only on its own terms but also as an exemplar of the broader process of sovereignty in transition and as a key testing ground for the intellectual debates concerning that transition. In pursuing these objectives, the volume seeks to be multi-perspectival in two senses and at two levels. First, at the conceptual level, it aims to expose and draw upon the diverse but intertwined disciplinary roots of the theoretical debate over sovereignty. Secondly, at the practical level, it seeks to examine the meaning and trajectory of sovereignty as a fundamental axiom of legal and political authority from the perspective of different authority sites within the EU.

The first part of the volume (disciplinary perspectives) opens with a series of essays by Neil Walker, Bert Van Roermund, Martin Loughlin and Hans Lindahl which approach the theme of sovereignty from the perspective of legal and constitutional theory. These are followed by two essays by international lawyers, one—Bardo Fassbender—considering the general evolution of the concept of sovereignty within international law, and the other—Ernst-Ulrich Petersmann—

considering sovereignty from the perspective of the 'international' relations of the EU. Thereafter, there are a number of contributions from scholars situated beyond the boundaries of legal scholarship. Richard Bellamy, Michael Keating and Jef Huysmans discuss the mixed legacy of sovereignty within political theory, political science and international relations respectively. Finally, Govert Buijs discusses the career of the sovereignty concept within the history of ideas, with particular reference to the traditions of Western theology. The reader will discover many overlaps but also many differences between these various perspectives, reflecting not only the divergence of disciplinary paradigms but also the very distinctive intellectual signatures of the authors themselves.

In the second part of the volume (constitutional perspectives) the major national and 'regional' doctrinal perspectives are covered, as is the view from the EU itself. Jacques Ziller, Miriam Aziz, Marta Cartabia and Kenneth Armstrong examine the development of constitutional theory and doctrine on the subject of the relationship between state sovereignty and EU membership in the four largest states of the EU—France, Germany, Italy and the United Kingdom. Bruno de Witte undertakes a similar analysis for two smaller but founding states—Belgium and the Netherlands, and Cezary Mik does the same for Poland, as the largest of the current accession states. These 'internal' examinations are complemented by two 'external' examinations—one by Anneli Albi looking at the shared sovereignty sensibilities of the Central and Eastern European accession countries, and the other by Jeff Goldsworthy examining continuities and discontinuities in the theoretical and doctrinal evolution of the concept of sovereignty between the federal United States of America and the 'quasi-federal' European Union. The volume concludes with three essays whose point of departure is the EU as a whole. Gráinne De Búrca assesses the sovereignty implications of the supremacy doctrine of the European Court of Justice, Jo Shaw examines how citizenship politics at state and supranational level are altering the contours of the European sovereignty debate, and Miguel Maduro, in a return to the themes explored in the opening essays, examines how claims to 'sovereignty' or fundamental legal authority at national and supranational level might be reconciled within a new pan-European constitutional sensibility.

The project that gave rise to this volume commenced with a workshop at the European University Institute on 21–22nd September 2001. It was apparent from the outset that the ambitious range of the projected volume would make it difficult to achieve an intensity of engagement with common themes across the individual contributions sufficient to ensure that the whole would at least be the equal of the sum of its parts. In order to minimise this danger, the workshop contributors—and, indeed, those authors who were kind enough to contribute to the final volume without attending the workshop—were asked to bear in mind the following series of questions:

• In what way have social, cultural, political and other historical factors contributed to changing conceptions of sovereignty today? • How are these changes variously conceived within different disciplinary traditions?

- How do these changes affect the explanatory and normative currency of the concept of sovereignty in general?
- How do these changes affect the explanatory and normative currency of the concept of sovereignty in the European Union in particular?
- To what extent do the various national constitutional traditions continue to inform member state attitudes to sovereignty vis-à-vis the European Union?
- To what extent and in what ways does the European Union (through its constituent institutions) conceive of itself as 'sovereign' in its treatment of member states?
- How has the concept of sovereignty been reshaped and how might it further be reshaped in the context of the European Union to take account of the novel circumstances of the world's first post-state polity? To what extent, if at all, can we talk about sovereignty being pooled, shared, divided or negotiated? To what extent can we talk about sovereignty being transcended or marginalised? How do or might changes in the concept of sovereignty alter the framework within which other deep institutional themes and constitutional values are protected or nurtured—including federalism, the separation of powers, decentralisation and subsidiarity, democracy, fundamental rights, citizenship and social justice?

Clearly, some of the above themes are more relevant to some contributions than to others, but it is a tribute to all the contributors that they strove so hard in the context of the workshop and post-workshop exchanges to find the common ground on which an inclusive conversation on 'sovereignty in transition' could take place. My first and foremost thanks, then, are to the contributors themselves for their serious engagement with the themes of the project. I would also like to record my special appreciation of the efforts of Bert Van Roermund, Martin Loughlin, Ernst-Ulrich Petersmann, Govert Buijs, Anneli Albi and Jeff Goldsworthy, each of whom generously agreed to contribute a chapter without the preparatory advantage of presenting a paper to the workshop. Many others contributed to the success of the workshop and the production of the final volume. Mike Wilkinson, Sean Loughlin and Wojciech Sadurski were excellent commentators and/or chairpersons at the original workshop, in the preparation and running of which Marlies Becker proved yet again her peerless organisational skills. The Research Council of the European University Institute were generous sponsors of the workshop, and the additional financial (and moral) support furnished by my close colleague Gráinne de Búrca also deserves special tribute. As the final drafts arrived, Mike Wilkinson (again) was an extremely knowledgeable, skilful and diligent editorial assistant. Finally, Richard Hart was as ever a model of patience, good humour and sound but unobtrusive advice, and I am greatly obliged to him for bringing the volume to publication.

Neil Walker
Fiesole, January 2003

About the Contribtors

Anneli Albi is a Lecturer in Law at the University of Kent, England.

Kenneth Armstrong is a Senior Lecturer in Law at Queen Mary College, University of London.

Miriam Aziz is a Marie Curie Fellow at the European University Institute, Florence.

Richard Bellamy is Professor of Politics at the University of Essex, England.

Govert Buijs is at the University of Amsterdam in the Netherlands.

Gráinne de Búrca is Professor of Law at the European University Institute, Florence.

Marta Cartabia is Professor of Law at the University of Verona, Italy.

Bardo Fassbender is Professor of International Law at the Humboldt University, Berlin.

Jeffrey Goldsworthy is Professor of Law at Monash University, Australia.

Jef Huysmans is a Lecturer in International Relations at the Open University, England.

Michael Keating is Professor of Politics at the European University Institute, Florence.

Hans Lindahl is Reader in Legal Philosophy at Tilburg University, the Netherlands.

Martin Loughlin is Professor of Law at the London School of Economics.

Miguel Poiares Maduro is Professor of Law at the University of Lisbon, Portugal.

Cezary Mik is Professor of Law, University of Cardinal S Wyszynski, Warsaw, Poland.

Ernst-Ulrich Petersmann is Professor of Law at the European University Institute, Florence.

Bert van Roermund is Professor of Philosophy at Tilburg University, the Netherlands.

Jo Shaw is Professor of European Law at Manchester University, England.

Neil Walker is Professor of Law at the European University Institute, Florence.

Bruno de Witte is Professor of Law at the European University Institute, Florence.

Jacques Ziller is Professor of Law at the European University Institute, Florence.

Part A

Disciplinary Perspectives

1

Late Sovereignty in the European Union[1]

NEIL WALKER

1. SOVEREIGNTY AND CONSTITUTIONAL PLURALISM

ABSTRACT DEBATE OVER whether sovereignty is alive or dead, or perhaps in the operating theatre undergoing radically reconstructive surgery, is both sterile and meaningless. To undertake an assessment of the contemporary resonance of the concept of sovereignty serves no purpose and permits no satisfactory conclusion in isolation from a broader set of concerns which define the explanatory or normative purpose of that assessment. This is not to say that sovereignty can mean whatever we want it to mean and can be given whatever diagnosis and whatever treatment we see fit, just provided that meaning passes the test of internal coherence within any particular intellectual scheme. Internal coherence is of course necessary, but it is also crucial that the knowledge claims that emerge from that scheme are more generally persuasive. It is important that those who are more generally interested in the continuing currency or otherwise of the concept of sovereignty are minded to conclude that the particular conception of sovereignty within the particular intellectual scheme in question helps to produce significant knowledge claims on behalf of the scheme as a whole. The external audience, in other words, must be persuaded that the conception of sovereignty proffered not only fits with the scheme as whole (internal coherence), but also does so in a way that enhances the explanatory and/or normative value of that overall scheme.

[1] Many thanks to the participants in the 'Sovereignty in Transition' conference for responding so thoughtfully to the early version of this paper I delivered at that event. Some of these responses they have pursued in their own contributions, others were developed in private correspondence. My views remain at odds with those of some of the participants, but each and every response was nonetheless invaluable to me in the preparation of the final text.

The debate over sovereignty, therefore, is not a debate over the capacity of a particular concept to capture some underlying trans-theoretical essence, but, rather, over the heuristic value of this or that conception of sovereignty (or its demise) as a way of enhancing the claims of a particular theoretical understanding of the world. In the present chapter, the particular understanding of the world that provides the theoretical context for discussion of sovereignty is that of constitutional pluralism.[2] Constitutional pluralism, which overlaps with at least some more general 'legal pluralisms,'[3] is a position which holds that states are no longer the sole locus of constitutional authority, but are now joined by other sites, or putative sites of constitutional authority, most prominently (though by no means exclusively) and most relevantly for present purposes those situated at the supra-state level, and that the relationship between state and non-state sites is better viewed as heterarchical rather than hierarchical. Constitutional pluralism, at least in the version to which I subscribe,[4] has both an explanatory dimension and a normative dimension. In explanatory terms, it holds that we can only begin to account adequately for what is going on within the new European constitutional configuration—and indeed the new global constitutional configuration to which the European configuration contributes—if we posit multiple levels of constitutional discourse and authority. In normative terms, constitutional pluralism welcomes the implications of the explanatory account, holding that the only viable and the only acceptable ethic of political responsibility for the new configuration is one which is premised upon mutual recognition and interpenetration of constitutional sites located at different levels. This configuration, it is argued, should lead neither to a new unity or fixed hierarchy of constitutional authority nor, at the other extreme, to a fragmentation of authority such that the sense is lost of there being distinctive units of constitutional authority at least some of which possess a broad influence over questions of social, political and economic organisation.

As our very vocabulary of constitutional analysis and design has been developed, or at least refined, in the context of the state and, indeed, of a one-dimensional international system of states, the articulation of an approach such as constitutional pluralism faces profound 'problem of

---

[2] For extended discussion, see N Walker, 'The Idea of Constitutional Pluralism' (2002) 65 *Modern Law Review* 317–59.

[3] See eg BZ Tamanaha, 'A Non-Essentialist Version of Legal Pluralism,' (2000) 27 *Journal of Law and Society* p. 296; for broader consideration of the relationship between constitutional pluralism and other forms of legal pluralism, see Walker, above n 2, esp. 340 *et seq.*

[4] For discussion of the different types of constitutional pluralism, and in particular of the variable relationship between explanatory, normative and epistemic claims, see Walker, above n 2, 336–38.

translation'[5] 'The touch of stateness'[6]—so familiar as to be 'often invisible'—affects our understanding of key ideas and institutional possibilities as diverse as democracy, fundamental rights, equality, security, citizenship, the separation and dispersal of powers, the rule of law and the independence of the judiciary, and, indeed, the general portmanteau idea of constitutionalism itself. Steeped in the traditions of the modern state, all of these terms pose significant challenges if we are to demonstrate their relevance to non-state polities and, indeed, to the new multi-dimensional configuration (no longer simply *inter*-national) in which state and non-state polities relate. Yet, as will hopefully become clear, nowhere are these problems more profound, and nowhere are the answers provided more indicative of the general prospects and shape of a defensible conception of constitutional pluralism than with regard to sovereignty and sovereign statehood—the very premise of fundamental authority that 'anchors our concept of modern politics.'[7]

How, then, against a background where the continuing currency of the concept of sovereignty *in general* is the subject of much scepticism and its meaning and import is much disputed, and where such scepticism and disputation assumes a particularly pressing significance in debate over the use-value of sovereignty in the immediately relevant context of the authority configuration of the European Union, can we develop a persuasive conception of sovereignty to underpin and reflect the idea of constitutional pluralism? The argument proceeds in a number of stages. In section two, a working definition of sovereignty is introduced as a way of responding to some of the more insistent general objections that have been levelled against the concept. In section three, the debate over sovereignty is resituated in the context of the shift to a post-Westphalian order and the emergence of post-state polities such as the European Union. In section four the ways in which various strands of constitutional scholarship, and the political positions associated with these strands, have treated sovereignty in the context of the emergence of the European Union are briefly assessed and subjected to critical scrutiny. In sections five and six we reach the crux of the argument and the idea of 'late sovereignty' is introduced and developed as a way of asserting, consistently with the general conception of sovereignty offered in section two, the continuing explanatory currency of sovereignty in the post-Westphalian context. Finally, in the conclusion, some of the normative implications of this position are sketched and offered in additional justification of the position adopted.

[5] JHH Weiler, *The Constitution of Europe* (Cambridge, CUP, 1999) 270.
[6] J Shaw and A Wiener, 'The Paradox of the European Polity' in M, Green Cowles and M Smith (eds) *State of the European Union 5: Risks, Reform, Resistance and Revival* (Oxford, OUP, 2000).
[7] R Jackson, 'Introduction: Sovereignty at the Millennium' (1999) 47 *Political Studies*, 423

2. THE CONCEPT OF SOVEREIGNTY

Sovereignty may be defined as *the discursive form in which a claim concerning the existence and character of a supreme ordering power for a particular polity is expressed, which supreme ordering power purports to establish and sustain the identity and status of the particular polity* **qua** *polity and to provide a continuing source and vehicle of ultimate authority for the juridical order of that polity.* This definition seeks to address and to answer a number of objections concerning the irrelevance, vagueness, incoherence and normative shortcomings of the concept of sovereignty.

The line of argument which seeks to reject or marginalise sovereignty[8] as irrelevant is based upon the premise that in a world in which many circuits of power operate beyond the direct control of the sovereign state, a trend which is clearly exacerbated by processes of globalisation or trans-nationalisation of productive forces, information exchange, political capacities, social identities etc., sovereignty figures lower and lower in the register of explanatory variables which may be invoked to make sense of that world. Certain fallacies and questionable assumptions lie behind this claim, and these may be exposed by developing the proposition, implicit in the above definition, that sovereignty involves a 'speech act'[9]—a *claim* to ordering power.

To begin with, the argument from irrelevance involves 'the descriptive fallacy'[10]—the notion that sovereignty should correspond to, be measurable against and be described in terms of an independent and objective reality. From this perspective, it is assumed that sovereignty denotes the actual capacity of a polity to retain full internal control and external independence, but that due to globalising trends, 'there is less and less in *reality* (emphasis added) that corresponds to the idea of a sovereign state.'[11] The empiricist assumption underlying this approach tends to go hand in hand with what may be termed a fallacy of abstraction. In this mode it is argued, or more often simply assumed, that because sovereignty is a very special medium of power in terms of the type and comprehensiveness of authority it claims—that is, in its assertion of *ultimate* ordering or regulatory power—then to the extent that it is rivalled in intensity by other forms of power (as on many reckonings it is) its very distinguishing characteristic, and so its very conceptual relevance, fades and becomes peripheral. Such an approach assumes that sovereignty's claim to be an overarching framework

---

[8] In his chapter in the present volume, Bert Van Roermund characterises—and criticises—this argument as the Argument from Redundancy.
[9] WG Werner and JH De Wilde, 'The Endurance of Sovereignty' (2001) 7 *European Journal of International Relations* 283–313, 277.
[10] *Ibid* 285.
[11] *Ibid.*

for power, to be the 'power over powers', means that an analysis of the concept of sovereignty must extrapolate to, and be tested in terms of the operation of power generally. It assumes, in other words, that 'power' is the key abstract concept of which particular modalities—'sovereign power', 'economic power', 'symbolic power' etc., are concrete instances, and as such are apt to be compared with and measured against one another in terms of a singular metric of 'power'. But this makes no more sense than to assert that the continuing relevance of the concept of law itself, namely its claim to provide an encompassing framework of normative order, depends upon its capacity to dominate and subsume all other forms of normative order. In neither case—and this is an insight which is available from a vast range of theoretical perspectives from systems theory through to legal positivism—does the framing and ordering claim and capacity of the core or axiomatic idea depend upon the environment or behavioural field contemplated by the core or axiomatic idea being directly or exhaustively controlled or determined by that idea.

At the root of both the descriptive fallacy and the fallacy of abstraction lies a category mistake. Sovereignty neither corresponds to some state of affairs in an independently verifiable material world, nor, relatedly, is it commensurable with other concrete articulations of the abstract concept 'power'. Rather, as a speech act, its capacity to make a difference to the world depends upon its plausibility and its acceptance as a way of knowing and ordering the world, which in turn depends upon its status as an *institutional* fact'[12]—a fact whose authenticity and credibility depends upon the internalisation by key actors of a complex of rules and expectations which support and subscribe to the sovereign claim.

A second line of criticism sees sovereignty as an irredeemably vague and polysemic concept, and so as lacking any conceptual common core. Thus Krasner talks about four different meanings of sovereignty which are 'not logically coupled, nor have they covaried in practice.'[13]—namely domestic sovereignty, interdependence sovereignty, international legal sovereignty and Westphalian sovereignty. In its equation of sovereignty not with a general ordering claim but with control over certain substantive practices rooted in other circuits of power, the idea of interdependence sovereignty—

---

[12] *Ibid.* 291. The ideas of 'speech acts:' and 'institutional facts' drawn on by Werner and DeWilde, and also adopted in the present argument, are derived from the well-known work of Austin and Searle: See JL Austin *Philosophical Papers* (Oxford, OUP, 1961); JR Searle *Speech Acts* (Cambridge, CUP, 1969); *The Construction of Social Reality* (New York, Free Press, 1995). The best known development of the theory of institutional facts within legal philosophy is that of MacCormick and Weinberger; see DN MacCormick and O Weinberger *An Institutional Theory of Law* (Dordrecht, Kluwer, 1986); see also DWP Ruiter, 'Structuring Legal Institutions' (1998) 17 *Law and Philosophy* 215–32.

[13] SD Krasner, *Sovereignty, Organised Hypocrisy* (Princeton, Princeton University Press, 1999) 9.

the capacity or otherwise of national authorities to regulate the flow of capital, goods, persons, services, pollutants, diseases, ideas etc. across national boundaries—tends to succumb to the fallacies of description and abstraction, and can for that reason be discounted. As regards the other three, while on one view they may be perceived as quite discrete ideas, in the sense that they are indeed neither functionally interchangeable nor enjoy relationships of logical entailment, this is not because they have quite separate conceptual roots but rather because they are diverse operationalisations of a single claim to the ultimate ordering power which constitutes and sustains the polity. Domestic sovereignty represents the working through of this core claim in the internal sphere,[14] international legal sovereignty represents its working through in the external sphere,[15] while Westphalian sovereignty, defined by Krasner as the principle of non-intervention, represents one key (but essentially derivative) aspect or incident, variously interpreted and qualified, of the claim to sovereignty in the external sphere.[16] Their true coherence lies not in their relationship *inter se* but in their separate relationships to and common derivation from a deep core claim to know and order the world in a particular way. To argue otherwise, and to suggest inherent vagueness or polysemy within the concept of sovereignty is to confuse the idea itself—indeed reduce it to—its various operationalisations.

Two further objections to the continuing currency of the concept of sovereignty are addressed more briefly here, as they are examined in greater depth below. The third conceptual argument against sovereignty concerns a more specific point of supposed incoherence;[17] namely the notion, central to my own definition of sovereignty as simultaneously source and vehicle of the juridical order, of a tension within its conceptual structure between legal and political registers—between the idea of law as foundation of the polity and the idea of law as the medium through which a non-legal or political foundation to the polity is given legal expression. As argued in section five below, this tension rather than undermining the idea of sovereignty, is actually key to the meaning and distinctive function of the *claim* to sovereignty.

As for the final objection to sovereignty, the critique of sovereignty as redundant and incoherent is often also seen as having a normative dividend, as an escape from the discourse of legalised violence and peremptory authority which attends political conflict-resolution in a world in which sovereignty is axiomatic. In the world of post-sovereignty or the marginal-

---

[14] That is to say, in terms of the definition provided in the text above, '. . . *to provide a continuing source and vehicle of ultimate authority for the juridical order of that polity.*'
[15] That is to say, in terms of the definition provided in the text above, '*to establish and sustain the identity and status of the particular polity . . .*'
[16] See further, Bardo Fassbender's contribution to the present volume.
[17] See further, Bert Van Roermund's contribution to the present volume.

isation of sovereignty that is heralded, dialogue, persuasion, consensus and compromise are celebrated as providing a more enlightened and beneficent normative grid of relations between polities and political actors. Again, however, if the emphasis shifts away from a conception of sovereignty as a certain fixed and ascertainable state of affairs and towards a conception of sovereignty as a discursive claim, then quite apart from raising a doubt over whether sovereignty is or is likely to become irrelevant, the emphasis on the form of the claim leaves open whether the content and consequences of that claim should be read in the negative terms that some of sovereignty's critics suggest.

Before pursuing these lines of thoughts further, however, it is important to focus in on the emergence of the European Union and of other post-state polities, and to show that the shift to a multi-dimensional configuration of authority which this portends deepens and sharpens the challenge to sovereignty. As we shall see, this more pointed challenge demands, at least, a radical overhaul in our understanding and conceptualisation of our key term, and at most, a renewed consideration of whether it is indeed facing redundancy.

3. TWO PHASES OF SOVEREIGNTY

A broad but important distinction may be drawn between two phases in the modern use of the language of sovereignty. There is, first, the earlier so-called Westphalian phase. This refers to the international order of sovereign states gradually and only very unevenly established after the Peace of Westphalia in 1648.[18] That international order was supported by two complementary frameworks of law; Constitutional law—the law governing the internal order of sovereign states; and international law, the law governing the relations between sovereign states. But despite this dual legal structure the Westphalian order was characterised by a one-dimensional configuration of legal authority. No claims to authority other than by or on behalf of the state were seriously countenanced, notwithstanding the best efforts a long and distinguished historical line of global idealists and liberal internationalists embracing Kant, Bentham and Kelsen.[19]

Today, however, we have reached, or at least are in a process of transition towards a second, or post-Westphalian phase, ushered in by the linked pres-

---

[18] See, for example, D Held, 'The Transformation of Political Community: Rethinking Democracy in the Context of Globalization', in I Shapiro and C Hacker-Cordon (eds) *Democracy's Edges* (Cambridge, CUP, 1999) 84–111.

[19] On Kelsen's theory of an international law-centred monistic order, see H Kelsen, *Introduction to the Problems of Legal Theory* (Oxford, Clarendon, 1992, tr. B and S Paulson) 120. These views were later modified; see n 23 below.

sures of globalisation on the one hand and multi-dimensionality and constitutional pluralism on the other. Globalisation of economic organisation,
transnational commerce, culture and travel, and the new communications
media, as we have already observed, challenges the effective political capacity of the state. And, in large part in response to, and as a means to contain
and capture the collective action problems precipitated by these movements,[20] we see the growth of polities which are not states but which rival
states in terms of legal and political authority—paradigmatically the EU, but
also international organisations such as the Council of Europe, UN, WTO[21]
etc., and even, perhaps, organisations growing within or around the EU in
its current moment of 'flexibility', such as Schengen and the 'Eurozone.'[22]

How does the use of the language of sovereignty differ between these two
phases? In a nutshell, in the earlier Westphalian phase, sovereignty forms a
confident part of the *meta-language* of political science, law, international
relations etc., and also provides a key reference point in their various
object-languages. That is to say, it is a concept typically used to explain and
to justify the world, as well as a concept regularly utilised as a discursive
claim and established as an institutional fact within that world. It is
acknowledged as a plausible mechanism to help make sense of the social
world, as well as forming part of the discourse and self-understanding of
social actors. By way of contrast, in the current post-Westphalian phase,
while sovereignty clearly continues to form part of the object-language, it is
no longer so widely or so confidently conceived of as part of the meta-
language of explanation and political imagination. This is, of course, in
some measure due to the cumulative effect of the four general criticisms
cited above, but scepticism about and disagreement over the conceptual
currency of sovereignty has deepened in the face of the more insistent challenge posed by the emergence of new forms of polity. What price sovereignty in a world in which states no longer hold a monopoly of credible
claims to wide-ranging forms of legal and political authority?

4. RECONCEPTUALISING SOVEREIGNTY IN THE EUROPEAN UNION

How, then, in the particular context of the European Union, has constitutional scholarship treated sovereignty in responding to the challenge of the

---

[20] See, for example, F Scharpf, *Governing in Europe: Effective and Democratic?* (Oxford, OUP, 1999).

[21] See, for example, N Walker 'The EU and the WTO: Constitutionalism in a New Key,' in G de Burca and J Scott (eds) *The EU and the WTO: Legal and Constitutional Aspects* (Oxford, Hart Publishing, 2001) 31–58.

[22] See, for example, N Walker, ' Sovereignty and Differentiated Integration in the European Union,' (1998) 4 *European Law Journal*, 355.

emergence of forms of polity that rival the state? Four very broad categories of approach may be distinguished.

In the first place, there remains considerable support for what might be termed the received unitary[23] or one-dimensional approach to sovereignty in the European Union.[24] This might seem a paradoxical state of affairs, given that it is precisely in the area of constitutional scholarship, its traditional focus on the self-contained legal order of the state polity unavoidably disturbed and distorted by the encroachment of a new supranational entity with its own distinctive legal order, that the received view of sovereignty would seem most likely to be posed its most direct and exacting challenge. But this would be to reckon without the particular relationship of legal academics to official legal doctrine and practice. For reasons of intellectual training, professional socialisation and associated normative commitment many doctrinal lawyers see their task as one of exposition, representation, organisation and refinement of the internal structure of the legal orders which are their object of study. They thus seek to understand the legal order from the internal point of view of its officials and its accepted institutional practice In this mode, domestic constitutional scholars will often assume the parameters of state sovereignty and sovereign authority—still fundamental to the object-language of domestic constitutional law—as their own

---

[23] Superficially, 'monist' might be considered the better term, as monism is the classic term within international law literature, and in certain domains of legal theory, to describe a view of law as a single system with a clear hierarchy, and so necessarily premised on the idea of final authority, or sovereignty, being located at one particular level. Moreover, the level in question is typically that of international law, although some writers, notably the later Kelsen, have argued that it is also possible to understand the unity of law from a state-centred monistic perspective (see H Kelsen, *The Pure Theory of Law* (Berkeley and Los Angeles, Cal., University of California Press, 1967) 333–9). However, in the move from meta-language to the object-language of constitutional law doctrine, the meaning of monism is transformed. Within constitutional law doctrine, monism, in conceptual opposition to dualism, speaks to the indivisibility of domestic and international law, to the applicability of international law in domestic law without the need for a domestic instrument of implementation, and, in varying degrees, to the recognition by domestic law of the normative priority of international law. Yet, paradoxically, the very fact of domestic recognition demonstrates the conditional quality of the priority of international law, and so the inevitable qualification of any meta-level thesis of international law centred-monism. For within the object-language of domestic constitutional law doctrine, 'monism' cannot but be a *position within and authorised by a domestic legal system*. In the very act of asserting the priority of international law, even a constitutional system such as the Dutch system which is quite unequivocal in its deference to a 'monist' international order— Art. 94 of the Dutch Constitution providing that self-executing treaty provisions should take 'precedence' even over duly entrenched constitutional law (for more details, see Bruno de Witte's chapter in the present volume)—necessarily qualifies its deferential posture by confirming its own final authorship and authority. Accordingly the language of monism is inexorably transformed in and inevitably confused by the move from meta-language to object-language, and for that reason is avoided in the present contribution.

[24] For a similar argument, dramatising the self-referentiality and mutual exclusivity of the two unitary perspectives on European sovereignty by reference to the conflicting world-views experienced by the 'alien' transported to the setting of the typical national Constitutional Court on the one hand and the ECJ on the other, see Miguel Maduro's chapter in the present volume.

intellectual parameters, and, indeed, in their task of refinement, often set out to provide the best sense and best defence of the resilient sovereign foundations of the domestic legal and constitutional order. From that state-centred perspective, it is still common to see the entire EU system relegated to the status of delegated authority,[25] a perspective often aided by the traditional language of international law in which the states still stand proud as 'masters of the treaties.'[26]

A similar if more nuanced picture can be painted of some aspects of European law scholarship. Here, too, the bold outline of a unitary perspective may be discerned, even if it may seem to steal many of the clothes of the state unitary perspective in order to set itself up in direct competition with that perspective. It is well-known that the European Court of Justice has been remarkably frugal in its discussion of sovereignty, and on those few occasions where it has engaged it has been more forthright in the view that the sovereignty of member states is limited by their implication in the EU order[27] than in the more radical claim that the EU itself possesses sovereign authority.[28] Yet the ECJ has been much more assertive—audacious even—in its development, and much more tenacious in its maintenance, of a doctrine of *supremacy*. And as Grainne de Burca demonstrates in her contribution to the present volume, while supremacy is clearly not identical with sovereignty, the assertion of original authority and of priority over domestic law contained in the doctrine of supremacy appears to presuppose—and implicitly confirm—the EU's sovereign status. So while, on the one hand, the virtual absence of an explicit discourse of sovereignty may acknowledge and seem to defer to state sovereigntist sensibilities, on the other hand, a deep presumption of sovereignty is implicit in the broader constitutional logic espoused by the ECJ and endorsed by the other European institutions. Just as in the domestic domain, there is a significant strain of EU scholarship which for reasons of intellectual training, professional socialisation and associated normative commitments is minded to

---

[25] For a recent robust defence in the UK context, see T Hartley, 'The Constitutional Foundations of the European Union' (2001) 117 *Law Quarterly Review* 225.

[26] See, eg A Pellet, 'Les Fondements Juridiques Internationaux du Droit Communautaire,' *Collected Courses of the Academy of European Law*, Volume V (1994), Book 2, 211. See also T Schilling, 'The Autonomy of the Community Legal Order: An Analysis of Possible Foundations,' (1996) 17 *Harvard International Law Journal*, 389, together with his 'Rejoinder: The Autonomy of the Community Legal Order,' (1996) *Harvard Jean Monnet Working Paper Series*; responding to Joseph Weiler's reply to Schilling's earlier article; Weiler, above, n 5. This position, which I label 'defensive internationalism,' is discussed in N Walker above n 2, 322. For a recent collection which shows the continuing strong currency of the idea of 'external sovereignty' within international law thinking generally, see G Kreijen (ed) *State, Sovereignty and International Governance* (Oxford, OUP, 2002); see further, Bardo Fassbender's contribution to the present volume.

[27] *Costa v ENEL* Case 6/64 ECR 585; *Van Gend en Loos*, Case 26/62 [1963] ECR 1; Opinion 1/91 *Agreement on the European Economic Area*[1991] ECR I-6079.

[28] *Costa*, above n 27; *Euratom Ruling* 1/78, [1978] ECR 2151.

embrace the official constitutional perspective and object-language of the EU as its own, and to develop the best sense and best defence of those of the ECJ's various doctrines of constitutional self-assertion—not just supremacy but also direct effect, implied powers etc.,—which seem to embrace and confirm a sovereigntist self-understanding.

Nevertheless, the political implications of such a position are far from straightforward. Whereas the unitary state sovereigntist perspective in constitutional law tends to sit comfortably—complacently even—with an idea of political community centred on the state, for those who endorse a unitary EU sovereigntist perspective in legal doctrine the political ramifications of such a perspective are less clear and are often ignored and left undeveloped. To be sure, such a position necessarily implies a robustly autonomous jurisdiction and political capacity for the EU, but many legal scholars who work with the sovereignty-presupposing object-language of the ECJ, draw no wider inferences about the overall configuration of constitutional authority in the European domain. One notable exception, which has few public sponsors but perhaps rather more private sympathisers, is the position which holds that legal supranantionalism should be accompanied by full federal statehood for the EU, with the member states relegated to a secondary role as mere glorified provinces.[29] Other more sophisticated positions exist, which, while not drawing the 'superstate' inference, seek to build on the distinctive and non-derivative standing of legal supranationalism to fashion an understanding of the entire structure of relations between the EU and the states as a complex and *sui generis* unity. Such perspectives, prominent amongst which is the 'multilevel constitutionalism' of Ingolf Pernice,[30] set out to reconcile the idea of a poly-centred structure of political authority with the idea of an encompassing EU-wide unity. Inevitably, though, sovereignty hovers as a somewhat disconcerting ghost at this particular conceptual feast. Legal unity appears to presuppose a single source of sovereign authority, but if so it is difficult to see how the idea of a genuinely poly-centred structure may be sustained, since the multiple

---

[29] See F Mancini, 'Europe: The Case for Statehood' (1998) 4 *European Law Journal* 43.

[30] For a recent statement, see I Pernice, 'Multilevel Constitutionalism in the European Union' (2002) 27 *European Law Review* 511–29. Other more sophisticated unitarian positions on the EU whose general premises are similar to those of Pernice include the 'supranational federalism' of Armin Von Bogdandy and the 'layered international organisation' of Deirdre Curtin and Igge Dekker; see, for example, Von Bogdandy, 'The European Union as a Supranational federation: A Conceptual Attempt in the Light of the Treaty of Amsterdam' (2000) 6 *Columbia Journal of International Law* 27–54; Curtin and Dekker, 'The EU as a "Layered" International Organization: Institutional Unity in Disguise' in P Craig and G de Burca (eds) *The Evolution of EU Law* (Oxford, OUP, 1999); 'The Constitutional structure of the European Union: Some Reflections on Vertical Unity-in-Diversity' in P Beaumont, C Lyons and N Walker (eds) *Convergence and Divergence in European Public Law* (Oxford, Hart Publishing, 2002) 59–78.

centres must, in the name of that unity, be reducible *in the final analysis* to one master principle or generative norm.[31]

For all that some constitutional scholars of both domestic and EU persuasion are happy to endorse the sovereignty-affirming or sovereignty-presupposing official discourses of national or EU constitutional actors, many others are uncomfortable with the myopic partiality of simple unitarian positions in the face of substantial evidence of growing constitutional plurality. Furthermore, as suggested above, many would also be doubtful of the capacity even of the more complex and sophisticated unitarianism of multi-level constitutionalism and its ilk to sustain robust pluralist political premises. These doubts help to explain the popularity of a second position, which views sovereignty in the European context in disaggregated terms. From this quarter, there is, and has been since the early days of Community law, much talk of pooled,[32] shared, divided, split or partial sovereignty, to name but some of the metaphors of disaggregation and

[31] The difficulty of reconciling his broader pluralism with a unitarian legal perspective is in fact reflected in Pernice's uncertain attitude towards sovereignty in the article cited above (see n 29 above). On the one hand we are told that 'sovereignty is pooled ([and] powers are shared at the European level' (511), suggesting a more disaggregationist approach to sovereignty (see text below). On the other hand we are told that in the light of Arts 6 and 7 TEU 'it is even doubtful whether we can still say that the Member States are each the sovereign masters of their constitutions' and, moreover, that, as the citizens of Europe taken as a whole are now Masters of the Treaties, no Member State, regardless of its own constitutional self-understanding, any longer has the right of unilateral withdrawal from the European Union (519). At least part of the reason for this ambivalence seems to be the well-known problem in federal theory of distinguishing the integrity of the system as a whole from the claims of either of the two levels (federal and state) which make up the system. If one is concerned with the integrity of the overall system, it is structurally difficult to avoid privileging the federal level, which, compared to the states, tends to have greater legal responsibility and capacity and greater political motivation to safeguard system integrity. So in accordance with a unitarian approach, authority within a multi-level system would seem inevitably to gravitate towards the federal level, even if, as with Pernice, it is the citizenry rather than the institutions which are seen as the fount of authority and the custodians of sovereignty. One does not overcome the problem of structural privileging by moving from the institutional level to the level of the citizenry since what counts as an authoritative expression of the views of the citizenry merely begs the question of what counts as the authoritative unit of expression, whether the national citizenries separately or the European *citizenry* collectively, which requires a prior privileging decision. Pursuing the idea of structural privileging further, we may in fact question whether and to what extent 'pooling' is indeed consistent with a disaggregationist approach. Certainly, it suggests a voluntary alienation and recombination of elements of national sovereign authority, which presupposes that national sovereign authority can be internally disaggregated in the first place, but, by the same token, the metaphor of 'pooling' does not easily suggest later reversibility. While not as final as a term such as 'merger', the idea of pooling sits uncomfortably with the prospect of later disaggregation of the centrally reaggregated elements.

[32] Although, as argued in n 31 above, 'pooling' has highly ambivalent connotations, and is just as capable of supporting an EU unitarian position as a disaggregationist position.

reaggregation[33] which have been deployed to grasp the poly-centred dimension of the new European configuration of authority. Yet for all its continuing popularity, the vulnerability and instability of this position is never far from the surface. Often the metaphorical language of sovereignty disaggregation is contained in self-consciously ironic quotation marks, a rhetorical flourish to highlight the oxymoronic suggestion in such strange couplings as 'shared' or 'divided' sovereignty, and thus to indicate the failing or bankrupt currency of the traditional explanatory language of sovereignty. Even where the attributions of divisibility, alienability, compossibility and mixity are not self-consciously deployed towards a critique of traditional sovereignty, it is nevertheless clear that they sit uneasily with the sense of sovereignty as a unifying and self-identifying claim made on behalf of the polity. For the theorists of disaggregated sovereignty, the concept of sovereignty is at best a somewhat awkward label, palpably incapable of filling the conceptual and discursive role it once did and now little more than a loose identifier of the different cloths in the patchwork of European legal and political power. If sovereignty is now everywhere, it seems that nowhere is it particularly important.

The difficulties with the notion of disaggregated sovereignty in turn accounts for the development of a third, post-sovereign position in the European context. If the idea of disaggregated sovereignty stretches any meaningful sense of sovereignty to breaking point, then perhaps, in a local echo of the more general critique of sovereignty as marginal or redundant, it is time to dispense with the concept itself. As Neil MacCormick, one of the most articulate defenders of this view, argues, should we not think of sovereignty against a background where it is no longer the exclusive preserve of the state as 'like virginity, something that can be lost by one without another's gaining it . . . ?'[34] The growing popularity of this position, which, as for MacCormick himself, is often seen as 'a matter of celebration' rather than grief—as involving the kind of normative approval of and commitment to a world no longer in thrall to sovereignty alluded to earlier—can be seen not only in the trend to confront the inadequacies of

---

[33] For discussion, see, for example, B De Witte, 'Sovereignty and European Integration: the Weight of Legal Tradition' in AM Slaughter, AS Sweet and JHH Weiler (eds) *The European Courts and National Courts: Doctrine and Jurisprudence* (Oxford, Hart publishing, 1998). As De Witte points out (302), the doctrine of divisible sovereignty gained support even within the ECJ as early as 1970, for which see the extra-curricular pronouncements of judge Pierre Pescatore in 'L'apport du droit communautaire au droit international public' *Cahiers de droit européen* (1970) 501. As De Witte also points out (303), the theory of divisible sovereignty is also central to the influential treatise of JV Louis, *The Community Legal Order* 2nd edn (Brussels, Office for official Publications of the EC, 1990)

[34] N MacCormick, *Questioning Sovereignty: Law, State and Practical Reason* (Oxford, OUP, 1999) 126.

sovereignty head-on, but also in the tendency both in the academy[35] and in some political circles[36] simply to ignore or dismiss sovereignty as an anachronistic irrelevance or a reactionary danger in discussion of the terms of the emerging European legal and political configuration.

Yet there are profound difficulties with this position too. If, like many political scientists and international relations scholars, at least those constitutional scholars and legal theorists who escape the confines and unitarian logic of a particular legal order no longer so readily favour sovereignty as a meta-concept—as a way of making sense of the world or of imagining improvements in that world—then perhaps they dismiss too easily the persistence of sovereignty in official constitutional discourse. For sovereignty-scepticism at the level of meta-language, I would contend, is to reckon without what Anthony Giddens calls the 'double hermeneutic'.[37] In human sciences, rather than natural sciences, to understand the world is to interpret not the inert world of nature—the single hermeneutic—but a world which has already been interpreted. It is an interpretation of an interpretation, a critical reading by experts, or so-called experts, of a prior reading by the social actors who make up the world. And, crucially, that prior reading is partly constitutive of the world to be explained. Social reality is not independent of the perceptions and beliefs of social actors or of the discursive claims in terms of which these perceptions and beliefs are articu-

---

[35] To take but one example, see O Gerstenberg and CF Sabel, 'Directly-Deliberative Polyarchy: An Institutional Ideal for Europe,' in C Joerges and R Dehousse (ed) *Good Governance in the European Union*, (Oxford, OUP, 2002). This contains an excellent treatment of the dangers of 'personification' in constitutional thinking, the taken-for-granted treatment of the boundaries of the sovereign polity as the proper focus and boundaries of political initiative, and suggests instead that a new commitment to bottom-up democratic experimentalism should be encouraged. It is possible to agree with much of this analysis but to question both the adequacy of its conception of *praxis*—how we get from where we are to where we want to be without working with the concept of sovereignty—and also, relatedly, its reluctance to see in at least some models of sovereign will-formation the resiliently affirmative possibilities of large-scale representation and political capacity. See further text below. In his contribution to the present volume, Richard Bellamy also defends a post-sovereign or rather, as he terms it, a pre-sovereign approach, albeit on somewhat different grounds. It is questionable, however, given his emphasis on a plurality of power-centres each making authoritative claims, whether his approach and its institutional implications is properly post-sovereign according to the terms here set out, or, rather, another variant of the constitutional pluralism defended in the present chapter.

[36] To take a topical example, at least until the end of 2002 the proceedings in the Laeken Convention on the Future of Europe, the self-styled 'constitutional convention' under the chairmanship of Valery Giscard D'Estaing, had largely by-passed the question of the proper allocation of sovereign authority in Europe and what, if any, would be the implications of adoption of a Constitutional Treaty for this question. On the perils and paradoxes of treating questions of fundamental law within a constitutional document whose *pouvoir constituant* remains highly contested, see P Craig, 'Constitutions, Constitutionalism and the European Union' (2001) 7 *European Law Journal* 125; see also N Walker 'The Idea of a European Constitution and the *Finalité* of Integration' in B De Witte (ed) *The Emergence of a European Constitution* (Oxford, OUP, forthcoming).

[37] See eg A Giddens, *The Constitution of Society* (Cambridge, Polity, 1984).

lated, but is in part constituted by and through them. So there is an internal relationship between the beliefs of the social actors who participate in the world and the beliefs of the experts who try to explain it. Or, in terms appropriate to our inquiry, there is an internal relationship between object-language and meta-language, and so between the concepts used in the object-language and in the meta-language. That is to say, a concept that retains significant discursive currency in the real world, such as sovereignty, must also continue to be taken seriously at the meta-level. The sovereignty beliefs and representations of actors, whether judges, civil servants, politicians or their 'publics'—cannot just be dismissed as so many self-delusions or so much self-interested rhetorical cover, because these beliefs help to constitute important institutional facts within that the world. Sovereignty may, as Krasner claims, be an example of 'organised hypocrisy,'[38] in that it can be invoked selectively and self-servingly, but that does not stop it from being taken seriously by significant political actors and audiences and from having real consequences for the overall configuration of authority and for the assertion of prior claims and the resolution of disputes within and across the institutions which make up this configuration. Sovereignty, in the final analysis is about a plausible and reasonably effective claim to ultimate authority, or in perspective theory a representation of authority made on behalf of a society which is (more or less successfully) constitutive of that society *as* a political society, or as a polity.[39] Sovereignty claims, when they achieve some measure of acceptance, continue to have profound political and social effects, and have to be taken seriously at the explanatory level for that reason.

This does not, of course, imply simple endorsement of this or that sovereignty claim, or even, in the long term, of the continuing currency of sovereignty claims in general. To enslave oneself to the current object-language of political and constitutional representation *just because it is* the current object-language of political and constitutional representation is no less an error—and one with inevitably conservative consequences—as it is to dismiss this language just because its prior explanatory and normative mould has been broken. Rather, to take sovereignty seriously implies accepting that any plausible explanatory or normative project must contend with its tenacious institutionalisation, and be prepared either to work with and within this institutional grid or, alternatively, to demonstrate how it is

---

[38] SD Krasner, n 13 above, 40.
[39] See, for example, Bert Van Roermund, 'Instituting Authority: Some Kelsenian Notes' (2002) 15 *Ratio Juris* 206, drawing on Panofsky; see also H Lindahl, 'Sovereignty and Symbolization,' (1997) 28 *Rechtstheorie* 3, drawing on Ernst Cassirer; see also H Lindahl and B Van Roermund, 'Law without a State: On Representing the Common Market,' in Z Bankowski and D Scott (eds) *The European Union and its Order: The Legal Theory of European Integration.* (Oxford, Blackwell, 2000). See also the respective contributions of Van Roermund and Lindahl to the present volume.

possible to think beyond this institutional grid in terms which nevertheless begin with this institutional grid and the forms and subjects of authority which it harbours and sustains.

But, how, precisely, is it possible to retreat from the assumptions of post-sovereignty without returning to the oxymorons of disaggregation or the myopia of the unitary approach? That some who have grown sceptical of the disaggregated approach and may have flirted with post-sovereignty seem to retreat in the final analysis to a form of unitarianism is tribute to the resilient attraction of the unitary approach in constitutional thought and language.[40] Yet if, as argued above, it is the case that no unitary approach, however nuanced, can adequately capture the diversity of the emerging constitutional order, the only remaining alternative is the kind of constitutional pluralism advertised at the beginning of this chapter. Constitutional pluralism, as a fourth approach to sovereignty in the context of the European Union, accepts that just as we cannot dismiss the constitutive power of those claims which continue to be registered in the language of sovereignty, we cannot either ignore the objective reality of globalisation and multi-dimensionality which has caused many at the meta level to forsake the claims of sovereignty. Constitutional pluralism attempts, therefore, to resolve the tension between the resilience of unitarianism in the object-language of sovereignty and the persuasiveness of pluralism in the meta-language of explanation and normative commitment precisely by taking *both* seriously.[41] In other words, constitutional pluralism stands beyond the perspective of any particular system in order to conceive of sovereignty in terms of a plurality of unities and in terms of the emergent possibilities of the relationships amongst this plurality of unities.

---

[40] For example, MacCormick himself, having abandoned sovereignty, may, as he in some measure acknowledges, have brought it in again through the back door when he opts for 'pluralism under international law . . . a kind of monism; in Kelsen's sense' in which international arbitration or adjudication provides the final recourse in cases of constitutional collision; above n 34, 121. So also, Bruno de Witte, despite finding traditional unitary approaches inadequate, having subsequently dismissed disaggregated approaches as incoherent finally reverts to a kind of unitarianism, asking whether with reference to the IGC process and national ratification sovereignty may 'lie with the peoples of the European Union taken together, rather than with each of these peoples separately?' above n 33, 304. While not as susceptible to a centralising tendency as Pernice's approach (see n 30 above), this approach still succumbs to the temptation of resolving the messy pluralism of the European configuration by academic fiat—and so by a unitarianism which resolves rather than accepts this pluralism. For a discussion of similarly unitarian candidate theories of sovereignty in the United States context, see Jeffrey Goldsworthy's contribution to the present volume.

[41] For work along similar lines see, for example, C Richmond, 'Preserving the Identity Crisis: Autonomy, System and Sovereignty in European Law,' (1997) 16 *Law and Philosophy* 377–420; M Kumm, 'Who is the Final Arbiter of Constitutionality in Europe?: Three Conceptions of the Relationship Between the German Federal Constitutional Court and the European Court of Justice,' (1999) 36 *Common Market Law Review*, 351–86, M La Torre, 'Legal Pluralism as an Evolutionary Achievement of Community Law,' (1999) 12 *Ratio Juris* 182–95. See also Miguel Maduro's contribution to the present volume.

5. LATE SOVEREIGNTY

How then, if we are to retain the language of sovereignty, are we to make it adequate to the changing configuration of authority in the European Union and beyond? I suggest that as a conceptual gambit—as a heuristic device—we adopt the language *of late sovereignty* to make sense of the new multi-dimensional order. The language of late sovereignty rather than sovereignty or post-sovereignty, like the language of late modernity[42] rather than modernity or post-modernity, or late capitalism[43] rather than capitalism or post-capitalism, suggests a number of things. First, it suggests fundamental *continuity* than discontinuity, that the basic conceptual apparatus of sovereignty can be adapted to understand the new order. Secondly, it suggests a *distinctive* phase in the discursive career of the term. That just as there are continuities in the meaning of sovereignty, there are also significant changes. Thirdly, it suggests *irreversibility*, that there is no way back to the world of early sovereignty and the one-dimensional system of states which it represented. Fourthly, it suggests *transformative potential*, that sovereignty has entered a final stage, that its capacity to represent the world of political authority is being tested to the limits, and even, possibly, that in that challenge there may be a transformation into an order of authority where sovereignty is of diminishing value, and where its continuing use both in the object-language of constitutional representation and in the meta-language of explanation and normative projection is tested to the limit. Let us assess these four characteristics of late sovereignty—continuity, distinctiveness, irreversibility and transformative potential—in turn.

First, there is continuity. We have already suggested that this lies in the resilient currency of self-identifying and self-sustaining claims made on behalf of legal and political communities whether state polities or post-state polities. In Michel Foucault's terms, sovereignty expresses both the power that enacts law and the law that restrains power—(political) ruler sovereignty and (legal) rule sovereignty—*pouvoir constituant* and *pouvoir constitué*.[44] For many, including Foucault, this double claim is testimony to the conceptual incoherence of sovereignty alluded to in section two, but it can also be viewed more constructively, as the conceptual key to sovereignty as a dynamic process of mutual constitution and mutual containment of

---

[42] See, for example, A Giddens, *The Consequences of Modernity*, (Cambridge, Polity, 1991) ch 4.

[43] See, for example, E Mandel *Late Capitalism* (London, Verso, 1985)

[44] See in particular. M Foucault *Governmentality* in G Burchell, C Gordon and P Miller (eds) *The Foucault Effect: Studies in Governmentality* (Hemel Hempstead, Wheatsheaf, 1991).

law and politics.[45] The claim to sovereignty is indeed inextricably tied to the paradox of *pouvoir constituant* and *pouvoir constitué*, but it is only if a claim is made on behalf of sovereignty either within a purely political register or within a purely legal register[46] that the sovereignty claim may be seen as *foundering* on that paradox. Instead, we should view the sovereignty claim as necessarily situated at the boundary between politics and law. If, then, we understand the use of the term sovereignty both as an expressive reminder of the indispensable legal context of politics and as an expressive reminder of the indispensable political context of law—that is to say as a claim which alternately connotes the ultimate dependence of all law on political forces—on acts of initiative, representation and sanction—and the ultimate dependence of all forms of political initiative and regime development on the justifying and stabilising representations of legal normative order, then, rather than founder on the paradox of ruler and rule power, sovereignty can be seen as a coming to terms with that paradox which provides the discursive resources to enable and account for order and change alike in and through the mutual signification of law and politics.[47]

In the context of the birth of a new polity, the idea of mutual constitution and containment allows us to understand the emergence of a sovereignty-presupposing claim to autonomy as a diachronic process, a process of construction over time. Of course, the assertion of sovereignty in political or legal discourse may present itself—and in many state contexts has presented itself—as a big-bang single moment, but this should never disguise the fact that such momentary claims are never more than provisional; instead they remain remorselessly dependent on an ongoing dialectic of law and politics in which the earlier claim in either political or legal register will inevitably be conditioned by and *re*presented, refined and perhaps significantly reshaped in the other register. In the case of the European Union, the political conditions for this kind of big-bang claim

---

[45] See, for example, Van Roermund, above n 39, and his contribution to the present volume. While my own understanding of sovereignty is informed by Van Roermund's views, in his chapter he takes issue with my conceptualisation of constitutional pluralism, and in particular with the idea of a plurality of overlapping sovereign orders which underpins it. This is not the place to pursue this argument in depth. In brief, Van Roermund views constitutional pluralism as no more or less than 'constitutional unitarianism deferred to times of crisis.' In philosophical terms, I can but agree, but I am more concerned with the overall implications in terms of a global political sociology. Some forms of relations between polities may stabilise short of crisis, other may not. However, the onset of crisis and the reassertion of unitarianism in any particular case does not, short of the successful assertion of a new world-hegemonic empire, change the general picture of a plurality of overlapping orders and the overall globalising dynamic which feeds that process. A particular set of inter-polity relations under constitutional pluralism may be precarious, but that does not mean that the pluralist syndrome or configuration as a whole is precarious.

[46] As indeed is often done within constitutional law and theory. See further, Martin Loughlin's contribution to the present volume.

[47] I am indebted to Hans Lindahl for some of the ideas here expressed.

have never been propitious,[48] but the absence (thus far)[49] of a self-conscious polity-defining event is no more fatal to the process of polity-construction than its presence is conclusive thereof. Regardless, therefore, of their historical antecedents, new claims to sovereignty need not be caught in Foucault's conceptual trap of being seen as merely legally derivative, and so not truly politically independent, nor as politically unconstrained, and so not truly legal—and so in neither case fulfilling the double condition of sovereignty, as mutually constituted through law and politics.

If we turn, then, to the particular historical antecedents of the EU, we may observe that its origins as a creature of state-based international law did not consign the EU for ever more to the status of a derivative polity, and so not truly sovereign. In time, as already noted, the ECJ in a famous line of cases asserted the direct and supreme authority of European law. In other words, a state-legally-derivative legal organ of the EU, the ECJ, backed up by other state-legally-derivative political organs, principally the Commission and the European Parliament, came in time through a series of political representations of the legal context of the Community and legal representations of the political context of the Community to reclaim and reconstitute the EC, and later the EU, as a different type of legal order, still bound by law but by a law now deemed to be autonomously rooted—to be 'autochthonous'[50]—and to be nested elsewhere than the state. The historically undeniable fact of derivative authority gave way to the claim to original authority—the 'international' institutions of the EU pulling themselves up by their own bootstraps to assert a new supranational order with themselves as it its sovereign representatives.[51] Thus a late sovereign polity such as the EU, like the state polities of early sovereignty, still makes the claim of ultimate authority and, like these state polities, does so through a complex of institutions which, however and wherever derived, comes to claim to be representative of the polity in question.

So much for continuity. What of distinctiveness? What are the objective differences in the claims that are made in late sovereignty? Now sovereign claims were always particularising, and this, crucially is a *constitutive* rather than a *limiting* feature of sovereignty. Sovereignty would not be sovereignty if it were not sovereignty 'over' something, if it did not *connote* that over which it was not sovereign in the very act of *denoting* that over which it was sovereign. Sovereignty is always a claim over a particular society, indeed—

---

[48] See, for example, on the necessary cunning of the Court of Justice in precipitating a 'quiet revolution', see JHH Weiler, 'Journey to an Unknown Destination: A Retrospective and Prospective of the European Court of Justice in the Area of Political Integration' (1993) 31 *Journal of Common Market Studies* 418.

[49] The draft Constitutional Treaty of the European Union promulgated in June 2003 may, of course, change matters. However, even if its text and import is not substantially altered during the 2004–5 Intergovernmental Conference, its 'revolutionary' credentials in the (re)making of the European polity will doubtless remain the subject of deep dispute for a long time to come.

[50] KC Wheare *The Constitutional Structure of the Commonwealth* (Oxford, OUP, 1960).

[51] See, for example, De Witte, n 33 above.

to repeat—a claim to constitute that society as a polity or political community, and so it always necessarily excludes as well as includes. The key to sovereignty is the double-claim to ultimate authority over where the boundary between the inside and the outside lies and to ultimate authority, to final power of decision which defeats any claim of 'external' encroachment, within that self-defined boundary.[52] The key difference in the claim made in the multi-dimensional post-Westphalian order is that the boundaries are no longer merely *territorial*, but, if in an increasingly permissive sense, also *functional*.[53] To be sure, states in the age of late sovereignty still make claims to territorial authority *tout court*, but non-state polities typically make claims to authority bounded by territory and by function. In other word, the political *societies* which non-state polities claim to constitute are no longer just territorial communities but also functional communities. But allowing for that difference, the same logic of inclusion/ exclusion applies as does in the traditional state context. The same claim to ultimate authority over where the boundary lies is made, even if, unlike the state order, the claim is restricted to one of 'judicial *Kompetenz-Kompetenz*' or 'interpretive autonomy'[54] over the precise extent of the functional boundaries, and cannot, just because of these textually ordained functional limitations, embrace the further claim to 'legislative *Kompetenz-Kompetenz*'. Equally, the same claim to ultimate authority in the face of any external encroachment within the self-determined boundary as traditionally asserted at the state level is now asserted at the suprastate level.

---

[52] This is linked to, and endorses, external sovereignty—Krasner's international legal sovereignty (n 13 above)—in a double sense. First, there should be no external curtailment of the power of decision within the self-defined boundary. Secondly, what lies within the self-defined boundary includes not only internal powers vis-a-vis the political community, but also the right to exercise powers on behalf of that community in the international domain, and this, too, should not be encroached upon.

[53] Here I acknowledge the strength of the arguments of Miguel Maduro and Gráinne de Búrca, both of whom are uncomfortable with the idea of functional limitation. For Maduro, the EU had gradually been transformed 'into a political community of open and undetermined political goals'; see 'Where to Look for Legitimacy?' in EO Eriksen, JE Fossum and AJ Menendez (eds) *Constitution Making and Democratic Legitimacy* (Oslo, Arena) ARENA Report No. 5/2002. 81. Similarly, for De Búrca in the present volume, the idea of the functionally limited sovereignty of the EU, 'if not oxymoronic, is somewhat meaningless'. In response I would make two points. First, limitation by function is rather different from, and less constraining than limitation by sector. It does not mean that there are sectoral policy areas from which the EU is necessarily excluded, but rather that the limitations of the EU's sovereign reach is merely the limitation of the (necessarily cross-sectoral) functional projects it has been mandated to pursue. Secondly, the existence of interpretive autonomy on the part of the EU means that this limitation is, finally, a form of *self*-limitation in accordance with a textual mandate. Self-limitation may be different from external limitation, and may be abused or, indeed, interpreted in very open-ended terms, but if we accept that even self-policed normative limitations can still constrain, just because they *are* normative limitations and they are construed by an interpretive community which internalises them in some measure, then the idea of functional limitation appears to retains some explanatory value.

[54] T Schilling, 'The Autonomy of the Community Legal Order: An Analysis of Possible Foundations,' (1996) 17 *Harvard International Law Journal*, 389, 389–90.

Yet the shift to functionally limited polities within a multi-dimensional order does require an adjustment to the deep conceptual structure of sovereignty. In its traditional statist version, the claim to sovereignty or ultimate authority implies both autonomy and territorial exclusivity. Autonomy or independence, because a derivative or dependent authority is by definition not ultimate. Exclusivity, because a world order of states is generally[55] one of discrete and mutually exclusive territorial jurisdictions. Within the symmetrical logic of such an order, a non-exclusive authority is typically a dependent one, in the sense that any other authority claim made over the jurisdiction can only be made by a rival state, which if plausible and effective, as in the tradition of Western imperialism, then becomes an extension of the exclusive claim to authority of that rival state, so defeating or debasing the indigenous claim.[56] In other words the mutual exclusivity of comprehensive territorial jurisdictions in the one-dimensional global map implies a corresponding mutual exclusivity of effective claims to sovereignty.

In the new post-Westphalian order, in contrast, with the emergence of functionally-limited polities which do not claim comprehensive jurisdiction over a particular territory *it becomes possible to conceive of autonomy without territorial exclusivity*—to imagine ultimate authority, or sovereignty, in non-exclusive terms. Crucially, the development of functionally limited claims is self-reinforcing to the extent that it allows of the possibility of territorial overlap without subsumption. To be sure, the boundaries between different polities are still deeply contested. Indeed, in a configuration in which overlap and intersection become the norm, these boundary disputes, whose only *legal* discipline is the self-discipline of highly open-textured functional limitations, as we shall see, become more systematic.[57] Yet even so, the advent of functionally limited polities co-existent within the same territorial space means that the assertion of authority around a disputed boundary does not necessarily impugn the integrity of the other polity *qua* polity. So, for example, to the extent that the claim to sovereignty of the European Union over a range of competences previously within the exclusive jurisdiction of the fifteen member states is plausible and effective, this does not seriously question the continuing sovereignty of

---

[55] The condominium, an arrangement in which sovereignty is jointly exercised over two or more states, provides an exception to this rule. Historically, condominia have existed from the Sudan to the New Hebrides.
[56] See eg R Jackson, 'Sovereignty in World Politics: A Glance at the Conceptual and Historical Landscape,' (1999) 47 *Political Studies*, 431.
[57] N Walker, above n 22, 375–8.

the fifteen member states as regards their remaining areas of territorial jurisdiction.[58]

What, now, of irreversibility? Why can late sovereignty not, in Martin Amis's phrase, reverse 'time's arrow'[59] and become again early sovereignty? There are two sets of reasons for this. First, there are macro-political reasons. The dynamic of globalisation, and of the response to globalisation through the formation of non-state polities, continues inexorably to unfold. The challenge of multinational capital, of global communications and of free movement of goods, services, persons and capital is beyond the regulatory grasp of the state, and the grant of regulatory authority to non-state polities consolidates and reinforces that process. Put starkly, the development of non-state polities cannot, except through the most obtusely state-reassertive perspective, be seen as a holding measure until states reassert their hegemony, but rather as a process of reallocation of regulatory authority which guarantees that states will never re-establish that hegemony. Alongside the macro-political considerations, the logic of sovereignty itself guarantees irreversibility, at least in the sense of the old retaining no residual claim over the new. As we saw earlier, the formation of new sovereign entities necessarily involves a claim to autonomy on the part of a putative polity and a process of mutual constitution of that autonomy through the twin poles of politics and law. In that process, the link to the original legal order is severed. The process of sovereignty-creation, provided it becomes an effectively legitimated legal and political claim to representation of and

---

[58] To the extent that such questioning does take place, it tends to derive at least in part from a confusion between legislative *Kompetenz-Kompetenz* and interpretive autonomy—or judicial *Kompetenz-Kompetenz*—and a consequential exaggeration of the significance of the ECJ's power to determine the boundaries of its own jurisdiction. So according to Lenaerts, there 'is simply no nucleus of sovereignty that the Member States can invoke, as such, against the Community.' This proposition tends to overlook two points (1); that as the jurisdiction of the Community/Union remains a textually limited one, even in the EU's own terms that which lies outside these textual limits presumably continues to be part of the nucleus of sovereignty of the Member States, albeit that they cannot as a matter of EU law invoke this authoritatively against the Community, and (2); that in any event, in line with the pluralist premises of the present argument, in their own constitutional terms rather than those of the EU, the Member States do retain a nucleus of sovereignty which they can invoke in their own courts; see K Lenaerts, 'Constitutionalism and the Many Faces of Federalism', (1990) *American Journal of Comparative Law*, 205–63, 220. See text below for further discussion of the relationship between sovereignty and interpretive autonomy.

The territorially non-exclusive representation of sovereignty by the EU is, however, not reciprocated by the Member States. Continuing claims of state sovereignty tend not to concede that any part of that sovereignty has been or is even capable of being irrevocably transferred to the EU, instead maintaining that in the final analysis the EU has no plausible or legitimate sovereign claim against the states as opposed to a plausible and legitimate claim to have been delegated certain substantial powers by the states. For a possible exception to or modification of this position in the case of The Netherlands, where the concept of sovereignty does not explicitly figure in official constitutional discourse, and where constitutional procedures are particularly receptive to the transfer of powers to the EU, see Bruno De Witte's contribution to the present volume.

[59] M Amis *Time's Arrow* (London, Penguin, 1991).

within that political space, necessarily breaks the link with the prior polity. This was true within the one-dimensional order of sovereign states, and it is just as true of a multi-dimensional order of states and other polities. The difference is that within the one-dimensional order such irreversibility simply meant that the birth and death of new sovereign states was not within the gift of old sovereign states, whereas within the multi-dimensional order what was true of *units* is now true of *categories*—the fate of the new category—or dimension—of non-state polities is no longer within the gift of the first category—or first dimension—of state polities. Sovereign entities—non-state as well as state—are much more than the sum of their antecedents and necessarily transcend the condition of their formation.

Let us turn, finally, to transformative potential. If late sovereignty cannot revert to early sovereignty, will it sustain and steady itself in its 'late' form? Or is there an unstable dynamic within late sovereignty which will lead to further transformations, and perhaps to a configuration of political authority where notions of sovereignty cease to be germane to the self-understanding of the actors involved, and so, finally, are no longer necessary or valuable within the meta-language of explanation?

6. THE PRECARIOUSNESS OF LATE SOVEREIGNTY

There are indeed arguments to suggest that late sovereignty contains the seeds of its own transformation. These arguments fall into three categories. There are arguments, first, about conflict and boundary maintenance, secondly, about diffusion of sovereign power, and thirdly, about reflexivity.

Let us deal first with conflict and boundary maintenance. To be sure, there were issues of boundary maintenance within the one-dimensional order of states. But since the only sovereign polities were states which were also territorial communities, these conflicts took a certain form and operated within certain limits. Jurisdictional boundaries were literally physical boundaries in a flat one-dimensional legal world and were resolved as minor border skirmishes[60] or by conquest and incorporation, by the categorical assertion of one sovereignty claim over another. In a multi-dimensional world there are more, and more subtle and complex boundaries.[61] Not only are there boundaries between states, but also between states and non-state polities, between different non-state polities or putative non-state polities, and even, as in the notorious Bananas litigation series involving the WTO, the EU and its Member States,[62] complex multiple intersections involving a plurality of non-state and state polities. The testing of the terms

---

[60] Whether conducted through law, diplomacy or physical force.
[61] See Walker, above. n 22.
[62] For discussion, see, for example, Miriam Aziz's chapter in the present volume.

and limits of sovereign authority—the *external* probing of the internal claim to sovereign authority—becomes the norm rather than the exception. To be sure, these different polities use their interpretive autonomy—their judicial *Kompetenz-Kompetenz*, as a way of retaining their integrity—their representational authority, but how resilient are these interpretive autonomies in the face of such pervasive boundary-probing?

Secondly, there is the problem of diffusion. In the world of multi-dimensionality there are many emergent, or putative polities. The WTO is one example,[63] NAFTA the Council of Europe and, perhaps, the United Nations,[64] are others, while other still may include entities such as Schengen or, more plausibly, the 'Euro' zone, which in their very different ways and through their different trajectories emerge from and interact with the EU itself. The mutual constitution of law and politics in these cases, least of all in the cases of the flexible margins of the EU, has not yet reached a stage where serious and potentially effective claims to sovereign or ultimate authority are being made. Will that stage ever be reached? There are countervailing forces at work here, which I have discussed elsewhere.[65] Flexibility within the EU, such as has produced Schengen and EMU, and which, particularly in the context of the present Eastward enlargement[66] may produce new variants of multi-speed convergence and variable geometry, is not marked by design, certainty and consensus, but by contingency, ambiguity and disagreement. For some, flexibility is about diluting the power of the EU, about putting in place additional, shallower, more state-centred and traditionally intergovernmental alliances to erode the core EU. For others, it is a way of strengthening the non-state level, of producing more supranational authority, perhaps in new supranational entities—a device to marginalise or outflank the state sceptics or relegate to a second tier those whose capacity for integration is less developed. So flexibility is a ubiquitous device which can serve different, even diametrically opposing ends, lying as it does at the intersection of two competing gambits. What this suggests is a process with profoundly unforeseeable and unintended consequences. More generally, both in the context of flexibility and in the wider framework of transnational political initiatives beyond the EU, the

---

[63] For an analysis of the WTO as a partially constituted constitutional polity, see Walker, above n 21

[64] See Bardo Fassbender's contribution to the present volume.

[65] See Walker above n 22; see also 'Flexibility within a Metaconstitutional Frame: Reflections on the Future of Legal Authority in Europe,' in G de Búrca and J Scott (eds) *Constitutional Change in the ECL: Between Uniformity and Flexibility?* (Oxford, Hart Publishing, 2000).

[66] Which has stimulated a new series of flexibility proposals. See in particular, the much discussed and controversial proposals of Joschka Fischer in 'From Confederacy to Federation: Thoughts on the Finality of European Integration', reprinted together with a series of responses in C Joerges, Y Meny and JHH Weiler (eds) '*What Kind of Constitution for What Kind of Polity? Responses to Joschka Fischer*' (Florence, Robert Schuman Centre, 2000).

unstable and shifting alliances and competitions between different geopolitical strategies and different substantive policy aspirations does not
suggest any smooth completion of new sovereign projects, but instead
further fragmentation, the emergence of more and more putative polities,
which precisely because of the remorseless dynamic of fragmentation are
not necessarily sovereign entities-in-waiting. Diffusion may give rise to—or
rather give way to—*defusion*, to a plethora of organisational fragments
which do not fit comfortably within the representational perspective of an
existing sovereign but which do not themselves, yet, or perhaps ever, make
independently effective sovereignty claims.

Thirdly, and finally, there is the question of reflexivity. In the very development of new and endemic boundary clashes and in the proliferation of
putative polities, the self-understanding of systems may be transformed.
The interrogative gaze of sovereign authorities may no longer be exclusively
directed outwards towards competing or putative sovereign orders, but, in
response to these competing claims, and also to the self-organising and self-
regulatory claims of communities of practice and interest which do not
define themselves as multi-functional polities,[67] may also turn inwards.
There may then, arguably, develop the momentum for a general trans-order
or trans-system shift in the understanding of legal and political authority,
one which continuously reflexively interrogates the pattern of sovereign
boundaries already drawn, and perhaps, some might suggest, even the idea
of bounded polities, and so of sovereign order, itself.

But against this, there is surely a limit to the internalisation of doubt.
Polities may constantly adjust to a changing environment, but it is a more
remote possibility to contemplate that, serially or simultaneously, such
actually existing polities might, with the assistance of a hostile and revolutionary citizenry, re-imagine themselves (or have themselves re-imagined)
out of existence, and out of power. Even if they did, to pursue this speculative hypothesis, what succeeded them would not, or no longer, be a sceptical anti-authoritarian, sovereignty-transcending 'view from nowhere'; it
would instead be a new entity, or new entities, which would necessarily seek
to adopt a settled frame of political organisation and so define and represent the political world in their own aspiringly authoritative, and thus putatively sovereign terms.

To retreat from this speculative hypothesis, it is much more likely as a
matter of political sociology, and, relatedly—if the threshold legitimacy of
the idea of multi-functional political capacity seeking to present a unity of
ordered normative expectations out of a diversity of constituencies and
tasks does indeed survive—it is then also *inevitable* as a matter of the epistemology of legal and political power, that reflexivity will lead not to the

---

[67] See, for example, Walker, above n 2.

demise of the sovereign polity but instead to a new order of relations between and amongst polities and putative polities, a new and enlarged zone of boundary politics, and a new set of approaches to negotiating these boundaries. And so finally, we may answer the charge of actual or anticipated redundancy by suggesting that the dynamic of transformation within late sovereignty will involve the continuous evolution rather than the demise of sovereignty.

What are the emergent properties of this new order of relations? Constitutional lawyers thinking along pluralist lines tend to emphasise the possibility of constitutional collision between the high judicial authorities of different polities as the major point of contestation and crucial axis of communication between sovereign polities in a multi-dimensional configuration of authority.[68] Certainly, if we think of the different norm types within constitutional orders in terms of polity identifying rules (rules of recognition, change and adjudication);[69] substantive rules (content of prescriptive norms); and structural rules (institutional architecture), then the key fault-line between different sites—the single cell in the matrix of possible relations between orders where their different points of departure are incommensurable and where conflict in principle most intractable, is where the polity identifying rules are at stake on either side. Each of the polity-identifying rules describes a normative context where, by definition, an autonomous sovereign order cannot defer to or accommodate the authority of another order if it is to consolidate or successfully assert its claim to sovereignty—(and where, it follows, deference can be viewed as a threshold test of the distinction between effectively sovereign and putatively sovereign polity). Precisely because there is no scope for mutual deference here, one order may claim sovereign authority over the other, or these claims may even be made reciprocally, but these sovereignty-encroaching claims can never be recognised as having trumping effect by the other sovereign. A sovereign order must assume its own continuing or self-amending sovereignty within its sphere of authority (rules of recognition and change) and must retain interpretive autonomy (rules of adjudication), deciding the boundaries of that sphere of authority. This is the irreducible core, the non-negotiable given of any sovereign order—in the words of Bert Van Roermund, the 'vanishing point' of perspective[70] from which its 'sovereign' vision of the world is constructed or assumed but which itself cannot be seen and cannot be questioned in the construction of that vision. Some of the most celebrated constitutional cases in the history of EU-state relations have been precisely about the contemplation of such collisions, and about

---

[68] See references at note 41 above.
[69] In Hart's famous formulation. See HLA Hart *The Concept of Law* 2nd edition (Oxford, Clarendon, 1994) ch 5.
[70] Above, n 39, drawing on Panofsky.

the strategic measure taken within different contexts to ensure the optimal assertion of the norms of the particular system without risking the 'mutually assured destruction'[71] that a direct clash would bring.[72]

Yet while these cases may be the most spectacular, they are merely the tip of the relational iceberg of constitutional pluralism. There are many other contexts of interaction between sites where the overlap of jurisdiction, interests and aspirations provides scope for competition and co-operation and where other mechanisms and practices of communication hold sway. Sometimes, as with the preliminary reference procedure under Article 234 EC, there is a formalised bridging mechanism at the level of structural rules which provides an authoritative resolution or avoidance of difference. Sometimes, as in the emerging interaction between fundamental rights charters at state and EU level, there is a relationship between substantive norms which is a complex mix of competition, emulation and complementarity. Clearly, too, the relations between sites are often structured only very indirectly by authoritative legal rules. So the structural constitutional rules concerning the political institutions of the EU and the member states, by the very act of creating and mandating the institutions in questions, set in train a whole complex of relations between national Parliaments and the European Parliament, between national executives and the Commission, between national banks and the European Central Banks etc., with the terms of these cross-site, inter-institutional relations subject to highly variable levels of specification within the constitutional rules of any particular site.[73]

Still in the institutional field, we can point to other circumstances where the relational dimension between sites, while still structured by the different sovereign self-understanding of the sites, contains the germ of a more radical transformation of the terms of exchange. Thus the contested margins of relations between sites can provide the structural dynamic for the emergence of new, and potentially more dialogical relations between actors across polities. One example is the Comitology committee structure.[74] Essentially a complex compromise between the 'intergovernmental' Council's need to delegate much of the administration of its legislative instruments to the 'supranational' Commission, the Council's desire nevertheless to limit the influence of the Commission bureaucracy, and the

---

[71] See Weiler, above n 5, ch 9.

[72] For discussion of many of these cases, see De Witte, above n 33.

[73] For example, under the EMU provisions of the EC Treaty there is complex and detailed regulation of the relationship between the European Central Bank and national banking institutions under the European System of Central Banks, whereas, by contrast, there are only very few and only very permissive institutional provisions linking the European Parliament with national Parliaments.

[74] See eg C Joerges ' "Good Governance" through Comitology?' in C Joerges and E Vos (eds) *EU Committees: Social Regulation, Law and Politics* (Oxford, Hart Publishing, 1999).

Commission's own dependence on state administrations for the detailed implementation of its policies, the Comitology system creates inclusive decision-making contexts which allow for mutual accommodation and mutual learning between different types of national, supranational and non-aligned actors. Similarly, the recent development of the Open Method of Co-ordination is in some measure at least in response to the indeterminacy and contestation of jurisdictional boundaries between state and EU in matters as diverse as employment policy and asylum policy.[75] The OMC responds by side-stepping the hard questions of competence and substituting for a compartmentalised decision-making hierarchy an inclusive policy cycle which lacks any authoritative end-point. In both of these cases, out of the novel, complex and untidy legal arrangements for the development of 'constitutional' relations between sovereign sites we can see the development of a dynamic in which actors with partial and interconnected governance projects in the same policy sectors can begin to imagine and reciprocally enact and co-ordinate polity-transcending comprehensive governance projects.[76]

It was argued in section two that those who doubt the explanatory relevance of sovereignty often do so against an analytical backdrop of false abstraction, tending to place sovereignty on the same conceptual plane as all other power relations and then declaring it wanting or marginal as a form of power in comparison with these other power relations. The answer to that criticism is to see sovereign not in competition with these other power relations but as a discursive factor in the framing and articulation of these other relations. The same caution applies in the altered context of late sovereignty. To argue that sovereignty has a general structuring effect on legal, political and economic processes as they flow within and between different polities and orders of polities in the multi-dimensional, complexly intersecting, post-Westphalian configuration is in principle to claim no more or less explanatory power than might have been made on behalf of the concept with regard to intra-polity and inter-polity relations in the more clearly delineated one-dimensional order of states that preceded it. Just how this structuring effect manifests itself in practice and how central it is to the ordering of power relations within any particular policy field and in relation to the interests and other regulatory influences in that field (private law, soft law, private ordering, custom, corporatist agreement, expert committees etc.) is a matter of empirical inquiry. What is undeniable, however, is that sovereignty, and, in particular, the indistinct, unresolved and continuously negotiated boundaries between different sovereign or aspirationally sovereign sites, remains a framework consideration within

---

[75] See for example, J Scott and DM Trubak, 'Mind the Gap: Law and New Approaches to Governance in Europe' (2002) 8 *European Law Journal* 1–18.
[76] See further, Walker, note 2 above.

our explanatory model, however heavily or lightly, directly or indirectly, that framework might impinge in any particular place at any particular time.

7. CONCLUSION: SOME NORMATIVE IMPLICATIONS

Having examined and defended the continuing explanatory currency of sovereignty, we are now at last in a position to address the normative question about the relationship between the heterarchically organised sovereignties of the world of constitutional pluralism on the one hand, and on the other, the rejection of the violence, peremptory authority and illegitimate domination often associated with the worst excesses of sovereign power and the nurturing instead of consensual and reasoned forms of legal and political communication. It follows from the argument developed above concerning the epistemological centrality of sovereignty to our understanding and framing of legal and political authority generally, that it makes no sense for sovereignty to be considered in any general way to be the enemy or rival of these forms of communication. Rather sovereignty, or at least a concept or a process which does the functionally equivalent work of representation of a polity, is presently and for as long as the very idea of multi-functional units of public authority is legitimately sustainable, one of their indispensable preconditions. The task, therefore, of political and constitutional theory in conditions of late sovereignty is not to imagine, or to anticipate, a world in which new political values and virtues flourish in the absence of sovereignty, but to imagine and anticipate ways in which such values and virtues may flourish *through* the operation of sovereignty.

But, in conclusion, if the epistemological embeddedness of sovereignty is not just about how the world is—about how the plausible claim to sovereignty can generate a self-fulfilling complex of institutional facts which order the world in accordance with that claim—but also about how it ought to be, then something more has to be said about the normative case for sovereignty and for the constitutional pluralism which, in an age of multi-dimensionality, sovereignty anchors. To begin with, as I have argued elsewhere, as one of the preconditions of polity formation generally, sovereignty is also by necessary inference one of the preconditions of *constitutional* polity formation.[77] The other sovereignty-dependent features and indices of constitutional polity formation against which both existing state polities and putative non-state polities such as the EU and WTO can be assessed include; first, the existence of a reflexive and publicly approbated constitutional discourse of responsible self-government associated with the

---

[77] See further, Walker, note 2 above.

polity; secondly, the existence of broad jurisdictional scope—not just the single-minded pursuit of a discrete regulatory goal but a general mandate of multi-functional governance and thus a capacity to consider, balance and co-ordinate the various public goods and private interests implicated in such a broad programme; thirdly, interpretive autonomy, which as well as being a necessary incident of sovereignty itself also provides the institutional space and encourages the institutional responsibility for the development of a judicial discourse and practice which highlights the 'rule of law' virtues of certainty, consistency and reasoned and accountable application of norms within the distinctive juridical order of the polity; fourthly, institutional depth and breadth, including the existence of well-defined legislative, executive and judicial organs and the promotion of the virtues of mutual restraint and efficient division of government labour associated with such a separation of powers; fifthly, citizenship, or the existence of a permanent membership for whose general well-being, however defined, the polity must function; and sixthly, representative mechanisms, through which the citizenry is constituted as a *demos* with the participatory, preference-identifying and accountability virtues that democracy entails.

Of course the assertion or even the establishment of a sovereign claim, particularly in the fragmenting post-Westphalian order, offers no guarantee as to the measure or quality of development of these associated constitutional values. As has already been argued, constitutional virtue on any account, is hugely underdetermined by the discourse of sovereignty. What is clear, however, is that in the absence of the ordering work of sovereignty, even in its late mode, in providing an enabling normative frame for constitutional polity formation, it is difficult to see how else the rich mix of ingredients of both 'input-orientated legitimisation' and 'output-orientated legitimisation'[78] associated with the constitutional polity at its best could remain available in the recipe book of global governance.

---

[78] Scharpf, above, n 20, 7–21.

2

Sovereignty: Unpopular and Popular

BERT VAN ROERMUND

"Ma i Soverani, i Soverani nostri? E la leggitimità dove va a finir—?"[1]

I. INTRODUCTION

THERE ARE TWO main arguments counting against the notion of sovereignty as the basic idea for a legal order in modernity: let's call them the Argument from Redundancy [R] and the argument from Incoherence [I]. I will briefly review them in section two. There I will submit that the conclusion of [R] often exceeds the scope of its premises, once these are stripped of some misunderstandings and misconceptions. Indeed, it will appear far from easy to substantiate the redundancy, for a legal order, of 1) some form of agency, 2) that conceives of itself as united in action, 3) by some form of representation. The real attack on sovereignty, then, comes from argument [I], which criticises the concept of sovereignty for wanting to have it both ways: it purports to express the idea of a power that sets law, and, at the same time, of a power that is restrained by law. I investigate several attempts to account for the core phrase 'at the same time'

Parts of this paper were discussed at various seminars and conferences. In particular, I want to mention a GLOBUS-seminar at Tilburg University in March 2000, where I received valuable criticism from Neil Walker as my discussant. I gratefully acknowledge support of the GLOBUS Institute (Tilburg University) in organising this two-day conference. I also thank my Tilburg colleagues Hans Lindahl and David Janssens, as well as my former colleague Mogobe Ramose, for their critical comments; the same goes for the participants in the seminar discussions (September 2000) of the Centre for Transboundary Legal Development (Tilburg University). I am indebted to Filip Buekens for guidance in the labyrinths of indexical knowledge. Papers on sovereignty I gave in Kraków (May 2000), Brussels (May 2001) and Amsterdam (June 2001) evoked so many questions that I was prevented from the serious error of publishing earlier versions of this one. A three months sabbatical granted by my Faculty of Philosophy gave me the occasion to complete it. Once more I thank Hans Lindahl and Neil Walker for their careful reading of the penultimate version.

[1] 'But the sovereigns, our sovereigns? And what, in the end, will happen to legitimacy?' G Tomasi di Lampedusa, *Il gattopardo*, Ed. conforme al manuscritto del 1957, (Milano, Feltrinelli, 1969 [1958]), p. 47 (my transl., BvR).

which are all, in my view, unsuccessful. These discussions confirm the three problems diagnosed in the analysis of [R]; moreover, they bring out the paradoxical rather than the incoherent character of sovereignty. In section three, I propose an alternative account, departing from the classical Rousseauist idea of 'popular sovereignty'. It aims to solve the paradox and to do justice to the three key-features a legal order cannot afford to waive as redundant. On the basis of contemporary philosophies of language and action, I present the first outlines of a formal scheme [LEX], with four different instances of the first person plural. These allow us to assign different predicates of sovereignty to different pragmatic functions in one and the same basic format of democratic law making. Then we may be able to see in what sense sovereignty appears both inside and outside the legal order, why it is a manifold and why it is a unity, why it is not redundant and why it is essential.

From the outset it should clearly be said that my contribution is very close to Hans Lindahl's. We are in an almost daily discussion about the contributions philosophy of law could make to the discussion on representation and authority in the modern legal order. Acknowledging that the empirico-legal analyses are entirely his, I largely share his diagnosis of the problems. [LEX] is an attempt to understand, from my own perspective and in my philosophical vocabulary, what Lindahl also points to as being the crucial point: the sustained intertwinement of constituent and constituted power in even the tiniest piece of law making. A lucid and critical insight into this dialectical relationship is itself constitutive of a legal order that acknowledges the ambiguity of its being 'modern'. It will not make sovereignty any more popular, but it may help to understand democracy and the rule of law.

2. TWO PROBLEMS OF SOVEREIGNTY

Let us look briefly at the argument from Redundancy [R] and the argument from Incoherence [I]. [R] is a normative argument. It states that the concept of sovereignty has become outdated. Sovereignty has allegedly proved to be no longer fit to clarify, let alone to guide, modern developments in the area of legal empowerment. The argument characteristically, and emphatically, tackles the idea of a monopoly of law-making in the hands of the nation state. It explains that the nation state is withering away, although not for the reasons Marx anticipated. It welcomes a host of alternatives: multi-party sovereignty, interlocking legal orders, negotiated law-making, soft law and their ilk, all of which strongly suggest that law-making in the modern era will be very much a matter of participation, communication, deliberation, mutual recognition and interdependence. The argument from Incoherence [I] holds that the notion of sovereignty is a conceptual failure. It has always been confused, if not contradictory. Most, though not all, of this alleged confusion can be captured by Foucault's observation that the concept of sovereignty embraces the ambiguity of a typically legal attitude towards power: it purports to express both the (political) power that enacts law and the law that restrains (political) power. Proposals to solve it invariably fall victim to the infamous Münchhausen-trilemma (Albert): they become involved in petitio principii, or infinite regress, or normative inference from facts.[2]

A. The Argument from Redundancy

As far as [R] is concerned, there is some mist around its premises, which make it hard to assess if the argument itself is in good shape. Some misunderstandings and misconceptions pervade its rhetorics. The misunderstandings are fourfold

> a) Suspicion against the monolithic picture of sovereignty is often rooted in an unwarranted equation of state authority with administrative authority, sometimes even the authority of a specific form of administration or government. From this perspective it is the absolute form of administrative authority, rather than sovereignty itself, that is the true target of the claim to redundancy. That an administration can exercise power over but without its citizens was not even believed during the high days of absolutism, when the 'parlemens' were as necessary as 'le sécret du roi'.[3]

---

[2] Note that these problems are far from academic: they are at the heart of politico-legal life, both national and international. Indeed, they become visible as soon as such life is exposed to conflict. Remember the two matters of principle involved in the so-called Kosovo debate concerning NATO's armed strike against Yugoslavia, which developed in the course of 1999–2000. In a slightly generalised form, the questions were: (i) If the official legal policy of a national state S becomes repressive towards large parts of the population to the point where S violates human rights, should the international community try to persuade the regime of S to change its policy, respecting S's sovereignty, i.e. its supreme power to enact and enforce what it claims to be law? Or should it intervene and coerce the regime of S to comply with international standards of law? (ii) If the international community does intervene to enforce compliance with international legal standards in S, though it may be in violation of internationally accepted rules that empower it to take such action, can it still claim to act on the basis of international law? Issues (i) and (ii) neatly reflect [R] and [I]. Issue (i), by its alternative format, demonstrates the received view that, having reached 'the end of history', i.e. universally acknowledged legal principles, we do not need the concept of sovereignty anymore. It cannot shield a state from intervention when gross violations of these principles are at issue, and it does not designate the instances that are to uphold them. Issue (ii) strongly suggests that there is some form of circularity hiding in the concept of sovereignty itself, regardless of whether it is applied on a national or a supranational level. The question is whether it takes legal rules to empower an agent (NATO) to act as an official, or a powerful agent (NATO) to really set and uphold some rules as legal in the first place? To the extent that the answer is uncertain, we must not be over-confident that, with the end of history, sovereignty has become an obsolete notion.

[3] See Machiavelli, *The Prince*, IX The Constitutional Principality, a.f.: 'I shall only conclude that it is necessary for a prince to have the friendship of the people; otherwise he has no remedy in times of adversity.' *Cf.* A Lebigre, *La justice du roi. La vie judiciaire dans l'ancienne France* (Paris, Albin Michel, 1988), p. 48ff; J Goldsworthy, *The Sovereignty of Parliament. History and Philosophy* (Oxford, Clarendon Press, 1999). p. 22ff.

b) Equally unwarranted, though widespread, is the belief that the nation state is the paradigm of states. Over the centuries, the state has been many things, from a tiny *polis* to a vast empire. If one were to give a general parameter for this variable, one could say that in western political thought, the concept of state has stood for that organisation of society that was believed to make a legal order stable in political space and sustainable over political time.[4] Since the beginnings of the 19th century, with the reshaping of Europe during the Restoration, there has been this specific belief that a people's collective awareness regarding its origin and destiny through history could be manipulated and applied as the basis for a balance of power between equally sovereign political entities called nation states. It can readily be admitted that the value of this variable 'state', replicated as it may be by separatist movements to this day, is rapidly falling outside the scope of its parameters. At present, the network of national states is much more a 'state' than the states it connects. But then it may also be much more sovereign, which is exactly what the European Community[5] is with regard to its member states.

c) I also want to set aside the idea that an account of law in terms of sovereignty amounts to a 'gunman theory' of law (Hart). It is almost trivial to stress that the only thing sovereignty asks us to grant is that law is, ultimately and in a variety of ways, prescriptive or normative. All the rest pretty much follows from this. If the synonym 'imperative' is sometimes used in this connection, we should take it in its logical sense (i.e. as a mode of practical thought), not in its socio-psychological sense (i.e. not as a kind of action). Logically, commands as well as advice, requests and exhortations are 'imperatives', expressing 'what is to be done' by someone.

d) Finally, let us put in perspective the somewhat surprising view that sovereignty has become redundant because now for the first time in history people have become subjects of different, intersecting legal orders. In fact there were hardly any long periods of time in European legal history that people were not at the crossroads of intersecting legal orders.[6] Historically, the rise of the notion of sovereignty can be explained to a large extent by the conflicts caused by people either profiting or suffering from this very situation.

There are also some serious misconceptions, of which I mention three.

a) The first is that the idea of sovereignty entails law being the arbitrary exercise of power by some body (king or assembly), whereas the modern legal order is based on the validity of some basic rules constraining the use of power. However,

---

[4] I refrain from elaborating on the exact implications of the spatio-temporal metaphor. Suffice it to say that its core issues are: maintaining a society as a distinct entity in its political environment and its political history.

[5] I still hesitate to write 'the Union' in this context.

[6] One should perhaps keep in mind what 'LLM' stands for, or why German students read 'iura' rather than 'ius'. After the decline of canonical, or rather papal, law, the problem of too many legal orders intersecting in every individual's sphere of rights and obligations was a major factor in the call for legal reform, for instance in post-revolutionary France (*cf.* Portalis's *Discours préliminaire*) and in counter-revolutionary Germany (Von Savigny's *Berufschrift*).

quite apart from the historico-conceptual error lurking in the background,[7] and quite apart from the importance of the rule of law, this form of 'constitutional-ism' (or 'rule sovereignty') tends to forget that even the rule of law has to be set, executed, applied and enforced in order for it to be a rule of law. This rule, or rather these rules, are not self-executing. Indeed, they are not even self-evident, unless they are formulated on such a high level of abstraction that nobody cares too much about their consequences. Although the ongoing debate on the content of law is important, the very point and purpose of law is not an issue for ongo-ing debate in the same way as is true of philosophy or science. The pursuit of justice requires some form of *agency* setting the norm for what justice is here and now.

b) The second misconception is that traditional theories of sovereignty, such as Bodin's or Hobbes's, are often taken to express a command theory of law in the quasi-psychological sense of equating law with the power of some individual king issuing his will and ordering 'do's and don'ts' to his subjects. They did not. What these theories really wanted to convey, basically, was that supreme power should be indivisible, not that it should be individual. They were happy to grant as much participation and deliberation as possible, as long as the warrant for the ultimate *unity* of law enactment and law enforcement was not in jeopardy.[8] The classical formula of 'the King in Parliament' expresses neatly what was at stake: for legal authority to be a final word to end conflict, there should be unity among the agents who set the law in the first place.

c) The last misconception is that attributing sovereignty amounts to organising (the threat of) coercion. In a sense it does: at the end of the day, justice is admin-istered by what a legal order acknowledges as legitimate violence. But the use of coercive force as *ultimum remedium* should not be confused with either the best or the normal way to exercise power, let alone to implement law in a society. In fact there is long tradition of writings, much older than constitutional democ-racy, in which it is argued that give-and-take, communication and persuasion, and welfarism as paradigm examples are far more effective than (the threat of) coercion.[9] Sovereignty is a force much closer to the 'productive' and 'normal' ways to arrange life in society than a constant threat of violence could ever become. It purports to convey the legitimate source for the *public* exercise of

---

[7] *Cf.* H Lindahl, 'Sovereignty and Symbolization', in (1997) 28 *Rechtstheorie*, 347–71.

[8] In *De Cive* (1642), a book more revealing of Hobbes's authentic views than the much more self-restrained *Leviathan* (1651), he even comes close to Rousseauist formulations when he says that 'The *People* rules in all Governments, for even in *Monarchies* the *People* Commands'. He remained convinced, however, that individuals only gained a corporate identity by being united under a sovereign, while Rousseau tried to argue that the reciprocity of the social contract itself constituted the sovereign in the first place. *Cf.* Noel Malcolm, 'Hobbes and Spinoza', in *The Cambridge History of Political Thought*, 1450–1700. (Cambridge, Cambridge University Press, 1996 [1991]), p. 541.

[9] A tradition that begins, of course, with Socrates' arguments against Trasymachus and Glauco; includes, for instance, remarkably different authors like Bodin, Machiavelli and Nietzsche; and is very much alive in contemporary writings, Foucault's most of all. See his *Power/Knowledge. Selected Interviews and Other Writings 1972–7*, C Gordon (ed.), (New York, Pantheon Books, 1980).

such productive powers. It thus *represents* the format of the common good in virtue of which such an enterprise as 'politics becomes possible'[10] and it does so in all meanings of 'representation': making present, depicting, showing and substituting.[11]

So is sovereignty a redundant notion? It would be, if it could be argued that law in modern society could do without (1) a norm-setting agency, (2) unity of agency, (3) representation of this unity, all with regard to the rules we regard as being 'legal'. This is a huge burden of proof, discharged by none of the arguments we reviewed. Most of them ground the conclusion of redundancy upon ominous premises that, on closer examination, turn out to be phantoms.

B. The argument from Incoherence

The argument from Incoherence [I] is much harder to deal with. In fact, some versions of [R] regain their punch under [I], as we shall see. A popular and succinct way of bringing out the core of the problem is to say, with Michel Foucault among many others,[12] that the concept of sovereignty expresses the oxymoron of (political) power constituting the law and the law restraining that very (political) power. On the one hand, it grants that the imperator is beyond his imperative (thus, *legibus solutus*) while, on the other, it wants the imperator's power to be legal power or competence. The implication is a real bug; for if X's claim to power is just, merely in virtue of X's power to sort out just claims, then, as far as X is concerned, there is

---

[10] One of the two 'bodies' of the king, as analysed by Kantorowicz, pertained to this ultimate format, while the other had to do with the king as a human individual. See E H Kantorowicz, *The King's Two Bodies: A Study in Mediaeval Political Theology* (Princeton, Princeton University Press, 1957).

[11] *Cf.* B Waldenfels, *Vielstimmigkeit der Rede. Studien zur Phänomenologie des Fremden*, 4. (Frankfurt a. M., Suhrkamp, 1999), p. 119.

[12] *Cf.* C Schmitt, *Politische Theologie. Vier Kapitel zur Lehre von der Souveränität*. 2. Ausg., 7. Aufl., (Berlin, Duncker & Humblot, 1996 [1934]), p. 13*f*; M Foucault, *Power/Knowledge*, in particular his 'Two Lectures'; G Agamben, *Homo Sacer. Sovereign Power and Bare Life*, (Stanford, Stanford University Press, 1998), ch. 1: 'The Paradox of Sovereignty'. In a very different tradition of thinking: P Scholten, 'Soevereiniteit' in *Verzamelde Geschriften*, I, 2. (Zwolle, Tjeenk Willink, 1949), (Scholten's Harvard Lecture in 1946), p. 506: 'Het recht schijnt in de macht op te gaan, doch tegelijkertijd is het het recht, dat bepaalt, hoe de Staat tot zijn regels komt (. . .).' In a different tradition again, recently Jules Coleman, acknowledging a fundamental problem in the Hartian rule of recognition (to which he claims to have 'a clear and decisive response'): 'The rule of recognition, we are told, exists only when officials act in a certain way; but whether or not individuals are officials in the relevant sense seems to depend on the existence of a rule of recognition. After all, people are officials in virtue of the laws that create officials.' *The Practice of Principle. In Defence of a Pragmatist Approach to Legal Theory*, (Oxford, Oxford University Press, 2001), p. 100–1.

no distinction between just and unjust claims to power. Indeed, the ideas of law and power become indistinguishable.

Three lines of argument attempt to escape from this predicament. The first is the self-subjection fallacy, which starts out from the dualism between facts and norms. The facts relevant here are the phenomena of power in a given society, power being defined (for instance with Max Weber[13]) as the chance to pursue one's will against the will of others, regardless of the ground on which this opportunity may rest. It may rest on brute force, tradition, money, arguments, or other things. Let us treat these as parameters of domination, i.e. of the chance to find persons ready to obey certain directives. Suppose now that some dominant agent purports to pursue his will by establishing *law*. Then, if he comprehends what he is doing, i.e. if he is familiar with the concept of law, he will also intend immediately to subject himself to the rule of law as soon as he himself has enacted a law. For, a priori, the concept of law entails the idea of power restrained by law. He will consequently comply with what he has established himself.[14] No doubt this line of thought is descriptively close to what goes on in socio-political life: law 'arises' from facts of domination being somehow acknowledged in a society. As a conceptual argument, however, it seems to fail. It presupposes that one can define 'rule of law' independently of sovereignty, and it conceives of the rule of law as a set of demands 'given' by our sense of justice. But this was what called out for proof in the first place. Our question was precisely whether or not the concept of law could be understood without the notion of sovereignty as norm-setting agency. So [I] survives. Yet, a possibly weak spot has become visible. What if the puzzle were not to be construed between the concepts of a power enacting law and a power being restrained by the very law it is supposed to enact, but between the act of making something and the concept of what is made? It requires a poet to make poetry, but only one who makes poetry is a poet. It is not that this puzzle is without problems, but at least it looks more like a paradox than like a conceptual bug. The second half of this chapter attempts to solve it.

The second possible means of escape comes from social contract theory, which begins by denying the cleft between facts and norms. The theory, which is in fact the principle of reciprocity writ large, dismantles the problem by stating that this principle requires us to acknowledge that power ultimately resides in 'all those involved'. We may call this 'the people', but

---

[13] *Wirtschaft und Gesellschaft*. Studienausg. in 2 Bdn., (Köln–Berlin, Kiepenheuer & Witsch, 1964 [1921]), Bd. 1, p. 38.
[14] This is more or less Jellinek's argument in his 'Zwei Seiten Lehre' of the state, with doubtful references to Kant's views on the autonomous self-subjection of the person to the moral law. For a both vehement and incisive critique of Jellinek's argument, see H Kelsen, *Hauptprobleme der Staatsrechtslehre*. 2. Neudr. der 2., verm. Aufl., (Aalen, Scientia Verlag, 1984 [1923]), kap. XIV.

only in a purely indexical sense, as it were. This all-inclusive people should be seen as 'the sovereign', in which case the power that enacts law is indeed identical with the law that restrains power. The rulers are identical to the ruled. This is, in principle, a promising line of thought to pursue and I will come back to it in the next section. But there is one problem that, at this stage of the argument, makes it beg our question. It is a general problem of contract theory, in all of its guises like Game Theory, Law & Economics, *Diskurs* Theory, etc.: Who are to be parties to the social contract cannot be decided in terms of the social contract. Who is to play the game, who will be recognised in debate, which interests are acknowledged such that their subjects will be involved—these are all questions that must be considered as 'asked and answered' before the contract can be made. They cannot be decided in a higher order contract without infinite regress. They cannot be decided by a pre-established rule without the *petitio principii* criticised under the fallacy of self-subjection. They cannot be decided on other grounds without admitting that the decision is arbitrary, since the contract was supposed to solve the problem of arbitrary power disguised as law in the first place. Nevertheless, 'the people' seems to refer to an already unified entity before the unification in terms of reciprocity has taken place. For the second time we are back with [I]. But also for the second time, the incoherence seems to have been tempered by the heat of a paradox: that between the concept of something and the concept of the framing identification of that very something. The frame is neither the painting nor some other 'thing' in the world different from the painting; but without framing there is no painting.[15]

A third way out is promised by the well-known distinction between internal and external sovereignty. It argues that the chicken-and-egg agony between political power enacting law and law restraining this very power only arises from a simple confusion between the two distinct ideas of sovereignty: final authority within a system of law and final autonomy with respect to other systems of law.[16] Alas, although this distinction is useful for the practical purposes of law, it underestimates the theoretical pertinence of

---

[15] J Derrida, 'Il y a du cadre, mais le cadre n'existe pas', *La vérité en peinture* (Paris, Flammarion, 1978), p. 93.

[16] This line of argument is all the more attractive as it promises a new future for [R]. First, we conceptually disentangle [I] by making a distinction between: (a) the autonomy of a legal order to make its own laws, independent of other legal orders (external sovereignty or factual power that enacts law); and (b) the authority structure of a legal order, the hierarchy of which enables it to decide, with final discretion, cases of conflict brought to it (internal sovereignty or the power restrained by law). The conceptual puzzle solved, we now can append an argument to the effect that sovereignty is definitively out of fashion. Cast in the mould of classical syllogism, it goes like this: (1) If a legal order is dependent on sovereignty, then it is (externally) independent and (internally) hierarchical. (2) Legal orders, at present, are in fact neither (externally) independent nor (internally) hierarchical. (3) Therefore, it makes no sense anymore to say that a legal order is dependent on sovereignty.

[I]. It does not ask from which point of view the distinction between external and internal sovereignty is made. Surely the two terms both flow from the idea of sovereignty being 'supreme power'. And what do we mean by that? We cannot possibly mean 'strongest power'. Strongest power is a matter of fact, to be established by empirical observation of the results of competition, conflict or war. No norms follow from these results which could oblige either the participants or the observers. What we do mean, however, is a power that is 'highest' in the normative sense: no power is higher in norm-establishing authority, neither inside nor outside the legal order. But this, of course, already presupposes the pertinence of an internal point of view: it is from within a legal order that this power is deemed to be 'highest'. Only from 'within' a legal order, i.e. in so far as we represent ourselves as part of that unity committed to norm enactment and norm compliance, can we actually *mean* something by saying that a certain power is 'supreme', in that it is both autonomous with regard to the outward world and authoritative with regard to the inward world. Far from defusing [I], the distinction between external and internal sovereignty reconfirms that sovereignty is situated always at both sides of the boundary between the legal and the non-legal 'from within' the legal. There is a preference in the difference here, as Waldenfels puts it.[17] This takes us right back to the conceptual puzzle that was behind the argument of Incoherence. But again, the puzzle is sized down to a paradox: self-representation never seems to capture the self that is representing itself.

In sum, discussing the arguments against [I] brings back the very same problems that seemed to be ignored by the arguments in support of [R]: the problems of law requiring norm-setting agency, unity of this agency and representation of this unity. But it also moderated these problems as deriving not from one big conceptual bug, but from some intriguing paradoxes that should be straightened out. With regard to agency the paradox is between the quality of the maker and the quality of what is made; with regard to unity, the paradox is between the frame of this unity of agency and the substance of it; with regard to representation, the paradox is between the representation of this unity and the self-representation of it. If these are not paradoxes of sovereignty, they are surely paradoxes of law.

3. AN ALTERNATIVE ACCOUNT

I think we can solve these paradoxes if we can show that they arise from mixing up distinct pragmatic functions in the speech act that is involved in 'setting the law'. Their nucleus can be found in Rousseau's idea of 'popular

---

[17] B Waldenfels, *Antwortregister*, (Frankfurt a.M., Suhrkamp, 1994), p. 223.

sovereignty', and the concept of law derived from it. I will gradually unfold the implications of his deceivingly simple formula and store these in an analytical scheme [LEX], which perspicuously caters to all the pragmatic functions involved.[18] I will have to insert some philosophy of language to underpin these functions.

(a) Identity, sameness and reflexivity

Recall that, in the *Social Contract* (II, 6), Rousseau gives what could be called a rule of recognition for law in modernity: a law is law only 'if the whole people rules ("statute") over the whole people'. This phrase is usually read in terms of the identity thesis [ID]. Roughly put, [ID] states that law can only be law if 'rulers' and 'ruled' are co-referential terms. They are the same bunch of people, who are supposed to rule what they want, and to do what they ruled. As they will not go against their own basic interests or values, democracy and the rule of law become one and the same idea.[19] In a slightly more sophisticated version [ID] would amount to:

> [ID] Both the normativity and the validity of law lie with its subjects being identical to its legislators.

Once Rousseau's definition is read along the lines of [ID], it becomes rather ethereal. In one fell swoop it turns both rule of law and democracy into a romantic dream of universal participation. On the rebound, one feels compelled to state the obvious: that universal participation cannot be realised in complex societies like ours; that we have to retreat to second best solutions (representation); that we must always be keen to switch to participation wherever we can afford to do so.[20]

But [ID] is not the only reading possible for Rousseau's phrase; a second, and much neglected, reading is as feasible as the first one. When, in lawmaking, the whole people rules over the whole people, this amounts to the whole people ruling on *itself*. Let us call this the Reflexivity Thesis [RF]:

> [RF] Both the normativity and the validity of law lie with its legislators ruling over themselves.

---

[18] Strictly speaking, Rousseau refers to 'a law', i.e. *a* rule of law. But this quasi-juristic parlance should be understood from a philosophical point of view as amounting to *the* rule of law, i.e. the law of laws.

[19] As Rousseau himself is quick to point out, albeit in his own vocabulary.

[20] The experience with the subsidiarity principle in the EU context reveals that the decision whether lower level participation is possible in a given case, necessarily involves the highest level of authority, in which prior decision (lower-level) participation is impossible. Though not unimportant in practice, I think this principle is theoretical humbug.

What difference does [RF] make? From a brief look[21] we may learn that there is a considerable logical gulf between the coreferential reading [1] and the reflexive reading [2]:

[1] The people P rules that φ with regard to the people P.
[2] The people P rules that φ with regard to itself*.

Let us assume that [1] and [2] are both utterances by a speaker S (say: a law professor) in front of an audience H (say: her class), and that the term 'rules that φ' here stands for a practical cognitive attitude, equivalent to 'endorses φ'.[22] Then [2] may be true about the people P, although P does not know or believe *that it is P*. Imagine P being S's name for a tribe that has never been in touch with other people, who think that they are the whole of mankind and therefore only refer to themselves as 'we'. Or they may simply have a name for themselves different from the one S uses. Being the speaker of [2], S leaves all of that out. All she expresses in [2] is that P has some idea of itself as a first person and that it refers to itself accordingly. Thus, the expression 'itself*' in [2] does not refer to the world as S sees it, but for S's attributing self-knowledge to P. Such expressions are called 'quasi-indicators', and I will use asterisks to signal them throughout the remainder of this chapter.[23] On the other hand, [1] may be true although P does not rule that φ with regard to *itself*. It may rule that φ regardless of whom it may concern. For instance, it may occur to S, as the speaker of [1], that the effects of P's policy are disastrous for *the same*, i.e. for P. Then [1] can be true or false, but not in the sense of [2]. In other words: identity is two things: sameness and selfhood, similarity and reflexivity.[24] Now my hypothesis is that the riddle of sovereignty could be solved if we understood the relationship between [ID] and [RF]. That is to say: if we could give an account, not only of who is in charge of the politico-legal order at the end

---

[21] To be sure: a brief philosophical look. In what follows I cover some ground that is pretty familiar to most philosophers, but completely foreign to most lawyers.

[22] I subscribe here to Castañeda's view as explained by Bratman: 'Believing and intending are not different types of propositional attitudes but, rather, the same type of attitude—namely, full endorsement—directed at different types of noemata: in the one case propositions, in the other case intentions.' See M Bratman, 'Castañeda's theory of thought and action', in J Tomberlin (ed.), *Agent, Language and the Structure of the World. Essays presented to H-N Castañeda, with his replies*, (Indianapolis, Hackett Publishing Company, 1983), p. 149.

[23] Ie they only refer to the antecedent 'We' in the direct clause, and do not refer to the outside world on their own account, as indicators (I, here, now, this) do. I am in fact applying H-N Castañeda's seminal papers on (quasi-) indexicality, transposing them from the philosophy of mind to political philosophy. The easiest access now available to his views is via some chapters in H-N Castañeda, *Thinking, Language and Experience*, (Minneapolis, University of Minnesota Press, 1989). From there one can follow the references to the early papers, dating from 1966. The posthumously published *Intentionality, Modality and Supervenience*, edited by M van den Hoven and GJ Lokhorst, (Rotterdam, Faculteit Wijsbegeerte, 1990), includes a chapter on 'Indexical Reference and Causal Diagrams in Intentional Action'.

[24] *Cf.* P Ricoeur, *Soi-même comme un autre* (Paris, Du Seuil, 1990), p. 12, where the Latin distinction is mentioned between *idem* and *ipse*.

of the day, but also of how there can be a reflexive relationship of this order to itself, despite the plurality of its representatives all Schmittian talk about 'unity', 'exception', 'limit' and 'exclusion' begins to make a lot more sense, if we consider it as an account of a reflexive relationship of a polity to itself that is inherent to any polity how ever organised, rather than of some specific, and of course highly suspect, organisation of the polity. We may even appreciate why, far from withering away, the problem of sovereignty emerges again and again in our discussions of democracy, where the relationship of 'the many' to 'the polity' is virtually challenged with every vote on the 'common' good. Let us try to flesh out what the hypothesis means, realising that its corroboration would require a long-term research programme.

The whole drift of a reflexive reading is, as said, the attribution of first person references to the agent of the main clause, P. This is the only sense in which S can 'enter' the content of the dependent that-clause. In all other respects, this clause is what philosophy of language calls an intensional or opaque context: S is either not in control of what P (endorsingly) thinks in ruling that φ, or she is not in control of what P refers to in ruling that φ. Phrase [1] on the other hand presents a transparent context: given that 'the people P' is a referential device used by S in her main clause, the second token of 'the people P' is equally hers, not P's. This device is not within the scope of the operator 'rules'. But S can only use it at the cost of losing what she can express in [2]: ascription of first person self-reference by P. This is far from indifferent from S's point of view, as two implications are to be derived from it. Firstly, by framing [2], S acknowledges that P is involved in intentional action and in the specific kind of commitment that goes with it. Secondly, by the same token, S acknowledges that P is, from its own perspective, some sort of unity. For the idea of unity is part and parcel of referring to oneself. Unity is, as it were, the format of the internal accusative of self-reference. There is, necessarily, only *one* self in oneself.[25] Where there is no unity to refer to, there is no self to refer to. In psychopathology, the multiple-self syndrome is precisely a pathological type of case, because the patient is involved in references to multiple selves that cannot be united. He or she recognises all of these selves, without being able to combine them into a unity as 'his' or 'hers'. This is quite different from recognising different 'aspects' of oneself. In political contexts, though the pathology (civil war) is perhaps only remotely analogous,[26] we have the same mechanism as far as self-reference is concerned: the reference postulates such unity that we can call a political self. Note that this unity is not primarily a function of

---

[25] I am aware that R.A. Posner takes the opposite view in 'Are We One Self or Multiple Selves?' in (1997) 3, *Legal Theory*, p. 23–35, but cannot argue against him within the framework of this paper. But what both of us do agree on, is that, one way or another, *authority* is involved in the reflexive relationship. See his p. 23.

[26] Note that Hobbes's notion 'warre' refers to *civil* war, i.e. a war on the self of a polity.

awareness. If that would be the case, the analogy between the self of a human individual and the self of a social group would break down immediately. The unity is a function of (self-)reference; and we will see below that such references can be made by different agents belonging (in some sense to be specified) to the group. It would also be false to conceive of the unity as some entity existing apart from the agents referring to it.

These two implications, I submit, are exactly what Rousseau must have had in mind. Not a coreferential reading, but only a reflexive reading of his definition underpins the idea of freedom under the law that—at least at this stage of his argument—he is carving out. Firstly, by conceiving of legislation as a first person commitment in the format of an intention, he can get rid of the idea of law being a prescription (whether command, advice or request) by someone other than the people.[27] Obeying law is a matter of doing what you, yourself, intended to do. That is why you remain free in complying with the law. Secondly, Rousseau acknowledges the role of unity as inherent to (the ascription of) self-reference. That is why, in his definition, he emphatically talks about 'the whole people', i.e. the people as a whole, a unity.[28] Contrary to what [ID] wants us to believe, his concern is not with numerical identity of rulers and ruled.[29] It is with the possibility of a people relating, for the sake of legislation, to the political self they claim to belong to as a whole. Only if there is this relationship can politics be situated in a public realm; only then can politicians and citizens use and understand notions like 'the public interest', 'the common good', 'national security', etc. Thus, rather than [ID], Rousseau asks us to accept what one may call the Reflexive Polity Thesis [RP]:

[RP]Legislation presupposes legislators to represent their polity as a set of agents with diverging interests that is for *itself* a distinct unity in action.

(b) Representations

If we now transform [2] into an expression, rather than an ascription, of a first person plural intention of P, we get a scheme like [INT$_L$]

[27] I skip the arguments against the view that intentions are reducible to prescriptions to oneself. See H-N Castañeda, *Thinking and doing, the philosophical foundations of institutions*, (Dordrecht-Boston, Reidel, 1975), ch. 6.

[28] This equation follows, I believe, from his definition of the sovereign and of the state in I, 7, as well as from II, 2, where it is argued that the sovereign is 'indivisible', as well as from various passages from which it is clear that the sovereign people is not just an aggregation of individuals.

[29] This type of identity is quickly ruled out in *The Social Contract*, Book III, where the government is introduced, in particular the chapter on 'democracy': identity of rulers and ruled will not work, Rousseau says, unless perhaps (he grants) in unrealistically small and simple communities. Note, however, that the argument is one of principle: democracy without representation would entail that everyone would have the right to rule on everyone's business, the result being a perfect mess.

[INT$_L$]   We intend/rule that we* (ourselves) φ with regard to ourselves*,

in which, again, the asterisk indicates that these referential devices are not used as indicators but as quasi-indicators, attributing first person reference. The speaker S of an utterance of the form [INT$_L$] is no longer this third person (the law professor) but someone within the group constituting the first person (for instance, a Member of Parliament). Her audience H is an unde-termined crowd of people who may or may not conceive of themselves as within the same group, depending on how S frames the use of the first person plural device. Let us now turn to the complications that enter this picture.

i) The first person plural

If legislation is guided by an intention, it should again be stressed that it is an intention in the plural we are talking about: law is a not a first person commitment, but a first person *plural* commitment. It is what we may call—with Bratman, for instance—a shared intention. It will readily be granted that an intention is not shared by virtue of the sole fact that more than one agent is involved in doing the same thing. To quote Bratman's simplest of examples: if you and I both have the intention of painting your house we do not have, yet, the shared intention to paint your house; and the same goes for you and I both being in the process of intentionally painting your house. We may not know that the other is doing the same, we may not care what the other is doing, as long as we can go on doing what we intend to do, or we may even be involved in mad competition, thwarting each other where we can. We only have a shared intention if and when we somehow fill in the unity of the 'we' that is the formal internal accusative of our self-reference. What fills in the unity, its epiphenomena so to speak, will be the kind of features Bratman analyses as characteristic of shared intentions: mutual responsiveness, commitment to a joint activity, commitment to mutual support in the process of the joint activity, the activity in legislative cases an instance of φ.[30] Whether the agent to whom self-reference is ascribed is 'in fact' a unity or not in the eyes of some third person (the speaker of [2], for instance) is entirely irrelevant. All that matters is that the agents involved in shared intentional action give shape to the unity they refer to in thinking, expressing and, indeed, living their intentions. Least of all would a shared intention imply '(. . .) an attitude in the mind of some superagent consisting literally of some fusion of two [or more; BvR] agents. There is no single mind that is the fusion of your mind and my mind.'[31]

---

[30] Bratman, above note 22, p p. 94–5. The whole of the paper is a finely grained and elegant argument for these three characteristics.
[31] ME Bratman, *Faces of Intention. Selected Essays on Intention and Agency*, (Cambridge, Cambridge University Press, 1999), p. 111.

ii) Actor and author

The speaker expressing an intention of the form [INT$_L$] is not identical with the 'we' that is the expressed subject of the intention.[32] The 'we' expressed as the subject of the intention is not, in fact, the agent who utters the intention, but the agent to whom the intention is ascribed by the speaker. As Waldenfels put it,

> 'The "we" that turns up within the content [of the utterance] is not identical to the performative "we" of the act [of uttering]. (. . .) Thus it is impossible for a we to say "we". (. . .) Saying "we" is done, rather, by someone who participates, directly or indirectly, in the act of constitutional legislation. A political group finds its voice only in spokesmen, who speak in its name and represent it *as a whole*.'[33]

It seems convenient to use different subscripts to denote these two instances of 'we' (the speaker-agent and the subject-agent). There are good reasons to pick abbreviations of the Hobbesian terms 'actor' and 'author' as they succinctly capture the relation of representation and authorisation that is at stake here. Thus we will distinguish between We$_{AC}$ and We$_{AU}$. The speaker-agent We$_{AC}$ will have to represent the subject-agent We$_{AU}$ in a double sense: she will pose as substituting the subject's authority, but in order to do so she will also have to picture this subject by identifying references, which again she can only do on the basis of her authority.[34] For example, if some gathering of people issues the declaration 'We the People of the United States (. . .) do ordain and establish this constitution for the United States of America', there is a double bind. The speaker We$_{AC}$ has to point out, before the audience H of her speech act, on whose behalf she is talking; and she will do so by making, either on her own account or on request, identifying references to the author of her authority We$_{AU}$. Only then she will be successful in posing as a substitute. Individuals in H will be judges of such success, provided that they derive their criteria from their vision of We$_{AU}$ and not from elsewhere. But in order to make these references, We$_{AC}$ must already begin by posing as a substitute for We$_{AU}$. Is this the conceptual paradox of sovereignty all over again? No, it is not; or if it is, it is now disguised as a quite normal feature of some human action. I can only walk a path if it is made, but I can only make it if I walk it. Inversely, I can only make the path if I take into account how it can be walked again and again; and walking it again and again will be the way in which the path is made over time. Now think of path making as a metonymy of arriving at institu-

---

[32] This is another problem Rousseau was very well aware of. For immediately after his famous definition of the law he goes on to ask—in a tone of despair, to be sure: 'How shall the people speak with one voice?'
[33] Above note 11. My translation [BvR]; italics in the original.
[34] *Cf.* Th Hobbes, *Leviathan* [1651], ch. 16.

tional action in general. With regard to authority, an actor can only represent an author if she is authorised, but she can only be authorised by representing the author (who, by definition, never speaks). She will only be successful if she takes into account how others (her audience) will be able to identify her author, as only these identifications will eventually uphold the authority she is representing. Which is not to deny that, in both cases (walking a path and mobilising an institution), *doing it for the first time* does bring some difficulties of its own. But constituent power is not only doing something for the first time; it is also making last what is brought about. In the case of law it is 'a plebiscite of every day', as Renan said about the nation.

A peculiar feature arises from this double bind: it is not at all necessary that the speaker be a group of individuals, she may be an individual speaking in the first person plural form, as long as she successfully represents the subject-author in the double sense of picturing and replacing. Outside the context of legislation we often see speakers quickly step from one representation to another within the range of a single sentence. For instance, the Prime Minister may say at his press conference:

> We$_1$ cannot discuss this issue right now here any further, but we$_2$ will send a proposal to Parliament one week from now, we$_3$ will discuss it amply within the next two months to take a decision; and then we$_4$ can have a more adequate exchange about it here.

The PM as an individual establishes four different relations by his use of 'we': he and the journalists present at the press conference, he and his government, his government in parliament, and he and some other bunch of journalists, or perhaps even the public at large, at a later date. For note that the audience of a speech act is not the people actually present and hearing it. It is the people listening to it (enemies included). Similarly in legislative speech acts, the speaker may use various ways of 'securing uptake' by her audience in the course of one and the same act.

One more complication to go. In [INT$_L$] the first person plural appears outside and inside the scope of the intentional attitude operator, as we saw. Outside the scope of the operator it appears at two positions: We$_{AC}$ and We$_{AU}$. They signal, respectively, the first person plural as the speaker of the utterance, and the first person plural as the subject of the intention uttered (who is the referent of the utterance). But inside this scope it appears at two positions as well. First as the self who is the agent of the intended action φ and, thus, the medial object for the subject of the intention. Typically, in intentions one pictures oneself doing something. Thus the 'self' is what one thinks about as acting and what is about to act. It is this position that first person references are supposed to refer to and reflexive unity is imposed on. Then, finally, the first person plural also appears towards the very end of the scheme, where 'ourselves' refers to 'we' in the mode of the object that is to profit from 'our' ruling φ and doing φ, i.e. the 'we' in whose interest ruling and doing φ is supposed to be. Now, interests are ambivalent relationships of a person to the world around her. In the sense of 'preferences', they are entirely subjective; in the sense of 'stakes', they are very much dependent on objective states of affairs.[35] For instance, I may believe that I have an overriding interest, thirsty as I am, in drinking this water in front of me, but what if it is poisoned? Or I may believe that I have a keen interest in getting a Juilliard scholarship, but do I really if I cannot tell minor from major? Interests, therefore, are of particular importance in bridging the gap between the opaque world in which everything is governed by We_{AU} and the transparent world that is common between the speaker We_{AC} and the audience of the speech act H. For the speech act to be successful the speaker has to pose as representing We_{AU} *before H's account of it in terms of H's interests.* As every politician knows: you can considerably enhance the chances of your claim to authority being found valid if you talk about 'we' in terms of the interests of your audience. But you can only do that by walking a fine line between leaving these interests entirely to them and showing them in the light of objective states of affairs beyond their unreflected preferences.[36] Your audience should come to believe that you see their interests in a better light than they themselves see them, and that, yet, they remain the judges of what light is better. Or, slightly cynical perhaps: an overriding interest of your audience is a better account of their interests.

Our scheme caters for this, too. To see how, let us go back, for just a moment, to the third person perspective on $[INT_L]$, which was [2]. A slightly extended version [2a] will clarify the point:

[2a] The people P rules that it(self)* does φ with regard to the best of its own* interests,

with the asterisks throughout signalling quasi-indicators within the scope of P's intention. In [2a], the phrase 'with regard to its own* interests' renders more perspicuously what is expressed in [2] by 'with regard to itself*'. Surely the quasi-indexical 'own*' is on a par with the quasi-indicator 'itself*'? These tokens do not have, necessarily, an indexical force of their own: rather, they take part in attributing first person reference to the people P. In this role they are within the opaque context created by the intentional operator 'rules that'. So the expression 'to the best of its interests' is a device that is within P's scope and not within the speaker's scope. It is used *de dicto* and not *de re*, to mention a closely related distinction. But one can also take the expression 'with regard to the best of its own

---

[35] Cf. J Feinberg, *The Moral limits of the Criminal Law, I, Harm to Others*, (New York, Oxford, OUP, 1984), p. 33–4.

[36] Cf. Raz's 'normal justification' thesis of authority, in *The Morality of Freedom*, (Oxford, Clarendon Press, 1986), p. 53.

interests' out of the scope of the intentional operator and apply a transparent *de re* reading by letting the speaker of [2a] reign over the relation between the people P and its interests, as in [2b]:

[2b] With regard to its own interests, the people P rules that it(self)* does φ. Now the expression 'with regard to its own interests' has dropped its quasi-indexical role and means nothing more or less that 'with regard to the interests of the people P'. Which means that now the speaker S makes reference to the interests of P on his own account of the matter, accessible also by his audience. For instance, he could add some form of innuendo like 'With regard to their own interests, these dummies of P . . .' Her hearers H may apply a similar transparent reading, and it may or may not tie in with S's. But the general point behind it is that S as well as H can switch between two registers in referring to the interests of P: taking his cue either from a framework common to him and his audience, or from the agency to whom he ascribes first person references. Little of this has to emerge to the surface of the language used: most of if it passes as possible readings to be negotiated and fine-tuned by S and H.

Likewise, the speaker involved in uttering some legislative speech act of the first person form [INT$_L$] can speak in different registers. She can take 'us' inside or outside the scope of the intentional operator and be heard as doing so—or not. In order to make the representational part of her speech act successful, We$_{AC}$ will have to tune her identifying references to the devices of her hearers. A number of observations obtain in such a case. Firstly, these are *de re* devices, as the hearers are outside the scope of the intentional operator as she herself is. Secondly, they will often be related to the way in which these hearers see their interests related to themselves as included in We$_{AU}$ or as related to the *de re* world they share with We$_{AC}$. Thirdly, We$_{AC}$ will also have to take her cue from hearers' references to their interests in order to fill in the unity of the first person plural self that she has to impose on them in order successfully to represent We$_{AU}$.

Let us now wrap up all these different appearances of the first person plural in one analytical scheme [LEX], which purports to lay out the full dimensions of Rousseau's concept of popular sovereignty. As [LEX] embraces 'the full speech act in the full speech act situation' from a theoretical point of view, I will have to add a notation for the speaker S and the audience H, whoever they may be.

[LEX]   We$_{AC}$ [We$_{AU}$ rule that We*$_{AU}$ φ with regard to Ourselves*$_{AC/AU}$] H

The slash in the subscript of (admittedly artificial) 'Ourselves' indicates the switch between the two registers, bringing the device into or out of the scope of the intentional operator. This distinction is exactly parallel to the one between Actor and Author, as two appearances of the first person plural in any legislative speech act based on popular sovereignty.

4. SOME CONCLUSIONS AND PROSPECTS

Towards the end of section three, the argument from Incoherence [I] had turned into three paradoxes of a legal order, which sovereignty was supposed to solve. The advocates of redundancy [R] would have us believe that we could do without sovereignty, but their pledge left us with the predicament of these paradoxes. We are now able to see how the structure of popular sovereignty, as accounted for by [LEX], offers a way out.

1) [LEX] maps out the difference between the first person plural as the agent setting the law and as the agent said to set the law. Their interdependence (representation as depiction and representation as substitution) is the solution to the paradox between the lawmaker who makes the law and the law who makes the lawmaker.

2) [LEX] accounts for the unity of the agent setting the law by seeing this unity as the attribute of the self reflexively involved in lawmaking as a first person commitment. The 'frame' of this unified agency as a format of shared intentions can be distinguished from its substance of mutual support in joint action.

3) [LEX] acknowledges the difference between the representation of this self as a unity and the plurality of identifying references made by different speaker-agents in their joint action, taking their cues from different interests in the audiences they are addressing in their speech acts.

Let me now try to tie [LEX] in with some of the positions on sovereignty issues taken in this volume, particularly in the context of EU law. First, in what sense is sovereignty in transition from a monist to a pluralist conception? My answer is that we have come to see, indeed to appreciate, the incongruity between the speaker-agent (the actor) and the subject-agent (author) of a legal order. The speaker-agents may be plural as long as they attribute singular unity to the subject-agent. Or, to use Bratman's vocabulary, actors may be involved in shared intentional activity, as long as they mesh subplans and are committed to mutual response and support in doing so, notwithstanding their distinct reasons and strategies. Thus, there may be radically different accounts of this unity, while the attribution of unity to the subject-agent as such is not contested. What does this mean in actual practice? It means that these actors will try to convince their audiences of their respective accounts, but not at the cost of using force or leaving the polity in case they fail. As long as they can make a distinction between opting out and walking away, the unity of the subject-agent retains a prima facie credibility. But they cannot make that distinction at will or make it a matter of unqualified negotiation without giving up their claims to representation: some forms of opting out will be regarded as walking away. The fact that some member states of the EU opted out with regard to the social or the monetary parts of the Treaty was a major contestation of what the European legal order was about in the eyes of the other member states. So were the (much earlier) *Solange* decisions by the German Constitutional

Court, when it was decided that the rulings of the European Court of Justice would only have direct effect in the BRD 'as long as' its performance in protecting human rights would meet the standards set by the German *Grundgesetz* (to be judged by the same German Court, to be sure). As long as these modes of opting out do not meet with a veto from other parties to the Treaty, and as long as a veto from other parties does not lead to going solo and leaving the Treaty, the format of ultimate unity is not simply negated by contestation; rather it is reconfirmed by a form of contestation that does not lead its protagonists to radical practical implications. Radically contesting what would count as the most acceptable account of the unity of the European legal order is, on the level of speech acts, one way of radically confirming that such unity is what counts at the end of the day.

Elsewhere in this volume Maduro explains how in particular the ECJ, over time, could only represent the European legal order as a whole by taking its cue from the various ways in which a large number of actors in the Community articulate its unity from their perspectives and their interests. He refers to this constitutional unity as the 'grammar' of diverging articulations, a term close to what I called above the 'internal accusative' of political self-reference. Thus he pictures European law as a 'discursive' product, preserving the process (of participation via diverging options) in the product that it makes (the underlying unity) and vice versa. And although he rejects hierarchy as the privileged model of unity, he accepts other metaphors like (contrapunctal) harmony to provide a more adequate picture of such unity. Even if it could be objected that counterpoint is based on hierarchy (both of scales and within scales), however playfully laid out, Maduro's point is well-taken: preservation of the precarious legal indeterminacy of the European legal order is contingent upon a specific *mise-en-scène*: to make each and every judicial body, domestic or European, account for its claims and decisions in terms of 'a coherent and integrated' European legal order.

But matters may not be as harmless as this.[37] What—and this is the second issue I pick from a very broad range—if different speaker-agents not only give different accounts of what unites them, but refer and, eventually, retreat to different subject-agents, i.e. authors, thus raising incompatible claims to final authority? Is there such a thing as author-pluralism—or in Neil Walker's terms: constitutional pluralism[38]—over and against actor-pluralism? And if so, does [LEX] account for it? The answer is: in a sense it does, in another sense it does not, which means that we should be suspicious about the latter. Let's take the affirmative answer first. Remember that

---

[37] Once again I am indebted to Neil Walker for pressing our point of discussion harder than I wanted it to be at first.

[38] See Walker's paper elsewhere in this volume; see also his 'The idea of Constitutional Pluralism' (2002) 65 *Modern Law Review* 317.

[LEX] takes the subject-agent of legislative speech acts as a focus of references by (a plurality of) speaker-agents (official bodies like parliaments, governments, member states, courts, politicians, citizens, companies, unions, NGOs, etc.). Such a focus does not have a separate existence as an entity over and against the entities who act as speaker-agents. It is not a transcendent unity that speaks for itself on a higher level of political organisation. As said before: though the speaker-agents derive their authority from 'that which unites them', they are the only ones exercising such authority. No authority speaks but through their mouths. Now the exercise of such authority may become institutionalised in greater or lesser detail (e.g. giving priority to the rulings of parliament over the claims of individual citizens). But suppose that such institutionalisation is not established yet, as is the case, often enough, in periods of politico-legal transition; and suppose that the speaker-agents act under no prior institution of authority. Then [LEX] still suggests two things: (a) that the 'sites' from which these authoritative agents speak are not identical with the 'sites' on which they ground their authority, and (b) that Bratman's reciprocity parameters of shared co-operative activity (to wit: mutual responsiveness and support in commitment to the joint activity) are crucial in determining if they acknowledge the difference between the two sites in their authoritative discourse. These parameters condition and constrain the negotiations between speakers and hearers of legislative acts. Of course, they do not impose a hierarchy on what they conceive as a set of reciprocal relations that only require meshing, not matching, of subplans, motives and grounds. As long as co-operation is the default setting, they will be happy to suspend hierarchisation, for the obvious reason that suspension enlarges their playing-field. It means, for instance, that the participating agents may take turns in who takes initiatives and who is responsive to the actions of the others, that they may each pursue their own justificatory discourses as long as they remain committed to the joint activity, that they may profit from other bargains in the course of their commitment to mutual support. Thus, a picture of 'functionally limited sovereignties' may take hold of our political retinas—a sense datum that De Búca, elsewhere in this volume, is justifiably critical about. I would call this *deferred* (rather than late) *sovereignty*, because such shared co-operative activity is a precarious equilibrium that continues to exist only by virtue of its meeting the Bratman parameters when push comes to shove. What [LEX] does not account for, however, is the situation in which speaker-agents can agree to retreat to radically incompatible sources of authority in their accounts of We_{AU}. This seems obvious. For instance, if one of the member states of the EU would systematically ignore the direct effect of directives, or flatly deny *acquis communautaire*, or the jurisdiction of the Commission in competition law (e.g. by giving massive governmental support to national companies facing insolvency), it will probably be taken to cancel its membership. In doing so, it may well further the cause of the Union and its legal order (causing the others to unite more strongly, or to think again); but not by exercising legal power in legislative intent, i.e. not by exercising sovereignty. In other words: on the basis of [LEX] constitutional pluralism is constitutional unitarianism deferred to times of crisis, when shared co-operative activity threatens to break down. As long as it lasts we can count our blessings. But we cannot organise or monitor its deference without anticipating making the most classical sovereignty claim possible: to announce crisis. One of the daunting experiences after 11 September 2001, is how quickly this claim can turn into real force. We restored the most classical form of sovereignty in days on a world-wide scale, even at the cost of national governmental crisis (Germany). Faced with the ruthlessness of terrorism, the global polity found shelter in the armour of the Leviathan. Faced with the ruthlessness of the global market, we or others may well do the same. It will not make sovereignty any more popular. It will make it more ambivalent.

3

Ten Tenets of Sovereignty

MARTIN LOUGHLIN

S OVEREIGNTY HAS BEEN given such a variety of ambiguous and
confused meanings that many have suggested that, in the interests of
precision and rigour the concept should be altogether abandoned.
This has been a recurrent refrain throughout the twentieth century. In the
early decades, for example, an influential movement aimed to jettison the
idea of sovereignty and, through the promotion of pluralism in political
thought,[1] sought to replace it with such notions as 'polyarchism'.[2] At mid-
century, the influence of positivism and behaviourism in legal and political
studies was such that, as an influential study of the concept acknowledged,
there was 'a tendency among present-day political theorists to work without the aid of the concept of sovereignty'.[3] And at the century's end, scholars seeking to explain the significance of contemporary trends, especially
those paraded under the labels of globalisation, flexibilisation and the

---

[1] See, eg, Francis W. Coker, 'The Technique of the Pluralist State' (1921) 15 *American Political Science Review* 186–213. The implications of pluralism for sovereignty had been illustrated in John Dewey, *Outlines of a Critical Theory of Ethics* [1891] (New York, Hilary House, 1957), 172: 'Every institution . . . has its sovereignty, or authority, and its laws and rights. It is only a false abstraction which makes us conceive of sovereignty, or authority, and law and rights as inhering only in some supreme organisation, as the national state'. (cited in Jens Bartelson, *The Critique of the State* (Cambridge, Cambridge University Press, 2001), 89).
[2] See, eg, Ernest Barker, 'The Discredited State' (1915) 5 *Political Quarterly* 101–21, at 120; Harold J Laski, *The Foundations of Sovereignty and other essays* (London, Allen & Unwin, 1921) 157. *Cf* Joshua Cohen and Charles Sabel, 'Directly Deliberative Polyarchy' (1997) 3 *European Law Journal* 313–42; Oliver Gerstenberg, 'Law's Polyarchy: A Comment on Cohen and Sabel' (1997) 3 *European Law Journal* 343–58.
[3] WJ Rees, 'The Theory of Sovereignty Restated' (1950) 59 *Mind* 495–521, at 495. See also Stanley I Benn, 'The Uses of "Sovereignty"' (1955) 3 *Political Studies*, 109–22, at 122: 'it would be a mistake to treat "sovereignty" as denoting a genus of which the species can be distinguished by suitable adjectives, and there would seem to be a strong case for giving up so Protean a word'. *Cf* Raia Prokhovnik, 'The state of liberal sovereignty' (1999) 1 *British Journal of Politics & International Relations* 63–83, at 63: 'The initial aim of this paper is to counter the claim that sovereignty is a bankrupt concept'.

emergence of multi-level governance, have argued that we were now living in an era of post-sovereignty.[4]

My argument in this chapter will be that such efforts to erode, to overcome, to evade or to move beyond sovereignty[5] are based on a misunderstanding of the nature of the concept and the roles that it performs in both political and legal discourse. Sovereignty is to be understood as a representation of the autonomy of the political, and as providing the foundational concept of the discipline of public law. Many of the difficulties that have been experienced in grappling with sovereignty thus flow from the inability of commentators to recognise public law as a practice with its own distinctive methods and objectives. And many of the resulting confusions stem either from attempts by lawyers and political scientists to fix the concept of sovereignty within a formal, analytical and positivist frame[6] or from efforts of political and legal theorists to devise some transcendental principles of right conduct to which legal and political behaviour must be subject.[7]

In order to explain and justify this argument, I will explicate sovereignty as a quintessentially political concept. I do so by presenting ten tenets of sovereignty. These tenets—ideas that have been translated into concrete practices—define the essence of the modern concept of sovereignty. My argument will be that, at base, sovereignty has been devised for the purpose of giving expression to the distinctively political bond between a group of people and its mode of governance. Sovereignty comes into existence through a process in which a group of people within a defined territory is moulded into an orderly cohesion through the establishment of a governing authority that can be differentiated from society and which is able to exercise an absolute political power. This concept of sovereignty is bound up with the emergence of the modern state and the establishment of an institutionalised form of government which is able to impose itself on society as an instrument of power. And the principal method by which this sovereign

---

[4] See eg Neil Walker, present volume.

[5] See, eg, Henry Shue, 'Eroding Sovereignty: The Advance of Principle' in Robert McKim and Jeff McMahon (eds), *The Morality of Nationalism* (New York, Oxford University Press, 1997), 340–59; Richard Falk, 'Evasions of Sovereignty' in RBJ Walker and Saul H Mendlovitz (eds), *Contending Sovereignties: Redefining Political Community* (Boulder, Colorado, Lynne Rienner, 1990), 61–78.

[6] The most egregious recent illustration from political science has been Krasner's labelling of sovereignty as 'organised hypocrisy': see Stephen D Krasner, *Sovereignty: Organized Hypocrisy* (Princeton, NJ, Princeton University Press, 1999).

[7] See, eg, Shue, above n 5, 349: 'I want to argue . . . against sovereignty directly. . . . I shall argue that there ought to be external limits on the means by which domestic economic ends may be pursued by states, limits that ought to become binding on individual sovereigns irrespective of whether those sovereigns wish to acknowledge them, just as sovereigns are already bound by both legal rights and moral rights against the domestic use of torture whatever their own opinions on the subject of torture may be'.

will is expressed is through the medium of the law. Sovereignty and law are inextricably linked.

Concepts lose their intelligibility when they are burdened with a plethora of contradictory meanings. By retrieving an understanding of the classical idea of modern sovereignty, I hope to show that, notwithstanding the potentially powerful impact of contemporary movements in governance, sovereignty can be understood to be a coherent concept of continuing relevance. This stance depends, however, both on an acknowledgement that sovereignty is socially constructed[8] and on a political commitment to continue to embrace modern sovereignty as an expression of contemporary juridico-political discourse.

1. SOVEREIGNTY IS A FACET OF THE MODERN STATE

Being 'entirely inseparable from the state',[9] sovereignty is a modern concept. Although the terminology of sovereignty was in use during the medieval period, the concept in a true sense did not then exist.[10] In the words of Bertrand de Jouvenel, although people in the Middle Ages had 'a very strong sense of that concrete thing, hierarchy; they lacked the idea of that abstract thing, sovereignty'.[11]

During the Middle Ages, sovereignty was used simply to signify a superior. But notwithstanding the common etymological root, sovereignty and suzerainty must be distinguished. Feudal power, the power of lordship or property, should not be confused with sovereignty. Although the Holy Roman Emperor might have been recognised 'as the suzerain of suzerains and the seignior of seigniors—as, it might even be said, the king of kings' this status only implied 'command over those who were best placed to disobey'.[12] For a variety of reasons of a technological, geographical, fiscal and military character, the central authority possessed only a limited hold over the governed. Until these rather basic obstacles could be overcome, the activity of governance could not emerge as an autonomous practice. This was achieved only as a consequence of the formation of the modern state. Being bound up with this movement, the assertion of sovereignty was part of an intrinsically modernising project.

---

[8] See, eg, Thomas J Biersteker and Cynthia Weber (eds), *State Sovereignty as Social Construction* (Cambridge, Cambridge University Press, 1996).

[9] Charles Loyseau, *Traicté des Seigneuries* (Paris, Abel l'Angelier, 1614), II. 4: 'la Souveraineté est du tout inseparable de l'Etat'.

[10] See Walter Ullmann, 'The Development of the Medieval Idea of Sovereignty' (1949) 64 *English Historical Review* 1; JW McKenna, 'The myth of parliamentary sovereignty in late-medieval England' (1979) 94 *English Historical Review* 481.

[11] Bertrand de Jouvenel, *Sovereignty: An Inquiry into the Political Good* JF Huntington trans. (Cambridge, Cambridge University Press, 1957), 171.

[12] Jouvenel, *ibid* 173.

This project was realised in stages. Royalty was first obliged to acquire the *plenitudo potestatis*, the supreme power, and this necessitated the destruction of all authorities that sought to challenge the power of the royal will. By breaking the political power of the feudal magnates, an internal coherence of governing authority was established. It might be noted here that the situation in England was unusual since, after the conquest, Norman statecraft ensured that, although the chief barons became major landlords, they did not assume the tasks of government; the conditions thus favoured the growth of a unified and highly centralised polity.[13] Elsewhere in western Europe, the struggle was longer drawn.[14]

The establishment of internal authority also had to be bolstered by the assertion of the territorial autonomy of the kingdom. This movement to acquire independence from external authority is best illustrated by the actions of those kings of England and France who, challenging the authority of the Pope and the Holy Roman Emperor, claimed to be emperor in their own realm.[15] The emergence of sovereignty thus manifests itself primarily as an assertion of royal authority and the subversion of the medieval order.

An especially important aspect of achieving these modernising objectives was the deployment of law as an instrument of royal power. In his analysis of the establishment of sovereignty in France in the early modern period, Bernard Durand highlighted the use of law as an instrument of authority in these terms:

> 'The central power', Mousnier wrote, 'only had a limited hold on the governed'. Distances (it took ten days to travel from Paris to Toulouse), the variety of spoken languages, the lack of administrators, the vague knowledge of the kingdom, everything contributed to the need for a strong message in order to compensate for material weaknesses. Only legal instruments (skilfully used) were able to bring cohesion to and ensure obedience from populations accustomed, since the Middle

---

[13] See WL Warren, *The Governance of Norman and Angevin England, 1086–1272* (London, Edward Arnold, 1987); James Campbell 'The Significance of the Anglo-Norman State in the Administrative History of Western Europe' in his *Essays in Anglo-Saxon History* (London, Hambledon Press, 1986), ch 11.

[14] See Wolfgang Reinhard (ed.), *Power Elites and State Building* (Oxford, Clarendon Press, 1996); Thomas Ertman, *Birth of the Leviathan: Building States and Regimes in Medieval and Early Modern Europe* (Cambridge, Cambridge University Press, 1997), chs 2,3,5.

[15] From the mid-thirteenth century onwards, jurists began to refer to the king's authority in terms of the maxim, *rex in regno suo imperator est* (a king is emperor within his own kingdom): see Gaines Post, *Studies in Medieval Legal Thought: Public Law and the State, 1100–1322* (Princeton NJ, Princeton University Press, 1964), 453–82. For the source of the maxim, see Peter N. Riesenberg, *Inalienability of Sovereignty in Medieval Political Thought* (New York, Columbia University Press, 1956), 82–3. The line of thought culminates in the opening words of the Act in Restraint of Appeals 1533 which declared that 'This realm of England is an empire, and so hath been accepted in the world, governed by one supreme head and king having the dignity and royal estate of the imperial crown . . .'. See Walter Ullmann, 'This Realm of England is an Empire' (1979) 30 *Journal of Ecclesiastical History* 175–203.

Ages, to a juridical message. Legislation, justice, law, were the instruments which made authority possible and efficacious. They showed themselves not only through the services they rendered and the rules they laid down but also through the justification they conveyed and the message they reinforced. The progress of state power was obviously made possible by these legal instruments: the very foundations of sovereignty were concerned, as well as the available instruments, justice and legislation.[16]

The project of forging a modern state required the promotion of a conception of law as an instrument of command. For this purpose, jurists drew heavily on such Roman law maxims as *quod principi placuit legis habet vigorem* (what pleases the prince has the force of law), which provided the intellectual source of such contemporary expressions as *si veut le roi, si veut la loi; car tel est notre plaisir* (what the king wills, the law wills; for such is our pleasure).[17]

Sovereignty thus emerges as an aspect of the formation of the modern state. Michael Oakeshott has indicated that the modern state was a 'free' or 'sovereign' association in respect of three main characteristics: first, because its government was 'not subject to any superior external authority'; secondly, 'in virtue of being an association in terms of law'; and thirdly because its government possessed 'the authority and the procedures to emancipate itself continuously from its legal past', in the sense that 'there was no law so ancient and so entrenched that it could not be amended or repealed'.[18] Put slightly differently, it might be said that sovereignty gives expression to three basic features of the modern state: internal coherence, external independence, and supremacy of the law.[19]

2. POLITICAL RELATIONSHIPS DO NOT DERIVE FROM PROPERTY RELATIONSHIPS

The roots of the argument that political relationships do not derive from property relationships lie in the struggle to differentiate the feudal patrimonial rights of monarchs from their political rights as sovereigns.[20] Because

---

[16] Bernard Durand, 'Royal Power and its Legal Instruments in France, 1500–1800' in Antonio Padoa-Schioppa (ed.), *Legislation and Justice* (Oxford, Clarendon Press, 1997) 291–312, at 293. The role of the common law in the processes of state formation in England was of particular importance. See, eg, Paul Brand, 'The Formation of the English Legal System, 1150–1400' in Padoa-Schioppa, *ibid* 103–21; RC van Caenegem, *The Birth of the English Common Law* 2nd edition (Cambridge, Cambridge University Press, 1988).

[17] See Digest of Justinian, 1. 4.1.

[18] Michael Oakeshott, 'On the Character of a Modern European State' in his *On Human Conduct* (Oxford, Clarendon Press, 1975), 182–326, at 229.

[19] See Blandine Kriegel, *The State and the Rule of Law* Marc A LePain and Jeffrey C Cohen trans. (Princeton, Princeton University Press, 1995), 29.

[20] See especially Kriegel, *ibid* ch 2.

the English monarchy centralised its power so early, it was able to prevent the build up of political feudalism which afflicted much of continental Europe.[21] And it is perhaps for this reason that English jurists undertaking their inquiries into the foundations of state power felt no great need formally to differentiate between political and proprietary power.

For an explicit acknowledgement of the importance of this distinction it is therefore necessary to turn to French scholars who grappled with the issue of sovereignty. In the works of jurists such as Bodin and Loyseau, the necessity of defining sovereign authority as a phenomenon that operated in direct opposition to the exercise of feudal power can be seen to form a central aspect of their endeavour.[22] Nevertheless, although Hobbes built upon and in certain respects radicalised the insights of the early-modern French jurists, he was able to develop his theory of sovereignty from basic precepts of political reasoning. Hobbes felt no need explicitly to unravel the proprietorial from the political. For Hobbes, a system of property (the rules of *Meum* and *Tuum*) is the product of the exercise of the sovereign power of prescribing the rules of civil law.[23]

This distinction between the political and proprietorial is one that was well rooted in classical political thought, with the Greeks differentiating between the spheres of the *polis* and the *oikos*, and the Romans between *res publica* and *dominium*.[24] And Hobbes too recognised this distinction between the household of the king and those that served the sovereign in the discharge of political responsibilities.[25] But this classical distinction

---

[21] The Norman kings also strengthened their position by requiring an oath of allegiance to be sworn by all holders of land and not simply the chief vassals. This ensured that, over and above the feudal relationship, a political bond of obedience between the subject and the crown was forged. See Émile Boutmy, *The English Constitution* Isabel M. Eaden trans. (London, Macmillan, 1891), 10.

[22] See Jean Bodin, *Six livres de la république*, Bk. I, esp. chs. 8–10; Loyseau, above n 9, chs 1 and 2. See also Charles Loyseau, *A Treatise of Orders and Plain Dignities* [1610] Howell A. Lloyd trans. (Cambridge, Cambridge University Press, 1994), VII. 2, 14 (pp. 138, 141–2): 'According to its true etymology, "prince" signifies the supreme head, that is, he who has the sovereignty of the state [but] the dukes and counts of France had long since called themselves princes because they had usurped the rights of sovereignty. Thus they were really subject princes'.

[23] Thomas Hobbes, *Leviathan* [1651] Richard Tuck ed. (Cambridge, Cambridge University Press, 1996), 125. For a contrasting interpretation, however, see CB Macpherson, *The Political Theory of Possessive Individualism: Hobbes to Locke* (Oxford, Oxford University Press, 1962), 265: 'For Hobbes the model of the self-moving, appetitive, possessive individual, and the model of society as a series of market relations between these individuals, were a sufficient source of political obligation'.

[24] See, eg, Aristotle, *The Politics* [c.335–323BC] TA Sinclair trans., Trevor J. Saunders ed. (Harmondsworth, Penguin, 1981), Bk. I, ii: 'It is an error to suppose, as some do, that the roles of the statesman, of a king, and of a household-manager and of a master of slaves are the same on the ground that they differ not in kind but only in point of numbers of persons . . .'

[25] Hobbes, above n 23, 166: 'they that be servants to them [the sovereign] in their naturall Capacity, are not Publique Ministers; but those onely that serve them in the Administration of the Publique businesse'.

seems subsequently to have been suppressed in English political thought, not least because of the Whig assumptions, underpinned by the work of Locke, that property is a pre-political category and that the chief end of government is to ensure its preservation.[26]

The maintenance of this distinction between political power and the power exercised through property is nevertheless essential to an understanding of sovereignty. It is one that is in need of particular reiteration today, largely because of a modern tendency to reduce all arguments of power to a matter of economics.[27] One particularly significant aspect of this propensity is that which conceptualises the modern state as an instrument of the dominant classes in society.[28] However, although this largely Marxist debate has generated an extensive literature,[29] it has never been able to provide an adequate account of political order that dislodges the underlying sense of the distinctive unity of the state.[30] From this perspective, the second tenet of sovereignty should be understood as a proposition which asserts the autonomy of the political in the face of such modern socio-economic reductionism.

3. PUBLIC POWER MUST BE DIFFERENTIATED FROM PRIVATE POWER

Although essentially a reformulation of the previous tenet, the idea that public power must be differentiated from private power enables us to highlight an especially important feature of the political relationship, one that lies at the core of sovereignty. This is that political power derives neither from force nor from the power that property confers. Political power cannot be possessed like property, nor applied like force. Political power, as

---

[26] See John Locke, *Two Treatises of Government*, II, §§ 28, 124. See *Entick v Carrington* (1765) 19 St. Tr. 1029, per Lord Camden CJ: 'The great end, for which men entered into society, was to secure their property. That right is preserved sacred'.

[27] See Kriegel, above n 19, 65–7, criticising the tendency of historians such as Perry Anderson whose 'economistic approach [to the development of the modern state] is preoccupied with surplus value and class struggle, but it is blind to the juridico-institutional forms that engendered a new state organisation at an early date in England and later on and only in part in France' (at 66).

[28] The classic expression is that of Marx in *The German Ideology*: 'Through the emancipation of private property from the community, the State has become a separate entity, beside and outside civil society; but it is nothing more than the form of organisation which the bourgeois necessarily adopt both for internal and external purposes, for the mutual guarantee of their property and interests'. (see Karl Marx and Frederick Engels, *Selected Works* (Moscow, Progress Publishers, 1969), vol. 1, 16–80, at 77).

[29] For an overview see Martin Carnoy, *The State and Political Theory* (Princeton, NJ, Princeton University Press, 1984). Although largely a debate within Marxism, it should be noted that it is not confined to that tradition of thought: see, eg, Charles A. Beard, *An Economic Interpretation of the Constitution of the United States* [1913] (New York, Macmillan, 1954).

[30] See Bartelson, above n 1, ch 4.

Hannah Arendt has argued, is always 'a power potential and not an unchangeable, measurable, and reliable entity like force or strength'.[31] Political power is 'to an astonishing degree independent of material factors', since the only material factor required in the generation of political power 'is the living together of people'.[32] And it is this political power that maintains the public realm.

Private power is the product of a relationship between a person and other persons in respect of an object, such as land and other forms of property. It is the power of mastery or *dominium*. Private power is exercised through the ownership and control of material resources. Political power, by contrast, is a product of a relationship between individuals (natural persons) that, in form at least, conceives them to be equals. This power, a product of the world-building capacity of humans, 'comes into being only if and when men join themselves together for the purpose of action'.[33] But this political power becomes public power proper only when taking some institutional form. As Arendt notes, the Romans

> knew that the principle of *potestas in populo* is capable of inspiring a form of government only if one adds, as the Romans did, *auctoritas in senatu*, authority resides in the senate, so that government itself consists of both power and authority, or, as the Romans put it, *senatus populusque Romanus*.[34]

Public power is formed by harnessing political power through the institutionalisation of authority.

Public power is thus the product of some form of partnership. This is what Oakeshott calls *societas*, which is a formal relationship constituted by a system of rules.[35] The power that is generated is therefore a consequence of the loyalty of individuals to the system. Public power may thus be said ultimately to rest on opinion and belief.[36] Even Hobbes, the greatest of the theorists of the authoritarian state, recognised

---

[31] Hannah Arendt, *The Human Condition* (Chicago, University of Chicago Press, 1958), 200.
[32] *Ibid* 200–1.
[33] Hannah Arendt, *On Revolution* (Harmondsworth, Penguin, 1973), 175. Arendt adds: 'The grammar of action: that action is the only human faculty that demands a plurality of men; and the syntax of power: that power is the only human attribute which applies solely to the worldly in-between space by which men are mutually related, combine in the act of foundation by virtue of the making and keeping of promises, which, in the realm of politics, may well be the highest human faculty'.
[34] *Ibid* 178.
[35] Oakeshott, 'On the Character of the Modern European State', above n 18, 199–203. Oakeshott here defines the state as *societas*, 'a formal relationship in terms of rules, not a substantive relationship in terms of common action' (201).
[36] James Madison, Alexander Hamilton and John Jay, *The Federalist Papers* [1788] Isaac Kramnick ed. (Harmondsworth, Penguin, 1987), No. 49 (Madison): 'If it be true that all governments rest on opinion, it is no less true that the strength of opinion in each individual, and its practical influence on his conduct, depend much on the number which he supposes to have entertained the same opinion'.

that 'the power of the mighty hath no foundation but in the opinion and belief of the people'.[37]

This distinction also suggests that, notwithstanding the Whig belief that the object of government is the preservation of property, the political relationship has no precise object at which it is aimed. Although some have expressed the objective rather grandiosely as being the maintenance and extension of human freedom, it is perhaps better summed up by the rather general and ambiguous idea that the object is to promote the *salus populi*.[38] But in formal terms, the political relationship is one that simply is born of 'the activity of attending to the general arrangements of a set of people whom chance or choice have brought together'.[39]

Seeking to fix on the defining characteristics of this public relationship, Oakeshott, following Aristotle, identified the four basic features of what he called 'the civil condition'. These are that it is a relationship of human beings, that it is a relationship of equals, that it is a 'constituted' condition, and that it is a self-sufficient relationship.[40] Following this line of argument, it is suggested that public power is a product of the civil condition and is generated by the establishment of a system of governance, the setting to work of an apparatus of rule.

4. PUBLIC POWER IS NOT PERSONAL BUT OFFICIAL

Charles Loyseau succinctly identified both the essence of this tenet and its connections with tenets 2 and 3 in the distinction he drew between lordship and office. Lordship, Loyseau argued, can be defined as 'dignity with power in property'; office, by contrast, connotes 'dignity with public function'.[41] This concept of office (*officium*) was derived from ecclesiastical institutions and it 'drew concurrently upon the dual Roman and canonical tradition of

---

[37] Thomas Hobbes, *Behemoth, or the Long Parliament* [1682] Ferdinand Tönnies ed. (London, Cass, 1969), 16. See also Joseph de Maistre, 'Study on Sovereignty' in Jack Lively (ed.), *The Works of Joseph de Maistre* (London, Allen & Unwin, 1965), 93–129, at 110: 'Any *institution* is only a political edifice. In the physical and the moral order, the laws are the same; you cannot build a great edifice on narrow foundations or a durable one on a moving or transient base. Likewise, in the political order, to build high and for centuries, it is necessary to rely on an opinion or belief broad and deep: for if the opinion does not hold the majority of minds and is not deeply rooted, it will provide only a narrow and transient base'.

[38] Hobbes, *On the Citizen* [1647] Richard Tuck and Michael Silverthorne eds (Cambridge, Cambridge University Press, 1998), 143: 'All the duties of sovereigns are implicit in this one phrase: *the safety of the people is the supreme law*'. This derives from Cicero, *De Legibus* [c.51BC] Bk. III. ch 6: *salus populi suprema lex esto*.

[39] Michael Oakeshott, 'Political Education' in his *Rationalism in Politics* (London, Methuen, 1962), 111–36, at 112.

[40] Oakeshott, 'On the Civil Condition' in his *On Human Conduct*, above n 18, 108–84, at 109–10.

[41] Loyseau, above n 22, I. 6.

service to the public realm and the common good'.[42] *Officium* signified a position of some permanence; the position assumes the status of an institution.[43]

This concept of office transforms our understanding of public power: power, it might be argued, vests not in the individual but in the office itself. The distinction between the personal and official nature of the task has deep medieval roots. It is, for example, manifest in the distinction that medieval jurists drew between the king's two bodies: between the natural and the politic, the private and the public, the personal and the official, the king and the crown. And the politic body, we are told, 'consist[s] of policy and government, and [is] constituted for the direction of the people, and the management of the public-weal'.[44] Once this stage of intellectual development is reached, it is but a short step to acknowledge that power is entrusted to the institutional framework of government.[45] Consequently, although in Britain we continue to pay lip-service to the notion that justice emanates from Her Majesty or that the Queen's fiat makes law, it is evident that this royal will is in no sense personal. This power can only be exercised through specific institutional and official forms.[46]

The official character of public power was fully understood by the early-modern theorists of sovereignty. Bodin, for example, argued that the sovereign can be identified essentially by knowing his attributes, these being those properties that are not shared by subjects. The principal 'marks' of sovereignty were defined by Bodin as: the power of law-making, the power to declare war and make peace, the power to establish offices of state, the ultimate right of judgment, the power of pardon, the right of coining money,

---

[42] Hélène Millet and Peter Moraw, 'Clerics in the State' in Reinhard (ed.), above n 14, ch 9 at 179. For the Roman influence see: Myron Piper Gilmore, *Argument from Roman Law in Political Thought, 1200–1600* (Cambridge, Mass, Harvard University Press, 1941), ch 3. And for the work of medieval publicists on the concept of office see Riesenberg, above n 15, ch 2.

[43] See Udo Wolter, 'The *officium* in Medieval Ecclesiatical Law as a Prototype of Modern Administration' in Padoa-Schioppa ed., above n 16, ch 2, at 23.

[44] *Case of the Duchy of Lancaster* (1561) 1 Plowden 212, 213. Note should also be made of the work of Sir John Fortescue in the fifteenth century who, in characterising the English regime as *dominium politicum et regale*, emphasised the fact that although the king possessed authority to rule, he was unable to pass whatever measures he pleased but was required to work through the institutional arrangements of Parliament. See Sir John Fortescue, *De Laudibus Legum Anglie* [1468–71] SB Chrimes ed. (Cambridge, Cambridge University Press, 1942).

[45] This is nevertheless a shift that, because of an inability to separate the king from his crown, the English have never been able cleanly to make. But many of seventeenth century constitutional conflicts can be understood in this light: see, eg, Janelle Greenberg, 'Our Grand Maxim of State, "The King Can Do No Wrong" ' (1991) *History of Political Thought* 209–28.

[46] See, eg, AV Dicey, *Introduction to the Study of the Law of the Constitution* 8th edition (London, Macmillan, 1914), 322: 'the Royal will can, speaking generally, be expressed in one of three different ways, viz. (1) by Order in Council; (2) by order, commission, or warrant under the sign-manual; (3) by proclamations, writs, patents, letters and other documents under the Great Seal'.

and the right of taxation.[47] The complex and sophisticated character of these attributes in themselves suggest that such rights and powers are unlikely to be personal; Bodin here seems to be contemplating the establishment of an elaborate institution. This point is developed by Hobbes, who insists that sovereigns are not proprietors of their sovereignty. Sovereign power is in no sense personal; it resides entirely in a representative office.[48]

The power that is exercised through this institutional framework of government is what we generally recognise to be the sovereignty of the state. Further (referring back to tenet 1), it would be inaccurate to suggest that this institutional notion of sovereignty came into being because parliament succeeded in wresting sovereignty from the king. Before the formation of this elaborate institutional framework of the state, sovereignty did not exist. In his study of the evolution of parliament, AF Pollard concisely captured this understanding of the concept. 'The crown', Pollard suggested,

> had never been sovereign by itself, for before the days of parliament there was no real sovereignty at all: sovereignty was only achieved by the energy of the crown in parliament, and the fruits of conquest were enjoyed in common.[49]

Sovereignty is a function of the institutional arrangements established as a consequence of the formation of the modern state.[50]

5. PUBLIC POWER IS A PRODUCT OF A POLITICAL RELATIONSHIP

Although public power vests in the arrangement of offices rather than the individuals who hold office (tenet 4), it has also been suggested, when distinguishing public and private power (tenet 3), that this apparatus of rule ultimately derives its power from the character of the political relationship between a government and its subjects. This aspect of sovereignty must now be directly addressed. Properly understood, political power does not reside in any specific locus, whether that be the king, the people or an institution such as parliament. Political power is generated from the particular quality of the relationship that evolves between the sovereign and subject, government and citizens. Political power generated through the apparatus of rule must be conceived as being relational.

---

[47] Bodin, above n 22, I. 10. *Cf* Hobbes, *On the Citizen*, above n 38, VI. 18.
[48] Hobbes, *Leviathan*, above n 23, ch 30: 'Of the Office of the Soveraign Representative'.
[49] AF Pollard, *The Evolution of Parliament* (London, Longmans, 1926), 230.
[50] This point provides one answer to Lord Cooper's puzzle, expressed in *MacCormick v Lord Advocate* 1953 SC 396, at 411: 'The principle of the unlimited sovereignty of Parliament is a distinctively English principle which has no counterpart in Scottish constitutional law ... Considering that the Union legislation extinguished the Parliaments of Scotland and England and replaced them by a new Parliament, I have great difficulty in seeing why it should have been supposed that the new Parliament of Great Britain must inherit all the peculiar characteristics of the English Parliament but none of the Scottish Parliament ...'

The basic point being highlighted here is that the state's capacity of effective command depends on its ability to establish its authority. This requires the harnessing of power, and this is derived from the degree to which the loyalty of citizens can be secured. Authority, notes Lester Ruiz,

> 'is the giving and receiving of confidence and commitment between persons who recognise and affirm a common community; it is not an independent variable that creates or imposes the values that constitute this common community'.[51]

Once authority is understood as such, it may be seen that legitimacy is conferred by authority, rather than the reverse, that authority precedes positive law, and that relationality precedes authority.[52] As Arendt explains, the term authority (*auctoritas*) is derived from the verb *augere* (to augment) and 'what . . . those in authority constantly augment is the foundation'.[53] Authority therefore 'has its roots in the past';[54] the question of authority 'is fundamentally a question of tradition' and 'the question of tradition is inextricably related to the question of *the people*'.[55]

This insight into the nature of authority helps us to appreciate the significance of a growing body of scholarly work that is concerned to analyse the processes of development of the modern state.[56] In the case of Britain, for example, the fact that a highly centralised agency of government was established at an early stage of development has been of critical significance. Consequently, when a parliament that was strongly linked to local government emerged, it found itself unable to prevent the process of state-building. Parliament therefore came to focus its activities on the necessity of ensuring that the central authority operated within an acceptable constitutional framework. And the framework of authority that was established has proved to be particularly effective and durable.[57] Historical work of this character—showing, for example, how the growth of representative assemblies became closely bound up with the furtherance of the state's objectives—suggests the need to revise some of the more idealised accounts that

---

[51] Lester Edwin J. Ruiz, 'Sovereignty as a Transformative Practice' in Walker and Mendlovitz (eds), above n 5, 79–96, at 85.

[52] See Ruiz, *ibid*.

[53] Hannah Arendt, 'What is Authority?' in her *Between Past and Future: Eight Exercises in Political Thought* (Harmondsworth, Penguin, 1977), 91–141, at 122.

[54] *Ibid*.

[55] Ruiz, above n 51, at 85.

[56] See, eg, Charles Tilly (ed.), *The Formation of Nation States in Western Europe* (Princeton, Princeton University Press, 1975); Otto Hintze, *The Historical Essays of Otto Hintze* Felix Gilbert ed. (New York, Oxford University Press, 1975); Michael Mann, *The Sources of Social Power. Vol. 1: A History of Power from the Beginning to AD 1760* (Cambridge, Cambridge University Press, 1986), *Vol. 2: The Rise of Classes and Nation-States, 1760–1914* (Cambridge, Cambridge University Press, 1994); Martin van Creveld, *The Rise and Decline of the State* (Cambridge, Cambridge University Press, 1999).

[57] This thesis is presented in Ertman, above n 14, esp. ch 4. See also John Brewer, *The Sinews of Power: War, Money and the English State, 1688–1783* (London, Unwin Hyman, 1989).

lawyers in particular have given of the system of parliamentary democracy. More generally, it helps us to bring authority and liberty into a more appropriate alignment. Contrary to certain interpretations, liberty and authority should not be conceived as being in direct antagonism. As Benedetto Croce put it: 'Liberty struggles against authority, yet desires it; and authority checks liberty, yet keeps it alive or awakens it, because neither would exist without the other'.[58]

The authority invested in the institutional framework of government rests on the foundation of a political relationship. Although the involvement of the people in the activity of government is an effective state-building strategy, once it is recognised that political power rests ultimately in the people, it becomes evident that this power must be actively managed. Governmental authority rests on the allegiance of the people; once support is withdrawn, the authority of governors dissipates.

6. SOVEREIGNTY IS AN EXPRESSION OF PUBLIC POWER

Public power, it has been argued, is to be differentiated from private power; it is a form of official power which is the product of a distinctively political relationship. It has further been argued that this type of public power acquires an autonomous status only with the establishment of the modern idea of the state. Once these tenets have been set in place, sovereignty can be understood to be an expression of public power.

In the formative period, the emergence of the concept of sovereignty, perhaps understandably, gave effect to a monistic conception of the state. Sovereignty, in the words of Jean Bodin, 'is the absolute and perpetual power of a commonwealth', it is 'the highest power of command'.[59] As the source of law, the sovereign cannot be subject to the laws.[60] Sovereignty thus seems to provide a justification for absolutism. If we focus solely on the monistic and absolutist features of sovereignty, however, we are liable to misunderstand its character. The concept certainly borrows some of its authority from such Roman law maxims as *princeps legibus solutus est* (the prince is freed from the laws) and *quod principi placuit legis habet vigorem* (what pleases the prince has the force of law).[61] The sovereign does indeed provide the source of all positive law. And sovereign authority possesses what in the German tradition of public law is called *Kompetenz-*

---

[58] Benedetto Croce, *Politics and Morals* [1925] Salvatore J. Castiglione trans. (New York, Philosophical Library, 1945), 14.
[59] Jean Bodin, *Six livres de la république*, [1576] Bk. I, ch 8: see Bodin, *On Sovereignty* Julian Franklin ed. (Cambridge, Cambridge University Press, 1992), 1.
[60] Bodin, *ibid* Bk. I. ch 8, at 12–3.
[61] Digest of Justinian (of n. 17), I. 3.31, I. 4.1.

Kompetenz, 'the competence of its competence', or the competence to determine the limits, if any, of its own competence.[62] But those who highlight its absolutist features generally fail to recognise that sovereignty is a concept which makes sense only once the public and official character of governmental power has been acknowledged.

Once this aspect of sovereignty is grasped, the classical categorisation of the forms of government must be placed in question. Within the modern state, Aristotle's widely accepted claim that there are three basic forms of government—monarchy, aristocracy and democracy[63]—can no longer be conceived as alternative forms of political rule. In the framework of the modern state these classical forms do not provide realistic alternatives: the notion that a single individual could be vested with a boundless right of rule is virtually incomprehensible, and the idea of direct democracy in the classical sense[64] has almost entirely been superseded by an indirect, representative version of that form.[65] Modern government is invariably of an aristocratic character. To the extent that the classical forms continue to be relevant they must now be conceived as three phases in the activity of ruling: consultation, which involves all; counsel, which involves few; and decision, which is singular.[66]

Understood as an expression of public power, sovereignty thus resides in the established institutional framework of the state. However, since it is accepted (tenet 5) that public power is an expression of a political relationship, it would be a mistake to assume that sovereignty resides in a specific locus, whether that be the king, the people or an institution such as parliament. Sovereignty ultimately inheres in the form which the political relationship takes.

7. SOVEREIGNTY IS RELATIONAL

Sovereignty is quintessentially an expression of a political relationship and, from a juristic perspective, sovereignty constitutes the essence of the modern state. The state, argued Hobbes, is the person that is created as a result of the authorisation through covenant of the people (a multitude). The sovereign is the representative of the person of the state.[67] Sovereignty,

---

[62] See, eg, Paul Laband, *Das Staatsrecht des Deutschen Reiches* (Tübingen, Mohr, 1901), vol. 2, 64–7, 85–8; Georg Jellinek, *Allgemeine Staatslehre* (Berlin, Springer, 1900), 483–4.
[63] Aristotle, above n 24, Bks IV–VI.
[64] See MH Hansen, *The Athenian Democracy in the Age of Demosthenes* (Oxford, Blackwell, 1991).
[65] See Bernard Manin, *The Principles of Representative Democracy* (Cambridge, Cambridge University Press, 1997).
[66] *Cf* Croce, above n 58, 17.
[67] Hobbes, *Leviathan*, above n 23, 120–1.

it follows, is the name given to express the quality of the political relationship that is formed between the state and the people, or the sovereign and the subject. This relational aspect of sovereignty is highlighted by Croce. 'In the relationship between ruler and ruled', he argues, 'sovereignty belongs to neither but to the relationship itself'.[68]

What is the precise nature of this relational aspect of sovereignty? Is it best expressed by focusing on the relation between sovereign and subject or between the state and the people? In Hobbesian theory this issue remains ambiguous, essentially because it is axiomatic that the state is able to act only through the person of the sovereign. But once a conceptual distinction is drawn between the state and the office of the sovereign, it is evident that this question may throw some light on two principal facets of sovereignty that have often provided a source of confusion. These two facets are generally called the legal and the political conceptions of sovereignty. At base these two conceptions of sovereignty reflect a differentiation that can be drawn between the public and the political.

It has been argued that public power is not personal but official (tenet 4), that public power is the product of a political relationship (tenet 5) and that sovereignty is an expression of public power (tenet 6). This suggests that sovereignty is both an expression of official power and is the product of a political relationship. The former, focusing on the institutional and public, depicts the legal conception of sovereignty; the latter expresses the political conception. These legal and political conceptions of sovereignty in turn reflect concerns about the issues of competence and capacity, or of authority and power.

Competence is an official or institutional matter. As a facet of sovereignty, competence is an expression of the absolute power of the state to enact law. In the technical sense of jurisdiction, competence reflects both internal coherence (that is, the existence of a viable system of rule) and external independence (the identity of the state as an entity in the international arena). The external aspect, which expresses the basic principle of state sovereignty, is widely understood.[69] But, especially from a British perspective, the internal aspect sometimes causes confusion. Under the British constitution, the internal aspect is classically understood as the right of the Crown in Parliament 'to make or unmake any law whatever', with no person or body being recognised 'as having the right to override or set aside the legislation of Parliament'.[70] This is commonly stated to be the legislative sovereignty of parliament. In the British context, the structure of official power is unusually simple. And the reason for this is that, as a

---

[68] Croce, above n 58, 17.
[69] See, eg, RBJ Walker, *Inside/Outside: International Relations as Political Theory* (Cambridge, Cambridge University Press, 1993).
[70] Dicey, above n 46, 38.

consequence of maintaining a Hobbesian framework, the Crown in Parliament—the ultimate law-making institution—is the sole representative of the person of the state. In this respect, the British constitution is almost unique.

Most modern states have, through the exercise of the constituent power of 'the people' or 'the nation', established a formal constitutional frame-work which allocates legislative, executive and judicial powers of the state to designated institutions. This constitutional framework generally defines and delimits the competence of the legislative assembly to enact laws and, if a federal regime is established, may divide legislative powers between federal and provincial institutions. Such a limitation or division of legisla-tive power does not, however, amount to a division of sovereignty: sover-eignty divided is sovereignty destroyed. The constitutional framework instituted for the exercise of governmental power of the state must be understood as an explication, rather than a division, of sovereignty. The supreme power to enact law is exercised through the power of 'the nation' to constitute a system of government. The constitutional framework provides the measure of internal coherence; the constitution can thus be understood to be an elaboration of legal sovereignty. In this arrangement, sovereignty understood as an expression of official power exists in the rela-tion between the form of institutional authority established and the subjects of that power (ie, the citizenry).

However, in addition to expressing a relation of jurisdictional compe-tence or authority, sovereignty is also an expression of the fundamental political relationship between the people and the institutional framework of state power. This is the aspect of sovereignty that is concerned not so much with competence but with capacity, not with authority but rather with power. This political conception of sovereignty focuses on the capacity of a people to overcome social division and conflict by establishing a sense of political unity. Political sovereignty is what George Lawson termed 'real sovereignty', which is 'the power to constitute, abolish, alter, reform forms of government'.[71] Real or political sovereignty, which is synonymous with what Sieyes called the 'constituent power',[72] is 'a power to model a state'.[73]

This underlying relationship between rulers and ruled is one that lawyers—working on the assumption of the ultimate authority of the normative framework—have a tendency to suppress. On rare occasions, as when a new state is formed through a process of decolonisation, the judici-ary is obliged to recognise that the doctrines of legal sovereignty must

---

[71] George Lawson, *Politica Sacra et Civilis or, A Modell of Civil and Ecclesiasticall Government* [1660] Conal Condren ed. (Cambridge, Cambridge University Press, 1992), 47.
[72] Emmanuel Joseph Sieyès, *What is the Third Estate?* [1789] M. Blondel trans. (London, Pall Mall Press, 1963), 124–8.
[73] Lawson, above n 71, 47.

march alongside political reality.[74] But this conception of political sovereignty generally remains below the level of juristic consciousness. It is nevertheless one that is basic to an understanding of sovereignty, even in the juristic sense. Political sovereignty provides the ultimate basis for the belief that, as Sieyes put it, the holders of official power 'do not exercise it as a right inherent in themselves, but as a right pertaining to other people; the common will is confided to them in trust'.[75]

The official power that is entrusted by the people is to be used to promote the well-being—to enhance the capacity—of the state. As has been argued (tenet 6), this capacity depends on strengthening the bonds of allegiance between governors and governed. Although this can be achieved in a number of ways, one of the most effective is to institutionalise checks on the exercise of governmental power. Such constraints, which ensure that public power is wielded only for public purposes, serve to bolster the confidence of the people in the integrity of government and this greatly enhances the capacity of public power. In this way, authority (competence) is directly linked to power (capacity), and legal sovereignty connected with 'real' sovereignty.

The relational aspect of the political conception of sovereignty is mainly concerned with elaborating the ways in which constitutional arrangements serve state-building purposes. This feature of political sovereignty is the product of the peculiarly communal character of political power, which requires that individuals act in concert. Political power, Arendt notes,

> 'can be divided without decreasing it, and the interplay of powers with their checks and balances is even liable to generate more power, so long, at least, as the interplay is alive and has not resulted in a stalemate'.[76]

Viewed in this light, constitutional constraints should not be seen simply as limitations on the exercise of public power; they simultaneously act as a method of generating political power.

8. RIGHTS ARE NOT ANTAGONISTIC TO SOVEREIGNTY BUT ARE THE PRODUCT OF ITS EXPRESSION

Classical political thought conceived of law as an expression of equity, of rightness, within the natural order of things. There was thus a correlation

---

[74] See, eg, *British Coal Corporation* v *The King* [1935] AC 500, 520: 'It is doubtless true that the power of the Imperial Parliament to pass on its own initiative any legislation it thought fit extending to Canada remains in theory unimpaired [as a consequence of the Statute of Westminster 1931]. But that is theory and has no relation to realities'. *Cf Madzimbamuto* v *Lardner-Burke* [1969] AC 645.

[75] Sieyes, above n 72, 122–3.

[76] Arendt, above n 31, 201. For an elaboration of this theme see: Stephen Holmes, *Passions and Constraint: On the Theory of Liberal Democracy* (Chicago, University of Chicago Press, 1995); Jon Elster, *Ulysses Unbound: Studies in Rationality, Precommitment, and Constraints* (Cambridge: Cambridge University Press, 2000).

between law and right. Classical political thought did not therefore possess any subjective concept of right, that is, of a right which an individual maintained against other individuals or the collectivity.[77] Although the status of subjective rights in medieval thought has been the subject of extensive debate,[78] the concept appears to receive its first systematic formulation by early modern writers who devised their political theories from the foundation of the individual as a bearer of rights. Such theories, however, should not be viewed as being antagonistic to the idea of sovereignty. Rather, the idea of rights which vest in individuals was generally elaborated in conjunction with the articulation of the concept of sovereignty.

This point is most clearly highlighted in the work of Hobbes, who constructed his entire system of political order from the foundation of natural rights. But what Hobbes argued was that the natural rights that inhere in the individual are relinquished in the process of covenanting to establish an all-powerful sovereign authority. These natural rights are alienated for the purpose of acquiring the security offered by the establishment of a common power. Consequently, the sovereign, as the bearer of supreme power, is not subject to any rights claims. To the extent that individuals hold rights under political order, then such rights are conferred purely through the law-making action of the sovereign. From the perspective of the theories of sovereignty, individual rights-bearers do not possess rights either because they are inscribed in nature or because they can be understood to be expressions of human reason, but only because they have been conferred as a product of the legislation of the sovereign.

Such notions as rights, duties and powers are thus to be understood essentially as relational concepts which operate within an institutional framework of sovereign authority.[79] Most modern accounts, even those which have provided the inspiration for modern liberalism, operate within the frame of sovereignty. Consider, for example, the work of Montesquieu, which has provided one of the most influential expositions influencing modern liberal thought. Reworking the classical forms of rule as aspects of the activity of ruling, Montesquieu argued that liberty is the product of those political and legal arrangements which operate to ensure that gover-

---

[77] See, eg, Michel Villey, 'L'idée du droit subjectif et les systèmes juridiques romains' (1946) *Revue historique de droit* 24–25, 201, who argues that the concept of ius in Roman law meant right in an objective sense: that which is right. *Cf* Richard Tuck, *Natural Rights Theories: Their Origin and Development* (Cambridge, Cambridge University Press, 1979), 7–13.

[78] See, eg, Tuck, *ibid Cf* Brian Tierney, 'Tuck on rights: some medieval problems' (1983) 4 *History of Political Thought 429*; Tierney, 'Origins of natural rights language: texts and contexts, 1150–1250' (1989) 10 *History of Political Thought 615*.

[79] For the classic juristic account within the frame of sovereignty see Wesley N Hohfeld, *Fundamental Legal Conceptions as Applied in Judicial Reasoning* (New Haven, Yale University Press, 1923).

nors do not abuse their powers. But Montesquieu is explicit in arguing that only in a system of state sovereignty governed by law is liberty able to flourish. Political liberty, Montesquieu contends, 'in no way consists in doing what one wants'; rather it must be seen as 'the right to do everything the laws permit'.[80]

Fundamental rights are often touted today as being the expression of universal moral claims, and therefore as claims which transcend and restrict the political. This claim must be recognised to be essentially rhetorical; rights claims are intrinsically partial and political.[81] Another way of expressing this would be to say that rights are a product of the expression of sovereignty. Rights are the result of certain political values being given legal recognition, whether by legislative enactment or designation in constitutional arrangements, and protected by the governing authorities.

9. THE SYSTEM OF PUBLIC LAW IS AN EXPRESSION OF SOVEREIGNTY

The absolutist aspect of sovereignty lies in danger of being misunderstood; it can properly be understood only from the perspective of law. Since sovereign authority is expressed through those established institutional forms which enable the general will to be articulated, that general will, although absolute, has nothing in common with the exercise of an arbitrary power.[82] Sovereign will is the antithesis of subjective will.[83] And since the expression of this will takes the form of law, sovereignty in reality means the sovereignty of law.[84]

There is, however, another aspect of the relationship between sovereignty and law which must be considered. In the perspective of sovereignty, law is the command of the sovereign. But since the sovereign is an office that exercises an official power, the will of the sovereign can be expressed only through certain institutional forms. And these institutional forms must also be laid down in law. The constitution of authority, it might be said, is conditioned by law. This means not only that the omnipotent power of the state

---

[80] Montesquieu, *The Spirit of the Laws* [1748] Anne M Cohler, Basia Carolyn Miller and Harold Samuel Stone trans. and ed. (Cambridge, Cambridge University Press, 1989), Bk. 11, ch 3.
[81] See Michael Ignatieff, *Human Rights as Politics and Idolatry* (Princeton, NJ, Princeton University Press, 2001), 3–52.
[82] This is one of the key themes of Montesquieu, who argues that, being rooted in fear, despotism is one of the least powerful forms of government: above n 80, Bk. 1, ch 9.
[83] Arendt expresses this point by drawing a distinction between power and violence: see Hannah Arendt, *On Violence* (San Diego, California, Harcourt, Brace & Co., 1970), 42: 'The extreme form of power is All against One, the extreme form of violence is One against All'.
[84] Bodin, above n 22, Bk. I, ch 8: 'For law is nothing but the command of a sovereign making use of his power'.

can be expressed only in the form of law but also that it can be expressed only through those institutional forms which are recognised by law. Sovereignty, in the words of Jellinek, 'has the exclusive capacity to determine itself and to restrain itself from the perspective of the law'.[85]

The capacities and restraints that give expression to a particular arrangement of the sovereign authority of the state form the subject matter of public law.

10. PUBLIC LAW IS NOT SOLELY A MATTER OF POSITIVE LAW

Many of the most intractable problems in juristic thought arise as a result of misunderstandings about the concept of sovereignty. Some of the difficulties emerge from a failure to recognise the official or institutional character of the exercise of sovereign authority, but often they stem from an inability to grasp the essentially relational character of sovereignty. As we have seen (tenet 7), sovereignty is doubly relational and these two aspects, the legal and political conceptions, reflect twin concerns with competence and capacity. It has been argued that the legal conception, which focuses on the authority of the sovereign to enact law, has the tendency to suppress the political conception, which is more concerned with the capacity to generate political power through the relationship between the state and the people. In order to understand the juristic significance of sovereignty, it is necessary to examine more closely a third relational aspect, that is, the relation between the legal and the political conceptions.

This issue is thrown into relief by reflecting on the theoretical framework of legal positivism, the predominant tendency in modern jurisprudence. In the English tradition, positivism has invariably accepted that the foundations of legal validity rest on the existence of political authority. Whether those foundations are expressed as habitual obedience to a sovereign power,[86] as 'ultimate legal principles' which have historical but not legal sources,[87] or as a 'rule of recognition' whose existence is 'an empirical, though complex, question of fact',[88] the legal is conceived ultimately as being based on the political. It is, however, in the characterisation of both the legal and the political, and hence of the relation between the two, that this tradition of thought falls into error. The legal error is to adopt an essentially command—or rule-based conception of law—law as the will of the

---

[85] Jellinek, cited in Kriegel, above n 18, 32.

[86] John Austin, *The Province of Jurisprudence Determined* [1832] Wilfrid E. Rumble ed. (Cambridge, Cambridge University Press, 1995), 166.

[87] John W Salmond, *Jurisprudence* PJ Fitzgerald (ed.) 12th edition (London, Stevens, 1966), 111–112.

[88] HLA Hart *The Concept of Law* (Oxford, Clarendon Press, 1961), 245.

sovereign—which is unable to provide an adequate account of the constitutive aspects of public law.[89] The error that is made concerning the political is to assume that political power is an empirical rather than a relational
phenomenon.

The consequential problems are highlighted in the work of Neil
MacCormick, who has recently engaged in a basic re-assessment of sovereignty from within the positivist tradition.[90] Starting from the standard
positivist account, which maintains that a 'political sovereign' undergirds
the 'legal sovereign', MacCormick suggests that, while this account may be
useful for 'some types of politico-legal order', it has been 'found wanting in
respect of those situations in which there is a standing constitutional tradition'.[91] This is a peculiar—and peculiarly English legal positivist—understanding of sovereignty. For MacCormick, once 'the powers of state are
effectively divided according to a constitutional scheme' then there is 'a
difficulty in identifying any sovereign being or sovereign entity holding
power without any legal limitation'.[92]

We can make sense of this argument only once it is recognised that it is
built on an Austinian definition of sovereignty as 'power not subject to limitation by a higher or co-ordinate power, held independently over some territory'.[93] From this rather loose formulation, which is applied both to legal and
political conceptions of sovereignty, a catalogue of errors flow. MacCormick
thus suggests that since 'all power holders', whether in a political or legal
sense, are subject to 'some legal or political checks or controls', it follows that
'there is no single sovereign internal to the state, neither a legal nor a political sovereign'.[94] Building on this erroneous assumption, MacCormick argues
that since a 'well-ordered Law-State or *Rechtstaat* is not subordinated to any
political sovereign outside or above the law', this shows 'that sovereignty is
neither necessary to the existence of law and state nor even desirable'.[95] He

---

[89] This error stems mainly from treating law as being founded on the bedrock of fact: see Dicey,
above n 46, 37: 'My aim in this chapter is . . . to explain the nature of Parliamentary sovereignty and to show that its existence is a legal fact'. See also HWR Wade, 'The basis of legal
sovereignty' [1955] *Cambridge Law Journal* 172–97, at 189: 'What Salmond calls the "ultimate legal principle" is therefore a rule which is unique in being unchangeable by Parliament—
it is changed by revolution, not by legislation; it lies in the keeping of the courts, and no Act
of Parliament can take it away from them . . . It is simply a political fact'.
[90] Neil MacCormick, *Questioning Sovereignty: Law, State and Nation in the European
Commonwealth* (Oxford, Oxford University Press, 1999), 75? 'I shall suggest that there is . . .
a theoretical structure available, one built out of different materials presented to us by other
strands within the positivist tradition'.
[91] *Ibid* 128.
[92] *Ibid*
[93] *Ibid* 129, 128.
[94] *Ibid* 129.
[95] *Ibid*

concludes his analysis by suggesting that we have moved 'beyond the sovereign state'[96] and into an era of 'post-sovereignty'.[97]

Many of these errors stem from a misconception concerning the nature of political power. MacCormick believes that political power is 'power-in-fact', that is, 'power to make sure that somebody in fact acts in a certain way'.[98] But this notion of power as coercive force overlooks the intrinsically relational aspect of political power.[99] And it is this failure to acknowledge that political power is generated by the relationship between rulers and ruled that lies at the root of the inability of positivists to accept the idea of the 'constituent power'—the people or 'the nation'—as being the repository of the office of the sovereign in those regimes that adopt formal constitutions and allocate legal authority to designated organs of government. For want of this concept of constituent power, constitutionalist regimes are assumed to have 'divided' or moved 'beyond' sovereignty. But if sovereignty is taken to provide a representation of the autonomy of the political, the problem for positivist jurisprudence is that of providing an answer to the question of what sort of political world we are inhabiting once sovereignty is eliminated from our conception of law and state.

Some, though not all, of these difficulties stem from the peculiarities of the English approach to legal positivism. But the general problem can be highlighted by briefly considering the more abstract, neo-Kantian version of positivism expounded by Hans Kelsen. In contrast to Austin and the English analytical jurists, Kelsen rejected the idea that law was based on state power. His objective was to present a theory of law as a normative order which was not only 'purified of all political ideology' but, since it did

---

[96] *Ibid* 133. See also Neil MacCormick, 'Beyond the Sovereign State' (1993) 56 *Modern Law Review* 1–18.

[97] MacCormick, above n 90, ch 8, 'On Sovereignty and Post-Sovereignty'.

[98] *Ibid* 12.

[99] In an earlier article on this subject, MacCormick, implicitly recognising the limitations of this empirical conception of political power, stated that 'political power, to be sustained over time, requires legitimacy. Law is a significant source of legitimacy'. See Neil MacCormick, 'Sovereignty: Myth and Reality' in Nils Jareborg (ed.), *Towards Universal Law: Trends in National, European and International Law-making* (Uppsala, Iustus Förlag, 1995), 227–48, at 235. This point has been subjected to critical analysis by Hans Lindahl, who argued that this means that political power must present itself as being conditioned and therefore not sovereign. Lindahl contended both that MacCormick's account contained a contradiction and that he had proved less than he claimed since the implication of his concession about legitimacy was that 'legitimate powers within a polity represent the sovereign'. Lindahl concluded, persuasively, that: 'While [MacCormick] has shown that there may be no individual or group of individuals in a legal and political order who enjoys undisputed superiority over all others, he has not demonstrated that sovereignty is contingent. In fact, his analysis suggests that sovereignty is a necessary legal and political concept'. See Hans Lindahl, 'The Purposiveness of Law: Two Concepts of Representation in the European Union' (1998) 17 *Law and Philosophy* 481–505, at 484–7. In rewriting this essay for *Questioning Sovereignty* (above n 90, ch 8), MacCormick seeks to evade this criticism by retreating to an essentially empirical conception of political power and omitting his original statement concerning the relationship between legitimacy and political power.

not rest on empirical phenomena, also of 'every element of the natural sciences'.[100] Since in Kelsen's universe, the state is conceived to be simply the personification of legal order, the dualism between state and law that underpins Austinian legal science is dissolved.[101] And since Kelsen's scheme rests legal order on a hypothesis—the basic norm as that pre-supposition which gives expression to the autonomy of legal order—his theory is left unaffected by historical or sociological investigation. While this may be acceptable as a theory of legal validity, on the vital question of sovereignty Kelsen's theory leads only to a circularity in which the state, which on the one hand apparently exists prior to law, also presents itself as a presupposition of law. As an insight into the juristic issues surrounding the concept of sovereignty, the pure theory has little to offer. Carl Schmitt's assessment—that Kelsen tried to resolve the issue simply by 'negating it'[102]—seems essentially correct. Focusing primarily on the issue of legal validity, Kelsen is able to maintain the purity of the normative order only after conceding that 'the concept of sovereignty must be radically repressed'.[103]

The fundamental difficulty with positivist theories of law is that they are more or less explicitly devised for the purpose of presenting positive law— law as a system of enacted rules—as an autonomous practice. And because sovereignty is an essentially political concept, this means that once such jurists come to provide an explanation of the foundations of legal author- ity, they almost inevitably distort or suppress this foundational concept. Thus, although Kelsen was able to finesse the law-state dichotomy, he was obliged to fall back on another distortive duality, that between the legal and the political. Kelsen was quite explicit about this; he recognised that the maintenance of a duality of the concepts of the legal and the political 'performs an ideological function of extraordinary significance'.[104] This, he suggested, was because legal theory is obliged both to assume that 'the state, as a collective unity that is originally the subject of will and action, exists independently of, and even prior to, the law' and also to recognise that the state 'is a presupposition of the law ... beholden to the law, because obligated and granted rights by the law'.[105]

---

[100] Hans Kelsen, *Introduction to the Problems of Legal Theory* trans. by Bonnie L. Paulson and Stanley L. Paulson of first edn. [1934] of *Reine Rechtslehre* (Oxford, Clarendon Press, 1992), 1.
[101] See Hans Kelsen, 'God and the State' [1922] in his *Essays in Legal and Moral Philosophy* Ota Weinberger intro. (Dordrecht, Reidel, 1973), ch 3.
[102] Carl Schmitt, *Political Theology: Four Chapters on the Concept of Sovereignty* [1922] George Schwab trans. (Cambridge, Mass, MIT Press, 1988), 21.
[103] Hans Kelsen, *Das Problem der Souveränität und die Theorie des Völkerrechts* (Tübingen, Mohr, 1920), 320; cited in Schmitt, *ibid.* 21.
[104] Kelsen, above n 100, 96–7.
[105] *Ibid*

The basic problem, it would appear, is that positivist theories of law focus almost entirely on the issue of competence. While this may help to explain positive law as a structure of civil obligations, it seriously distorts the attempt to understand law's role in establishing and maintaining the state. In relation to this latter function—the singular undertaking of public law—the issue of capacity must be drawn into an appropriate relation to that of competence; the political aspects of sovereignty must not be suppressed.

Within the security of a stable political order, within what MacCormick calls a 'standing constitutional tradition',[106] it is evident that law has 'its own relatively independent domain . . . [which] can be utilised to support or refute other domains'.[107] But it should not be forgotten that this legal sovereignty of competence is linked to a political sovereignty of capacity. When Schmitt commenced his study of sovereignty with the now notorious claim that 'sovereign is he who decides on the exception'[108] he was doing little more than stating the basic principle of the political conception of sovereignty. 'The rule proves nothing', claimed Schmitt with marked exaggeration, and 'the exception proves everything: It confirms not only the rule but also its existence, which derives only from the exception'.[109] It might be said, more prosaically, that whenever critical issues concerning the interests of the state are presented as matters of law, we should not forget that law's function—and the duty of all officers of the law—is to maintain and bolster the sovereignty of the state. The constitution, as Justice Robert Jackson once explained, is not a suicide pact.[110]

This type of explanation may disconcert those who seek some insurance against the threat of abuse of official power. Although their concerns are not unfounded—and certainly we should not overlook the state's potential to act as a force of domination—the standard remedy proposed by many, that of maintaining faith in the transcendent quality of law, is misconceived. To the question of how in practice sovereign authority can be prevented from using public power oppressively, it must openly be acknowledged that ultimately there can be no juridical solution.

---

[106] Above, at 75.
[107] Carl Schmitt, *The Concept of the Political* [1932] George Schwab trans. (Chicago, University of Chicago Press, 1996), 66.
[108] Schmitt, *Political Theology*, above n 102, 5.
[109] *Ibid* 15.
[110] *Terminiello v City of Chicago* 337 US 1 (1949), at 37(diss). *Cf* Koskenniemi's synopsis of Jellinek's views: 'The State . . . is a purposeful community. Among its purposes is the wish to engage in contacts with other States. To break one's compacts would go against this. It would make social life impossible. To have a purpose is to will the presence of the conditions under which the purpose may be fulfilled. If a State can fulfill its purpose only by participating in international life, then it must keep its promises unless there is a reasonable motive . . . for disregarding them. No State can be reasonably assumed to commit suicide'. See Martti Koskenniemi, *The Gentle Civilizer of Nations: The Rise and Fall of International Law* (Cambridge, Cambridge University Press, 2001), 205–6.

This does not mean that the institutional arrangements of law offer no protection. To the contrary, once sovereignty is properly understood, it must be evident that law performs a vital role in seeking to ensure that such power is properly exercised. For sovereignty, though absolute (ie, absolute from the perspective of its own particular way of conceptualising the world) incorporates certain intrinsic constraints. Such limitations are derived from the basic tenets of sovereignty, which identify sovereignty as being generated through an institutional framework that is established for the purpose of maintaining and promoting the peace, security and welfare of citizens. Without the limits implied by those tenets, sovereignty could not be identified as a representation of the autonomy of the political and thereby distinguished from the power that economic wealth, feudal dominion or despotism confers.[111]

Law plays a critical role in explicating in the form of rules, regulations, rights and responsibilities the character of sovereign authority. But if we are to take seriously the nature of public law, it must be recognised that, notwithstanding certain rhetorical flourishes about the appeal to 'higher', 'fundamental' or even 'natural' law, the determination of the limits to sovereign authority, even when articulated by courts, must be political.[112] It is political because it is in the nature of sovereignty that a political system must be capable of authoritatively expressing its will on any issue. This sovereign will is expressed through institutional forms and arrangements which are generally laid down in law, and adherence to these forms gives meaning to the idea of the rule of law. But thus constituted, there can be no legal limitation on competence, and in this sense it might be said that the sovereign is above the law.[113] Between these two basic propositions,

---

[111] *Cf* Montesquieu's project in *The Spirit of the Laws* (above n 80) which can be understood as an extended essay on the threat that despotism poses to sovereign authority: 'republican government is that in which the people as a body, or only as a part of the people, have sovereign power; monarchical government is that in which one alone governs, though by fixed and established laws; whereas, in despotic government, one alone, without law and without rule, draws everything along by his will and his caprices' (Bk. 2, ch 1). Despotism is the 'other'—a deviant form which lacks law, counsel and politics and eradicates the distinction between public and private—which Montesquieu uses to throw into relief the achievements of political order. Nevertheless, it might be noted that, by projecting an Oriental image of despotism, Montesquieu the aristocrat masks the degree to which it flourished in Europe as feudal dominion: on which see Kriegel above n 18, 18–9. *Cf* Arendt, above n 31, 202: 'Tyranny prevents the development of power . . . it generates, in other words, impotence as naturally as other bodies politic generate power'.

[112] In *The Concept of the Political* (above n 107), Schmitt illustrates this point at the same time as highlighting the limitations of his interpretation of Hobbes. He states (at 67): '[Hobbes] has emphasised time and again that the sovereignty of law means only the sovereignty of men who draw up and administer this law. The rule of a higher order, according to Hobbes, is an empty phrase if it does not signify that certain men of this higher order rule over men of a lower order'. What Schmitt here overlooks is the intrinsically representational aspects of Hobbes's sovereign, which have the effect of impressing public responsibilities in that institution.

[113] The complexity of this formulation can be discerned by considering the history of the maxim that 'the king can do no wrong': see Greenberg, above n 45.

however, lies a sphere of ambiguity. On the one hand, it could be said that since the sovereign will is omnipotent there can be no legal limitations whatsoever, because established institutional forms can always be changed. On the other hand, it might be argued that the sovereign is above law only in the way that a building is above its foundation; tamper with the foundation (the fundamental laws/the distinctive political relationship) and the building could collapse. Utilising this architectural metaphor, some try to transform these foundational issues into matters of law (hence the point about transcendence). But these issues, going to the core of the relational aspect of sovereignty must be acknowledged to be political. Cicero might say that such issues are resolved by *prudentia*, Acquinas by practical reason, and Montesquieu by the necessary relationships which stem from the nature of things. Whatever the precise characterisation, the point is that these are not matters which are susceptible to formulaic, rule-based prescription. To pretend that there are answers above the cut and thrust of the necessity of decision in the face of conflicting views, is to do a disservice both to the value of law and the art of politics.

CONCLUSION: SOVEREIGNTY IN TRANSITION?

By explicating the concept of sovereignty, my objective has been to show that sovereignty is the foundational concept that underpins modern juridico-political order. Thus understood, sovereignty stands as a representation of the autonomy of the political. By drawing on an intrinsically collective notion of political power—what Arendt referred to as 'the worldly in-between space by which men are mutually related'[114]—sovereignty can be recognised to be a relational phenomenon. This relational idea of sovereignty enables us to identify both the public and political aspects of the concept, which concern the issues of competence (authority) and capacity (power) respectively. Lawyers in particular need to be able to locate the authority structure of the state with some precision. When focusing on the issue of jurisdictional competence, however, it should never be forgotten that the regime draws its power from a political relationship between state and citizens; the issues of competence and capacity are inextricably linked.

Once sovereignty is understood in this light, it is difficult to conceive how, as many now claim, the present era is one that may be characterised as moving 'beyond' sovereignty. Such analyses are, for the most part, based on a misunderstanding of the concept. But since the contemporary trends in governance that provide the basis for such an assessment are of undoubted

---

[114] Arendt, above n 33, 175.

importance, the potential impact of these developments on the idea of relational sovereignty must be examined.

Most analyses focus on the likely impact of newly emerging institutional configurations on the status of the modern, territorially organised, state. The tendencies of states to promote greater institutional differentiation in the domestic sphere, leading to a devolution of authority from the centre,[115] and greater institutional integration in the international arena, leading to transfers of jurisdictional competence to supra-national bodies,[116] both appear to challenge their pre-eminent position. As has already been implied (tenet 7), however, such responses to contemporary political challenges should not be treated as amounting to a division or transfer of sovereignty; in principle, such developments can just as easily be explained as an extension or augmentation of sovereignty. The general point to be made is that, provided the question of 'ultimate' authority is not significantly affected by these novel institutional arrangements, they do not entrench on sovereignty. That is, provided these institutional arrangements can be explained as an elaboration of internal coherence or as the promotion of more efficacious external action, the basics of sovereignty remain unaffected. And the reason for this is that issues of jurisdictional competence are generally not determinative of questions of sovereignty.

This point may be illustrated by briefly considering the most innovative arrangement, that of the evolving structure of the European Union (EU). The project now known as the EU was formed by states in western Europe, essentially for the purpose of better advancing their traditional objectives of maintaining the security, prosperity and welfare of their citizens.[117] For these purposes, an elaborate supra-national authority structure was established. In the words of the European Court of Justice (ECJ), one of the newly-formed institutions, the Union constitutes 'a new legal order of international law for the benefit of which the states have limited their sovereign rights'.[118] But shared competence or transferred jurisdiction does not entail shared or transferred sovereignty, even if, with the acquiescence of the

---

[115] Note, eg, recent reforms affecting the governmental arrangements of the several parts of the United Kingdom: see Alan J. Ward, 'Devolution: Labour's Strange Constitutional "Design" ' in Jeffrey Jowell and Dawn Oliver (eds), *The Changing Constitution* 4th edition (Oxford, Oxford University Press, 2000), ch 5.

[116] See, eg, David Held, Anthony McGrew, David Goldblatt and Jonathan Perraton, *Global Transformations: Politics, Economics and Culture* (Cambridge, Polity Press, 1999).

[117] See Alan S. Milward, *The European Rescue of the Nation-State* re. edn. (London, Routledge, 1994), esp. ch 1.

[118] Case 26/62, *Van Gend en Loos v Nederlandse Administratie der Berlastingen* [1963] ECR 1, 12. See also Case 6/64, *Costa v ENEL* [1964] ECR 585, which asserts the supremacy of European Community law over the domestic law of member states (EC law cannot 'be overridden by domestic legal provisions, however framed, ... without the legal basis of the Community itself being called into question') and declares that state accession entails 'a permanent limitation of their sovereign rights'.

member state, European law assumes priority in any conflict with a provision of domestic law.[119] With the extending range of EU competences, however, deliberation over the autonomy of the EU legal order has been transmuted into a debate over the 'constitutionalisation' of the entity[120] and this has generated analyses concerning the formation of a 'post-state polity'.[121] Despite this flurry of activity, the critical question of sovereignty remains that which was most directly addressed by the German Federal Constitutional Court in 1993 in the case of *Brunner*.[122] In *Brunner*, the court declared that, with respect to matters of German constitutionality and sovereignty, it was for the constitutional court, and not the ECJ, to determine the limits of the powers of the EU.[123] The court also stated that, 'given the right [of the people] guaranteed by Article 38 of the Constitution to participate in the legitimation of state power'[124] (the principle of democracy), it followed that:

> If the peoples of the individual States provide democratic legitimation through the agency of their national parliaments (as at present) limits are then set by virtue of the democratic principle to the extension of the European Communities' functions and powers.[125]

Although the court did not preclude the possibility of the democratic bases of the EU being built up in tandem with continuing integration, it maintained that presently

> 'the exercise of sovereign power through a federation of States like the European Union is based on authorisations from States which remain sovereign and which in international matters generally, act through their governments and control the integration process thereby'.[126]

What the German constitutional court here recognised was the essentially political character of sovereignty. Sovereignty, it implied, is not directly affected by increasingly elaborate institutional arrangements of governance, since sovereignty, at its most basic, is an expression of a political relation-

---

[119] See Bruno de Witte, 'Direct Effect, Supremacy, and the Nature of the Legal Order' in Paul Craig and Gráinne de Búrca (eds), *The Evolution of EU Law* (Oxford, Oxford University Press, 1999), 177–213.

[120] See JHH Weiler, *The Constitution of Europe: 'Do the New Clothes have an Emperor?'* (Cambridge, Cambridge University Press, 1999); Dieter Grimm, 'Does Europe Need a Constitution?' (1995) 1 *European Law Journal* 282–302; Jürgen Habermas, "Remarks on Dieter Grimm's 'Does Europe Need a Constitution?" ' (1995) 1 *European Law Journal* 303–7.

[121] See Neil Walker, 'The Idea of Constitutional Pluralism' (2002) 65 *Modern Law Review* 317–59.

[122] *Brunner v European Union Treaty* [1994] 1 CMLR 57.

[123] *Ibid* para. 49.

[124] *Ibid* para. 34.

[125] *Ibid* para. 44.

[126] *Ibid* para. 46.

ship between the people and the state.[127] Jurisdictional questions of competence ultimately rest on political issues of capacity, the norm on the exception. And in an exceptional state of crisis, there seems little doubt that the state retains ultimate power and authority.

Concerns about sovereignty that are geared to issues of competence presented by the emergence of new institutional frameworks of governance thus turn out generally to be misplaced. But this is not to say that contemporary trends do not present major challenges for the idea of sovereignty. Such challenges, however, are not focused primarily on institutional matters. Rather, they are threats to capacity which are directed fundamentally at the political conception of sovereignty. This is a much more serious threat, one that presents a challenge to the continuing viability of the modern political project.

This radical challenge to the concept of sovereignty is rooted in an analysis of power in the contemporary world. The argument here is not merely that, as a consequence of new institutional configurations, the power of the modern state to impose its authority is diminishing. Although significant economic limits to the conduct of modern politics undoubtedly exist,[128] so long as the political realm is able to be conceptualised as a discrete sphere of human activity, such economic constraints do not directly undermine the idea of sovereignty. The argument is that power in late modernity has so fundamentally altered in character that the modern concept of sovereignty as a transcendent and representational idea founded on the autonomy of the political is now redundant.

This radical claim is most closely associated with the work of Michel Foucault, who argues that, as a consequence of technological, economic and social change, the political power generated by sovereignty has, through the processes of bureaucratisation, been transformed into a general economy of discipline that now pervades society.[129] This is what Foucault refers to as 'the paradox of the relations between capacity and power'.[130] A

---

[127] In this sense, the 'devolutionary' arrangements of the Scotland Act 1998, which establish a Scottish parliament able to give institutional expression to Scots political identity, potentially provide the more radical challenge to the sovereignty of the United Kingdom state. For comparison with the Canadian situation, see *Reference by the Governor in Council, pursuant to section 53 of the Supreme Court Act, concerning the secession of Quebec from Canada* [1998] 2 SCR 217; Mark D. Walters, 'Nationalism and the Pathology of Legal Systems: Considering the *Quebec Secession Reference* and its Lessons for the United Kingdom' (1999) 62 *Modern Law Review* 371–96.

[128] See John Dunn (ed.), *The Economic Limits to Modern Politics* (Cambridge, Cambridge University Press, 1990).

[129] Michel Foucault, 'Governmentality' in Graham Burchell, Colin Gordon and Peter Miller (eds), *The Foucault Effect: Studies in Governmentality* (Hemel Hempstead: Harvester Wheatsheaf, 1991), 87–104.

[130] Michel Foucault, 'What is Enlightenment?' in Paul Rabinow (ed.), *The Foucault Reader* (Harmondsworth, Penguin, 1986), 32–50, at 47.

synthesis having been effected between political and economic power, Foucault contends that disciplinary power not only shapes social and political practices but is able also to structure human thought.[131] As a consequence, the relationship between society and power—between the people and government—has been inverted and the regulatory force of governmental power, as a form of bio-power, is now applied to humanity itself.[132] This new paradigm of governance without government marks the death of the subject, the destruction of the autonomy of the political and the end of sovereignty.[133]

The juridical implications of Foucault's thesis have recently been examined by Michael Hardt and Antonio Negri.[134] Hardt and Negri argue that this decline in the modern political conception of sovereignty as a result of the emergence of 'governmentality' is better conceived 'as a passage *within* the notion of sovereignty'.[135] Sovereignty, they claim, should now be understood to have assumed a new form 'composed of a series of national and supranational organisms united under a single logic of rule'.[136] And this 'new global form of sovereignty' is what they call 'imperial sovereignty' or simply 'Empire'.[137]

Imperial sovereignty presents itself as the nemesis of modern sovereignty: imperial sovereignty reflects a fusion of economic and political power (*cf* tenet 2),[138] the elimination of the distinction between public and private (*cf* tenet 3),[139] the erosion of civil order which underpins the idea of official power (*cf* tenet 4),[140] and the disintegration of a distinctive political relationship (*cf* tenets 5 and 6).[141] More generally, it signals the end of the idea

---

[131] Michel Foucault, *Discipline and Punish: The Birth of the Prison* Alan Sheridan trans. (Harmondsworth, Penguin, 1977).

[132] Michel Foucault, *The History of Sexuality* Robert Hurley trans. (New York, Vintage, 1978), vol. 1, 135–45.

[133] Michel Foucault, *Power/Knowledge* (Brighton, Harvester, 1980), 121: '[Political] theories still continue today to busy themselves with the problem of sovereignty. What we need, however, is a political philosophy that isn't erected around the problem of sovereignty, nor therefore around the problems of law and prohibition. We still need to cut off the King's head: in political theory that has still to be done'.

[134] Michael Hardt and Antonio Negri, *Empire* (Cambridge, Mass, Harvard University Press, 2000).

[135] *Ibid* 88.

[136] *Ibid* xii.

[137] *Ibid* xii, 8.

[138] *Ibid* 354: 'Empire constitutes the ontological fabric in which all the relations of power are woven together—political and economic relations as well as social and personal relations'.

[139] *Ibid* 188–9.

[140] *Ibid* 187: 'In the imperial world, this dialectic of sovereignty between the civil order and the natural order has come to an end'.

[141] *Ibid* 307: 'Today a notion of politics as an independent sphere of the determination of consensus and a sphere of mediation among conflicting social forces has very little room to exist. . . . Politics does not disappear; what disappears is any notion of the autonomy of the political'.

of the modern state (*cf* tenet 1)[142] and of a relational sovereignty based on a territorial unit (*cf* tenet 7).[143] Imperial sovereignty marks the triumph of institutional competence, of legal sovereignty severed from political capacity, and, in a return to classical political thought (*cf* tenet 8), to the emergence of 'imperial right'.[144] Empire is the sovereign power that governs the world, the consummation of a capitalist project of fusing economic and political power. And in the process, the modern idea of public law is replaced by a systems-orientated framework of regulatory law operating in accordance with this 'single logic of rule' (*cf* tenets 9 and 10).[145]

Imperial sovereignty presents a challenge to modern sovereignty in the starkest of terms. Modern sovereignty is a juridico-political fiction that no longer is able adequately to represent the realities of power in late modern societies; it therefore serves the function of masking and legitimating an authority structure whose dynamic it is unable to grasp.[146] If modern sovereignty symbolises the past, then imperial sovereignty, a process that 'is materialising before our very eyes',[147] represents the future. Hardt and Negri believe not only that the emergence of Empire is inevitable, but that it should be embraced. Since Empire is a concept—an alternative theoretical construction to that of modern sovereignty—the question of whether the shift should be effected is essentially one of political judgment. But this political judgment is of major juristic significance, not least because lawyers, who tend to focus solely on issues of competence and jurisdiction, are likely to be unwittingly seduced by the universalising proclivities of imperial right.

Hardt and Negri promote Empire essentially because they place their faith in the constituent power of the multitude.[148] The emergence of Empire,

---

[142] *Ibid* 306: 'the state has been defeated and corporations now rule the earth!'

[143] *Ibid* 139–40: 'there is no longer an outside that can bound the place of sovereignty. . . . In this smooth space of Empire, there is no *place* of power—it is both everywhere and nowhere'.

[144] *Ibid* 62, referring to 'the frustration and continual instability suffered by imperial right as it attempts to destroy the old values that served as reference points for international public law (the nation-states, the international order of Westphalia, the United Nations and so forth) along with the so-called turbulence that accompanies this process'. From this perspective, it seems clear that bodies such as the European Court of Justice are to be conceived as being agencies of imperial right.

[145] *Ibid* 13–4: 'The new paradigm is both system and hierarchy, centralised construction of norms and far-reaching production of legitimacy, spread out over world space. It is configured *ab initio* as a dynamic and flexible systemic structure that is articulated horizontally. We conceive the structure in a kind of intellectual shorthand as a hybrid of Niklas Luhmann's systems theory and John Rawls's theory of justice. . . . The development of the global system (and of imperial right in the first place) seems to be the development of a machine that imposes procedures of continual contractualisation that lead to systemic equilibria—a machine that creates a continuous call for authority'.

[146] *Ibid* 375: 'European virtue—or really its aristocratic morality organised in the institutions of modern sovereignty—cannot manage to keep pace with the vital powers of mass democracy'.

[147] *Ibid* xi.

[148] See Antonio Negri, *Insurgencies: Constituent Power and the Modern State* Maurizia Boscagli trans. (Minneapolis, University of Minnesota Press, 1999).

they argue, highlights the fact that 'the multitude is the real productive force of our social world' and that Empire is 'a mere apparatus of capture that lives only off the vitality of the multitude'.[149] Empire therefore creates a greater potential for revolutionary action—constituent power in all its radicalness and strength—as 'all the exploited and the subjugated' come face to face with 'the machine of command' with 'no mediation between them'.[150] However, for those who lack such faith, who reach different judgments over the risk calculation, or who believe that the theoretical construct of imperial power is contradictory,[151] the neutralisation of the transcendental imagination that the abandonment of modern sovereignty signifies may simply be too great. Notwithstanding its limitations, abandonment of a representational political discourse founded on a public identity, and the jettisoning of a public law discourse rooted in political equality, in the face of a rapid agglomeration of global economic power does not seem ultimately to make much sense. Properly conceived, modern sovereignty continues to be a potent force.

---

[149] Hardt and Negri, above n 134, 62.
[150] *Ibid* 393.
[151] See, eg, Charles Taylor, 'Foucault on Freedom and Truth' in his *Philosophy and the Human Sciences: Philosophical Papers, vol. 2* (Cambridge, Cambridge University Press, 1985), 152–84.

4

Sovereignty and Representation in the European Union

HANS LINDAHL*

1. INTRODUCTION

S OVEREIGNTY IS NOT only a political concept but also a highly politicised concept. Indeed, the contemporary discussion about this concept is largely dominated by the question whether one is 'for' or 'against' sovereignty. While the partisans of sovereignty are increasingly isolated on a theoretical level, they continue to carry considerable weight in politics, as witnessed, amongst others, by *les souveranistes* in France. Conversely, opposition to sovereignty is particularly strong in the academic field but still relatively weak in politics. Given this state of affairs, a theoretical inquiry into sovereignty that does not a priori assume that this concept is a thing of the past, or something we need to move beyond, exposes itself to the charge of championing a form of *souveranisme*. This charge is particularly damning for an inquiry that, as is the case with this chapter, examines whether the concept of sovereignty remains apposite to the process of European integration. For, it will be said, an approach that refuses to accept in advance that sovereignty is an outdated concept merely deploys a nostalgic rearguard action, blind to the bold innovations that have led the European polity to where it now stands. Bluntly, such an inquiry smacks of crypto-Europhobia.

These preliminary considerations suggest that a philosophical reflection about sovereignty— i.e. an inquiry that seeks to understand what sovereignty is about rather than to justify why one is either 'for' or 'against' it— has become difficult and for this reason all the more necessary. For could it be that sovereignty is the name of a *problem*, far more than its solution? If so, would attempts to move 'beyond' sovereignty unwittingly reintroduce

* I appreciate helpful comments on this paper by Gráinne de Búrca, David Janssens, Bert van Roermund, Jo Shaw and Neil Walker.

the problem in another guise? Might not calls to proscribe the word 'sovereignty' from our legal and political vocabulary simply conceal the problem it names, thereby failing to deal with it?

Philosophically speaking, the question about sovereignty begins as a question about the structure of political power: Does sovereignty pertain to an aspect of political power as such and in general? Or is sovereignty only germane to a historically determinate structure of power? The answer to this query is at first sight obvious: as Bodin's *Republic* makes clear, sovereignty refers to a typically modern way of organising political power in a community. Yet, at second sight, Giorgio Agamben traced back the problem of sovereignty to Pindar, Solon and Hesiod, a problem he summarises under the title *'nomos basileus'*.[1] Nevertheless, one can and should retort, at third glance, that Agamben's analysis of these authors is thoroughly governed by the modern consciousness of the problem of sovereignty. So we need to reformulate the point of departure of our inquiry: In what way, or better, under what conditions could sovereignty at all become a problem for modern philosophy?

I submit that a philosophical elaboration of the concept of sovereignty is intimately bound up with the acute existential problem that is constitutive for the modern age, namely *contingency*. Bodin's standard reading has him devising the concept of sovereignty to hold at bay the disintegration of society in the face of bitter religious wars. Yet, this reading falls far short of explaining why sovereignty only became a philosophical theme at the threshold of modernity; after all, there was no dearth of civil wars prior to Bodin's time. The point, rather, is that these wars acquired their acute existential significance for Bodin in the framework of what Blumenberg called the experience of 'loss of order' that inaugurates modernity.[2] This inaugural experience draws the concept of sovereignty into the very heart of early modern philosophical reflection. By implication, and this is a hypothesis I will continuously test throughout the chapter, an inquiry into sovereignty provides the key to understanding in what sense our political communities are contingent.

Let me be more specific about contingency: Sovereignty is the concept by means of which modern political and legal philosophy elaborates the problem of the contingent *unity* of a political community. Paraphrasing Leibniz's principle of sufficient reason, the question challenging modern political and legal philosophy is the following: Why this political unity and not another?

---

[1] G Agamben, *Homo Sacer: Sovereign Power and Bare Life*, translated by D Heller-Roazen (Stanford, Stanford University Press, 1998), 30 *ff.*
[2] H Blumenberg, 'Ordnungsschwund und Selbstbehauptung: Über Weltverstehen und Weltverhalten im Werden der technischen Epoche' in H Kuhn and F Wiedman (eds.), *Das Problem der Ordnung* (Meisenheim, Anton Hain Verlag, 1962), 37–55. See also H Blumenberg, *The Legitimacy of the Modern Age*, translated by RM Wallace (Cambridge, Mass., The MIT Press, 1986).

At issue here is not simply opposing unity and plurality, as many contemporary interpretations of sovereignty would have us believe, but understanding the conditions under which political unity can and ought to be instituted, given a plurality of (competing) views of the good. This problem lay at the heart of Bodin's interpretation of the concept of sovereignty, as expressed in the canonical form 'After God, the king'; it continues to govern, amongst others, Jürgen Habermas's effort to reformulate the concept of popular sovereignty in terms of a 'discourse principle'. Thus, far from disappearing from philosophical discussion, the concept of sovereignty remains to this day the privileged locus for reflecting on the problem of the contingent unity of political communities. By implication, and this is decisive for our inquiry, although the aforementioned problem reached the threshold of philosophical reflection together with the appearance of the modern *state*, the latter by no means exhausts its scope. In effect, the contingency of political unity pertains to the concept of a *polity* as such and in general. I aim to show, in particular, that the problem of contingent unity remains very much alive in the process of constituting and maintaining the European polity, a polity that, according to many, marks the decisive passage beyond sovereignty.

In short, the problem of sovereignty, as a philosophical problem, points to four different but interrelated questions:

(1) Under what conditions does a political community constitute and maintain itself as a *unity*? (2) In what way do these conditions reveal that political unity is *contingent*? (3) What structure of *power* manifests itself in the process of constituting and maintaining a contingent political unity? (4) Finally, in what way does the structure of power, by constituting and maintaining a contingent political unity, shed light on the concept of *sovereignty*?

These questions animate the forthcoming analyses, even though they are not always explicitly raised in this way or addressed in this order.

The central thesis developed in this chapter is that the connection between sovereignty and the problem of contingent political unity can best be approached by way of a reflection on representation. Drawing on the well-known opposition between direct and representative democracy, section two probes the argument in favour of a direct or 'participative' model of democracy for the EU, showing that all deliberation between the members of a polity presupposes an operation of inclusion and exclusion that constitutes a group of individuals as a unity. Subsequently, section three analyses the logic of representation and discusses the implications of the insight that political unity is always a represented unity. After discussing how the logic of political representation is at work in the Treaty of Rome, section four makes explicit the link between sovereignty and the representation of unity, showing that a dialectic between *pouvoir constituant* and *pouvoir constitué* is at work in the ECJ's constitutionalisation of the

Community Treaties. Finally, section five briefly returns to examine the relation between sovereignty and contingency.

2. THE STANDARD PICTURE ABOUT SOVEREIGNTY

Something approaching a standard picture has emerged concerning sovereignty. This standard picture has become so ubiquitous and powerful that no attempt to consider the problem of sovereignty afresh can ignore it, other than at the risk of being itself ignored, misunderstood or boxed into this picture. So, let us briefly sketch out its main lines.

Contemporary political and legal developments, it is held, reveal two opposed models of government and two conflicting normative approaches to the exercise of power. On the one hand, we find 'state-centrism', the organisation of power germane to the modern sovereign state. State-centrism is characterised by the centralisation and concentration of power, typically in the hands of a parliament and a corresponding majority government. The hoary doctrine of the sovereignty of parliament in British constitutional law is but an extreme example of the fact that the sovereign state concentrates ultimate power over the polity in the hands of a single, clearly localised organ. This top-down, command-and-control approach implies that the central lawmaker issues general legal norms, which are subsequently applied by local organs. These features of the sovereign state render lawmaking vulnerable in two ways. First, the law, by dint of its generality, cannot accommodate the differentiation required by an increasingly fragmented and complex society. This has led to a significant erosion of the effectiveness of lawmaking. Second, the generality of the law leads to democratic distortions when the majority view in the localities in which the law must be applied conflicts with the majority view at a national level. Under these conditions, the centralisation of lawmaking power in the hands of a representative organ leads to a distinct loss of legitimacy. In sum, 'state-centrism' is shorthand for the composite of centralism, verticality, representation, command and monism.

So much for the first term of the standard picture. Its second term, we are told, is the 'multi-level' polity. If we take the EU as an example, however embryonic and imperfect, of this kind of polity, 'multi-level' means that decision-making involves the participation of supranational, national and sub-national actors in such a way that neither the supranational nor the sub-national actors can be viewed simply as agents of national authorities. The rise of comitology, for example, has meant that the European Commission often consults sub-national actors directly, bypassing the governments of member states. More generally, sub-national actors, such as regions, interest groups and private persons, have acquired a direct role in at least some fields of European lawmaking. This feature contrasts with the centralisation and concentration of lawmaking in national parliaments: representation makes way for citizen participation. By implication, the 'multi-level' polity is also 'multi-centred': it moves away from a single, centralised lawmaker, as in the sovereign state, towards a manifold of power sites. Consequently, and in contrast with the sovereign state, sovereignty is now 'shared' or 'pooled'. The multiplication and decentralisation of power-sites in the multi-level polity promotes two features of lawmaking that are the inverted images of the disadvantages of lawmaking in the sovereign state. First, decisions are taken much closer to the concrete issues that require regulation. By virtue of its sensitivity to context, lawmaking in a multi-level polity is more effective. Second, direct citizen participation greatly enhances the legitimacy of lawmaking, as now also the citizens themselves engage in lawmaking by way of deliberation. In sum, 'multi-level' governance is shorthand for the compound of decentralisation, horizontality, participation, deliberation and pluralism.

This, roughly, is the standard picture that dominates current discussions about sovereignty. Its influence is by no means restricted to academia; with some refinements, the standard picture has played a decisive role in the process of drafting the European Commission's White Paper on European Governance. Recent developments in the EU, it is asserted,

> ... mark *a break* with the position where representatives are democratically elected, formulate broad policies in legislative chambers and oversee their detailed implementation by administrative departments or the smooth running of the free market. Instead, the process of policy formation and implementation is increasingly understood as a more collective effort with public actors playing a more enabling role—neither imposing a particular understanding of the problems to be tackled nor of the means by which they might be resolved.[3]

This citation is important, for it suggests that what is at stake in the passage from 'state-centred' to 'multi-level' governance is no merely functional adaptation of ageing political structures to new social and economic circumstances. First and foremost, the erosion of the sovereign state has a normative interest, namely seizing the opportunity to breathe new institutional life into the idea that the people are the ultimate lawmaking authority of a democratic community, its *pouvoir constituant*. In its most elemental and politically pregnant formulation, popular sovereignty means that all power in the community emanates from the people. By the same token, the legislative, the executive and the judiciary are *pouvoirs constitués*, having received their powers from the people. Accordingly, the standard picture does not strike out sovereignty from the vocabulary of politics

---

[3] N Lebessis and J Paterson, 'Improving the Effectiveness and Legitimacy of EU Governance: A Possible Reform Agenda for the Commission', Working Paper, European Commission, Forward Studies Unit, CdP (99) 750, at 26.

and law; it argues that current transformations in 'governance' imply a *diffusion* of sovereignty. To diffuse—and defuse—the exercise of political power is to realise the democratic principle of popular sovereignty.

Thus, the unquestioned presupposition without which a confrontation between 'pluralists' and 'monists' could not even get off the ground is that two fundamentally different models of democratic government are at stake in the discussion about sovereignty, namely representation and participation. If practical considerations hitherto justified a division of political labour, whereby the few govern on behalf of the many, this very argument now militates against representation. As strictly empirical reasons motivate the passage from participation to representation, supervening empirical reasons can reverse or temper this passage: 'the complexity of problems and the diversity of [European] society mean that it is no longer sufficient to look for inspiration to the model of representative democracy.'[4]

My critical questioning begins at this point. The implicit assumption underpinning the standard picture's opposition between representation and participation is that the *citizens* of a community are the sovereign people. While this assumption is a truism of political and legal theory, it marks the point at which conceptual obfuscation about the concept of popular sovereignty sets in. To reveal where things go awry, let us briefly discuss a recent and influential defence of popular sovereignty, which has been widely welcomed as a plausible and normatively attractive model of democracy for the EU.

Joshua Cohen and Charles Sabel defend a participatory model of democracy called 'directly-deliberative polyarchy'. As they put it, directly-deliberative polyarchy '. . . is an attractive kind of radical, participatory democracy with problem-solving capacities useful under current conditions and unavailable to representative systems'.[5] This model advocates collective decision-making by citizens who are at the receiving-end of public services, in a deliberative process that takes into account the experiences of similar deliberative arenas. The authors advance two arguments in support of participatory democracy, both of which echo familiar features of the standard picture. The first is functional, and refers to the greater problem-solving capacity of participation; the second is normative, and points to the greater legitimacy of lawmaking through participation. According to Oliver Gerstenberg, who defended the relevance of this model for the European Union, 'directly-deliberative polyarchy . . . insists that sovereignty resides with the problem-solving units themselves as the political substrate of radical democracy'.[6]

---

[4] *Ibid*, at 11.
[5] J Cohen and C Sabel, 'Directly-Deliberative Polyarchy', 3 (1997) *European Law Journal*, 313–42, at 313.
[6] O Gerstenberg, 'Law's Polyarchy: A Comment on Cohen and Sabel' in 3 (1997) *European Law Journal*, 343–58, at 357.

Gerstenberg's comment is illuminating, not so much because it links popular sovereignty to 'problem-solving units' rather than to 'the people', but because it seems to ascribe sovereignty to a *unity*. For a 'problem-solving unit' is, minimally, a unity. But can we make sense of this unity in terms consistent with the requirements of a theory of 'radical' democracy? Can, namely, the foundation of a problem-solving unit be viewed as a deliberative act? More concretely, who are the members of the problem-solving unit? A related question concerns the way in which the problem that requires deliberation is to be defined. In sum, how are the boundaries of unity to be determined?

Cohen and Sabel are well aware of this problem, as they explicitly pose the question concerning 'the circle of membership' of problem-solving units. Their answer is that 'directly-deliberative arenas are to be open to providers and parties affected by the extent and manner of provision'.[7] But this response falls short of the strict requirements posed by a theory of 'radical' democracy. For should not the criteria determining who is 'affected' by provisions be the outcome of deliberation? Notice the predicament: who is affected and what is the problem to be solved are matters of substance that require deliberation, yet deliberation cannot kick off without a prior determination of the members and the problem of the deliberative body. Reason-giving presupposes an act that is not itself a reason-giving; the act of 'opening up' a deliberative arena is not a deliberative act.

This insight returns us to the distinction between constituting and constituted power at the heart of popular sovereignty. If, as asserted by democratic theories, the *pouvoir constituant* is sovereign, and if problem-solving units must be *constituted* to be able to function, can one still assert, as Gerstenberg does, that 'sovereignty resides with the problem-solving units themselves'?

This problem resurfaces when one turns to the highest problem-solving unit in which lower-order units operate, namely a polyarchy. For, whatever the criteria that must be met, such that a polity can qualify as a 'polyarchy', the latter is a *unity*. Significantly, Cohen and Sabel assume, for the purposes of their analysis, that 'the institutions of polyarchy are in place'.[8] Obviously, this also involves assuming that unity is 'in place', i.e. has been instituted. However, should not the foundation of a polity be the subject matter *par excellence* of deliberation? This question becomes all the more urgent when Cohen and Sabel assert that democracy '[opens] debate to all'.[9] For their statement in fact means that democracy opens debate to all *citizens*, i.e. to the members of the polity. Deliberation presupposes a prior act of inclusion

---

[7] Cohen and Sabel, n 5 above, at 332.
[8] *Ibid* at 326.
[9] *Ibid* at 320.

and exclusion, which brings about the fundamental political distinction between citizen and alien. More pointedly, the act that opens political debate for some perforce closes it for others. There is no deliberation without inclusion, but also no deliberation without exclusion. Unity is always a *constituted* unity, and deliberation by citizens cannot begin without the constitution of unity. Does it make sense, then, to assert that the ensemble of citizens is the sovereign people?

It is instructive to see how this problem reappears in Habermas's interpretation of popular sovereignty in terms of what he calls a 'discourse principle'. For, despite the substantial differences between Habermas, on the one hand, and Cohen and Sabel, on the other, the problem concerning the unity of a community also crops up in Habermas's definition of the discourse principle: 'Just those action norms are valid to which all possibly affected persons could agree as participants in rational discourses'.[10] Here again, the question about unity looms large: Who counts as a 'possibly affected' person? Habermas answers: '. . . anyone whose interests are touched by the foreseeable consequences of a general practice regulated by the norms at issue.'[11]

In a penetrating critique, Bert van Roermund exposed the shortcomings of Habermas's approach to the aforementioned problem:

> Without a standard of normality, which in turn refers to what a certain group values as 'normal' in the light of its own beliefs and preferences, the [notion of the foreseeable] will not work. So the act of a group uniting into one group is already presupposed in [the discourse principle].[12]

He then goes on to show that the same quandary applies to Habermas's further specification, 'anyone whose interests are touched'. Whether or not someone's interests are touched is a thoroughly normative question that can only be answered by reference to a group that has already been constituted as a unity. To borrow Alfred Schütz's vocabulary, the terms 'concerned' or 'affected' (persons) are variations on the general phenomenon of *relevance*, and who or what is relevant or irrelevant can only by determined by reference to a constituted order.[13]

In sum, the contractarian interpretation of popular sovereignty encounters an insurmountable obstacle in its effort to account for the unity of a polity: social contract will not even function as the 'virtual' foundation of a community because who ought to participate in its founding act can only

---

[10] J Habermas, *Between Facts and Norms*, translated by W Rehg (Cambridge, Mass., The MIT Press, 1996), at 107.

[11] *Ibid*

[12] B van Roermund, *Law, Narrative and Reality: An Essay in Intercepting Politics* (Dordrecht, Kluwer Academic Publishers, 1997), at 151.

[13] A Schütz, *Reflections on the Problem of Relevance*, translated by RM Zaner (New Haven, Yale University Press, 1970).

be settled by already presupposing the polity's normative foundation. To put it another way, all deliberation between the members of a polity about the latter's normative principles and institutions presupposes an operation of inclusion and exclusion that constitutes a group of individuals as a unity.

This insight has a far-reaching implication for the standard picture's opposition between a 'command' and 'deliberation'. Indeed, does not an immanent critique of social contract theory reveal that a command, defined as a claim about unity that escapes justification through deliberation between 'all those concerned', not only survives in the foundation of every polity, democratic or otherwise, but proves to be a *necessary condition* for its foundation? Is not a command, in the aforementioned sense, a necessary condition for deliberation? Yet more sharply, if there is no deliberation without a prior command, is deliberation ever *purely* deliberation, even when the participants engage in it with a 'good will'?[14]

3. THE LOGIC OF POLITICAL REPRESENTATION

Abstracting from all nuances and conceptual refinements, normative theories of popular sovereignty endeavour to generate unity from plurality, that is, to explain 'the people', in the singular, beginning from 'people', in the plural. Although they fail in this attempt, there is a good reason for their reluctance to postulate unity as the necessary presupposition of democratic politics. For this presupposition all too easily boils down to a form of *reification*.

An exchange between Dieter Grimm, justice of the German Federal Constitutional Court, and Jürgen Habermas neatly illustrates this point.

---

[14] I envisage here not only a critique of Habermas's discourse principle but also of Gadamer's interpretation of the role of 'good will' in a dialogue (*Gespräch*); see H-G Gadamer, 'Und dennoch: Macht des Guten Willens' in P Forget (ed.), *Text und Interpretation: Deutsch-französische Debatte* (München, Wilhelm Fink Verlag, 1984), 59–61, at 59. Whatever the differences between Habermas and Gadamer, both stand on the same side of the debate about pluralism and monism. While both staunchly defend pluralism, they do so in view of generating an encompassing unity from plurality by way of discourse (Habermas) or dialogue (Gadamer). This point is important because, paradoxically, *the standard picture's critique of sovereignty in the name of pluralism is profoundly monistic*: deliberation and participation do not merely expose social division but aim to overcome it, to reconcile difference in a higher unity. Plurality, for the advocates of the standard picture, is always a provisional plurality, even if unity must be forever postponed given the vicissitudes of real-life politics. The truly fundamental normative challenge facing a reflection on sovereignty, a challenge I can only point to here without developing it, is to think and deal with plurality in a strong sense of the term, namely a 'difference' that cannot be integrated into the legal order without either neutralising the former or destroying the latter. Unity and plurality are neither simply disjunctive terms nor terms that can be fully reconciled within an all-encompassing polity as 'internal difference', plurality within unity. This, as I see it, is the challenge that Neil Walker seeks to address under the general rubric 'constitutional pluralism' (see, amongst others, his contribution to the present volume).

Implicitly referring to the conceptual underpinning of the well-known 'Maastricht' decision of the Constitutional Court, Grimm noted that

> The [European] Community, for lack of a pre-existing social substrate that could give it unity, exists only as a legal unity.[15]

Firmly rejecting the idea of a primordial substrate as the basis of a legal order, Habermas retorted that political integration

> . . . in no way [requires] a collective identity that is *independent of the democratic process itself* and as such existing prior to that process.[16]

Habermas was right to criticise Grimm's reification of political unity. But his normative account of popular sovereignty falls prey to the difficulty we have discovered with respect to the 'discourse principle': unity cannot be generated from plurality without already presupposing unity.

(a) Presence and Absence

Why is the hypostasis of the people a risk that haunts popular sovereignty? The answer, I believe, is that every legal order necessarily presents itself as legitimate, and this is another way of saying that the law always claims to be grounded. Again, every legal order avers that it is the institutionalisation of a higher order. This thesis obviously does not entail that every legal order is legitimate, for the law's claim is always challenged with varying degrees of intensity; instead, it makes a point about the logic at the heart of lawmaking. This logic is *representational*: the law claims to express—represent—a pre-legal unity.

Returning to our question about hypostasis, the theory and practice of democracy are constantly in danger of reifying the people because this danger is rooted in representation itself. In effect, what seems more obvious than that the people, as a unity, exists *independently* of its legal representations and that, at decisive moments of a polity's existence (e.g. at its foundation or, later, in elections and sundry forms of citizen participation), the sovereign people is *itself present* in the political arena? The logic of representation seems to require that there first be a sovereign people, as a unity, and, subsequently, that this people enact a legal order. This, in a nutshell, is Grimm's argument about the EU.

Although commonsensical, this understanding of the logic of representation boils down to a form of 'originalism' or, if you wish, a metaphysics of

---

[15] D Grimm, 'Does Europe Need a Constitution?', 1 (1995) *European Law Journal*, 282–302, at 289.
[16] J Habermas, 'Remarks on Dieter Grimm's "Does Europe Need a Constitution?"', 1 (1995) *European Law Journal*, 303–07, at 305.

presence. In effect, the postulate that a people exists independently of its (legal) representations implies the primacy of presence over representation; it assumes that the representation of the sovereign people leads back to an original presence, which can always be actualised by suspending representational practices. On this view, the ever-actualisable return to an original presence justifies designating the people as the 'ground' or 'bearer' of a legal order. The spell of a metaphysics of presence cannot be broken by simply abjuring the concept of representation nor, in terms of politics and political theory, by playing off political representation against participation. Instead, it requires a fundamentally different approach to the logic of representation. If, at a minimum, representation means that something absent is rendered present, then we need to carry further this idea by arguing that absence is not merely provisional but *definitive*. I suspect that celebrations of philosophical radicalism always come too soon, but if, nonetheless, one were to qualify a theory of democracy as 'radical', then such a theory should begin by recognising that the sovereign people is absent, not merely for empirical reasons associated with the political division of labour, but because it never is nor can be present. In other words, the people, as a unity, is never directly accessible; unity is always a *represented unity*. Why?

Claude Lefort provides an answer to this question in the framework of his analysis of the symbolic structure of power:

> The fact that [a polity] is organized as one despite (or because of) its multiple divisions and that it is organized as the same in all its multiple dimensions implies a reference to a place from where it can be seen, read and named. This symbolic pole proves to be power, even before we examine it in its empirical determinations . . .; power makes a gesture towards an *outside* (*un dehors*), whence [a polity] defines itself. Whatever its form, [power] always refers to the same enigma: that of an internal-external articulation, a division which institutes a common space . . .[17]

---

[17] C Lefort, *Democracy and Political Theory*, translated by D Macey (Cambridge, Polity Press, 1988), at 225. This, of course, is the domain that Lefort calls 'the political' (*le politique*) as opposed to 'politics' (*la politique*). The reduction of politics and law either to the subject matter of applied moral philosophy (normative approaches to popular sovereignty) or to empirical studies of political and legal institutions (political science) systematically blocks access to *le politique* and, with it, to the general and necessary conditions of the acts that structure a political community. A good example of the limitations of the purely institutional approach of political science is the article by G Marks, L Hooghe, and K Blank, 'European Integration from the 1980s: State-Centric v. Multi-level Governance', 34 (1996) *Journal of Common Market Studies*, 341–78. The authors distinguish between two concepts of the 'state', the first of which is so capacious that it defines the domain of political science proper: '. . . a particular constellation of formal (and informal) rules that specify the location, extent and basis of legitimate authority in a society' (*ibid*, at 347). While this definition is no doubt adequate to the institutional analyses of political science, its reference to a 'particular constellation' of rules raises a fundamental question: Under what conditions can a manifold of rules be viewed as a *unity*, in the singular and determinate? This question cannot be answered at the level of 'politics'; it leads straight to the domain of 'the political'. However fashionable, the term 'governance' cannot make the problem of unity disappear; it can only briefly camouflage it.

Lefort's insight debunks the widely held view that the sovereign people can be equated with a group of individuals. The sovereign people is not a real entity but a symbolic pole lying 'outside' the community of individuals, and by reference to which these individuals can recognise themselves as the members of a polity. In effect, 'people', in the plural, is an aggregate or numerical concept; as such, it implies precisely the opposite of unity, namely division and particularity. Evidently, no political community is possible without citizens, but the people, as a unity, does not coincide with an ever-changing set of citizens. Accounting for this distinction in a way that avoids reifying unity requires recognising that only *individuals* are and can be present, whereas the people is always absent as a *unity*, i.e. as the 'bearer' or 'subject' of a legal order.

Yet, Lefort only takes us part of the way in understanding the logic of political representation. For what concrete sense can we make of political representation as the relation between presence and absence? In what way is this relation effectual in the institutional forms of political representation as we know them?

David Plotke's article, 'Representation Is Democracy', provides an illuminating clue. A representative, Plotke notes,

> . . . cannot only say: I support Y because I am bound to do so by an agreement with my constituents. He or she must say: Y, which is a matter of great concern to my constituents, is crucial to the public good. Political debate contests that claim.[18]

Plotke's point is that political representation creates a tension between a particular interest and the 'public' good. Now, what characterises the good as 'public' is its *commonality*. In other words, political representation perforce presents a particular interest as concretising the common good. This is another way of saying that the relation between a particular interest and the common good is itself *representational*. What is perhaps most interesting about Plotke's remark is that it suggests that political representation unfolds a relation of *interdependency* between the representation and the represented. On the one hand, a particular interest can only raise a claim to legitimacy by asserting that it represents the common good. In this sense, the representation—a particular interest— depends on what it is claimed to represent—the common good. On the other hand, although Plotke himself does not draw this conclusion, the common interest is equally dependent on its particularisations: *there is no direct access to the common good; it is only accessible by way of its representations.* The common good remains forever absent and this means that, deprived of particularising representations, it would remain an empty normative signifier that provides no

---

[18] D Plotke, 'Representation Is Democracy', 4 (1997) *Constellations*, 19–34, at 33.

normative orientation whatsoever. And as the common good is the way of conceiving the people as a *unity*, to argue that the common good is only accessible through its particularisations is to assert that unity is necessarily a represented unity.

In sum, if political representation always involves the danger of hypostasis, by suggesting that unity exists independently of and prior to its legal representations, the reformulation of the concept of representation developed heretofore counters hypostasis, by showing that unity is never given directly, but only by way of its particularisations. This, I submit, is the concrete political meaning of the representational relation between presence and absence.

(b) Two Implications

The structure of political representation has a far-reaching implication for the standard picture about sovereignty. Although the latter recognises that, in practice, a democracy always combines representation and participation, it assumes that, at least in principle, the sovereign people can either delegate lawmaking power to its representatives or suspend representative practices in view of intervening directly, 'in person', in the political arena. The foregoing analyses dispute the very possibility of drawing a conceptual distinction between representation and participation. If unity is necessarily a represented unity, then, whatever its form, *citizen participation is perforce political representation*. The standard picture operates with a reductive concept of representation, namely *parliamentary* representation. Yet, the members of parliament are not the sole political representatives of a polity, nor, for that matter, does one succeed in grasping the comprehensiveness of political representation by merely extending this term to include, say, the executive and the judiciary. For whenever they cast a vote, also the citizens represent the people by indicating which political programme in their view best expresses the common good. And the same logic is at work in all modes of citizen participation: to participate in the political life of a community, is, ultimately, to engage in the ongoing process of giving a content to the common good, that is, of representing it.[19]

In short, all attempts to interpret popular sovereignty in terms of 'direct' democracy either reify unity—as is the case with political 'originalism'—or

---

[19] Accordingly, calls for introducing mechanisms of citizen participation into European decision-making actually advocate new forms of political representation. For example, Christian Joerges's proposal to introduce a deliberative model of decision-making into comitology in fact outlines a model of political representation sensitive to the constraints imposed by market regulation in the EU; see, amongst others, C Joerges, ' "Good Governance" Through Comitology?' in C Joerges and E Vos (eds.), *EU Committees: Social Regulation, Law and Politics* (Oxford, Hart Publishing, 1999), 310–38.

are internally inconsistent—as is the case with normative theories of popular sovereignty. The distinction between direct and indirect democracy is a particularly stubborn political manifestation of a metaphysics of presence: the people is never immediately present to itself as a unity, not in so-called 'primitive' democracies, nor in 'deliberative' democracies; the relation to self of a political community is inevitably indirect, mediate, representational. Paraphrasing Derrida's remark about the Leitmotif of phenomenology—*zu der Sache selbst*, to things themselves—one could say that '[C]ontrary to what our desire cannot fail to be tempted into believing, the [people] itself always escapes'.[20]

A second implication of the structure of political representation concerns the tension between its two terms. For the one, there is no simple disjunction between 'either' interest representation 'or' representation of the common good. All attempts to merely oppose these two terms, such that representing the people, as a whole, would require resolutely banishing interest representation from democratic politics, lose sight of the fact that the common good is only accessible through its particularisations. There is no 'neutral' political representation; by concretising the common good, every representation always proves to be more or less interested.[21] For the other, the common good does not simply coincide with any of its manifold concretisations, precisely because it is only accessible through the latter. The 'whole' people calls forth a surplus of normative meanings that is never exhausted by any representation. Accordingly, the tension between particular interest and common good determines every act of political representation as a *contestable claim*. Periodic elections are one way of institutionalising the contestability of representational claims. Precisely for this reason, gaining political representation is of such vital importance; this, ultimately, is what the desideratum of greater citizen participation is all about.

This tension can also be expressed in terms of inclusion and exclusion, a theme that we encountered in the immanent critique of normative accounts of popular sovereignty. In effect, every representation of the common good necessarily implies the inclusion and exclusion of values. As such, representation is a thoroughly ambiguous achievement. On the one hand, it would be a mistake to view the exclusion of values merely as a 'privation', as a defective form of political representation. First and foremost, exclusion is a

---

[20] J Derrida, *Speech and Phenomena and Other Essays on Husserl's Theory of Signs*, translated by DB Allison (Evanston, Northwestern University Press, 1973), at 104.

[21] This point impugns Schmitt's attempt to oppose interest representation and representation of the people, when he argues that, given the crisis of parliamentary democracy in Weimar, only the president of the Republic, as a 'neutral power', was capable of representing the people; see C Schmitt, *Der Hüter der Verfassung* (Berlin, Duncker & Humblot, 1931), 132 *ff*. By the same token, it contests all claims that party politics *eo ipse* threatens democratic political representation, that is, representation of the people as a *whole*.

positive feature of representation, for closure is a necessary condition for the disclosure of a common or public space. On the other hand, the operation of normative inclusion and exclusion implies that political representation always brings about a normative reduction: the disclosure of the common good as embodied in 'this' or 'that' interest necessarily involves a normative closure of the good. Political representation reveals and conceals, actualises a normative meaning of the common good by eliding other possible meanings.

Evidently, the values excluded by political representation do not simply vanish into thin air. They are *marginalised*, that is to say, they remain at the fringes of a polity, embodied in forms of behaviour that retain the potential of subverting the representations of the common good positivised in the legal order. No polity can establish itself without a representation of unity, but the representation of unity also guarantees that no polity ever succeeds in establishing itself definitively. The same logic that moves political power to claim that it represents the 'whole' people ensures that the 'whole' people cannot be definitively contained within the forms of any legal order. The disturbances during the meeting of the European Council in Göteborg are a particularly stark reminder of the fact that, with varying degrees of intensity, a polity always finds itself in a 'state of emergency'; a 'state of normality' is a borderline case that a polity can only approach, without ever attaining. Waxing pathetic, the representational act that gives birth to a polity inevitably creates the conditions for its possible revolutionary overthrow and replacement by a new polity. The contingency of a polity and its contestability are two sides of the same representational coin.

4. SOVEREIGNTY AND THE REPRESENTATION OF UNITY

We can now enter the final and decisive stage of our inquiry. What are the implications of the logic of political representation for the concept of sovereignty in general and popular sovereignty in particular? In what way does the insight that unity is always a represented unity shed light on the role played by sovereignty in the process of European integration?

(a) 'An Ever Closer Union Among The Peoples of Europe'

The foregoing analyses of the logic of political representation situate the discussion with the standard picture there where this picture is strongest, namely its insight that the debate about sovereignty ultimately hinges on the concept and the problem of *unity*. Indeed, the whole weight of the series of oppositions set up by the standard picture comes to bear on the oppositions between monism and pluralism, unity and plurality. The normative interest in moving away from 'state sovereignty' towards a 'post-sovereign' polity is to invent new institutional venues for democratic pluralism.

Such venues are no doubt welcome; but can they do away with the problem of unity? More pointedly, can one scrap the people, in the singular and determinate, from the concept of popular sovereignty? To be sure, one can eschew altogether defining democracy in terms of popular sovereignty, in the hope that deleting the label will also delete the problem. One could then go on to set up a checklist of features, procedural or otherwise, that must be met, such that a polity can be granted the quality predicate 'democratic'. But this strategy only postpones the problem. For, under what conditions is a polity, hence a *unity*, at all possible? This is not to say that the procedural features traditionally associated with a democracy are unimportant; it is to assert that these features draw their meaning from a specific way of dealing with the problem of unity. In effect, such features are democratic because they institutionalise the insight that unity is always a represented—contestable—unity.

But does this objection hold for the European Union? Does not the European polity mark a definitive break with the claim to unity that characterises the modern nation state?

To address this question, let us scrutinise the Treaty of Rome, concretely showing how the logic of political representation is at work in the founding act of the European Economic Community. Consider, in particular, the famous passage of the Preamble to the Treaty of Rome, which provides the most general formulation of the project of European integration: '. . . to lay the foundations of an ever closer union among the peoples of Europe.' Great importance has been attached to the fact that the Preamble refers to 'the peoples of Europe', in the plural, rather than to 'the people of Europe', in the singular. Not only is the plurality of European peoples the point of departure of an integrative process, but also retaining this plurality is a desideratum of integration, as witnessed, amongst others, by the principle of subsidiarity, the EU's obligation to 'respect the national identities of its Member States', and the Treaty of Amsterdam's caveat to the effect that European citizenship 'shall complement and not replace national citizenship'. It would seem, therefore, that the Preamble to the Treaty marks a fundamental rupture with the founding acts of nation states, which, paradigmatically, commence with 'We the people . . .' By implication, the Treaty of Rome seems to confirm the pluralistic vocation of the European enterprise, as opposed to the nation state's penchant for unity.

Are things so simple? Notice, to begin with, that by referring to 'Europe', the Preamble postulates a *unity*. It would be a mistake, moreover, to think that, in the context of the preamble, 'Europe' merely denotes a geographic region; first and foremost, the term is used to denote a *normative* unity. Crucially, the Preamble's reference to an ever closer union of European peoples presupposes that there *already* was a union at the time of laying its legal foundation in the Treaty of Rome, a community of peoples that, by virtue of their shared values, can go further together, engaging in a process of legal and economic integration. Hence, and paradoxically, the very treaty that comes first, by virtue of founding the European Economic Community, claims to come *second*: a prior normative unity is held to be the starting point of a process of integration. In the same stroke by which the Preamble to the Treaty of Rome recognises a plurality of European peoples, it also presupposes their shared identity. In this minimal sense, the Treaty claims that a European people, *in the singular*, is the starting point of the integrative process as a whole, regardless of the institutional form that might be given to the relation between that greater unity and its constituent parts.[22] Hence, the Preamble to the Treaty of Rome confirms what we already learned from the failure of social contract theories: unity cannot be generated from plurality without already presupposing unity.

Let me briefly discuss two decisive ways in which the Treaty of Rome confronts the EU with the problem of unity in the very same way that unity is an unavoidable problem for *any* polity, including the modern nation state:

1) Notice, first, that in the closing consideration of the Preamble to the Treaty of Rome, the founding parties '. . . [call] upon the other peoples of Europe who share their ideal to join in their efforts . . .' At one level, of course, this consideration expresses the openness of the EC to other potential member states. At a deeper level, however, it reminds us of the fact that, while the six founding member states claimed to represent European unity, they had received no mandate from 'all possibly affected' parties, whether states or individuals, to found a European Community. Bluntly, the founding states are the *self-proclaimed* representatives of European unity. It is tempting to interpret this fact as an additional confirmation of the dubious democratic credentials of the Treaty of Rome and of the European Union as a whole. But, prior to all normative qualifications, whether 'positive' or 'negative', the Treaty of Rome illustrates something that is far more fundamental: there is no genesis of a polity, democratic or otherwise, without a representation of unity, but this initial representation is not mandated because, by effecting a normative closure, it provides a first determination of the actors that, actually or potentially, are entitled to participate in and mandate political representation.[23] Accordingly, *there is a core of irre-*

---

[22] Obviously, the representational claim to unity presupposed in referring to a European *Community*, or for that matter to a European *Union*, does not imply the additional (and unwarranted) assertion that the EU is already a federal polity or is necessarily moving towards a form of federalism. European integration is not a zero-sum game between either a European 'people' or European 'peoples'.

[23] This, in my view, is a specific illustration of the thesis, formulated in various ways by authors such as Heidegger, Merleau-Ponty, Foucault and Derrida, that '[t]he event (*Ereignis*) of the foundation of an order is not part of the founded order'; B Waldenfels, *Verfremdung der Moderne: Phänomenologische Grenzgänge* (Essen, Wallstein Verlag, 2001), at 139 (my translation). I am indebted here to Bert van Roermund, who links this theme to the structure of representation in his article 'Constituerende macht, soevereiniteit en representatie' (64 (2002) Tidschrift voor Filosofie 509–532).

ducible groundlessness at the heart of the EU, a representational claim that cannot be justified in terms of deliberation between 'all those concerned', yet without which 'reasongiving' in the EU cannot even begin. The standard picture notwithstanding, a command, in the sense noted at the end of section two, proves to be a necessary condition for deliberation in the EU and, more generally, for the very possibility of European integration.

2) Moreover, the Treaty of Rome illustrates the logic of political representation because, in the same stroke by which it claims to express a pre-legal normative unity, it also assigns content to this unity. To cite the original wording of Article 2 EC Treaty, '. . . a harmonious development of economic activity, a continuous and balanced expansion, an increase in stability, an accelerated raising of the standard of living and closer relations between the States belonging to [the EEC]' are not merely technical objectives to be achieved by the creation of a common market and the approximation of economic policy. Instead, these tasks provide the common good with a content, which must itself be further concretised by the European legal order.[24] As a representational act, the Treaty is an act of normative inclusion and exclusion. The Treaty brings about a normative closure by opting, amongst others, for a market economy: the common *market*, it is claimed, represents the common *good*. Thus, the founding act of the European polity is thoroughly ambiguous. On the one hand, it opens up a common space that enables individuals to recognise themselves as members of one and the same community; on the other, it can only open up this common space by marginalising competing values. The Treaty's representation of unity—and each of the representations that followed it—is an ambiguous achievement because it both integrates and disintegrates, because it sows division in the very process of instituting community. If the tension between unity and division, between centripetal and centrifugal forces, is what drives politics, then *politics was made possible and rendered inevitable by the representational structure of the act that founded the European polity.*

In short, the representational logic at work in the Treaty of Rome shows that a claim to unity is constitutive for the European Union, no less than for all of its member states, independently of whether the organisation of power in the EU is or is not reducible to that of its member states. Here lies the crux of the matter: the logic of political representation dislocates the standard picture by *displacing* the locus of sovereignty. If, as the standard picture asserts, sovereignty is linked to the notion of unity, then sovereignty does not only pertain to the first term of the opposition between 'state-centric' and 'multi-level' polities; sovereignty is apposite to the notion of a

---

[24] See H Lindahl and B van Roermund, 'Law without a State? On Representing the Common Market' in Z Bankowski and A Scott (eds.), *The European Union and Its Order: The Legal Theory of European Integration* (Oxford, Basil Blackwell, 2000), 1–16.

polity as such and in general. While the standard picture correctly links sovereignty to unity, this linkage guarantees that sovereignty cannot be restricted to the 'sovereign state'.

By the same token, the standard picture's pat opposition is misleading because it conceals the fact that political power always claims to represent a unity, whether in a 'state-centric' or in a 'multilevel' polity. The logic of political representation, which cannot include without excluding, implies that, at all levels of the legal order, a polity is continuously confronted with the question about unity. This is not a question that a polity can choose to leave unanswered, invoking the need to cultivate pluralism. To the contrary, every polity must time and again take up a position regarding the legal content of its unity, precisely because it is confronted with a plurality of representations of unity. That a polity must determine the legal content of its unity means that, in the case of competing and irreconcilable representations thereof, there has to be an organ that concretely and conclusively establishes the meaning of unity for the situation at hand. At the end of the day, 'governance' is government, and there is no government without a sovereign in the sense of a final arbiter in the event of an irresolvable conflict about the content of unity.[25]

(b) The dialectic between *pouvoir constituant* and *pouvoir constitué*

But in what way is the representation of unity concretely related to sovereignty? And in what way does the representation of unity shed light on the role of sovereignty in the process of European integration?

It is instructive, in view of answering these questions, to examine the constitutionalisation of the Community Treaties by the European Court of

---

[25] I submit that Miguel Poiares's excellent contribution to the present volume is a case in point. Poiares develops a normative model for disciplining the relations between the European legal order and the legal orders of the member states. These relations need to be disciplined to prevent as far as possible normative conflicts between these orders and to deal with conflicts when they arise. He rejects—correctly, I believe—a 'hierarchical' solution to this problem, 'hierarchical' in the sense of instituting a general rule that requires either European or national law to give way in case of conflict. Instead, he puts forward a set of 'principles of contrapunctual law' that make it possible to safeguard legal pluralism and (he implicitly argues) keep out sovereignty. While his normative model for dealing with the contrapunctual character of European and national law is highly perceptive and persuasive, I believe that it reintroduces sovereignty and hierarchy rather than disposing of these terms. First, the principles of contrapunctual law amount to a *higher-order normative unity* that, however 'thin' in content, encompasses both the European and national legal orders, and to which these are subordinate. Accordingly, he advocates legal pluralism *within* unity. No less importantly, it does not suffice to account for these principles in terms of '*legal* sovereignty', because conflict about the meaning of these rules is of course possible (and in due course inevitable). Consequently, a form of '*ruler* sovereignty' is indispensable, ie an organ that, in the case of conflict, conclusively determines the meaning of these principles, hence of higher-order unity.

Justice. For the issue of sovereignty acquired concrete significance for European integration with *Van Gend & Loos* and the ECJ's subsequent landmark rulings. Notice, to begin with, that the doctrine generally uses the term 'constitutionalisation' with some conceptual trepidation (by placing it in quotation marks!), despite the fact that these rulings became part of the *acquis communautaire* that was formally incorporated into European law. Indeed, the enactment of a constitution, according to the generally accepted view, is a political decision by a people to organise itself as an autonomous legal order. Dieter Grimm, as we have seen at the outset of section three, contends that the EU is a legal community, not a political community, because there is no European people, in the singular and determinate, that could serve as the 'substrate' of an autonomous legal order. Inevitably, this assumption leads Grimm to rejecting the constitutional status of the Treaties:

> To the extent that constitutions are concerned with legalizing political rule, the Treaties leave nothing to be desired . . . The Treaties are not however a constitution in the full sense of the term. The difference lies in the reference back to the will of the Member States rather than to the people of the Union . . . The European public power is not one that derives from the people, but one mediated through States. Since the Treaties thus have not an internal but an external reference point, they are also not the expression of a society's self-determination as to the form and objectives of its political unity.[26]

As Grimm sees it, a constitution, in the 'full sense of the term', can only be enacted by the people, as a political unity. For, so his argument runs, the enactment of a constitution is the manifestation *par excellence* of popular sovereignty, that is, the exercise of the people's *pouvoir constituant*. Whereas the modern nation state meets this condition, the EU does not (yet).

Grimm by no means stands alone in defending this position. Steve Boom summarises the prevalent view when noting that

> . . . a constitution by definition establishes the basic principles and laws of a *nation* or *state;* an international treaty, on the other hand, specifies the contractual rights and duties of . . . distinct sovereign states.[27]

As a constitution gives expression to a people's self-determination, the Community Treaties cannot be a constitution because they 'do not refer to a singular European people; rather, the many peoples of Europe are recognized as distinct groups'.[28] Boom's argument that the 'constitutionalisation' of the Treaty of Rome (the quotation marks are his) precludes dealing with

---

[26] Grimm, n 15 above, at 291.
[27] SJ Boom, 'The European Union after the Maastricht Decision: Will Germany Be the "Virginia of Europe"?', 43 (1995) *American Journal of Comparative Law*, 177–226, at 209.
[28] *Ibid*, at 208.

the Treaty of Maastricht as a 'traditional, "run of the mill" international treaty'[29] provides no solace, for the German Court challenges the constitutional status of the Treaty of Rome. To reiterate the fundamental objection, a European constitution presupposes a European people that can act as *pouvoir constituant*, either by directly enacting a constitution or by mandating a body—say a 'European Constituent Assembly'—to enact a constitution on its behalf.

Here we touch the bedrock of the discussion on sovereignty in general and popular sovereignty in particular, namely *self-determination*. In effect, expressions such as 'state sovereignty' or 'sovereign polity' imply an autonomous legal order; they refer to *political* unity understood as collective self-legislation. By qualifying the European Community as a 'new legal order of international law' and as 'an own legal system', the *Van Gend & Loos* and *Costa v. ENEL* rulings of the European Court of Justice determined that, in view of the objectives set out in the Treaty, the Community was an independent legal order. By qualifying the Community as a 'new' and 'own' legal order, the ECJ asserts what Grimm denies, namely that lawmaking in the Community takes place by virtue of an 'internal reference point', as a result of which Community law is the expression of collective self-legislation. If we return to the standard picture, it by no means suffices to say that, in contrast with the 'single' or 'exclusive' sovereignty of the nation state, sovereignty is 'shared' or 'pooled' in the Community. Instead, the constitutionalisation of the Treaties implies that, within the scope of its objectives, the EC is a sovereign polity. Grimm's objection effortlessly exposes the implications of asserting that sovereignty is 'shared' or 'pooled'. For if such were the case, this would be tantamount to acknowledging that the Treaty has an 'external reference point', namely the member states. By implication, these states could at any moment abrogate their participation in the EC, recovering legislative autonomy in the spheres in which they had agreed to act together.

The difficulty, rather, is that, according to the tradition of democratic theory, the autonomy of a legal order implies that this legal order must be referred back to a people as its ground or bearer, which means that a people exercises its *pouvoir constituant* by directly enacting a constitution or by mandating a body to do so on its behalf. This, precisely, is the gist of Grimm's allusion to the 'internal reference point' of a constitution. Hence, the question concerning the link between sovereignty and the representation of unity can also be stated as follows: What is the relation of collective self-determination to representation? In particular, if, as argued hitherto, unity is always a represented unity, what sense can we make of the enactment of a constitution as an act of *self*-determination?

---

[29] *Ibid*, at 209.

The essential point, I believe, is that the reflexivity implied in 'self-determination' is not the expression of identity, if by this we mean the immediate presence of a people to itself, but of a representational relation, whereby a manifold of individuals is revealed as comprising 'this' or 'that' unity. The enactment of a constitution is a representational act that inevitably introduces an interval, a gap, between the represented and the constitutional representation. There is no people, in the singular and determinate, in the absence of constitutional representations of unity, yet the logic of political representation also ensures that the people is not exhausted by any of its constitutional representations. Waldenfels expresses a similar idea when noting that

> [t]he 'We' that constitutes itself in such declarations [e.g. 'We the People of the United States . . .'] and enacts a constitution for itself, eludes itself (*entgleitet sich selbst*). Linguistically speaking, this means that the 'We' of the utterance content does not coincide either with the 'We' of the utterance process that speaks about the We or with the 'I' that speaks for the We.[30]

It would therefore be ingenuous—and on occasion disingenuous—to view the enactment of a constitution as being simply the exercise of the *pouvoir constituant* of the people. Rather, the logic of political representation requires reinterpreting the relation between *pouvoir constituant* and *pouvoir constitué*. On the one hand, the notion of representation implies that, as constituted powers, all representative organs within the community are subordinated to a highest power. This idea belongs, as we have seen, to the basic repertoire of democratic theory. On the other hand, the critical reformulation of the concept of political representation also implies that unity is only given indirectly, through its particularisations. In other words, unity depends on its representations. In this sense, the representative is a *pouvoir constituant*, such that representation constitutes 'We the [European] people.' Any simple opposition between constituting and constituted power loses sight of the fact that, in the same stroke by which political representation claims to articulate the values that define the identity of a community, it also determines *that* there is a community and *what* constitutes it as a unity.[31] The representational movement that depletes power, by turning our gaze away from it in the direction of its alleged source, also intensifies power, by opening up and closing what we see—unity. In short, the logic of political representation unfolds a dialectic between *pouvoir constituant* and *pouvoir constitué*.

---

[30] B Waldenfels, *Topographie des Fremden: Studien zur Phänomenologie des Fremden* (Frankfurt, Suhrkamp, 1997), at 149 (my translation).
[31] This insight would have to be the point of departure for a more detailed discussion of and debate with Schmitt's thesis that representation and self-determination ('identity', as he calls it), are opposed principles for the formation of political unity; see C Schmitt, *Verfassungslehre* (Berlin, Duncker & Humblot, 1928), 204 *ff.*

These ideas shed light on Grimm's objection that only a European people, either directly or by way of a 'European Constituent Assembly', could legitimately enact a European constitution and, therewith, an autonomous legal order. This move, which is dictated by the presuppositions of 'political originalism', loses sight of two points. First, the demand that the people mandate a constituent assembly if the democratic principle of popular sovereignty is to be satisfied, forgets that all mandating leads back to a representational claim that is not itself mandated. If a 'European Constituent Assembly' were ever convened to formally enact a European constitution on behalf of the European people, such a mandate would be 'contaminated' by the core of irreducible groundlessness of the representational claim raised by the six founding states of the EEC. This fact is not a blemish that characterises the EU as a *'sui generis'* polity, and that justifies setting it off from the 'self-determination' of a nation state; it is a necessary feature of *every* polity, including nation states.

Second, and no less importantly, the problem is not whether a body has or has not been mandated to produce a constitution on behalf of the people; it is that, regardless of the body that enacts a constitution, the logic of political representation dictates that this body both claims to being mandated *and* determines the meaning of its mandate. To borrow the vocabulary of speech act theory, representation deploys a *performative force*.

This feature of representation is particularly clear in *Costa v. ENEL*, the ruling whereby the ECJ introduced the doctrine of the supremacy of Community law. The following consideration is the cornerstone of the reasoning that justifies the supremacy of European law over national law:

> The law stemming from the Treaty, an independent source of law, could not because of its special and original nature, be overridden by domestic legal provisions, however framed, without being deprived of its character as community law and without the legal basis of the Community itself being called into question.[32]

Notice the circularity of the ECJ's reasoning. For the one, the ECJ categorically asserts that the Treaty is an 'independent source of law', i.e. that the European legal order is not derived from the legal orders of the member states. The ineluctable consequence of the Treaty's autonomy is that, within the scope of the Treaty, Community law enjoys supremacy over national legal orders. For the other, the ECJ argues that, unless Community law enjoys supremacy over national law, the 'legal basis of the Community itself', hence the Treaty's independence, would be compromised, or as the Court puts it, 'called into question'. Precisely what could be 'called into question' (as the *Bundesverfassungsgericht* later did!), namely the Treaty's autonomous status, *cannot* be called into question, because the ECJ has already asserted that the Treaty is 'an independent source of law'.

---

[32] Case 6/64 [1964] ECR, 585–615, at 594.

One would entirely miss the point if one were to conclude that the reasoning which justifies the ECJ's constitutionalisation of the Treaty is specious, for something far more fundamental is at stake here. In effect, the Court's circular reasoning illustrates in a concrete manner how the logic of political representation unfolds the dialectic of *pouvoir constituant* and *pouvoir constitué:* in the same stroke by which supremacy is held to flow from the 'special and original nature' of the Treaty, the Treaty acquires a 'special and original nature' because the ECJ grants its provisions supremacy over national law.

A comparable operation is at work in the ECJ's earlier *Van Gend & Loos* ruling, when the Court established that

> [t]he objective of the EEC Treaty, which is to establish a Common Market, the functioning of which is of direct concern to interested parties in the Community, implies that this Treaty is more than an agreement which merely creates mutual obligations between the contracting States.[33]

For the ECJ's claim that the Treaty is more than an ordinary treaty under international law only holds if one presupposes that the functioning of a Common Market is not of direct concern only to the states, that is, only if one presupposes that the Treaty is not an ordinary treaty under international law.

To repeat my point, the Court's tautology is not simply an example of flawed reasoning, but of the performative force involved in the representation of unity. Collective self-determination always involves a representation of political unity, and thus an ineradicable moment of performativity that, paradoxically, '. . . excludes that a We says "we"'.[34] From this perspective, and returning to Grimm's objection to the Community Treaties, a constitution, including the constitution of a nation state, is *never* such 'in the full sense of the term'.[35] Positively expressed, the Community Treaty is, from the point of view of the structure of an act of collective self-determination, as much (or as little) a constitution as that of a nation state.

---

[33] Case 26/62 [1963] ECR, 1–30, at 12.
[34] Waldenfels, n 23 above, at 140, (my translation). It would be possible to show, for example, that the American Supreme Court played a decisive role in the process of constituting the United States as a federal political unity. As detailed historical studies have made clear, the reference in the Preamble of the American Constitution to 'We the people of the United States' was no less consistent with a confederation than with a federation of states. I have dealt with this example at greater length in my article 'European Integration: Popular Sovereignty and a Politics of Boundaries', 6 (2000) *European Law Journal*, 239–56, esp. 252–53.
[35] Were this not the case, were there no gap between the represented people and its constitutional representation, we could not even begin to make sense of the trivial fact that constitutions also need to be modified nor, for that matter, of the fact that the constitutional status of a body of norms can be disputed.

(c) Seizing the Initiative

To conclude this section, the Court's constitutionalisation of the Treaties points to what I take to be the fundamentally reductive character of a 'deliberative' approach to politics in general and the question about sovereignty in particular. In effect, the Court's rulings illustrate the fact that no polity and no politics is possible without acts of *seizing the initiative* with respect to unity and its content. The notion of a *pouvoir constituant* ultimately points to this capacity to commence things, where the reference to 'capacity' precedes any evaluation, whether positive or negative, of power. Certainly, the idea of a pure commencement in politics—a *creatio ex nihilo*—is untenable, as witnessed by the dialectic of constituting and constituted power. Moreover, a commencement can only be recognised as such when it has 'caught on', that is to say, when the claim about political unity is accepted by other actors as the basis for further political action.[36] Yet, no appeal to a procedural model of political rationality and no reference to (the normative idea of) 'deliberation' between citizens can either explain or substitute for the act of seizing the political initiative; to the contrary, they presuppose it.

The foregoing analysis attempts to recover this moment of seizing the initiative in terms of a *performative force* of the constituting power, a force that manifests itself in the capacity to create and shift the normative boundaries of a polity. In some aspects, this analysis is akin to Hannah Arendt's discussion of 'action' as a fundamental feature of political life.[37] Yet, I would suggest that we need to go further than Arendt. No less important than the capacity of commencing things is the fact that the political initiative is always *seized*. In this specific sense, constituting power is *legibus solutis*. Yet, it would be a grave distortion of the political significance of constituting power to simply reduce it, as deliberative models of democracy do, to a merely deficient form of political action, namely political action that does not meet the formal requirements of deliberative rationality. In contrast to the reductiveness of such an approach, my analysis points to the ambiguity of constituting power. Indeed, two aspects go into the latter's single performative *force*: the impetus that is required to set something new

---

[36] In this sense, Miguel Poiares is entirely right in stressing that it would be a mistake to think that the ECJ could have constitutionalised the Treaties on its *own*. Not only was the cooperation of other actors required in creating an autonomous legal order, but this cooperation effectively meant that the process of constructing European law does not simply unfold in 'top-down' fashion but also—and decisively—'bottom-up' (Poiares, present volume). I would add that this is an implication of the representational structure of lawmaking: the dialectic of *pouvoir constituant* and *pouvoir constitué* is no exclusive prerogative of the ECJ; see my article 'Authority and Representation', 19 (2000) *Law and Philosophy*, 223–46, for a discussion of the representational relation between the norms of a legal order.

[37] H Arendt, *The Human Condition* (Chicago, Chicago University Press, 1958), 175 *ff.*

on its way always involves a rupture, a breach, and, in this sense, an inevitable moment of violence. To 'seize' and to 'commence' are welded together into one and the same performative 'force'.[38] These two features, I would argue, determine the exercise of the constituting power as an *act of sovereignty*.

My key contention is, therefore, that the standard picture's opposition between 'commands' and 'deliberation' systematically conceals the structure of the exercise of the *pouvoir constituant* as an act of seizing the initiative. In terms of the genesis of the European polity, the standard picture cannot even begin to make sense of the fact that the enactment of the Treaty of Rome and the ECJ's *Van Gend & Loos* and *Costa v. ENEL* rulings seize the political initiative and are, as such, acts of sovereignty.

5. XENONOMOUS AUTONOMY

At the outset of this chapter, I suggested that addressing sovereignty as a philosophical problem required addressing four distinct yet interrelated issues, namely political unity, contingency, power and sovereignty. In the context of the logic of political representation developed heretofore, these questions can be answered most generally as follows: (1) A polity constitutes and maintains itself as a political *unity* by way of representational acts. (2) Political unity is *contingent* because unity is always a represented unity. (3) *Power* unfolds a representational logic in the process of constituting and maintaining political unity. (4) The representational logic deployed by political power manifests itself as a dialectic of *pouvoir constituant* and *pouvoir constitué*. I would like to conclude this paper by briefly showing how these four different strands of the foregoing analysis flow together into a specific interpretation of the contingency of political unity.

I hope, in the course of doing so, to at least begin to answer a question Jo Shaw raised about this paper. 'What about my aliens?', she asked, where the reference to 'my' aliens was meant to articulate her concern about and research in alien policy in the EU.[39] Rather than a query about specific and concrete recommendations for alien policy in the EU, I take her question to be an invitation to explain in what way an inquiry into sovereignty and representation could contribute to the debate about the foundations of alien policy in the EU, in particular about electoral rights for aliens. Shaw's question about aliens is particularly apposite if we remember the wording of the ECJ's *Costa v. ENEL* ruling, which introduces the doctrine of supremacy by

---

[38] This analysis of the *pouvoir constituant* stands close, I believe, to Derrida's discussion of the 'force of law'; see J Derrida, *Force de loi: Le 'Fondement mystique de l'autorité'* (Paris, Galilée, 1994), esp. 32–34, 83 *ff*.

[39] See Jo Shaw's contribution to the present volume

referring to European law as an 'own' legal order. This 'ownness', as we have seen, refers to the autonomy the ECJ claims for the European legal order *vis-à-vis* the legal order of the member states. To reformulate Shaw's question as sharply as possible, does not all talk about sovereignty, representation and autonomy ultimately lead back to a conception of politics that derives the alien from a more original sphere of 'ownness'? Does not the alien thereby become a purely residual category, negatively defined as 'not-own'? Is not this view of politics the price to be paid for an approach that insists on granting such importance to the conditions whereby political unity is constituted and maintained? *Souveranisme*, after all is said and done?

Yet, might not the insistence on an inquiry into the conditions whereby political unity is constituted and maintained lead to an entirely different outcome, namely to the insight that political unity is contingent in a way that *debars* any appeal to an original sphere of 'ownness'? In effect, the foregoing analysis returns time and again to the idea that unity cannot be derived from plurality without already presupposing unity. I have argued that this problem is intimately bound up with the representational structure of power: political unity is always a represented unity. Moreover, and crucially, all representations of political unity lead back to a representational act that is not mandated, yet without which no genesis of a polity is possible. Not only does this suggest, as mentioned in section four, that there is a core of irreducible groundlessness at the heart of every political community, but also that *no polity is contemporaneous with its own genesis.*

These two features cast new light on the claim to collective self-determination. As we have seen, this claim is one and the same with the claim to sovereignty of a polity. In particular, these features call attention to a peculiar ambiguity in the hyphen between 'self' and 'determination'. For if no polity, including the EU, is contemporaneous with its own genesis, does this not mean that there is no determination *by* a self that is not preceded and conditioned by the determination *of* a self? Does not the dialectic of constituting and constituted power disclose *a necessary alterity within ipseity?* Instead of deriving the alien from a sphere of ownness, the logic of political representation suggests that while every polity necessarily refers to its origin as 'its own', this origin remains forever alien to it. It is in this sense, then, that political unity is not only contingent, but also radically contingent. Thus, I not only welcome Shaw's reference to 'my aliens' but would also like to generalise it as follows: The fact that political unity is always a represented unity confronts the members of a polity with 'our (own) alienness'. There is a long way to go from this paradoxical intertwinement between the 'own' and the 'alien' to specific policy recommendations for alien policy; but the aforementioned insight could contribute to critically reconsidering how the terms of this distinction are used by policy-makers in this field.

Sovereignty is a fundamental problem for politics and law because it suggests that, to borrow the Greek root of the word 'alien', xenonomy is inscribed in the very act of saying 'we' as the precondition for exercising political autonomy. Sovereignty confronts us with the inevitability of xenonomous autonomy.

5

Sovereignty and Constitutionalism in International Law

BARDO FASSBENDER*

1. INTRODUCTION

T HE IDEA OF sovereignty is amongst the oldest concepts of modern international law; it accompanied and fostered the rise of the modern state. The 'sovereign state' is still the standard member of the international community. International law endeavours to maintain a uniform global system of sovereign states, and therefore sometimes generously attributes sovereignty to entities whose independent statehood is doubtful not only in actual, but also in legal terms. Throughout its long history, the concept of sovereignty has proved highly adaptable. It has survived many premature obituaries, and the charge that it stands in the way of a system of international governance adequate to ensure the future existence of humanity. Through the centuries, it has acquired an almost mythical quality.[1] Sovereignty is usually claimed, or rejected, in times of political crisis, party strife, war and civil war. Although (or perhaps just because) its contours are so blurred, it played, and continues to play, a prominent role in modern constitutional and international legal theory, as well as in politics.

We are concerned here with sovereignty as a legal notion and concept, but as such it integrates a political dimension which paradoxically often defies legal control. In other words, sovereignty as a legal concept is characterised by an uneasy tension between an effort legally to define, and therefore limit, the powers of the person or body who claims to be sovereign, and that sovereign's (at least occasional) efforts to evade the control exerted by legal rules and procedures, or to change the law according to his

---

* This paper is dedicated, as a sign of gratitude, to my dear teacher Ernst Portner, Professor of Modern History at the University of Bonn, who first spoke to me of sovereignty.
[1] See L Henkin, 'The Mythology of Sovereignty', in RStJ Macdonald (ed.), *Essays in Honour of Wang Tieya* (The Hague, Martinus Nijhoff, 1993), 351.

interests. The latter aspect refers us back to the origins of the concept, when sovereignty was all about claims—the assertion of a right or an alleged right, or of something ('sovereign power') as a fact. Since the French jurist and philosopher Jean Bodin introduced the notion into the theory of state in the sixteenth century, it has been resorted to as an argument in a concrete political struggle—as a description of what was desired or aspired to rather than of what really existed. At the beginning of the modern European system of states, the notion was used in order to establish and defend the independence of the French King from the Pope and the Emperor of the Holy Roman Empire, and the supremacy of his orders over those of particularistic powers in what became France. From time to time, this original meaning, political in nature, comes to the surface, and more so in the international affairs of a state than 'at home' where (at least in the Western world) constitutional restraints are more fully developed. To fail to appreciate this untamed side of sovereignty is to misunderstand the concept.

2. SOVEREIGNTY IN THE 'INTERNATIONAL LAW OF COEXISTENCE'

According to a widely shared view, sovereignty has two complementary and mutually dependent dimensions: Within a state, a sovereign power makes law with the assertion that this law is supreme and ultimate, *i.e.* that its validity does not depend on the will of any other, or 'higher', authority. Externally, a sovereign power obeys no other authority. As the modern state began to develop, the internal dimension of sovereignty addressed the prob lem of 'intermediate' powers within a certain territory, independent in a legal or actual sense, which an emerging 'central' power sought to subjugate. The external claim to sovereignty was directed against powers outside the territory.[2] This latter dimension is also referred to as 'sovereignty in international law' or 'independence'.[3]

---

[2] For the history of the concept of sovereignty, see FH Hinsley, *Sovereignty* 2nd edition (Cambridge, Cambridge University Press, 1986), H Quaritsch, *Staat und Souveränität: Die Grundlagen* (Frankfurt/Main, Athenäum, 1970), id., *Souveränität: Entstehung und Entwicklung des Begriffs in Frankreich und Deutschland vom 13. Jahrhundert bis 1806* (Berlin, Duncker & Humblot, 1986). Of the older literature, I mention CE Merriam, Jr., *History of the Theory of Sovereignty since Rousseau* (New York, Columbia University Press, 1900) (*Studies in History, Economics and Public Law*, vol. XII no. 4). For the etymology of the word, see D Klippel & H Boldt, 'Souveränität', in O Brunner *et al.* (eds.), *Geschichtliche Grundbegriffe*, vol. 6 (Stuttgart, Klett-Cotta, 1990) 98. For a fresh look of a political scientist at the history of sovereignty in political practice, offering an analysis of a whole spectrum of mechanisms of intervention made use of by the major powers since the nineteenth century, see SD Krasner, *Sovereignty: Organised Hypocrisy* (Princeton, NJ, Princeton University Press, 1999).
[3] See, *e.g.*, *Interpretation of Peace Treaties with Bulgaria, Hungary and Romania*, ICJ Reports (1950) 65 at 98, 99 *et seq.* (sep. opinion Zoričič): sovereign equality as 'the corollary of independence'.

The modern centralised territorial state appeared in Europe due essentially to the fact that the idea of (internal) sovereignty, as propounded by political philosophers and legal scholars, had been generally accepted in state practice. The entire legal order, including the powers of 'public' persons and communities subordinated to the central authority, was constructed as deriving from the will of the sovereign. The medieval concept of personal jurisdiction was augmented by a territorial jurisdiction, consolidating fragmented regal rights into a unified sovereign power as a source of comprehensive and exclusive authority. Externally, sovereignty was understood as legal independence from all 'foreign' powers, and as impermeability—protecting the relevant territory against all outside interference. The medieval universalism of the Empire and the Roman Catholic Church was superseded by the new concept of the 'international legal community' proclaimed by Spanish theologians.[4]

According to the doctrine of sovereignty prevailing in the nineteenth and the better part of the twentieth century, states were only bound by those rules of law to which they had agreed, either by the conclusion of treaties or customarily. There existed a presumption in favour of 'unrestrained sovereignty'. In the *Lotus* case, the Permanent Court of International Justice held that 'restrictions upon the independence of States cannot . . . be presumed'.[5]

The *jus ad bellum*, or right to go to war, had been claimed by factually independent powers long before the concept of sovereignty was formulated;

> 'but just as it was consolidated by the rise of the modern state, so it was freed from external moral and theological sources of restraint and made into the most basic of all the rights of the sovereign state . . . In the international law of the modern international system it was a legal right . . . [S]tates clung tenaciously to this right, believing it to be fundamental to their sovereignty.'[6]

Wolfgang Friedmann identified the classical system of international law as a 'law of coexistence'. This law he juxtaposed with a newer 'international law of co-operation' the beginnings of which he recognised in the period between the two World Wars of the twentieth century:

---

[4] See A Verdross & B Simma, *Universelles Völkerrecht* 3rd edition (Berlin, Duncker & Humblot, 1984), at 8 *et seq.*, 11–3; A Nussbaum, *A Concise History of the Law of Nations* (New York, The Macmillan Company, rev. ed. 1954), at 79–91.
[5] See *Lotus* judgment, PCIJ, Series A, No. 10 (1927), at 18: 'International law governs relations between independent States. The rules of law binding upon States therefore emanate from their own free will as expressed in conventions or by usages generally accepted as expressing principles of law and established in order to regulate the relations between these co-existing independent communities or with a view to the achievement of common aims. Restrictions upon the independence of States cannot therefore be presumed.'
[6] See Hinsley, above n 2, at 230.

'This move of international society, from an essentially negative code of rules of abstention to positive rules of co-operation . . . is an evolution of immense significance for the principles and structure of international law.'[7]

The principle of non-intervention in the internal affairs of other states, the rule that in the territory of a foreign state sovereign power may not be exercised,[8] and the concept of state (or 'sovereign') immunity[9] are primary examples of Friedmann's 'rules of abstention'. The principle of external sovereignty determined the overall structure and virtually the entire substance of the international law of coexistence.[10] Max Huber's famous definition of sovereignty in the *Island of Palmas* arbitral award (1928) is a perfect expression of the negative or exclusive quality characteristic of the concept in the period of 'coexistence':

'Sovereignty in the relations between states signifies independence. Independence in regard to a portion of the globe is the right to exercise therein, *to the exclusion of any other state*, the functions of a state.'[11]

An individual state's internal order was not only shielded from intervention by other states but also from any uninvited 'intrusion' by international law. The concept of the 'impermeability of the state' protected a domestic legal order like a shield through which international law could not pass.[12] It led to Heinrich Triepel's doctrine of 'dualism'—a strict separation of international and domestic law—,[13] and also to the idea that in its external relations a state should only speak with 'one voice', namely that of the central government and its minister of foreign affairs.

---

[7] See W Friedmann, *The Changing Structure of International Law* (London, Stevens & Sons, 1964), at 62. In 1970, the General Assembly proclaimed the duty of states 'to co-operate with one another, irrespective of the differences in their political, economic and social systems, . . . in order to maintain international peace and security and to promote international economic stability and progress, the general welfare of nations and international co-operation free from discrimination based on such differences' ('Friendly Relations Declaration', below n 49).

[8] See *Lotus* judgment, above n 5, at p. 18 *et seq.*: '[A State] may not exercise its power in any form in the territory of another State. In this sense jurisdiction is certainly territorial; it cannot be exercised by a State outside its territory except by virtue of a permissive rule derived from international custom or from a convention.'

[9] See, eg, I Brownlie, *Principles of Public International Law* 5th edition (Oxford, Clarendon Press, 1998), at 327: Sovereign immunity rests on the principle, 'expressed in the maxim *par in parem non habet jurisdictionem* [and] concerned with the status of equality attaching to the independent sovereign, [that] legal persons of equal standing cannot have their disputes settled in the courts of one of them'.

[10] See A Bleckmann, *Völkerrecht* (Baden-Baden, Nomos, 2001), at 60–71.

[11] For text of the award, see 22 *American Journal of International Law* (1928) 867 at 875; 2 *UNRIAA* 829 at 838 (emphasis added).

[12] See A Bleckmann, *Grundgesetz und Völkerrecht* (Berlin, Duncker & Humblot, 1975), at 264–73.

[13] See H Triepel, *Völkerrecht und Landesrecht* (Leipzig, CL Hirschfeld, 1899), and id., 'Les rapports entre le droit interne et le droit international', 1 *Recueil des Cours: Collected Courses of the Hague Academy of International Law* [hereinafter *Recueil des Cours*] (1923–I) 77.

International law was considered as a body of norms exclusively regulating relationships between states, so that only states could be subjects of international law. It was generally denied that the individual could enjoy such status,[14] and only in the age of the League of Nations was the possibility of international legal personality of international organisations composed of states reluctantly accepted.[15]

In the nineteenth century, the ideas of sovereignty, the nation state and imperialism had been joined, reinforcing each other and leading to an 'anarchy of sovereignty'.[16]

'[T]he concept of sovereignty, being made to serve the state or the nation regarded as an absolute end, was interpreted as justifying the use of absolute power or symbolising the actual possession of it.'[17]

Only in these circumstances, after the decline of the doctrine of natural law, was a claim to a power unrestrained by law derived from the concept of sovereignty. The emphasis shifted from building and perfecting an effective state authority to a fierce competition with other nations. 'Sovereign nation states', constructed and understood as closed, self-contained entities facing one another, fought over political, economic and military power. To preserve, strengthen or, if lost or impaired, reestablish 'national sovereignty' became the ultimate foreign policy goal, and thus thinking in terms of sovereignty was intimately linked with power politics. In this period, 'sovereignty in international affairs could never be conceived apart from a confusion of it with arbitrary power'.[18] A state's sovereignty was not conceived of as a power to be used towards a 'common good' of the international community but as a subjective right to be exercised in that state's own interest. International law was essentially bilateral, and was not considered to go beyond the correlative rights and obligations of its subjects.[19] It was only later that states came to realise, and acknowledge, a need for cooperation for the furtherance of community goals, and to assume that all members of the international community should take into account the valid interests of the other members in exercising their respective sovereignty.[20]

---

[14] See Verdross & Simma, above n. 4, at 255 *et seq.*, 264, and Friedmann, above n. 7, at 232–42, 245–9.

[15] See B Fassbender, 'Die Völkerrechtssubjektivität internationaler Organisationen', 37 *Österreichische Zeitschrift für öffentliches Recht und Völkerrecht* (1986), 17 at 18–25.

[16] See O Kimminich, *Einführung in das Völkerrecht* 6th edition (Tübingen, Francke, 1997), at 66.

[17] See Hinsley, above n. 2, at 217.

[18] See G Butler, 'Sovereignty and the League of Nations', 1 *British Year Book of International Law* (1920–1) 35 at 42.

[19] See B Simma, 'From Bilateralism to Community Interest in International Law', 250 *Recueil des Cours* (1994) 217 at 230–3.

[20] For an exposition of shifts in the understanding of external sovereignty 'in the age of co-operative international law', see A Bleckmann, 'Commentary on Art. 2(1) of the UN Charter', in B Simma (ed.), *The Charter of the United Nations: A Commentary* (Oxford, Oxford University Press, and Munich, CH Beck, 1994), 77 at 84–7.

Understandably, in retrospect, the idea of sovereignty was seen as having supported political developments eventually leading to the two world wars. The idea entered a state of crisis in the 1920s, and in particular after 1945, when legal science reacted to the adoption of the UN Charter by gradually redefining sovereignty and advancing the notion of solidarity, of all member states of the international community. In Western Europe, cooperation under the umbrella of a 'supranational' organisation replaced national sovereignty as the central theme of international relations. The new approach found a characteristic expression in the preamble of the 1951 Treaty of Paris:

> 'The Heads of Government and State,
> . . . Considering that world peace can be safeguarded only by creative efforts commensurate with the dangers that threaten it,
> . . . Resolved to substitute for age-old rivalries the merging of their essential interests; to create, by establishing an economic community, the basis for a broader and deeper community among peoples long divided by bloody conflicts, and to lay the foundations for institutions which will give direction to a destiny henceforward shared,
> Have decided to create a European Coal and Steel Community . . .'[21]

After 1945, sovereignty was only emphasised by 'latecomers' (the new states which, having emerged from decolonisation, sought to consolidate their fragile independence) and states feeling unsure of themselves (in particular the Soviet Union and its satellite states).[22]

3. EQUALITY OF STATES

The legal principle of equality of states is so closely connected with that of sovereignty that the fusion in the UN Charter of the two terms into one ('sovereign equality', Art. 2(1)) suggested itself. But still, the history of the concept of equality in modern international law cannot be told as a similar story of rise and fall. It seems that, compared to sovereignty, the equality of states was always more disputed in state practice as well as legal doctrine. This is understandable because sovereignty was a principle defended by all states, including the powerful, which often played a leading role in this regard, whereas equality was generally invoked by smaller states (and their

---

[21] Treaty of Paris Establishing the European Coal and Steel Community, 18 April 1951, preamble, 261 UNTS 140. For the historical context, see, e.g., B Fassbender, 'Zur staatlichen Ordnung Europas nach der deutschen Einigung', 46 *Europa Archiv* (1991) 395 at 397.
[22] See, e.g., N Mugerwa, 'Subjects of International Law', in M Sørensen, *Manual of Public International Law* (London, Macmillan, and New York, St Martin's Press, 1968), 247 at 253–5; RP Anand, 'Sovereign Equality of States in International Law', 197 *Recueil des Cours* (1986) 9; Akademie der Wissenschaften der UdSSR—Rechtsinstitut, *Völkerrecht* (L Schultz transl., Hamburg, Hansischer Gildenverlag Joachim Heitmann, 1960), at 91–109.

lawyers) against the actions, aspirations and presumptions of a mighty neighbour state or the 'Great Powers' together.

As a principle of modern international law, the equality of (Christian) states was recognised in the Peace of Westphalia of 1648; regardless of their Catholic or Protestant faith, and of their monarchical or republican form of government, their statehood was equally recognised and protected. The treaties formally bade farewell to the medieval conception of a society of states organised hierarchically, *i.e.* on the basis of inequality.[23] At the same time, this recognition of equality resulted from a political compromise in favour of peace—an agreement henceforth to ignore, from a legal point of view, certain actual differences which before had been of legal relevance.

The most widely read book on international law in the eighteenth century, written by Emer de Vattel—a foremost representative of the natural law school of the period—was based on the idea of a *société des nations*, the members of which enjoy an equal status. In his introduction, Vattel said: 'A dwarf is as much a man as a giant is; a small Republic is no less a sovereign state than the most powerful kingdom.'[24] In the age of Enlightenment the idea of the equality of states was based on an analogy with the 'natural' status of men which, a century earlier, Thomas Hobbes had described as follows: 'Nature hath made men so equall, in the faculties of body, and mind'.[25] In the same spirit of natural law, the Virginia Bill of Rights of 1776 proclaimed in its very first sentence that '[a]ll men are by nature equally free and independent and have certain inherent rights . . .'[26] In accordance with the said analogy, the Articles of Confederation between the thirteen United States of America of 1777 then provided that '[i]n determining questions in

---

[23] See L Gross, 'The Peace of Westphalia, 1648–1948', 42 *American Journal of International Law* (1948) 20 at 33, and B Fassbender, 'Die verfassungs- und völkerrechtsgeschichtliche Bedeutung des Westfälischen Friedens von 1648', in I Erberich *et al.* (eds.), *Frieden und Recht* (Stuttgart, Richard Boorberg, 1998) 9 at 21–33.

[24] See E de Vattel, *Le droit des gens, ou principes de la loi naturelle, appliqués à la conduite et aux affaires des Nations et Souverains*, vol. 1 (London, Tutior, 1758), at 11. Translated as *The Law of Nations, or the Principles of Natural Law, applied to the Conduct and to the Affairs of Nations and of Sovereigns* by CG Fenwick ('The Classics of International Law', Washington, DC, The Carnegie Institution of Washington, 1916); quotation at 7. For a summary of Vattel's principal ideas, see Nussbaum, above n. 4, at 156–64, and E Reibstein, *Völkerrecht: Eine Geschichte seiner Ideen in Lehre und Praxis*, vol. 1 (Freiburg and Munich, Karl Alber, 1958) at 571–609.

[25] See T Hobbes, *Leviathan, or The Matter, Forme, & Power of a Common-Wealth Ecclesiasticall and Civill* (London, A Crooke, 1651, CB Macpherson (ed), London, Pelican Books, 1968), part 1, ch. XIII. For the history of the notion of equality in the modern age, see O Dann, 'Gleichheit', in *Geschichtliche Grundbegriffe* (above n. 2), vol. 2 (1975), at 997–1046.

[26] For text, see SE Morison (ed.), *Sources and Documents Illustrating the American Revolution 1764–88 and the Formation of the Federal Constitution* 2nd edition (London, Oxford University Press, 1929) at 149. For an explanation of the historical and philosophical context, see G Kleinheyer, 'Grundrechte, Menschen – und Bürgerrechte, Volksrechte', in *Geschichtliche Grundbegriffe* (above n. 2), vol. 2 (1975), at 1047–82.

the United States in Congress assembled, each state shall have one vote'.[27] Here, the idea of equality in legal status was translated into equal voting power.

Inspired by Vattel and the thinking of the Enlightenment, the theorists of the French Revolution also equated states with individuals having the same rights and duties. In a representative statement, the Abbé Grégoire said in his draft declaration of the rights of peoples of April 1793:

'. . . 2. Peoples are independent of each other and sovereign, irrespective of the number of individuals they comprise and the extent of the territory which they occupy. 3. One people has to act in relation to others as it wants others to act in relation to itself; what one man owes another one people owes the other.'[28]

As Wilhelm Grewe concluded, the ideas of the Revolution about the law of nations were a precise reflection of its philosophy of individualism at the level of inter-state relations,[29] a philosophy that remained influential.[30] In this context, the principle of equality of states was related to, and partly deduced from, the ideas of democracy, popular sovereignty and the self-determination of peoples, and today it is still situated in that same conceptual field or milieu.

In the nineteenth century, the principle was upheld as a matter of law, but beginning with the defeat of France by the anti-Napoleonic coalition and the Congress of Vienna (1814–15) the 'Great Powers' actually exercised a hegemony over the other European states. It was they that took the decisions they deemed necessary for maintaining the European order and the balance of power in Europe.[31] Those powers were called *puissances à intérêts généraux* because they were thought to be concerned with all international

---

[27] Art. V para. 4. For text, see *Sources and Documents, ibid.* 178 at 179.

[28] '. . . 2° Les peuples sont respectivement indépendants et souverains, quel que soit le nombre d'individus qui les composent et l'étendue du territoire qu'ils occupent. 3° Un peuple doit agir à l'égard des autres comme il désire qu'on agisse à son égard; ce qu'un homme doit à un homme, un peuple le doit aux autres'. See WG Grewe (ed.), *Fontes Historiae Iuris Gentium: Sources Relating to the History of the Law of Nations*, vol. 2 (Berlin and New York, Walter de Gruyter, 1988), at 660. See also the draft declaration of the member of the National Assembly, Comte de Volney, of 18 May 1790; reprinted in B Mirkine-Guetzévitch, 'L'influence de la révolution française sur le développement du droit international dans l'Europe orientale', 22 *Recueil des Cours* 22 (1928) 299 at 309.

[29] See WG Grewe, *The Epochs of International Law* (Berlin and New York, Walter de Gruyter 1984), at 415.

[30] Consider only the preamble of the UN Charter which speaks of 'the equal rights of men and women and of nations large and small'.

[31] For the history of the 'European Concert', see K Wolfke, *Great and Small Powers in International Law from 1814 to 1920* (Wrocław, Société des Sciences et des Lettres de Wrocław, 1961), at 9–49, and S Verosta, *Kollektivaktionen der Mächte des Europäischen Konzerts, 1886–1914* (Vienna, Verlag der Österreichischen Akademie der Wissenschaften, 1988). For the notion of hegemony as a legal term, see, in particular, H Triepel, *Die Hegemonie. Ein Buch von führenden Staaten* 2nd edition (Stuttgart, W Kohlhammer, 1943). See also A Randelzhofer, 'Great Powers', in R Bernhardt (ed.), ii *Encyclopedia of Public International Law* (Amsterdam, Elsevier, 1995), 618.

affairs even if their immediate interests were not affected.[32] In a tone of British self-assurance, the 1947 edition of Oppenheim's treatise still read:

> 'Arrangements made by the body of the Great Powers tend to gain the consent or the acquiescence of the minor States. The Great Powers are the leaders of the Family of Nations, and every advance of the Law of Nations during the past has been the result of their political hegemony . . .'[33]

On the other hand, smaller powers were able to participate on an equal basis in international conferences on technical matters (such as postal services) and the codification of international law, the number of which grew rapidly in the second half of the century.[34]

Dickinson concluded in 1920 that the 'equality of states' was actually the expression of two distinct legal principles, namely 'the principle of equal protection of the law or equality before the law, and that of equality of rights and obligations or simply equality of rights'. To him, the first principle was 'absolutely essential to a stable society of nations', whereas the second 'has never been anything more than an ideal' and was even dangerous when applied to the participation of states in international organisations.[35] State practice of the time does not suggest that anything more was protected than an equality of formal legal status, in particular the same political independence and territorial integrity, and the same freedom to act in a legally relevant way on the international plane.[36]

As far as 'procedural equality' in international law was concerned, *i.e.* equality in representation, voting, and active participation in international organisations and conferences, the Covenant of the League of Nations (1919) made it clear that it was only guaranteed to a limited extent. On the one hand, the Covenant confirmed the principle of equality of states by opening the League to '[a]ny fully self-governing State' (and even any such 'Dominion or Colony'),[37] and by making the unanimity rule the basis of its voting arrangements.[38] As a subcommittee of the League's Assembly

---

[32] See H Mosler, *Die Grossmachtstellung im Völkerrecht* (Heidelberg, Lambert Schneider, 1949), at 22 *et seq.*

[33] See L Oppenheim, *International Law: A Treatise*, vol. 1 6th edition (London, Longmans, Green & Co., 1947, H Lauterpacht, ed.), at 244. The eighth edition (1955) retained only the first sentence of this statement (at 275).

[34] See Wolfke (above n. 31), at 47–78.

[35] See E de W Dickinson, *The Equality of States in International Law* (Cambridge, Mass., Harvard University Press, 1920), at 334–6.

[36] *Cf.* the formulation in Art. 4 of the Montevideo Convention on the Rights and Duties of States of 26 December 1933 (28 *American Journal of International Law* (1934), Suppl., 75 at 76): 'States are juridically equal, enjoy the same rights, and have equal capacity in their exercise. The rights of each one do not depend upon the power which it possesses to assure its [sic] exercise, but upon the simple fact of its existence as a person under international law.'

[37] See Art. 1(2) of the Covenant.

[38] See Art. 5 of the Covenant: 'Except where otherwise expressly provided in this Covenant or by the terms of the present Treaty, decisions at any meeting of the Assembly or of the Council shall require the agreement of all the Members of the League represented at the meeting.'

declared, '[t]he essential characteristic of the unanimity rule . . . is that it serves as the safeguard of the sovereignty of states.'[39] But at the same time, and more importantly, the existence of leading powers and their special role was given a formal legal expression—the 'Principal Allied and Associated Powers' were assigned permanent seats in the League's Council.[40]

> 'The Paris Conference of 1919, confirming and consolidating the leading position of the great Powers, which stretched back to the first years of the previous century, marked the close of an important stage in the development of . . . international law.'[41]

This did not happen by chance. Unlike a legal system which is without any permanent institutional structure, a constitutional order such as that built by the Covenant cannot ignore actual differences among its constituent members which bear strongly on the political and legal course the community is steering. However, the four or five major powers elevated to the rank of permanent members never constituted a majority of the Council. The number of non-permanent members was raised from four originally, to six in 1922, nine in 1926, ten in 1933 and eleven in 1936. An observer critically noted in retrospect: '[I]t was the unworkable nature of the doctrine of equal rights that caused power, like water, to find its level, and the real decisions to be made outside Geneva.'[42]

4. SOVEREIGNTY SINCE 1945: THE CONCEPT OF 'SOVEREIGN EQUALITY'

Since the United Nations Organisation was founded in 1945, the traditional notion of sovereignty has experienced a profound modification and limitation. Step by step, and following the experience of a steadily increasing interdependence of states, the 'sovereign state' of the past turned into a (primarily territorially defined) organisation with a large number of international legal obligations (arising with, without, and even against its will)—an organisation which in the complex structure of the universal legal order is endowed with, comparatively, the highest degree of autonomy. In 1934, Hermann Heller still referred to sovereignty as a 'highest, exclusive, irre-

---

[39] See Records of Second Assembly, Meetings of Committees, I, pp. 177 *et seq.*, quoted in DP Myers, 'Representation in League of Nations Council', 20 *American Journal of International Law* (1926) 689 at 703.
[40] See Art. 4(1) of the Covenant.
[41] See Wolfke (above n. 31), at 125.
[42] See HW Briggs, 'Power Politics and International Organization', 39 *American Journal of International Law* (1945) 664 at 670.

sistible and independent power' of a state.[43] Today, such a power no longer exists, neither in a factual nor in a legal sense.

A. 'Sovereign Equality' in the UN Charter

The Charter of the United Nations does not speak of 'sovereignty' as such but proclaims the 'principle of the *sovereign equality*' of all members of the UN (Article 2(1)). By referring to the concept of sovereignty, it seems, those drawing up the Charter sought to link their project to earlier periods of the international legal order, and make it appear less of a break with the past than it actually was. However, the phrase 'sovereign equality', newly introduced into international law by the Charter, is already a signal indicating profound change. 'Sovereign equality' is not simply the addition of 'equality' and 'sovereignty' of states in a traditional sense. It is not an expression which would have transposed the old concepts into the Charter. Instead, the year 1945 constitutes a deep dividing line in the history of sovereignty. Pre-Charter explanations and definitions of sovereignty must be approached carefully in order to evaluate their relevance in the age of the UN.

The notion of 'sovereign equality' first appeared in the Moscow Declaration (or 'Declaration on General Security') of 30 October 1943, in which the governments of the United States, the United Kingdom, the Soviet Union and China pronounced

> '[t]hat they recognise the necessity of establishing at the earliest practicable date a general international organisation, based on *the principle of the sovereign equality of all peace-loving states*, and open to membership by all such states, large and small, for the maintenance of international peace and security'.[44]

In Committee I/1 of the San Francisco Conference, '[s]everal delegates expressed disapproval of the phrase sovereign equality and suggested replacing it with juridical equality or some similar term' because other parts of the Charter (*i.e.*, the provisions concerning the Security Council) would not be consistent with the concept of equal sovereignty.[45] The rapporteur of the committee felt that

---

[43] See H Heller, *Staatslehre* 6th edition (Leiden, AW Sijthoff's, 1934, Tübingen, JCB Mohr, 1983), at 246 and 278, respectively: 'Die Staatsgewalt ist souverän, das heisst sie ist auf ihrem Gebiete oberste, ausschliessliche, unwiderstehliche und eigenständige Macht.'

[44] Paragraph. 4. For text, see UNYB 1946–47 at 3. For the drafting history of Art. 2(1) UN Charter, see B Fassbender, 'Commentary on Art. 2(1) of the UN Charter', in Simma, *The Charter of the United Nations* (above n. 20), 2nd ed. 2002. The phrase 'sovereign equality' apparently was first used in the context of inter-American relations before and in World War II; see RA Klein, *Sovereign Equality Among States: The History of an Idea* (Toronto, University of Toronto Press, 1974), chapters 5 and 6, in particular pp. 104, 108, 113.

[45] See Summary Report of Eighth Meeting of Committee I/1, 17 May 1945, in VI United Nations Conference on International Organization [UNCIO] at 310. See also Summary Reports of Seventh Meeting, 16 May 1945, *ibid*. 303 at 304, and of Eleventh Meeting, 4 June 1945, *ibid*. 331 *et seq*.

'Article 1 ['Purposes'] should be re-worded to include the three ideas that (1) members are juridically equal, (2) all enjoy the rights inherent under [*sic*] sovereignty, and (3) they all should act in accordance with their duties under the Charter; Article 2 ['Principles'] should be eliminated. . .'[46]

However, the drafting subcommittee decided to leave the text of Chapter II (the later Article 2), paragraph 1 as proposed by the Four Sponsoring Governments.[47] In its report of 1 June 1945 the subcommittee included an interpretive statement that was an amalgam of the various suggested amendments to Chapter II, paragraph 1:

'The Subcommittee voted to keep the terminology, 'sovereign equality,' on the assumption and understanding that it conveys the following:
(1) That states are juridically equal;
(2) That they enjoy the rights inherent in their full sovereignty;
(3) That the personality of the state is respected, as well as its territorial integrity and political independence;
(4) That the state should, under international order, comply faithfully with its international duties and obligations.'[48]

Because of its careful preparation and adoption by consensus, the 'Friendly Relations Declaration' of the UN General Assembly of 1970[49] can be relied upon almost as a text enjoying binding force.[50] Among the seven principles considered to constitute the groundwork of international law in the era of the United Nations, the 'principle of sovereign equality of States' is set forth as the penultimate. It is significant that the principle is only mentioned after five fundamental duties of states arising from their membership in the international community have been stated (namely the duties to refrain from the threat or use of force, to settle disputes by peaceful means, not to intervene in domestic matters of other states, to cooperate with other states, and to promote the realisation of the principle of equal rights and self-determination of peoples), and that it is followed by the statement of yet another duty (to fulfil international obligations in good faith). The principle of sovereign equality is explained as follows:

'All States enjoy sovereign equality. They have equal rights and duties and are equal members of the international community, notwithstanding differences of an economic, social, political or other nature.

---

[46] *Ibid.* (Eighth Meeting), at 311.
[47] See Text of Chapter II as Agreed upon by the Drafting Committee, 28 May 1945; VI UNCIO at 687.
[48] See Report of Rapporteur of Subcommittee I/1/A to Committee I/1: Chapter II, 1 June 1945; VI UNCIO at 717 *et seq.*
[49] Annex to GA Res. 2625 (XXV). For text, see UNYB 1970 at 788.
[50] See the *Nicaragua* judgment of the International Court of Justice, ICJ Reports 1986, 14 at 107: '. . . the Declaration . . . which set out principles which the General Assembly declared to be 'basic principles' of international law'.

In particular, sovereign equality includes the following elements:
(*a*) States are juridically equal;
(*b*) Each State enjoys the rights inherent in full sovereignty;
(*c*) Each State has the duty to respect the personality of other States;
(*d*) The territorial integrity and political independence of the State are inviolable;
(*e*) Each State has the right freely to choose and develop its political, social, economic and cultural systems;
(*f*) Each State has the duty to comply fully and in good faith with its international obligations and to live in peace with other States.'

In conformity with Article 5 of the 1949 Draft Declaration on Rights and Duties of States elaborated by the UN International Law Commission,[51] the principle of sovereign equality is primarily understood as assuring states a right to equality in law. The specification, which opens with the words 'in particular' to express its non-exhaustive character, then essentially repeats the interpretive statement of the San Francisco Conference. Compared to that statement, only the right defined under (e) was added, and the duty to live in peace with other states under (f). Whereas the latter simply reinforces the first two principles of the Friendly Relations Declaration, the former is a consequence of the recognition of the right to self-determination of peoples in the era of decolonisation—a right which is not lost once a people has established its own independent state. However, the inclusion of the right stated under (e), a right the existence of which was simply taken for granted in the framework of the international law of coexistence, shows that in the first two-and-a-half decades after 1945 the traditional understanding of what constituted the *domaine reservé* of states, closed to an international exertion of influence, had considerably changed.

Apart from accentuating the legal equality of states, the Declaration's definition of equal sovereignty is as unspecific as that of 1945. The difficulty of defining sovereign equality is manifested by the circular explanation, also taken from the San Francisco formula, that this equality amounts to the enjoyment of 'the rights inherent in full sovereignty'.

B. Sovereign Equality as a New Concept

In isolation, the term 'sovereign equality of states' makes little sense. As an adjective, 'sovereign' means 'supreme, paramount, principal, greatest, most notable' or 'having superior or supreme rank or power'.[52] Accordingly, 'sovereign' cannot meaningfully be applied to equality in terms of a state's quality of being equal with every other state. In the drafting history of the

---

[51] For text, see UNYB 1948–9 at 948 *et seq.* and 44 *American Journal of International Law* (1950), Suppl., at 15–8. For analysis, see Fassbender, 'Commentary', above n. 44.
[52] See *Oxford English Dictionary*, 2ⁿᵈ ed., vol. xvi (1989) at 77 *et seq.*

UN Charter, 'sovereign equality' was first used with regard to nations, not states, and the first formulation simply spoke of the 'principle of equality of nations'.[53] When the term was applied to states, as the established holders of external sovereignty, the emphasis on equality in law was not changed, but supplemented with an adjective reminiscent of the traditional status of states in international law. The word 'sovereign' appeared, but not in formulations like 'the principle(s) of equality and sovereignty of states' or 'the principle of equal sovereignty', which were intentionally avoided.

At the San Francisco Conference, 'sovereign equality' was deliberately adopted as a 'new term'.[54] Its purpose was clear: The idea of equality of states in law was given precedence over that of sovereignty by relegating the latter to the position of an attributive adjective merely modifying the noun 'equality'. In this combination, sovereignty was meant to exclude the legal superiority of any one state over another, but not a greater role played by the international community vis-à-vis *all* its members.[55] The new term proved to be an accurate description of a development characterising the international legal order in the age of the League of Nations and, in partic- ular, the UN: From the two elements (sovereignty and equality), 'sover- eignty is in a process of progressive erosion, inasmuch as the international community places ever more constraints on the freedom of action of States'. We witness a 'development towards greater community discipline . . . driven by a global change in the perception of how the right balance between individual State interests and interests of mankind as a whole should be established'.[56]

C. Sovereign Equality as Constitutional Autonomy

In an article entitled 'The Principle of Sovereign Equality of States as a Basis for International Organisation' written in 1944, Hans Kelsen defined sover- eignty as follows:

---

[53] A first draft of the Moscow Declaration (see above n. 40) made in the US State Department had referred to an organisation 'based upon the principles of equality of nations and of univer- sal membership'. It was later revised to read 'based on the principle of the sovereign equality of all nations', with the intention to indicate that the equality referred to was legal rather than factual. See RB Russell & JE Muther, *A History of the United Nations Charter: The Role of the United States 1940–5* (Washington, DC, The Brookings Institution, 1958) at 111, 120.

[54] See the statement of the Rapporteur of Committee 1, discussing 'amendments to determine the meaning of *the new term 'sovereign equality'*: 'When the Committee was considering this subject, it passed the article, the paragraph before you as it stands . . . *The term 'sovereign equality' was kept as a new terminology'*. Verbatim Minutes of Second Meeting of Commission I, 15 June 1945; VI UNCIO 65 *et seqq*., at 69 (emphasis added).

[55] See B Fassbender, *UN Security Council Reform and the Right of Veto: A Constitutional Perspective* (The Hague, Kluwer Law International, 1998) at 109 *et seq*.

[56] See C Tomuschat, 'Obligations Arising for States Without or Against Their Will', 241 *Recueil des Cours* (1993) 195 at 292.

'[S]overeignty of the States, as subjects of international law, is *the legal authority of the States under the authority of international law* . . . [T]he State is then sovereign when it is subjected only to international law, not to the national law of any other State. Consequently, the State's sovereignty under international law is its legal independence from other States.'[57]

In other words, sovereignty is a collective or umbrella term, denoting the rights which, at a given time, a state is accorded by international law, and the duties imposed upon it by that same law. These specific ('sovereign') rights and duties constitute 'sovereignty'; they do not 'flow from' it.[58] Sovereignty is the legal status of a state as defined (and not *only* 'protected')[59] by international law.[60] Accordingly, sovereignty is neither 'natural' nor static. In a process that has placed ever more constraints on the freedom of action of states, its substance has changed, and will further change in the future. For that reason, the unspecific and open-ended definitions of the San Francisco statement[61] and the Friendly Relations Declaration,[62] which at first glance seemed rather unsatisfactory, are fully accurate.

Under the rule of the UN Charter, the most important limitation of the rights formerly collectively addressed as sovereignty is the abolition of the *jus ad bellum*, or the right to wage war against another state. The Charter has put the international use of force under the exclusive control of the Security Council, the only exception being a state's temporary right to self-defence according to Art. 51 of the Charter. In the words of FH Hinsley, this acceptance by states that war has ceased to be a legalised form of force constitutes 'a greater displacement of assumptions about relations between states than any that has ever taken place' since the rise of the state in human

---

[57] See H Kelsen, 53 *Yale Law Journal* (1944) 207 at 208 (emphasis added). See also id., *Principles of International Law* (New York, Rinehart, 1952) at 155–7, 438–4, and id., 'The Draft Declaration on Rights and Duties of States: Critical Remarks', 44 *American Journal of International Law* (1950) 259 at 268 *et seq.*, 276.

[58] See also IL Claude, Jr., 'Foreword', in MR Fowler & JM Bunck, *Law, Power, and the Sovereign State: The Evolution and Application of the Concept of Sovereignty* (University Park, PA, Pennsylvania State University Press, 1995), at x: Sovereignty 'is the essential indicator of the currently asserted and currently accepted implications of the status enjoyed by the units that give the system its multistate character: the rights, immunities, responsibilities, and limitations attributed to states.'

[59] But see H Steinberger, 'Sovereignty', in iv *Encyclopedia of Public International Law* (above n. 31), 500 at 518: 'As a juridical status protected by international law, [sovereignty] is embedded within the normative order of this law.'

[60] See also L Wildhaber, 'Sovereignty and International Law', in RStJ Macdonald & DM Johnston (eds.), *The Structure and Process of International Law: Essays in Legal Philosophy, Doctrine and Theory* (Dordrecht, Martinus Nijhoff, 1986), 425 at 441: 'Authoritative writers agree that sovereignty is a relative notion, variable in the course of times, adaptable to new situations and exigencies, a discretionary *freedom within, and not from, international law.*' (Emphasis added.)

[61] See above text accompanying n. 48.

[62] See above text following n. 49.

history.[63] Today, the Charter's ban on the use of force is understood not so much as a limitation of sovereignty but as a necessary prerequisite for a de facto enjoyment of sovereign equality by states. A state's sovereign equality depends on a comprehensive prohibition of the use of force and on an effective mechanism to implement and enforce this prohibition.[64] An equally important limitation of traditional sovereignty is the obligation of any state to protect the fundamental rights of all individuals subject to its jurisdiction, and the concomitant legal interest of the international community and all its members in their protection.

'If mankind is to achieve a more effective international organisation [. . .] the development must be from international towards constitutional law'.[65] Quite in line with this remark by W Friedmann, a more recent school of thought in international law understands the development of the law of nations, since the foundation of the League in 1919, as a process of constitutionalisation.[66] The adoption of the Covenant and, later, the UN Charter is seen as a gradual effort to give the international community a constitution expressing systematically and in writing its fundamental values and the rules and procedures which shall protect them, so that the peaceful coexistence and cooperation of all nations of the world is ensured. The international community is not just perceived as a sum, or addition, of the interests of the individual states but as an entity committed to humankind as a whole, having its own legal personality and purposes which it can set against the opinion and action of a recalcitrant state.[67] This constitutional approach to international law seeks to reestablish a category of superior norms based on the collective will of the international community as a whole. The approach recognises a hierarchy of rules of international law in which those rules having the quality of constitutional law of the international community enjoy the highest rank and greatest firmness. At the same time, the notion of constitution takes up elements of organisation and

---

[63] See Hinsley, above n. 2, at 232.

[64] See Fassbender, *UN Security Council Reform*, above n. 55, at 111 *et seq.*

[65] See Friedmann, above n. 7, at 113 *et seq.* (with reference to the evolution of the European Communities as a possible 'prototype of developments that may . . . eventually extend to the international community as a whole').

[66] For an analysis of the different constitutional concepts, see, in particular, P-M Dupuy, 'The Constitutional Dimension of the Charter of the United Nations Revisited', 1 *Max Planck Yearbook on United Nations Law* (1997) 1; B Fassbender, 'The United Nations Charter as Constitution of the International Community', 36 *Columbia Journal of Transnational Law* (1998) 529 at 538–68; A Paulus, *Die internationale Gemeinschaft im Völkerrecht* (Munich, CH Beck, 2001) at 285–328; R Kolb, *Théorie du ius cogens international. Essai de relecture du concept* (Paris, Presses Universitaires de France, 2001) at 100–8 (with an emphasis on the doctrinal history).

[67] See Tomuschat, 'Obligations', above n. 56, at 209–40; Simma, 'From Bilateralism', above n. 19, at 229–84. For a comprehensive study of the idea and reality of the international community in contemporary international law, see Paulus, *Die internationale Gemeinschaft* (above n. 61).

institutionalisation characteristic of modern state constitutions. It is this constitutional view of the present international legal order which, following Kelsen's approach, leads to an understanding of sovereign equality that is in accordance with an orientation, so strongly strengthened in the past fifty years, of the individual state towards community values and goals: *Sovereign equality is the legal authority and autonomy of a state as defined and guaranteed by the constitution of the international community.* It denotes the entitlement of a state, and the people constituting it, to autonomous development and self-responsibility within the limits set by international law.

5. 'SOVEREIGN RIGHTS' OF STATES UNDER THE CONSTITUTION OF THE INTERNATIONAL COMMUNITY

That legal equality of states is the gist of the principle of sovereign equality was already emphasised in the proceedings of the San Francisco Conference as well as in the Friendly Relations Declaration of 1970,[68] which opens its explanation of the principle, it will be recalled, with the words: 'All States . . . have equal rights and duties and are equal members of the international community, notwithstanding differences of an economic, social, political or other nature.' One may add: notwithstanding, in particular, differences in the size of territory and population, and in political, economic and military power.

But what exactly are those 'equal rights and duties'? In the words of Christian Tomuschat, 'every State, large or small, enjoys the rights which international law grants to States as subjects of international law'.[69] As equality as such does not, and cannot, define what these rights are, we are referred back to the above definition of the sovereign equality of states under the authority of international law. Accordingly, equal rights are the 'sovereign' rights equally enjoyed by states, as defined by international law or, more exactly, the constitution of the international community. If at times we speak of sovereignty, and then again of equality, we in fact address the same legally defined status of states. What differs is only the perspective, or the accent which is placed either on the autonomy of a state, understood as its legally defined capacity for self-determination, or its status in relation to that of other members of the international community and that community itself. Understood this way, the principle of 'sovereign equality' is indeed an apt representation of the identity of 'sovereignty' and 'equality' of states in the age of the United Nations.

---

[68] See above text accompanying n. 49.
[69] See C Tomuschat, 'International Law: Ensuring the Survival of Mankind on the Eve of a New Century', 281 *Recueil des Cours* (1999) 1 at 189.

In accordance with these two perspectives, the 'sovereign rights' presently accorded to states by international constitutional law are, first, the legal protection of a state's autonomy as a space of self-determination and, secondly, rights ensuring a state's equal membership in the international community. None of these rights 'flow' or 'derive from' sovereignty, equality, or sovereign equality as legal concepts or super-norms. On the contrary, it is they, as rights defined by norms of the positive constitutional law of the international community, that make up what can be addressed as the 'sovereignty', 'equality', or 'sovereign equality' of states.

A. Rights Protecting Constitutional Autonomy

As regards the constitutional rights in the service of state autonomy, a state is protected by the prohibition of the threat or use of force (Art. 2(4) of the UN Charter). If, nevertheless, an armed attack occurs, the attacked state has the right of individual or collective self-defense until the Security Council has taken the measures necessary to maintain international peace and security (Art. 51). A state is further protected by the duty of the other states and the organised international community not to intervene in matters within its domestic jurisdiction.[70]

> 'A prohibited intervention must . . . be one bearing on matters in which each State is permitted, by the principle of State sovereignty, to decide freely.'[71]

Within the limits of international law, a state is entitled freely to determine its constitution and its political, social, economic and cultural order, which the other members of the international community must respect. If a state has a democratic constitution, its sovereignty protects a space of democratic self-determination. A sovereign state possesses jurisdiction over its citizens as well as over foreigners present in its territory (albeit limited by the obligation to safeguard their fundamental human rights and freedoms), and an exclusive power to use physical force to enforce its law within its territory. Further, a sovereign state has the right to determine its future legal status. It can, for instance, decide to form a union with, or to become an integral part of, another state, and thus relinquish its sovereignty. The details of all these rights and entitlements are controversial and dynamic, and must be studied with the help of treatises, manuals and casebooks of international law.

---

[70] For an overview of the contemporary rules of jurisdiction, in particular extraterritorial jurisdiction, see *ibid.* at 195–202.
[71] See the *Nicaragua* judgment of the International Court of Justice, ICJ Reports (1986) 14 at 108.

B. Rights of Participation in the International Community

The rights ensuring equal membership in the international community are principally rights of participation in the exercise of the functions of governance of that community, that is to say, in making and applying international law and adjudicating international legal claims.[72] Traditional formal rights of participation—which are also means of pursuing and enforcing the substantive rights of autonomy—are the rights to conclude international treaties, to send and receive diplomatic envoys (right of legation), and to make diplomatic claims. A sovereign state enjoys a principally unlimited international legal personality and capacity to perform international legal acts. This distinguishes it from other subjects of international law, in particular intergovernmental organisations, which have a limited legal personality defined by the respective founding treaty. It used to be said that sovereign states are the only 'born' or 'natural' persons of international law, whereas all others are 'made' in the sense that they are brought into existence as legal persons by an action of states.

According to traditional doctrine, equality in legal status does not mean that every state is entitled to join treaties purporting to set up universal regimes, or law-making treaties laying down general rules of conduct for an unspecified number of states. Even the organised international community is said to be under no obligation to open access to the treaties drawn up under its auspices to all states.[73] This view is highly objectionable.[74] It means that individual states can be excluded from treaties effectively serving as legislative instruments of the international community. In fact, if a certain subject has been dealt with in a multilateral treaty with general or even quasi-universal participation, an excluded state is effectively barred from regulating this subject by means of bilateral or multilateral treaties. To that extent, that state is actually deprived of its treaty-making capacity. It is submitted that this is incompatible with the idea of equal membership of all states in the international community—an idea suggesting, contrary to the above, a right of every state not only to join such general treaties but also to participate in their negotiation.[75] In accordance with this view, Art. 10 of

---

[72] For the system of governance established by the UN Charter, see Fassbender, *Columbia Journal of Transnational Law*, above n. 66, at 574–6.

[73] See Tomuschat, 'International Law', above n. 69, at 189 et seq., and for the category of 'law-making treaties' R Jennings & A Watts (eds.), *Oppenheim's International Law*, vol. 1, 9th ed. (London and New York, Longman, 1992), at 1203–6. In its 1962 Draft Articles on the Law of Treaties the International Law Commission defined a 'general multilateral treaty' as 'a multilateral treaty which concerns general norms of international law or deals with matters of general interest to States as a whole'.

[74] *Cf.* Simma, 'From Bilateralism', above n. 19, at 325 *et seq.*

[75] See, e.g., V Pechota, 'Equality: Political Justice in an Unequal World', in *The Structure and Process of International Law*, above n. 58, 453 at 467.

the Charter of Economic Rights and Duties of States[76] provides that 'as equal members of the international community, [all States] have the right to participate fully and effectively in the international decision-making process in the solution of world economic, financial and monetary problems'.

Today, all states are equally obliged to heed the rules of the UN Charter. Consequently, all states are also equally entitled to membership in the permanent organs of the international community. The 'principle of universality' of the UN follows from the constitutional character of the Charter.[77] Art. 4(1) of the Charter must therefore be read as entitling every sovereign and 'peace-loving' state to membership in the United Nations.[78] The latter requirement is met if a state credibly accepts the fundamental constitutional principles of the international community as enshrined in the Charter and other instruments. This right to membership is especially momentous if one recalls that today 'in most instances membership in the United Nations determines the existence of a State, irrespective of any additional unilateral acts of recognition on the part of States'.[79] Since the 'package deal' of 1955, UN practice has generally recognised the constitutional right of states to UN membership.

A (temporary) suspension of a state which has seriously violated the rules of the Charter 'from the exercise of the rights and privileges of [UN] membership' (Art. 5 of the Charter) is acceptable from a constitutional point of view.[80] However, it seems inadmissible *permanently* to exclude a state from the organic structure of the community as established by the Charter. To prevent a state permanently from participating in the work of the community organs is incompatible with the very idea of an international community living under a constitution. In fact, in the history of the UN, not a single member state has been expelled from the Organisation.

C. Sovereign Equality in the United Nations

The records of the San Francisco Conference and the preceding diplomatic negotiations demonstrate that the prerogatives which the leading powers were given in the UN Charter—in particular permanent membership in the

---

[76] General Assembly Res. 3281 (XXIX), 12 December 1974; UNYB 1974 at 402.
[77] See Fassbender, *Columbia Journal of Transnational Law*, above n. 66, at 610–3, and id., 'Universality', in H Volger (ed.), *A Concise Encyclopedia of the United Nations* (The Hague, Kluwer Law International, 2002) at 576–8.
[78] See *Conditions of Admission of a State to Membership in the UN* International Court of Justice Reports (1947–8) 57 at 71 (indiv. opinion Alvarez). See also the amendments and comments of states concerning UN membership submitted at the San Francisco Conference: Department of State (ed.), *The United Nations Conference on International Organization: Selected Documents* (Washington, D.C., Government Printing Office, 1946), at 111 *et seq.*
[79] See J Dugard, *Recognition and the United Nations* (Cambridge, Grotius, 1987), at 167.
[80] See Fassbender, *Columbia Journal of Transnational Law*, above n. 66, at 613–5.

Security Council and the right of veto according to Art. 27(3)—were regarded as painful, albeit necessary, exceptions to a true equality of status of all member states in the new Organisation. So much was even admitted by the major powers themselves. The first leading commentary on the Charter could do no more than state the contradiction between the promise of Art. 2(1) and the provisions of Arts. 23(1) and 27(3) by saying:

'In the Charter the principle of equal legal rights is recognised . . . The Charter does, however, recognise the inequality of Members in respect to power and political influence by according the 'Great Powers' permanent membership in the Security Council and the so-called 'right of veto'.'[81]

As far as a contradiction is recognised between the terms of the Charter on the one hand, and sovereign equality as a principle of general international law on the other, a purely contractual view of the Charter has no difficulty in resolving it: It is exactly their sovereignty which is said to enable states to enter into international agreements which may, or may not, provide for unequal rights and obligations of the parties. This argumentation, however, is no longer viable if the Charter is seen as the constitution of the international community.[82] Since this view dissolves the dualism of 'general international law' and the law of the Charter,[83] exceptions to legal equality in the latter can no longer be justified by having recourse to the former category. Instead, an attempt to read the Charter in a way that reconciles its seemingly contradictory pronouncements is necessary.

An answer to the problem may be sought by recalling once again that in the Charter the traditional concepts of sovereignty and equality of states were replaced with a new principle—with a different, 'community-oriented' content—that of sovereign equality. In line with this orientation, '[t]he rule of state equality could be understood as coherently modified by a rational principle of distinction: that states bearing the greatest institutional responsibility should also have the greatest say in critical disputes'.[84] In the form of sovereign equality, formal equality of states has been qualified to the extent necessary for achieving the common interests of the international community.[85] This common interest requires furnishing certain states,

---

[81] See LM Goodrich & E Hambro, *Charter of the United Nations: Commentary and Documents* 2nd edition (Boston, World Peace Foundation, 1949), at 100. Similarly PC Jessup, *A Modern Law of Nations: An Introduction* (New York, Macmillan, 1948), at 30.

[82] For a fuller exposition of the following reasoning, see Fassbender, *UN Security Council Reform*, above n. 55, at 287–95.

[83] See Fassbender, *Columbia Journal of Transnational Law*, above n. 66, at 585–8.

[84] See TM Franck, *The Power of Legitimacy Among Nations* (Oxford, Oxford University Press, 1990), at 177.

[85] For an analysis of the place and role of the 'common interest' in current international law, see B Fassbender, 'Zwischen Staatsräson und Gemeinschaftsbindung: Zur Gemeinwohlorientierung des Völkerrechts der Gegenwart', in H Münkler & K Fischer (eds.), *Gemeinwohlkonkretisierungen und Gemeinsinnerwartungen: Zur Relevanz unbestimmter Rechtsbegriffe* (Berlin, Akademie Verlag, 2002).

whose extraordinary commitment to community goals is indispensable, with special rights if otherwise their support cannot be enlisted.[86] It must also be taken into consideration that the prohibition of the use of force in international relations is a prerequisite for an enjoyment of sovereign equality by states,[87] and that, in turn, the effectiveness of this prohibition depends on a working institutional arrangement—a necessary part of which is the special position given to the major powers in the Security Council.

Thus the principle of sovereign equality recognises as necessary a relation between responsibilities (or duties) and rights in an institutional structure established with the principal purpose of maintaining international peace and security (*cf.* Art. 1(1) of the Charter). At San Francisco, this consideration of responsibility in the understanding of equality found expression in Colombia's proposal for a preamble of the Charter as follows:

'The High Contracting Parties,

. . .,

Agree that the following are necessary:

. . .

VI. To establish the principle of the equality before Law of all States, whatever their population, their wealth, their strength or their territorial extent, but to admit, at the same time, that the Great Powers, because they have greater international responsibility, must likewise exert a greater functional influence in the organization of the world.'[88]

D. Sovereign Equality of States in Their Mutual Relations

In their mutual relations, states must treat each other as equals. The practical importance of that principle is, however, limited. In spite of several provisions in the UN Charter about the international cooperation of states (*cf.* Arts. 1(3), 11, 13, 56), and the 'duty of States to co-operate with one another . . . in the various spheres of international relations' proclaimed in the Friendly Relations Declaration,[89] states are still considered free not to maintain relations (of a diplomatic, political, economic or other character) with other states at all. If such relations are maintained, a state may differentiate between states in the treatment it accords to them.[90] In particular,

---

[86] Colin Warbrick speaks of a 'functional' reason for providing certain states with a preferential status. See C Warbrick, 'The Principle of Sovereign Equality', in V Lowe & C Warbrick (eds.), *The United Nations and the Principles of International Law: Essays in Memory of Michael Akehurst* (London and New York, Routledge, 1994), 204 at 211, 215.

[87] See above text accompanying n. 64.

[88] See proposal of May 11, 1945; VI UNCIO at 528.

[89] See above n. 49. See also many other resolutions of the General Assembly to that effect, for instance the Charter of Economic Rights and Duties of States (above n. 76).

[90] See *Oppenheim's International Law*, above n. 73, at 376–9. However, the authors add that 'in some particular respects a rule of non-discrimination may exist, within limits which are not clear'.

states can, when entering into international treaties, agree on an unequal treatment of parties to the treaty. Trade agreements can, for instance, provide for an unequal access to the respective markets. Likewise, there is no general right to most-favoured-nation treatment. When establishing international organisations, states can arrange for differentiated responsibilities and rules of weighted voting which take account of the factual importance of a country in a certain respect (like its economic strength, or its importance as a maritime power). In short, sovereign equality is not a rule of *jus cogens* (as defined by Art. 53 of the 1969 Vienna Convention on the Law of Treaties)[91] from which no derogation could be permitted,[92] notwithstanding its character as a fundamental principle of the constitutional law of the international community.

Therefore, in the relations between states, the principle of sovereign equality remains essentially confined to its formal dimension.[93] It means that '[e]ach State has the duty to respect the personality of other States', as the Friendly Relations Declaration puts it. A procedural consequence is emphasised by the Manila Declaration on the Peaceful Settlement of Disputes of 1982, which formulates the rule that '[i]nternational disputes shall be settled on the basis of the sovereign equality of States'.[94]

In addition, states are obliged to comply, in their relations with each other, with a number of specific 'rules of abstention'[95] which—as in a mirror image—arise from the rights protecting the constitutional autonomy of states. In fact, the autonomy accorded to states by the constitution of the international community only becomes effective because of corresponding obligations imposed on the same states. The rules prohibiting the threat or use of force, and intervention in matters within the domestic jurisdiction of other states, and the right to self-determination imply, on the one hand, rights of any one state vis-à-vis the other states—*i.e.* 'sovereign rights' intended to protect a state's autonomy under international law. On the other hand, the same rules constitute obligations on every state vis-à-vis any other state, obligations intended to ensure the sovereign equality of states in their mutual relations.

Whether, and to what extent, these obligations are actually fulfilled is, of course, a different question. It is the answer to that question which decides

---

[91] For text, see 1155 UNTS 331, 63 *American Journal of International Law* (1969) 875, 8 *International Legal Materials* (1969) 679.

[92] See Tomuschat, 'International Law', above n. 69, at 193; Wildhaber, above n. 60, at 442, 444; A Cassese, *International Law* (Oxford, Oxford University Press, 2001), at 110. *Cf.* Kolb, above n. 66, at 115 *et seq.*, 172–81 ('la nécessité de distinguer entre *ius cogens* et ordre public international').

[93] See Tomuschat *ibid.*

[94] Annex to General Assembly Res. 37/10, 15 November 1982, para. I 3; UNYB 1982 at 1372.

[95] For this term, coined by W Friedmann, see above text accompanying n. 7.

how wide and deep the gap is between international law and reality, or the legal ownership and the real holding of sovereign equality. It is obvious that today the autonomy actually enjoyed by the large majority of states almost entirely depends on the functioning of an organised international community which patiently strives

> 'to replace unlimited and, ultimately, destructive national competition and freedom of action by international co-operation'.[96]

E. Sovereign Equality of States and Supranationalism

Under present international law, sovereign equality (namely the rights of participation and rights protecting autonomy) is only enjoyed by sovereign states and not by intergovernmental or 'supranational' organisations, even if they have been granted far-reaching governmental powers and approach a state-like quality. As long as such an organisation has not constituted itself, and has not been recognised, as a 'sovereign state', its status in international law remains a derivative one. Internally, *i.e.* in the relations between the organisation and its member states, sovereignty may be 'divided', 'shared' or 'mixed', but in international law an all-or-nothing approach to sovereignty is still operative. Doctrine and legal practice follow the route once fixed to identify the 'seat of sovereignty' in federal associations and unions of states (the distinction between *Bundesstaat* and *Staatenbund*).[97] However, while it was in the past political communities below a 'central' level of territorial government that were declared non-sovereign on the basis of this theory, it is now the case that communities are vaulting the 'sovereign' states and partially replacing them in the exercise of governmental functions.

It is a characteristic shortcoming of the present constitution of the international community that it defines, in the form of 'sovereign equality', the constitutional status of ('sovereign') states but not that of international or supranational organisations, despite the importance they have won in the international legal order. Instead, it is still left to the member states of such an organisation to define in each case its international legal position. On the other hand, it is testimony to the dissolution of 'sovereignty' traditionally understood in a number of variable ('sovereign') rights that a body like the European Union has little difficulty in asserting, in its relations with non-member states, the rights necessary for the performance of its functions. In other words, in its regular business the EU does not miss 'equal sovereignty' all that much.

---

[96] See W Friedmann, 'General Course in Public International Law', 127 *Recueil des Cours* (1969) 39 at 243.
[97] See Merriam, above n. 2, ch. X (pp. 185–216) about 'federalism and continental theory'.

6. SOVEREIGN EQUALITY IN AN AGE OF GLOBALISATION

Some authors argue that contemporary international law has surpassed Friedmann's 'law of cooperation'. To Tomuschat, for instance, today the international legal order is in the third stage of its development: the law of coexistence and the law of cooperation are followed by a period of 'international law as a comprehensive blueprint for social life', the chief characteristic of which is a 'further intrusion of international law into matters previously thought to be shielded from any outside interference'. In particular, the author emphasises the obligations imposed on states with regard to human rights, democracy as a form of government, and 'good governance'.[98] He concludes that international law, '[i]nstead of being a set of rules limiting and guiding States in their foreign policies, . . . has become a multi-faceted body of law that permeates all fields of life . . . [W]e are facing today a totally new international law which has lost all of its former inhibitions.'[99] Accordingly, it is stated that, juridically, little remains of the traditional sovereignty of states.

As regards the principle of sovereign equality of states, the development described in those terms can be explained as a further reduction of the space of autonomy accorded to states by international law. In other words, the boundary between matters left to the exclusive control of states, and those which are a concern of the international community and can be regulated by international law, has moved further, extending again the space of international competence. This shift does not, however, simply amount to a greater restriction of the sovereign equality of states. Rather, it involves an increase in importance of the 'second pillar' of sovereign equality, namely the rights of participation in the international community. A certain loss of autonomy of states—in particular in the legislative field, but also with regard to the executive and the judicial functions—can thus be compensated for by increased participatory rights at the international level.[100]

However, contemporary international law is also regarded as being challenged from a different perspective:

[G]lobalisation has rendered the traditional assumption of an inter-statal society problematic . . . [It] seems to diminish the role of the state and to open up international society for new actors, both economic and altruistic non-governmental organisations . . . Some observers . . . see the state squeezed between globalisation from above (business) and below (NGOs). . . [G]lobalisation has also curbed the

---

[98] See Tomuschat, 'International Law', above n. 69, at 63–70.
[99] *Ibid.* at 70 *et seq.*
[100] This process is reminiscent of the constitutional development in federal states like Germany and Switzerland where the individual states (*Länder, Kantone*) have lost legislative powers but won participatory rights at the federal level. Similarly, the loss of independent powers of EU member states to the advantage of the Union is said to be (at least partially) offset by a gain of rights of participation at the EU level.

belief in the benefit of governmental institutions, be they national or global. Liberals and Neoliberals demand a reconstruction of international law on an interindividual basis.'[101]

Whether these partially contradictory trends and aspirations—which are discussed mainly in the current international relations literature—will prevail is as yet uncertain.[102] But we may well be moving in the direction of a more diverse or fragmented international order in which states no longer play the leading role—and in which international law as hitherto defined (*i.e.* law principally governing the intercourse between states) can no longer claim to be the primary regulatory code of international affairs.[103] Perhaps there is indeed an international system of 'interlocking communities'[104] looming on the horizon, made up of individuals, organisations (economic and others) and states with overlapping memberships and allegiances.[105]

For the principle of sovereign equality, as a cornerstone of contemporary international law, such a development would raise complex problems which can only be indicated here. Sovereign equality is a principle which applies to the relations between states and the organised international community, and between states in their mutual relations. If the relations between these 'public' actors become less important because of privatisation, deregulation (on the national or international level) and a proliferation of other international actors, the scope of application of the principle of sovereign equality diminishes accordingly. Within its respective autonomous space, each state is free to remove regulatory controls from economic, social and other activ-

---

[101] See Paulus, above n. 66, at 439, 441, 443. For studies focusing on the issue of sovereignty which generally support this description, see, *e.g.*, RBJ Walker & SH Mendlovitz (eds.), *Contending Sovereignties: Redefining Political Community* (Boulder, Col., Rienner, 1990); JA Camilleri & J Falk, *The End of Sovereignty? The Politics of a Shrinking and Fragmenting World* (Aldershot, Elgar, 1992); MSM Mahmoud, 'Mondialisation et souveraineté de l'État', 123 *Journal du droit international* (1996) 611; S Sassen, *Losing Control? Sovereignty in an Age of Globalization* (New York, Columbia University Press, 1996); B Badie, *Un monde sans souveraineté. Les États entre ruse et responsabilité* (Paris, Fayard, 1999). See also WH Reinicke, *Global Public Policy: Governing without Government?* (Washington, DC, Brookings Institution Press, 1998).

[102] For a cautious prognosis, based on historical analysis, 'that in many respects the contemporary state system is becoming more firmly entrenched rather than declining', see H Spruyt, *The Sovereign State and Its Competitors: An Analysis of Systems Change* (Princeton, NJ, Princeton University Press, 1994) at 192. For a similar appraisal from a legal point of view, see N Schrijver, 'The Changing Nature of State Sovereignty', 70 *British Year Book of International Law* (1999) 65 at 95–8. For a more determined judgment, see Krasner, above n. 2, at 223: 'There is no evidence that globalisation has systematically undermined state control or led to the homogenization of policies and structures. In fact, globalization and state activity have moved in tandem.'

[103] For a sketch of an international legal framework based on a greater diversity of actors, see C Schreuer, 'The Waning of the Sovereign State: Towards a New Paradigm for International Law?', 4 *European Journal of International Law* (1993) 447.

[104] For this phrase, see J Thompson, *Justice and World Order: A Philosophical Inquiry* (London and New York, Routledge, 1992), at 171, 180, 183. *Cf.* Paulus, above n. 61, at 161 *et seq.*

[105] See Paulus, *ibid.* at 446.

ities; acting jointly, states may also engage in 'international deregulation'. It is as yet unclear what forms of new structures and decision-making processes could emerge under such changed conditions. Perhaps the concept of equal rights of peoples, already familiar to international law in connection with the right of self-determination, could take over some of the functions until now performed by the principle of sovereign equality of states—especially that of giving individuals and groups the possibility of 'mak[ing] a difference in a structured political space'.[106]

7. THE UNTAMED SIDE OF SOVEREIGNTY

In international law, we concern ourselves with sovereignty as a legal notion. We engage in an effort to define its contents and borders, and to relate it coherently to other notions, principles and rules of international law. Why has this, when we look back on the literature of the past, always been so difficult, much more so than in the case of other concepts of international law?

Since it was invented, sovereignty has had a strong political dimension—it has, in fact, been more about making claims for a change of the *status quo*, or claims to power, than a careful observation of legal rules. JL Brierly once spoke of 'the impulse to power that we call sovereignty when we see it manifested in the conduct of states'.[107] The clearest manifestation of that impulse is still war. War, the historian Golo Mann once said, was the '*ultima ratio* of kings'; 'there were no kings without war'.[108] The UN Charter notwithstanding, the bond between sovereign statehood and war has remained close.

The international law of coexistence was a rather loosely woven fabric, offering states many opportunities for action not, or not strictly, based on the authority of law. In contrast, the present international legal order aspires comprehensively to regulate social life on all levels of governance. In this transformed environment, the sovereignty of states stands out as a legal concept which exposes one of its flanks to politics and power. 'It has

---

[106] For a well-founded warning that discarding sovereignty in favour of a multifaceted, functional-contractual system of rule-making in a diverse international community could lead to larger inequalities in and between societies, and a legitimisation of 'interventionist or otherwise coercive activities in other countries that reflect struggles and dilemmas in politics in the West', see B Kingsbury, 'Sovereignty and Inequality', 9 *European Journal of International Law* (1998) 599.
[107] See JL Brierly, 'The Sovereign State Today' (1949), in id., *The Basis of Obligation in International Law and Other Papers* H Lauterpacht & CHM Waldock (eds), (Oxford, Clarendon Press, 1958), 348 at 352.
[108] See G Mann, 'Krieg', in id. & H Pross, *Aussenpolitik* (Frankfurt am Main, Fischer, 1957), 143 at 159.

frequently had to serve as a juridical cover to mere power politics.'[109] In other cases, it provided, or rather channelled, legal arguments which, having found acceptance by other states, eventually led to a change in the law. What has made the concept in that respect especially convenient (or, in a different perspective, vulnerable) is a certain fuzziness resulting from its long history and the many different uses made of it in the past. In particular, sovereignty's original meaning as 'supreme authority' has asserted an indistinct presence, notwithstanding the efforts—mere attempts as well as achievements—of legal science to domesticate the notion and define it as the legal autonomy of a state under international law. Sovereignty still

'stands for freedom of action by states when the need is for central coordination and control, and it evokes the fear of unpredictable and irresponsible state behaviour instead of progress toward the international rule of law'.[110]

There is an untamed side of sovereignty—characteristic, one could say, of the international system as a political system *sui generis*—[111] which one can deplore or disapprove of, but which to ignore in legal analysis would be a mistake.

In the late 1920s, Kelsen referred to his time as a transitional period in the history of international law, and saw this character reflected in the 'contradictions of an international legal theory which in an almost tragic conflict aspires to the height of a universal legal community erected above the individual states but, at the same time, remains a captive of the sphere of power of the sovereign state'.[112] Almost forty years later, W Friedmann arrived at a very similar conclusion when he said:

'In terms of objectives, powers, legal structure and scope, the present state of international organisation presents an extremely complex picture. It reflects the state of a society that is both desperately clinging to the legal and political symbols of national sovereignty and being pushed towards the pursuit of common needs and goals that can be achieved only by a steadily intensifying degree of international organisation.'[113]

And where do we stand today? The UN Charter was a bold effort to end the transitional period recognised by Kelsen in favour of a lasting international constitutional order no longer dependent on the capriciousness of sometimes well-meaning, sometimes egoistic states. But more than fifty years after the 'constitutional moment'[114] which gave rise to the Charter, the

---

[109] See Steinberger, above n. 59, at 501.
[110] See Claude, above n. 58, at ix.
[111] See Hinsley, above n. 2, at 229.
[112] See H Kelsen, *Das Problem der Souveränität und die Theorie des Völkerrechts. Beitrag zu einer Reinen Rechtslehre* (Tübingen, JCB Mohr (Paul Siebeck), 2ⁿᵈ edition 1928), at 320.
[113] See Friedmann, *The Changing Structure*, above n. 7, at 293 *et seq.*
[114] The term is borrowed from B Ackerman, *We the People: Foundations* (Cambridge, Mass., and London, Harvard University Press, 1991), *passim*.

contradictions have not disappeared. Behind sovereign equality, sovereignty lingers on. Or rather: Images of sovereignty constructed in past centuries remain, much longer than was expected, or hoped for, in 1945. It seems that the power of those images was underestimated, a power, admittedly, perhaps greater than that of sovereignty's tamed version.

6

From State Sovereignty to the 'Sovereignty of Citizens' in the International Relations Law of the EU?

ERNST-ULRICH PETERSMANN

1. INTRODUCTION: SOVEREIGNTY IN INTERNATIONAL LAW AND IN CONSTITUTIONAL DEMOCRACIES: TOWARDS CONVERGENCE?

FROM THE PEACE treaties of Westphalia (1648) to the UN Charter (1945), the *international law of coexistence* evolved as a system of rights and duties of states regulating the 'external sovereignty' of states and their 'sovereign equality' (Article 2:1 UN Charter) based on effectiveness of government control over a territory and a population. The internal structure of states was considered to be a matter of domestic affairs ('internal sovereignty'). Inside *constitutional democracies* (such as the USA), popular sovereignty was construed as entailing that the validity of law depended on respect for human rights and for democratic self-determination. The validity of classic international law, however, and the recognition of states as subjects of international law into whose 'domestic jurisdiction' other states must not intervene, did not depend on respect for human rights and democratic legitimacy of the governments concerned. Due to its power-oriented character, the lack of legitimacy of classic international law has long been criticised (eg by colonial and other suppressed people) and has rendered a worldwide rule-of-law system impossible. In the USA, for instance, numerous intergovernmental treaties were not ratified by the US Senate (which earned the reputation as a 'graveyard of treaties'); the US Congress insisted on legal primacy in US law of 'later-in-time legislation' over prior international treaties so as to ensure democratic legitimacy of the domestic implementation and application of intergovernmental rules.

State sovereignty continues to be a universally recognised principle of public international law protecting a state's freedom of action by specifying rights and obligations of states under international law. Since the fall of the Berlin Wall (1989), however, human rights and popular sovereignty have become universally recognised by all UN member states not only as part of international treaty law (eg in the UN human rights covenants of 1966 and the 1989 UN Convention on the Rights of the Child, ratified by 191 states), but also of international customary law and of the 'general principles of law recognised by civilised nations' (Article 38, Statute of the International Court of Justice). The universal recognition of inalienable human rights to self-government legally limits state sovereignty by requiring respect for personal autonomy ('individual sovereignty') as well as for popular sovereignty, including rights to individual and democratic participation in the exercise of government powers. The history of 'human rights revolutions' illustrates, however, that transforming 'legal' into 'real sovereignty' of citizens over the state involves persistent bottom-up struggles for rendering human rights and democracy effective not only in principle, but also in the day-to-day exercise of national and international government powers. For the required structural reforms of state powers and also of oppressive *civil society* traditions (such as abuses of economic power, privileges for certain social classes, other social injustice), equal human rights, popular sovereignty and the 'sovereign equality' of states can and should serve complementary functions, for instance by defining equal freedoms and legal boundaries that may not be crossed by other individuals and states without the consent of the respective subjects of sovereign rights (eg individuals, peoples, states).

The legal evolution of concepts of sovereignty and democracy, and the democratic exercise of government powers defining, balancing, protecting and promoting human rights, legitimately differ from country to country. The human rights objective of maximising equal freedoms and social welfare across frontiers requires, however, a reallocation of sovereign powers in supranational organisations (like the EU) and worldwide organisations (like the WTO) with far-reaching repercussions on traditional, national concepts of popular sovereignty and state sovereignty. Regional and worldwide integration law (such as EU and WTO law) has established new legal frameworks for welfare-increasing cooperation among individuals and democratic self-development and experimentation. The adoption by all countries of written or unwritten national constitutions reflects the universal historical experience that individual and popular self-government and 'sovereign equality' of states can be achieved only in a framework of mutually consistent constitutional rules which protect individual and democratic freedom against their inherent tendencies to destroy themselves through abuses of power (the 'paradox of freedom').[1] The globalisation of

---

[1] See e.g. EU Petersmann, 'Constitutionalism, International Law and "We the Peoples of the United Nations"', in: HJ Cremer, T Giegerich, D Richter and A Zimmermann (eds.), *Festschrift für H Steinberger*, (Springer Verlag, Berlin, 2002) 291–313.

economics, politics, law and the environment calls for new forms of *cosmo-politan democracy* maximising equal human rights and real autonomy for personal and democratic self-development across the traditional boundaries of local and national democracies.

2. PRINCIPLES AND PROCEDURES FOR RECONCILING 'INDIVIDUAL SOVEREIGNTY', POPULAR SOVEREIGNTY, STATE SOVEREIGNTY AND SOVEREIGN POWERS OF INTERNATIONAL ORGANISATIONS

National and international human rights instruments base the universal recognition of inalienable human rights on the premise of 'human dignity', i.e. the insight that values can be derived only from the individual and only if individual autonomy is legally protected. The emerging human right to democratic self-government is based on the similar value premise and historical experience that human dignity and personal autonomy also require democratic procedures for the supply of 'public goods' (such as peace and social justice), supplementing the spontaneous supply of 'private goods' and limiting 'market failures' as well as 'government failures'. Human rights and democratic procedures can be combined in numerous ways which legitimately differ from country to country.[2] Yet, only together can they ensure that *government of the people* is also *government by the people* and *for the people*. Human rights are important not only for 'input-oriented legitimacy' of democratic decision-making processes (*government by the people*) but also for output-oriented effectiveness of *government for the people* and for promoting access to, and growth of, scarce economic resources (eg through division of labour and voluntary market exchanges based on liberty rights and property rights) which are essential precondi-tions for protection and enjoyment of most human rights. The main empir-ical finding and policy conclusion of this contribution is that the EU's unique focus on equal individual rights appears justified by the fact that the larger the people (EU citizenship) and the markets for mutually beneficial cooperation become, and the more remote government institutions are from their constituents (i.e. the people in a delimited territory), the less effective *procedural citizen rights* for democatic participation, representation and accountability risk becoming. This is particularly true in the area of state-centered, power-oriented foreign policies which, for centuries, have been dominated by discrimination against foreigners and by other welfare-reduc-ing interest group politics, as illustrated by European history prior to World War II.

---

[2] See e.g. D Held, *Models of Democracy*, 2nd ed. (Blackwell, Cambridge, 2000).

The UN's *international law of cooperation* includes intergovernmental rights and obligations to mutually beneficial cooperation and protection of human rights across frontiers which enable a challenge to power-oriented concepts of state sovereignty ('L'Etat, c'est moi') as being inconsistent with universal human rights and popular sovereignty. UN practice (eg regarding admission of states to the UN, supervision by UN bodies of UN human rights conventions) tends to favour state sovereignty and has only rarely (eg in the UN Security Council authorisation to intervene in Haiti) forced member governments to stop human rights violations.[3] Membership in the intergovernmental UN bodies is not limited to democratically elected representatives of 'We the Peoples of the United Nations'; and the International Court of Justice has no worldwide compulsory jurisdiction for the protection of the rule of law and human rights. As long as a large number of UN member states do not effectively protect human rights and democratic governance, the 'human rights deficit' and 'democracy deficit' of UN law continue to undermine the democratic legitimacy of international law in the name of the 'sovereign equality' asserted by dictatorial regimes.

In European integration, respect for human rights and democracy is a condition of membership of the EU (*cf*. Articles 6,7, 49 EU Treaty) and of the Council of Europe. The EC Treaty also explicitly recognises that respect for international treaties (*cf*. Articles 300, 307 EC Treaty) and membership in international organisations (*cf*. Articles 302–6) are indispensable for the rule of law in a globally integrated world. Human rights, democratic self-government and compliance with international law are mutually complementary principles of EU constitutional law.[4] The European Court of Justice has confirmed long since that 'fundamental human rights (are) enshrined in the general principles of Community law and protected by the Court',[5] and 'respect for human rights is a condition of the lawfulness of Community acts'.[6] The European Court of Human Rights has likewise emphasised that the human rights obligations of the more than 40 member states of the European Convention on Human Rights (ECHR) apply not only to national measures but also to *collective* rule-making in international organisations and to the domestic implementation of international rules:

'Where States establish international organisations, or *mutatis mutandis* international agreements, to pursue cooperation in certain fields of activities, there may

---

[3] *Cf*. EU Petersmann, 'Constitutional Primacy and Indivisibility of Human Rights in International Law? The Unfinished '"Human Rights Revolution" and the Emerging Global Integration Law', in S Griller (ed.), *International Economic Governance and Non-Economic Concerns*, (Springer Publishers, Vienna, 2002).

[4] *Cf*. EU Petersmann, 'Human Rights in European and Global Integration Law', in A Bogdandy, P Mavroidis and Y Mény (eds.), *Festschrift für CD Ehlermann*, (Kluwer Publishers, Doordrecht, 2002).

[5] Case 29/69. *Stauder*, ECR 1969. 419, para. 7.

[6] *Opinion 2/94*, ECR 1996 I-1759, para. 34.

be implications for the protection of fundamental rights. It would be incompatible with the purpose and object of the Convention if Contracting States were thereby absolved from their responsibility under the Convention in relation to the field of activity covered by such attribution.'[7]

Human rights and democracy, as constitutional principles of the law of international organisations (such as the EU and the Council of Europe), have legal implications beyond those in national parliamentary democracies, as illustrated by the limited legislative and other powers of the European Parliament and the lack of a single 'European *demos.*' Using equal human rights for the necessary specification of the legal and democratic framework for mutually beneficial cooperation is much more difficult in *transnational* relations than within local and national communities with stronger participatory processes and solidarity traditions.

Regional and worldwide *integration law* (such as EU and WTO law) differs from the intergovernmental *international law of coexistence* and *international law of cooperation* in its focus on reciprocal liberalisation of welfare-reducing market access barriers for the benefit of transnational movements of private persons and of goods, services, capital and payments demanded and supplied by individuals.[8] Since protection and enjoyment of human rights depend on scarce economic resources and on individual access to foreign markets (eg for goods and services like food, medicines and information), the individual and social welfare gains made possible by *integration law* are of constitutional significance. The mutually beneficial, citizen-oriented legal structures of *integration law* have enabled legal guarantees of freedom, non-discrimination, rule of law and compulsory jurisdiction (eg in WTO, EU and NAFTA law) that go far beyond those of the power-oriented UN law.

The international relations law of the EU[9] illustrates the *interface problems* between state-centered international law rules and modern integration

---

[7] European Court of Human Rights, Third Section Decision as to the Admissibility of Application No. 43844/98 by T.I. against the United Kingdom, 7 March 2000, at page 16 (nyr). In *Matthews v UK*, the European Court of Human Rights found the United Kingdom in violation of the human right to participate in free elections of the legislature even though the law which denied voting rights in Gibraltar implemented a treaty concluded among EU member states on the election of the European Parliament: 'there is no difference between European and domestic legislation, and no reason why the United Kingdom should not be required to "secure" the rights (under the ECHR) in respect of European legislation in the same way as those rights are required to be "secured" in respect of purely domestic legislation'. *Cf.* European Court of Human Rights, judgment of 18 February 1999 on complaint No. 24833/94, see: Europäische Grundrechtszeitschrift (EUGRZ) 1999, 200.
[8] See EU Petersmann, 'From the Hobbesian International Law of Coexistence to Modern Integration Law: The WTO Dispute Settlement System', (1998) 1 *Journal of International Economic Law*, 175–198.
[9] See eg A Dashwood and C Hillion (eds.), *The General Law of EC External Relations* (Sweet & Maxwell, London, 2000); D McGoldrick, *International Relations Law of the EU* (Longman, London, 1997).

law focusing on individual citizens (eg in their roles as producers, investors, traders and consumers) and on extending voluntary market exchanges and civil society cooperation across frontiers. European integration law protects fundamental rights in international *economic* relations no less than in *political* relations. The UN Covenant on Economic, Social and Cultural Rights (UNCESCR), by contrast, offers much looser legal and institutional safeguards for economic and social human rights compared with the UN Covenant on Civil and Political Rights (UNCCPR).[10] By omitting reference to property rights and 'safeguarding fundamental political and economic freedoms to the individual' only in an indirect and inadequate manner (*cf.* Article 6:2), the UNCESCR does not protect the legal preconditions for creating the economic resources necessary for effective enjoyment of human rights.

3. THE EU: AN *INTERNATIONAL DEMOCRACY* BASED ON HUMAN RIGHTS

European integration law offers EU citizens more individual rights for the free movement of goods, services, persons, capital and payments, as well as for democratic participation and access to courts at local, national and European levels, than European citizens ever enjoyed in earlier European history. EU constitutional law also takes into account Europe's historical experience that democracy—in the sense of individual and popular self-government—can effectively protect the human rights of citizens only if majority decisions and the exercise of collective powers (eg to tax citizens, regulate private behavior, redistribute income) are constitutionally restrained and subject to institutional 'checks and balances'.[11] The comprehensive *substantive fundamental rights* in EU law compensate, to some extent, for the weak *procedural democratic participation* of EU citizens in EU institutions.[12] The substantive rights not only define and protect fundamental citizen interests (e.g to extend market exchanges and voluntary cooperation in a European *civil society* across frontiers) and empower citizens to control and challenge abuses of powers (eg through freedom of

---

[10] *Cf.* eg K Arambulo, *Strengthening the Supervision of the International Covenant on Economic, Social and Cultural Rights*, (Oxford, Hart Publishing, 1999); EU Petersmann, 'Time for a UN "Global Compact" for Integrating Human Rights into the Law of Worldwide Organisations', *European Journal of International Law (2002)* 621–650.

[11] See eg K Lenaerts, P Van Nuffel and R Bray, *Constitutional Law of the EU*, (Sweet & Maxwell, London, 1999).

[12] *Cf.* F W Scharpf, *Governing in Europe: Effective and Democratic?*, (OUP, Oxford, 1999), at 7: input-oriented legitimisation (eg through 'participation' and 'consensus') is easier in local contexts where all persons affected by a decision, or representatives closely associated with

opinion, freedom of the press, individual access to information and to courts so as to hold public decision-makers accountable); they also specify the constitutional limits of government powers (eg minority protection vis-à-vis majority decision) and give more specific meaning to the common *public interest*. In 'international democracies' like the EU, fundamental citizen rights offer indispensable preconditions and countervailing powers for *government by the people* as well as *for the people*, for instance by means of consumer-driven market competition and democratic and judicial control of abuses of supranational government powers in remote governance institutions.

Human rights theory and democratic theory have so far focused on challenges to human rights and to democracy emerging from *within* national boundaries, and within the EU, much more than on challenges arising from the globalisation of markets, politics, communications, law and the environment. Individual freedom and 'rule by the people' across frontiers cannot be secured solely by national constitutions and unilateral power politics without effective *international constitutional constraints* on foreign policy powers to tax and restrict domestic citizens (eg by means of trade policy powers, war powers).[13] Modern constitutions, such as the 1949 Basic Law for the Federal Republic of Germany, abandon reference to the notion of 'state sovereignty' and authorise the transfer of 'sovereign powers to international organisations' subject to respect for inalienable human rights and other constitutional safeguards (*cf.* Articles 23, 24 Basic Law). The EU Treaty, likewise, does not mention 'state sovereignty' and instead authorises the legal self-limitation of the EC as well as of the EU by international law and international adjudication (such as the compulsory jurisdiction of WTO dispute settlement bodies and the Law of the Sea Tribunal).[14] The EU Charter of Fundamental Rights of December 2000[15] is another recent attempt at reconciling individual and democratic self-determination by committing the EU to the protection of human rights and democracy across frontiers. The Charter's guarantees of Dignity (Chapter I), Freedoms (Chapter II), Equality (Chapter III) and Citizens' Rights (Chapter V) recognise EU citizens as legal subjects of EU law and ultimately the best judges of their own interests. By also protecting fundamental rights to Solidarity (Chapter IV) and Justice (Chapter VI), and providing for common EC policies necessary for correcting 'market failures' (see eg Articles 81 *et seq.* on competition law and policy, Articles 136 *et seq.* on social policy, Articles

---

[13] This important insight by the philosopher I Kant is explained by Petersmann (note 1). For a modern political explanation see eg J Nye, *The Paradox of American Power: Why the World's Superpower Can't Go It Alone*, (OUP, Oxford, 2002).

[14] On the recent conclusion of the first international agreement by the EU (rather than the EC) see the editorial comment on 'The EU—A New International Actor' in: 38 *Common Market Law Review (2001)*, 825–8.

[15] Official Journal of the EC C 364/1 of 18.12.2000.

174 *et seq.* on environmental policy), EU law recognises that individuals, to be 'free and equal', must be capable ('sovereign') of exercising human rights and developing personal autonomy in economic, social and political affairs across frontiers.

The EU's *common foreign and security policy* (CFSP) is constitutionally committed 'to develop and consolidate democracy and the rule of law, and respect for human rights and fundamental freedoms' in compliance with international law (Article 11:1). Does this symmetry between internal and external human rights objectives of the EU, and the constitutional requirements (eg in Article 300:7 EC Treaty, Article 11 EU Treaty) to comply with international law, conflict with the political reality that human rights are not yet effectively integrated into the law of worldwide organisations and are not effectively protected by national and international courts outside Europe in most foreign policy areas? Could and should the EU rather follow the 'realist' concept of American hegemonic power politics and unilateralism vis-à-vis non-democratic foreign states? Since EU member states have transferred only limited powers to the EU whose joint exercise and legitimacy depend on respect for the rule of law: Is the unusual focus on human rights, the rule of law and *civilian power* (rather than *military power*) in the EU's *foreign policy constitution* a necessary consequence of the weak parliamentary control of the CFSP, of the strong constitutional rights of EU citizens in the EU's internal market, and of the residual sovereign rights of EU member states to democratic self-government? Why are human rights and the legal empowerment of EU citizens so crucial for 'participatory democracy' across frontiers and for the representativeness and accountability of supranational organisations far away from the homes of most citizens?

4. RE-ALLOCATION OF SOVEREIGN RIGHTS IN THE *INTERNATIONAL RELATIONS LAW* OF THE EUROPEAN UNION: THE EU'S INEFFECTIVE *FOREIGN POLICY CONSTITUTION*

Modern *globalisation* with its diversity of power centers outside the direct control of a single state illustrates the need for new forms of *cosmopolitan democracy*.[16] The foreign relations law and policy of the EU reflects the manifold tensions in the transition from state-centered traditional international law towards multi-level constitutionalism based on fundamental individual rights, popular sovereignty and sovereign powers of national and international organisations. As noted by Advocate-General Tesauro, 'the Community legal system is characterised by the simultaneous application of provisions of various origins, international, Community and national; but

---

[16] See eg D Held, above note 2, chapter 9.

it nevertheless seeks to function and to represent itself to the outside world as a unified system'.[17] As regards *domestic law and policies* of the EU, European constitutional law has succeeded in integrating national and EU constitutional guarantees of human rights, democracy and the rule-of-law, notwithstanding the lack of a 'European people', the still limited powers of the European Parliament and the frequent lack of democratic transparency of EU rule-making and decision-making processes.

The *foreign relations law and policy* of the EU, by contrast, continues to be characterised by incoherence. The EU's *foreign policy constitution* requires respect by all EU institutions for international law (see eg Article 300:7 and Articles 302–7 EC Treaty).[18] Yet, notwithstanding more than 30 GATT and WTO dispute settlement findings of violations of GATT and WTO rules by the EC, the EC Court of Justice (ECJ) has de facto refrained from exercising judicial review regarding the question of whether EC institutions are in compliance with their GATT/WTO obligations of protecting freedom, non-discrimination and the rule of law in international trade.[19] Even though EU law nowhere authorises the EU Council and Commission to violate international treaties ratified by the EU and its member states, the practice of openly violating GATT/WTO obligations has prompted an increasing number of politicians and academics to affirm executive EU powers to overrule treaties ratified by parliaments in the EU,[20] without regard to parliamentary democracy and the rule of law in the EU. The ECJ's recognition of individuals as legal subjects entitled to invoke and enforce the *internal* customs union obligations among EU member states (eg Articles 25, 28 EC Treaty), and the Court's persistent treatment of the same citizens as mere legal objects who are *not* entitled to invoke the *external* customs union obligations vis-à-vis third countries (eg Article 23 EC Treaty in connection with GATT Articles II, XI, XXIV), is another illustration of the tension between *citizen-oriented* interpretation of internal EU rules and state-centered interpretations of the EU's foreign policy powers.

The common foreign policies of the EU (eg for agricultural and commercial policies) are not yet effectively constitutionally constrained by the consent of national parliaments and EU citizens. All too often, the limited 'sovereign powers' conferred on the EU institutions are exercised by the EU beyond the limited mandate granted by national parliaments and by EU citizens in a manner reducing equal citizen rights, parliamentary

---

[17] Case C-53/96, *Hermès*, ECR 1998 13603, para 21.
[18] *Cf.* EU Petersmann, 'The Foreign Policy Constitution of the EU: A Kantian Perspective', in U Immenga, W Möschel and D Reuter (eds), *Festchrift für EJ Mestmäcker*, (Nomos Verlag, Baden-Baden, 1996) at 433–448.
[19] *Cf.*: EU Petersmann, 'Darf die EG das Völkerrecht ignorieren?', *Europäische Zeitschrift für Wirtschaftsrecht* (1997), 325–31.
[20] See e.g. C Schmid, 'Multi-Level Constitutionalism and Constitutional Conflicts', EUI Florence 2001 (doctoral thesis) who claims that the EU Council may decide by majority to violate WTO rules (p. 280).

democracy and economic welfare.[21] In the context of the EU's common policies, sovereign powers are being transferred 'upwards' to regional and world-wide organisations (eg to the WTO Dispute Settlement Body) without adequate safeguards of their transparent and democratic exercise. The CFSP is even less constitutionally constrained and remains based on the intergovernmental 'second pillar' provisions in Title V of the EU Treaty which do not provide for effective citizen participation and judicial protection of citizen rights (*cf.* Article 46).

A. Empowerment of EU Citizens—Not vis-à-vis the EU's Compliance with International Law

In the relations between EU member states, the progressive realisation of a customs union, an internal market, monetary union and, now, an 'area of freedom, security and justice' (Article 61 EC) was characterised by constitutional limitations on discretionary national foreign policy powers through EC Treaty guarantees of fundamental individual rights, such as rights to free and non-discriminatory movement of goods, services, persons, capital and related payments, non-discriminatory conditions of competition, stable money, the rule of law, democratic participation in the exercise of EU government powers, and individual access to justice across frontiers. This enlargement of 'individual sovereignty' and the empowerment of EU citizens vis-à-vis EU member states has, however, not been applied to the EU's external relations.

Even though the EU's customs union rules (Articles 23–31 EC1) and their underlying GATT and WTO guarantees of freedom, non-discrimination and the rule of law tend to be precise, unconditional and judicially enforceable, the ECJ has not so far dared to resist the protectionist requests from the Commission and Council that the customs union prohibitions of non-tariff trade barriers vis-à-vis third countries must not be construed as conferring *individual freedoms of trade* similar to the freedoms of trade inside the EU (eg in Article 25 EC). Only in the context of reciprocal free trade area and customs union agreements between the EU and third countries have prohibitions on non-tariff barriers been construed as constituting individual rights to freedom and non-discrimination enlarging the 'individual sovereignty' of EU citizens.[22] The frequent violations of GATT and

---

[21] On this latter aspect, which is not pursued in this contribution, see e.g. PA Messerlin, *Measuring the Costs of Protection in Europe*, (Institute of International Economics, Washington, 2001).

[22] See notably the *Kupferberg case*, 104/81, ECR 1982,3659, where the ECJ rightly emphasised that the reciprocity principle does in no way hinder EC and national courts to apply precise and unconditional treaty guarantees of freedom and non-discrimination directly for the benefit of EU citizens.

WTO rules by the Council and Commission, the persistent disregard by the ECJ of legally binding GATT/WTO law and related GATT/WTO dispute settlement rulings, and the existence of only one single ECJ judgment—over a period of 45 years—establishing a violation of international law by the EC,[23] illustrate the failure so far of the EU to ensure that, in the international relations of EU citizens with third countries, 'the law is observed' (as required by Article 220 of the EC Treaty).[24]

B. Limited Delegation of 'Sovereign Rights' to the EU and Their Joint Exercise

According to the ECJ:

> 'the Community constitutes a new legal order of international law for the benefit of which states have limited their sovereign rights, albeit within limited fields, and the subjects of which comprise not only Member States but also their nationals.'[25] 'The transfer by the States from their domestic legal systems to the community legal system of the rights and obligations arising under the Treaty carries with it a permanent limitation of their sovereign rights, against which a subsequent unilateral act incompatible with the concept of the Community cannot prevail.'[26]

The EU competencies are described by the ECJ as 'sovereign rights' notwithstanding the EU's lack of legislative 'competence-competence'. Paradoxically, the progressive expansion of EU competencies and sovereign rights exercised collectively by EU institutions, with corresponding *legal limitations on state sovereignty*, has dramatically increased 'individual sovereignty' for voluntary citizen cooperation across frontiers.

In both its internal and external relations, the EU 'has only those powers that have been conferred upon it'.[27] The EC Treaty provisions on the external relations powers of the EC are scattered (*cf.* Articles 111, 133, 170, 174, 181, 3000, 302–4, 310) and incomplete. For instance, there are numerous foreign policy provisions (eg in Articles 61 *et seq.*, 71, 95, 137, 149–52, 155, 310) that do not specify the EC treaty-making powers necessary for the realisation of the foreign policy objectives. The ECJ has construed Article 281 to the effect that the EC has general international legal capacity to exercise rights and obligations under international law within the limits of the EC Treaty objectives and of the limited powers conferred on it explicitly or implicitly by the EC Treaty.[28]

---

[23] Case T-115/94, *Opel Austria*, C.M.L.R. 1997, 733.
[24] See Petersmann, above note 19; and also: 'International Activities of the EU and Sovereignty of Member States,' in E Cannizzaro (ed.), *The EU as an Actor in International Relations*, (Kluwer Publishers, Dordrecht, 2002).
[25] Case 26/62, *Van Gend en Loos*, ECR 1963, 1, 12.
[26] Case 6/64, *Costa v ENEL*, ECR 1964 585, 593–4.
[27] *Opinion 2/94*, ECR 1996 I-1759, para. 23.
[28] *Cf.* Case 22/70, *ERTA*, ECR 1971, 263.

i) Exclusive EU competencies in the foreign policy area

As a matter of principle, external EU competencies are based on specific and limited conferment of powers (*cf.* Article 5 EC). Exclusive foreign policy powers of the EU exist in the following five areas:[29]

(a) Common commercial policy (Article 133);[30]

(b) Common fisheries conservation (Article 102 of the First Act of Accession 1973);[31]

(c) Common transport policy (Article 71) and other policy measures, even outside the framework of 'common policies',[32] to the extent that the EU institutions have exercised their powers in the internal sphere and complementary external measures are necessary for attaining the objectives of the EC Treaty objectives concerned ('ERTA principle'), or where the EC Treaty objective can only be attained by conclusion of an international agreement by the EC even if internal EC rules have not yet been adopted in the policy area concerned;[33]

(d) Monetary policy so far as participants in the European Monetary Union (EMU) and its single currency are concerned (eg EURO exchange rates);

(e) Relations between the EC and other international organisations (*cf.* Articles 302 *et seq.*) to the extent that they are based on exclusive 'community agreements' (eg on participation of the EC in the North Atlantic Fisheries Organisation).

Exclusive EC competencies for the common commercial policy and for the conservation of sea resources have been construed to preempt state actions even in the absence of secondary EC regulations. Exclusive EU competencies based on the 'ERTA principle' or on the 'Opinion 1/76 principle' intrude less into state sovereignty because they block state actions only if Community legislation has been adopted, or if national legislation would otherwise 'affect the Community rules or alter their scope'.[34]

ii) Concurrent foreign policy powers

In other fields (such as international movement of persons and services, intellectual property rights, environmental policy, development aid), the

---

[29] For detailed analyses with references to the jurisprudence see: A Dashwood and C Hillion, note 9 above.
[30] See notably *Opinion 1/94*, ECR 1994 I-5267.
[31] See notably cases 3,4 and 6/76, *Kramer*, ECR 1976, 1279.
[32] Opinion 23/91, *ILO*, ECR 1991 I–1061.
[33] Opinion 1/76, *Rhine Navigation Agreement*, ECR 1977, 741.
[34] *ERTA Case*, above note 28, para. 22.

external EU competencies tend to be of a concurrent nature and subject to Community obligations of close cooperation between national and EU authorities. This concurrent nature (eg of treaty-making powers) is explicitly emphasised in certain EC Treaty provisions, eg, on monetary policy (Article 111:5), environmental policy (Article 174:4) and development aid (Article 181). The *Bangladesh Case*[35] illustrates that, if the member states elect to take a decision in the field of shared competence by means of an *intergovernmental agreement* rather than through EU procedures, the decision may not be considered to be an 'act' for the purpose of complaints pursuant to Article 230 EC and thus may not be amenable to judicial review by the ECJ. Yet, in the *EDF Case*,[36] the ECJ asserted jurisdiction to rule on whether a contested act was within the scope of the EC Treaty or encroached upon the powers conferred by the EC Treaty on the Community.

iii) Progressive extension of the EU's foreign policy powers

The Maastricht, Amsterdam and Nice Treaties reflect a progressive extension of EU foreign policy powers through amendments of EU primary law. The Nice Treaty amendments of Article 133 illustrate the possibility of more flexible procedures (eg a unanimity decision by the Council) on enlarging the treaty-making powers of the EU and on promoting the coherent exercise of mixed EU and national treaty competencies; the new paragraph 6 of Article 133, however, explicitly protects the national competencies of EU member states in the fields of cultural and audiovisual services, educational services, social and health services. Articles 61–9 EC on visa, asylum and immigration policies further show that foreign policy powers coordinated in the intergovernmental 'third pillar' of the EU may later become incorporated into the supranational 'first pillar' of EU law. The evolving borders between supranational EC law and intergovernmental EU law reflect the changing borders between national sovereignty and sovereign rights collectively exercised in the EC/EU. Even where EC Treaty provisions explicitly exclude 'any harmonisation of the laws and regulations of the Member States' (eg in Article 149, 151, 152), EC law imposes obligations on member states for the exercise and international coordination of their national powers (eg EC Treaty obligations regarding non-discrimination on grounds of nationality).

---

[35] Joined Cases C–181/91 and C–248/91, *European Parliament v Council and Commission*, ECR 1993, 3685.
[36] See Case C–316/91, *European Parliament v Council*, ECR 1994, 625: 'an action taken by the Parliament against an act of an institution intended to have legal effects is admissible irrespective of whether the act was adopted by the institution pursuant to Treaty provisions.'

C. Joint Exercise of National Foreign Relations Powers in the EU Framework

In the second, third and 'fourth pillar'[37] of the EU, certain member state competencies are jointly exercised, eg, by means of 'common strategies', 'joint actions', 'common positions' (*cf.* eg Articles 12–5 EUT) and international agreements by the Council in the 'second pillar' of the EU (Article 24 EUT). According to Article 11:1 EUT, the common foreign and security policy of the EU shall cover 'all areas of foreign and security policy' without mentioning exceptions. Member states 'shall refrain from any action which is contrary to the interests of the Union or likely to impair its effectiveness as a cohesive force in international relations' (Article 11:2). The broad scope of the 'second pillar' is in line with the requirement of Article 3 EUT that the 'Union shall . . . ensure the consistency of its external activities as a whole in the context of its external relations, security, economic and development policies'. Where national foreign policy powers are not exercised jointly in the EU framework, EU law may impose obligations on member states, eg, to 'inform and consult one another within the Council on any matter of foreign and security policy of general interest' (Article 16) and 'coordinate their action in international organisations and at international conferences' (Article 19 EUT). For instance, due to the so far limited scope of the EC's common commercial policy, various trade-related national competencies (eg for the regulation of foreign investments and intellectual property rights) have been coordinated in the past or exercised jointly in the EU Council.

D. National Foreign Policy Actions outside the EU Framework

Many national government policies (eg regarding education, health, public transport, labor, social and defense policies) continue to be determined by member states outside the EU institutions. The incorporation, by the Amsterdam Treaty, of part of the Schengen Agreement into the EC Treaty (Protocol No.2) is an example of the transformation of intergovernmental cooperation outside the EU framework into supranational Community law. Article 297 EC Treaty illustrates that, even in very exceptional situations such as civil war or other internal disturbances, EC law requires member states to consult and cooperate.[38]

---

[37] The frequent coordination and joint exercise of national competences inside the EU's institutional framework, but outside its first, second and third pillars has been described as a 'fourth pillar' of the EU by R Torrent, 'The fourth pillar of the EU after the Amsterdam Treaty', in Dashwood and Hillion, above note 9, 221–35.

[38] *Cf.* P Koutrakos, 'Is Article 297 EC a "Reserve of sovereignty"?' in (2000) 37 *Common Market Law Review,* 1339.

The economic, political and military actions with regard to the former Yugoslavia offer an example of simultaneous, complementary foreign policy measures based upon 'pillar I' (eg trade sanctions), 'pillar II' (eg the 'European administration' of the town of Mostar), 'pillar III' (eg 'joint actions' and 'common positions' pursuant to Articles 14 and 15 EUT vis-à-vis refugees from the former Yugoslavia), 'pillar IV' and member state actions *outside* the EU institutions (eg WEU and NATO military interventions). Whereas the legal boundaries of the supranational 'pillar I' are strongly defended by the Commission and the ECJ, member states appear to view the legal demarcation lines between coordination and joint exercise of national foreign policy powers inside pillars II to IV or outside the EU framework in a pragmatic and progressively evolving manner.

5. EU PARTICIPATION AND COLLECTIVE EXERCISE OF SOVEREIGN RIGHTS IN INTERNATIONAL ORGANISATIONS

The EC Treaty (eg Articles 300, 302–7) and the EU Treaty (eg Articles 6, 11) require the EU to comply with international law and to participate in the activities of other international organisations.

A. Different Forms of EU Participation in other International Organisations

Due to the limited competencies of the EU, different forms of EU participation and of foreign policy coordination in international organisations have emerged in a pragmatic manner:[39]

(a) Exclusive EU competencies may lead to exclusive EU membership in an international organisation (such as the North Atlantic Fishery Organisation) without simultaneous membership of EU member states.

(b) 'Mixed' EU and national competencies may lead to different forms of 'mixed' membership of both the EU and EU member states in an international organisation. The external and internal legal obligations of such membership depend on whether EU membership has been expressly limited to the field of EU competencies (as in the Food and Agricultural Organisation and the Law of the Sea Convention) or whether the EU and EU member states have become members of the international organisation concerned without limiting their international obligations to their respective fields of competencies, as in the World Trade Organisation (WTO). The exercise of international rights by the EU and its member states differs accordingly: alternative exercise of membership rights in the FAO,[40] but joint representation of the collective rights of the EU and its member

---

[39] For a survey see R Frid, *The Relations between the EC and International Organisations*, (Kluwer Publishers, Dordrecht, 1995).

states by the Commission in most areas of WTO activity (except the WTO's Budget Committee).

(c) Multilateral treaties or organisations (eg a treaty with Switzerland negotiated in the context of the Rhine Navigation Commission) may provide for 'mixed' participation of the EU and of only some of the EU member states.

(d) In some state-centered international organisations (eg the IMF), EU competencies (eg for the European Monetary Union and its EURO) and national competencies (eg for economic policy) are coordinated pragmatically. International agreements may be concluded inside such organisations by the EU member states as 'trustees' of the EU (eg conclusion of conventions in the International Labor Organisation) if the EU cannot itself exercise its competencies in an organisation of which the EU is not a member.[41] Even though state sovereignty may thereby be preserved to a greater extent than in the case of EU membership, the citizen's interests in maximum equal freedoms ('individual sovereignty') may be more effectively protected through EU membership than in the case of membership of EU states and their pursuit of diverse national policy objectives.

(e) In many other international organisations (such as the UN) which barely affect EU competencies, national foreign policies of EU member states continue to be coordinated pragmatically. The EU often intervenes in such organisations through the member state exercising the EU presidency and speaking on behalf of the EU (rather than through use of the observer status of the EU in such organisations).

B. The EU's International Relations Law as a Catalyst for Changing the State-Centered Structures of the Law of International Organisations

The *external* forms of EU participation in international treaties and international organisations, and the integration of EU law into the constitutional systems of EU member states, have not only changed concepts of state sovereignty inside the EU; the EU has also increasingly succeeded in adjusting state-centered structures of international law to the needs of regional integration (eg by allowing full EU membership in FAO, WTO, NAFO and the European Bank for Reconstruction and Development), thereby contributing to the emergence of new forms of intergovernmental cooperation and acting as an agent for 'the international law of the future'.[42]

Especially where the EU is the dominant partner in bilateral and multilateral treaty relationships (eg in the 'Europe agreements' and 'association agreements' with more than twenty European and Mediterranean countries,

---

[40] *Cf.* Article II:8 of the FAO Constitution: 'A Member Organisation shall excercise membership rights on an alternative basis with its Member States that are Member Nations of the Organisation in the areas of their respective competences and in accordance with rules set down by the Conference.'

[41] See Opinion 2/91, *ILO-Convention*, ECR 1993 I–1061.

[42] See e.g. McGoldrick, above note 9, at 210.

or the 'Cotonou Agreement' with 77 developing countries), such agreements are often inspired by substantive EU rules, such as human rights clauses and democracy clauses permitting suspension of treaty cooperation and development aid in case of grave human rights violations. The global integration law of the WTO is likewise increasingly influenced by pertinent experiences of European integration law (eg regarding mutual recognition of different but equivalent national standards, competition-oriented deregulation of trade in services). The limitations of state sovereignty inside EU law (eg as a result of the EU's customs union law, competition law and human rights law) have prompted an increasing number of *third countries* to accept, in their treaty relationships with the EU, similar legal limitations on their national regulatory powers. The international relations law of the EU thereby acts as a driving force in adjusting traditional international law concepts of state sovereignty to modern integration law focusing on human rights, democracy and compulsory international adjudication (eg in the WTO).

6. THE NEED FOR STRENGTHENING MULTI-LEVEL CONSTITUTIONALISM AND HUMAN RIGHTS IN THE INTERNATIONAL RELATIONS LAW OF THE EU

Human history remains characterised by only very slow progress in limiting abuses of power through constitutional safeguards of equal liberties and other human rights. The moral and human rights objective of maximising equal liberties of citizens across frontiers (including 'positive' freedoms) continues to be inadequately protected in EU law as well as in the foreign relations law of most states. Defining equal human rights ever more precisely across frontiers and protecting citizen rights through democratic national and international implementing legislation and judicial protection of human rights offer the most powerful, but also the most difficult strategies for strengthening the sovereignty of citizens in foreign policies and international organisations. The less effective democratic procedures, 'participatory democracy' and 'deliberative democracy' are likely to be in remote international organisations, the more important *substantive* civil, political, economic and social human rights and their judicial protection by national and international courts become.

A. The Need for a Multi-Level Constitutional Approach based on Human Rights

Constitutional democracies and EU law have been most successful in those areas (such as human rights, competition law and common market law) where individual rights were protected by the courts and by other independent 'guardians of the law' (like independent competition authorities, central banks) on the basis of 'multi-level guarantees' of equal liberties and non-discriminatory competition (eg in federal states, EU law, human rights law). Individual and democratic sovereignty cannot remain effective without national and international guarantees of human rights and their constitutional protection (eg by rule of law requirements, primacy of constitutional over post-constitutional rules, horizontal and vertical separation of powers, judicial protection of human rights and other 'checks and balances'). As violations of international law by EU institutions overstep the limited EU competencies and encroach on the powers reserved to national parliaments, EU citizens must be enabled to counteract as guardians of the law and to challenge violations of precise and unconditional international guarantees of freedom and non-discrimination in the courts.

B. National and International Law as Divided Power Systems for the Multi-Level Protection of Human Rights and of Popular Sovereignty

Constitutional democracies, EU law and modern international law derive their democratic legitimacy from their common functions to protect human rights and limit abuses of power. From a citizen and human rights perspective, national and international law constitute and limit horizontally and vertically divided government powers designed to protect, promote and regulate the human rights of citizens across frontiers. In a globally integrated world, foreign policy and international law are no less important for the protection of human rights and the democratic self-determination of peoples than domestic law and policies. Foreign policy and international law therefore require constitutional restraints and judicial protection of individual rights no less than does domestic law.[43] In view of the 'constitutional functions' of international law for protecting freedom, non-discrimination and other human rights and 'democratic peace' across frontiers,[44] it is an important constitutional achievement that EU law recognises international law as an 'integral part of the Community legal system' with legal primacy over autonomous 'secondary' Community law. The requirement of designing European integration in compliance with the international legal obligations of the EU has contributed to making the EU one of the most important driving forces for the necessary adjustment of the state-centered structures of international law to citizen-oriented integration law.

---

[43] From a constitutional law perspective, foreign policy and international organisations should therefore be conceptualised as a 'fourth branch of government', cf. Petersmann, above note 1.
[44] Cf. EU Petersmann, *Constitutional Functions and Constitutional Problems of International Economic Law*, (Fribourg, Fribourg University Press, 1991).

The ECJ has rightly emphasised that member states owe compliance with international law not only to third states but also to the EU (*cf.* Article 300:7 EC).[45] Yet, the EU likewise owes respect for international law not only to third states but also, first and above all, to EU citizens and to their democratically elected governments and parliaments which have ratified international agreements (eg on the WTO) for the benefit of their citizens. Manifest violations of international law by the EU have not been authorised by any parliament and encroach on the powers reserved to national parliaments and EU citizens. Contrary to the ECJ judgment in *Portugal v Council*,[46] EU citizens and EU member states must have effective judicial remedies against the frequent violations of international law by EU institutions. Respect for 'human dignity', as the universally accepted 'Grundnorm' of national and international human rights law, requires treating individuals as legal subjects rather than mere objects equally in the *international relations law* of the EU. National and international civil, political, economic, social and cultural guarantees of freedom, non-discrimination and the rule of law (eg including the EU's 'market freedoms' and corresponding WTO guarantees) should be interpreted as parts of a coherent 'multi-level constitutional system' designed to protect human rights, popular sovereignty and democratic self-government across frontiers.[47] Legally binding WTO dispute settlement rulings protecting freedom and non-discrimination across frontiers should be respected by the EU and national judges no less than judgments of the ECJ.

C. Advantages of Cooperation and Constitutional Dialogues between National and International Courts

Notwithstanding the EU principle of limited attribution of powers and the lack of 'legislative *Kompetenz-Kompetenz*' of the EU, the EC Treaty (eg Articles 220 *et seq.* on the jurisdiction of the ECJ) and its interpretation by the ECJ assert the constitutional primacy of EU law over national law and 'judicial *Kompetenz-Kompetenz*' of the ECJ for the interpretation of EU law.[48] Several Supreme Courts and Constitutional Courts of EU member states, by contrast, have inferred powers from their respective national constitutional systems to review whether secondary EU law—especially in

---

[45] See the *Kupferberg case*, above note 22.
[46] Case C–149/96, *Portugal v Council*, ECR 1999 I–8395.
[47] My concept of multi-level national and 'international constitutional law' protecting human rights and popular sovereignty (*cf.* Petersmann, above note 44, chapters VII–IX) avoids the 'concept of divided sovereignty' as used by I Pernice, 'Multilevel Constitutionalism and the Treaty of Amsterdam: European Constitution-Making Revisited?', (1999) 36 *Common Market Law Review*, 703–50.
[48] *Cf.* e.g. JHH Weiler, *The Constitution of Europe*, (OUP, Oxford, 1999), at 286–323.

case of EU acts that are *ultra vires* and conflict with fundamental rights and democratic legitimacy—violates national constitutional law and is therefore not legally binding for national authorities.[49] So far, the theoretical risk of conflicting assertions of jurisdiction and of mutually inconsistent ECJ and national judgments has been avoided through pragmatic cooperation between national and European judges focusing on effective protection of human rights rather than on formal claims of legal hierarchy and 'autonomy'. This served as an incentive for European judges to take human rights and the constitutional limits of EU law more seriously.[50] Vice versa, it also helped national judges to respect the primacy of EU law and promote the coherence of European and national constitutional law.[51] Rather than endangering the rule of law or the 'autonomy' and supremacy of EU law, dialogues between national and European judges promote deliberative democracy and the coherence of national and European constitutional law for the benefit of citizens.

D. How to Promote 'Dual Federalism'?—Substantive and Procedural Approaches

Like most federal states, the EU is characterised by the progressive expansion of legislative and executive powers at a higher level at the expense of lower levels of government. State sovereignty and the Community principle of limited attribution of powers (*cf.* Article 5 EC) can assist in protecting 'dual

---

[49] *Cf.* M Kumm, 'Who is the Final Arbiter of Constitutionality in Europe?' (1999) 36 *Common Market Law Review* 351–86.

[50] In Opinion 2/94, ECR 1996 I–1759, for instance, the Court ruled that Article 308 EC was not a sufficient legal basis for accession by the EC to the European Convention on Human Rights. In a judgment of 5 October 2000 (case C–376/98, nyr), the EC Court annulled EC Directive 98/43/EC on the approximation of national laws and provisions relating to the advertising and sponsorship of tobacco products for lack of EC competence.

[51] In its decision of 7 June 2000 (2 Bvl. 1/97) on whether the application in Germany of the EC regulations on the common market for bananas was compatible with the German Basic Law (notably Articles 3,12 and 14), the German Constitutional Court concluded that, as long as the EC and the ECJ continued to protect fundamental rights as effectively as in Germany, the Federal Constitutional Court would not exercise its jurisdiction over the applicability of secondary Community law in individual cases and would consider referrals under Article 100 of the German Basic Law inadmissible. Even though the illegality of the EC banana regulations had been authoritatively established through legally binding WTO dispute settlement rulings, the German Constitutional Court did not refer to its earlier doctrine (developed in its 1993 Maastricht judgment) of legal acts ultra vires ('ausbrechende Rechtsakte') and did not examine whether EC regulations in manifest violation of the international legal obligations of the EC and of all its member states exceed (are 'breaking out' of) the limited Community competences consented by the German Parliament when it ratified the EU Treaties. As the ECJ has so far never taken into account GATT and WTO dispute settlement rulings on the numerous GATT and WTO violations by the EC, the judicial self-restraint by both the German and the EC Court are regrettable because—rather than acting as guardians of EC law—both courts contribute to the lack of the rule of law and democratic self-determination in the international relations of the EC.

federalism', *i.e.* the need for limiting EU competencies to transnational tasks and for protecting state sovereignty from progressive erosion by the unnecessary expansion of EU powers (notably in *internal* policy matters such as police powers, education and cultural policies). In its Maastricht judgment of October 1993, the German Federal Constitutional Court emphasised the distinction between 'interpretation' and 'amendment' of EC law and the need for a restrictive interpretation of Community competencies based upon Article 308 of the EC Treaty.[52] Proposals for replacing the interrelated Articles 3 and 308 of the EC Treaty by catalogues of mutually exclusive national and EU competencies are confronted with numerous political and legal problems (eg due to the imperfect, dynamic and open-ended nature of integration in the EU). *Procedural* methods for promoting 'dual federalism' appear politically more flexible and legally easier to realise than incorporation into the EU Treaty of catalogues of exclusive national and EU competencies.

Potential conflicts between national and EU competencies can be reduced by additional *democratic procedural safeguards*, such as making the exercise of EU powers (notably under Article 308 EC) conditional on the consent of the European Parliament and subjecting member state representatives in the EU Council to stricter control by national parliaments. Conflicts between the *judicial Kompetenz-Kompetenz* of the ECJ in the interpretation of EU law and the judicial *Kompetenz-Kompetenz* of national constitutional or supreme courts for the interpretation of their respective national constitutional laws could be reduced by more effective *judicial cooperation* (e.g., requests by national constitutional courts for preliminary rulings pursuant to Article 234 EC if the EU does not comply with WTO dispute settlement rulings) or by submitting conflicts over the delimitation of national and EU competencies to a new 'Constitutional Council' composed by judges from the ECJ and national constitutional courts.[53] Judgments by international courts binding on the EU and EU member states (e.g. WTO dispute settlement rulings) should be observed both by the ECJ and by national courts. Incorporation of the newly adopted EU Charter of Fundamental Rights into the EU Treaty, perhaps at the EU's Intergovernmental Conference scheduled for 2004, could give more specificity to the constitutional limits of EU law and encourage a more coherent constitutional discourse on the human rights and popular sovereignty of EU citizens, and on the legitimate goals and limited discretion of EU rule-making.

---

[52] Bundesverfassungsgericht, judgment of 12 October 1993, English translation in Common Market Law Reports 1994, 57: 'in future it will have to be noted as regards interpretation of enabling provisions by Community institutions and agencies that the Union Treaty as a matter of principle distinguishes between the exercise of a sovereign power conferred for limited purposes and the amending of the Treaty, so that its interpretation may not have effects that are equivalent to an extension of the Treaty. Such an interpretation of enabling rules would not produce any binding effects for Germany.'

[53] *Cf.* Weiler note 48, at 322.

7

Sovereignty, Post-Sovereignty and Pre-Sovereignty: Three Models of the State, Democracy and Rights within the EU

RICHARD BELLAMY[1]

1. INTRODUCTION

F EW WOULD DENY the established pattern of sovereign states faces practical and normative challenges. The capacity and right of existing states to exercise supreme authority within their territory, control access to it, and speak for their citizens outside it, have all become harder to sustain and justify. The related processes of globalisation and social differentiation have enhanced interconnectedness at an international level while producing greater heterogeneity at regional and local levels. These forces have reduced the ability of states either to frame independent socio-economic, foreign and defence policies, or to draw on or forge a national identity capable of sustaining an allegiance to the public good and the political institutions and decisions that define and uphold it. Increasingly, if to varying degrees and with many qualifications, citizens question not only the functional competence of states to provide for their economic and personal security, but also the legitimacy of even democratic states to define and uphold, let alone override, their rights.

Though most people concede these problems exist, both academics and the general public debate their severity and implications. There are two main views. The first view contends that states either have retained their sovereignty but developed new strategies to defend it, or are in the process

[1] Research for this essay was supported by an ESRC Grant L213 25 2022 on 'Strategies of Civic Inclusion in Pan-European Civil Society'. I am grateful to Dario Castiglione, Ian Hunter, Philip Pettit, Jim Tully and Neil Walker for their comments on an earlier version.

of transferring it to other bodies.[2] Either way, sovereignty remains central to the nature of politics. The second view argues that we both are and should be going beyond the sovereign nation state towards a post-national politics based on human rights.[3] Sovereign authority is being curtailed, both formally and in fact, without it passing to other bodies. A government that is bound by domestic and international human rights charters can no longer claim to be entitled to do whatever it wishes with its population, even if its policies are democratically sanctioned. If sovereignty is by definition inconsistent with such limitations, then these arrangements must entail its transcendence. For sovereignty has not been embodied in the law or the courts. Their authority is normative rather than political, grounded in justice rather than the command or force of those in power.

These two views involve contrasting perspectives on the relationship between the state, democracy and rights. The first, pro-sovereignty, view treats state and popular sovereignty as mutually dependent. People can only rule themselves if they, usually through their representatives, possess supreme authority within a given domain, albeit indirectly through controlling those who govern in their name. Consequently, any weakening of state sovereignty either undermines democracy, or involves a transfer of sovereign power elsewhere and so requires a parallel shift of democratic control. Meanwhile, rights only have standing through being enshrined in law by the sovereign body—which in a democracy is the legislature. Thus, state sovereignty defines the demos and its ability to rule, and popular sovereignty defines rights. By contrast, the second, post-sovereignty view, sees both forms of sovereignty as a potential threat to rights. State sovereignty can hinder humanitarian intervention against oppressive regimes, and popular sovereignty can produce tyrannous majorities. As a result, they have to be limited (and, in consequence, their claims undermined) by rights mechanisms, such as constitutional and international charters. On this account, state and popular sovereignty possess no intrinsic worth or legitimacy. They are only instrumentally valuable as a means for the protection and promotion of rights. Indeed, pre-political rights—which attach to individuals by virtue of their humanity, provide the very basis for politics. So,

---

[2] Eg Robert Jackson, 'Sovereignty in World Politics: a Glance at the Conceptual and Historical Landscape'; Alan James, 'The Practice of Sovereign Statehood in Contemporary International Society' and Georg Sørensen, 'Sovereignty: Change and Continuity in a Fundamental Institution', all in Robert Jackson (ed.), *Sovereignty at the Millenium*, Special Issue, (1999) 47 *Political Studies* 423, 457 and 590 respectively.
[3] Eg D Held, *Democracy and the Global Order: From the Modern State to Cosmopolitan Governance* (Cambridge, Polity, 1995), p. 135; Andrew Linklater, *The Transformation of Political Community: Ethical Foundations of the Post-Westphalian Era* (Cambridge, Polity, 1998), pp. 29, 32, 34, 50–1 and L Ferrajoli, 'Beyond Sovereignty and Citizenship: a Global Constitutionalism' in R Bellamy (ed.), *Constitutionalism, Democracy and Sovereignty: American and European Perspectives*, (Aldershot, Avebury, 1996), J Habermas, *The Inclusion of the Other: Studies in Political Theory*, (Cambridge, Polity, 1999), pp. 118–20.

rights define both the polity, as a convenient functional unit for fostering rights, and democracy, through providing the rationale for the right to vote.[4]

There is a certain symmetry about these two views. Both are premised on sovereignty being fundamentally political, supreme, and agent or agency-based. Hence, if political sovereignty has not been defended or transferred it must have evaporated. This chapter disputes this common premises. Sovereignty and allegedly post-sovereignty views turn out to be two sides of the same coin. Neither the rule of persons nor the rule of law can be sustained without the other. Therefore, attempts to make one or other supreme will become locked in a vicious circle. Consequently, the contrast between sovereignty and post-sovereignty turns out to be overdrawn. Sovereign power never has been, nor indeed could be, purely political, in the sense of ruler-based. Sovereignty has always required normative recognition of some kind which both constrains and facilitates its exercise.[5] Law and rights standardly provide such a normative basis for political power. Yet, contrary to the claims of post-sovereigntists, sovereignty does not thereby dissolve but becomes vested in these fundamental norms and those charged with their interpretation and implementation. For rights can clash and may be subject to conflicting interpretations over their application to particular cases, so a 'supreme' court may have to exercise finality of decision of a direct or more indirect kind and rely on political authorities to back its decisions. These arrangements may tame sovereignty and reduce the opportunities for certain kinds of oppression, but they can also create new problems associated with weak governance and a lack of democratic accountability. Meanwhile, the normative basis of the law's sovereign authority remains contested, apparently resting more on might—the power to enforce a particular view—than consensus on the right. So, the transfer thesis errs through not recognising that political sovereignty is not self-sufficient and that legal norms alter its basis, manner of application and areas of competence, while the evaporation thesis is mistaken in its turn in denying that key elements of sovereign political power still persist, being both necessary to and unsettling the normative sovereignty of the law.

However, it would be mistaken to believe that some form of sovereignty is unavoidable. We are apt to forget how recent the doctrine of sovereignty is, originating only in the sixteenth and seventeenth centuries to buttress the novel claims of absolute monarchs. As such, it involved a conscious and, at the time, contentious and contested, critique of an alternative view that was concerned with the maintenance of a pre-sovereignty condition and a corre-

---

[4] Eg T Pogge, 'Cosmopolitanism and Sovereignty' in C Brown (ed.), *Political Restructuring in Europe: Ethical Perspectives* (London, Routledge, 1994).
[5] HLA Hart, *The Concept of Law*, (Oxford, Clarendon Press, 1961), Chs IV and VI.

sponding form of politics.[6] According to this republican theory, power was best distributed and shared rather than concentrated. So republicans advocated a mixed constitution, involving a balance of powers between different political institutions and sections of the community. The aim of these arrangements was to ensure no person or body had the capacity to act in an arbitrary manner. To the extent finality of decision existed in this set up it was a systemic feature, requiring the co-operation of all relevant agents and agencies, rather than residing in any one of them. As a result, all collective decisions had to be negotiated by citizens or their representatives to show they were publically justifiable and treated the values and interests of those they affected with equal concern and respect. So, the rule of law results from the rule of persons, but without invoking either the sovereign will of a *demos* or assuming consensus on a sovereign *Grundnorm*. Rather, its basis and safeguard lies in negotiated agreements between heterogeneous persons located within different levels and branches of government. Because no group or person is sovereign over any other, the tyranny of any minority or majority must give way to deliberation and the construction of laws that deal fairly with others. Within this scenario, therefore, democracy and rights finally come together.

In what follows, I shall defend both the theoretical coherence and the practical plausibility of the pre-sovereignty approach. Updated as a theory of 'mixed sovereignty', its division of sovereign power proves curiously suited to a world where conflicting claims to sovereignty abound. As debates about the character and future of the EU illustrate, this issue is of more than academic interest. The EU is seen by many as a test case for whether, and if so in what ways, state and popular sovereignty are being transformed. Proponents of the sovereignty view, interpret the EU as either an intergovernmental organisation that allows its constituent states to maintain their prerogatives in new circumstances,[7] or a federal state in the making that shall ultimately take on the powers hitherto held by its members.[8] By contrast, others see the EU as potentially a new kind of post-sovereign entity, that might regulate solely on the basis of rights,[9] although left and right disagree over how far these rights are positive as well as negative. However, I shall argue that it also has many of the characteristics of the 'pre-' or 'mixed' sovereignty conception of a polity and that republican

---

[6] For a useful historical account, see Julian H Franklin, 'Sovereignty and the Mixed Constitution: Bodin and his Critics' in JH Burns and Mark Goldie (eds), *The Cambridge History of Political Thought 1450–700*, (Cambridge, Cambridge University Press, 1991).

[7] Eg A Moravcsik, 'Preferences and Power in the European Community: A Liberal Intergovernmentalist Approach', (1993) 31 *Journal of Common Market Studies* 473.

[8] Eg J Pinder, 'Building the Union: Policy, Reform, Constitution' in A Duff, J Pinder and R Pryce (eds.), *Maastrict and Beyond: Building the European Union*, (London, Routledge, 1994).

[9] Eg above n 3 Linklater, *The Transformation of Political Community*, Ch 6.

constitutional arrangements offer the most normatively attractive way to ensure its complex structures meet the twin demands stemming from democratic politics and legal rights.[10]

I begin, in section two, with an analysis of the relations between political and legal sovereignty that provides the framework for an assessment of the transformation from sovereignty to post-sovereignty in section three. Both have drawbacks and advantages, while sharing a fundamental incoherence. Section four then outlines and defends the pre-sovereignty conception of the mixed constitution as the true alternative to a sovereignty based political system. Throughout I will refer to developments within the EU to illustrate aspects of my argument.

2. POLITICAL AND LEGAL SOVEREIGNTY

The rationale for sovereignty lies in the supposed need for some ultimate adjudicator of all conflict in a world where consensual agreement on the right and the good cannot be counted on. The sovereign is the agent or agency where the buck stops and a final decision gets made. The only alternative is said to be an anarchic state of war.[11] Therefore, the core element of sovereignty is the possession of 'supreme authority'. However, theorists from Bodin and Hobbes onwards have argued that to secure this supremacy sovereignty must be unlimited and hence in certain crucial respects 'absolute' and 'unitary' or 'indivisible' as well.[12] For a start, it is claimed the status cannot be partial. As Georg Sørensen has put it, sovereignty is like being married, you either possess this status or you do not, one can no more be 75 per cent sovereign than 75 per cent married.[13] Similarly, sovereignty cannot be shared or distributed, because then no one agent or agency will have finality of decision. Still, it need not involve total power in the sense of directly co-ordinating everything, an impossible task in a society of any size and complexity. Many tasks can be delegated and some left to semi-autonomous authorities. All that sovereignty requires is that in the event of a clash of authorities the sovereign's decision prevails. In this respect, it can

---

[10] See too R Bellamy and D Castiglione, 'Democracy, Sovereignty and the Constitution of the European Union: The Republican Alternative to Liberalism' in Z Bankowski and A Scott, *The European Union and its Order: The Legal Theory of European Integration*, (Oxford, Blackwell, 2000).

[11] Eg T Hobbes, *Leviathan*, ed. R Tuck, (Cambridge, Cambridge University Press, 1991), p. 90, who links plurality in judgements with the 'war of every man against every man' and argues only a 'common power' can establish both 'right and wrong' and legal order in such circumstances.

[12] J Bodin, *On Sovereignty* ed. JH Franklin, (Cambridge, Cambridge University Press, 1992), pp. 1–4 (Bk 1 Ch 8 of *The Six Books of the Commonwealth*).

[13] Above n 2 Sørensen, 'Sovereignty: Change and Continuity in a Fundamental Institution', 593.

operate as a 'threshold concept'.[14] Nevertheless, in a sovereign system power can only be devolved vertically and in a hierarchical manner. Delegated authorities, be they officials or agencies, remain under the control of the sovereign, who sets and can change their terms of reference, remove them from office and even abolish the position altogether. Likewise, the sovereign decides which areas can be governed by the autonomous decisions of individuals or private agencies. Even federal arrangements must leave finality of decision with a superior body at the centre. From this sovereignty perspective, a system based on a horizontal distribution of power is tantamount to anarchy, lacking coherence and consistency. Yet, as we will see, this is the very arrangement proposed by pre-sovereignty theorists.

Such supreme authority was traditionally associated with the political sovereignty of a ruler. However, a problem arises at this point, that brings us to the central dilemma surrounding the practice of sovereignty noted in the introduction. For it is doubtful that political sovereignty could be sustained or consistently exercised without the support of law, or that law, contrary to Hobbes's and Austin's view,[15] be reduced to the commands of the sovereign. Sovereignty must be de jure as well as de facto. The sheer political capacity of a government to exert power over a community, or of the populace—in the case of popular sovereignty—to assert their interests, will not ensure they are regularly obeyed or listened to. If only might decides who has the right to command, then unless an agent is so powerful as to be truly unassailable, their supremacy will always be subject to fluctuations in the prevailing balance of power. Moreover, an omnipotent authority would raise even more serious concerns. Any sovereign powerful enough to rule by might alone would have no incentive not to be so tyrannous as to make the uncertainty of a sovereignless world more preferable to the certainty of oppression.[16] So political sovereignty is legitimated and exercised through domestic and international law. Legal institutions establish the right of sovereigns to rule and systematise their ruling by embodying it within legal rules. However, if political sovereignty is constituted and regulated by law, its absoluteness, indivisibility and supremacy seem called into question. Political sovereignty appears to be limited, shared or even supplanted by legal sovereignty. Yet legal sovereignty in its turn seems compromised. For law, while a semi-autonomous system, also needs political power in its turn to render it effective and legitimate, most typically within a democracy through the direct or indirect tacit and active consent

---

[14] Steven Lee, 'A Puzzle of Sovereignty' (1997) 27 *Californian Western International Law Journal* 241, 245 cited in N Walker, 'Sovereignty and Differentiated Integration in the European Union' in Bankowski and Scott (eds), *The European Union and its Order*, above n 10 pp. 33–4.

[15] Above n 11 Hobbes, *Leviathan*, p. 80.

[16] The classic statement of this objection is of course J Locke, *Two Treatises of Government*, ed. P Laslett, (Cambridge, Cambridge University Press, 1960), II 93 p. 328.

of those to whom it applies. Thus, law and politics appear deeply inter-twined. Each supports the other but in so doing seems caught in a vicious circle that challenges the very logic of sovereignty.[17]

One attempt to unravel this dilemma is to distinguish the 'polity' and the 'regime' dimensions of sovereignty, treating the former as the primary, polit-ically 'constitutive' element, and the latter as the secondary, legally 'regula-tive' aspect.[18] That way politics provides the basis and raw material for law. In this account, the polity dimension of sovereignty concerns where, over whom and by who power is exercised. In other words, it defines the func-tional and territorial 'spheres' where politics can operate, and the 'subjects' who rule or are ruled through the established political procedures within these spheres. As such, it involves both the internal exercise of power over and by subjects within certain domestic spheres, and the foreign employ-ment of power to defend or extend the polity externally. The regime dimen-sion of sovereignty concerns how and when power is exercised. It refers to the extent or 'scope' of politics, for example whether it entails intervention and redistribution or simply regulation, and the 'styles' of politics, such as the type of electoral system, the form of democratic decision-making and so on. Regimes too are not only domestic, within a polity, but also increasingly well-developed in foreign affairs between polities.

Following Georg Sørensen, we can align this distinction between 'polity' and 'regime' with a division between the 'constitutive' and 'regulative' rules of sovereignty.[19] Constitutive rules define the aims, actors and possible moves within any activity, while regulative rules govern how such a consti-tuted activity might be carried out. Thus, the constitutive rules of soccer differentiate it from rugby, and various regulative rules structure how soccer should be played. It is possible to change a regulative rule, like the off-side rule or the number of yellow cards needed to be sent off or suspended, without altering the constitutive rules either at all or so much that one effectively invents a new game. Yet, as the games analogy reveals, the distinction between the two is not hard and fast. Changes in the one have knock-on effects for the other, with modifications in the regulative rules often having the incremental effect of changing the game. Sørensen

---

[17] For this intertwining of law and politics, see N MacCormick, 'Sovereignty, Democracy and Subsidiarity', in R Bellamy, V Bufacchi and D Catiglione (eds), *Democracy and Constitutional Culture in the Union of Europe* (London, Lothian Foundation Press, 1995) pp. 95–100 and M Loughlin, *Sword and Scales: An Examination of the Realtionship, Between Law and Politics*, (Oxford, Hart Publishing, 2000).

[18] As I understand it, Bodin attempted to make this move by distinguishing what is standardly translated as 'state' ('polity') from 'government' ('regime'), and arguing the Prince could be sovereign over the one while limited in the other. Though Bodin ultimately abandoned this argu-ment, rightly noting its incoherence, it was taken up by others, such as Pufendorf, later. See above n 6 Franklin, 'Sovereignty and the Mixed Constitution: Bodin and his Critics', pp. 307, 317.

[19] Above n 2 Sørensen, 'Sovereignty: Change and Continuity in a Fundamental Institution', 591–7.

argues the constitutive elements of sovereignty consist of 'states with a delimited territory, a stable population, and a government', possessing 'constitutional independence' and operating in the context of the 'international society of states'.[20] He claims this basic model has remained essentially unchanged since the seventeenth century. What has altered are the regulative rules, most particularly via the development of more extensive international regimes to regulate trade, security and human rights, most of which have internal implications for the domestic sovereignty of states as well as their external relations with each other.[21] Even as closely integrated a regime as the European Union can still plausibly (if not uncontentiously) be seen as having sovereign states as its constitutive units, though he grants that this may turn out to be a case where alterations of the regulative rules ultimately undermine the sovereignty game.[22]

This historical analysis provides an interesting interpretation of the supposed transition from sovereignty to post-sovereignty, examined in the next section, that apparently reconciles the primacy of political sovereignty with the growing role of a putative post-sovereign legal challenge to its constitutive supremacy. However, I believe it ultimately fails. Sørensen likens sovereign states to elements of an antecedent activity, such as driving cars, and regulative legal rules to the Highway Code.[23] Thus, the political sovereignty of a territorially located *demos*, who make up the 'polity', is 'constitutive' of its own legal regulatory 'regime'. For the former is presupposed by, establishes and ultimately legitimates the latter. In this way, it appears one could have a sovereign political 'polity' which nonetheless provides its own limited legal 'regime'. Yet by what right does the *demos* possess such constitutive power? As Sørensen also notes, the external status of sovereign states rests on their mutual recognition and collective agreements as mediated by international law.[24] Internally too, constitutional norms identify and can reconfigure the right of any *demos* to rule. Think of the way excluded groups, women, workers, religious and ethnic minorities, came to be recognised as part of the *demos*.[25] So regimes, both external and internal, are also constitutive—they provide the Hartian 'rules of recognition' or Kelsenian *Grundnorm* that authorise and facilitate the exercise of sovereign power.[26] Thus the distinction between 'constitutive' and 'regula-

---

[20] *Ibid* 592–3.
[21] *Ibid* 596–8.
[22] *Ibid* 602–4.
[23] *Ibid* 595.
[24] *Ibid* 593.
[25] See R Bellamy and D Castiglione, 'Normative Theory and the European Union: Legitimising the Euro-polity and its Regime, in Lars Trägårdh (ed.), *After National Democracy: Rights, Law and Power in America and the New Europe*, Onati International Series in Law and Society, (Oxford, Hart Publishing, 2003).
[26] Above n 5 Hart, *The Concept of Law*, Ch. VI, above n 17 MacCormick, 'Sovereignty, Democracy and Subsidiarity', 98.

tive' rules refers to elements of both the 'polity' and the 'regime', returning us once more to the vexed relations between de facto and de jure sovereignty, politics and law, democracy and rights, and the original dilemma of political and legal sovereign power.

3. FROM SOVEREIGNTY TO POST-SOVEREIGNTY

Taking the above analysis into account, the alleged shift from sovereignty to post-sovereignty can now be more fully described and assessed, and compared with an account of pre-sovereignty in the following section. A sovereignty based system assumes an autonomous polity possessing an independent regime with a single supreme authority exercising finality of decision over all issues at the apex of a vertical and hierarchical distribution of power. Sovereignty so conceived is standardly thought to be fundamentally political, being exercised either by a single unelected ruler, or the people—usually through their elected representatives. Law is required to stabilise any regime, giving it the coherence and consistency needed for the efficient exercise of power, but its source must ultimately lie in the commands of the de facto ruler—be that a person or the people. Such power is said to possess three defining characteristics—it must be 'absolute', because independence cannot be qualified or limited, 'unitary', because it must apply to all matters and cannot be shared or divided, and 'supreme', because it must be final. As a result, sovereignty is linked to a territorial nation state as the only viable context for such power to be exercised. Only here can rulers claim a monopoly of decisional power over a given sphere and its subjects that admits of no higher or superior authority or limitation. The sovereignty of states and their rulers is even said to be self-constituting—deriving from their mutual recognition within the society of states.

Post-sovereignty theorists believe this account presents a relatively easy target, with both the absolute and unitary conditions having been so weakened as to have fatally weakened claims by any political agent or agency to supremacy of the requisite kind.[27] With regard to absoluteness, I have already remarked how they can point out the ways law is semi-autonomous from the state—constituting its very existence and establishing the norms and rules that define the rights and duties of states and their office holders towards their citizens and those of other states or none. The *Rechtsstaat* is not only domestic but international, with international law an explicitly non-state system of law. As a result, the constitutional independence of states has come to be regarded as 'absolute' only to the extent it meets certain

---

[27] For a good overview, above n 3 Held, *Democracy and the Global Order*, Chs 5 and 6.

formal and substantive conditions of legitimacy—otherwise there would be no grounds for humanitarian intervention. International agreements and organisations have also reduced the autonomy of states to act in certain important spheres in ways that affect the 'unitary' condition. Though states and their representatives are the prime actors within organisations such as NATO, the WEU, or the EU, their interactions and collaborations are so numerous and intense as to have profoundly modified their independence of action. Sovereignty has been to a degree 'pooled' or shared with other states and partly divided, with finality of decision over clashes with regard to certain economic, strategic and even social and civil policies passing to bodies such as the WTO, the UN or the European Court of Human Rights. Such pooling and dispersing of power is of course particularly intense in the European Union,[28] but exists to a degree for almost all states. Finally, increased regional autonomy has increasingly challenged the hierarchical pattern of standard federal systems, pushing them closer to confederalism or consociationalism where shared decision-making is the norm in crucial or sensitive areas, with vetoes or opt-outs challenging 'finality' at the centre.

The pro-sovereignty theorist's fall back position in the face of these developments is to assert that ultimately states can always withdraw from such arrangements or choose not to comply. For example, though the Treaty on European Union has no formal provision for secession, it is generally granted that this possibility exists. It is this option that leads Sørensen to assert that though the regulative rules governing the normal exercise of sovereignty may have changed, the constitutive rules of sovereignty remain the existence of states with the de facto political capacity to act as supreme authorities.[29] Yet, practically neither the one hegemonic economic and strategic super power, the United States, nor pariah states, such as Libya or Iraq, can totally disengage and still act effectively or even, in the case of the latter, have their statehood respected. If sovereignty has not been totally eroded, therefore, even at the constitutive level it has been profoundly weakened and changed in character. In particular, states have to recognise the legal sovereignty exercised by various domestic and international courts, the supreme authority in certain areas of various international organs that they have created through their agreements, and a more general need to negotiate with other states, bodies, regions and even ordinary citizens in order to act.

Nonetheless, it remains true that, contrary to the claims of post-sovereignty theorists, sovereignty has not thereby passed away. For domestic and international courts, regulatory agencies, intergovernmental organisations

---

[28] See William Wallace, 'The Sharing of Sovereignty: The European Paradox', (1999) 47 *Political Studies* 503.
[29] Above n 2 Sørensen, 'Sovereignty: Change and Continuity in a Fundamental Institution', 603.

and the like, can all operate as supreme authorities in discreet areas without being either absolute or unitary. For example, the European Court of Human Rights is the ultimate forum for deciding whether the law of signatory states infringes the European Convention, but its manner of operation and competences are strictly circumscribed. In other words, though there has been a parcelling out of sovereign powers and changes in their mode of operation, this process has involved the piecemeal transfer and weakening of sovereignty, not its demise. The result has been a fragmentation of the comprehensive polity and associated regime typical of the nation state into a number of different policy or functional 'polities', each working at different levels of aggregation and with its own distinctive 'regime'.[30] This development reduces certain sorts of abuses associated with the concentration of sovereign power, with regulators and the courts promoting procedures and policies that can lead governments to take rights more seriously. It also means that law can be tailored to local preferences and circumstances. However, there are also drawbacks to this development. When there is a single and powerful locus of sovereignty the lines of responsibility are clearer; it is easier to prioritise policies and consider how they fit together, noting the ways tackling one issue in a certain way may facilitate or hinder efforts elsewhere; and delivery can be more effective through being more direct. The task of ensuring democratic accountability is also simplified, as is the process of collective deliberation amongst a people in order to negotiate agreement on which public goods should be supported, by whom and why. In a dispersed system, there are more opportunities for free riding and compliance may be harder to monitor, while officials and politicians can find it easier to escape scrutiny and control.

In a recent essay, Jim Tully has noted three trends whereby many of the global economic and legal processes that are undermining or weakening state sovereignty have also damaged democratic government and the rule of law.[31] The first trend arises from the manner in which international legal and regulatory regimes foster certain of the worst as well as the better features of global capitalism. They protect the rights underlying free trade but often in ways that disadvantage poorer countries and persons, especially as powerful states are usually in a position, as the prime enforcers of these regimes, to defect from or fail to comply with measures that go against their interests. Even within advanced capitalist states, there has been an erosion of socio-economic and cultural rights. For these processes of global juridification rarely bring in their wake parallel mechanisms for

---

[30] Again, this development has gone further within the EU than elsewhere. See G Marks, L Hooghe and K Blank, 'European Integration from the 1980s: State-Centric *v* Multi-level Governance' (1996) 34 *Journal of Common Market Studies*, 341.

[31] J Tully, 'The Unfreedom of the Moderns in Comparison with the Ideals of Constitutional Democracy', (2002) 65 *Modern Law Review*, 204.

maintaining democratic accountability. Yet, democracy has been the prime mechanism whereby people have attempted to ensure that law-makers and enforcers treat their views and interests on these issues with equal concern and respect. It has been through democratic contestation, for example, that women and workers won the vote and obtained important rights protecting them at home and in the work place. Instead, power increasingly passes to democratically unaccountable bodies, such as international corporations and tribunals, technical regulatory authorities, and so on.

The second trend refers to the ways the devolution of power within established states not only increases the opportunities for democratic self-governance for regions and minority nations, but also produces weaker political units that are unable to challenge the global pressures for economic deregulation, low taxation and flexible labour markets. As a result, there is a further reduction in the resources available for these political units to provide the public goods and services required to secure the well-being of their citizens. Education, health, the environment, and the infrastructure all suffer. All too often, what coercive power these small political units do possess is dedicated largely to suppressing the social unrest and criminal behaviour associated with the growing inequality and poverty produced by indiscriminate policies of economic liberalisation.

Finally, the third trend concerns the growth of executive power and the decline of democratic deliberation and decision-making within traditional representative institutions. The growth of global regulatory regimes and intergovernmental organisations, on the one hand, and the privatisation of many public services or their contracting out to semi-autonomous agencies and QUANGOs, on the other, has removed many areas of decision-making from adequate scrutiny by domestic legislatures. In any case, representatives remain too dependent on parties that, with the decline of mass membership, are ever more tools of the leadership, to wield much influence. By contrast, well-organised interest groups, media corporations and unelected experts are increasingly influential. Not surprisingly, citizens have become less attached to parties and more motivated by sectoral concerns and single causes, issues and campaigns. Some of these developments have been both beneficial and successful, contributing to the creation of transnational movements in areas such as the environment. But they also reflect a general privatising of political life and a move away from a concern with the public good and integral collective agreements.

The EU reflects both the positive and the negative aspects of this passage from sovereignty to post-sovereignty. Positively, European integration has promoted peace and prosperity between the member states, with increased interaction modifying national self-interest and fostering co-operation to tackle transnational problems such as cross border pollution. The commitment to certain standards of liberal democracy has also bolstered the new democracies of Spain, Greece and Portugal, while often prompting progressive reforms within the more established democracies in areas such as the equal treatment of men and women. Negatively, however, the removal of barriers to the free movement of goods, services, capital and persons, and the enshrining of these 'four freedoms' within European law, has had certain of the deleterious effects associated above with the trend towards global juridification: threatening local self-determination, linguistic and cultural diversity, and risking a 'race to the bottom' in certain welfare provisions and employment and social security rights. Clashes between the European Court of Justice and national constitutional courts over the interpretation and ranking of rights in these areas have been common, with no settled procedure for their satisfactory resolution. Intergovernmental agreements have enhanced executive power, removing certain crucial economic and security decisions from effective parliamentary or popular control at the national level without, as the EU's notorious 'democratic deficit' attests, establishing effective forms of accountability at the supra-national level. Meanwhile, the EU remains a 'weak' polity—lacking the legitimacy to engage in redistributive and interventionist as opposed to regulatory policies, and often not possessing the capacity to implement and secure compliance for even these measures. Yet little support exists for remedying these defects by turning the EU in its turn into a sovereign political unit. For example, though national identities have to some degree fragmented, with people showing increasing regional and transnational allegiances, very few people claim to have a European identity or would welcome EU-wide collective decision-making.[32]

The move towards a condition beyond or post-sovereignty poses in a new form the paradox surrounding the purpose and practice of sovereignty examined in the last section. For the very processes that have tamed sovereignty have also rendered it both necessary and no longer possible. Though the heightened complexity and social differentiation of contemporary societies constrain the ability of sovereign states to dominate their citizens, they also enhance both value pluralism and the oppressive power of private institutions, thereby raising the problems of deep disagreement, free-riding and the powerlessness of the weak before the strong which sovereignty claims to resolve by authoritatively defining right and wrong, acting as the supreme arbiter, and compelling all to obey. Post-sovereignty theorists seek to overcome this difficulty by arguing there can be agreement on rights— the framework within which we resolve our disagreements about the nature

---

[32] For example, a recent Eurobarometer Report (52 April 2000—based on research October-November 1999) records that while an average of 46% of European citizens believe their country has benefited from the EU, only 4% see themselves as exclusively European and 6% as European and nationality (eg European-Irish or European-British). Most, 42%, regard themselves at best as nationality and European (eg as French-European or Danish-European). Earlier polls produced very similar results.

of the good life—and indeed that without such an agreement no use of sovereign power can ever be legitimate. So conceived, post-sovereignty takes us not beyond sovereignty, so much as towards a basis for the legitimation and limitation of sovereign power. Yet in the process it empowers the judiciary, creating a legal sovereignty that is often as arbitrary as, if generally weaker, but also less accountable, than the political sovereignty it displaces. For rights to property, privacy, freedom of speech, bodily integrity and so on are deeply contentious, yielding disputes every bit as heated as (and usually linked to) those occasioned by people's more comprehensive beliefs—as debates over such matters as welfare, freedom of the press, pornography and abortion amply show. Therefore, the challenge has to be to retain certain key elements of, and offer a coherent basis for, a sovereign system, notably effective and democratic government, within the new conditions of a post-sovereign world of multiple polities, regimes and identities and without losing some of the welcome curbs on arbitrary power these developments have produced. Put another way, a legitimate unity has to be constructed out of plurality without creating 'a common Power to keep them all in awe'.[33] The next section proposes the arrangements of a pre-sovereign system as being best suited to this task.

4. FROM PRE-SOVEREIGNTY TO MIXED SOVEREIGNTY

The arguments for sovereignty developed by Bodin and Hobbes, which so many commentators on this issue take as their starting point, involved the conscious criticism of what had hitherto been the standard view—namely, that even within monarchical systems power should be mixed in ways that blocked any one agent or agency acting in an arbitrary manner.[34] A view associated with the Roman constitution and republicanism, its central tenet was that a well-ordered political system rests on the 'the Empire of laws and not of men'.[35] However, this condition does not replace political with legal sovereignty. Not only is the idea of a putatively non-political judicial branch a largely post-sovereignty notion, but also it was clear to these theorists that even natural law has to be interpreted and applied, thereby giving discretionary power to those charged with doing so. If laws were not to reflect the mere whim or will of the ruler, thereby dominating and potentially oppressing the ruled, but to apply equally and consistently to all, so none could be above the law, while being so formulated as to show all citizens

---

[33] Above n 11 Hobbes, *Leviathan*, p. 88.

[34] Above n 6 Franklin, 'Sovereignty and the Mixed Constitution: Bodin and his Critics', pp. 301–5; Above n 12 Bodin, *On Sovereignty*, Bk 2 Ch 1, especially pp. 103–5; Above n 11 Hobbes, *Leviathan*, p. 225.

[35] See James Harrington, translating Livy, *The Commonwealth of Oceana*, ed. JGA Pocock, (Cambridge, Cambridge University Press, 1992), pp. 8, 20.

equal concern and respect, then rule by an agent or agency over others had to be replaced by a system of popular self-rule.[36] Yet, this proposal should not be equated with popular sovereignty. Republican theorists did not conceive of 'the people' as a homogeneous group. Quite the contrary, they were well aware of their class and religious divisions. So the system they advocated was one where each person was to count equally with others. As the seventeenth century neo-Roman republican theorist James Harrington put it, in an explicit critique of Hobbes, it is only when all are equal in the making of the laws that they will be 'framed by every private man unto no other end (or they may thank themselves) than to protect the liberty of every man'.[37]

Thus, a pre-sovereignty system involves bringing together democracy and the rule of law in such a way that there is neither legal nor political—including popular—sovereignty. Instead, citizens have to engage with each other as political equals and negotiate collective agreements that embody reciprocity and a willingness to 'hear the other side', neither ignoring nor overriding other people's concerns so long as these too embody mutual respect. The key to promoting such dialogue lay in the idea of a 'mixed' constitution that both distributed and shared power: the very two devices that the sovereignty theorists were to criticise, though they acknowledged both could be found in the Roman and other constitutions. Two central mechanisms within this peculiarly republican regime facilitate the distribution and sharing of power: the 'separation of powers' and the 'balance of power'.[38] The first, distributive, mechanism reduces the discretionary aspect of the law, preventing it degenerating into a mere command. The second, sharing, mechanism encourages the law to track the interests of those to whom it applies and gives them a sense of ownership over it. Taken together, they serve to remove the sovereignty of any agent or agency, thereby blocking the abuse of power while facilitating and legitimating its constructive and more differentiated use. As a result, the law becomes more sensitive to the diversity of ideals, interests and situations within the polity.

Though the institutional forms taken by the mechanisms for distributing and sharing power may require adjustment to reflect new social and political problems, cleavages and structures, the logic behind them remains much the same. The 'separation of powers' distributes sovereignty by dividing the legislative from the executive and judicial functions to prevent any person or group becoming a judge in their own cause. Separating those who formulate the laws from those entrusted with their interpretation, application and

---

[36] Q Skinner, *Liberty Before Liberalism*, (Cambridge, Cambridge University Press, 1998), pp. 74–5.
[37] Above n 35 Harrington, *The Commonwealth of Oceana*, pp. 19–20.
[38] R Bellamy, 'The Political Form of the Constitution: the Separation of Powers, Rights and Representative Democracy' (1996) 44 *Political Studies*, 436.

enforcement brings all within the law. The legislators are constrained in their ability to decree ad hoc or self-serving laws by the judiciary's role in applying the law to all in an impartial and consistent manner. Meanwhile, the discretionary and interpretative powers held by the executive and judicial branches are checked because exercised under laws they do not make. However, there are two well-known problems with this thesis. The first concerns the conceptual and practical difficulty of separating functions. For example, when judges adjudicate on which rules apply in given cases, they often end up setting precedents that come to constitute new rules. Similarly, officials frequently create rules in the course of implementing a law, while legislators are inevitably concerned with how the laws they frame will be interpreted and applied to specific cases. Thus, the three functions are inter-related, with each branch of government engaged to some degree in the activities of the other. The second problem arises at this point. For the constraints imposed by whatever functional separation is possible will be undermined if all branches of government represent similar groups and interests. Having each function run by different people will not necessarily prevent their working for a partial interest if all belong to the same party or class. This problem has been particularly acute in systems, such as the British, where the executive controls the legislature and can exert direct and indirect influence over the judiciary through appointments or other ways.

The notion of the 'balance of power' comes in here. This device seeks to share the various functions between different groups and classes of people. Historically, the various branches of government were assigned to different classes. For example, in Montesquieu's famous depiction of the British constitution, executive power belongs to the Crown, the legislative lies largely with the Commons and partly with the Lords, who also control the judicial branch through the law Lords. The sharing of power is more usual today through systems of representation that ensure a variety of different constituencies can obtain an equal voice, and by multiplying the sites of decision-making. Thus, bi-cameral systems typically employ different methods of election for the two houses, while corporatist and consociational systems share powers amongst different functional, cultural or religious groups. Likewise, federalism, workplace democracy and associationalism provide ways of multiplying the sites and levels of decision-making, be they factories, schools, neighbourhoods or regions. Through sharing and distributing power, a balance is produced between the various interests and values of individuals and groups within the polity, obliging them to interact in ways that oblige them to treat each other fairly and with reciprocity. Harrington famously expressed this point in terms of the fable of the girls and the cake, who ensure a fair division by having the one who cuts the cake take the last slice.[39] A mixed constitution similarly divides sovereign

---

[39] Above n 35 Harrington, *The Commonwealth of Oceana*, pp. 22–5, 64–7.

powers so as to avoid the possibility of any person or group being able to pass public measures for personal or sectional advantages.

Because no body can get their way without the support of others, the mixed constitution obliges citizens and governments to engage in a process of public justification to show why the policies they advocate truly promote public interests. Republicanism is committed to a conception of dialogical reason. The watchword of such reasoning is to 'listen to the other side' (*audi alterem partem*), which carries with it 'a willingness to negotiate over rival intuitions concerning the applicability of evaluative terms'.[40] Such public justification involves more than a lowest-common denominator test, whereby the only legitimate collective rules relate to goods that de facto are in everyone's rational interest to have publically provided. In this case, those able to provide for themselves could object to supporting collective arrangements and even standard public goods might be deemed unacceptable. Instead, public justification entails the giving of reasons that are shareable by others and so carries with it a commitment to dialogue and mutual understanding.[41] Common rules should not only treat all individuals as moral equals capable of autonomous action, but also be attentive to the variety of circumstances in which they find themselves and the diverse forms of practical reasoning they adopt. Consequently, legislators must drop purely self-interested and self-referential reasoning and look for forms of argument that could be accepted by other individuals who are similarly constrained. In other words, there will be an assumption that in evaluating laws we start by taking into account the effects of their general performance for securing the various generic goods that one could expect individuals to value in the different situations they might find themselves. This assumption implies neither that all are similarly situated nor that they value the same goods. On the one hand, it would exclude any arguments that failed to heed the plight or concerns of others and could not be plausibly shared. So, self-serving arguments by the prosperous that there could never be grounds for mutual aid would be unlikely to pass this test. On the other hand, it merely requires that arguments be made in terms all could relate to. This requirement is consistent with groups or individuals either pointing out how their peculiar circumstances create special demands which would be felt by others in their place, or requesting their currently ignored claims be recognised on grounds of fairness by drawing parallels with certain exist-

---

[40] Q Skinner, *Reason and Rhetoric in the Philosophy of Hobbes* (Cambridge, Cambridge University Press, 1996), pp. 15–6 and P Pettit, *Republicanism: A Theory of Freedom and Government*, 2nd edition, (Oxford, Clarendon Press, 1999).

[41] This is a deliberate weakening of the formulation of T Scanlon, *What we Owe to Each Other*, (Cambridge MA, Harvard University Press, 1999), whose account of public reasoning I otherwise follow. It arises from thinking that pluralism requires greater flexibility and compromise than he believes necessary. See R Bellamy, *Liberalism and Pluralism: Towards a Politics of Compromise*, (London, Routledge, 1999), Introduction and Ch 3.

ing entitlements of others. When incommensurable goods and values are in play, it also allows for collective agreements to take the form of a compromise involving reciprocal concessions of various kinds.[42]

A critic might argue that this system smuggles in both a sovereign *Grundnorm* of 'hearing the other side', along with the values of reciprocity and equality of concern and respect that derive from it, and a sovereign 'people', who ultimately decides. Being essentially an argument from democracy, it must surely rest on both a set of constitutional democratic rights and a *demos*. But the norms do not in any sense precede or frame the practice of dialogue, they are intrinsic to it and only emerge within it. Thus, there is no pre-existing consensus on rights. Rather, rights—including those on which the democratic process itself rests, are identified through contestation, negotiation and compromise, often between highly divergent views. Likewise, there is no unitary *demos* but rather multiple *demoi* who must make their claim to be recognised and listened to through dialogue with others. Is the process as a whole to be regarded as sovereign then? Only in a sense that renders the term meaningless. No agent or agency holds the power of supreme authority. Unity here depends not on an authoritative *command* but on normative *agreement* between the various parties. Indeed, it is the inability of any agent or agency to force a decision that partly motivates the search for such an agreement. It might still be objected that even if the internal regime lacks a sovereign, the polity must operate as a sovereign unit. Even if true, in foreign as in domestic affairs the executive must be accountable to the system as a whole, so external sovereignty is also not the prerogative of any agent. However, the external sovereignty of a polity is standardly balanced and increasingly shared with other polities. Mixed international regimes can complement their domestic counterparts, which, as we shall see, the EU illustrates. After all, early modern mixed constitution theorists had the German Empire as their model.

Because the mixed constitution privileges neither rights nor democracy, it undermines both legal and political sovereignty. Demands for new rights highlight this mutual dependence of rights and democracy and its essentially pre- and anti-sovereignty logic.[43] It is sometimes argued that progressive change depends on either a political sovereign able to compel powerful social groups to give up their privileges, or a legal sovereign able to curb majority or minority tyranny by upholding individual rights. But arguably quite the opposite is the case. Calls for new rights generally challenge the

---

[42] Above n 41 Bellamy, *Liberalism and Pluralism*, Ch 4.

[43] What follows draws on and develops themes in J Tully, 'The Agonic Freedom of Citizens' (1999) 28 *Economy and Society* 161 and R Bellamy, 'The "Right to have Rights": Citizenship Practice and the Political Constitution of the EU' in R Bellamy and A Warleigh (eds) *Citizenship and Governance in the European Union*, (London, Continuum, 2001) and Tully, 'The Unfreedom of the Moderns' above n 31.

prevailing ways politics and law are constituted. Standardly, they involve political recognition for new categories of people and legal recognition of new types of claim, both of which are linked to altering the way power is shared and distributed by reconstituting the 'polity' and 'regime'. From this perspective, sovereignty merely entrenches the domination of hegemonic groups. Therefore, widening the practice of dialogue involves further fragmenting rather than strengthening sovereignty. For example, the demand for workers' social and economic rights went hand in hand with the demand for the vote. They claimed these rights on the basis of an entitlement to citizenship, as being capable of taking part in a process of public justification concerning the ways they should be treated equally or unequally to others. As a result, they criticised the prevailing definitions of both people and rights for being inconsistent with the practice of dialogue. They questioned property as a qualification for voting and a largely negative conception of rights that blocked interfering with the ways property-owners conducted their business. The constitutive and regulative rules of the dialogical game were dramatically changed as a result. Thus, the nature of the 'polity' altered as the economy became a legitimate sphere for political regulation and workers were recognised as active rather than passive subjects. The character of the 'regime' similarly altered as new 'styles' of politics, such as mass parties and union activism, became accepted, and the 'scope' of politics came to embrace more interventionist and redistributive policies. These alterations to the 'polity' and 'regime' produced new forms of sharing and distributing power through schemes such as industrial democracy and corporatism. For it is only through dispersing power in this way that rights gains can ultimately be secured and maintained. Later movements for women's and multicultural rights have followed a very similar trajectory.

Law and politics play complementary roles in these campaigns. The judiciary and legal system operates as an important counter to democracy, ensuring that legislation is consistently applied and forms part of a coherent body of law. It stabilises the *status quo*, so that citizens know where they stand and can plan ahead, and can even be the starting point for an internal critique of the existing system when it fails to live up to its own standards. Though distinct, however, law does not have an authority that is entirely separated from or superior to politics, based on some putative fundamental values that are immune to political criticism. For it is through politics that law, including constitutional law, is promulgated and legitimised. So rights campaigns are first and foremost political in nature, seeking to change the political and hence the legal constitution of the system, opening both to fuller forms of public justification. As we saw, these changes generally involve introducing greater diversity in both the loci and forms of civic participation. These innovations include multiplying the sites of legal decision-making and rendering legal procedures more consultative and accessible. In some circumstances, limited entrenchment of certain rights may be advisable to guard against myopia or carelessness on the part of the legislature, but this too must involve some form of democratic entrenchment. Meanwhile, appeal to democracy does not rest on the sovereignty of any given *demos* because the construction of the people is also contested within these democratic dialogues, and new forms of civic identity asserted that multiply the range of *demoi* participating within the system. Think of the way transnational social movements have challenged the sovereigntist's view of the *demos* as territorially located.

A mixed constitution is well suited to pluralist and complex societies, allowing policies to be responsive to local difference without the weakening of governance or concern with the common good that sovereignty theorists fear. Dispersing power obtains a hearing for the diverse preferences and reasons of different individuals, ensuring the peculiar circumstances of particular contexts get taken into account. General rules can be tailored to a wide variety of objects and concerns, and their implementation and monitoring enacted to meet the special requirements of a given situation and constituency. In certain cases, specific norms can even be established to meet special circumstances and relevant differences. However, respect for plurality is always balanced against the need to engage with the collectivity. Sharing and distributing sovereignty not only gives minorities a degree of autonomy, but also curbs their ability to act arbitrarily or independently, thereby promoting collaboration that recognises difference. Consequently, strong government action is fostered rather hindered. Because positive measures must be devised in ways that take into account the variations typical of highly differentiated societies, they are both fairer and more efficient. As a result, they have greater legitimacy and are more likely to be undertaken and implemented.

It might be argued that talk of pre-sovereignty seems at best misleading and at worst impractical and incoherent after three centuries when politics has been dominated by claims to sovereignty. But in circumstances in which these claims have proliferated and entered into conflict with each other, the republican approach is effectively to mix these different quasi-sovereign agents and agencies so they cancel each other out, thereby de-sovereigntising sovereignty. The potential for a shift to a mixed sovereignty system is well illustrated by the EU. I remarked earlier how the EU has been portrayed as betwixt and between a sovereign and a post-sovereign system, being both intergovernmental and federal, on the one hand, and a regulative rights-based legal regime, on the other. Yet some of these apparently paradoxical features, along with many of its achievements, arguably arise from the EU's having evolved into a mixed sovereignty system. Recent analyses of the EU have stressed its 'multi-level' nature, involving a mixture of sub-state, state, and supra-state actors and decision-making fora. As a result, authority is now shared (and contested) between national executives and actors operating above and below the state, such as the European Parliament and the regions respectively.[44] Moreover, these multiple levels coalesce in different ways according to the policy area. No one set of institutions is ultimately responsible for all competences, whilst the membership and character of these institutions varies. For example, foreign, monetary and social policy require different types of agreement between different sorts of actors concerning different policy spheres and affecting different sets of people. This multi-levelled structure is also reflected in the interaction between EU law and that of the member states. At least since 1964, the European Court of Justice has considered the Community (now Union) as constituting a distinct legal order, with its own internal norms of validity.[45] However, there is no European *Grundnorm* or *demos* underlying this European constitutional order, qualifying it as a 'higher' order to those of the member states. Rather, it exists along side, and occasionally in tension with, the legal orders of the member states, each of which also possesses distinct norms of validity, including distinct criteria concerning the relevant situations where EU law applies and is valid. The application and enforcement of rights and obligations under EU law remain matters for the authorities of the member states. Each must individually obtain democratic approval either directly, through referenda, or indirectly, through the national parliament, for any major legislative changes arising from further European integration, and national courts justify their acceptance of Community law by reference to these domestic processes.[46]

From the perspectives of the sovereignty and post-sovereignty positions, the EU structures can appear messy and incoherent. On the one hand, political supremacy appears to lie with neither the member states nor the supra-state organs of the EU, but between them all in differing ways and combinations according to the policy area. On the other hand, the juridification of this regime is similarly partial and unclear. European legal norms exist, but they do not have a clear-cut constitutional supremacy as a 'higher law' above the legal norms or even the political decisions of the member states. By contrast, from a mixed sovereignty point of view, this situation represents a highly desirable state of affairs. It represents a distribution and sharing of sovereign power between the different peoples of Europe that obliges them to negotiate collective policies in ways that reflect the various interests and values of those concerned. Thus, Neil MacCormick has seen the sharing of legislative authority between the European Parliament, the Council and the Commission as conforming to the rationale of a mixed

---

[44] Above n 30 Marks, Hoogue and Blank, 'European Integration from the 1980s', 341–2.
[45] See *Costa v ENEL*, [1964] ECR 585.
[46] See N MacCormick, 'The Maastricht-Urteil: Sovereignty Now' (1995) 1 *European Law Journal* 255 and J Weiler, 'European Democracy and the Principle of Toleration', in F Cerutti and E Rudolph (eds.), *A Soul for Europe: Vol 1 A Reader*, (Leuven, Peeters, 2001)

constitution—producing a healthy balance between transnational, national and supranational interests.[47] It could be added that their deliberations are increasingly supplemented by other channels of representation for other sorts of political subjects, with selected functional interests being represented in the Economic and Social Committee (ESC) and the obscure comitology process, sub-national interests in the Committee of the Regions (CR), and so on.[48]

Of course, there is no denying the many shortcomings of these arrangements—the purely consultative role of the ESC and the CR, the imperfect balance between large, medium and small states, the difficulties of getting transnational interests represented, and the relatively weak democratic accountability of government representatives on European matters, amongst other failings.[49] But these problems should not obscure the central achievement of this mixed sovereignty system—namely, the reciprocal modification of national interests, both vis-à-vis each other and increasingly with regard to their sub-national communities, and their collaboration in promoting collective interests. This process of negotiation and compromise has been as true of the development of EU law, where human rights policy evolved through successive challenges by various national constitutional courts to the ECJ, as it has been of EU politics.[50] A reassertion of sovereignty at either the national or the European level would not only remove this delicate balance but also be deeply delegitimising. For if integration has not created a European identity, it has produced a profound modification and partial Europeanisation of national identities. At the same time, the weak governance and poor accountability typical of a largely regulatory and juridical regime remain the EU's chief shortcoming, and would only be intensified by it moving further towards a post-sovereign system. Instead, attention should be focused on improving the EU's mixed constitution in ways that further enhance the reciprocal interaction and dialogues between its multiple *demoi* and levels of governance.

---

[47] N MacCormick, 'Democracy, Subsidiarity, and Citizenship in the "European Commonwealth" ' (1997) 16 *Law and Philosophy* 33. See too P Craig, 'Democracy and Rule-making Within the EC: An Empirical and Normative Assessment' (1997) 3 *European Law Journal* 105 and Bellamy and Castiglione, 'Democracy, Sovereignty and the Constitution of the European Union' above n 10.

[48] D Curtin, *Postnational Democracy: The European Union in Search of a Political Philosophy* (The Hague: Kluwer Law International, 1997).

[49] PC Schmitter, *How to Democratize the European Union . . . And Why Bother?* (Maryland: Rowman and Littlefield Publishers, Inc., 2000).

[50] Eg *Internationale Handelsgesellschaft* Case 11/70 [1970] ECR 1125 p. 1134, *Internationale Handelsgesellschaft* [1974] 2 CMLR 549., *Nold v Commission* [1974] ECR 503, *Frontini v Ministero delle Finanze* [1974] 2 CMLR 372, *Rutili v Minister for the Interior* Case 36/75 [1975] ECR 1219, *Nicolo* [1990] 1 CMLR 173.

5. CONCLUSION

This chapter has challenged the contrast between sovereignty and post-sovereignty. If the one prioritises politics, the other makes law supreme. Each has its drawbacks, and neither ultimately proves possible. The first risks equating might with right, while the second overlooks how right needs the might resulting from the assent of those to whom it applies to be effective and legitimate. Both wrongly assume that sovereign power cannot be divided—in the first case thereby justifying a concentration of power, in the second ignoring the power wielded by organs other than the state—including the courts. Finally, though each presents itself as a solution to the problem of an absence of unity, each ends up proposing a unity as the source of political or legal sovereign authority—be it a homogenous *demos* or a consensus on rights. A pre-sovereign system escapes these difficulties. It shares and distributes sovereignty in ways that remove the arbitrary power of any single agent or agency. Through the resulting democratic negotiation between peoples, laws have to be publically justified in ways that give due recognition to difference. The multiplicity of sites of governance and decision-making also enables them to be implemented more efficiently and with greater sensitivity to local variations. Thus, unity is constructed via a dialogue amongst a plurality, with the one being continually challenged, renegotiated and reconstructed as the other evolves and becomes more diverse. The doctrine of sovereignty was developed alongside the development of the modern state. As that political formation begins to fragment, it seems highly appropriate to return to the ideas and institutional structures it sought to supplant.

8

Sovereignty and Plurinational Democracy: Problems in Political Science

MICHAEL KEATING

1. THE ELUSIVE CONCEPT OF SOVEREIGNTY

THIS CHAPTER HAS two aims. The first is to discuss the concept of sovereignty within the discipline of political science, and how political scientists have sought to come to terms with 'late sovereignty'. The second is a discussion of one aspect of this, the rise of new claims on the part of stateless nations, challenging not only the state in which they are located but the very idea of the sovereign nation-state itself. My argument is that these may provide examples of new forms of politics with a democratising potential and an ability to contribute to thinking about the restructuring of political authority in late modernity.

It is a great paradox that the discipline of political science, so concerned with the distribution of power and legitimate authority, has given rather little attention to the concept of sovereignty. Political scientists have thus found themselves ill equipped to address issues of sovereignty in transition. They talk rather more about the state but here too there is a great deal of semantic confusion and a lot of unquestioned assumptions by political scientists brought up within a national tradition and unable to escape from its assumptions. Two of these are particularly problematic. The first is the connections between concepts of the state and sovereignty. For some, sovereignty is a predicate, whose addition to the noun 'state' amplifies or qualifies its meaning. For others, sovereignty seems to be a defining characteristic of the state. If we follow the logic of the former we should be able to talk of sovereign non-state entities and of non-sovereign states. If we follow the latter, we have a terminological redundancy. A second redundancy arises in the expression nation-state, often used to refer simply to the state itself rather than as a way of adding something or of distinguishing nations and states. Reduced to tautological or purely formal conceptions of sovereignty, political science has proved unable to come to terms with its subtleties, its variations and its transformations in late modernity.

Some of the reasons for this are to be found in the mundane matter of the division of labour within the social sciences; others within the national traditions in which political science has emerged; and others in the historical epoch in which political science came to maturity coinciding with a specific phase in the evolution of the sovereign state. There is a long-standing division of roles among scholars of international relations; of political theory (or as it used, more accurately, to be called, political philosophy); and of comparative politics (the heart of 'political science'). For international relations specialists, the sovereign state is the central object of analysis, so much so that any suggestion that it may be transcended is sometimes seen as a threat to the discipline itself. While this gives sovereignty a central place in IR analysis, it does not always encourage an analysis of the concept itself. Political theorists have given a great deal of attention to the idea of sovereignty as a normative concept and have been able in recent years to engage in a fruitful dialogue with legal scholars. Yet they have struggled to reconcile their universalist normative principles with a world in which authority is divided into separate jurisdictions which, according to the principle of sovereignty, are ultimately self-validating. Comparative political scientists have tended to give such normative matters a wide berth, leaving them to the theorists. This in turn is explicable by the positivistic bias of political science since its emergence in the late nineteenth century and particularly since the 'behavioural revolution' of the 1960s, with its search for universal rules and forms of explanation.

Political science grew up along with and within the modern state and, when it has not simply taken it for granted, has tended to celebrate it. The political development school of the 1960s and 1970s rather explictly saw the western state as representing a higher stage of political evolution and a norm to which other polities should aspire. Modernisation (itself a rather loaded concept), economic progress, liberalism and democracy were all presented not merely as coinciding with the consolidated territorial state but as the product of it. Counter-tendencies could be dismissed as part of the 'revolt against modernity'[1] in much the way that opposition to market economics is treated in the early twenty-first century. This tendency also allowed political scientists to handle the problem of legitimacy, distinguishing it from mere legality, which could be the product of a backward regime, as well as from mere power. Legitimacy remained a difficult issue but could be brought within the positivistic and behaviourist fold by treating it as a function of the consent of the governed and the satisfaction of the criteria

---

[1] Seymour Martin Lipset, 'The Revolt against Modernity', in *Consensus and Conflict. Essays in Political Sociology* (New Brunswick, NK, Transaction, 1975).

of political modernisation. This in turn reinforced the statist assumptions since the state came, *faute de mieux*, to be the sole fount of legitimate authority.

Within this broad consensus, there were certainly national variations, although political science has been dominated to probably a greater degree than any other discipline except economics, by the United States and so has absorbed American national traditions into the comparative mainstream. In the United States, the issue of sovereignty was definitively resolved by 1865 and no-one has been willing to question it since. This has allowed the issue to fade into the background so that domestic politics is treated as a pluralistic game in which groups trade off gains and losses in a form of mutual accommodation.[2] It is as though the state was not there, although the 1980s saw a rather extraordinary (to European eyes) debate about 'bringing the state back in' to analysis. American international relations specialists tend to the other extreme, reifying the state, treating it as a unitary actor, and endowing it with an interest and a strategy. The yawning gulf between these two perspectives has been perpetuated by the existence of separate disciplines, with all the infrastructure of university departments, journals and conferences and the general process of socialising emerging generations. The division has in recent years been brought over to Europe by US scholars studying European integration, and has revived the old debate between neo-functionalists and intergovernmentalists. Among European scholars there is a division between the British, who have tended, like the Americans, to assume the state away in analysis of domestic politics, and continentals who have elevated it to a mystical status, largely beyond question. None of these approaches has equipped political scientists for a world in which the sovereign state is challenged from above and below, in relation both to its functional capacity and to its normative claims. These problems can be illustrated through an examination of three issues: the Westphalian paradigm; the concept of the nation-state; and the debate on the transformation of the state.

2. THE WESTPHALIAN PARADIGM

It is a staple of international relations and of most political science that the system of sovereign states was established by the Peace of Westphalia (often

---

[2] Thinking in the heyday of behaviouralism is summed up in Nettl's critical comments, 'The concept of the state is not much in vogue' (p.559) and 'nowadays the problem of sovereignty is, for social scientists, a dead duck' (p.560). Nettl did add that the state nevertheless 'retains a skeletal, ghostly existence largely because, for all the changes in emphasis and interest of research, the thing exists and no amount of conceptual restructuring can dissolve it' (p.559). JP Nettl, 'The State as a Conceptual Variable, (1968) 20 *World Politics*, pp. 559–92.

referred to erroneously as the Treaty of Westphalia) which ended the Thirty Years War in 1648. Unfortunately, neither the Treaty of Munster or that of Osnabrück contains any reference to sovereignty or to anything like the sovereign state.[3] It did provide for the 'nationalisation' of religion as a way of coping with a problem that had threatened public order over the previous hundred years but this can scarcely be its main legacy since European countries have long abandoned the idea that religious uniformity is a defining task of the state. It did not establish the present system of European states, and indeed the only state which still has its 1648 borders is Portugal. On the contrary, its main achievement was the prolongation of the Holy Roman Empire for another 150 years. The Westphalian fallacy seems to arise from a teleological interpretation of what happened in the subsequent three hundred years and an assumption that the seeds must have lain in this event. This is unfortunate since it appears to close off other possible historical trajectories and obscure other traditions which may be of relevance in our present day circumstances of 'late sovereignty'.

Leaving these issues aside for the moment, Westphalian scholars generally hold that state sovereignty is absolute and indivisible, and has an external dimension and an internal one.[4] The external dimension is summarised by Held[5] in seven propositions:

> The world consists of, and is divided by, sovereign states which recognise no superior authority.
> The process of law-making, the settlement of disputes and law enforcement are largely in the hands of individual states.
> International law is orientated to the establishment of minimal rules of co-existence; the creation of enduring relationships among states and peoples is an aim, but only to the extent that it allows national political objectives to be met.
> Responsibility for wrongful cross-border acts is a 'private matter' concerning only those affected.
> All states are regarded as equal before the law; legal rules do not take account of asymmetries of power.
> Differences among states are ultimately settled by force; the principle of effective power holds sway. Virtually no legal fetters exist to curb the resort to force; international legal standards afford minimal protection.
> The minimisation of impediments to state freedom is the 'collective' priority.

Internal sovereignty means that the state has complete control over its territory and ultimate authority within it. The external sovereignty argument is an important foundation for the 'realist' school in international relations and their assumption that the state has an interest in maintaining

---

[3] A Osiander, *The States System of Europe, 1640–1990. Peacemaking and the Conditions of International Stability* (Oxford, Clarendon, 1994).
[4] Robert Jackson, 'Sovereignty at the Millenium', (1999) 47 *Political Studies*, pp. 423–30.
[5] David Held, *Democracy and the Global Order* (Cambridge, Polity, 1995), p.78.

its own sovereignty and autonomy and expanding its influence. The internal sovereignty argument is the basis for most political science, which sees states as self-contained self-regulating systems.

Yet there are serious problems with both dimensions of the state sovereignty paradigm. A common one is that some states lack the power and resources for any kind of autonomous action, while other non-state entities may have a great deal of power. Westphalians will dismiss this objection easily by pointing out that sovereignty is a legal principle which has nothing whatever to do with power, which is another matter altogether. A slightly different way out is to distinguish between *de facto* and de jure sovereignty[6] where *de facto* sovereignty appears to mean de jure sovereignty plus the ability to exercise it in practice. In one sense, they are of course right since power and legitimacy are two different things, but in an other the response is too facile. If sovereignty is a legal principle, it must surely be rooted in a system of law and, according to the Westphalian paradigm, there is no system of international law to sanction it. Indeed, if there were such a system one might argue that it and not the individual states, was the repository of sovereignty. Resorts to recognition by the United Nations or by other states merely beg the question. Once we bring in a distinction between factual power and legitimate power or sovereignty, we are on the slippery ground of normative concepts, a terrain in which political scientists are all too prone to fall down. As for international relations, there is surely something anomalous in scholars subscribing to a 'realist' perspective on world politics appealing to essentially normative principles to distinguish the state from other forms of organised power.

On the internal dimension of sovereignty, an objection is often lodged by federalists who note that certain states divide sovereign power among two levels of government, neither of which is competent to trespass in the reserved fields of the other. The answer of the Westphalians is that this is merely an internal matter, which leaves the external dimension of sovereignty and thus the sovereignty of the state in its entirety unchanged. Yet this is to evade the question. It does not address the issue of internal sovereignty directly and, in so far as there are implications for the 'internal' doctrine it implies that violations of federal order have no remedy. In particular, federated units whose powers are curtailed by federal governments cannot seek redress in secession or in appeals to outside powers.

3. THE NATION-STATE

Further confusion is introduced into the debate by the term 'nation-state'. For many political scientists and IR scholars, this is synonymous with the

---

[6] *Ibid* p.82.

sovereign state, and the term itself is often used as an inseparable compound. This is confusing indeed since if states are by definition sovereign, then no prefix at all is needed. If we want to emphasis sovereignty, on the other hand, why resort to the prefix 'nation' which introduces another whole set of ideas and associations altogether? Where it does not stem from simple confusion or sloppy thinking, the term nation-state may refer to two quite separate ideas; that states are in practice made of nations; or the basis for endowing the state with sovereign authority lies in the nationality principle. One is an empirical argument and the other a normative one. The normative argument is that political authority must rest upon consent and that the national community is the best basis for this. Self-determination, the principle that states should reflect communities of consent, is thus a foundation for democracy. Shared national identity is also, for some liberals like J.S. Mill, a condition for a liberal democracy, since it provides the shared values and trust that are needed to underpin a liberal order. Closing the circle, it is then possible to argue that the sovereign nation state in which the boundaries of the demos correspond to those of political authority is a necessary if not sufficient condition for democratic life. Unfortunately, as Jáuregui[7] notes, this ensures democracy within the nation state only at the cost of a complete absence of democracy in the international order.

The most common objection to the principle of basing sovereign statehood on nationality, however, is that nationality is itself impossible to define or agree on. Gellner, Connor[8] and many others have recounted that there are thousands of 'nations' in the world and not enough states to go around. For the most part these objections can be dismissed as resting on another conceptual confusion, between ethnic groups or even language groups, and nations, and on the assumption that every group will wish to constitute itself into a sovereign state. In fact, many nations are ethnically heterogeneous, including some with extremely strong national identities (like the United States). As for language this is just one possible criterion on which national identity might rest; there are nations without their own language and language groups without their own nationality. Nationality cannot be defined as a descriptive category or reduced to some other, measurable attribute like language. It is rather a normative concept, combining elements of objective criteria with a subjective sense of common identity, and the demand to be treated as a distinct entity with its own collective rights. Groups defining themselves as nations are thus advancing a claim to

---

[7] Gurutz Jáuregui, *La democracia planetaria* (Oviedo, Nobel, 2000).
[8] Ernest Gellner, *Nations and Nationalism* (Oxford, Blackwell, 1983); Walker Connor, 'A Nation is a Nation is a State, is an Ethnic Group, is a . . .' (1978) 1 *Ethnic and Racial Studies*, pp. 379–400.

self-determination and to be constituted as a subject in the political order. To put it slightly differently, then, they are making claims to sovereignty.

Political science and international relations have had considerable difficulty in coming to terms with this issue, since they once again identify sovereignty with the state and assume that the only means for its exercise lies in secession and the creation of a new state. For the IR mainstream new states may be created by secessions or decolonisation but this merely confirms the validity and ubiquity of the principle of sovereign statehood itself. Indeed for James[9] it appears that recognition by the original state is the key criterion for the transfer of sovereignty. Comparative politics specialists have written a great deal on nationalism and secession as a problem of political stability and management but have also tended to take their units of analysis for granted. Political theorists are tied to a universalist form of reasoning in which no principle is valid unless it can be applied everywhere in a consistent manner. Since there is no agreement on what constitutes a nation, what the boundaries of nations are, or how many nations exist, we cannot construct a general right of self determination on such a flimsy basis.[10] Consequently political scientists, including IR specialists, theorists and comparativists have been almost unanimously opposed to the idea of secession, since they have been unable to find a political principle to justify it. Yet they have been almost equally unanimous in not feeling any need to justify the existing state system or pattern of sovereign authority.

The result is to reinforce the conservative status and role of political science. The existing state system is taken as not only a constellation of power but as embodying powerful normative principles such as sovereignty and nationality. Yet these are the very principles whose incoherence and lack of operational application are used to knock down arguments for other forms of political order including secessionist states or the relocation of sovereignty. Now it may be that a Hobbesian argument can be made to the effect that present states and boundaries at least guarantee order and that to change them risks destabilising the whole social system. Secession might be imprudent, or bad policy, but this is not a fundamentally ethical matter. It would not justify the whole ideological apparatus constructed by political science to defend the nation state unless we assume that political scientists are the organic intellectuals whose role is to legitimate the power structure.

---

[9] Alan James, 'The Practice of Sovereign Statehood in Contemporary International Society', (1996) 47 *Political Studies*, pp. 457–73.
[10] Wayne Norman, 'The Ethics of Secession as the Regulation of Secessionist Politics' in Margaret Moore, (ed.), *National Self-Determination and Secession* (Oxford, Oxford University Press, 1998).

4. CHALLENGES TO SOVEREIGNTY

None of this mattered a great deal in the heyday of state-centred political science in the twentieth century, especially during the Cold War. It has, however, left political science ill-prepared for a new order in which the relationship between state and nation is called into question and in which new normative orders are emerging, above, below and beyond the state.

Scholars have given a lot of attention to the functional restructuring of the state, its supposed loss of decisional autonomy and the fragmentation of public power. The panoply of effects caught by the term globalisation includes economic, cultural and political changes. Rapid capital mobility and the rise of transnational corporations are said to constrain the power of states to manage their national economies and to undermine the very notion of national economies. The ability of capital to opt out of social responsibilities by relocating is said to undermine national welfare states and force governments into similar programmes of restructuring. Cultural globalisation, or perhaps just the extension of American cultural norms, are seen to threaten national cultures, ways of life and even identity. Consequently, the whole social and political balance underpinning the mixed economy welfare state is disintegrating. This has spawned a huge literature pitching globalisation theorists against those who insist that nothing much has changed; and economic determinists for whom states must bow to global markets, against those who still believe that states can act to promote their own distinctive goals. This is not the place to resolve these arguments, although I believe that while globalisation does matter, its use by economic and political elites to construct a world vision in which other policy options are closed is even more important. Globalisation has coincided with an ideological assault on the state by neo-liberals. Either way, globalisation and its interpretation have helped break the mystique of the state and forced a reconsideration of the structures in which politics is conducted. Whether they represent the end of sovereignty[11] is another matter.

A second set of factors is represented by institutional change. States have conceded powers and authority to transnational bodies in a range of areas, including economic regulation, human rights and security and, in Europe, are in the process of constructing a whole new polity. At the same time, many states have been devolving power to lower levels so that all the large European states now have an intermediate or 'meso' level of government. These devolved or federated governments have in turn started to engage in politics at the European level and to conduct a variety of 'paradiplomatic'

---

[11] J Camilleri, and J Falk, *The End of Sovereignty? The Politics of a Shrinking and Fragmenting World* (Aldershot, Edward Elgar, 1992).

activities beyond the state borders. As the old model of state economic management breaks down, regions are increasingly seen as productive systems in their own right and pitched directly into global markets in competition with each other for capital, markets, technology and labour.

These changes pose serious challenges to traditional thinking about states, nations and sovereignty, but there has been a variety of responses. For some, functional restructuring and institutional change do not fundamentally alter the nature of the state or its sovereignty, since sovereignty is about something else. So there is nothing to stop states using their sovereign authority to reject globalisation, although there may be a heavy cost. Membership of the European Union, still less of other transnational organisations, does not curtail sovereignty since states can always withdraw and in any case these organisations are based precisely on the existence of state sovereignty and draw their authority from it. Devolution to sub-state governments can be reversed either by a simple state law (in the United Kingdom) or by constitutional amendment elsewhere. There is more difficulty in the case of federal states like Germany or Canada, where the central government owes its existence to the same constitutional document as the federated units but, as noted above, the supporters of the state sovereignty principle manage to evade this issue by insisting that 'external' sovereignty is still absolute.

Another group appears to identify the loss of functional authority as a loss of sovereignty itself. There is a whole raft of books on the demise of the nation-state including Kenichi Ohmae's piece of functional reductionism, which equates the rise of regional economies with the end of the nation-state itself, without the need even of a question mark.[12] In his vision, the end of the state and its sovereignty is a thoroughly good thing, allowing the market to remain as the sole principle of legitimacy. This chimes with public choice analysis which has become very influential in political science in recent years, and which holds that the sole principle of legitimation is individual self-gratification. States are mere mechanisms for facilitating this and have no special status above other forms of social organisation. Indeed, public choice advocates tend to be very suspicious of states and conceptions of sovereignty as obstacles to the expression of individual preferences and interests. Others are more concerned about the loss of sovereignty. Guéhenno writes of the end of the nation-state, a phenomenon which in the French version had been described as the end of democracy itself.[13] David Held moves from a discussion of sovereignty through the question of state autonomy to argue that at some point the principle of state sovereignty

---

[12] Kenichi Ohmae, *The End of the Nation State. The Rise of Regional Economies* (New York: Free Press, 1995).
[13] Jean-Marie Guéhenno, *Fin de la démocratie* (Paris, Flammarion, 1993); *The end of the nation-state* (Minneapolis, University of Minnesota Press, 1995).

itself is undermined.[14] Others have questioned the usefulness of the doctrine of sovereignty if it is progressively emptied of substantive content.

A third group have opted for a form of neo-pluralist analysis in which the sovereign state, seen as based on principles of hierarchy, gives way not to unbounded markets but to self-regulating networks. The term 'multilevel governance' has been applied to a way of thinking about the European Union that rejects both the intergovernmentalist and the neo-functionalist visions, as well as to the rise of regionalism and the increasing interpenetration of the public and private sectors.[15] This has its origins in organisational theory, which refuses to accord the state a privileged place in the analysis and sees sovereign authority as no more than one power resource among others, to be used in a process of mutual accommodation and bargaining.

All of these approaches raise serious problems at two levels, the analytical and the normative. The analytical need is for principles and concepts allowing us to explore issues of power and legitimacy. Normatively, the problem is how to find the bases of democratic community and control over government.

Simply denying that shifting constellations of power and functional capacity have anything to do with sovereignty is unhelpful. We can cope with some disjuncture between the formal claim of sovereignty and the real functional autonomy of the state, but if these become totally disconnected then the analytical value of the concept of sovereignty must come into question. It would also render discussion about the use of sovereign authority as the basis of democratic political control almost meaningless. The normative claims of sovereignty have always rested on a certain mystification of the state and both functional restructuring and ideological challenges have begun to break this too. The magic gone, people just stop believing in the absolute claims of the state.

As for the neo-liberal prophets of the end of sovereignty, they too are trapped in a contradiction. They may celebrate the end of state control of economic management and welfare but their followers in the political world tend to be well aware that maintaining a neo-liberal order requires a large repressive apparatus, combining the 'free economy and the strong state'.[16] Indeed the British Conservative Party in recent years has sought to combine a programme of rigorous anti-statism in economic matters with an increase in the repressive capacity of the state and an obsession about

---

[14] David Held, above, n 5.
[15] Gary Marks, Liesbet Hooghe and Kermit Blank, 'European Integration since the 1980s: State-centric Versus Multi-Level Governance', (1996) 36 *Journal of Common Market Studies*, pp. 343–78.
[16] Andrew Gamble, *The Free Economy and the Strong State. The Politics of Thatcherism* (London, Macmillan, 1988).

maintaining sovereignty in Europe. Sovereignty does seem to matter after all. Public choice advocates, who tend to be of a more libertarian disposition than the average British Tory, prefer to assume away the question of who will be making the rules, how they will be enforced and within what units they will operate.

Neo-pluralists in the multilevel governance school similarly tend to avoid questions about order and the maintenance of the rules of the game. By reducing the state to just one actor among many, they sidestep the question of legitimacy. Instead, the legitimacy of the process seems to be determined purely by its outcomes, or by the presence of multiple 'stakeholders' or, as they would have been called in the old days, interests. This violates a fundamental principle of liberal democratic order, that the process by which decisions are taken also matters a great deal too. As with other forms of pluralist analysis and organisation theory, the methods and choice of units of analysis preclude them from looking at these issues.[17]

5. STATELESS NATIONS AND SHARED SOVEREIGNTY

For some observers, the decline of the sovereign state represents a setback for democracy so that there is an urgent need to re-establish it or save it in something like its traditional form.[18] Others like Held[19] have called for new forms of global democracy. The problem is that most efforts to create this have involved somewhat improbable mechanisms at the global level, although one might think that the problems facing the old state would resurface again at this level, notably those of lack of power and the basis of legitimacy. Jáuregui is on firmer ground, arguing for a 'planetary democracy' based in emerging realities.[20] These include states but also the European Union and the claims of stateless nations.

Minority nationalism within democratic states has generally had a bad time from political scientists, regarded at one time as a pathology of the body politic, evidence of 'failed' state-building or retarded modernity or at best a 'problem' to be dealt with. Faced with the prestige and power of the sovereign state, minorities were required to demonstrate good reason for existing as collectivities, let alone making demands for self-government. They were caught in a conceptual trap in which, to gain any recognition they had to demonstrate that they were 'different'; but their very difference

---

[17] It is not adequate, as some have now proposed, to bolt on a normative dimension to organisationally based analysis, since the very framework rules out the big questions about sovereignty and authority that we are trying to address here.

[18] Ralph Dahrendorf, 'La sconfitta della vecchia democrazia', *La Repubblica*, 12 January 2000.

[19] David Held, above n 5.

[20] Gurutz Jáuregui, above n 7.

was then used to suggest that they failed to meet the universal liberal democratic criteria. In recent years, however, minorities in western European states (as well as other places like Canada) have been able to turn the tables on the states, themselves suffering from increasing problems of democratic performance and legitimacy. Minority nationalisms have tended to de-ethnicise, adopting the same inclusive and civic discourse that was previously the property of state-nationalism. They have, with some notable exceptions, tended to move towards the progressive side of politics and make common cause with new social movements. They have accepted globalisation less as a threat than an opportunity, and they have wholeheartedly embraced European integration.[21] Nor are the minorities marked by pronounced social and political 'difference'. Minority nationalism has increased in importance, although values have continued to converge between state majorities and minorities and, more generally, across Europe as a whole, an affect recalling de Tocqueville's paradox.[22] Nationalist movements have to a greater or lesser degree moved from demanding their own sovereign state to seeking a place in the new order of diffused authority and shared sovereignty.

In some ways, this makes the nationality issue more tractable, especially within the European political space. Yet on the other hand, it raises new and difficult issues. If stateless nations are no longer making particularist demands for special treatment, they are making broad claims to constitute the primary framework for social regulation. They are, as Langlois puts it, becoming 'global societies' rather than ethnic fragments.[23] They are also making claims to sovereign authority, not necessarily in the old exclusive manner of the nation-state, but to a sufficient degree to constitute themselves as subjects and not objects of constitutional debate. Usually this is expressed as a demand for self-determination, meaning not necessarily the right to establish their own state, but the demand to negotiate their own position within the emerging state and transnational order. So in the United Kingdom, Spain, Belgium and France, we see strong nationalist movements with substantial public support, none of which is seeking a state on traditional lines. Quebec nationalists have consistently linked their demand for 'sovereignty' with support for continued links to the rest of Canada. Flemish nationalists tend to support secession only in so far as they can be

---

[21] Michael Keating, *Nations against the State. The New Politics of Nationalism in Quebec, Catalonia and Scotland*, 2nd edition (London, Palgrave, 2001); *Plurinational Democracy. Stateless Nations in a Post-Sovereignty Era* (Oxford, Oxford University Press, 2001).
[22] Stéphane Dion, 'Le nationalisme dans la convergence culturelle. Le Québec contemporain et le paradoxe de Tocqueville', in R Hudon and R Pelletier (eds), *L'engagement intellectuel. Mélanges en l'honneur de Léon Dion* (Sainte-Foy, Presses de l'Université de Laval, 1991).
[23] Simon Langlois, 'Le choc des deux sociétés globales', in Louis Balthazar, Guy Laforest and Vincent Lemieux, *Le Québec et la restructuration du Canada, 1980–92* (Saint-Laurent, Septentrion, 1991).

absorbed into a tighter European union. Catalonia's dominant coalition, Convergència i Unió is quite forthright in rejecting independence and ties this to a historic vision of Catalonia before 1714 as a self-governing trading nation within the Crown of Aragon, linked to Spain and operating in the wider Mediterranean and European arenas. Even the more independence-minded Esquerra Republicana de Catalunya wants separation from Spain only when a European federation is available to take its place. Basque nationalists tend to be more separatist but are still mostly in favour of a post-sovereign order similar to the Catalan vision. The most classically statist is the Scottish National Party, which seeks independence within the European Union, but even it is divided between those who want full statehood and a post-sovereigntist wing. The Welsh nationalist party, Plaid Cymru, has eschewed independence in favour of Welsh self-government within the emerging European order. Public opinion in these places generally follows a similar line, refusing to make a hard and fast distinction between home rule and independence, favouring more self-government but not interested in taking on all the classical functions of statehood, such as defence and security or monetary autonomy.[24]

Their justifications for their demands are based on two grounds, which are not always deployed together or, where they are, not always in a consistent manner. These are that they are historically constituted nations with original rights which were never surrendered to the state; and that they are a self-conscious community expressing a democratic demand. So one leg of the argument rests in the past and the other in the present. Now it is easy to mock the idea of historic rights and to point to the degree of invention in nationalist historiography. It is also easy to say that if we were to concede self-determination to any group that expressed a desire for it, the world would be unmanageable. These are indeed the standard answers in the political science literature. Yet these two grounds are, if we are to be candid, the very bases upon which political science upholds the sovereignty of the existing states (or fails to question it). Now that the states are losing their mystique and are challenged from above and from below, they are being forced to justify their own sovereign claims, and do so in rather different ways.

Stateless nations with their own governments have now consolidated the argument as modern institutions have claimed to custodianship of these historic rights. The Scottish Parliament, according to the continuing Westminster doctrine, is the creature of British statute and could be abolished tomorrow with a one-line bill. Yet almost nobody in Scotland believes this.[25] Quebec politicians are almost unanimous that the Canadian federa-

---

[24] A fuller analysis is given in Michael Keating, *Plurinational Democracy*, above n 21.
[25] The Labour Party has faced both ways, signing the Declaration of Right of the Scottish Constitutional Convention, that sovereignty rests with the Scottish people, and then insisting in the Scotland Act 1998(s.27) that Westminster sovereignty is as absolute as ever.

tion is based upon a bargain between the French Canadian (now Quebec) nation and English Canada so that repatriation of the constitution in 1982 without the assent of the Quebec National Assembly was illegitimate. Basque politicians claim that their historic rights, or fueros, are original rights prior to the 1978 Spanish constitution, while their counterparts in Madrid insist that they are the gift of the Spanish state. Catalan politicians have less by way of legal continuity on which to base their claims, but will insist that Catalonia never surrendered its sovereign rights and can therefore negotiate its own place in Spain and Europe. It is not just the nationalists in these cases who are making these claims; they are shared also by those who would use their self-determination to remain within the host state.

We thus have a paradox, that sovereignty is said to be ebbing away, but new sovereignty claims are being made all the time. Yet these, by and large, are not the expansive claims of the classic 'nation-state' but claims rather to recognition as legitimate actors in complex systems of authority. If historic rights have gained new currency in the argument over power and authority, it is not because people are looking to the past as a model for the future, but because these are ways of establishing their credentials. As Herrero de Miñon puts it, they are claims not to do but to be.[26]

Political science has not yet developed the conceptual tools to address this constellation of authority but there are some elements that might be pressed into service. Rokkan and Unwin identify the 'union state' as a category distinct from both federal and unitary states. In the union state, the various parts or some of them, came into the union on special terms and retain elements of their old rights and institutions.[27] The concept, never developed further by its authors, has been taken up in recent years in relation to the United Kingdom and particularly the case of Scotland.[28] Elazar's concept of unions as a distinct form of state picks up the same idea.[29] An earlier formulation was Jellinek's idea of 'fragments of state' recently brought into the Spanish debate by Herrero de Miñon.[30] A fragment of state is an entity with some of the attributes of a state (territory, subjects and government in Jellinek's formulation) and the idea was clearly inspired by the crownlands and other territories of the Habsburg empire in the nineteenth century. It could equally apply, however, to Scotland, Catalonia, Quebec or the Basque Country.

---

[26] Miguel Herrero de Miñon, 'Estructura y Función de los Derechos Históricos: un problema y siete conclusiones', in Miguel Herrero de Miñon and Ernest Lluch (eds), *Foralismo, Derechos Históricos y Democracia* (Bilbao, Fundación BBV1998).
[27] Stein Rokkan, and Derek Urwin, *Economy, Territory, Identity. Politics of West European Peripheries* (London, Sage, 1983).
[28] James Mitchell, *Strategies for Self-government. The Campaigns for a Scottish Parliament* (Edinburgh, Polygon, 1996).
[29] Daniel J Elazar, *Exploring Federalism* (Tuscaloosa University of Alabama Press, 1987).
[30] Miguel Herrero de Miñon, *Derechos Históricos y Constitución* (Madrid, Tecnos, 1998).

So we have new ways of thinking about sovereignty, but these are also rooted in historic doctrines and practice, notably the notion of constitutions as a form of pact. Modernists have tended to dismiss these notions as part of the ancien régime, or as a feudal, mediaeval hangover having no place in mature constitutionalism. There is a certain metropolitan or statist bias here too, as when scholars dismiss the Scottish Declaration of Arbroath (1320) with its doctrines of Scottish sovereignty and limited kingship, as nothing more than a fabrication of monks at the behest of mediaeval barons, but laud Magna Carta as the foundation of English and, by extension, British democratic liberties. There is a similar tendency in Spain.[31] Centralists have taken the constitution of Cadiz (1820) as the foundation of the democratic Spanish nation, claiming that this over-rides pre-existing forms of sovereignty just as the French Revolution swept away the ancien regime and its privileges to focus sovereignty in the people. The demystification of the state stemming from its loss of functional capacity and the rise of other forms of normative order have made it less easy to make this sort of case, but such is the dependence of political science (and much other social science besides) that we do not yet have a new paradigm to encompass the new dispensation. I have, with some trepidation, used the term 'post-sovereignty' to capture that which is both new and old. Social scientists are given to resolving this type of terminological conundrum by resorting to the prefixes 'neo' and 'post', not abandoning the old terms but incorporating them in the new. The term 'post-industrial', for example does not denote the abandonment of industry—all post-industrial societies are industrial—but refers to a stage in which industrialism no longer provides the sole or main social paradigm. Post-modern, according to the Cambridge English Dictionary, 'includes features from different periods in the past or in the present and past.' So, unable to find a better alternative, I have been using the term 'post-sovereignty' not to denote an era in which sovereignty has disappeared but rather to denote its transmutation into other forms.

6. PLURINATIONAL DEMOCRACY AND THE FUTURE OF EUROPE

Political science has been very concerned with the question of democratic order, but has tended to see the sovereign nation-state as the sole possible container for it. It has therefore struggled with the normative aspects both of plurinationalism and of European integration. Proposals for democratising Europe have tended to take the form either of constituting it as a new form of state, albeit a federal one, or of strengthening the role of member states within it. Neither adequately responds to the needs of democratic development in contemporary conditions. It is well known that Europe does not possess a single demos such as might underpin a democratic order

[31] Mikel Sorauren, *Historia de Navarra, el Estado Vasco* (Pamplona, Pamiela. 1998).

modeled on the nation-state and, indeed, one of the main objects of the European project was to transcend this type of nationalism whose other side is aggression and xenophobia. Were it to become a state, or even to aspire to being one, then it would provoke a reaction from both state and stateless nationalists, who would resent it as a new form of domination. It would also rigidify its institutions and ways of working, depriving it of the flexibility that has proved its strength. A European state or federation would have to follow a specific model, as we see from the different visions of what it might look like coming from French and German enthusiasts.

Going back to the old sovereign-nation-state model is also ruled out, since I have been arguing that the three elements in this compound are separable in principle and increasingly separated in practice. Yet there is a democratic deficit. Complexity and the proliferation of levels of decision making do reduce democracy as power seeps from elected institutions into networks. If multilevel governance means anything, it is surely a highly undemocratic order in which organisational elites and those with the skills, time and resources to operate in complex sectoral and territorial networks have immense advantages over their fellow citizens. Democratic and accountable government is a complex matter but there would seem to be two basic requirements. The first is the existence of deliberative spaces for the formation of a democratic will. I am assuming here, against the Public Choice school, that citizens' democratic preferences are not the mere sum of individual desires, which could be left to the market or to referendums, but result from deliberation and exchange. It is these deliberative spaces that need to correspond to a sense of common or shared identity, or to a demos, if not an exclusive one. The second requirement is a system of accountability corresponding to the areas of decision making in the emerging functional systems. In a complex system with functional and territorial divisions, these can no longer always be done by the same institutions.

For example the European Parliament is probably as good as most national parliaments (admittedly not a difficult test) in scrutinising executive institutions and holding them to account (the fall of the Santer Commission is exemplary). It does not, on the other hand, sustain a pan-European deliberative community or help form a pan-European democratic will. It probably never will, and possibly never should. We may therefore need to delink these activities. Accountability and scrutiny may take a variety of forms—audit, legal control, parliamentary investigation, adversary politics—and work at various levels. Deliberative democracy and will formation can similarly occur at various levels. In some cases, the state remains the main focus. This is clearly so in Denmark, Portugal and Ireland, and is still largely true in the larger states of France and Germany. In Belgium, on the other hand, deliberation is increasingly confined to the two main linguistic communities. In the multinational states of Spain and the United Kingdom there are deliberative communities within the nations of

Catalonia, the Basque Country, Scotland and Wales, as well as at the state level. Northern Ireland presents further complexity, caught as it is between a UK community with which its links are weakening, an all-Irish community, and an Ulster or Northern Irish community.

There is in parts of the social science community a residual prejudice against recognising national communities other than states as deliberative communities or as the building blocks of democracy. Siedentop for example, referring to the historic regions of Europe insists that 'few such regions have any civic tradition, any tradition of democracy or citizenship in working order'.[32] Dahrendorf calling for a renewal of democratic citizenship in the face of transnationalism, insists that this should not rest on communities like Wales, Quebec or Catalonia on the grounds that these are divisive and produce rigidities.[33] Like Habermas[34] these writers seem to favour a kind of deracinated democracy, ignoring the specific cultural bases of their own societies or confusing them with a kind of cosmopolitan virtue. This amounts to a form of evasion, shirking the need to democratise communities of will where they exist and to embrace new forms of citizen involvement. Similarly, the frequent description of the emerging order as 'postnational' repeats the old conceptual confusion of nation and state. We may, I have argued, be in a post-sovereign era if sovereignty is identified with the old absolutely sovereign state. Nationality, on the other hand, is very much with us and remains one of the structuring principles of modern societies. What we need are new ways of connecting it to political order and a reformulated conception of sovereignty.

Stateless nations are not, of course, the only possible deliberative communities. Elsewhere, the pressures for participation and democratisation have favoured deliberative communities at the city level. This is notably the case in France, where decentralisation has strengthened the local level as a political arena, and in Italy, where the crisis of the central state has coincided with a revalorisation of the local level. In other cases again, the deliberative community might be a large region, beyond a city but without the characteristics of a stateless nation. In the limiting cases, democratic will and identity may be located at a very small scale, as in the small communes of many countries, which are too small to correspond to any functional system.

Deliberative democracy may therefore be located at various levels and stateless nations, far from being a problem for Europe, may serves as exem-

---

[32] Larry Siedentop, *Democracy in Europe* (London, Allen Lane, 2000), p. 175. Even more contentiously, Siedentop compares European regions unfavourably with the original American colonies, without mentioning slavery or the disenfranchisement of women.

[33] Ralph Dahrendorf, 'Preserving Prosperity', *New Statesmen and Society*, 13/29 December, 1995, pp. 36–40.

[34] Jürgen Habermas, 'Die postnationale Konstellation und die Zukunft der Demokratie', in *Die postnationale Konstellation. Politische Essays* (Frankfurt, Suhrkamp, 1998, pp. 91–167).

plars of such communities. Yet to create a democratic commonwealth, these communities must be linked and not isolated. This inter-communicative aspect of democracy is essential, with ideas and practices flowing from one to another and a continuing debate on the common good articulated at various levels.[35] Pillarised societies are ill-equipped to do this, as critics of consociational democracy have often pointed out. The relationship between English and French Canada has often been described as one of two solitudes, a tendency that may increase with the reassertion of nationalism on both sides. Belgium is in the process of falling into the same problem, as inter-communication between the two communities declines; it is fortunate in this case that both communities are part of a broader European communicative order. Northern Ireland is a deeply divided society, but there is now a conscious policy of building links across the communities, to the Republic, to the United Kingdom and to Europe. There is a historic fear in Scotland of parochialism, and this has placed a barrier in the path of home rule; it is greatly lessened in the European context. Similarly, the traditional isolation of much of Basque society is being overcome by linking it to other European communities. In this vision, the democratisation of Europe would come not through strengthening summit-level institutions on the assumption that they correspond to a unitary demos, but through a whole system of parliamentarism, linking Europe, states and sub-state levels.[36] Here again, Europe has a role to play, not as a hierarchically superior level of government or proto-state, but as an open and plural system underpinned by some shared values. European integration may not involve a direct assault on state sovereignty since, as has often been noted, it is the creation of states themselves. Yet it may permit a loosening of state monopolies and facilitate asymmetrical constitutional arrangements to allow the expression of multiple identities since it ensures that matters like market regulation and human rights will not diverge excessively.

Plurinational democracy is thus more than multilevel governance or anarchic pluralism. It rests on some structuring principles at both analytical and normative levels, locating democracy in communities of will, incorporating historic rights and current demands and recognising the needs of mutual accommodation. It assumes a body of shared democratic principles and human rights. It is not a blueprint for a new world, but a way of doing politics in a complex world where not only functional capacity but also normative claims to authority are dispersed.[37]

---

[35] James Tully, *Strange multiplicity. Constitutionalism in an age of diversity* (Cambridge, Cambridge University Press, 1995).
[36] Jean-Marc Ferry, 'Quel patriotisme au-delà des nationalismes? Réflexion sur les fondements motivationnnels d'une citoyenneté européenne', in Pierre Birnbaum (ed.), *Sociologie des nationalismes* (Paris, Presses Universitaires de France, 1997).
[37] These arguments are developed at greater length in Michael Keating, *Plurinational Democracy*, above n 21.

9

Discussing Sovereignty and Transnational Politics

JEF HUYSMANS

1. INTRODUCTION

T HIS CHAPTER FOCUSES on how imaginations of transnationalism raise questions about the concept of the political. What and where is politics in the context of transnational practices? More specifically, the chapter deals with the question whether transnational practice defies the assertion of sovereignty in international politics.

The point of departure of my argument is that the important question concerning the challenge posed by transnational developments to sovereignty is not whether transnational developments limit the degree of state authority and state control. Rather, the key question is to what extent re-imaginations of the location and nature of politics dilute or re-articulate the *matrix* of sovereignty. The matrix of sovereignty refers to a particular way of framing *the question* of the political. This conceptualisation of sovereignty emphasises that what is fundamentally at stake is not whether the state is withering away under the pressure of transnational developments but rather whether transnational developments facilitate a reworking of the framework of sovereignty.

I focus on two readings of how transnational developments re-articulate understandings of the 'international political'. To an extent both conceptualisations rework concepts of the political. However, the spectre of sovereignty does rise in the context of this reworking of the political. In itself this is not surprising. The framework of sovereignty is, after all, at the heart of modern imaginations of the political.[1] It is a political spectre—a haunting, ideational presence in reflections about the transformation of politics.

The first reading focuses on how transnational flows challenge the sovereignty of the state. Usually this means that flows of goods, people, capital and services defy control by the state and therefore limit the autonomy of state authority to govern its territorially conscripted society. For example, the argument that big companies need to be pampered because otherwise they will relocate their business to more beneficial locations assumes that governments have only limited control over the global movement of the means of production and that big companies can easily relocate their business. Loss of political control follows from the capacity of the industry to relocate its capital relatively quickly. In this understanding, the transnational flows are not in themselves political. They are economic, social and/or cultural. Their political significance follows from the incapacity of political authorities to meet the demand for political control of these flows. In so far as the demand and the incapacity to meet it exist, a political question, or more precisely, a question about the political arises: what and where is *politics and political authority in a transnationalising world?*

The second reading focuses on a more directly political understanding of transnationalism. Transnational political and social movements fight for a particular definition of the common good across territorial states. Their political significance does not derive primarily from a challenge to the capacity of the state to control flows of goods, capital, services, and people. Rather, they challenge the authority of the state to decide and sustain a definition of the common good by means of the formation of transnational political spaces and activities. In other words, transnationalism refers here to a relocation of politics itself. A classic example is an environmentalist movement mobilising consumers against particular oil companies in the name of the need to protect the environment, if need be at a serious economic cost. The environmentalist movement is most unlikely to be politically authorised in a traditional way (for example, through free elections) to decide the common good. These transnational *politics* also raise a question of the political, but one which is slightly different from the previous question: what and where is *transnational politics?*

The two questions are not the same. In the former case transnational developments trigger a question about conventional understandings of politics but they do not consist themselves in a reimagination of the political as transnational. The latter occurs in the second case when transnational practice articulates a transnational understanding of the political.

But, before presenting how the spectre of sovereignty may enter each of these understandings of transnationalism, I need briefly to indicate a few key elements of the spectre of sovereignty.

2. THE SPECTRE OF SOVEREIGNTY AND THE POLITICAL

Sovereignty is not first of all a principle of international law or a condition of territorially bound authority but it is a specific matrix that defines

---

[1] See R Walker *Inside/Outside: International relations as Political Theory*, (Cambridge, Cambridge University Press, 1993).

parameters that structure variations in the imagination of what constitutes proper politics. The spectre of sovereignty refers to the difficulty, if not, the impossibility, of escaping the matrix of sovereignty when imagining the political.

In this section, I wish to highlight two key dimensions of this matrix. The first is that the question of the political is a question of 'the possibility of contingent unity'.[2] The second is that sovereignty is tightly connected to a specific form of political governance, the rule of law. In addition, I wish to indicate how International Relations fixes problems of the political as they are raised within the matrix of sovereignty.

A. Sovereignty and unity

In a world of different opinions about what is right and wrong and what is good and bad the question arises of how some form of unity can be created among the diversity of opinions and people. In so far as common definitions of the good and/or of what is right and wrong cannot be established, the human world remains radically pluralistic. It consists of random encounters of diverse opinions.

The problem of the political in the matrix of sovereignty is how to create and sustain unity in a pluralistic world so as to overcome the problem of anomie—the absence of shared moral standards. By implication, any political community, which expresses and sustains unity, is a contingent, human creation that needs to be justified and reproduced. Why are national states the proper form of political community? Why not a form of world government? Why not define political unity in functional terms, such as the unity of the firm, or the unity of farmers, or the community of people wearing glasses?

Historically sovereignty has developed into a two-faced problem of unity. The immediate problem is the unification of the state, that is *the imposition of authority* to define common rules of what is right and wrong, what is good and bad.[3] This is the question of domestic politics and of the unification of the political community. This understanding of the question of the political produces another question: the nature of the plurality that exists in the relations between the authorities imposing unity among the different opinions, or in other words, the question of international politics.[4] One solution is to see relations between political communities as a practice of survival in the absence of a highest—that is sovereign—authority that defines and sanctions the rules of proper foreign policy. The political

---

[2] See Hans Lindahl's essay in the present volume.
[3] *Ibid* for extensive treatment.
[4] See R Walker, above n 1.

communities act on the basis of their own opinion and capabilities and therefore the inter-community interaction is radically plural. In the modern age—late 18th and 19th Century onwards in Europe and the US—however, the international system became increasingly a system of defining and sustaining the plurality of states. The international system becomes a political system which makes it possible for states to exist as sovereign states and thus for the plurality of opinion between political communities to continue.[5] In other words, the problem of the international political is not simply a question of the existence of a radical pluralism but is first of all a question of unity—of the common understanding of international politics within which the existence of a plurality of states is guaranteed.[6]

The invention of the international as a particular sphere of the political implies that the problem of political unity consists of two questions of unity. In the domestic sphere the problem of unity refers to maintaining the rule of law, retaining a monopoly of the legitimate use of violence, and binding people into an imaginary community. In the international system the problem of unity is the question of guaranteeing the existence of a plurality—the international society of sovereign states[7]. International politics draws boundaries between who is in the system and who is out (eg only those deemed civilised could be part of international society at some point). It also defines legitimate rules of engagement (eg the balance of power in post-Napoleonic Europe).[8]

In the modern age, the matrix of sovereignty defines the political as a two-faced question of the constitution and support of unity, which is therefore also a double question of authority to constitute and sustain unity and a double question of representation of this unity.[9] It separates the domestic from the international and thereby frames the political as a question of the unity of the state and the unity of the international system of sovereign states. In both cases sovereignty defines the question of the political as a question of establishing unity in a world of plural opinions.

---

[5] See, for example, J Der Derian, *On Diplomacy: A Genealogy of Western Estrangement*, (Oxford, Basil Blackwell, 1987); J Bartelson, *A Genealogy of Sovereignty* (Cambridge, Cambridge University Press, 1995).

[6] See also H Bull, *The Anarchical Society. A Study of Order in World Politics*, (London, Macmillan, 1977); H Bull and A Watson (eds) *The Expansion of International Society* (Oxford, Clarendon, 1984).

[7] This is the key political issue in much of the Classical Realist literature in International Relations. See, for example, H. Morgenthau, (1948) *Politics Among Nations* (New York, McGraw-Hill, 1948); H Kissinger, *A World Restored* (Boston, Houghton Mifflin, 1957) Bull above n 6. For an extremely interesting interpretation of classical realism along these lines, see M Williams (1998), 'Identity and the Politics of Security', (1998) 4 *European Journal of International Relations*. No. 2, pp. 204–25; *Wilful Realism. The Realist Tradition and the Limits of International Relations* (2002, unpublished manuscript).

[8] See Kissinger, above n 7.

[9] See Lindahl's contribution to the present volume for a more elaborate exposition of the link between the questions of unity, authority and representation.

B. Sovereignty and the law

Sovereignty also refers to a particular technique of constituting and governing unity among free individuals. The rule of law and the creation and reproduction of legal order constitute the particular technique of sovereign governance. In relation to this technique of governance, the question of the political—of what and where politics is—relates to the question of the limit of law.[10] The political emerges when the rule of law cannot account for the definition and implementation of the common good and the distinction between what is right and wrong. In the matrix of sovereignty, defining politics is fundamentally connected to the tension between politics and law and between being inside and being outside of the law. In other words, in the framework of sovereignty concepts of the political articulate particular ways of dealing with this tension.[11] This understanding sides with the view Neil Walker articulates in his contribution to this book: the tension between politics and law is a defining element of the question of sovereignty.

The key to the question of the nature of the rule of law is the question of the power of deciding what is right and wrong and of commanding obedience. Does the rule of law derive its authority to command from a proper application of legally defined procedures which allow 'judges' to derive law and judgement about what is right and wrong from constitutionally given fundamental principles and existing law? Or, does the law's authority to command and be obeyed derive from extra-legal political and sociological determinants such as charisma, courage to stand up to enemies, tradition, the monopoly over the means of violence?[12] In other words, is the rule of law a question of the legality of deciding and implementing law or is it a question of the legitimacy of political decisions declaring law and commanding obedience?[13]

---

[10] See, for example, D Dyzenhaus 'Legality and Legitimacy. Carl Schmitt, Hans Kelsen and Hermann Heller' in *Weimar* (Cambridge, Cambridge University Press, 1997); H Morgenthau, *La notion du 'politique' et la théorie des différends internationaux* (Paris, Recueil Sirey, 1933); W Scheuerman, *Carl Schmitt: The End of Law* (Lanham, Rowman & Littlefield Publishers, 1999).

[11] See, for example G Agamben, *Homo Sacer. Sovereign Power and Bare Life* (Stanford, Stanford University Press, 1995); Morgenthau, above n 33; C. Schmitt, *Political Theology. Four Chapters on the Concept of Sovereignty* (London, MIT Press, 1985[1922]). Foucault's work is particularly instrumental in demonstrating that the matrix of sovereignty is not the only mode of organising unity and governing modern societies. His work on normalisation and discipline and on governmentality and biopolitics demonstrates alternative techniques of governance in modern Western societies; see M Foucault *Surveiller et punir* (Paris, Gallimard, 1975); *Histoire de la sexualité. 1. La volonté de savoir* (Paris, Gallimard, 1976); *'Il faut défendre la société'* (Paris, Gallimard Seuil, 1997); *Les Anormaux* (Paris, Gallimard Seuil, 1999).

[12] The classic reference is M Weber *Economy and Society* Guenther Roth and Claus Wittich, (eds) (Berkeley, University of California Press, 1978).

[13] Dyzenhaus, above n 10.

The distinction between legality and legitimacy primarily refers to the constitution and protection of legal order. A legal order can be grounded in natural law and the methodical derivation of other laws from it. The authority to decide law and to command obedience to that law are grounded within law itself, that is within legal procedures and principles. But, the decision to create law—and, legal procedures and principles—can also be a political decision, that is a decision to impose a definition of the good and the right in a struggle between opinions. Political decisions derive their authority from sources other than legal principles and procedures (eg charisma, tradition or effectively preventing societal disintegration). In other words, the debate about the legality and legitimacy of the rule of law is a debate about whether the rule of law constitutes the legal practice or whether legal practice is constituted by political practice. Political practice refers to decisions in situations of uncertainty and is informed by opinion. It is contrasted with a legal practice that consists of the technical application of law in particular cases.[14]

The difference—and, the tension—between the legality and the legitimacy of the legal order and the authority to defend it points towards a fundamental difference and tension within the rule of law: the difference between constituted and constituting power and the tension between the legal order and political decisions. As Lindahl excellently demonstrates in this volume, the question of the political is never just the question of constituted authority but always implies the question of a constituting power, of seizing the initiative, of 'commencement'. As he shows with reference to a few landmark decisions of the European Court of Justice, even within the judicial institutions, political moments are moments of seizing the initiative and constituting legal order.

The political emerges in this matrix either as administration of social relations within a constitutional framework—politics as legality—or as a decision to construct legal order. I do not have time to go into further details about the peculiar nature of the latter understanding of politics. Neither is there any need for this, as both Neil Walker's and Hans Lindahl's contributions have developed this extensively. However, one further dimension needs to be raised.

The question of sovereignty emerges in situations when the rule of law reaches its limit. Under normal circumstances the rule of law refers to making and implementing law within the constitutional framework. However, there are situations in which the law does not provide answers and during which the political community defined by the constitutional framework is severely challenged. The most radical manifestation of this limit is civil war and societal and political disintegration. This is a situation

---

[14] See further Dyzenhaus above n 10; Scheuerman above n 10.

in which the unity has dissolved or risks dissolving into a radical plurality. During these exceptional circumstances the rule of law can no longer be the procedural, technical formulation and implementation of law. The exceptional circumstances call for and legitimate a legally ungrounded decision by an authority to preserve and/or re-establish unity.[15]

In this framework the question of the political arises at the interstice between the legality of sovereign power and the legitimacy of sovereign decisions when the law does not provide an adequate answer.[16] The political is ultimately the question of the gap between the normal and the exceptional. Often the political is then contrasted with legal, procedurally informed decisions by defining it as the activity deciding on the exception, to use Schmitt's infamous definition of sovereignty.[17] Deciding on the exception does not only refer to the need to decide what to do when exceptional circumstances arise but it also refers to the decision that there is an exceptional situation. In this reading, the political is constituted in the legal, constitutional framework around the question of who and how one decides that an exceptional situation exists and thus that the normal rule of law does no longer hold.

More generally however, within the framework of the rule of law, the question of the political emerges from a tension between legality and legitimacy and a gap between the normal and the exceptional.

C. Inside/Outside

The split between international politics and domestic politics is a particular solution to the question of where politics is within the framework of sovereignty. It externalises the question of the exception and the decision it requires. In other words, the split between inside and outside *territorialises* the key problem of the rule of law. The normal and legal are contained within a territorially defined state. In the state authority is defined and bound by the rule of law. This territorial sphere is defined as the constitutional order. The exceptional and the extra-legal legitimacy are moved to the space of international relations, or the relations between states with

---

[15] For a radical—and, also worrying—interpretation of authentic politics along these lines see Carl Schmitt's work, especially Schmitt above n 11; *The Concept of the Political* (Translated and with an introduction by George Schwab) (Chicago, The University of Chicago Press, 1996[1932]); *The Leviathan in the State Theory of Thomas Hobbes. Meaning and Failure of a Political Symbol* (Westport, Greenwood Press, 1996[1938]).

[16] As Lindahl demonstrates convincingly in his contribution to the present volume, one does not have to read the interstice necessarily in Schmittean terms, in which the interstice arises when a community faces a mortal threat in the form of an external or internal enemy. He identifies the interstice not with an encounter with an enemy threatening the survival of the community, but with an act of seizing the initiative.

[17] See Schmitt, above n 11.

different opinions about what is the common good. International politics, thus, is the politics within a space that lacks a constitutional order. Authority does not derive from law but from a capacity to act in situations where the rule of law has reached its limits. Domestic politics is a normal politics grounded in the rule of law. International politics is a politics in exceptional circumstances in which there is no rule of law and therefore a decision by political leaders, or, the sovereign, is called for. The situation is one in which the unity of the state is continuously threatened by an externally existing plurality of opinion. In other words, the international is the game in which the exception in domestic politics becomes the normal condition of politics.

This rendering of the matrix—to an extent—solves the problem of the political as it arises in relation to the matrix of sovereignty. The gap between the normal and the exceptional is no longer a problem in terms of deciding where it exists. The normal and the exceptional are located in two different planes of existence: the domestic and the international. As a consequence the gap dissolves into two separate notions of the political: a legalistic notion emphasising the rule of law and a political realist notion emphasising the decision in the absence of a constitutional order. Moreover, each of the concepts of the political is located within a specific space of politics: the territorial state and the international system, respectively.[18]

If the divide between the international and the domestic is a particular rendering of the matrix of sovereignty which defines two problems of unity, two forms of authority and two spaces of politics, then the disciplinary divide between political science and international relations reflects this particular fix. It is important, however, to understand this as a particular fix within the matrix of sovereignty. In other words, the question of sovereignty is not the issue of whether the territorial state can maintain its unity and authority to command domestically against a radical plurality which may emerge in international politics (for example, through the rise of revolutionary power which has the capacity to call into question a particular international order). Rather, the question of sovereignty is the question of how to create unity and authority through the rule of law in a radically plural world.

From this perspective, the question- whether sovereignty is withering away or not in a transnationalising world- may well be the wrong question. Challenges to the control and to the authority to command of the territorial state do not necessarily challenge the matrix of sovereignty. What they may do, however, is to lead to the re-emergence of the question of the political: that is, where and what is politics? This question can and usually does re-emerge within—or, at least in relation to—the matrix of sovereignty. In

---

[18] See R Walker, above n 1.

other words, the question of the political emerges because the question of unity, the question of authority and its legality and legitimacy, and the gap between the normal and exceptional are re-orientated towards and re-articulated within transnational developments. The key point is that if this is the case, then imagining transnational politics is not imagining the end of sovereignty but, first of all, re-introducing the very question of sovereignty which is the question of imagining the political within the matrix of sovereignty. From this perspective, a challenge to sovereignty is not a challenge to the territorial state but a challenge to the construction of the question of the political *within* the framework established by the matrix of sovereignty. In the next section, I will try to illustrate that although readings of transnational developments rework aspects of the concept of the political, they have a difficulty escaping the matrix of sovereignty. Or, in other words, I will look at how the spectre of sovereignty may arise in relation to some interpretations of transnational developments.

3. TRANSNATIONAL FLOWS AND THE POLITICAL

Let us start by briefly indicating key elements of how transnational flows are seen to raise particular questions for state authority in the international society of sovereign states. One of the key elements is that transnational societal flows are expected to challenge the capacity of the public authority of the state to control societal dynamics for political purposes. Economic, financial and population flows across states impede adequate governmental responses to the demands of people. The welfare demands of people put a lot of pressure on governments to deliver social and economic entitlements. But the transnationalisation of the economic and financial basis for providing entitlements partly escapes the control of a single government. For democratic governments of welfare states—that is, states for whom political legitimacy has become dependent on the provision of welfare—this causes a political problem. Their legitimacy considerably depends on delivering social goods and on expanding the scope of their care for society. How can a state claim to be sovereign when many societal and economic flows that the government is required to govern escape state control?[19]

Transnational developments are also seen as diluting the traditional hierarchy of policy areas in the international society of states. According to neo-realist analyses international politics is dominated by a concern for survival of the state which means that military issues dominate the agenda.[20] In a

[19] See, for example, K Kaiser 'Transnationale Politik. Zu einer Theorie der multinationalen Politik', in Czempiel, Ernst-Otto (ed.) *Die anachronistische Souveränität*, (Köln, Westdeutscher Verlag, 1969) pp. 80–109.
[20] See, for example, K Waltz, (*Theory of International Politics* (Reading, Addison-Wesley, 1979).

political system that lacks an authority that has the monopoly over the legitimate use of violence, the units have to rely upon themselves to survive. Before they should be concerned about things like welfare they have to be capable of defending themselves against potential aggressors. The literature on complex interdependence, however, has highlighted that this hierarchy of policy concerns which puts defence issues automatically at the top of the agenda no longer holds.[21]

The observation that economic concerns, for example, can prevail over military concerns is in itself—that is, outside of the clash of schools in the discipline of International Relations—not that important. The key aspect of this observation is that it points towards a functionally differentiated international society. States act in different functional arenas, eg economics, the environment, defence, which are not related in a strict hierarchical way. This means that military security is not a condition for economic and environmental concerns and policies to develop independent policy arenas. Moreover, the functional differentiation of state activity relates to a functional differentiation of power. According to this reading, states can be powerful actors in one arena (eg the WTO) but not in another (eg in the second Gulf War). In most Realist conceptualisations—a most interesting exception being Aron[22]—which are strongly embedded in the particular fix of the question of sovereignty and the political that I sketched in the previous section, this is not possible. Power is an aggregated concept that functions as a measure of a state's security and position in international society. Accepting the thesis of a functionally differentiated international society implies that the state may have to rely on different capabilities to be empowered in different arenas. For example, does a large, hi-tech military capacity make a key difference in global trade negotiations? If different functional systems require different capabilities and strategies, then one's power in one arena cannot necessarily be transferred to another policy arena. As a result, some functionally specialised agencies and states may be key actors in a particular arena without being important actors in other arenas and without having the capacity to defend themselves militarily. The unitary international society breaks apart into multiple systems of functionally defined interaction.

Finally, transnational developments are seen to multiply the number and kind of politically significant actors. Regions, sections of national bureaucracies, social movements and firms can be politically significant actors in these functional arenas. If a wide diversity of political and social agencies plays an important role in defining the common good in international or transnational relations, the capacity of the public authority of the state to

---

[21] See, for example, R Keohane and J Nye, *Power and Interdependence* (Boston, Little, Brown & Company, 1977).
[22] R Aron *Paix et guerre entre les nations* (Paris, Calman Lévy, 1962).

speak with one voice representing the position of that state may be seriously challenged. In a complex interdependent world the unity of governance fragments into cross-national policy relations between sub-sections of the bureaucracy, between non-governmental agencies and particular bureaucratic actors, between regions, and so on.[23] From this view, the diplomatic system that ruled the international society of sovereign states becomes part of a fragmented world in which multiple non-state and sub-state actors develop transnational activities and policy networks. These views of transnational developments picture a world that is functionally differentiated. The power capacity, the nature of agents, and the stakes differ according to the nature of the game.

The political significance of these developments follows from the assumption that sovereign states cannot effectively govern transnational societal and economic flows on their own.[24] To regain control, state authorities will co-operate in institutionalised settings. These can be of a supra-national nature such as the EU or of an inter-national nature such as international regimes. Often this view emphasises that interdependence and transnational developments facilitate institutionalised co-operation between sovereign states in an anarchical system—that is, a system that lacks a legitimate highest authority that can guarantee a rule of law. However, the more interesting aspect of this view is that it fragments governance and international politics into a myriad of policy arenas in which governments and other political actors try to define common rules of proper state practice in these policy areas. The result is a fragmented international system that consists of functionally defined policy arenas which institutionalise decision-making procedures and rules defining proper practice in the area. The scope can range from global human rights regimes or environmental protection regimes to regional free trade areas.

The concept of political rule within these functional arenas, however, does not seem to move beyond the parameters of political rule as defined by the matrix of sovereignty. The key political problem in these arenas is the construction and reproduction of a unity of procedures and beliefs about what is right and wrong. The technique of governance is very similar to a rule of law. Within these institutionalised forms of co-operation rules define the right procedures for taking binding decisions and for sanctioning deviation from the rules. In that sense authority to command depends on a quasi-constitutional framework that defines the parameters of rule within

---

[23] For an excellent example focusing on the construction of an internal security field in Europe see D Bigo *Police en réseaux. L'expérience européenne* (Paris, Presses de Sciences Po., 1996). Other examples include V Guiraudon Guiraudon, V (ed.) 'Sociologie de l'Europe.' *Cultures et Conflits.* No. 38–9. (2000), J Cesari (ed.) 'Les Anonymes de la Mondialisation.' In: *Cultures et Conflits,* No. 33–4 (1999).
[24] See Kaiser, above n 19.

the functional arena. The question of unity looms large: the political actors share an understanding of proper practice.[25]

This is the normal situation in which procedures allow for the proper formulation of rules defining what is right and what is wrong. In other words, a unity in the form of shared expectations and rules has been institutionalised. However, such an understanding of the political invites the question of the limit of the law and the question of the legitimacy of the original creation of the institutionalised arena. If one is interested not primarily in the issue of co-operation but in the concept of the political that is expressed in these views, the tension between legality and legitimacy of the authority to rule and the gap between the normal and the exceptional are never far away. How does one guarantee the unity of the system of rules when challenged by particular agencies? One solution, which clearly demonstrates to what extent the question of the political remains locked within the matrix of sovereignty, is that a hegemonic power will ultimately re-establish order and unity, possibly by destroying or excluding the challenging actors. In this view, the hegemonic agency also explains the origin of international regimes, that is the origins of the unity that they represent in plural international systems.[26] Such an interpretation of course raises the question of the legitimacy of both hegemonic acts of creation and the system of public authority and rule.[27]

The bottom line of my argument is that the most interesting aspect of these views on how transnational flows and developments affect public political authority is not that they may trigger co-operation between public authorities and political communities which otherwise would not have existed. This focus does not really add something to or even is concerned with the matrix of sovereignty and the way in which it frames the question of the political. In relation to the question of the challenge to sovereignty, the more important aspect is that it pictures a fragmented public authority in international politics, which is spread over different, not necessarily related, institutionalised policy arenas and policy networks. It fragments the international society of sovereign states into functionally defined arenas and consequently challenges the neat fix that territorialised the tension and the gap that characterise the matrix of sovereignty.

---

[25] For example, Krasner's definition of international regimes: '[Regimes are] sets of implicit or explicit principles, norms, rules and decision-making procedures around which actors' expectations converge in a given area of international relations. Principles are beliefs of fact, causation, and rectitude. Norms are standards of behavior defined in terms of rights and obligations. Rules are specific prescriptions or proscriptions for action. Decision-making procedures are prevailing practices for making and implementing collective choices.' S Krasner 'Structural causes and regime consequences: regimes as intervening variables', (1982) 36 *International Organisation* Vol. 36, No. 2, pp. 185–205, 186.

[26] See R Keohane *After Hegemony* (Princeton, Princeton University Press, 1984).

[27] See, for example, S Strange 'Cave! Hic Dragones: A critique of regime analysis,' (1982) 36 *International Organisation* pp. 479–96.

4. TRANSNATIONAL POLITICS AND THE SPECTRE OF SOVEREIGNTY

In this section I want to reflect on a second link between transnational developments and the re-articulation or questioning of sovereignty. To do this, I turn to a view that starts from a deconstruction of sovereignty and then tries to re-imagine the political as transnational politics. The main reference is a chapter on democracy and territoriality by William Connolly.[28]

In International Relations, sovereignty has been deconstructed in several ways. For example, sovereignty has been denaturalised by demonstrating its historical contingency. By demonstrating that the notion of sovereignty refers to a particularly modern way of organising political unity within a plurality of opinion, which itself has changed over time, the concept of sovereignty changes from a descriptive category to a category which is part of a political history characterised by a struggle between different imaginations of the political.[29] Another approach has emphasised that the notion of sovereignty and the concept of political community it supports is sustained by institutionalised rituals representing the particular framework of the political as a universal, and sometimes also eternal, truth.[30]

However, deconstruction of international politics and sovereignty is not just a critique which tries to demonstrate the historical specificity of sovereignty and the institutionalised, ritualised reproduction of concepts of the true political. It is also a strategy to make room for imagining a transnationalisation of the political within a democratic framework. At least, that seems to be a key concern for Connolly and RBJ Walker.[31] The empirical reference for this imaginary endeavour is the daily politics of, eg, social movements, civil services, and firms struggling for competing definitions of a common good across the traditional boundaries of states.

In contrast to the interpretation outlined in the previous section, here the focus is on transnational agencies acting politically, that is struggling over the definition of the common good and/or what is right and wrong, in a transnational political space. However, the notion of a transnational political space itself is not the main focus of Connolly's work. Rather, his first concern is to address the question of how to imagine the nature of politics in this transnational space. More specifically, the normative project is to imagine a politics which emphasises the nurturing of difference rather than the need for unity, which is the key to the matrix of sovereignty. To that

[28] W Connolly *The Ethos of Pluralisation* (Minneapolis, University of Minnesota Press, 1995) pp. 135–61.
[29] See, for example, R Walker, above n 1; Bartelson, above n 5.
[30] R Ashley, 'The geopolitics of geopolitical space. Toward a critical social theory of international politics.' (1987) 12 *Alternatives* pp. 403–34.
[31] See Connolly, above n 28; R Walker above n 1; see also S Guzzini 'Maintenir les dilemmes de la modernité en suspens: analyse et éthique poststructuralistes en relations internationales', in Klaus-Gerd Giesen (ed.) *L'éthique de l'espace politique mondial* (Bruxelles, Bruylant, 1997) pp. 247–85.

purpose, politics beyond the state and the international society of states is presented as an open confrontation between antagonistic forces with different opinions about what is right and wrong and with different concepts of the good life in a less homogenous space. In other words, the kernel of the political is an open struggle over beliefs and values and its outcome is therefore inherently uncertain. Transnational politics is presented as a politics that sustains radical antagonism between beliefs and uncertainty about outcomes and ways of reaching these outcomes. In relation to the topic of this chapter, the question has to be asked to what extent introducing radical antagonism—that is opposition of opinion in an arena which is not defined by particular procedures aimed at reaching consensus—moves the concept of the political beyond the matrix of sovereignty.

Transnational politics seem to be conceptualised as a practice of radical plurality. Developing a concept of the political that refers to a condition and process of radical plurality challenges the spectre of sovereignty. The problem of sovereignty is not in the first place the problem of supporting radical plurality. Rather the question of the political is first of all a question of constructing and sustaining a *contingent unity* in a condition of radical plurality. Thus, the question is one of sustaining unity in the face of plurality rather than sustaining plurality and difference in the face of unifying pressures.

In that sense the post-structural view of the political is not politically realist in a Schmittean way. It shares with political realist views an emphasis on power politics and on the need to make decisions in situations of conflict between competing views and interests. Both views also criticise concepts of the political that focus on the declaration and implementation of universal rules. Politics is not implementation of rules but first of all competition between particular notions of the common good and/or of right and wrong. Finally, both argue against a procedural understanding of politics—that is, politics as the production of legitimate consensus by the following of particular procedures. However, in Schmittean political realism the concept of the political is born out of exceptional circumstances in which the rule of law is in crisis. It is the gap between the normal rule of law and the exception that is the condition of possibility of the political. The authentic sovereign practice in the Schmittean scheme is always an act of closure, of re-establishing unity and order in situations threatening unity. In contrast, the post-structural concept of the political seems to focus on the need to create and maintain radical difference in conditions of unity. So, the political is not primarily about creating and maintaining unity but about creating and supporting difference.[32]

---

[32] See also, for example, D Campbell *National Deconstruction. Violence, Identity, and Justice in Bosnia.* (Minneapolis, University of Minnesota Press, 1998); Connolly above n 28; M Dillon *Politics of Security.* (London, Routledge, 1996); J Edkins, N Persram, V Pit-Fat, (eds), *Sovereignty and Subjectivity* (Boulder, Lynne Rienner, 1999).

Does a political scenery which is radically diversified by transnational agencies who challenge the monopoly of sovereign states on the definition of what is right and wrong and/or good or bad, reduce the presence of the spectre of sovereignty? Emphasising the creation of difference rather than unity does not necessarily eliminate the question of how unity is legitimately constructed. The call for plurality does not exclude the recognition that politics is fundamentally about the confrontation between different claims about the common good. That means that the question of the creation of a common good defining a particular comm-unity is not absent. However, the problem is that a consensus about the common good always excludes particular groups of people who have another opinion about the common good. Connolly's project searches to conceptualise a political space that guarantees that the excluded groups can challenge the consensus. That means that the unity of the community—that which connects the people sharing the consensus and those challenging it or being excluded from it—cannot be substantially defined, that is in terms of a particular understanding of the common good. The usual solution to this problem is to define politics procedurally. The unity of the community and the political space depends on following rules and procedures which stipulate the proper way for different opinions to engage politically in the struggle for the definition of the common good. Liberal democracy is a particular historical answer in line with such a procedural definition of politics.

The problem for someone like Connolly is that he wishes to separate the democratic form of politics from its particular historical institutionalisation in sovereign states. The concept of democratic rule is firmly tied to the concept of the democratic sovereign state which is territorially defined and includes a particular institutionalisation of the democratic rule of law, manifested in, eg, elections, a Parliament, an independent judiciary. However, the sovereign democratic state is constructed upon and through a radical exclusion of competing interests, opinions and identities. In other words, some opinions or groups are not allowed to emerge within the political space. Connolly uses the extermination of American Indians as a classic example.

This results in an interest in developments supporting a transnational form of democratic political practice, that is democratic practice which is not caught within the image of the sovereign, the territorial state and the traditional democratic institutions guaranteeing a democratic rule of law. The question becomes how to conceptualise transnational politics as democratic without defining it on the basis of the institutions and procedures which are historically and conceptually tied to the invention of the democratic territorial state.

As a solution Connolly separates two dimensions of the concept of democracy: democracy as a form of rule and democracy as an ethos. It is the latter which allows him to define the democratic nature of transnational antagonistic struggles for the definition of the good life. In other words, transnational democratic politics is not defined by the presence of particular institutions, such as a parliament, and particular procedures of representation such as elections but by sharing a particular ethical pre-disposition. The democratic ethos is defined as one of respecting difference and openness—as

> '[A]n ethos through which newly emerging constellations might reconstitute identities previously impressed upon them, thereby disturbing the established priorities of identity/difference through which social relations are organised.'[33]

By separating democratic ethos from democratic institutions and rule of law Connolly can define democratic politics in what seems to be the under-institutionalised space of transnational politics. In that way, he tries to transnationalise the concept of the democratic political, that is, retaining a democratic politics beyond the traditional institutions that guarantee the democratic nature of politics while avoiding a return to wars between opinions in conditions of radical plurality. In Connolly's own words

> [a] democratic ethos balances the desirability of governance through democratic means with a corollary politics of democratic disturbance through which any particular pattern of previous settlements might be tossed up for grabs again.'[34]

This notion of the political is very interesting but not unproblematic. The image of the political is one of agencies struggling for the definition of a common good across national boundaries and outside of traditional political institutions. However, as with any social practice, these social practices do not operate at random, that is, without being embedded in particular institutional settings. Although emphasising the importance of a shared democratic ethos is an important move in imagining a transnational concept of the political, it does not delete the question of institutions within which the democratic ethos articulates itself in an antagonistic practice for defining a common good. Connolly does not provide an answer. This does not devalue in any way the sharpness of his analysis and importance of his way of imagining the transnationalisation of democratic politics. However, from the perspective of this chapter, the question of the institutionalisation of political space and practice is quite important because it is one of the issues where the spectre of sovereignty can loom large. What form of rule do these antagonistic struggles define when they make a decision about how to rule an issue? Do they rely on rule of law implemented by states and/or international organisations? How are the arenas of struggle constructed? Who can participate and who cannot?

---

[33] Connolly, above n 28. 153.
[34] *Ibid* 154.

The last of these questions prompts a second remark. The concept of the transnational political is defined by the concept of a democratic ethos. That means that a unity is established among those who can 'legitimately' participate in democratic transnational politics. Any question of unity, whether defined through the rule of law or through an ethos, triggers a question of limits. Who defines and protects the community of those who share a democratic ethos when the community faces a fundamental challenge that cannot be dealt with within the confines of an antagonistic respect for difference? It is one of the questions through which the spectre of sovereignty tries to impose itself upon modern imaginations of the political. As remarked in the first section, this is the theme of the gap between normal political practice and exceptional political practice. Although Connolly does not go into this in any detail, the question of how his conceptualisation of the political imagines the gap still stands. The gap must be crucial for these imaginations of the political because they emphasise the need for breaking open existing unity. The possibility for doing this relies on the gap because the gap defines the possibility to transform an existing unity of belief. And as Lindahl argues in this volume that is precisely what sovereignty refers to. But, there is also the more radical interpretation of the gap along Schmittean lines in which the gap is defined by the identification of an enemy. Taking the presence of enemies seriously usually leads to the definition of two spheres of politics: a politics of the rule of law and a politics of the defence of the rule of law against its enemies. Given that Connolly's conceptualisation of transnational politics is defined as an antagonistic politics articulating a democratic ethos, the question arises whether the radical formulation of the limit as enemy is important for defining the political. Can Connolly's position avoid positing two kinds of transnational political spaces: one in which the democratic ethos articulates peaceful antagonistic politics and one in which the democratic ethos is radically challenged and therefore needs to be defended?

To summarise, the transnationalisation of politics introduces an anatagonistic concept of the political that is enacted across state boundaries. The focus is on maintaining plurality in the face of the pressure to create unity. It presents politics as a power struggle with an inherently uncertain outcome. Politics is an open battle between different agencies. This is an important starting point for reworking the matrix of sovereignty, especially if combined with the view that stresses a functionally differentiating international system. However, an important issue needs to be addressed in more detail: the institutionalisation of such a transnational politics. By re-introducing the question of democratic rule as a system of governance of a plurality of opinions and people, the questions connected to the institutionalisation and justification of unity, and consequently the spectre of sovereignty, will re-emerge. Reworking the matrix of sovereignty, therefore, cannot be avoided by asserting an antagonistic notion of democratic politics that builds on a democratic ethos.

5. CONCLUSION

The first argument of this chapter is that challenges to sovereignty should not be read in terms of the withering away of the state or the loss of control over societal flows by public authority. Sovereignty is a matrix of framing questions of the political. Reworking and challenging sovereignty has to be interpreted as reworking and challenging the particular way in which the matrix frames the possible imaginations of the political. I also called it a spectre because the matrix is difficult to escape in any rethinking of politics.

The question of sovereignty refers to the problem of creating unity in an inherently plural world. It also refers to two key issues with regard to the rule of law, which is a particular technique of governing the conduct of free individuals. The first issue is the tension between legality and legitimacy of the rule of law. Sometimes this tension is also translated as the tension between law and politics. However, it is a tension that is internal to the question of ruling by and through law. It is the tension between the law circumscribing the proper way of politics and politics circumscribing the proper rule of law. The second issue is the gap between normal rule and exceptional rule. The gap emerges when politics is required but the rule of law cannot provide the answer. In some conceptualisations, that is when authentic politics emerge. But, the more interesting issue is that the matrix of sovereignty seems to include two spheres of politics: a sphere of normal politics that develops within the rule of law and a sphere of exceptional politics that develops in the absence of the rule of law.

The matrix of sovereignty also includes a territorial fix to the questions raised above. It consists of defining a plural international system of sovereign states. At least since the 19th Century, the matrix of sovereignty articulates a double problem of unity: unity in the domestic realm and unity in the system of states. It also fixes, to an extent, the tension between legality and legitimacy and the gap between normal politics and exceptional politics by locating the sphere of legality and normal politics within the state and the sphere of legitimacy and exceptional politics in the system of relations between states.

In later sections, the essay dealt briefly with two ways in which transnational developments are expected to re-articulate the question of the political as it is framed within this matrix of sovereignty. First, transnational developments are expected to fragment the international system into functionally defined arenas of politics. A process of functional differentiation within the international system challenges the unity of the international system of sovereign states. However, I briefly indicated that the technique of governance in the functional arenas is similar to the rule of law. Consequently, the question of the unity of the functional sphere, the tension between legality and legitimacy of the authority to rule and the question of the limit of the rule of law, loom large. By focusing on co-operation between states, most of the literature on international regimes in a functionally differentiated international system does not really raise the question of the political and of the extent to which the spectre of sovereignty reigns in the imaginations of alternative political spaces. However, once the question of the political is raised, the spectre of sovereignty will emerge. The question then becomes whether a functionally differentiating international system articulates a transformation of the matrix of sovereignty or whether it transforms a particular fix of the problems without re-articulating the particular formulation and framing of the question of the political in the matrix of sovereignty.[35]

Similar questions were raised with regard to a literature that deconstructs sovereignty and tries to imagine the nature and space of the transnational political. Through reading Connolly, I tried to indicate that the transnational political is conceptualised not on the model of the rule of law but as an antagonistic competition between different opinions. The political question is the inverse of the question of sovereignty: how to create plurality in a world of unity instead of how to create contingent unity in a plural world? However, I have tried to indicate that although these are interesting ideas, they do not necessarily eliminate the questions that the matrix of sovereignty raises for conceptualisations of the political. Also in relation to Connolly's imaginative way of defining some key elements of conceptualising transnational politics, one of the most interesting questions with regard to the matrix of sovereignty is not further developed. Does transnational politics based on a democratic ethos transform the way of framing the question of the political or will the spectre of sovereignty still rule the imaginations of the political once the question of how to institutionalise this form of antagonistic politics is raised?

Whatever the answer, it seems that both the concept of a functionally fragmenting international political system and the concept of the political as pluralisation instead of unification, at least facilitate an explicit identification and re-working of the framework through which the concept of sovereignty shapes the question of the political. And that is the second argument of this chapter. The spectre of sovereignty is difficult to escape but interpretations of transnational developments and their political implications are instrumental in raising and highlighting the question of sovereignty as one concerning the ways of framing the political and in providing building blocks for reworking some important dimensions of the matrix of sovereignty.

---

[35] Neil Walker's chapter more extensively develops the significance of functional differentiation for the question of sovereignty.

10

'Que les Latins appellent maiestatem': An Exploration into the Theological Background of the Concept of Sovereignty

GOVERT BUIJS

1. INTRODUCTION

FROM THE OLD Sumerian, Akkadic and Egyptian times until at least the early modern period, the period in which the first formulations of the political symbol of sovereignty occur, a long tradition of linkages can be established between the language of power and the language of the divine. Following an old suggestion from Plato's *Politeia*, the Roman author M Terentius Varro coined the phrase 'political theology' for this tradition.[1] The symbol of 'sovereignty' does appear to be intimately connected to this tradition.[2] Is the symbol simply a continuation of this immemorial tradition of 'political theology'? Or is there something distinctively new about it, new also in its politico-theological aspects in such a way that it prefigures a final departure from, if not a radical break with this tradition? Or is this dichotomy too crude altogether and do we have to allow for a more subtle configuration of change and continuity regarding the place of the symbol within this tradition? If so, what are the 'politico-theological' roots of the notion of sovereignty?

---

[1] Plato, *Politeia*, II, 379a, speaks of 'different patterns of speaking about the gods' (*typoi peri theologias*). Not all the 'patterns' may be correct from a political point of view. According to St Augustine it was Marcus Terentius Varro (116–27 BC), a very prolific author almost none of whose writings have survived, who refined the Platonic notion of 'types of theology' into a distinction between three types of theology, ie mythical, physical and political (in Latin *theologia fabularis, theologia naturalis, theologia civilis*). See St Augustine, *De civitate dei*, VI, 5–12.
[2] JN Figgis, *The Divine Right of Kings*, (Cambridge, Cambridge University Press 1922 [1896]), p. 237: 'The Divine Right of Kings on its political side was little more than the popular form of expression for the theory of sovereignty'.

These are the central questions of this chapter. To obtain a sharper focus I start with some quotes that seem to attest to the great continuity of this age-old tradition right unto the first formulations of the symbol of sovereignty, although in the course of this article the initial suggestion of continuity will be qualified:

'When kingship was lowered from heaven, kingship was first in Eridu . . . . .'[3]

Thus opens one of the oldest documents of political theology still extant, the so-called Sumerian King List dating probably from around 2050 BC. The opening sentence is a standard formula in the self-presentation of kings in the Ancient Near East.[4] In these and similar documents the kingship is symbolised almost as a tangible 'object' that in spite of its apparently universal significance is located at one specific place and vested in one specific person, the divinely chosen ruler. Was he 'sovereign'?

The force of this type of symbolism can be sensed in the following declaration by the Egyptian Queen Hatshepsut (reigning from 1486–69 BC) almost a century after the violent Hyksos occupation of Egypt had come to an end:

Hear all ye people and folk as many as they may be I have done these things through the counsel of my heart. I have not forgetfully slept, but I have restored that what had been ruined (T)hey [the Hyksos, GJB] ruled without Re, and he (Re) did not act by divine command down to (the reign of) my majesty. Now I am established on the thrones of Re.

(T)his is the precept of the father of my fathers, who comes at his appointed times, of Re, and there shall not occur damage to what Amon has commanded. My own command endures like the mountains—The sun-disk shines forth and spreads rays over the formal titles of my majesty, and my falcon is high above my name-standard for the duration of eternity.[5]

The Queen is thus appointed one of the gods—she is a god herself. Her commands and the commands of Re are of a piece. She represents the divine order in the world. Was she 'sovereign'?

'Seeing that nothing upon earth is greater or higher, next unto God, than the maiestie of kings and soveraigne princes; for that they are in a sort created his lieutenants for the welfare of other men; it is meet diligently to consider of their maiestie and power, as also who and of what sort they be; that so we may in all obedience respect and reverence their maiestie, and not to think or speake of them otherwise than of the lieutenants of the most mightie and immortal God: for that he which speaketh evill of his prince unto whome he oweth all dutie, doth iniurie

---

[3] James B Pritchard (ed)., *Ancient Near Eastern Texts, Relating To The Old Testament* (2nd ed)., (Princeton, Princeton University Press 1955), p. 265.
[4] See Henri Frankfort, *Kingship and the Gods. A Study of Ancient Near Eastern Religion as the Integration of Society and Nature*, (Chicago, University of Chicago Press, 1978) [1948], p. 237f.
[5] James B Pritchard, *o.c.*, p. 231.

unto the maiestie of God himselfe, whose lively image he is upon earth. As God speaking unto Samuel, of whome the people of Israel had unadvisely asked a king, *It is not thee* (saith God) *but me whome they have despised.*[6]

Here we have, albeit in an early translated form, one of the very first theoretical statements of the modern concept of sovereignty still extant (and the most famous one as well). The common historiography of political ideas has it that this modern notion starts with Jean Bodin and this seems hardly contestable.[7] And Bodin is known to have been a very religious man indeed, though not in any dogmatic but more in a mystical sense.[8] But how this relates to his concept of sovereignty is not immediately apparent.

> Kings are the authors and makers of laws, and not the laws of the kings. (T)he state of monarchy is the supremest thing upon earth: for kings are not only God's lieutenants upon earth, and sit upon earth and sit upon God's throne, but even by God himself they are called Gods.
>
> (T)hat which concerns the mystery of the kings' power is not lawful to be disputed; for that is to wade into the weakness of princes, and to take away the mystical reverence that belongs unto them that sit in the throne of God.[9]

The above is a statement in which a king, an 'absolute king' that is, states his self-interpretation during the first high tide of concrete national sovereignty. James I of England (who was also James VI of Scotland) has been

---

[6] Quoted from *Of the Lawes and Customes of a Commonwealth, learnedly discoursing of the power of Soveraignety and Majestracy, and of the Orders and degrees of Citizens, with the priviledges of Corporations and Colleges: and other things pertinent to Estates and Societies. Written by J. Bodin, a famous Lawyer, and a man of great experience in matters of State. Out of the French and Latin copies, done into English, by Richard Knolles*, London 1606, p. 153. The French original (1577) reads: 'Puis qu'il n'y a rien plus grad en terre apres Dieu, que les Princes souverains, & qu'ils sont etablis de luy, comme les lieutenants, pour commander aux autres hommes, il est besoin de prendre garde à leur qualité, afin de respecter, reverer leur maieste en toute obeissance, sentir & parler d'eux en tout honneur, car qui mesprises son Prince souverain, il mesprise Dieu, duquel il est limage en terre. C'est pourquoy Dieu parlant à Samuel, auquel le peuple avoit demandé un autre Prince, Cést moy, dit-il, à qu'ils ont fait iniure.'

[7] George H Sabine and Thomas L Thorson, *A History of Political Theory*, (Orlando, Holt, Rinehart and Winston 1973) 4th ed., 372. Quentin Skinner, *The Foundations of Modern Political Thought*, Vol. 2 *The Age of Reformation*, (Cambridge, Cambridge University Press 1978, p. 284 *ff*. Strangely enough in the ambitious *History of Political Philosophy* edited by Leo Strauss and Joseph Cropsey (Chicago, University of Chicago Press 1987[1963]) the name of Bodin is not once mentioned.

[8] Bodin's letter to Jean Bautru is often cited as an indication of this mystical orientation. Here Bodin gives his famous description of true religion: 'Vera religio intentio aliud nihil esse quam purgatae mentis in Deum veram conversionem'. (True religion intends nothing else than the true conversion of a purified mind toward God). Bodin actually wrote as much or even more on religious issues as he did on political issues. His Demonology and Heptaplomeres (a long debate about the truth of different religions) have not attracted the attention that they deserve. In recent decades this has started to change.

[9] The quotes are to be found in George H Sabine and Thomas L Thorson, *A History of Political Theory*, (Orlando, Holt, Rinehart and Winston 1973) 4th ed. 368f. They are taken from *The Political Works of James I* CH McIlwain, ed. (Cambridge, Mass., 1918).

one of the most outspoken rulers with respect to his self-interpretation as a divinely appointed king. He clearly must have been 'sovereign'. But what then does sovereignty mean?

2. SCHMITT'S THESIS: SOVEREIGNTY AS A SECULARISED THEOLOGICAL CONCEPT

It has been observed quite often that the emergence of the concept of sovereignty and the place of the divine are intimately linked in Western culture. Van Creveld in his recent study *The Rise and Decline of the State* says, referring to Jean Bodin:

> 'In a world where God is no longer capable of providing a consensual basis for political life, Bodin wanted to endow the sovereign with His qualities and put him in His place, at any rate on earth and as pertained to a certain well-defined territory'.[10]

The interest in the theological background of the symbol of sovereignty, however, has probably received its strongest stimulus through the work of the famous—or infamous—German theorist of law Carl Schmitt. In his *Politische Theologie* of 1922, subtitled *Vier Kapitel zur Lehre von der Souveränität*, he launched the intriguing thesis that 'all the key concepts of modern political theory are secularised theological concepts' ('Alle prägnanten Begriffe der modernen Staatslehre sind säkularisierte theologische Begriffe').[11] In this respect Schmitt refers to two different levels, the first being historical derivation, the transfer of concepts from theology to legal theory, and the second being the structural similarity between theological and political concepts. The most important (and virtually the only) example that he discusses at some length is precisely the concept of 'sovereignty': sovereignty is a secularised theological concept.[12]

However, if one looks at the extant philological evidence (the first level identified by Schmitt), his thesis is open to objections. The concept of sovereignty itself does not carry the awesome weight of a longstanding theological tradition. In western theology the concept arises relatively late. Etymologically, the word seems to be derived from the medieval Latin

---

[10] Martin Van Creveld, *The Rise and Decline of the State*, (Cambridge, Cambridge University Press 1999), 177. *Cf* Sabine/Thorston, *o.c.*, 372 *ff.*
[11] The opening sentence of chapter 3, Carl Schmitt, *Politische Theologie*, subtitled *Vier Kapitel zur Lehre von der Souveränität*, (München/Leipzig, Duncker & Humblot, 1934) [1922], p. 49.
[12] See Th.WA de Wit, *De onontkoombaarheid van de politiek. De soevereine vijand in het denken van Carl Schmitt.* (Ubbergen, Pomppers 1992). De Wit shows in great depth that Schmitt's thesis is not a mere exercise in the history of ideas but that it is grounded in a deep theological critique of the modern immanence that ends up in Weber's 'iron cage' of bureaucracy and technicism. The concept of sovereignty for Schmitt retains as much of its theological lineage to be defended by him as a bulwark against further immanentisation.

adjective *superanus*, which means something like 'being above' and it is not found in classical Latin.[13] In the 12th century AD the term '*sovrainetez*' occurs meaning simply 'the top', the highest point, for example of a mountain. So the first known use of the word appears to have been 'secular'. In the same century now and then a religious use of the concept is found in phrases like 'God is the sovereign father' (*le soverain pere*). And very shortly thereafter a political, hence a 'secular', use can already be established and this appears to have been much more widespread.

Not only do the extant philological data seem to preclude a bold conclusion like Schmitt's, but in his thesis he also seems to have overlooked the basic problem of all religious language: that it always is somewhat lacking in appropriate vocabulary. As Aquinas said, the language of the divine is always metaphorical. Very often something known is taken as a symbol for the divine (for example 'God is a rock'). So throughout history one can expect that political symbols are used to denote the divine—God is King—as well as the obverse phenomenon that religious symbols inform political symbols—the King is God. So in itself the transfer of theological concepts to the political sphere does not mark a movement toward secularisation. The key phrase of late Roman imperial theology, stating that the emperor was *dominus et deus*, may illustrate the problem. Here in one phrase a 'secular' term (*dominus*) is exalted to the sphere of the divine and a term denoting the divine (*deus*) is politicised.[14]

This mutual interpenetration of the divine and the political spheres is also notable in the early development of the word sovereignty. The significantly theological use of the concept of sovereignty even seems to be of a later date than the well-established political use. In the work of John Calvin, one of the crown witnesses for Schmitt's thesis, a theological concept of sovereignty does not hold centre place and as far as it does occur it seems to have been developed as a polemical counterpoint to all political claims of sovereignty. God is called 'sovereign' in order to ward off claims of absolute

---

[13] Helmut Quaritsch, *Souveränität. Enstehung und Entwicklung des Begriffs in Frankreich und Deutschland vom 13.Jh. bis 1806*, (Berlin, Duncker & Humblot 1986), p. 13f.
[14] Schmitt shows himself to be aware of the problem however in the book that he wrote much later, *Politische Theologie II. Die Legende von der Erledigung jeder politischen Theologie.* (Berlin, Duncker & Humblot 1970), p. 40f.

sovereignty by earthly princes.[15] So the first conclusion, on a more philological level, is that the concept of sovereignty is not in itself a 'secularised'
theological concept.

The other line suggested by Schmitt is what he calls a 'sociology of law'.
In order to understand the dominant political and legal concepts of an age,
one has to relate these concepts to the dominant metaphysics of that age,
Schmitt claims. According to him, in this way it can be made clear why
some political or legal concepts are almost self-evident in a certain period
but are experienced as strange and abstruse in another. Examples given by
Schmitt include the following: in the legal theory of the 17th century the
monarch fulfills the same function as God does in the Cartesian world
system;[16] and in the modern concept of sovereignty the divine attribute of
omnipotence has been transferred to the state or to the political sovereign.[17]
So this second approach does not search for a continuity of concepts (for
example 'sovereignty') of which the referent changes (from God to the king)
but it searches for a specific configuration of theological and political
concepts and images within a certain period so that the theological and
political meanings of the concept are mutually illuminating. Only after

---

[15] Gisbert Beyerhaus, *Studien zur Staatsanschauung Calvins. Mit besonderer Berücksichtigung
seines Souveränitätsbegriffs*, [Berlin 1910], (Aalen, Scientia Verlag 1973). In *Der Leviathan in
der Staatslehre des Thomas Hobbes. Sinn und Fehlschlag eines politischen Symbols* Schmitt
explicitly refers to Beyerhaus' study to underpin his own thesis, but as far as I can see
Beyerhaus stresses much more the 'de-legitimising' use of the concept of sovereignty in Calvin.
Most of the quotes from Calvin given by Beyerhaus convey this central thrust: God is called
sovereign because the prince is not. Although Beyerhaus claims 'das die Lehre von der
Souveränität Gottes, ihrem Ursprunge nach eine rein theologisch-dogmatische Vorstellung ist'
(p. 84), sovereignty is not one of the 'classical' theological attributes of God. It only seems to
become a divine attribute in a polemical theological context. See Beyerhaus, *o.c.*, 86 *ff*, 108 *ff*.
The 'classical' theological attributes of God that can be regarded as coming closest to the later
concept of sovereignty are *simplicitas, aseitas* and perhaps *omnipotentia*, but the actual
content of these concepts differs significantly with the concept of sovereignty. See FG Immink,
Divine Simplicity, (Kampen, Kok 1987), (however, apparently unaware of the specific history
of the concept of sovereignty, Immink occasionally uses the concept of sovereignty as a mere
synonym for simplicity and aseity) and Gijsbert van den Brink, *Almighty God. A Study of the
Doctrine of Divine Omnipotence*, (Kampen, Kok Pharos 1993).
[16] Carl Schmitt, *o.c.*, p. 60f.
[17] *Ibid*, 49, 51.

these synchronic configurations have been identified does it become possible to draw conclusions regarding certain diachronic developments.[18]

3. TOWARD AN ARCHAEOLOGY OF SOVEREIGNTY

In spite of the philological problems surrounding it, Schmitt's thesis can hardly be contradicted if one takes into account the history of early modern political thinking as a whole. The ultimate justification of the political order did shift from the theological to the secular, from transcendence to immanence. Schmitt's secularisation thesis as a whole stands. Moreover, the concept of sovereignty does indeed somehow play a key role in this movement. So perhaps Schmitt's thesis must be amended as follows: sovereignty is not in itself a 'secularised' theological concept but it is a political concept used specifically to carry out, to execute, the secularisation of the political sphere. So I suggest tentatively that the development of a new concept was needed to articulate a new conception of political order.

To demonstrate this amended version, Schmitt's second line of investigation remains promising. Partly adopting that second approach I would suggest identifying different strands of meaning in the concept of sovereignty. So the concept can be taken as a meeting point, a nodal point of different strands that come together at a specific juncture in Western history. Taken separately these strands may have come to their full expression at different times and in different contexts and they may have been related to different types of 'metaphysics'. Probing these different layers, we find that it is impossible to force them into one diachronic line of a secularisation process. Rather there seems to be a kind of back and forth between theological and political experiences. The net result may turn out to be a secularised political order, but while this secularisation is in some respects theologically grounded, in other respects it is an unintended consequence of certain theological insights, and in still other respects indeed a result of a quite deliberate process of 'secularisation'.

---

[18] *Ibid*, 49, 51. Schmitt provides a more elaborate exposition of this type of diachronic analysis of the Western secularisation process in his essay on 'Das Zeitalter der Neutralisierungen und Entpolitisierungen' that forms the second part of his *Der Begriff des Politischen* (1932 versions). Here Schmitt uses the conception of a 'central sphere' (Zentralgebiet), which is the sphere of life that shapes the basic perspective of the dominant elites in a society in a given age. For all the major problems in a society in that age the solution will be sought in a direction that is given with this basic perspective. Problems of other spheres of life become secondary. The 'humanitarian-ethical' perspective of the dominant elites in the 18th century render the vexing theological and metaphysical problems of the 16th and 17th century obsolete. The economic perspective of the 19th century has the same result regarding ethics. Finally, the technical perspective of the 20th century renders everything else obsolete: all problems become technical problems, for which technical solutions have to be found. However, the authority of every central sphere is for Schmitt essentially 'religious': one can speak of a 'religion of economics' and a 'religion of technicism' etc.

This 'multidimensional approach' can also be helpful to shed some light on the problem of the alleged newness of the concept of sovereignty.[19] In the seminal work of Bodin the problem can already be felt very clearly. On the one hand the concept is one among several others that are used inter-changeably. Bodin himself is strongly aware of this. When he introduces the word 'sovereignty' in his *Six livres de la république* he refers to similar concepts in Roman antiquity ('que les Latins appellent maiestatem'), to the Israelite scriptures ('*tomeed sjéfèt*': he that holds the sceptre[20]), to classical Greek equivalents like *akra exousia* (highest power), *kuria archè* (masterly or highest rule) and *kurion politeuma* (masterly or highest government). On the other hand Bodin holds that nobody before him had a clear view of what sovereignty really is. As long as one operates with too monolithic a notion of sovereignty one faces the dilemma of either flatly denying Bodin's claim of continuity or playing down the novelty of his conception.

Analysing the theological roots of the different layers of meaning also supplies the opportunity to dig into some of these related concepts that together seem to constitute a family: 'highest power' (*summa potestas, plena potestas, plenitudo potestatis*), 'absolute power' (*potentia absoluta* or perhaps *omnipotentia*), 'being above the law' (*legibus solutus*), 'majesty' (*maiestas*) and imperial rule (*imperium*). They are all concepts that are or have been used as synonyms or as interpretations of the concept of 'sover-eignty'. And these are all concepts with strong theological overtones or reminiscences.

So what are these 'layers of meaning'? The most frequent definitions of sovereignty run along the lines of 'the highest authority to issue laws within a certain territory'. If one ponders this rough description in a phenomeno-logical manner, some characteristics emerge that one can tentatively single out. Together they seem to be specific to the modern notion of sovereignty compared to earlier politico-theological symbolism.

> The *first* element concerns unifying a realm and organising it into one political entity.
> The *second* element is the presence of one subject, one representative centre of power, one agent, who has his/her place vis-à-vis this entity, for example to issue laws.
> The *third* element of the concept of sovereignty concerns its voluntaristic over-tones. The sovereignty is mostly couched in terms of a will, of an almost personal character.

---

[19] See for this problem in the context of a 'history of ideas' FH Hinsley, *Sovereignty*, (London, CA Watts 1966, p. 15–26.

[20] The Hebrew equivalent that Bodin gives ('tomeed sjéfèt': he that holds the scepter) is some-what puzzling. In the Old Testament it is found only in the book of Amos and there it occurs only twice (1: 5, 8). The highly specific, technical-legal meaning that Bodin attributes to this expression cannot be inferred from these places. Did a Talmudic or other tradition develop later on in which this notion of 'scepter-bearer' has acquired a specific role to which Bodin alludes?

The *fourth* element is the territorial limitation. Compared to older symbolisms like the Sumerian King List mentioned above, the modern notion of sovereignty seems rather awkward: the highest power, but only in a limited territory. It is somewhat like calling a person 'world famous in his own village'.

These four elements—internal unification, agency, voluntarism and external limitation—I take to be characteristic of the modern notion of sovereignty. Having identified these four 'layers' I can now elaborate upon my initial question: can specific politico-theological changes be identified that at least partially account for the emergence and subsequent changes in all these four layers separately and which made them susceptible to being appropriated in the new concept of sovereignty? Or, stated somewhat differently: what steps had to be taken successively in order to arrive at this notion? And very important as well: did the development of the symbol of sovereignty have a free ride or were there counter-movements?

In the process of answering these questions successively I intend to develop what can be called an archaeology of sovereignty. To make clear: an archaeology is not a historical narrative nor an exercise in the history of ideas (both would far exceed the limits of this chapter, and I have to ask the masters of these genres to make allowances for what I am undertaking here and for the mistakes and overhasty conclusions which are inherent in my approach). It is rather an attempt to investigate historical materials in order to uncover the different layers of meaning that have gone into the shaping of a certain concept. In order to acquire a keen sense of what is theologically at stake in the symbol of sovereignty, attention will be paid also to the articulation of a 'counterposition' (section 6). Of course the politico-theological developments only partly account for the emergence of the symbol of sovereignty. Political, social, economic and perhaps still other factors should be taken into account as well but that would bring me far beyond the scope of the present chapter.[21]

4. THE FIRST LAYER: 'REX EST IMPERATOR'

A very intriguing formula that became fashionable among jurists in the period in which the concept of sovereignty was gradually articulated has it that 'the king is emperor in his own realm' (*rex est imperator in regno suo*).[22] Here we hit upon the first layer of meaning of the concept of sovereignty, the transfer of imperial claims. What were these claims and more specifically, what were their politico-theological implications?

[21] For a broader account see for example Helmut Quaritsch, *Staat und Souveränität*, (Frankfurt, Athenäum verlag 1970). Hendrik Spruyt, *The Sovereign State and its Competitors*, (Princeton, Princeton University Press 1994;) Daniel Philpott, *Revolutions in Sovereignty. How Ideas Shaped Modern International Relations*, (Princeton, Princeton University Press 2001).

[22] Piet Leupen, *Keizer in zijn eigen rijk. De geboorte van de nationale staat.* (Amsterdam, Wereldbibliotheek 1998), 100–11.

A first entry is offered by the opening quotes of this chapter. In the symbolism of the Sumerian King List we encounter the conception of what can be called 'imperial kingship' as it occurred in the Ancient Near East and as it may occur as well in many other historical symbolisms of 'empire' or unified world rule. A characteristic of the oldest imperial symbolisms is that they represent the empire as an analogy of the order of the cosmos. From the center the rule of empire extends over 'the Four Quarters (author's note: of the world—East, West, North and South)'.[23] Generally speaking, the empire is a *representation* of cosmic order. And this implies at the same time that the imperial society has to conform to the cosmic order. So there is a double movement: from the cosmic order downward into society and from society upward into the cosmic order. It is the king who is actually the play-ground of this double movement. The person of the king or the emperor becomes a mediator between the cosmic scene and the mundane world. He is the one who actually brings the cosmic order into the political order. And at the same time he represents the political order before and between the gods.[24]

This could be a time-consuming job for a king. In Assyrian times, Frankfurt relates, 'his time was largely taken up with penitence and prophy-lactic magic'. He had to rely heavily on the advice of the soothsayers and priests who were responsible for interpreting the signs of the celestial bodies and for instructing the king accordingly. For example a letter has been preserved in which the king is summoned to stay in a reed hut for seven consecutive days, submitting to purifying rites all the time. The king repeat-edly complains about all his cosmic duties, but his complaints are in vain. He sometimes even has to hire a 'stand-in' who performs the rites when these are considered too dangerous—but take place they must. This performer of cosmic rites is a far cry from a sovereign ruler.

So the king (or in the case of Hatshepsut, the queen) is not sovereign. He has indeed contracted power in one center, from which laws and measures are issued. But at the very same time in this center he is only considered to be a deputy of the gods. If one can speak of 'sovereignty' at all in this context it is only present among the gods, where for example Marduk is chosen by the other gods as their leader and vested with absolute power.

> 'Marduk, thou art of consequence among the elder gods;
> Thy rank is unequaled and thy command is Anu's.
> From this day onward shall thy orders not be altered;
> To elevate and to abase—this be within thy power.
> What thou hast spoken shall come true, thy word shall not prove vain.
> Among the gods none shall encroach upon thy rights!'[25]

---

[23] H Frankfurt, *a.w.*, p. 228.
[24] *Ibid*, p. 252–61.
[25] H Frankfurt, *o.c.*, p. 325.

So in what sense can it be maintained that the imperial theology is still a 'layer of meaning' in the modern notion of sovereignty? It lies in the awareness, or at least the claim, that a unified political entity is a necessary precondition for survival in the world. The political order provides shelter in an otherwise threatening world. To have a unified power structure, concretely to have a king, means to be able to endure in the world and to be protected. This stability in the world is always precarious. Therefore it has to be secured in a relation that transcends society proper. The stability of society has to be safeguarded vis-à-vis the 'outside'.[26]

Our conclusion in regard to this first layer of meaning can be that the imperial theologies represent a type of symbolism that expresses the experience of a unified political power structure as a shelter in an otherwise threatening cosmos.

As a corollary the following observations can be added. The constancy of this layer can easily be discerned in the modern contract symbolism of Hobbes, Locke and Rousseau. Without a unified political order the world is experienced as horrific and threatening (Hobbes) or as lacking in stability (Locke) or as a loss of man's pristine origins (Rousseau). The very high expectations that still surround the political sphere in modern times can perhaps be understood from the background of the age-old efficacy of this symbolism.

However—and here Schmitts's observations are to be recalled—the direction of the imperial symbolism has almost made an about-turn: no longer is this 'kingship lowered from heaven' but it is erected from below. It is a human artefact. Against this background a unified power structure can perhaps still be called a 'god', but it has became a 'mortal' one (Hobbes) or the symbolism of the divine gifts recedes from the public sphere altogether and is drawn into the private sphere (as in Locke, for whom God is the dispenser of private property rather than of a political power structure) or, reminiscent of the later phases of the Roman Empire, the symbolism of the divine becomes explicitly an intra-political invention to boost the social-psychological stability of the political structure (Rousseau's *religion civile*).

---

[26] This 'transcendental' structure of a political order is quite visible in the cases mentioned in the text. In recent years attention has been drawn to the fact that this kind of relation in a formal sense is somehow constitutive for any political order. What varies from one political order to the other is the content of what is regarded as 'outside'. See Eric Voegelin, *The New Science of Politics. An Introduction.* (Chicago, University of Chicago Press 1952), pp. 52–75; Claude Lefort, 'The Permanence of the Theologico-Political in: *Democracy and Political Theory*, (Minneapolis: University of Minnesota Press 1988), pp. 213–55, esp. pp. 219–26. (Orig. in: *Essai sur le politique. XIXe-XXe siècle.* (Paris, Seuil 1986); Hans Lindahl, 'Vorst, op God na. Politieke macht en de symbolisering van souvereiniteit', in: *Nederlands tijdschrift voor rechtstheorie en rechtsfilosofie*, vol. 26, nr. 2, 1997, pp. 122–36; Gerhard Hoogers, *De verbeelding van het soevereine. Een onderzoek naar de theoretische grondslagen van politieke representatie.* (Deventer, Kluwer 1999).

5. THE SECOND LAYER: MONOTHEISM

In the early empires the 'centre of power' is a condensation of powers in the cosmos. The centre is not that of an individual with a responsibility towards the political community to issue laws—and this is a presupposition of any notion of sovereignty. In the centre there is not a 'personal' being but a relationship between a representative and a represented pre-existing order.

When the formula *rex est imperator* is used by the medieval jurists they are of course not referring directly to the empires of the Ancient Near East but to a symbol that has received its specific connotations through the filter of the Roman empire. That is where we have to look for articulations of a more 'agency-like' conception of rulership, as is contained in the *rex est imperator* formula. What exactly did the symbol *imperator* mean in the Roman Empire? What were the connotations of the symbol *imperium*?

Of course it is not possible to draw general conclusions here. One has to take into account the specific phase of the empire. The meaning of the key symbols changes drastically whether one considers the republican phase, the period of the Principate or the phase after Diocletian of the Dominate. Originally, *imperator* was not a title that carried heavy implications. An army awarded it to its general after an important victory. There could be several *imperatores* at any given time. Later on, in the time of the Principate, the title was monopolised by the emperors and used as a proper name to enhance their splendor and glory, without explicitly referring to specific victories and without well-defined legal consequences. The same holds true *mutatis mutandis* for the symbol *imperium*, which originally referred to the highest military command and developed into a synonym for *potestas* which could refer to legally granted powers to execute what the law prescribes. The title *princeps* originally did not denote any sort of sovereignty either. It merely meant a prominent or front-rank citizen. There could be many *principes* at the same time. When Caesar Augustus founded the Principate he intentionally chose this title to avoid the impression of absolute rulership. His Principate was not based on his *potestas*, the actual legal powers which he allegedly shared with the senate, but on his *auctoritas*, his personal authority.

However, the title of *princeps* developed into a virtual synonym of the monopolising *imperator* and gained more and more monarchical-absolutistic connotations.[27] It comes as no surprise then that later a kind of competition with the designation *dominus* can be discerned. Sometimes the terms are used interchangeably. Sometimes a definite distinction is made as some

---

[27] Paulys and Wissowa, *Real-Encyclopädie der classischen Altertumswissenschaft*, (Stuttgart: JB Metzlersche Verlagsbuchhandlung), s.v. *princeps*, 2057–68, 2100. *Cf* Theodor Mommsen, *Römisches Staatsrecht*, vol. 2, pt. 2 (1876–88), (Basel, Benno Schwabe Verlag), 1952, pp. 749vv.

emperors consciously either refused or adopted one or other title. *Princeps* was then preferred to express the more 'senate-oriented' conception of imperial power. *Dominus*, originally a term of the private sphere denoting the absolute power of the father over his family (*pater familias, potestas patria*), implied that the emperor regarded the empire as his personal property. It is at this later stage that the material content of some aspects of what would later be called sovereignty is actually articulated. The two most famous phrases in this respect come from the lawyer Ulpian. *Princeps legibus solutus* (the emperor is not bound by the law) and *quod principi placuit legis habet vigorem* (what pleases the emperor has the force of law)—phrases to which I will return below. Here we get an impression of the notion of free, self-responsible law-giving that is a key element of sovereignty.

The full politico-theological meaning of the imperial rule in Rome can perhaps best be sensed in the symbols of *maiestas* (the very term that Bodin took as the precursor of his concept of sovereignty) and *auctoritas*. The symbol of *maiestas* would have a prodigious career: it became the key term in the legal articulation of treason as *crimen laesae maiestatis*. The word itself means literally 'highness' or 'sublimity'. 'What the Latins called *maiestatem*' refers to the specific position Rome held in the world as the divinely appointed leader of the *orbis terrarum*, the unified world. Therefore Rome had *maiestas*, a right to be revered, honored and obeyed by all the peoples of the earth.[28] For Ovidius *Maiestas* is the offspring of *Honor* and *Reverentia*. It is both power and glory, splendor and prestige. Those vested with *maiestas* are the gods as compared to the mortals, but also the *pater familias* as compared to the members of his family, and above all the Roman state and its representatives (*magistratus populi Romani* and later the *Princeps*) as compared to its own citizens and, especially, as compared to the other nations. *Maiestas* in the Roman Empire was never a well-defined legal concept. However, the number of offences that were covered by the *crimen laesae maiestatis* was gradually extended while at the same time the 'referent' of this crime was more and more reduced to one single person: the emperor. As the emperor became more and more a divine figure the *maiestas* became more and more the divine glory of the emperor and the corresponding crime became something akin to sacrilege. Greek translations then render the offence as 'impiety' (*asebeia*).

The *auctoritas* of the *princeps* initially seems to refer to something Max Weber would have called 'charisma'. It is not in any way a legal term but refers to personal influence that is assigned to the *princeps* by the people and especially by the representatives of the people, the senate. The key point here is the voluntary submission to what is supposed to be the emperor's

---

[28] *Ibid* Paulys and Wissowa, *Real-Encyclopädie*, s.v. *maiestas*, 27e Halbband, pp. 542–59.

wisdom or genius, based on the notion or the expectation that he will know what is best. But the term 'charisma' in this respect has to be qualified inasmuch as for Weber it is in contrast to 'traditional authority'. In the Roman *auctoritas* these two sources of authority merge. It links the present with the sacred past of the ancestors and founders of Rome. He who has *auctoritas* embodies the spirit of the *auctores*, the founders, who are the *maiores*, the older and hence greater ones.[29] He embodies the spirit and essence of Rome and becomes its unique representative.

Throughout the shifts in meaning of the key concepts in the Roman empire there is the issue of the increasing divinisation of the emperor. Shortly after his assassination on March 15, 44 BC Julius Caesar was already declared to have been divine. Augustus quickly arranged to be called 'son of the divine Caesar' and actually established a cult of worship centred around his own *genius*, which spread rapidly throughout the empire.[30] However, as *pontifex maximus* the emperor, notwithstanding his own divinity, still had the sacred duty to ensure the proper worship of all the traditional deities. Later on, emperor worship more and more functioned as the one overriding public cult for the entire empire (while at the same time allowing ample room for local and private cults). This development was enhanced strongly by the growing influence of the East in the empire: the city of Rome experienced an influx of Eastern religions and simultaneously the gravitation point of the empire moved toward the Eastern regions. So Rome lessened its resistance against the Eastern conceptions of kingship harking back to the old Mesopotamian and Egyptian empires and transferred by Alexander the Great into Hellenistic kingship. The growing emphasis on the divinity of the emperor and on his cult also coincided with syncretistic, monotheistic tendencies. More and more the view that there was only one *summus deus* became fashionable while all the other deities were gradually regarded as his manifestations.[31] And this in turn seems to have coincided with a change of emphasis from *auctoritas* to *maiestas*.[32]

---

[29] Th. Mommsen, *o.c.*, vol. 1, p. 309, vol. 3, pt. 2, p. 1038v. *Cf* Hannah Arendt (referring to Mommsen), 'What is Authority?', *Between Past and Future. Eight Exercises in Political Thought* [1961], (Harmondsworth/New York, Penguin 1987), pp. 91–141, esp. pp. 121–6.

[30] Until very recently the majority of Roman historians, echoing Kurt Latte, considered the importance of the Imperial Cult in classical times to be quite marginal. Thanks to the impressive work of eg Fishwick this opinion is changing drastically. See Duncan Fishwick, *The Imperial Cult in the Latin West. Studies in the Ruler Cult of the Western Provinces of the Roman Empire.* (Leiden, EJ Brill 1987–92) (4 vols.)... See also Allen Brent, *The Imperial Cult and the Development of Church Order. Concepts and Images of Authority in Paganism and Early Christianity before the Age of Cyprian.* (Leiden, Brill 1999).

[31] See Allen Brent, *o.c.*, pp. 251–309.

[32] See Paulys and Wissowa, *Real-Encyclopädie*, s.v. *maiestas*. Very infamous became the so-called *Lex Quisquis* of 397 which not only prohibited action dangerous to the state but also the planning of such action, which opened the door widely for all kinds of unprovable accusations against almost anyone.

The *auctoritas*, which is, as it were, a 'horizontal' concept, linking the present with the past, seems to have been replaced more and more by the 'vertical' concept of *maiestas*, which binds the present to the heights of the divine. And the *auctoritas*, precisely because of its 'horizontality', still carried the possibility of some *public* accountability. For the past is known to everybody, but who knows or can interpret the divine heights? Only a god can know a god. Only the divine emperor can gaze into the divine *arcanum*. But who is able to judge independently what he sees and whether he interprets rightly what is to be seen? The *maiestas* appears to have developed into the symbol of unaccountability and indemnity to criticism.

6. THE FORMATION OF A COUNTERPOSITION: TRANSCENDENCE

Exploring the relationship between different 'theological' conceptions and the emergence of the concept of sovereignty Hans Kelsen posited that

> 'Während die Mythologie als Theologie des Polytheismus hinter die eine Natur eine Vielheit von Göttern setzt, begnügt sich die Theologie des Monotheismus mit einer einzigen Hypostase. Und darum entspricht der Begriff des einig-einzigen Staates der Rechtslehre vor allem und insbesondere dem Begriff des einig-einzigen Gottes der jüdisch-christlichen Theologie'.[33]

So for Kelsen monotheism provides the metaphysical framework for the articulation of the key elements of the notion of sovereignty. Kelsen is not very positive about this marriage of monotheism and state sovereignty, because the modern notion of sovereignty itself is very problematic to him. He even states that 'Das Souveränitätsbegriff muss freilich radikal verdrängt werden'.[34] And because of this close relationship he draws the bold conclusion that in order to restore, or even to establish properly for the first time the unity of law and state, one has to resort to 'pan-cosmic pantheism' that does not allow for the ontological differentiations that Kelsen blames for the articulation of a conception of the state vis-à-vis the law.[35]

Yet, as was indicated above, monotheistic tendencies are not confined to the Jewish-Christian orbit, as Kelsen claims. It has even been questioned whether unqualified monotheism represents the orthodox Christian position at all. In his famous tractate on *Der Monotheismus als politisches Problem*, the German theologian Erik Peterson has claimed the contrary.

---

[33] Hans Kelsen, *Der soziologische und der juristische Staatsbegriff. Kritische Untersuchung des Verhältnisses von Staat und Recht*. [1922], (Aalen, Scientia Verlag 1962), 219f.

[34] Hans Kelsen, *Das Problem der Souveränität und die Theorie des Völkerrechts*, (Tübingen 1920), p. 320; 'The concept of sovereignty must of course be radically superceded.'

[35] Above n 3 Hans Kelsen, *Der soziologische . . .*, p. 247 *ff*.

Unqualified monotheism, according to Peterson, will always be liable to become a handmaiden to the powers that be. The attraction and perhaps unavoidability of representational images within the realm of the political is an invitation to complement the symbol of 'One God' (*eis theos, monarchia*) with the formula of 'One Emperor and One Empire'.[36] As a consequence the state becomes an all encompassing unity comparable to the Ancient Eastern Empires. For Peterson this tradition starts with Aristotle's quote from the Iliad at the end of the twelfth book of the *Metaphysics* which reads that 'the rule of many is not good; one be the lord'. This is then elaborated in the famous sixth chapter of the (pseudo-) Aristotelian *De mundo*, where the rule of God in the universe is compared with the rule of the Persian emperor.[37] Inspired by this work Philo in his turn imported the symbol of *monarchia* into the Christian orbit where it came to its ominous fruition in the works by eg Origen and Eusebius, who were also prone to some form of heresy. So for Peterson it is only the Western Christian tradition with its emphasis on the Trinity that shows itself immune to politicisation and prevents the emergence of a political theology—at least in principle. Three persons cannot be represented by one emperor.

Of course we should note that the key problem for Kelsen and Peterson is exactly the opposite. For Kelsen the problem of sovereignty is that it poses a person-like state over the law. He wants to establish the unity of state and law and therefore needs a 'unifying metaphysics'. For Peterson the problem is precisely the lack of distinction. So for Kelsen monotheism invites some form of separation of the political order. For Peterson monotheism is an element that prohibits making key separations. So both want to do away with monotheism, but for very different reasons.

Is there a way to clarify this puzzle? The key problem is that the two thinkers attach quite different meanings to monotheism. For Kelsen monotheism apparently is associated with transcendence, with a rift between the world and something 'outside' this world. Peterson associates monotheism with numerical oneness and therefore the tendency to confuse all differences and distinctions in the immanent one-ness of the cosmos. Precisely in their opposite positions Kelsen and Peterson point to a key problem in medieval (political) theology. In Christian theology God, as the Creator of the cosmos, is not part of the cosmos. And yet, He cannot be cut loose from the cosmos entirely either (as ancient Gnosticism attempted). So

---

[36] Erik Peterson, *Der Monotheismus als politisches Problem. Ein Beitrag zur Geschichte der politischen Theologie im Imperium Romanum*, [1935]; repr. in *Theologische Traktate*, (München: Kösel Verlag 1951), pp. 45–147.

[37] The argument for the Aristotelian authenticity of *Peri tou kosmou* or *De Mundo* has been brought forward with new vigour in recent years by G Reale and AP Bos. See for a short introduction into the present state of the debate the Introduction in AP Bos' Dutch translation of *De Mundo, Aristoteles. Over de kosmos*, (Amsterdam, Boom 1989), pp. 9–25. So it seems that after many centuries we can finally drop the disturbing prefix 'pseudo-'.

there is a certain differentiation between God and the world and at the same time a certain intimate connection. It was Thomas Aquinas who coined for this the symbol of *analogia entis*, the analogy of being, which expresses in one phrase difference and sameness. Masterful as the Thomasian symbol might be, it could not put all the tensions to rest (as will be elaborated in the next section).

To put the problem in a larger context it is helpful to call upon the work of the Israeli sociologist SN Eisenstadt. Over the last twenty years he has revived the concept of 'Axial Age' (Achsenzeit) as it was coined by Karl Jaspers.[38] 'Axial civilisations' for Eisenstadt are civilisations within which 'new types of ontological visions, of conceptions of a basic tension between the transcendental and the mundane orders emerged and were institutionalised'.[39] This distinction has important political consequences, especially for the symbolism of divine kingship. The cosmic oneness of things divine and human is broken. Groups or classes come into being that challenge the existing order and hold rulers accountable for either fulfilling the transcendent expectations or failing to do so. The earlier natural bond between the divine and the king or emperor is challenged fundamentally. Other groups, 'proto-intellectuals' like clerics and priests, claim the right either to judge the king or emperor or to regard themselves as basically free from the mundane world and its rulers. They in principle become dissidents, without striving simply to replace the worldly ruler. In their judging acts they somehow remain outside society. Moreover, the tension holds both with respect to ontology (no mundane order can be equated with the transcendental) and with respect to chronology or eschatology (the transcendental order will never be reached in history, but only beyond history proper).

Returning to the relation between monotheism/transcendence and sovereignty, one can say that indeed the notion of a transcendent and hence free Creator-God loosened the cosmic ties between the divine and the political and established the emperor or the king as a figure in his own right under

[38] Karl Jaspers, *Vom Ursprung und Ziel der Geschichte*, (Zürich, Artemis 1949). For Jaspers the 'Achsenzeit' is the period from 800 to 200 BC, with a high point around 500 BC, a period in which very diverse and remote regions in a rather similar fashion radical questions were asked about man and his place in the cosmos. In this period in China (Confucius, Lao-Tse), India (Buddha), Iran (Zoroaster), Israel (the prophets) and Greece (the philosophers) the basic categories were articulated with which we still interpret our own existence, according to Jaspers.

[39] Compared with Jaspers, one can note that for Eisenstadt the emphasis should not be on a certain chronological period, but on the basic ontological distinctions that are articulated whenever and whereever they may occur. See SN Eisenstadt (ed)., *The Origins and Diversity of Axial Age Civilisations*, (New York, SUNY Press 1986), especially the introductions by Eisenstadt. More recent: Chapter 16 'Japanese Historical Experience in a Comparative Framework' of the Japan monograph *Japanese Civilisation. A Comparative View*, (Chicago, University of Chicago Press 1996). Most recent, also very clear, *Fundamentalism, Sectarianism and Revolution. The Jacobin Dimension of Modernity*. (Cambridge, Cambridge University Press 1999). I quote from the latter publication, p. 4.

God. In this sense Christianity deepened and provided a new articulation for the late-Roman development of a more agency-like type of rulership. It comes as no surprise then that the ideal of rulership in medieval times changed from the cosmic suncult of the late Roman empire to the historical example of Israel's king David. In this respect Kelsen's observation makes sense.

But this very same transcendence prevented any notion of absoluteness of king or emperor and hence provided a critique of this late-Roman conception. Peterson is right in stating that indeed in the West a full-fledged political theology, establishing and defending the ruler's absolute claims, has encountered severe obstacles (though Peterson's term 'Erledigung' [emptying], might be an exaggeration).[40] In the West imperial and royal rulership became an office, a *charisma* within the societal order of the *corpus mysticum*.[41] And the way this office was carried out was in principle subject to criticism. Allowing for all kinds of nuances it can be said that in this respect there is a long and straight line between the famous dictum of Pope Gelasius (492–6) that there are 'two powers by which the world is chiefly ruled, the sacred authority (*auctoritas*) of the Popes and the royal power (*potestas*)' on the one hand and on the other hand the formulation of cardinal Bellarminus around 1610 of the *potestas indirecta in temporalibus*. The spiritual authority concerns the ethical and religious aspects of earthly rule (*pro ratione peccati*), but it does not aim to replace by itself the earthly ruler in case of misbehavior.[42] So the notion of oneness is not what has become characteristic for the West, but that of a double representation, the double and mutually irreducible representation of man by church and empire.[43]

---

[40] To be sure, this is partly due to different reasons than Peterson thought. There might have been a softening influence of the symbol of the Trinity in as far as this emphasises that in the one God there is a communication, a dialogue between three persons and hence none of them is 'absolute' in a strict sense (notwithstanding the fact that at the same time it is held that the *opera ad extra sunt indivisa*: the works in which the Triune God manifests Himself display oneness). But the transcendence of God seems to be a more important factor. And it is especially God's transcendence that is emphasised less in the Eastern branch of the early church. In the theologies of Origenes and other Eastern theologians the Christian Creator-God is to a great extent part of the one cosmos. God is the point of departure and the point of return of the cosmos in one 'natural' movement. *Cf* the still valuable study by H Berkhof, *De kerk en de keizer. Een studie over het ontstaan van de byzantinistische en de theocratische staatsgedachte in de vierde eeuw.* (Amsterdam, Holland 1946.) For a detailed, also philological, critique of Peterson's thesis see Alfred Schindler (ed.), *Monotheismus als politisches Problem? Erik Peterson und die Kritik der politischen Theologie*, (Gütersloh, Gerd Mohn 1978), esp. pp. 23–70.

[41] Erich Voegelin, *Rasse und Staat*, (Tübingen, JCB Mohr 1933), p. 137f. *Cf* Alois Dempf, *Sacrum Imperium. Geschichts- und Staatsphilosophie des Mittelalters und der politischen Renaissance*. (München, R Oldenbourg 1962), p. 136: 'Zugleich ist durch den sakramentalen Akt der Salbung das Königtum zu einem Amte und Dienste, zu einem *officium* und *ministerium* innerhalb der ecclesia geworden. Es hat damit völlig seine absolutistische Alleinherrlichkeit im spätantiken Sinn verloren'.

[42] John B Morrall, *Political Thought in Medieval Times*, (Toronto, University of Toronto Press 1980), p. 22f.

[43] Eric Voegelin, *The New Science . . .*, p. 104–6.

Vis-à-vis Peterson it seems more likely that the frictions surrounding imperial theology in the West have more to do with the transcendence of God than with a specific emphasis on trinitarian theology.

The conclusion regarding the concept of sovereignty has to be rather mixed. On the one hand the transcendence of the Christian God strips the ruler of his divine qualities. He becomes a responsible agent under God in his own right. So it seems to be a defensible claim that Christianity provided another and actually more fitting 'metaphysics' for the position the emperor had obtained in the late-Roman empire, as someone who does not carry out divine orders (as Hatshepsut claimed) but is a self-responsible law-giver for the empire. During the time of what Berman has called the 'Papal Revolution' this was even enhanced by the image of God as a 'lawmaker'.[44] At the same time however Christianity retained and actually institutionalised the 'Axial differentiation' between transcendence and immanence and so made the ruler accountable to God and to his fellow-Christians as represented by the church. It may be clear that in order to arrive at the modern notion of sovereignty this 'Christian qualification' would have to be removed. This is what happens implicitly in the work of Bodin and explicitly in the work of Th. Hobbes.[45] The longest chapter by far in his *Leviathan* is entirely devoted to the refutation of the *potestas indirecta* as formulated by Bellarminus.[46] And yet, while the transcendence of the Christian God vis-à-vis the ruler is 'taken back' by Hobbes, the transcendence of the ruler vis-à-vis society is strongly affirmed. In Hobbes we encounter the figure of the sovereign who is himself somehow 'transcendent in the immanence'.

6. THE THIRD LAYER: THE INSCRUTABILITY OF GOD

In his Latin translation Bodin begins his eighth chapter as follows: *Maiestas est summa in cives ac subditos legibusque soluta potestas.* The phrase is a rather free translation of the French original where it was said that 'sovereignty is absolute and permanent power'. The Latin rendering adopts without any reservation the famous dictum of Ulpian already mentioned above, the *princeps legibus solutus est*.

---

[44] Above n 26 Harold J Berman, *Law and Revolution. The Formation of the Western Legal Tradition.* (Cambridge MA, Harvard University Press 1983), p. 521: 'Law came to be seen as the very essence of faith. "God is himself law, and therefore law is dear to him", wrote the author of the *Sachsenspiegel*, the first German lawbook, about 1220'.

[45] *Cf* in this respect St L Collins, *From Divine Cosmos to Sovereign State. An Intellectual History of Consciousness and the Idea of Order in Renaissance England,* (Oxford, Oxford University Press 1989).

[46] Th. Hobbes, *Leviathan or the Matter, Forme and Power of a Commonwealth Ecclesiastical and Civil,* ed. (Michael Oakeshott, New York/London, Collier-Macmillan 1962), pp. 359–423 'Of Power Ecclesiastical'.

The history of the *legibus solutus* is in fact the history of a curious misunderstanding.[47] Before Ulpian—indeed as early as the time of the Roman republic—the senate in exceptional cases allowed someone by *legibus solutio* dispensation from a specific positive law. Later on emperors sometimes made use of this clause, for example to circumvent the existing laws of succession in order to adopt their successor as their son. Gradually however the phrase began to take on a life of its own and acquired a more general meaning, as a description of the legal position as such of the emperor. A curious development in this respect was that the emperor himself acquired the legal competence to declare his own *legibus solutio*. Even then the *legibus solutio* was still balanced by a certain awareness of *legibus obligatio* of the emperor. By the time of Ulpian however it had already acquired the meaning of 'not bound by any existing law'.

The phrase is also a telling example of the mutual penetration of theological and political symbols. With Ulpian, the phrase was clearly a political one. But in late medieval times it was taken up in philosophy and theology to become a centrepiece of the emerging nominalism. One can safely say that this theological and philosophical reworking of the concept in its turn became a strong reinforcement of a renewed political use and thus of its transformation into a key element of the concept of sovereignty. Such pivotal figures of the nominalist movement as Duns Scotus and William of Ockham did not shy away from political problems and in their treatment of the problems they showed themselves very aware of the consequences of their philosophical approach.

The late-medieval rise of nominalism is in fact, as Louis Dupré has emphasised, part of the rise of a new conception of freedom. In the classical conception freedom was always somehow limited by the rational order of the universe. Freedom always had something to do with the unhampered unfolding of the nature or essence of something. A conception of absolute freedom, as the possibility to do everything imaginable without restriction, was simply not conceivable. And this was exactly what the new meaning of freedom was all about.[48]

Nominalism can be seen as the most articulated and most telling expression of this deep change in social and political ontology. The single most important distinction that nominalism elaborated was that between *poten-*

[47] Paulys/Wissowa, *Real-Encyclopädie*, s.v. *princeps*. Dieter Wyduckel, *Princeps Legibus Solutus. Eine Untersuchung zur frühmodernen Rechts- und Staatslehre*. (Berlin, Duncker & Humblot 1979), p. 48 *ff*.
[48] Louis Dupré, *Passage to Modernity. An Essay in the Hermeneutics of Nature and Culture*, (New Haven, Yale University Press 1993).

tia absoluta and *potentia ordinata*.[49] In retrospect, the emergence of this distinction is not difficult to understand. According to the Christian view God is the transcendent, personal creator of the cosmos (see above). But if this is true the world can not be conceived of as a necessary outflow or emanation of God's rational being. He apparently must have *decided* to create it. Although the existence of the world could still be considered an analogy of God's rationality, on a more basic level it turns out to be based upon an act of divine free will. But then God could have decided otherwise as well (or else his will would not be free and hence God would not be really transcendent). So God in his *potentia absoluta* apparently must have all kind of possibilities that He for one reason or the other has chosen not to realise. God's chosen order is based upon his revealed *potentia ordinata*. So this existing order, ordained by God, does not reflect God's essence, but is an outcome of his will. So if God's essence is goodness, love, etcetera, and the existing order is not a reflection of his essence, is the existing order then good, is it trustworthy? In the nominalist conception it is, not because of an ontological warrant but because of God's *promissio*, his promise to uphold the existing order. God also has freely chosen to bind his will to the existing order. And the symbol in which this faithfulness of God towards the existing order is expressed is the *pactum*, the covenant or contract.[50] So the nominalist God is *legibus solutus* though He may choose freely to bind himself to an actual order—and according to the nominalist theologians He has in fact done so.

The significance of the nominalist movement can be found in four closely interrelated elements. The first element, as pointed out by Heiko Oberman, who inspired a re-evaluation of nominalism in recent decades, is that the thrust of nominalism was to bring about a new relation between the sacred and the profane, between transcendence and immanence.[51] Nominalism broke away from the symbolism of the 'chain of being', in which the world in its entirety is a necessary outflow of divine substance.[52] In this symbolism the divine is the Highest Being and everything else is necessarily of less

[49] A renewed attention to this distinction has been triggered by Heiko A Obermans, *The Harvest of Medieval Theology. Gabriel Biel and Late Medieval Nominalism*, (Cambridge MA, Harvard University Press 1963). For a short overview of the history of this distinction in medieval and early reformational theology see Gijsbert van den Brink, *o.c.*, 68–92. On the later development of the distinction see Marin Terpstra, *De wending naar de politiek. Een studie over de begrippen 'potentia' en 'potestas' bij Spinoza*, (Nijmegen, University of Nijmegen Diss. 1990), pp. 146 *ff*.

[50] See for this intimate connection between will, promise and covenant in late-medieval theology the study of Berndt Hamm, *Promissio, Pactum, Ordinatio. Freiheit und Selbstbindung Gottes in der scholastischen Gnadenlehre*, (Tübingen, JCB Mohr (Paul Siebeck), 1977).

[51] Heiko A Oberman, *The Dawn of the Reformation. Essays in Late Medieval Thought*, (Edinburgh, T & T Clark 1986), p. 25f.

[52] On this symbolism see the study in the fashion of a history of ideas by Arthur O Lovejoy, *The Great Chain of Being*, (Cambridge MA, Harvard University Press, 1936).

value. At the same time the divine remains somehow tied to this order of lesser value and hence is not in a position of free transcendence, as the Christian notion of free creation of the world requires. Nominalism attempted to restore God's freedom and transcendence vis-à-vis the world. So the Israelite-Christian Axial differentiation is re-articulated and thus re-affirmed: this world as it is, is not a necessary and unchangeable world. It can in principle be criticised and altered.

But at the same time, as Steven Ozment observes, nominalism attempted to restore the integrity and autonomy of the world in its own right.[53] Thus the second element is the re-affirmation of the world.

A third element can be called an uninvited guest of nominalism. If a distinction is indeed to be made between the *potentia ordinata* and the *potentia absoluta* in God, then doubts can arise concerning the reliability of the ordained, the given order. If God can do something entirely different than He has done (according to Occam God can even give orders to hate Him), what basis do we have to trust the given order? It has no goodness in itself, but only in its 'being ordered by God'. So the net outcome of nominalism is the spread of fear and uncertainty—contrary to its own intentions. The appeal of nominalism certainly had something to do with the fact that it somehow articulated the all-pervasive fear and uncertainty of the age.[54] Although it intended to overcome this fear by the stress on God's *promissio* and *pactum* nominalism simultaneously expressed this 'existential' fear of the world. In this way it created an issue that, as Hans Blumenberg has shown, has had enormous consequences for the beginning of the modern age: the problem of the unreliability and inscrutability of God and hence the uncertainty concerning man's place in the cosmos.[55]

Fourthly, and last but not least, there is the new emphasis on the role of the will. The creation of this world (*de potentia ordinata*) is an act of divine will. This basic viewpoint affects the entire nominalistic outlook upon the

---

[53] Steven Ozment, *The Age of Reform 1250–550. An Intellectual and Religious History of Late Medieval and Reformation Europe*, (New Haven, Yale University Press 1980), p. 180v. Strangely enough Ozment takes issue here with Oberman's interpretation but he must have been misled by a specific formulation of Oberman's; for Oberman in his essay quoted above 'takes a position that basically concurs with Ozment's findings. However, Ozment's further conclusion that 'the late Middle Ages attest the final division of the sacred and the profane' would indeed not have been acclaimed by Oberman.

[54] Above n 51 See Heiko Oberman, *The Dawn . . .*, p. 25 *ff*. Cf for the role of fear in the 14th century and in subsequent centuries, which has been noted by quite a few analysts and can be sensed for example in the drawings of Hieronymus Bosch, Hans Achterhuis, *De erfenis van de utopie*. (Amsterdam, Ambo 1998), 94 *ff*; Jean Delumeau, *La peur en occident. XIVe-XVIIIe siècles*, (Paris, Fayard 1978). And of course Johan Huizinga's *Waning of the Middle Ages/Herfsttij der Middeleeuwen* (Harmonds-worth, Penguin, 1955 (trans. F Hopman)) still makes arresting reading.

[55] Hans Blumenberg, *Die Legitimität der Neuzeit*, (Frankfurt am Main, Suhrkamp 1966), 1999, pp. 205–33, about 'Die Unentrinnbarkeit eines trügerischen Gottes'.

world. The role of the will becomes primordial in all areas of life. A new voluntarism pervades theology, law and politics.

This brings us to the political implications of nominalism. As indicated above, people like Scotus and Occam were quite conscious of the political consequences of their *via moderna*.[56] An interesting case of the changing climate of opinion is the following quote from Duns Scotus, where he uses the political sphere as an example for his theology that would apparently be perfectly understandable to his readers:

> 'We should state that when an agent acts in conformity with a right law or rule he can, if he is not limited and bound by that law, but if that law is subordinate to his will, out of a *potentia absoluta* act otherwise. For example, supposing that someone (like a king) is free to make a law and change it, he can act apart from that law by means of his *potentia absoluta*, because he can change the law and institute another one . . . And so it is clear how it must be understood that God can make *de potentia absoluta* what He cannot make *de potentia ordinata*.'[57]

The first political implication of nominalism was just mentioned: the voluntarist conception of law and government.[58] Law and government lose their legitimacy as a reflection of divine reason but now come to be regarded as based on an essentially arbitrary *decision (quia voluntas est voluntas)*. So the law-giver is essentially free from any pre-given law, he is *legibus solutus*. This voluntarist conception of law and politics is fully present in the great theoreticians of sovereignty, Bodin and Hobbes (and in their precursors like Marsilius of Padua).[59] Especially in Hobbes the consequences of this new outlook are weighty: the Hobbesian universe seems to be characterised in its entirety as a clash of wills.

The second, and rather paradoxical, political consequence is that it leaves no possibility to appeal from what is actually ordained by a lawgiver. This is a very counter-intuitive outcome, for we just noted that nominalism somehow restored the 'Axial differentiation' that made it possible to criticise the established order. However, at the same time nominalism cuts off (rational or mystical) access to a higher, transcendent order that provides the actual ammunition to criticise the existing order. The *potentia absoluta* does not provide for a standard to measure the actual order. He who has

---

[56] On the very significant reception of the theological distinction between the *potentia absoluta* and the *potentia ordinata* see Francis Oakley, 'Jacobean Political Theology, The absolute and Ordinary Powers of the King', *Journal of the History of Ideas*, 29, 1968, pp. 323–46.

[57] Quoted in Gijsbert van den Brink, *a.w.*, 78 to be found in J Duns Scotus, *Lectura* I 44 q.un., n 3, 5 (*Opera omnia* XVII, ed. Vaticana, 535f)..

[58] See Dieter Wyduckel, *o.c.*, pp. 124–9.

[59] For Bodin's voluntarism see Margherita Isnardi Parente, 'Le Volontarisme de Jean Bodin: Maïmonide ou Duns Scot?' in Horst Denzer (ed)., *Jean Bodin. Verhandlungen der internationalen Bodin Tagung in München*, (München, CH Beck 1973), pp. 39–51. For Hobbes see eg Sheldon Wolin, *Politics and Vision* (Boston, Little Brown, 1960). On Hobbes and natural right see Leo Strauss, *Natural Right and History*, (Chicago, University of Chicago Press 1952).

the power at the same time has the *ius non appellandi*. Hobbes, a self-proclaimed nominalist, articulated this in the very concise formula *auctoritas, non veritas facit legem*. So doubt about the existing order is the only thing left without there being a basis for this doubt in the (inner) experience of a superior order. The 'Axial rupture' is somehow aborted.

A third consequence is the emergence of the contract-symbol. In nominalism proper the symbol of the covenant is elevated to an all-encompassing ontological category. However, a contract is not a covenant. A contract is a covenant where fear of consequences has replaced trust in promises as its basis. So the contract symbol is the nominalist covenant washed in late-medieval and early-modern fear. It is the mutually agreed ceasefire between otherwise inscrutable wills. It comes as no surprise then that the master of the contract symbol, the nominalist Thomas Hobbes, said of himself: 'Fear and I were twins'.[60]

In conclusion: admittedly, in Bodin's view the law-giver is still bound by the laws of nature and the divine law. But the thrust of the new symbol of sovereignty is to ascertain that no one else has access to these laws or to this God. To be sure, Lindahl is right in claiming that the representative structure of political order is not altered by Bodin.[61] The sovereign exercises his rule 'in the name of . . . (something higher). . .'. However, the distance between the sovereign and this higher authority is virtually abandoned, for no-one else has access to this higher authority in order to 'check' the claims of the lawgiver. God has become inscrutable, *legibus solutus*, He hides in the darkness of his *potentia absoluta*, He cannot be appealed to—and the same applies to the sovereign.

7. THE FOURTH LAYER: 'IN REGNO SUO' AND THE PARTICULARISATION OF GOD

And yet . . . even when we have identified the three layers as analysed above, it still remains to be explained why these notions somehow lost their universal reference (as it is still present in Dante's symbol of 'monarchia'). It is the rise of rival claims of empire that has to be taken into account here: the king becomes emperor, but in his own realm (*in regno suo*). It is this somewhat unexpected twist that endows the modern notion of sovereignty with its peculiar awkwardness: the highest power, but only in a limited territory.[62]

---

[60] Hans Achterhuis, *Het rijk van de schaarste. Van Thomas Hobbes tot Michel Foucault*, (Baarn, Ambo 1988), p. 19 *ff*.

[61] Hans Lindahl, *o.c.*, pp. 122–36. Just to make clear: Lindahl uses the concept of sovereignty as part of a political ontology (on which see also Lindahl's contribution to the present volume) and therefore somewhat 'de-historicises' the concept. In this chapter I am interested in certain conditions that made possible the historical rise of the concept.

[62] The ideal of 'universal rule' resurfaces only with the articulation of the great modern ideologies.

The central interest of the very diverse symbolisms of empire is the universality of rule. The kingship that is lowered from heaven in the Sumerian King List is not the governance of one or the other city, or any other specific territory, but concerns universal rule. Eric Voegelin, who made extensive study of this early symbolism, remarks: 'Cities exist in the plural, the empire and its kingship only in the singular'.[63] So the 'lowering of the kingship from heaven' implies that although divine rule on earth may be located in a specific place, it is universal in scope. The city—to use another frequently articulated symbol—is the *omphalos*, the center out of which the light of rulership spreads all over the earth.[64] Exactly this connotation of the symbolism is still present in later Roman imperial theology. 'What the Latins called *maiestatem*' is not limited to a specific realm but has a universal or rather an 'imperialistic' thrust: Rome was destined by the gods to be the leader of the *orbis terrarum*.[65] So when Bodin takes *maiestas* as his preferred synonym for sovereignty he obviously does not refer to this universal connotation.

The famous phrase *imperator in regno suo* is of course directed against the emperor's universal claims.[66] However, the phrase is more often and with greater poignancy used vis-à-vis the claims of the universal church and its head, the papacy. And yet, curiously enough, the papacy had contributed very much to the 'decentering' of the empire. For it was the papacy that had claimed the *plenitudo potestatis*, the fullness of power both spiritual and temporal. By consequence, all earthly rulers, both emperor and kings, were placed on an equal footing, as 'vicars of God'. So the universal claims of the emperor, too, were diminished and the different *regna* were acknowledged in their own right. But once they actually claimed this own right for themselves, they still encountered the same rival the emperor had faced: the papal claims.

So the spiritual unity somehow had to be relocated on a regional level. The one universal *ecclesia* had to be transformed into a national political 'church'. This process was analysed beautifully and in great depth by Kantorowicz, who called it the development toward 'polity-centered kingship' in which the particular political community was to become a *corpus reipublicae mysticum* in its own right.[67] The national community now

---

[63] E. Voegelin, *The Ecumenic Age*, (Vol. IV of *Order & History*), (Baton Rouge LA, Louisiana State University Press 1974), p. 95.

[64] *Cf* Mircea Eliade, *Patterns in Comparative Religion. A Study of the Element of the Sacred in the History of Religious Phenonomena*, (Cleveland, Meridian Books/World Publishing Company 1963), p. 231 *ff*.

[65] See above par. 5.

[66] On these claims see Robert Holzmann, *Der Weltherrschaftsgedanke des mittelalterlichen Kaisertums und die Souveränität der europäischen Staaten*, (Darmstadt, Wissenschaftliche Buchgesellschaft 1953).

[67] Another very lucid study of this process are the two books by Piet Leupen, *Gods stad op aarde. Eenheid van Kerk en Staat in het eerste millennium na Christus*, (Amsterdam, Wereldbibliotheek 1996) (esp. the Epilogue) and the already mentioned *Keizer in zijn eigen rijk*.

began to be seen as an organic unity, consisting of a head and members. The body metaphor, derived from St Paul's Letter to the Corinthians where he compares the church to a body of which Christ is the head and the believers are the members, is now transferred to the political community.[68] Moreover, contrary to the New-Testament Letter to the Hebrews which states that 'a better, a heavenly fatherland' awaits the believer, the earthly political community is now seen as *patria*, an 'object of political devotion and semi-religious emotion', worth fighting for, worth crying for, worth dying for.[69] In this rekindling of the Roman word *patria* it is attested more clearly than anywhere else how in the late Middle Ages the Christian version of the Axial differentiation is reversed. Even the key Christian virtue of *caritas* was now redirected toward the fatherland.[70]

This loss of universality corresponds to the breaking down of the symbolism of the 'chain of being' according to which the cosmos is one hierarchically ordered whole with one highest, divine center (as described in the last section). The universality that can be articulated on the basis of a radical transcendence of God is not that of one cosmic hierarchy that binds God to the world but it is the universality of 'equidistance': all that exists has the same distance, or for that matter the same closeness, to the transcendent God. There is no *omphalos*, no privileged divine center of the world. The world is not a hierarchy but a co-ordinative whole of many *regna*. The key question in such an 'equidistant' universe becomes whether all these different *regna*, cut loose from one unifying representation of the divine on earth and hence cut loose from the representation of one universal normative orientation, will start to regard themselves as closed in themselves and as carrying their normative orientation within themselves. And if so: how then is the difference between the normative orientation and the actual power structures represented?

The sovereign is 'under God' but at the same time there is no extra-political, independent representation of God left. So the concept of sovereignty acts as a means to do away with all imaginable political representations of extra-political horizons. Or to put it somewhat differently: all extra-political horizons are drawn into the political community as represented by its sovereign. While the basic representative structure of the pre-modern political order is somehow maintained, its content is turned upside down. While 'God' in the Christian orbit was a critical counterweight, the notion of sovereignty intends to make Him part of a particular political order. God is particularised, not in theory, but in practice. He becomes the center of as many 'civil theologies' as there are *civitates*.

---

[68] Ernst H Kantorowicz, *The King's Two Bodies. A Study in Medieval Political Theology.* (Princeton NJ, Princeton University Press 1957, pp. 207–32.
[69] Kantorowicz, *o.c.*, 232 *ff.*
[70] Id., p. 242f.

That indeed the concept of sovereignty intended to seal off any possibility of a higher appeal vis-à-vis the given order of the state can be illustrated by another fascinating quote from James I.

> 'It is Atheisme and blasphemie to dispute what God can doe: good Christians content themselves with his will revealed in his word. So, it is presumption and high contempt in a subject, to dispute what a King can doe, or say that a King cannot doe this, or that: but rest in that which is the King's revealed will in his Law'.[71]

The first key phrase here is 'content with the revealed will'. It is the echo of the nominalist *potentia ordinata* applied to the earthly king: no questions are to be asked about the kingly rule. The second key phrase seems to me here the indefinite article 'a' that is repeated twice. No longer does James I describe himself as 'the king' but as 'a king': there might still be one God, but there are many kings. But all these kings require from their subjects that they 'rest in that which is the King's revealed will' as if it is God's will. God is particularised.

8. CONCLUSION: SOVEREIGNTY AS A CONCEPT OF CLOSURE

I set out to discuss the thesis that, although on a philological level sovereignty is not a secularised theological concept, it somehow has become the locus, the point of expression of a secularising movement. Precisely the relative novelty of the symbol attests to the occurrence of new 'secularised' conceptions of the political. I use the quotation marks to indicate that the secularisation of the political order does not necessarily entail a farewell to the language of the divine. It may also mean drawing the divine into the existing political order in a way that blurs the distinction between God and His representative, the king. Moreover, different motives can be discerned in the secularising development. The break with the symbolism of the 'chain of being' and the subsequent revaluation of earthly existence as a free creation of God was not in itself a secularising movement. It also entailed a new awareness of the world's being divinely created. The affirmation of the inscrutability of power and the emergence of fear that went with it were unintended consequence of a new awareness of both divine transcendence and divine covenantal faithfulness. The blurring of the distinction between God and the earthly king and the 'particularisation of God' may be called political secularisation proper in the sense that Schmitt probably intended.

As a net result, the modern notion of sovereignty can be described as one of a threefold closure: 'metaphysically' vis-à-vis any overriding universal authority (either God, a universal natural law or more recently universal

---

[71] Quoted by Francis Oakley, *o.c.*, p. 337 from the *The Political Works of James I*, p. 333v.

human rights), externally vis-à-vis other states and internally vis-à-vis its own political community.

Quite a few commentators emphasise that sovereignty in itself does not mean absolutism. For Bodin, Hobbes and others the sovereign remains bound to the laws of nature or the divine law. In one sense this is correct. However, to me the crux seems the degree of identification between the sovereign and the overriding laws or authorities. When this identification is almost complete, this *legibus obligatio* does not provide any ground for a higher appeal from the sovereign to the divine or natural law. The notion of sovereignty tends to replace representation by identification.

In this respect it is fascinating to see how in the post Second World War situation something like a *potestas indirecta* has re-emerged. In many situations the Universal Declaration of Human Rights has acted as an unenforceable moral judgment upon regimes, not curbing their actual power but eventually undermining their legitimacy. A similar role is frequently played by what is nowadays called 'civil society': in a strict sense it is powerless but it appeals to higher moral standards than 'sovereign regimes' are willing to acknowledge.[72]

Right into the 20th century the close identification between God and a 'representative' has annoyed quite a few Christian theologians and political thinkers, who mostly kept a sense of the 'Axial differentiation' and who allowed their political thinking to be informed by their 'theological' presuppositions or rather by their Christian convictions. This already started with the work of Theodor de Beze, it continued in the work of the so-called Monarchomachen[73] and in the work of Johannes Althusius. Althusius, though not abandoning the notion of sovereignty altogether, defended the position that sovereignty was always vested in the people: 'Bodin clamours that these rights of sovereignty cannot be attributed to the realm or people. I maintain the exact opposite'.[74]

These 'theological' or perhaps just Christian objections—for many of the spokesmen for this position were not theologians—gained a new urgency during the 20th century, since the symbolism of national sovereignty in several respects seemed to have lost its power. To conclude I briefly present the positions of two Christian thinkers, Herman Dooyeweerd and Jacques

---

[72] The implications of the emergence of all kinds of 'socio-ethical' movements for the concept of sovereignty are analysed in Joseph A Camilleri and Jim Falk, *The End of Sovereignty. The Politics of a Shrinking and Fragmenting World*, (Aldershot, Edward Elgar 1992).

[73] JW Sap, *Wegbereiders der revolutie. Calvinisme en de strijd om de democratische rechtsstaat.* (Groningen, Wolters-Noordhoff 1993) Engl. translation *Paving the Way for Revolution. Calvinism and the Struggle for a Democratic Constitution.* (Amsterdam, Free University Press 2001).

[74] See Brian Tierney, *Religion, Law and the Growth of Constitutional Thought 1150–1650*, (Cambridge, Cambridge University Press 1982), p. 71–9, esp. 73f.

Maritain, one from the Protestant and the other from the Catholic tradition, who formulated critiques of the notion of sovereignty itself.[75]

Herman Dooyeweerd, a Dutch philosopher of law, objected to the modern notion of sovereignty because it did not recognise any inherent limits to the powers and the competencies of the state. A starting point of his analysis is that from a Christian point of view only God can properly be called 'sovereign'. On earth there can only be something like secondary or derivative sovereignty. He therefore advocates a notion of broken or fragmented sovereignty, which he calls 'sovereignty in spheres'. According to this conception different kinds of institutions in society have their own God given, and at the same time essentially limited sovereignty. According to Dooyeweerd no modern theory of sovereignty has been able properly to articulate the ontological independence of different institutions within the political order.[76] So a principled pluralism replaces the notion of sovereignty.

Jacques Maritain, the Catholic theologian and political philosopher, launched an all-out critique of the concept of sovereignty in his Chicago Walgreen Lectures, published as *Man and the State*. The notion of sovereignty stands in the way of any kind of accountability of states with respect to other states or with respect to the community of states. As such sovereignty claims a power that is only God's. It turns states into a 'monadic whole superimposed on the body politic or absorbing it in itself'. According to Maritain, there is a flat-out contradiction between the notion of sovereignty and any form of principled accountability. 'If the state is accountable and subject to supervision, how can it be sovereign? (T)he two concepts of Sovereignty and Absolutism have been forged together on the same anvil. They must be scrapped together'.[77]

---

[75] A comparison between the two is given by HES Woldring, 'Herman Dooyeweerd en Jacques Maritain: de strijd om een sterke staat en een vitale civiele samenleving' in: GJ Buijs/HES Woldring (ed)., *Grote politieke denkers. Hun strijd tussen goed en kwaad.* (Zoetermeer, Meinema 2001), pp. 129–43.

[76] Herman Dooyeweerd, *De strijd om het souvereiniteitsbegrip in de moderne rechts- en staats -leer,* (Amsterdam, HJ Paris 1950).

[77] Jacques Maritain, *Man and the State,* (Chicago, University of Chicago Press 1951), pp. 28–53, esp. 51–3.

Part B

Constitutional Perspectives I: The View from the States

11

Sovereignty in France: Getting Rid of the Mal de Bodin

JACQUES ZILLER

1. INTRODUCTION

I F WE LOOK at the French debate on sovereignty over the past decades,[1] two somewhat contradictory impressions emerge. On one hand, an important trend seems to resist transformation, as demonstrated by the lasting passion with which so-called sovereignists—be they politicians, journalists or academics—persist in defending a concept of France that in their view is being endangered by the current evolution linked to European integration and globalisation. On the other hand, European integration and decentralisation are not only welcomed but even fostered by a majority of the French public as well as of politicians, journalists and academics, while developments in constitutional law show that attitudes and concepts as regards sovereignty are changing. My view—which cannot be neutral as I do not share the views of sovereignists—is that France is indeed getting rid of 'Bodin's Evil'[2] (*Le mal de Bodin*)—to use the seductive expression of the sociologist Henri Mendras.[3] Whereas for two centuries the French debate on sovereignty has been centred around the opposition between national sovereignty and popular sovereignty—*souveraineté nationale et souveraineté populaire*—when sovereignty was unanimously considered as inherent to the French state and French society, the discussion is nowadays shifting towards a transformation of the major features of sovereignty: is it possible to divide or share sovereignty?

One way of describing this evolution would be to sum it up into four major directions:

---

[1] See *Pouvoirs*, n¡ 67, 1993 : *La Souveraineté.*
[2] Translations from French to English are by the author.
[3] Henri Mendras, 'Le mal de Bodin', *Le Débat*, 105, May-August 1999, p. 71–89.

—after the institutional transformations linked to the Fifth Republic since 1958, the demise of lego-centrism was long resisted, mainly but not only in French constitutional doctrine; but since the eighties this resistance seems largely overcome;

—while France has had a leading role in European integration since even before World War II, there has been a long-standing resistance—on the side of some institutions like the *Conseil d'Etat* and in certain areas of legal doctrine—to accept the consequences of integration; while this resistance gained ground in the seventies and eighties and peaked at the time of ratification of the Maastricht treaty (1992), it seems now to be fading away;

—transformations linked to decentralisation—overseas but also in the European part of the French Republic—have fostered resistance to an emergent French federalism amongst some politicians and academics, while others accept it as a specific form of shared sovereignty;

—strangely enough there has been little debate in legal doctrine and even less in politics as regards the shift from dualism to monism in the field of international law that took place after World War II, if one excepts the comments that accompanied the decision of the *Conseil d'Etat* in the *Sarran* case of 1998.[4]

From a lawyer's point of view, it should be added that, due to the development of judicial review by the Constitutional Council since the seventies, the nature of the debate on sovereignty has also changed from controversies in legal theory and politics (national sovereignty v. popular sovereignty) to a discussion centred around judicial benchmarking (what are the essential conditions of the exercise of sovereignty?).

The aim of this chapter is not to describe in detail how this evolution has occurred and is progressing, but rather to try and find general explanatory factors for the set of inter-related changes in the hope that this might contribute to a broader debate on shifting perceptions of sovereignty.

2. THE ROOTS OF FRENCH SOVEREIGNTY

Generation after generation, French academics and politicians have been educated in thinking about sovereignty according to a tradition that sees it as a Franco-English invention, with some very specific features that, in the French case, are due to the Revolution. A good way to understand this tradition is to read Jean-Jacques Chevallier's '*Les Grandes Îuvres politiques de Machiavel à nos jours*',[5] a book which has been the key to political philosophy in law faculties and at the *Institut d'Etudes Politiques de*

---

[4] Conseil d'Etat, 30 October 1998, *Sarran, Levacher et autres*. For the text of the decision and references of comments, see Marceau Long et al. *Les grands arrêts de la jurisprudence administrative* 13th edition (Paris: Dalloz, 2001) p. 818 *ff*.

[5] For the most recent edition see Jean-Jacques Chevallier and Yves Guchet, *Les grandes œuvres politiques de Machiavel à nos jours* (Paris, Armand Colin 2001).

Paris ('*Sciences-po*'.—the main gateway to the *Ecole Nationale d'Administration*) since its first edition in 1949. This handbook analysed sixteen classical political theorists through their major works, in chronological order: Machiavelli, Bodin, Hobbes, Bossuet were presented under the heading 'Serving Absolutism' (*Au service de l'absolutisme*); Locke, Montesquieu, Rousseau and Siéyès under the heading 'Fighting Absolutism' (*L'assaut contre l'absolutisme*); Burke, Fichte and Tocqueville under the heading 'The Revolution's Consequences—1789–1848' (*Suites de la Révolution*); Marx and Engels, Sorel, Lenin and Hitler under the heading 'Socialism and Nationalism 1848–1927' (*Socialisme et Nationalisme*). The book's structure shows how central the 1789 Revolution has remained in French political culture, and the selection of authors also indicates the central place of the concept of sovereignty next to that of democracy.

Doubtless many academics and even more politicians would struggle to quote the exact title of Jean Bodin's 'The Six Books of the Republic' (*Les six livres de la République*[6]) and the date (1576) of its first edition. Some would probably wrongly associate him with Philippe Le Bel (1268–1314), whose *légistes* reworked the Roman law *imperium* to the benefit of the French monarch.[7] But the vast majority would be able to quote a number of famous sentences of one of the first important books in political thinking that had been written in plain French and not in Latin: '*Le Roi ne tient sa couronne que de Dieu seul*' (the King owes his Crown to God alone) and even more: '*Le Roi est empereur en son royaume*' (the King is an Emperor in his Realm). Thus French political and legal elites immediately associate the concept of sovereignty with the independence of France as against the Church and the Holy Roman German Empire, an association that was reinforced during the first half of the 20th century in the context of the French Republic's struggle against the Church and its wars with Germany. This explains the resilient strength of Bodin's concepts four centuries later.

Nevertheless it has to be understood that the French domination of Europe during the 17th and 18th century is far less of a presence in French culture than the Revolution, which is conceived as a major worldwide event. 1789 is perceived as the year of Human Rights—*Déclaration des Droits de l'Homme et du Citoyen* of 26 August—and the abolition of privileges—in the night of 4 August. It is also the starting point of a specifically French debate which has dominated constitutional thinking for two centuries: a debate opposing Siéyès—considered to have invented the concept of National Sovereignty (*Souveraineté nationale*)—to the followers

---

[6] Jean Bodin, Les six livres de la République (1576) (Paris, Fayard, 1986).
[7] As a matter of fact, these *légistes*' battle against the Pope to foster the King of France's autonomous power was not restricted to the field of legal theory: in September 1303 Guillaume de Nogaret also organised the attack of Anagni against Pope Bonifacius VIII.

of Rousseau—the father of the idea of popular Sovereignty (*Souveraineté populaire*).

3. NATIONAL SOVEREIGNTY V. POPULAR SOVEREIGNTY

Whereas a number of Frenchmen quote Bodin without ever having read him, they would have read Siéyès' pamphlet '*Qu'est-ce que le Tiers-état?*' the manifesto of bourgeois revolutionaries in 1789. Siéyès (1748–1836) had a major influence on the wording of French constitutional texts from 1789 to 1799. He is considered to have put forward the concept that enabled the reconciliation of the democratic ideas of the Revolution with the maintenance of a key role for the Monarch. This concept is expressed in two of the most famous French constitutional provisions, well known to generations of students:

> —Article 3 of the Declaration of Human and Citizen's Rights of 26 August 1789, which is still formally part of the French Constitution: 'The principle of all sovereignty lies essentially in the Nation. No body, no individual may exercise any authority that does not expressly emanate from it'[8] and;
> —Title III Articles 1 and 2 of France's first written Constitution of 3 September 1791: 'Sovereignty is one, and cannot be divided, alienated or extinguished. It belongs to the Nation, and no section of the people, nor any individual, may claim its exercise.
> 'The Nation, from which all powers stem, may only exercise them by delegation'.[9]

The concept of national sovereignty (*souveraineté nationale*) is defined quite precisely in French constitutional law and is usually[10] considered as having four major characteristics:

> —Sovereignty is indivisible, it is a whole that allows no subdivision. This concept is mainly derived historically from the fear of partition of the Kingdom into smaller parts and is the basis of the concept of the French state as a unitary system.
> —Sovereignty cannot be alienated, neither to a single person nor to any family (the first Constitution was still that of a monarchy, but the Nation rather than the King was sovereign) nor any foreign power.
> —National sovereignty finds its institutional manifestation in parliamentary sovereignty; it is directly linked to a representative regime, and as a constitutional consequence any imperative mandate is forbidden.
> —As sovereignty belongs to the nation, elections are only a technique to make the will of the nation known. Democracy is deemed compatible with limited suffrage.

---

[8] *Le principe de toute souveraineté réside essentiellement dans la nation. Nul corps, nul individu ne peut exercer d'autorité qui n'en émane expressément.*
[9] *La Souveraineté est une, indivisible, inaliénable et imprescriptible. Elle appartient à la Nation, aucune section du peuple, ni aucun individu, ne peut s'en attribuer l'exercice. La nation, de qui seule émanent tous les pouvoirs, ne peut les exercer que par délégation.*
[10] See for instance Jean Gicquel, *Droit constitutionnel et institutions politiques*, 15th edition (Paris, Montchrestien, 1997) p. 198–200.

Hence also the possibility of a specific representation of the nation by a single person acting as the Head of State: the King in 1791, the Emperors Napoleon I from 1804 to 1814 and Napoleon III from 1852 to 1870, and again the President of the Third Republic[11] and the Fifth Republic. This was very much the view of Charles De Gaulle, as stated during his famous press conference of 31 January 1964: 'The indivisible authority of the state is given to the President by the people who elected him and there is no other authority, neither of ministers, nor of the civil service, nor of the army, nor of the judiciary that would not be devolved and maintained by him'.[12] While this definition was highly debatable and has been criticised as barely compatible with democracy, it was clearly linked to the tradition of national sovereignty—an apparent paradox in the light of the fact that De Gaulle inspired the Constitution of the Fifth Republic, which contributed to the restoration of the concept of Popular sovereignty in French constitutional law.

The concept of popular sovereignty (*souveraineté populaire*) is considered as Jean-Jacques Rousseau's idea. It was developed in 1762 in 'The social contract' (*Le contrat social*) with formulations that are not easy to understand even in the French language. The previously quoted book by Chevallier succeeds quite well in summarising Rousseau's thought.[13] He first quotes Rousseau himself

'each of us puts in common his person and all his power under the supreme direction of the general will, and we as a body treat every member as an indivisible part of the whole'.[14]

In order to explain how Rousseau's concept is compatible with democracy, Chevallier then quotes Montesquieu, whose works preceded those of Rousseau and whose language is much clearer:

'In democracy the people are in some respects the monarch and in other respects the subject. They can only be the monarch through their votes, which are the expression of their will. The will of the sovereign is the sovereign itself'.[15]

Chevallier continues:

'Rousseau shows, less succinctly and less clearly, that each member of the political body is at the same time citizen and subject. Citizen—member of the sover-

---

[11] This was the concept of the constitutional texts from 1873 onwards, but as soon as 1879 a major shift in political tradition considerably reduced the role of the President under the Third Republic, a tradition that was maintained by the Constitution of the Fourth Republic of 1946.
[12] *L'autorité indivisible de l'Etat est confiée tout entière au président par le peuple qui l'a élu, il n'en existe aucune autre, ni ministérielle, ni civile, ni militaire, ni judiciaire, qui ne soit conférée et maintenue par lui.*
[13] Chevallier, p. 145–53.
[14] *Chacun de nous met en commun sa personne et toute sa puissance sous la suprême direction de la volonté générale, et nous recevons en corps chaque membre comme partie indivisible du tout.*
[15] *Le peuple dans la démocratie est à certains égards le monarque, à certains autres il est le sujet. Il ne peut être monarque que par ses suffrages, qui sont ses volontés. La volonté du souverain est le souverain lui-même.*

eign—insofar as he participates in the activity of the political body (called 'sovereign' when it is active and state when it is passive). Subject—insofar as he obeys the laws that have been voted by the political body, this 'sovereign' of which he is a member. Shedding light on this entire debate, and sometimes confusing it, is a true metaphysic, even a theology, of the general will: those two words inscribed in the definition of the social pact'.

And further on:

'Absolute, infallible, indivisible and inalienable—to which one may add sacred and inviolable—does it not have the most prestigious attributes, this sovereignty according to Rousseau? It has been aptly remarked that after *L'esprit des Lois* [Montesquieu], which put the accent on other values, the *Contrat Social* is sovereignty's revenge'.

Much better in my view than a long sociological-historical explanation, this quotation of Chevallier points to the semantic vagueness that made Rousseau's thinking so appealing to generations of politicians—and sometimes, alas, also academics. The first to take it up was the republican majority of the Convention, who translated it into articles 25 and 26 of the democratic Constitution of 24 June 1793:[16] 'Sovereignty rests with the people . . . no part of the people may exercise the power of the entire people; but each section of the sovereign assembled shall enjoy the right to express its will with absolute freedom'.[17]

The concept of popular sovereignty (*souveraineté populaire*) is also quite precisely defined in French constitutional law and is usually[18] considered as having the following major characteristics:

—The voting function (*électorat fonction*) is directly linked to the universal suffrage of the population (male until 1945; and with exception of the slaves in the colonies until 1848); remarkably, foreigners were allowed to vote at the beginning of the Revolution.

—A republican regime (as opposed to a monarchy); hence the constitutional reform of 1884 that ordained the abolition of monarchy by the Third Republic (1870–1940) added the provision of article 30 to the constitutional acts of 1875, according to which 'the republican form of government shall not be subject to amendment'—a clause that has been taken up by the Constitutions of the Fourth Republic (1946) and Fifth Republic (1958).

—Semi-direct democracy: the constitution of 1793 envisaged a generous use of referendums. But the abuse of plebiscites by the two Napoleons shed suspicion on

---

[16] Due to the war with other continental countries, the Constitution of 1793 was suspended immediately after it came into force and has never been applied. This has been one of the reasons for the longstanding mythical appeal of the text in French political thinking and legal theory.

[17] *La souveraineté réside dans le peuple . . . Aucune portion du peuple ne peut exercer la puissance du peuple entier; mais chaque section du souverain assemblée doit jouir de son droit d'exprimer sa volonté avec une entière liberté.*

[18] See for instance Gicquel, (n 10, p. 200–3).

referenda in French constitutional law until 1945, and not until the Constitution of 1958 was its use for (ordinary)[19] legislation again endorsed.

The debate on sovereignty during the Third Republic—considered as the golden age of French classical constitutionalism—was almost entirely centred around the opposition between national sovereignty and popular sovereignty, at a time when there was no judicial review of legislation, but when the *Conseil d'Etat* as supreme administrative court developed techniques of judicial review of the executive which enabled the scrutiny of delegated legislation. In his famous pamphlet of 1931 *La loi, expression de la volonté générale* (The law as expression of the general will)[20] Raymond Carré de Malberg (1861–1935) showed how the political class, with the help of a major section of academia, had confiscated the ideas of the Revolution in order to foster a lego-centrism which gave a free hand to members of Parliament. Carré de Malberg is now considered as one of the great classics of French legal theory but was severely criticised by a majority of his colleagues during his life. His ideas found solid ground twenty three years after his death in the Constitution of 1958; this was due, *inter alia*, to the fact that one of his pupils who became a professor of constitutional law—René Capitant (1908–1996)—also came to exercise a major influence on Charles De Gaulle's constitutional thinking.

Hence the formula of Article 3 of the Constitution of the Fifth Republic of 4 October 1958, which achieved a compromise between the tenets of national sovereignty and those of popular sovereignty:

> 'National sovereignty belongs to the people who exercises it through its representatives and through referendums. No section of the people and no individual may purport to exercise it'.[21]

The old debate was thus closed, but the rise of judicial review by the Constitutional Council led this sentence to become the basis for new debates mainly centred on legal rhetoric. While it was clear in 1958 for lawyers like René Capitant, that the new constitution would put an end to the domination of members of Parliament, nobody at that time could have foreseen that the Constitutional Council would develop into a true constitutional court,[22] thus also drawing a line under the lego-centrism asso-

---

[19] As opposed to constitutional legislation.

[20] Raymond Carré de Malberg, *La loi, expression de la volonté générale* (Paris, Economica, 1984 reprint).

[21] *La souveraineté nationale appartient au peuple qui l'exerce par ses représentants et par la voie du référendum. Aucune section du peuple ni aucun individu ne peuvent s'en attribuer l'exercice.*

[22] See Marie-Claire Ponthoreau and Jacques Ziller, 'The Experience of the French Conseil Constitutionnel: Political and Social Context and Current legal-theoretical Debates' in Wojciech Sadurski, (ed)., *Constitutional Justice, East and West—Democratic Legitimacy and Constitutional Courts in Post-Communist Europe, in a Comparative perspective*, (Kluwer, Dordrecht, 2002).

ciated with the French classical concept of sovereignty. As the Council stated in its decision on New Caledonia in 1985: 'The law, once voted . . . is the expression of the general will, but only with due respect of the Constitution'.[23]

4. THE EXTERNAL DIMENSION OF SOVEREIGNTY

Since Bodin's 'The King is an Emperor in his Kingdom' the French debate on sovereignty had been entirely centred on its internal dimension until the early 1950s when European integration, itself largely due to French initiatives, reopened the discussion. In order to understand fully this particular aspect of French political and legal thinking, due attention should however be given to the idea of France as an 'Imperial Republic',[24] an expression that seems quite appropriate, if only because the expression French Empire (*Empire français*) had been used not just by the autocratic constitutions of the two Napoleons, but also to designate the colonies of the Third Republic.

Curiously enough, the traditional school programmes on France's history—which has had a major role in shaping the French political culture since 1880—only gave a very small place to colonial history. Nevertheless, the two waves that marked that history are a key factor to understanding the French approach to sovereignty. The first one led to the establishment of French colonies in the West and East Indies, in some small coastal spots of Africa, and also in the Indian Ocean during the 17th Century; this phase was dominated by the struggle with England and the Netherlands for sovereignty over these areas. The remains of this part of the colonial Empire (after a number of defeats at the hands of the English) are mainly to be found in the present day 'Overseas Departments' (*départements d'outremer*), which have been on an equal footing with the other French departments since 1946. Their history has been very closely linked to the developments of the French Republic, as slavery was abolished in 1794 and citizenship given to all inhabitants of the French West Indies and Indian Ocean Isles. Slavery was however re-established in those colonies by Napoleon in 1802 and only definitively abolished in 1848. These so-called 'old colonies' (*vieilles colonies*) fully participate in French universalism, a

---

[23] *La loi votée . . . n'exprime la volonté générale que dans le respect de la constitution.* Decision 85–197 DC of 23 August 1985.

[24] This expression is due to Raymond Aron who used it in analysing the United States' foreign policy in *The Imperial Republic: the United States and the Modern World 1945–73*, (London, Weidenfeld & Nicolson, 1974).

cultural fact that explains why the French West Indies[25] and Indian Ocean Isle[26] have remained fully part of the Republic, as opposed to their British equivalents. To a certain extent, it could be argued that this is an illustration of the notion of popular sovereignty. The second wave of colonisation started during the restoration of the monarchy (1816–48) with the conquest of Algeria, but mainly resulted from the foreign policy of the Third Republic at the end of the 19th century. The indigenous inhabitants of those territories (in Africa, Southeast Asia and the Pacific) acquired full French citizenship only after World War II, and did not win full equality of political rights until 1956, a few years before the de-colonisation which signalled the demise of the 'French Community' (*Communauté française*) that had replaced the Empire in 1946. Although an entire rhetoric centred on France's colonial mission as the Fatherland of Human Rights (*Patrie des Droits de l'Homme*) was developed by the governments of the Third and Fourth Republics, this second wave of colonisation was still very close in spirit to that of the other big European colonial powers at the turn of the 20th century.

Although French legal theory gave little attention to the consequences of colonisation before the end of World War II, and while legal doctrine had largely lost interest in the questions relating to overseas until very recently, it seems to me that for a century and a half there was a major flaw in the French approach to the concept of sovereignty—whether conceived of as national or popular sovereignty. How could the Fatherland of Human Rights and the self-designated home of equality reconcile it's own sovereignty with a domination of other people and nations? At the beginning of the 21st century, the only remaining legacies of this second wave of colonisation are New-Caledonia and French Polynesia—two territories where a new approach to shared sovereignty is being pursued, and the micro-region of Wallis and Futuna—a territory with less than 10 000 inhabitants in total.

While France struggled with the premises of de-colonisation in the fifties, it also started to take initiatives in the field of European integration—initiatives that are far better known today than its colonial history, to French citizens and foreigners alike. The old rhetoric opposing popular sovereignty to national sovereignty finds an echo in two opposed conceptions of French policy with regard to European integration. In the case of the more integrationist tendency, led by Christian Democrats and in particular by Robert Schuman and Jean Monnet, the European Communities have been described by its sponsors as 'People's Europe' (*l'Europe des peuples*), a concept clearly underpinning the reasoning of the European Court of Justice in the famous *Van Gend & Loos* and *Costa* cases—two decisions made under the presidency of Judge Robert Lecourt, a French Christian

---

[25] Guadeloupe, Guyane, Martinique.
[26] La Réunion.

Democrat. The more intergovernmental tendency, initiated by Charles De Gaulle as soon as he returned to government in June 1958, was labelled by De Gaulle himself as 'Europe of the Fatherlands' (*l'Europe des patries*) or even sometimes as 'Europe of the Nations' (*l'Europe des nations*). To French minds the somewhat amorphous phrase—'Federation of Nation-States'—so trendy in the perspective of the current Convention on the Future of Europe—in its combination of nationalism with the idea of a federation of European citizens echoes the compromise of the Constitution of the Fifth Republic: 'National sovereignty belongs to the people'.

5. THE END OF LEGO-CENTRISM AND THE LIMITS OF SOVEREIGNTY

The end of lego-centrism in the face of the development of constitutional review has not fore-closed all debate on the relationship between sovereignty and law making. An echo of the old nation v. people debate can be found in the discussions concerning the limits of judicial review by the Constitutional Council.

Clearly in line with the tradition of popular sovereignty, a very significant part of legal doctrine continues to hold that while the Constitution of 1958 has indeed put an end to the supremacy of Parliament, sovereignty and thus supreme law-making power rests with the constitution-maker (*le constituant*). This generates the so-called theory of the pointsman (théorie de l'aiguilleur),[27] according to which the constitutional judge cannot definitively prohibit law making, but may only indicate which way ought to be taken at an unclear juncture: legislative or constitutional procedure. As Vedel puts it, '[I]f judges do not govern, it is because the sovereign can at any moment repeal their decisions as long as it appears in all its majesty of constitution making power'.[28] The powers that are instituted by the constitution (*pouvoirs constitués*) have to follow the will of constitution-making power (*pouvoir constituant*). One could argue that the theory of the pointsman is also in line with the tradition of national sovereignty, as it provides for the nation's representatives jointly to exercise the supreme power: much more emphatically than the ordinary legislative procedure, the procedure for constitutional amendment as laid down in Article 89 of the Constitution needs the joint approval of all representatives: the National Assembly, the Senate and the President of the Republic.

On the other hand, there is a minor tendency in the doctrine that defends the idea of supra-constitutionality by resort to a new form of natural law,

---

[27] The theory has been fully developped in Louis Favoreu, 'Le Conseil constitutionnel et la cohabitation', 135 *Regards sur l'actualité*, (1987). See also Ponthoreau and Ziller, n 22 above.
[28] Georges Vedel, 'Schengen et Maastricht. A propos de la décision 91–294 DC du 25 juillet 1991' (1992), *Revue française de droit administratif*, p. 180.

and according to which there would be inherent limits to law-making, even through constitutional amendment. Their main argument is based on the last indent of Article 89 of the Constitution—the article that lays down the procedure for constitutional amendments—which states that 'The republican form of government shall not be subject to amendment'.[29] According to this tendency, the 'republican form of government' covers a number of features including the rights laid down in the Declaration of 1789 and a certain number of fundamental principles established by legislation since 1880, especially that of *laïcité*.

Yet there are two technical legal arguments firmly opposed to the idea that Article 89 might create a system of supra-constitutionality similar to that of the 'eternity clause' of the German Fundamental Law of 1949 (which prohibits any constitutional amendment that would interfere with a series of principles relating to representative democracy, federalism and fundamental rights). The first argument is based on the fact that the drafters of the 1958 Constitution only repeated the formula of the 1884 amendment, whose sole purpose was to prohibit the restoration of monarchy. The second argument is based upon the fact that the 1958 Constitution does not provide for any remedy that would enable the Constitutional Council to quash an amendment—unlike the German Fundamental Law which allows reference to the Constitutional Court even before such an amendment is submitted to final vote by the Bundestag. An additional argument—based both on legal theory and the wording of the Constitution—stresses the fact that, unlike Members of Parliament and the President of the Republic, the members of the Constitutional Council are not representatives; thus they are not empowered to go against the will of the sovereign, as long as it has been expressed according to the procedures laid down in the Constitution. As in other countries, this debate on the limits of judicial review is not divorced from politics: the majority of advocates of supra-constitutionality have voiced their theories at a moment where the government of the day was not their favourite political coalition.

The debate seemed totally disconnected from practice until 1992, when the Constitutional Council had to decide three times upon the Maastricht Treaty.[30] In Maastricht II, the Members of Parliaments who referred the case

---

[29] *La forme républicaine du gouvernement ne peut faire l'objet d'une révision.*

[30] Decisions 308 DC of 9 April 1992, known as *Maastricht I* (the Council had been asked by the President of the Republic whether the Maastricht Treaty could be ratified without prior amendement of the Constitution), 312 DC of 2 September (*Maastricht II*—the Council had been asked by members of Parliament if the Maastricht Treaty was compatible with the Constitution which had in the meantime been revised), and 313 DC of 23 September (*Maastricht III*—the Council had been asked by members of Parliament if the Act, approved by referendum, that allowed for the ratification of the Maastricht Treaty was compatible with the Constitution). For the text of those decisions, comments and further references, see Louis Favoreu and Loïc Philip, *Les grandes décisions du Conseil constitutionnel* 11th edition (Paris, Dalloz, 2001) p. 781 *ff.*

to the Council claimed that the Treaty was not compatible with Article 3 of the Constitution (on sovereignty), notwithstanding the fact that Article 88 had been specially amended in June in order to pave the way for ratification of the Treaty. The Council rejected the claim by arguing that the

> 'constitution making power is sovereign; it may repeal, modify or complement clauses that have constitutional value in the form it deems appropriate; and thus nothing opposes the introduction of new clauses in the Constitution which derogate from a rule or principle of constitutional value in the circumstances it refers to; and such a derogation may be explicit as well as implicit'.[31]

This might have put an end to discussions around supra-constitutionality. However, the Council deemed it necessary to elaborate upon this clear statement by specifying the limitations of the sovereign constitution-making power. First, it recalled the fact that constitutional amendments are forbidden in certain periods or circumstances resulting from Article 89 (procedure and time limits for amendments) but also 7 and 16 (prohibition of amendments while the Presidency of the Republic is vacant or in the case of exercise of plenary powers by the President in exceptional circumstances); in the latter case the Council inferred from the Constitution something which is not explicitly stated in the text. Secondly, it also recalled and reaffirmed the prohibition of amendments to the 'republican form of government', without detailing precisely what this should cover. One could argue that the Council merely re-stated something that was commonly understood. But the mere fact that it made that statement—even although, according to the traditional style of French supreme courts, its decisions tend to be short and lacking in detail[32]—seems to indicate that the Council would be ready to review constitutional amendments. It does not say according to which remedy: there are indeed remedies for checking Acts of Parliament that follow constitutional amendments, and this might lead to an indirect review of the amendment itself, but there are no explicit remedies associated with and founding a direct review of the amendment.

The ultimate key to this discussion has probably been given by the Council in Maastricht III, where it reaffirmed the fact that it is strictly bound by the system of remedies provided by the Constitution and thus not allowed to review any piece of legislation that has been approved by refer-

---

[31] '[*considérant que . . .] le pouvoir constituant est souverain; qu'il lui est loisible d'abroger, de modifier, ou de compléter des dispositions de valeur constitutionnelle dans la forme qu'il estime appropriée; qu'ainsi, rien ne s'oppose à ce qu'il introduise dans le texte de la Constitution des dispositions nouvelles qui, dans le cas qu'elles visent, dérogent à une règle ou à un principe de valeur constitutionnelle; que cette dérogation peut être aussi bien expresse qu'implicite*' (indent no. 19).

[32] See Michel Troper and Christophe Grzegorczyk, 'Precedent in France', in D. Neil McCormick and Robert S. Summers (eds) *Interpreting Precedents—A Comparative Study* (Dartmouth, Ashgate, 1997) p. 103 *ff*.

endum (indent n° 5). The question before the Council concerned the law allowing for ratification of the Treaty which had been approved by referendum on 20 September. Maastricht II made it clear that the Council was not ready to find the Treaty contrary to the Constitution, and it was apparent that the members of Parliament who referred to the Council[33] did so mainly in order to make their point one last time in the realm of public opinion. It gave the Council the opportunity to reaffirm its longstanding jurisprudence according to which it was not allowed to review any acts adopted by referendum—whether they are ordinary legislation, they authorise the ratification of an international treaty, or they provide for a constitutional amendment—as 'with regard to the balance of powers established by the Constitution' they 'constitute the direct expression of national sovereignty' because they 'have been adopted by the French People by referendum'.[34] Paradoxically, due to the wording of Article 3 of the Constitution, the Council has to quote this power as the direct expression of national sovereignty, whereas it is de facto clearly a triumph for the concept of popular sovereignty. Acts adopted by the people's representatives—the clear expression of national sovereignty—are by contrast usually susceptible to judicial review, except far constitutional amendments (Decision on decentralisation, March 2003).

6. TRANSFERS OF SOVEREIGNTY V. SHARED EXERCISE OF COMPETENCIES

The development of European integration, and more recently, some elements of globalisation, have generated a somewhat Byzantine debate on the possibility of transferring sovereignty.

Carré de Malberg in his 'Contribution to General Theory of the State' (1922)[35] argued that the legal expression of sovereignty was to be found in the discrete competencies of the state, a position that earned him wide criticism in French doctrine as it could lead to a splitting up of sovereignty. Whereas under the Third Republic this had no clear consequence, the adoption of the Constitution of 1946 provided room for an in-depth change. Indent 15 of the Preamble provided for the possibility that 'under condition of reciprocity, France consents to those limitations of sovereignty that are

---

[33] Led, as in the case of Maastricht II, by the two main sovereignist opponents of the Treaty of Maastricht—the Gaullists Charles Pasqua and Philippe Séguin.

[34] *Au regard de l'équilibre des pouvoirs établi par la Constituent, les lois que celle-ci a entendu viser dans son article 61 sont uniquement les lois votées par le Parlement et non point celles qui, adoptées par le Peuple français à la suite d'un référendum contrôlé par le Conseil constitutionnel au titre de l'article 60, constituent l'expression directe de la souveraineté nationale.*

[35] Raymond Carré de Malberg, *Contribution à la théorie générale de l'Etat* (Paris, Sirey, 1920–2 [reprint Paris: CNRS 1985]).

needed for the organisation and defence of peace'.[36] Furthermore Article 55
of the Constitution of 1958 clearly states that

'Treaties or agreements which have been legitimately ratified or approved have an
authority superior to that of laws as soon as they have been published, conditional in the case of each agreement or treaty on its application by the other
party'.[37] This confirms the choice of a monist approach to the relationship
between municipal and international law, contrary to the traditional French
approach until 1946. The somewhat unrefined wording of those provisions—as
shown by the lack of due consideration for multilateral treaties in Article 55—and
the need to also take into account the wording of the Preamble of 1946 have
generated changes in the Constitutional Council's jurisprudence—or at least in its
wording—to the great delight of many constitutional lawyers.

In 1970, the Council was presented with its first opportunity to contrast
the consequences of European integration with the Constitution's procla-
mation of indivisibility of sovereignty when asked to review the Act of
Parliament authorising the ratification of the Treaty of 22 April 1970 and
the (EC) Council decision of 21 April 1970, which revised the EC treaties
in order to provide for Communities' 'own resources'. The Constitutional
Council stated that 'in this specific case, neither on account of its nature nor
on acount of its importance, it cannot impinge upon the essential conditions
of the exercise of national sovereignty'.[38] This clearly meant that the
Council was reserving cases where the importance of transferred powers
would run against the Constitution. The key question for future case law
was to draw the boundary between permitted transfers on the one hand,
and, on the other, those which would 'impinge upon the essential conditions
of the exercise of national sovereignty' and so necessitate a constitutional
amendment before being ratified.

In 1976, however, the Council changed its formulation when asked to
review the act authorising ratification of the (EC) Council decision of 20
September allowing for direct elections to the European Parliament. It
affirmed that

'no provision of a constitutional nature authorises transfers of the whole or part
of national sovereignty to any international organisation'.[39] This sentence has
been heavily criticised in different strands of doctrine, both for ignoring the

---

[36] *Sous réserve de réciprocité, la France consent aux limitations de souveraineté nécessaires à l'organisation et à la défense de la paix.*

[37] *Les traités ou accords régulièrement ratifiés ou approuvés ont, dès leur publication, une autorité supérieure à celle des lois, sous réserve, pour chaque accord ou traité, de son applica-tion par l'autre partie.*

[38] Decision 70–39 DC of 19 June 1970 'Community resources': *dans le cas d'espèce, elle ne peut porter atteinte ni par sa nature, ni par son importance aux conditions essentielles d'exer-cice de la souveraineté nationale.*

[39] Decision 76–71 DC of 30 December 1976: *aucune disposition de nature constitutionnelle n'autorise des transferts de tout ou partie de la souveraineté nationale à quelque organisation internationale que ce soit.*

Preamble of 1946 and, mainly, for using the provocative term 'transfer' of sovereignty. Criticisms were also addressed to the Council for the very complicated exercise in dualism it had to go through in order to accept direct election of the European Parliament as not impinging upon French sovereignty. A majority of French academics, indeed, consider that sovereignty cannot be transferred as it is by nature not divisible: the external dimension of sovereignty is subject to limitations due to the nature of international society, and the Preamble of 1946 only provides for the possibility of transferring the exercise of some of the state's competencies to international organisations.

The Council seems to have been sensitive to these criticisms[40] as it has not used the same formula again. Since 1985 it has claimed only to check whether a treaty which transfers powers does impinge upon the 'essential conditions of the exercise of national sovereignty'. It has tried to defined these essential conditions in the decisions concerning the death penalty (1985), the Schengen agreements (1991), the Maastricht Treaty (1992— Maastricht I), the Amsterdam Treaty (1997) and the Treaty of Rome establishing the International Criminal Court (1999).[41] According to the 1985 decision, these essential conditions include: respecting the Republic's institutions, the 'continuity of national life' (*continuité de la vie de la Nation*) and the guarantees of fundamental rights and liberties (*garantie des droits et libertés des citoyens*). Whenever a treaty is found to be impinging upon these conditions, its ratification needs a previous constitutional amendment. The French system of remedies for constitutional review is particularly well adapted for this, as the Council may be asked to directly examine the treaty at any time before ratification or to review the constitutionality of the Act of Parliament authorising ratification as soon as voted. In the case of an executive agreement that needs no authorisation for ratification, the classical remedy for review of legality of executive decisions (*recours pour excès de pouvoir*) is available, which allows the *Conseil d'Etat* to provide for the same type of control.

The only case where no remedy is available in order to stop a transfer of powers is that of a referendum authorising ratification, as in the case of the Maastricht Treaty in 1992. This explains why French politicians and academics so readily envisage a referendum in order to approve a future new European Constitution that might come out of the 2004 IGC.

---

[40] Some commentators see no contradiction between the different decisions of the Council, like for instance Favoreu and Philip (n 30 above) p. 803–5. But a former Secretary General of the Council seems to share the majority doctrinal view: Bruno Genevois, *La jurisprudence du Conseil Constitutionnel—Principes directeurs* (Paris, S.T.H., 1988) p. 365.

[41] For all those decisions see Favoreu and Philip (n 30 above).

7. TOWARDS SHARED SOVEREIGNTY

The most recent French debate on sovereignty addresses the notion of shared sovereignty. This concept is heavily criticised in much legal doctrine as being contradictory in terms, due to the fact that sovereignty—like the French Republic—is one and indivisible (*une et indivisible*); it is often said that sovereignty cannot be shared (*la souveraineté ne se partage pas*). This debate is linked to the evolution of the concept of citizenship and is far from being clearly structured, let alone generally acknowledged in academia. This is why this chapter only aims at presenting the terms of the discussion in a schematic way.

As far as the external dimension of sovereignty is concerned, the notion of shared sovereignty was used for the first time (to my knowledge) by the leading French scholar on constitutional review, Louis Favoreu, in an article in *Le Figaro* of 22 April 1992; he introduced the idea of the coexistence of two constitutions since the Treaty of Maastricht:

> 'one that corresponds to the traditional concept of national sovereignty and its indivisible exercise by the representatives of the French people and the other that introduces the idea of a shared sovereignty and of a member state of a larger aggregation of a quasi-federal type'.

While some authors like Jean Gicquel[42] retain the idea of a dual constitution and others like Henri Oberdorff[43] insist on the notion of state membership of a larger polity, it is however striking that neither notion has generated deep discussion, let alone a solid corpus of doctoral research. It is not even apparent whether—as one might be tempted to see it—the use of 'dual constitution' corresponds rather to a nostalgia of the good old times where sovereignty was a crystal clear concept and France undoubtedly a large sovereign nation, or whether the use of 'shared sovereignty' instead suggests a more positive and less tradition-bound attitude towards present-day developments.

As far as the internal dimension of sovereignty is concerned, the situation seems clearer. The concept of 'shared sovereignty' appeared first in the Noumea Agreements (*Accords de Nouméa*) of 5 May 1998, which were signed by the representatives of the indigenous *Kanak* population of New Caledonia, those of the descendants of European settlers (so called '*caldoches*') and the French government. The agreements provided for a new form of autonomy for New Caledonia, which includes the creation of a double citizenship—French citizenship plus Caledonian citizenship—for natives and settlers as well as the possibility for Caledonian institutions to

---

[42] Gicquel (n 10 above), p. 514 *ff.*
[43] See Henri Oberdorff, 'Des incidences de l'Union rueopéenne et des Communautés européennes sur le système adminsitratif français', (1995) *Revue du droit public*, p. 25–49.

adopt 'laws of the land' (*lois de pays*). The agreements have been incorporated into the constitution via quotation by the constitutional amendment of December 1998, introducing the new Articles 76 and 77 in the Constitution. To sum up in a few words, France now belongs to the category of asymmetric federations or composite states that also includes the United Kingdom since the enactment of a devolved Parliamant for Scotland in 1998. A reform of the same kind was also started in 1999 concerning French Polynesia, and has not yet been concluded only because of the interference of other political debates on the French agenda. With the dust settling on the 2002 elections, an early agreement is now likely. Few French constitutional commentators have given the necessary attention to this major institutional evolution.[44] Many others seem to have ignored it—often due to lack of interest in overseas matters, but sometimes in a quite deliberate way, as this evolution seems offensive to their understanding of the logic of legal theory, or, more pragmatically, because they fear that this change might precipitate the transition of France towards federalism in its European territory too—starting soon with Corsica. While shared sovereignty has formally become part of French constitutional vocabulary by virtue of the reference to the Noumea agreements in Article 76 of the Constitution, a number of academics[45]—quite opposed to the evolution in New Caledonia—still consider this concept as totally meaningless, whereas a few others—including myself[46]—welcome the potential of an idea which helps to explain and to guide European integration as well as the evolution of state forms away from a unitary model in a growing number of national jurisdictions.

---

[44] To my knowledge, the majority of these contributions are to be found in Jean-Yves Faberon & Guy Agniel (eds.) *La Souveraineté partagée en Nouvelle-Calédonie et en droit comparé* (Paris, La Documentation française, 2000) and in issue n°1009/1010 of the *Revue Politique et Parlementaire*: *Quel Etat pour des 'régions singulières'*, Nov. 2000-Feb. 2001.

[45] See amongst others the contributions by Alain Moyrand, p. 29 and *ff*, Olivier Gohin, p. 387 and *ff* or Mathias Chauchat, p. 411 and *ff* in Faberon and Agniel, cit., p. 447–58.

[46] See Jacques Ziller, 'Partager la souveraineté, ici et ailleurs' in Faberon and Agniel, cit., p. 447–58.

12

Sovereignty Über Alles: *(Re)Configuring the German Legal Order*

MIRIAM AZIZ*

1. INTRODUCTION

S OVEREIGNTY IN POST-WAR Germany has been a highly constrained and contested concept, understood as something aspired to, rather in the way that one desires that which one does not have. If one can legitimately speak of 'desiring sovereignty' in the German context, then it makes sense to distinguish two forms of aspiration: either, a longing for that which was once possessed but which was lost, or a longing for that which was never possessed. In the case of Germany, the reclaiming or claiming of sovereignty[1]—however it is understood—has traditionally been aspired to by constitutional lawyers, who regard it as the quintessential prerequisite to independent state formation.[2] The consequences of this aspiration post-1945 have been mainly two-fold.

First, much significance has been attached to internal sovereignty, that is to say, the state's power of self-determination. Secondly, external sovereignty, namely the state's ability to act in the world arena, has been regarded as paramount. The word paramount is used specifically to denote the particularity of the German case because it is the recognition by other states

* LLB, PhD, Barrister-at-Law currently a Marie Curie Fellow at the Robert Schuman Centre for Advanced Studies, the European University Institute, Florence. I am grateful to Bardo Fassbender, Matthias Mahlmann, Bruno de Witte, James Hughes and Peer Zumbansen for their comments on earlier versions of this article. I am also indebted to Matthias Geis who provided assistance by way of materials. The usual disclaimer applies.
[1] The distinction being made here is that the *Kaiserreich* and the Third Reich were sovereign states. By contrast, the Federal Republic of Germany was never a fully sovereign state.
[2] According to M Usteri, *Theorie des Bundesstaates* (Zürich, 1954) who cites Gierke, Haenel, Waitz, Heller, von Seydel, Stier-Somlo and Zorn as representing supporters of this view. See also M Stolleis, *Geschichte des öffentlichen Rechts in Deutschland* (Munchen, CH Beck, 1992).

of Germany as a sovereign state which has both formed and informed the German juridical debate concerning sovereignty. It is of interest to note that, prior to (re)unification, both German states, that is to say, the Federal Republic of Germany and the German Democratic Republic (GDR), responded to the constraints enforced by limited sovereignty (West Germany to the Four Powers, the GDR to the Soviet Union under the so-called *Brezhnev* doctrine[3]) in a similar manner, albeit in different contexts. Indeed, a comparison between the two sheds considerable light on the ambivalence of their aspiration for sovereignty and what that meant once it was attained, thereby bringing out the complicated relationship between people, territory and the state. As this paper will show, external recognition of statehood was of paramount—perhaps even exaggerated—importance for both states. Social, cultural, political and historical factors have each contributed to what must be regarded as part of an evolution. In the German case, however, it is not the conceptions of sovereignty which have changed but the parameters within which the concept has evolved. Thus, in 1990, when Germany was (re)unified, and the reserved rights of the Four Powers (France, the United Kingdom, the Soviet Union and the United States) for Berlin and Germany as a whole were relinquished, Germany was regarded by many German jurists as being once again, or for the first time—again, depending on how one wants to regard it—sovereign. This new lease of life captured the constitutional imagination of many jurists, as the attempt to enact a new constitution illustrates.[4] For both German states, the drafting of their constitutions was 'supervised' closely—by the Americans, in the case of West Germany,[5] and by the Russians, in the case of the German Democratic Republic.[6] Evidently, the power base from which both documents were framed in 1949 was military occupation, the legacy of which had far reaching influences on German legal thinking. In the case of West Germany, the national division, the disappearance of Prussia, the attendant alteration of boundaries, the creation of the new *Länder* consti-tutions, the introduction of judicial review, federalism, democratisation,[7] presidentialism, changes in local government practice, rules for a state of emergency and changes in cultural politics laid the entire groundwork for West German national existence after 1945.[8]

---

[3] After the events of Spring 1968 in Prague.
[4] See UK Preuß, B Guggenberger and W Ullmann (eds), *Eine Verfassung für Deutschland. Manifest, Text, Plädoyers* (München, Hanser, 1991).
[5] B Fait, 'In einer Atmosphäre von Freiheit: Die Rolle der Amerikaner bei der Verfassunggebung in den Ländern der US Zone 1946' (1985) 33 *Vierteljahrshefte für Zeitgeschichte* 420.
[6] See S Mampel, *Die sozialistische Verfassung der DDR* (2nd edn) (Frankfurt am Main, Metzner, 1982) at pp. 56–7.
[7] See R Merritt, *Democracy Imposed: US Occupation Policy and the German Public, 1945–9* (New Haven, Yale University Press, 1995).
[8] CJ Friederich, 'The Legacies of the Occupation of Germany' (1968) 27 *Public Policy* 1.

Ironically, the (re)gaining of sovereignty in 1990 took place against the backdrop of the introduction of the European single currency which goes some way towards qualifying the sovereignty of the German state. One might conject, what was given with one hand, was taken away with another. As state sovereignty has evolved into a relative concept,[9] a significant portion of the German juridical debate has responded by over-emphasising the sovereignty of the German state over and above its European and international commitments as part of its crusade against what is seen by many as the 'withering away' of the state.[10] The issue of loss informs much of the debate concerning the effects of European integration on sovereignty, a trend which goes hand in hand with the debate concerning the effects of globalisation on the sovereign state.[11] Generally speaking, regarding sovereignty and the EU, loss has also been instrumentalised by some who seek to initiate what in law is sometimes referred to as a 'claw back' process or, to draw from Milton, to regain that which has been 'lost'. Thus, the age of absolute sovereignty is regarded as an age which is rather akin to 'paradise lost'.[12] What is significant in the German case is the obsession by German jurists with the issue of the ultimate arbiter in relation to the impact of European law on German law. Indeed, the very wording, *the impact of European law on German law* could be attributed to those jurists who regard EU law and German law as representing two separate legal orders. Those jurists who regard European integration as giving rise to one legal order represent a minority in a debate which, as I have addressed elsewhere, is extremely divisive.[13] Indeed, the pragmatic view of 'pooled' sovereignty[14] in the light of the increasing interdependence between states[15] and the supra-national level represents a conceptualisation of sovereignty which is underrepresented in the German legal debate.[16]

---

[9] See J Isensee, 'Der Förderalismus und der Verfassungsstaat der Gegenwart' (1990) 115 *Archiv für Öffentliches Recht* 248 at p. 268.

[10] *Ibid*.

[11] See, for example, S Sassen, *Losing Control? Sovereignty in an Age of Globalisation* (New York, Columbia University Press, 1996).

[12] See J Milton, *Complete Poems and Major Prose* Merrit Y Hughes (ed) (Indianopolis, Policy Press, 1957).

[13] M Aziz, 'Sovereignty Lost, Sovereignty Regained? The European Integration Project and the *Bundesverfassungsgericht*' (2001) EUI, Florence Working Paper, RSC No. 2001/31.

[14] N MacCormick, 'The *Maastricht-Urteil*: Sovereignty Now' (1995) 1 *European Law Journal* 259. See also N MacCormick, *Questioning Sovereignty: Law, State and Nation in the European Commonwealth* (Oxford, Oxford University Press, 1999).

[15] See, for instance, the concept of interdependence sovereignty espoused by SD Krasner, *Sovereignty: Organic Hypoerisy* (Princeton, University Press, 1999).

[16] See J Schwarze, 'Concept and Perspectives of European Community Law' (1999) 5 *European Public Law* 227 at 236 and also D Grimm, 'Die Zukunft der Verfassung' in UK Preuß (ed.), *Zum Begriff der Verfassung: Die Ordnung des Politischen* (Frankfurt am Main, Fischer, 1994) at p. 279. See also the interview with Germany's Federal Constitutional Court Justice, Professor Udo Di Fabio, (2001) 2 *German Law Journal* (June 1 Issue) available at http://www.germanlawjournal.com.

The absence of pragmatism is partly explained when the historical context is taken into account. The Treaty of Versailles (1919) which severely constrained Germany's powers was regarded by even the most level-headed of German jurists as a provocation. Herman Heller, for example, viewed the effects of the Treaty as leaving the German people 'defenceless and plundered',[17] a position which fuelled appeals for a strong version of German nationalism—upon which Hitler was only too willing to capitalise.

The purpose of this paper is to evaluate the concept of sovereignty in the German legal order in connection with socio-political and historical parameters with the aim of situating the German juridical debate within a wider context. This wider context includes an assessment of the legacy of certain theories of the state in German constitutional law as well as a brief appraisal of the concept of sovereignty in the former German Democratic Republic. In so doing, I will attempt to provide a suitable framework within which the German constitutional tradition as regards the attitudes to sovereignty in the European Union may be addressed.

2. SOVEREIGNTY AND THE FEDERAL REPUBLIC OF GERMANY POST—1945

The West German state was accorded a particular status under public international law after the second World War.[18] Subsequent to the German capitulation on May 8, 1945, the Four Powers (France, the Soviet Union, the United Kingdom and the United States) assumed the supreme authority in Germany as provided by the Allied Declaration of June 5, 1945.[19] In effect, the military commanders of the four Allies administered their respective zones and acted jointly through the Inter-Allied Control Council regarding all matters which related to the country as a whole.[20] The 1952 'Settlement

---

[17] See P Caldwell, *Popular Sovereignty and the Crisis of German Constitutional Law. The Theory and Practice of Weimar Constitutionalism* (Durham, Duke University Press, 1997) at p. 128 who refers to 'Heller's Critique of Versailles: (Diktat): Die politischen Ideenkrise der Gegenwart' (1926) in H Heller, *Gesammelte Schriften* C Müller (ed.) (Tübingen, Mohr, 1992) I: 359.

[18] See the case of *Prince Hans-Adam II of Liechtenstein v Germany* (Application no. 42527/98), Judgement of July 12, 2001 in which Germany's position under public international law is outlined.

[19] Declaration regarding the defeat of Germany and the assumption of supreme authority in Germany and the assumption of supreme authority with respect to Germany by the Governments of the United States of America, the Union of Soviet Socialist Republics, the United Kingdom and the Provisional Government of the French Republic, UNTS 68, p. 190 *et seq.* See generally I von Munch (ed.), *Dokumente des geteilten Deutschlands: Quellentexte zur Rechtslage des Deutschen Reiches, der Bundesrepublik Deutschland und der Deutschen Demokratischen Republik* (Stuttgart, Kröner, 1968–74).

[20] Such as military matters, transport, finance, economic affairs, reparations, justice, prisoners of war, communications, law and order as well as political affairs.

Convention'[21] was designed to end the Occupation Regime.[22] Article 1 of Schedule I of this Convention provides that the Federal Republic of Germany is accorded 'the full authority of a sovereign State over its internal and external affairs'. However, article 2 provides that the Three Powers retain their rights 'relating to Berlin and to Germany as a whole, including the reunification of Germany and a peace settlement'.

This had considerable consequences for the administration of justice. Thus, for example, whereas the Federal and the Land authorities were given powers to repeal or amend legislation enacted by the Occupation Authorities, rights and obligations created or established by or under legislative, administrative or judicial action of the Occupation Authorities remained valid for all purposes under German law.[23] Furthermore, there was a bar on the prosecution of persons by actions of German courts or authorities on the ground of having sympathised with or aided or furnished with information or services the Three Powers or their Allies. The exclusion of German jurisdiction was to ensure that acts undertaken by the Allies dating back to the time of the German occupation were not retroactively questioned.[24] In order to regain the full authority of a sovereign state, Germany had to accept, both in 1954[25] and in 1990, restrictions on the jurisdiction of their courts over such matters. The limitation of its jurisdiction was absolute and a *force majeur*.[26] Germany had very little choice in the matter.[27]

The reservation by the Three Powers challenges concepts of sovereignty old and new. One of the basic principles of medieval theories of sovereignty, namely, *par in parem imperium non habet* (an equal cannot exercise power and jurisdiction over an equal),[28] defined and conditioned the authority of

---

[21] The Convention on the Settlement of Matters Arising out of the War and the Occupation which was one of the 'Bonn Conventions' signed by France, the United States of America, the United Kingdom and the Federal Republic of Germany at Bonn on May 26, 1952. See the BGBl II, 31 March 1955 at p. 405 *et seq*.

[22] The Bonn Conventions did not enter into force but were amended in accordance with the five Schedules to the Protocol on the Termination of the Occupation Regime in the Federal Republic of Germany which was one of the 'Paris Agreements', signed in Paris on October 23, 1954.

[23] The same applied to rights and obligations arising under treaties or international agreements which had been concluded on behalf of the three Western Zones of Occupation by the Occupation Authorities or by the Governments of the Three Powers.

[24] This exclusion was maintained in the Agreement of September 27 and 28, 1990 following the Two-Plus-Four Treaty.

[25] In the Protocol on the Termination of the Occupation Regime in the Federal Republic which was signed in Paris on October 23, 1954 and which revised the Bonn Conventions of May 26, 1952. Note that it was as a consequence of this document that the Allied High Commission was abolished.

[26] *Ibid.*

[27] See the concurring opinion of Judge Ress and Judge Zupancic in the case of *Prince Hans-Adam II of Liechtenstein v Germany* (Application no. 42527/98), Judgement of July 12, 2001.

[28] See Guido's second part of his Gloss in which he commentates on Justinian's Digest.

a ruler to change, promulgate, or abolish law in the jurisprudence of the *Ius Commune*.[29] This was reformulated in the 19th Century during the period of state formation in which the belief in the autonomous and omnipotent authority of the state and the power to regulate all its matters came to be regarded as paramount.[30] Sovereignty to administer justice remains central to German administrative law to this day with the emphasis placed by some German constitutional lawyers on the unity of the state,[31] having been transposed from constitutional law into the debates concerning German administrative law.[32]

It was in 1990 that the Four Powers negotiated to end their reserved rights for Berlin, and Germany as a whole. The Treaty on the Final Settlement with respect to Germany (the so-called 'Two-Plus-Four Treaty') signed in Moscow on September 12, 1990[33] confirmed the definite nature of the borders of the united Germany (article 1), ended the rights and responsibilities of the Four Powers relating to Berlin and to Germany (article 7) and in effect gave Germany full sovereignty over its internal and external affairs. The shift from what was referred to in 1955 as 'rights inherent in a sovereign state' to Germany being referred to as a 'sovereign state' gave rise to a distinction made between de facto and de jure sovereignty,[34] a distinction which is reminiscent of Calhoun's delineation between sovereignty and the exercise of sovereign rights.[35] What is instructive about Calhoun is that he embraces a conceptualisation founded on the division of powers which accrue to sovereignty while expressly refuting bthe notion of divided sovereignty, which, as he argued, would destroy it.[36] The difficulty in the German case is that sovereignty has always been fragmented.

The main characteristics of sovereign states have customarily been held to be territory, people and a government.[37] The German case is interesting because the territory was contested (particularly as regards the German Democratic Republic) and the powers of the German Government were

---

[29] Note that *Nec magistratibus* and *Tempestiuum* were two of the *loci classici* where the jurists discussed this doctrine of legislative sovereignty.
[30] See O Lepsius, *Steuerungsdiskussion, Systemtheorie und Parlamentarismuskritik* (München, JCB Mohr, 2000) at p. 17 *et seq*. See also L Ferrajoli, *La sovranità nel mondo moderno* (Roma-Bari, Laterza, 1997) at pp. 29 *et seq*.
[31] See J Isensee, 'Staat und Verfassung' in J Isensee & P Kirchhof (eds), *Handbuch des Staatsrechts der Bundesrepublik Deutschland* (CF Müller, Heidelberg, 1987) at § 13.
[32] See C Möllers, 'Braucht das öffentliche Recht einen neuen Methoden und Richtungsstreit?' (1999) 99 *VerwArch* 187 at p. 198.
[33] BGBl of October 13, 1990 at p. 1308 *et seq*. The Treaty entered into force on March 15, 1991.
[34] Which is referred to in German as *faktische* or *rechtliche Souveränität*.
[35] This is not to be confused with divided sovereignty. See F Mayer, *Kompetenzüberschreitung und Letztentscheidung* (München, CH Beck, 2000) at p. 286 *et seq*.
[36] See J Calhoun, *A Disquisition on Government and a Discourse on the Constitution and Government of the United States* (South Carolina, 1851) at p. 146.
[37] MR Fowler and JM Bunck, *Law, Power and the Sovereign State. The Evolution and Application of the Concept of Sovereignty* (Pennsylvania, University Press, 1995) at p. 33.

constrained by the Allies; both were, for a large part of the 20th century, occupied territories. One of the effects of locating sovereignty in the people—as provided by article 20 (2) of the Basic Law (*Grundgesetz*)—[38] was that it circumnavigated the territorial obstacle to 'full' sovereignty to the extent that the sovereign right to define the German people through citizenship laws remained untouched. This, as we shall see, was the case as regards both the FRG and the GDR.

3. POPULAR SOVEREIGNTY AND GERMAN NATIONHOOD

In the attempt to found a nation state, the *kleindeutsche* origin of German statehood in 1871 created confusion over the meaning of citizenship, since state (*Bundesstaat*) citizenship was prior to federal citizenship. Of considerable importance was the large number of Germans living outside German territory. Thus, a nation was evoked in Germany before a state was constructed, as nationhood revolved around the notion of common descent and culture.[39] The enactment of the Citizenship Law of 1913 (*Reichs- und Staatsangehörigkeits-Gesetz*) led to the notion of citizenship being reinterpreted by the Nazis in terms of 'ethnoracial' instead of 'ethnocultural' terms.[40] A distinction was drawn between Reich and State citizenship, the former being available only to persons 'with German blood'. Formal inclusion in the state was restricted to Reich members. Those who could be stripped of their State citizenship, like the Jews, lost their legal protection from persecution.[41] Nationalism came to be regarded as self-explanatory and natural, in other words, as an objectively pre-given reality.[42]

A conception of nationality based on the *ius sanguinis* was instrumental in the German process of nation building[43] which was regarded as a genet-

---

[38] Which provides that, 'All public authority emanates from the people. It shall be exercised by the people through elections and referendums and by specific legislative, executive and judicial bodies.' See *Basic Law for the Federal Republic of Germany* (Official Translation, Press and Information Office, Bonn, 1995).

[39] J Halfmann, 'Immigration and Citizenship in Germany: Contemporary Dilemmas' (1997) 105 *Political Studies* 260 at p. 267.

[40] Halfmann, above n 39 above at pp. 268–9.

[41] After the Second World War, the notion of Germans abroad again surfaced with the enactment of article 116 of the Basic Law which refers to a person who 'has been admitted to the territory of the German Reich within the frontiers of 31 December 1937 as a refugee or expellee of German stock (*Volkszugerhörigkeit*) or as the spouse or descendent of such a person. Two further categories of Germans abroad consisted of *Aussiedler* in the former Soviet Union who were treated as expellees due to their persecution under Stalin and the †bersiedler (citizens of the German Democratic Republic) who received a Western German passport on managing to cross the Border successfully.

[42] See J Willms, *Nationalismus ohne Nation. Deutsche Geschichte von 1789 bis 1914* (Düsseldorf, Claassen, 1983) at p. 10.

[43] See R Grawert, *Staat und Staatsangehörigkeit* (Berlin, Duncker Humblot, 1973) at p. 190 *et seq.*

ical-cultural organic unit and moreover, as a community based on blood, tribal and family bonds.[44] Homogeneity of the people of a State was defined in terms of a spiritual, social and political bond.[45] This is a recurrung theme in the writings of the German constitutional theorist Carl Schmitt[46] particularly in his use of the distinction between friend and enemy and the threat of the withering away of the state or *Entstaatlichung*, as he refers to it, if the distinction is not upheld.[47]

For Schmitt, political democracy is anchored in belonging to a particular people or *Volk*. In other words, the state form of democracy can only be grounded in a specific and substantive conception of equality,[48] and conversely, this equality is only bestowed on members of a state.[49] *Schmitt* regards treating foreigners or *Fremde* 'equally' as a matter of liberal rights to freedom which *he* does not classify as being political considerations. Thus, equality is not defined legally, politically or economically but belongs, as far as constitutional theory is concerned, to liberal individualism and the principle of basic rights.[50] Whereas this formulation may look harmless, it in effect justifies the exclusion of those not belonging to the state from the 'inner circle' of political participation by reference to an *a priori* metaphysical notion of a *Volk*.[51] In effect, the suspicion that this political communitarianism gives rise to a dubious conceptualisation of democracy is, in the German case, passed off as a supposedly value—free articulation of popular sovereignty—as shown by the foreigners' voting rights decision of the German Federal Constitutional Court.[52]

---

[44] See J Stahl for a typical 19th century statement concerning the *ius sanguinis*. *Rechts und Staatslehre auf der Grundlage christlicher Weltanschauung. Die Staatslehre und die Prinzipien des Staatsrechts* (Tübingen, 1878) at p. 161 *et seq*.

[45] 89 BVerGE 155 at 186.

[46] See J Habermas, 'Carl Schmitt in the Political Intellectual History of the Federal Republic' in J Habermas, *A Berlin Republic: Writings on Germany* (trans by S Rendall) (Cambridge, Polity Press, 1997) at p. 107 *et seq*.

[47] See M Zuleeg, 'The European Constitution under Constitutional Constraints: The German Scenario' (1997) 22 *European Law Review* 19 at p. 27 who cites Paul Kirchof in *Handbuch des Staatsrechts der Bundesrepublik Deutschland* (2nd edn) (CF Müller, Heidelberg, 1995) Vol. I. at p. 855–7.

[48] C Schmitt, *Verfassungslehre* (Berlin, Duncker & Humblot, 1928) at p. 226.

[49] '[w]er nicht Staatsangehöriger ist, kommt für diese demokratische Gleichheit nicht in betracht.' above n 48 at 227.

[50] above n 48 at 226.

[51] See H Heller, *Staatslehre* (Tübingen, JCB Mohr (Paul Siebeck), [1934] 1983) at p. 166–96. Heller saw the inherent dangers arising out of this naturalistic conceptualisation of the people in conjunction with a link with membership of a state, preferring an interpretation of membership of a community such as membership of civic organisations ranging from bowling clubs to the church of '*von Kegelklub zur Kirche*' as opposed to membership of a state. Heller, however, was not as persuasive as Schmitt in influencing German juridical thought.

[52] See generally GL Neuman, ' "We are the People": Alien Suffrage in German and American Perspective.' (1992) 35 *Michigan Journal of International Law* 237.

Legislation was enacted in certain *Länder*, namely, Hamburg,[53] Schleswig-Holstein,[54] and Bremen,[55] at the end of the 1980s to allow third country nationals to vote in local elections. However, this legislation was held to be irreconcilable with the Basic Law (in particular article 28) by the Federal Constitutional Court.[56] The court's reasoning was somewhat constrained by Article 116 of the Basic Law which defines German nationals. Nevertheless, the judgement illustrates the link between sovereignty, citizenship and identity.[57]

In the Schleswig-Holstein case, for example, it was argued that the constituency allowed to vote in local elections referred only to those holding German nationality in other words *das deutsche Volk*. Article 17 (2) sentence 2 of the Weimar Constitution (WRV) was recalled, which referred to *reichsdeutschen Männer und Frauen*. Being a member of a state was characterised by an insoluble bond of personal rights between the state and the citizen.[58] It was argued that foreigners could return to their homeland at any time.[59] Moreover, foreigners might also leave the region at any time without having to suffer the consequences of their decision.[60] (The fact that a German could do the same does not seem to have troubled the court).

The arguments in favour of upholding the right of foreigners to vote in local elections were made with reference to an inclusive conception of democracy. Thus it was argued that the model for the Basic Law was one based on a broad conception of the people and not on the notion of a collective nation. Thus, discrimination between people belonging to the state and those outside it (*Untertanen Verband*) was unacceptable. The People or *das Volk* was a concept more concerned with the legitimacy of decision-making and the sovereignty of the people rather than being a nationalist definition. In short, the people did not necessarily mean the *German* people.[61] The court decided otherwise, electing to adopt a somewhat essentialist conception of 'the People'. It favoured, particularly in the case of Hamburg, not only a local nexus but a local nexus of a *Staatsbürger* or citizen of the state, in other words, German nationals. Here we see the

---

[53] GVBl. 1989, Teil 1, s 29.

[54] GVBl. 1989, s 12.

[55] GVOBl. 1989, s 241.

[56] Case of the Federal Constitutional Court from 31. 10. 90, 2 BvF 2/89, 6/89; 2 BvF 3/89. Note that this case was somewhat overtaken by the event of the EC Treaty which provided EU nationals with the ability to vote and stand in local elections (Article 19 EC).

[57] For an insightful discussion of these cases, see JHH Weiler, 'Does Europe Need a Constitution? Demos, Telos and the German Maastricht Decision' (1995) 1 *European Law Journal* 219.

[58] This ethnic conception of 'the People' was also followed in the Hamburg case. See 2 BvF 3/89 at 71.

[59] 2 BvF 3/89 at p. 40.

[60] *Ibid* at p. 41.

[61] *Ibid* at p. 44.

'identity politics' nexus of the sovereignty debate in Germany which can be summarised thus: we are who WE say we are and reserve the ability to define who we are (whether it is by reference to the 'Other' or otherwise). This power of definition is our *sovereign right*. In the German case, this sovereign right has been central in 'constructing' the unity of the state. The last point is particularly important given that it draws upon Gellner's position that the state builders of early modern Europe articulated an engineered sense of nationhood and identity to forge societal cohesion.[62]

A more state centred view of the state, which may be referred to as 'etatist'[63] emphasises the distinctiveness of a state which is perceived as being based on a *Staatsvolk*[64] as well as culture, which is defined in terms of language, religion, art and history.[65] Moreover, this distinctiveness is instrumentalised in order to draw boundaries which must be protected in the face of European integration. Indeed, law is viewed as pivotal in enabling the state to maintain an openness towards the European ideal (*Europaoffenheit*) whilst, at the same time, ensuring that the state does not 'dissolve',[66] which clearly illustrates the defensive tenor of the 'etatist' position[67] despite appearances to the contrary. Thus, whilst appeals to the capacity of constitutional courts to listen, to question and to understand regarding the debate concerning the European integration project[68] are articulated—thereby appearing to be inclusive—the position is, in effect, exclusive as it is precisely language and culture which is instrumentalised in order to demarcate boundaries and to erect borders.[69]

Aside from cultural influences, and the different historical processes which led to the drafting of the respective constitutions, the assumption which prevails is that the conceptions contained therein are so distinct or 'essential' that they merit vigorous protection, a position which is supported by certain strands of German state theory. Thus, Hegel writes of the special historical role of people in history,[70] which is a consequence of

---

[62] See E Gellner, *Nations and Nationalism* (Oxford, Blackwell, 1983).

[63] See Aziz, above n 13 at pp. 4–5.

[64] That is to say, people who are related by birth and origin.

[65] See P Kirchhof, 'Europäische Einigung und der Verfassungsstaat der Bundesrepublik Deutschland' in J Isensee (ed.), *Europa als politische Idee und als rechtliche Form* (Berlin, Duncker & Humblot, 1993) at 79.

[66] *Ibid* at 64.

[67] Indeed, *Kirchhof* uses the term as a heading for a section which begins with the following: 'Die Staatlichkeit Deutschlands steht im Rahmen der europäische Einigung nicht zur Disposition'. above n 65 at 95.

[68] See P Kirchhof's editorial in (1999) 12 *Europaisches Zeitschrift für Wirtschaftsrecht* 353.

[69] This is not uncommon practice in German discussions concerning integration as a whole. A central element in a debate concerning Germany's 'leading culture' or *Leitkultur*, which occurred in the autumn of 2000, was the way in which the elements which were reputed to make up this culture were used as criteria for exclusion. See *Frankfurter Allgemeine Zeitung* from October 30, 2000 at p. 1.

[70] GWF Hegel, *Grundlinien der Philosophie des Rechts* (Frankfurt am Main, Suhrkamp, 1970) at § 344.

the dialectical development of Spirit. There are the *Völkergeister*[71] which denote the special differentiated modes of the existence of people, that is to say, there is such a thing as the 'Germanness' of Germans, the 'Englishness of the English' and so on which play their role on the stage of world history.[72]

To allow for 'outside' influences would further contribute to the 'withering away' of the state's sovereignty. As explained below, when translated into the register of constitutional debate, much of this argument is coded in the language of human rights. It does not involve a rejection of the universality of human rights as such, but is premised on the position that some states protect human rights more vigorously than others. Moreover—so the argument continues—some states have protected certain rights which are, as in the case of the protection of economic rights in the German Basic Law, for example, not to be found in the constitutions of other states, a position which must, in order to be understood more fully, be viewed in relation to the context of the German juridical debate concerning European integration.

4. THE CHALLENGE TO SOVEREIGNTY POSED BY EUROPEAN INTEGRATION

The nation-state is a vital premise of the legal reasoning upon which the reception of EC law into the jurisdictions of the member states is based. The underlying tension is as follows: either a state's membership of the EU entails categorical acceptance of the supremacy doctrine, which is, in itself, an endorsement of the hierarchical model of law. Or, alternatively, the state retains the right, in certain cases, to set the supremacy doctrine aside. Thus, even if it is accepted that the sovereignty of a member state has been qualified by its membership to the EU, it is a form of qualification which is by no means unconditional. These two positions represent two versions of events, so to speak, of the relationship between EC law and national law and constitute competing schools of thought in the German juridical debate concerning European integration. The term 'German juridical debate' is used to denote the legal academic community[73] which acts, in contrast to

---

[71] *Ibid* § 352.

[72] Thus, in Hegel's terms, unfolding the full world of the Spirit. above n 70 at § 274 regarding the nature of the constitution and the special nature of a people.

[73] Which Kokott refers to as *La Doctrine* which, in her opinion, is composed of professors of public, European and international law including former and future justices. The fact that Kokott does not include academics from the lower ranks of academia says much about the hierarchical structure within which German academia is entrenched. See J Kokott, 'Report on Germany' in A-M Slaughter, A Stone Sweet and JHH Weiler (eds.), *The European Courts and National Courts: Doctrine and Jurisprudence* (Oxford, Hart Publishing, 1998) at 79.

other member states of the EU, as a source of influence on the jurisprudence of the *Bundesverfassungsgericht* or German Federal Constitutional Court ('FCC')[74] which is, in turn, an actor in the European integration process of some influence. The role of the court should not be overestimated, particularly given the institutional constraints within which judges are obliged to operate. However, it is the national constitutional courts of the member states of the EU which are obliged to articulate the rapport between EC and national law in an ongoing debate which is characterised by changing normative relationships predicated on the issue of the fundamental legitimacy of political power. Moreover, as this next section will show, the judges of the FCC have managed their institutional constraints in such a way as to appear as 'apolitical' participants in the political debate on European integration. In particular, whereas most of its decisions regarding the European integration project are not explicitly about sovereignty, the court has managed to frame its judgements in such a way as to issue edicts which have considerable implications for the concept of sovereignty.

A. The *Bundesverfassungsgericht*'s Decisions as Regards European Integration: 'Sovereignty by any Other Name'

The jurisprudence of the *Bundesverfassungsgericht* concerning European integration is prolific. A detailed appraisal of its decisions would be not only be impossible for reasons of space but would detract from the focal point of the discussion at hand. Suffice to say that the cases referred to below must not be regarded as an exhaustive evaluation of the FCC's jurisprudence regarding European integration.[75] Rather, they serve to illustrate the finesse with which the FCC has developed the concept of sovereignty in such a way as to carve out a role for itself as guardian not only of the German constitution, but also of the identity—or 'distinctiveness'—of the German state.

One way in which it has been able to engineer this is through the concept of human rights. Thus, in its *Solange I* decision,[76] the court held that as long as ('*solange*') the EC has not proved itself to provide adequate protection of

---

[74] Indeed, the extent of the influence exercised by German legal academia on judicial decisions may be regarded as surprising by common law lawyers. It is often the case in Germany that judges are also academics. Historically, universities played an important role in the development and the systemisation of German law. Academic opinion, outlined in periodicals and commentaries (*Kommentare*) is regarded as persuasive authority. This is in direct contrast to the position in common law jurisdictions. See Lord Goff's *dicta* in *Spiliarda Maritime v Consulex Ltd* [1987] 1 AC 460 at 488. The position in Scotland can be distinguished on the grounds that it is more common to cite opinions of academics, which may influence the outcome of litigation.

[75] See, however, n 73 above at pp. 77–131.

[76] BVerfGE 37, 271.

basic rights, the Federal Constitutional Court would remain the ultimate arbiter concerning issues of human rights and would assess the level of protection afforded to human rights in *specific*[77] contexts. In the later *Solange II*,[78] the EC was now held to protect human rights in line with the protection of fundamental rights enshrined in the German Basic Law, enabling the FCC to relax its jurisdictional hold over questions of basic rights. Accordingly, as long as the general level of protection was secured by the ECJ, the FCC would not review the level in specific cases. The fundamental rights issue was not directly relevant for the later, and even more famous, *Maastricht*[79] judgement.[80] One can only speculate as to the effect of the judgement on the human rights issue. One reading of the case[81] is that the FCC reaffirmed the position it adopted in *Solange II*, that is to say that the FCC would only look at general cases in the event of a decrease in the general level of human rights protection. It was this interpretation[82] of the *Maastricht* decision which was of particular significance regarding the most recent instalment of the FCC's jurisprudence concerning European integration, namely, the *Banana* case[83] which was based on a challenge made by a group of third country banana importers[84] before a Frankfurt Administrative Court regarding the constitutionality of the conditions of trade for third countries imposed by virtue of an EU Regulation. In Germany, prior to the enactment of the regulation, the majority of the bananas on the market emanated from third countries.

According to the FCC in this case, fundamental rights in the EC, as the ECJ's decisions indicate, are still sufficiently protected.[85] That is to say, this protection is commensurate with the protection guaranteed by the provisions of the German Basic Law. As long as this continues to be the case, the FCC shall not exercise its jurisdiction concerning the applicability of secondary EC law. The FCC shall therefore not review secondary EC law[86]

---

[77] Ie on a case-by-case basis.

[78] BVerfGE 73, 339.

[79] BVerfGE 89, 155 or *Brunner v European Union Treaty* [1994] 1 CMLR 57.

[80] It is important to point out that the *Maastricht* decision was based on arguments concerning democratic legitimacy and competence-competence. The human rights nexus of the case is *obiter dicta* only.

[81] Indeed, there are several. See, for example, above n 47 above and also P Kirchhof, 'The Balance of Powers Between National and European Institutions' (1999) 5 *European Law Journal* 225.

[82] A plethora of interpretations of the effect of the *Maastricht* decision were offered as regards the human rights issue.

[83] Decision of June 7, 2000–2 BvL 1/97.

[84] Referred to as the Atlanta Group.

[85] The FCC has thereby reaffirmed its *Solange II* decision. See BVerfGE 73, 378–81.

[86] Or 'Solange dies so ist, wird das BVerfG seine Gerichtsbarkeit uber die Anwendbarkeit von abgeleitetem Gemeinschaftsrecht nicht mehr ausuben. Vorlagen von Normen des sekondären Gemeinschaftsrechts an das BVerfG sind deshalb unzulässig.' Here the court cross- referred to its Solange II decision. See BVerfGE 73, 339.

unless and until the ECJ fails to protect fundamental rights to the degree envisaged in *Solange II*.[87]

It is important to draw attention to the fact that the FCC's judgment was consistent with the provisions of the Basic Law. An amendment to the Basic Law (Article 23 (1) Sentence 1),[88] which was enacted prior to both the *Maastricht* decision and the ratification of the Maastricht Treaty, provides constitutional limits to European integration. Thus, the EC Treaties and any secondary legislation arising therefrom should be read in the light of other provisions of the Basic Law, such as the provisions falling under the so-called 'eternity clause'[89] which contains a reference to human dignity and the value of human life[90] as well as to the federal, democratic and social principles upon which the Federal Republic of Germany is founded.[91] The eternity clause provides that these principles may not be set aside by the legislature.[92]

In order for a challenge to succeed before the FCC, a court must prove that European legal development, which includes the decisions of the ECJ taken after the Solange II decision, has sunk below the necessary level of basic rights protection.[93] This necessitates reconciling basic rights protection at the national level with the European level according to the method envisaged by the FCC in *Solange II*. The FCC held that not only had the administrative court (*VG*) failed to undertake such an assessment but also the ECJ's case law illustrated that basic rights are sufficiently protected at the level of the EU.[94]

---

[87] above n 83 at paragraph 60.

[88] As amended on 21 December 1992. Article 23 (1) of the Basic Law provides that, '(1) To realise a unified Europe, Germany participates in the development of the European Union which is bound to democratic, rule of law, social, and federal principles as well as the principle of subsidiarity and provides a protection of fundamental rights essentially equivalent to that of this Constitution. The federation can, for this purpose and with the consent of the Senate, delegate sovereign powers. Article 79 (2) & (3) is applicable for the foundation of the European Union as well as for changes in its contractual bases and comparable regulations by which the content of this Constitution is changed or amended or by which such changes or amendments are authorised.'

[89] Article 79 (III) of the Basic Law.

[90] Article 1 of the Basic Law.

[91] See Article 20 of the Basic Law.

[92] In the event of conflict, the competing constitutional principles must be balanced in accordance with the principle of maximum effectiveness or 'practical concordance'. See K Hesse, *Grundzüge des Verfassungsrechts der Bundesrepublik Deutschland* 20th edn (Heidelberg, Müller, 1995) at 28 and 72. For a succinct yet informative outline of the applicability of article 23 of the Basic Law, see C Schmidt, 'From Pont d'Avignon to Ponte Vecchio: The Resolution of Constitutional Conflicts between the European Union and the Member States through Principles of Public International Law' in P Eeckhout and T Tridimas (eds.) (1998) 18 *Yearbook of European Law* 415 at pp. 418–9.

[93] above n 83 at paragraph 62.

[94] Such as the right to property, the right to economic activity, freedom of association, the right to equality and the prohibition against arbitrary conduct, freedom of faith, the protection of the family and the principle of proportionality. above n 83 at paragraph 58.

The questions addressed in the *Maastricht* decision do, to some extent, overlap with those raised in the *Banana* case. The judgements are, however, by no means interchangeable. *Maastricht* concerned the issue of competence of the German state, under its constitution to ratify the Maastricht Treaty. By contrast, the *Banana* case was based on the issue of fundamental rights. Yet both cases raise the question of the ultimate arbiter and by implication, the doctrine of sovereignty. It is of interest to note that the ease with which the FCC ranged beyond its basic remit in the *Maastricht* case, dealing with the human rights issue in a case which was essentially based on competence—albeit *obiter dicta*—was noticeably absent in the *Banana* case.[95] That is to say, in the latter case it elected not to address the issue of competence by way of *obiter dicta* in a case based on fundamental rights, a move which would have been in line with the tactics it adopted in its *Maastricht* decision. What begins to emerge is a picture of the court's power of definition, the way in which it reserves the right to interpret the issues which it deems most salient in a case. Thus, whilst appearing to address fundamental rights protection, it has in effect developed its 'sovereignty jurisprudence', based on a vision of itself as the ultimate guardian of the unity of the German state. The 'Euro' decision is a further case in point[96] of a tactic which would be surmised thus: *sovereignty by any other name*. Interesting historical parallels arise, such as the German general strategy in 1948–9 to regain full national sovereignty within parameters framed by military occupation by the Allies in which tactics were adopted to preserve as much national unity in the country as possible,[97] an issue which engages and is engaged by German state theory.

B. The Influence of German State Theory

The German debate concerning the need for a European constitution is a good illustration of the extent to which theories of the state both form and inform the discussion concerning the European integration project.[98] Broadly speaking, two schools of thought may be distinguished. The first school of thought contends that the European Union is unable to have a constitution in view of it not being a nation state.[99] The state is thereby

---

[95] See also BVerfG NJW 2000, 3124 and BVerfG EuZW 2001, 255.
[96] *Ibid.*
[97] See E Spevack, *Allied Control and German Freedom: American Political and Ideological Influences on the Framing of the West German Basic Law (Grundgesetz)* (Münster, Hamburg, 2001) at pp. 322–3.
[98] See the symposium reproduced in (2001) 2 *German Law Journal* (Issue of September 1) available at http://www.germanlawjournal.com; see also JE Murkens, 'The Integrative Function of a European Constitution (Discussion of Chr. Dorau: Die Verfassungsfrage der Europäischen Union' (2002) 3 *German Law Journal* (Issue of Feburary 1, 2002).
[99] See D Grimm, 'Does Europe need a constitution?' (1995) *European Law Journal* 282.

viewed as being both the object and the prerequisite of a constitution.[100] Moreover, a constitution must be authorised by the ultimate bearers of state authority, the people (*Staatsvolk*). The *pouvoir constituant* is viewed as being absent in relation to the EU in view of the lack of a European *Staatsvolk*.[101] The second school of thought, which I have elected to entitle 'post-etatist', contends that a prerequisite for a constitution is merely the existence of a political community, whether or not crystallised in the form of a nation state.[102] On this view, the state, or indeed any other political system, is shaped by the constitution, which is defined as the basic legal order of any authoritative political system.[103]

The schools of thought also have different interpretations of the concept of sovereignty. According to the first view, legal sovereignty is linked to the nation-state. The EU is viewed as 'supra-national' or even intergovernmental[104] and only legitimate to the extent that it provides a mechanism for furthering the interests of the nation-state, including those associated with fundamental rights.[105] The second view is arguably tantamount to a cosmopolitan position given it is intrinsically a 'post-sovereignty' position. Accordingly, rights are not tied to culture or territory; thus, it is perfectly possible to have a legal system which is transnational or 'trans' state-like which is focussed on the interpretation and elaboration of these fundamental principles.

The ultimate arbiter debate in Germany is underpinned by a tension between these two versions of events which are retold in what Ladeur has referred to as a, 'traditionally state-determined discourse'.[106] Thus, the 'etatist' view provides that EC law normally prevails over national law; there are, however, exceptions, and the ultimate source of authority remains national law. The 'post-etatist' view categorically accepts the order of precedence of EC law. Academic opinion in Germany amongst jurists falls into

---

[100] See J Isensee, 'Staat und Verfassung', above n 31 at ¤ 13. Para 1. See also C Dorau and P Jacobi, 'The Debate over a "European Constitution": Is it Solely a German Concern?' (2000) 6 *European Public Law* 413.

[101] See A Augustin, *Das Volk der Europäischen Union* (Berlin, Duncker & Humblot, 2000).

[102] See P Häberle, 'Die Europäische Verfassungsstaatlichkeit' in P Häberle *Europäische Verfassungslehre in Einzelstudien* (Baden-Baden, Nomos, 1999) at p. 65 *et seq*. See also N Walker, 'Beyond the Unitary Conception of the United Kingdom Constitution?' (2000) *Public Law* 384 at 399.

[103] above n 92 at paragraph 17.

[104] See, for example, M Pechstein and M Koenig who view the European Union as being established by international treaties. See *Die Europäische Union. Die Verträge von Maastricht und Amsterdam* 2nd edn (Tübingen, Mohr, 1998) at 275.

[105] See below.

[106] K-H Ladeur, 'Towards a Legal Theory of Supranationality—The Viability of the Network Concept' (1997) 3 *European Law Journal* 33 at 34.

precisely these two positions.[107] The positions represent competing schools of thought in a debate which is highly vitriolic, defensive, confrontational and rhetorical—in effect, the customary ingredients of legal debate. However, *the way in which* the main protagonists of each school of thought claim to hold the ultimate truth does little to foster open debate and even less to discount the accusation that amongst the protagonists are in effect polemicists disguised as legal scholars. Many would no doubt attribute this deep and resilient tension to the link between law and society which was never severed. Thus, the recognition of the state as having legal personality by jurists such as Jellinek[108] went some way towards linking a legal conception of the state with a sociological conception of the state. Thus, the concept of the state is juxtaposed with constitutional law on a basis which constitutional law is unable to cope with, given that societal expectations extend beyond the legal parameters provided by constitutional law.[109]

No appraisal of the concept of sovereignty would be complete without a reference to two leading state theorists, Carl Schmitt and Herman Heller, who are customarily presented as expressing two opposing strands of the German theoretical debate concerning sovereignty. Thus, Schmitt is cited as the advocate of a strong, unified state which can not bear the strain of pluralism.[110] Indeed, in his view, Weimar's failure was predicated on the demands from municipalities and the *Länder* which threatened the unity of the German state.[111]

The insistence on the concept of unity is instructive as it goes to the heart of the tension between the dichotomy of 'pro-nation State' versus 'pro-integration' positions[112] or what I have referred to as the 'etatist' and the 'post-etatist' schools of thought.[113] The tension somewhat oversimplifies the debate. It does, however, underline the importance afforded to the concept—or perhaps even *myth*—of unity[114] in German juridical thought in

---

[107] *Pro* the FCC being the ultimate arbiter R Scholz, *Neue Juristische Wochenschrift*, 1993, 1690 and *contra* G Hirsch, *Neue Juristische Wochenschrift* 1996, 2457. See also an article by the latter, a former judge at the ECJ, G Hirsch in the *Frankfurter Allgemeine Zeitung* on 9.10.1996 at p. 15.

[108] See G Jellinek, *Gesetz und Verordnung Staatsrechtliche Untersuchungen auf rechtsgeschichtlicher und rechtsvergleichender Grundlage* (Freiburg, 1887) at p. 192 *et seq.*

[109] See C Möllers, *Staat als Argument* (München, CH Beck, 2000) at p. 23 and also P Zumbansen, *Ordnungsmodelle im modernen Wohlfahrtsstaat. Lernerfahrungen zwischen Staat, Gesellschaft und Vertrag* (Baden-Baden, Nomos, 2000) at pp. 90–2 and also 286–94.

[110] See P Zumbansen, 'Carl Schmitt und die Suche nach politischer Einheit' (1997) 30 *Kritische Justiz* 63.

[111] above n 17 at 112.

[112] See A von Bogdandy, 'The Science of European Law' (2000) 6 *European Law Journal* 208 at p. 213.

[113] above n 13.

[114] above n 112 at 213: ': is the unity of politics and law as realised in the traditional nation state something to be protected and maintained as far as possible? Or does the European Union offer a historical new alternative to be realised and developed into a new form of political and legal governance according to its own singular logic?'

the face of European integration. It would be easy to try to transpose this dichotomy to the 'Schmitt-Heller' debate. The transposition, however, is incomplete as both agree on certain issues.

Where Heller and Schmitt meet is in their insistence on sovereignty representing the primacy of the will of nation-states. Heller, for instance, justifies state-actions against existing international and national law on the basis of the state's right to self preservation. It is when one reads Heller's account of the state as an entity which stands above the law that one sees the similarities with Schmitt. According to Heller, the state is a living will which exists prior to international law. However, his conception of the state may be distinguished from Schmitt's to the extent that sovereignty may not, as Schmitt maintains, be localised in an individual organ but rather is constituted through a dynamic process of national regeneration in an ongoing dialectic of institutional assertion and interaction. It is *Heller*'s emphasis on organisation, or what he referred to as an 'ordered structure for acting' (*geordnetes Handlungsgefüge*) which enables co-operation between the different levels of governance, not unlike the contemporary conceptualisations of multi-level governance.

The Schmitt/Heller debate has been taken up more recently, particularly regarding the substantive notions of unity, the concept of political democracy and German nationhood in the debate concerning German unification.[115] Schmitt's influence on German legal thought is, however, limited and it is questionable whether he has anything to offer as regards the juridical debate concerning European integration. The current vogue amongst scholars to draw from Schmitt would seem to be rather more a case of tasting the 'forbidden fruit' than anything else.[116] The ostensible reason he has been discussed in the European integration debate is to substantiate those conceptions of the state that stress the importance of unity and impermeability from outside influences. The fixation with unity, however, predates Schmitt. Locating sovereignty in the state was one of the most compelling ideological tools of state formation during the earlier nineteenth century, which perhaps explains why it has been coveted by German lawyers. They view sovereignty as the essential characteristic of state formation in the tricky task of reconciling territory with identity, particularly given the presence of two German states prior to reunification[117] and the wish to reconcile this division with the the idea of the resilience of a single nation.[118]

---

[115]   above n 17.

[116]   above n 110.

[117]   Although some would no doubt dispute the reference to the former German Democratic Republic as a 'German' state. See below and also generally A Grunenberg, 'Zwei Deutschlands—zwei Identitäten?' in G-J Glaeßner (ed.), *Die DDR in der ra Honecker* (Opladen, Westdeutscher Verlag, 1988) at pp. 94–107.

[118]   See S Meuschel, 'Zur Konzeption der Nation und Nationalgeschichte,' above n 117 at 79.

5. SOVEREIGNTY AND THE FORMER GERMAN DEMOCRATIC REPUBLIC (GDR)

The concept of sovereignty was understood and applied very differently in the 'other' Germany, the former German Democratic Republic (GDR). In the GDR the link between sovereignty and the dominant state ideology was overt. The standard view of the totalitarian school in Western communist studies is that sovereignty was not a legitimate subject for discussion among East German legal scholars and practitioners. Any perusal of the leading GDR law textbooks demonstrates that it did not enjoy the same standing as it did in West German legal scholarship. It is argued that the only form of research which was seen to be legitimate[119] was research which would aid the Socialist Unity Party (*Sozialistischer Einheitspartei* or SED) to assert its 'right to rule', to establish the recognition of the GDR on the international stage, and to legitimate the GDR socialist state as distinct from its West German capitalist counterpart. Legal academics were compelled to conduct research within ideological parameters that conformed to the Party line. Thus, it is maintained that freedom of research was virtually non-existent in the GDR, thereby inhibiting, as in the case of Soviet legal scholarship,[120] candid debate. It is often observed that there was no commentary on the GDR's constitution equivalent to those published about the West German constitution.[121] While the GDR had a Supreme Court, it did not have a constitutional court, nor an administrative court, where the mechanism of judicial review would normally be located. Citizens of the GDR were unable to rely on provisions of the constitution in order to appeal to their rights vis Ë vis the State, and, in any event rights were tied to the fulfilment of certain responsibilities to the state order.[122] The law and the legal system were subordinate to Party control and discretion, mirroring the position in the Soviet Union.[123] Thus, the terms democracy, election, parliament, federalism, trade-union and collective agreement must be interpreted differently in the GDR context because of the 'leading and guiding role' of the commu-

---

[119] Research in the GDR mirrored the position in the Soviet Union where legal research enjoyed vast government support and was closely linked to the themes prioritised in the Congresses and Programme of the Communist Party and in the State five year plans for economic and social development. See WE Butler, *Soviet Law* (London, Butterworths, 1983) at p. 71.

[120] AL Unger, *Constitutional Development in the USSR. A Guide to the Soviet Constitutions* (New York, Pica Press, 1981) at 219.

[121] A commentary compiled by a West German academic does, however, exist. above n 6.

[122] See E-W Böckenförde, *Die Rechtsauffassung im kommunistischen Staat* (München, Kösel, 1967).

[123] See OS Ioffe, *Soviet Law and Soviet Reality* (Dordrecht, Martinus Nijhoff Publishers, 1985) at 13. The explicit affirmation of the role of the Communist party was also incorporated in the constitutions of the former Yugoslavia (Introduction Part VIII), Czechoslovakia (article 4), Mongolia (preamble), Romania (articles 3 and 26), Bulgaria (article 1), Hungary (article 3), Cuba (article 5) and Albania (article 3).

nist Party.[124] Indeed, the fundamental concept of state organisation and sovereignty must be understood very differently in communist societies.

A. The Concept of the State

The concept of the state in the communist countries of Eastern Europe was based on Marxist-Leninist theory and Soviet practice. Both theory and Soviet practice underwent significant changes in the course of the 20th Century and especially in the post-Stalin period under Khrushchev, Brezhnev and Gorbachev. Political, ideological and constitutional changes in the Soviet Union were subsequently reflected in similar developments in the socialist bloc of states. According to Marxist-Leninist state theory, the state is an instrument of class domination,[125] which under socialism becomes the dictatorship of the proletariat (*Diktatur des Proletariats*). Accordingly , the state will inevitably wither away under socialism as part of the process of building communism. Historically, Marxism-Leninism distinguished between three types of state: the slave state (*Sklavenhalterstaat*), the feudal state (*Feudalstaat*) and the capitalist state (*kapitalistischer Staat*). All were held to share the common characteristic of domination by an exploitative class (hence the term exploitative state or *Ausbeuterstaat*). The GDR was founded in the Stalinist era and its first constitution of 1949 enshrined the Stalinist notion of the dictatorship of the proletariat. Following 'destalinisation' in the Khrushchev era, the state concept of the dictatorship of the proletariat was changed to 'people's democracy' or *Volksdemokratie*,[126] which was used in conjunction with Khrushchev's concept of the state as the 'whole people' or *allgemeiner Volksstaat*.[127] *With Khrushchev's fall to a neo-Stalinist revanchism in the Soviet Union in October 1964 there was a re-emphasis on the class nature of the state concept in the GDR. In the GDR constitution of 1968 the socialist state was regarded as an instrument of class power which was led by the communist party on behalf of the working class and the co-operative farmers (Genossenschaftsbauern)* (Article 1 of the 1968 constitution).[128] This ideological conservatism continued even through the Gorbachev era of Perestroika in the Soviet Union to the collapse of the GDR and the communist bloc in 1989.

---

[124] *Ibid* at p. 2.
[125] *DDR Handbuch* (Vol 2) (3rd edn) (Köln, Verlag Wissenschaft und Politik) at 1297. See also generally *Staatsrecht der DDR* (Berlin [Ost], 1977).
[126] A concept derived by the 1961 party program of the Communist Party of the Soviet Union. See generally H Weber, *Die DDR 1945–86* (München, R Oldenbourg Verlag, 1988) at pp. 23 *et seq*.
[127] See the party program enacted by the VI. Party conference of the SED in January 1963.
[128] Consolidated in 1974.

B. Popular Sovereignty, Socialism and East German Nationhood

The distinguishing feature of the language of sovereignty in the GDR legal system was that, although it was regarded as a general principle of public international law, its substantive and ideological content was derived from the unitary political organisation of the state and claims about its class basis. Article 47 (2) of the 1968 constitution provides that, 'The sovereignty of the working people, which is realised on the basis of democratic centralism is the fundamental principle of state structure'. In the GDR, distinctions were made between the sovereignty of the state, nation and people (or popular sovereignty). State sovereignty referred to legal competences as regards the territory and people of the state in international relations with other states and international organisations, such as participation in the production of public international law norms.[129] This was based on the basic principle of equal sovereignty espoused in the declaration of principles of the 25th UN General Assembly on October 24, 1970. After the USSR nominally granted the GDR 'full' sovereignty as part of the first measures of destalinisation reforms in March 1954, the task of public international law jurists in the GDR and other socialist bloc countries was to underpin the international recognition of the GDR as a 'sovereign' state based on the rights of self-determination and general interests of nations and people (*Völkerschaften*). Those states which refused to recognise the GDR as a sovereign state were regarded by the GDR as violating the principle of non-interference in a state's domestic affairs. The paradox of the assertion of state sovereignty in the GDR was that, as in its West German counterpart, sovereignty was severely constrained by the victorious allied powers of the Second World War and their military occupation of national territory.

The character of the internal sovereignty of the state is largely fixed by the power of the state to determine what its identity is, and who its constituents are, through citizenship laws. As a socialist state, the GDR established strong bonds between citizenship, nationality, and ideology. The relationship between citizenship and sovereignty was explicitly recognised by the GDR as it regarded the enactment of its citizenship regulations (the *Staatsbürgerschaftsgesetz (StBG)* in 1967 as a 'self-evident sovereign right'.[130] The GDR's citizenship law was fundamentally different in concept and application from its West German counterpart (which restated the 1913 regulation, paragraph 4 of the StBG, on *ius sanguinis, ius soli*). In contrast to the concept of *ius sanguinis, ius soli* citizenship of the GDR could be revoked by the state, for example, if a citizen left the GDR. On the other hand, a GDR citizen settling in the FRG was treated by right of

---

[129] See *Völkerrecht. Lehrbuch* edited by an author's collective, T. 1 (Berlin [Ost] 1973) at p. 278. Note that the GDR joined the United Nations in 1973.
[130] StaatsR DDR, LB, p. 160. See GBl DDR II 1967, p. 3.

German blood as an automatic citizen, without having to satisfy any citizenship requirements.[131] Furthermore, one of the key aspects of the GDR's citizenship law was that it made loyalty to the socialist state and its foundations and goals a statutory requirement.[132] The claim was that the GDR's 'Other', namely West Germany, was a bourgeois nation or *bürgerliche Nation*,[133] whereas the GDR constituted a new type of nation—a socialist nation.[134] The state-controlled socialisation mechanisms of education, the mass media, and culture meant that teachers, journalists, artists and intellectuals in general were duty-bound positively to reinforce this claim on a continuous basis. Thus, culture was instrumentalised[135] in order to forge a separate identity (symbols, myths, rituals, and collective memory) for the new state.[136] In 1974, the socialist ideological norms of the GDR's constitution were strengthened by amendments that expunged all the references to a German nation and replaced them by socialist rhetoric and claims to a socialist state of workers and farmers.[137]

Developments in international relations in Europe in the early 1970s had a significant impact on how sovereignty was perceived in the GDR. Membership by the GDR and the FRG of the United Nations in 1973 consolidated international recognition of a divided Germany and the delineation between the FRG and the GDR.[138] While the GDR recognised the

---

[131] See the judgement of the Federal Constitutional Court in 1973 in the so-called *Grundlagenvertrag* Judgement. BVerfGE 36, 1 = (1973) *Neue Juristische Wochenschrift*, 1539 *ff*. See also BVerfGE of October 21, 1987 in (1988) *Juristen Zeitung* at p. 144 *et seq*.

[132] H Roggemann, *Die DDR—Verfassungen. Einführung in das Verfassungsrecht der DDR* (Berlin, Arno Spitz, 1989) at p. 181 *et seq*.

[133] On the distinction between the *bourgeois* law and *socialist* law see G Ajani, *Diritto del Europa Orientale* (Torino, UTET, 1996)) at p. 50.

[134] Comments by Honecker during the VIII. Party Conference. See Protocol of the VIII. Party Conference at p. 56 reproduced in D Staritz, *Geschichte der DDR 1949–85* (Frankfurt am Main, Suhrkamp, 1985) at p. 211. See also E Honecker, *Aus meinem Leben* (Frankfurt am Main [DDR], 1980) at p. 391.

[135] See M Jäger, *Kultur und Politik in der DDR. Ein historischer Abriß* (Gütersloh, Edition Deutschland Archiv, 1982).

[136] Or what the sociologist Edgar Morin has referred to as collective memory, common norms and rules, the past with all its experience, tests, pain, joy, victories and defeats which is taken up by generation upon generation through their parents and their schools and are internalised. See E Morin, *Europa Denken* (Frankfurt am Main, Suhrkamp, 1988) at p. 168. In the case of the former GDR, however, it was issues such as a common history which were subject to revisionism to suit party ends. See H Weber, *Die DDR 1945–86* (München, R Oldenbourg Verlag, 1988) at pp. 108–9 where he writes about the 'disappearance' of certain controversial figures such as Khrushchev after his deposition in 1964 in history books.

[137] K Sorgenicht, *Staat, Recht und Demokratie nach dem IX. Parteitag der SED* (Berlin, Dietz Verlag, 1976) at pp. 80–1.

[138] After the ratification of Basic Contract or the *Grundlagenvertrag* which was enacted in 1972 between the German states by the GDR parliament (*Volkskammer*) in June 1973 and by the West German parliament (*Bundestag*) in May 1973 which formalised relations between the FRG and the GDR and which was founded on the Agreement between the Four Powers (*Viermächte-Abkommen über Berlin* (September 1971), the *Berlin-Transit-Abkommen* between East Berlin and Bonn (December 1971) and the Treaties between West Germany, Poland and the Soviet Union (May, 1972). above n 134 at 209 *et seq*.

FRG as a fully sovereign state,[139] it also aspired to extend its own sovereignty over the FRG. Until the early 1970s, GDR leaders argued that the relations between the two German states could only normalise after a GDR-led unification which, as Ulbricht stated to the GDR's parliament in May 1965, would be based on a process of 'democratisation and the resistance against imperialism and monocapitalism'.[140]

Ironically, in spite of the formal distinction between the states created under international law, travel restrictions between both states were relaxed leading some, like Bahr, the architect of the East-West dialogue, to say that 'Nation means a coming together'.[141] This interchange helped to undermine the attempt by the SED to develop a separate identity and distinguish the GDR on theoretical grounds, namely, on the basis of socialism and class conflict.

Finally, popular sovereignty rested with two strictly defined groups: the workers and the farmers. This form of sovereignty in the GDR is distinguished from that of West Germany both in its class nature, and to the extent that it established a state monopoly of ownership of capital and large-scale property (*Monopolkapital und Großgrundbesitz*).[142] Be that as it may, the appeals to unification in 1989 made during the demonstrations in Leipzig were not 'We are the People' but 'We are one People'.[143]

C. Limited Sovereignty

Sovereignty did not, however, play a central role in the relations between the GDR and other socialist bloc countries. Thus, the principles of equality, territorial integrity, independence and non-interference in domestic affairs were regarded as important principles but were subject to particular interpretation in the interests of what is referred to as 'fraternal assistance' towards other Eastern bloc countries.[144] Support for Soviet interventionism was justified on the grounds of the need to protect the socialist community

---

[139] See T Vogelsang *Das geteilte Deutschland* (10th edn) (München, DTV, 1980) at p. 331.
[140] *Ibid.*
[141] 'Nation ist, wenn man sich trifft'. above n 134 at p. 210.
[142] above n 125 at 1151. Note that class consciousness appears in many of the constitutions of the former communist world. See eg the Polish Constitution, the preamble of which provided, 'The Polish People's Republic is a republic of the working people'. See WB Simons (ed.), *The Constitutions of the Communist World* (Alphen aan den Rijn, Sijthoff & Noordhoff, 1980) at p. 288 or the Czechoslovak Constitution, article 1 (1) of which provided that, 'The Czechoslovak Socialist Republic is a socialist state founded on the firm union of the workers, peasants, and the intelligentsia, with the working class at its head'. *ibid* at p. 142. The Soviets also officially distinguished between workers, peasants and intelligentsia. See article 1 of the 1977 Constitution.
[143] B Zanetti, *Der Weg zur deutschen Einheit* (München, Goldmann, 1991) at p. 31.
[144] above n 125 at 1152.

of states or *sozialistischen Staatengemeinschaft*.[145] This rhetoric of self-imposed limitation on state sovereignty in the socialist bloc was a device to cloak Soviet interventionism to sustain its hegemony in Eastern Europe, and in particular its military occupation of the GDR.[146] The Soviet military interventions in Hungary in 1956, Czechoslovakia in 1968, Afghanistan in 1979, and the pressures on Poland in 1980, were seen as legitimate measures to defend the socialist bloc. Those socialist states which did not accept the hegemony of the Soviet Union, such as Yugoslavia (which broke with Moscow under Tito in 1948) and Albania, were isolated on the grounds that they had pursued the road of 'nationalism'—the ultimate form of deviation from the socialist cause.[147] The Soviet Union, as its interventions in Hungary and Czechoslovakia illustrate, was unable to accept a 'national' form of communism. For to do so would have called into question its hegemony over the socialist bloc and even its leadership of the Warsaw Pact.[148] Consequently, in the aftermath of the crushing of the Hungarian revolution of 1956, the Soviet Union imposed a doctrine of limited sovereignty on the socialist bloc of states, which was referred to as 'proletarian internationalism'.[149] Thereafter, any development of national forms of communism which was perceived as a threat to Soviet hegemony was met with the 'fraternal assistance'[150] of military intervention, most starkly in the Warsaw pact invasion of Czechoslovakia in 1968. This so-called *pax sovietica* was also secured by a process of integration in the socialist bloc whereby ruling elites (the communist party nomenklatura), economies, militaries, and national interests were locked into Soviet controlled supranational organisations such as Comecon and the Warsaw Pact.[151] The notion of limited sovereignty, sometimes referred to as the 'Brezhnev doctrine', was embedded in Article 30 of the 1977 Soviet Constitution (the so-called 'Brezhnev Constitution'), which committed the Soviet Union to 'friendship, cooperation and comradely mutual assistance' in accordance with the

---

[145] See generally V #akSitov, *Socialist"#akceskij internacionalism i patriottism* (Moscow, 1971) at pp. 55–6.

[146] A 'special relationship' which was maintained until the end as the discussions between Gorbachov and Honecker illustrate. See D Küchenmeister (ed.), *Honecker-Gorbatschow. Vieraugengespräche* (Berlin, Dietz, 1993) at pp. 92–3.

[147] See H Schulze, *Staat und Nation in der Europäischen Geschichte* (München, CH Beck, 1994) at p. 323.

[148] *Ibid.*

[149] As proclaimed in Moscow in October 1957 in the declaration of the communist parties in power to commemorate the 40th anniversary of the October 1917 Russian Revolution. The full text of 'the twelve' is reproduced in *The Communist Manifesto and Related Documents* in DN Jacobs (ed.) 2nd edn (New York, 1962) at p. 176.

[150] See generally *Das System der sozialistischen Gesellschafts-und Staatsordnung. Dokumente. Deutsche Demokratische Republik* (Berlin, Deutsche Demokratische Republik, 1969) at p. 267.

[151] *Sozialistischer Staat und staatliche Leitung. Aktuelle Probleme der Tätigkeit der Staatsmacht in der DDR* (Berlin, Staatsverlag der DDR, 1976) at p. 15.

principle of 'socialist internationalism,' and also to participate in 'economic integration'.

The GDR constitution locked the state into this wider system of limited sovereignty. Article 7 (2) of the GDR's constitution provided that it was an 'inseparable' element of the socialist community of states or *Staatengemeinschaft*. Furthermore, it committed itself to uphold the principles of socialist internationalism which, as article 7 (2) provided, refered to reciprocal support between all states of the socialist community. What is of particular interest is that a model for the special relationship or the 'brotherly friendship'[152] between the GDR and the Soviet Communist party was never explicitly further developed, nor indeed was it addressed beyond the 1964 Treaty which placed the relationship on a legal footing.[153] In effect, the Treaty was a mutual assistance pact in the event of any attack by another country or force.[154] Indeed, the Treaty went further in providing that if any state which was a signatory to the Warsaw Pact came under attack, the others were obligated to give immediate support.[155] The 'brotherly friendship' also extended to economic matters. Thus, states were obliged to help each other through economic aid and the exchange of economic and technical know-how in order to facilitate the co-ordination of their planned economies. This would be achieved by convergence and agreement between states in order to attain the highest degree of productivity.[156] Even right up to the dissolution of the Eastern bloc, vague references were made to a 'confederation'[157] based on a 'Marxist-Leninist' model. Article 16 of the proposed Russian Freedom Treaty even formally upheld the possibility of a multi-party system in the GDR. The relationship between the GDR and the USSR is viewed in the West as one of forced dependency or a *Zwangsverhältnis*. The relationship was not regulated by transparent legal norms or the courts, but by non-transparent formal and informal agreements between communist party leaderships. Silence on a division of competences, however, is something with which EU lawyers are very familiar.

---

[152] Referred to as 'comradely cooperation' in the Czechoslovak Constitution (article 14 (2) at 145, 'friendship and cooperation' in the Polish Constitution (article 6 (2)) and 'friendship, cooperation, and mutual assistance' in the Bulgarian Constitution (article 3 (1) above n 142.

[153] Vertrag über Freundschaft, gegenseitigen Beistand und Zusammenarbeit zwischen der Deutschen Demokratischen Republik und der Union der Sozialistischen Sowjetunion vom 12 Juni 1964 (GBl. I S. 132).

[154] *Ibid.*

[155] See article 5 of the Vertrag über Freundschaft, gegenseitigen Beistand und Zusammenarbeit zwischen der Deutschen Demokratischen Republik und der Union der Sozialistischen Sowjetunion vom 12 Juni 1964 (GBl. I S. 132).

[156] See article 8 of the Vertrag über Freundschaft, gegenseitigen Beistand und Zusammenarbeit zwischen der Deutschen Demokratischen Republik und der Union der Sozialistischen Sowjetunion vom 12 Juni 1964 (GBl. I S. 132).

[157] See *Willy Brandt: Die Spiegel Gespräche 1959–92* (Stuttgart, Deutsche Verlags-Anstalt, 1993) at p. 27.

6. CONCLUSION

The two German states of the post-war era provide good case studies of the relationship between the triumvirate of sovereignty, identity and citizenship. In many respects the two states were mirror images of each other. Both had limited sovereignty de jure and de facto—the West to the Four Powers, the GDR to the Soviet Union—and both their constitutions (Basic Laws) were framed by external powers who transplanted their own political models. Both states considered external recognition of statehood of paramount importance and invested significant resources in the attempt to build separate state identities based on reconstructed national myths. The citizenship provisions of both states illustrate their respective state ideologies, with the FRG seeking continuity with the pre-war German legacy of nationhood through the *ius sanguinis* while the GDR attempted to underpin a new national identity based on socialist ideals coupled with an adherence to *ius soli* citizenship.

Sovereignty has been coveted by German jurists in the post-war era, because it is regarded as the essential characteristic necessary for independent state formation. It is a reflection of a deeply held aspiration to return as a full member of the Westphalian international system of nation-states, free from foreign domination. Although German unification is now a decade past, the current German legal debate concerning sovereignty in conditions of European integration is entrenched in language derived from the pre-unification era. Thus, this debate is state fixated and stale, as opposed to being driven by newer, more innovative, non-statist and post-statist positions. Whilst, however, German jurists continue to bicker about the terms of reference for the debate, politicians have seized the initiative in formulating a vision of Europe which moves well beyond classical conceptions of constitutionalism umbilically linked to the state.[158]

---

[158] See Joschka Fischer's speech at the Humboldt University in Berlin on 12 May 2000 and Jacques Chirac's speech before the German *Bundestag* on 27 June 2000. See also *Frankfurter Allgemeine Zeitung* of both 15 May 2000 and 28 June 2000. Fischer's speech is reproduced at http://www.auswaertiges-amt.de/6_archiv/2/r/r000512b. See also C Joerges, Y Mény and JHH Weiler, *What Kind of Constitution for What Kind of Polity? Responses to Joschka Fischer* (Florence, Robert Schuman Centre for Advanced Studies, 2000).

13

The Legacy of Sovereignty in Italian Constitutional Debate

MARTA CARTABIA

1. INTRODUCTION: THE 'POLYSEMIC' AND EVOLVING NATURE OF SOVEREIGNTY

AN OVERVIEW OF the Italian legal literature immediately reveals that the debate on sovereignty has continued uninterrupted at least since the foundation of the Republic in 1948. During the first years of the Republic, founded under the Constitution of 1948, the debate was particularly lively because it aimed at providing a critique of the constructions of sovereignty that were derived from the previous regime and tended towards a recovery of the democratic principles rooted in the liberal idea of the Sovereignty of the People. Later, the idea of sovereignty was set aside in legal and political studies because it sounded old-fashioned and exhausted from a theoretical point of view; the only exceptions were the studies concerning the relationship between the State and the European Communities, where a reference to sovereignty remained necessary in order to highlight the incremental reductions in State sovereignty caused by the growing powers of European institutions. In recent times, the *fin de siècle* studies, and the new wave of legal literature at the beginning of the present century, present an interesting revival of the debate about sovereignty, in connection both with the new developments in the European Union— linked to the perspective of enlargement and the constitutionalisation of the Treaties—and the globalisation of economics, information, communication and other activities that seem to reduce the importance and the powers of nation states to the point of questioning their survival.

In each phase of the Italian debate, sovereignty has been taken into consideration from different points of view, charged with different meanings and related to different provisions of the Italian Constitution.

At first, the debate was mainly focused on the provision of article 1 of the Constitution: 'Sovereignty belongs to the people, who exercise it in the

manner, and within the limits, laid down by the Constitution'. This principle of *popular* sovereignty marks a great divide between the republican and
democratic era, on the one hand, and the previous totalitarian regime, on
the other. The totalitarian regime had relied instead upon the sovereignty of
the *State*, considered as a legal person, in order to justify the concentration
of all power in the Government. In this period, the problem of sovereignty
in Italy coincided with the problem of the absence of democratic legitimation of public powers within the State.

Later, attention turned to the international sphere and the discussion was
centred instead on article 11 of the Constitution: 'The Republic [. . .] gives
its consent to all the limitations of Sovereignty necessary to ensure peace
and justice among the Nations, and fosters and promotes the international
organisations oriented toward those purposes'. This is the constitutional
provision which allowed Italy's entry into the European Community, and
which continues to provide a constitutional ground for membership of the
EU today. Because of its broad wording, article 11 was also considered as
the legal basis for Italian membership of the United Nations and other relevant international organisations.[1]

Occasionally, article 7 of the Constitution has also spurred scholars to
reflect upon some aspects of state sovereignty, in so far as it affirms that the
Italian Republic and the Catholic Church are to be considered as two independent and Sovereign legal orders. Although it may sound odd to a foreign
observer, articles 7 and 11 of the Constitution are so similar in structure
that the interpretation of one has often influenced the interpretation of the
other, especially in the case law of the Italian Constitutional Court.[2]

So, even at a first glance, it seems that the notion of Sovereignty is so
complex and disputed, yet still so important, that the discussion about it
will probably be unending and, of course, this is not typically or uniquely
Italian. After all, one of the most ancient and common ideas is that sover-

---

[1] It should be noticed that the original intent of the founding fathers of the Italian Constitution
was primarily directed to alliance with the USA and with all the international organisations
belonging to the occidental world, Nato in particular. European integration could hardly have
been the main concern of the constituent assembly, because at that moment the European
Communities were not yet born or even envisaged. The historical background of article 11 of
the Italian Constitution was the division of the world into spheres of influence dominated by
the USSR and the USA, and the Italian choice to follow the American pattern. The use of article 11 for the purposes of European integration emerged at least ten years later, after the signa-
ture of the treaty of Rome in 1957, and more precisely with the first decision of the
Constitutional Court regarding the European Community of 1964, in the *Costa* case. See
Constitutional Court dec. n 14 of 1964. On this subject see A Cassese, *Art. 11*, in G Branca
(ed), *Commentario della costituzione*, vol. I, (Bologna-Roma, Zanichelli, 1975) 579 ss.
[2] See for example Constitutional Court decisions n 30 and 31 of 1971, n 169 of 1971, n 195
of 1972, 175 of 1973, n 18 of 1982, n 421 of 1993.

eignty has at least two different faces: the internal and the external. Even considered from a primitive, basic, elementary perspective—typically taught in all first year classes of constitutional law—sovereignty displays an ambivalent nature. When it refers to the internal affairs of the State it is linked to the problem of ultimate power. When it refers to the international context it is connected rather to the problem of the independence of the State, in order to prevent all other subjects from interfering with the State's internal political choices. Although, evidently, the present debate on sovereignty goes much further than that, it is still useful to recall the original dichotomy in the idea of sovereignty, because it provides evidence that sovereignty has been genetically marked by a 'polysemic' nature.

The debate is therefore fragmented. The idea of sovereignty appears as a puzzle that is almost impossible to assemble. Of course, this situation is due partly to the fact that the idea of sovereignty has evolved throughout history. Consequently, some of the historical problems involved in the debate on sovereignty have, over time, become obsolete and can safely be consigned to the past. This is certainly true, for example, of the idea of sovereignty as absolute power. Today every kind of power suffers limitations, in either the internal constitutional order or the international one, so that the problem of sovereignty is no longer a problem of the exercise of power without any constraints. Centuries ago, Benjamin Constant had already stated that 'La souveraineté n'existe que d'une manière limitée et relative'.[3] Nowadays, it is simply inconceivable that sovereignty evokes one single almighty sovereign. As has been said, in the contemporary world *the* Sovereign no longer exists. Nevertheless we still have *acts of Sovereignty*.[4] And this is not to deny, but rather to affirm, that sovereignty still deserves our interest and attention, especially in relation to the anticipated evolution of the European, international and global contexts.

At the same time it must be said that the meaning of sovereignty has continually evolved. Under the label of sovereignty a variety of very different things are described; in other words, it seems that sovereignty is a prism through which many different legal or political problems might be examined. Sovereignty raises issues of ultimate power, but also of the defence of territory; of military power, as well as of the government of money; of *kompetenz-kompetenz*, as well as of constituent power, and so on and so forth.

That the meaning of sovereignty is constantly shifting is clearly demonstrated in the case law of the Constitutional Court. At times, the Court uses

---

[3] B Constant, *Cours de politique constitutionnelle*, (Paris, Guillaumin 1982) vol. I, 9.
[4] See M Fioravanti, *Costituzione e popolo sovrano*, (Bologna, Il Mulino, 1998) 47 ss., especially 61, who stresses that from the historical point of view the age of constitutionalism has marked a shift from the idea of sovereignty as attributed to one sole subject—the Sovereign—to the idea of the distribution of sovereign powers among different institutions.

the concept in order to distinguish the state from regions and other territorial polities (for example, municipalities and provinces), which, while enjoying a certain degree of *autonomy* can never attain a sovereign character;[5] at other times the Court uses the idea of (popular) sovereignty as equivalent to *democracy*[6] and has characterised the right to vote in political elections and referendums as an expression of popular sovereignty, in the form of either representative or direct democracy. Sometimes sovereignty seems to denote *typical functions* of the State, which are represented by symbols such as money, the flag, the sword, and the gown.[7] At other times the Court, working with the idea that state sovereignty is now shared among several constitutional bodies—including Parliament, the Judiciary, the Head of State, the Government, the Constitutional Court itself—infers that some *privileges* are to be awarded to all of these sovereign organs:[8] eg Parliament's classical immunities, 'locus standi' before the Constitutional Court for conflicts of powers, the capacity for self-rule, and so on. In other cases, the Court stresses the territorial dimension of state sovereign powers, drawing a link between territory and sovereignty[9]—a link which is all the more significant in an age of globalisation.

The use of the word sovereignty in the case law of the Constitutional court surely reflects the diversity of views in the Italian legal debate. However, the Italian Constitutional Court does not seem to have fully elaborated its own doctrine of sovereignty, except in the case of article 11 of the Constitution as applied to the European Union. In all other cases, the use of the concept of sovereignty appears random. It plays the role of a cultural or rhetorical decoration rather than a true 'ratio decidendi'. For this reason I will consider closely only the constitutional case law as far as article 11 of the Constitution is concerned.[10]

However, before departing from the Constitutional Court's wider jurisprudence, we need to highlight one point. Since, to judge by the case law of the Constitutional Court, sovereignty appears to be a remarkably rich,

---

[5] Among several examples are decisions n 245 of 1995, n 209 of 1994, 171 of 1989, n 35 of 1981, n 110 of 1970, n 49 of 1963. The Court has often denied sovereignty to the regions and in consequence has also denied that regions are vested with foreign powers and even that they are subjects in international relations. A recent interesting decision on this matter is n 106 of 2002, where the Court declared null and void a Regional act aimed at changing the denomination of the representative assembly of the region, in order to call it 'Regional Parliament'. The Court affirms that in Italy there is a single Parliament, which is the national one, and relies on the idea of popular sovereignty in order to deny this possibility for the Regions.
[6] See, for instance, decisions n 68 of 1978, n 35 of 1981, n 79 of 1988, n 429 of 1995, n 49 of 1998.
[7] See for the judicial function eg decision n 127 of 1977.
[8] See eg decisions n 111 of 1963, n 15 of 1969, n 154 of 1985, n 9 of 1997, 417 of 1999.
[9] See eg decisions n 509 of 1988, nn 122 and 233 of 1989.
[10] See below sections 3 and 4.

polysemic or polymorphic term it might best be understood as *a relational idea*, one that cannot be grasped except in relation to other concepts. Sovereignty needs to be located within a context and its meaning changes when the context of reference changes.

For example, one aspect of Sovereignty is related to the idea of democracy, another aspect is addressed to European integration, another touches the international dimension, while yet another relates to the constitutional identity of the demos, and so on.

In this chapter, I will briefly outline the various meanings of sovereignty within the Italian debate. I will take into consideration the following themes:

a) *Sovereignty and the people*: the debate on direct and representative democracy.
b) *Sovereignty and legal norms*: the debate over the problem of the supremacy of international and European law.
c) *Sovereignty and values*: the Italian version of the theory of constitutional identity.
d) *Sovereignty and competences*: the theory of shared sovereignty in a multilevel system of government.
e) *Sovereignty and globalisation*: the quest for the legitimation of power in the global context.

Of course, the evolving nature of sovereignty—like many other legal and political concepts—warrants the existence of several different theories. However, some of these theories seem to have lost all connection with the original meaning of sovereignty. For instance, when one speaks of the sovereignty of substantive constitutional values or fundamental rights, what connection remains with the historical concept of sovereignty à la Bodin, Hobbes, and so on?

In my view the idea of sovereignty, although transformed and adapted to the reality of contemporary political societies, can still play a role. It still has something of significance to say. Sovereignty's legacy—or remainder—is preserved in contemporary states, and will remain so. Thus, on the one hand we have to accept that, historically speaking, sovereignty has lost some of its original features, as is the case with other significant legal and political concepts such as democracy, constitution and so on. On the other hand, we should not allow the word 'sovereignty' to embrace any meaning whatsoever; otherwise it becomes merely a label to be applied indiscriminately. Even in the contemporary world sovereignty has to remain faithful to its original roots, alongside other basic concepts such as 'power', 'State', 'demos', and 'democracy'. In other words, the use of sovereignty in contemporary legal and political theory and practice is still fruitful provided that it is located within a context consisting of the aforementioned elements. By contrast, any other use (or misuse) of the word renders the idea of sovereignty completely barren.

2. SOVEREIGNTY AND THE PEOPLE

At the dawn of the constitutional era in Italy, the first problem to be confronted resided in the question: 'who is the Sovereign' within the state? (ie the problem of identifying the subject vested with Sovereignty within the sovereign state).[11]

Once upon a time there was a King. At first, there could have been no doubt whatsoever that the King was the Sovereign. But the question—'who is the Sovereign?'—became both problematic and unavoidable during the age of the Constitutional monarchy, which in Italy lasted from the unification of 1861 until the constitutional crisis caused by the fascist regime.[12] For decades, this question had, in some way or another, been avoided. During the nineteenth century, in order to limit the King's position, but without going to the extreme of recognising the sovereignty of the people, the idea spread that the Sovereign could only be the state. State sovereignty was a generic and vague answer that disguised the paradox of two Sovereigns—the King and the Parliament—living together as roommates during the Constitutional monarchy. Sovereignty was attributed to an abstract entity— the State—and apparently neutralised.[13] This thesis clearly presupposed the personification and anthropomorphic conception of the state which arrived in Italy from Germany during the nineteenth century,[14] and which influenced political theory and practice up to and including the time of the fascist regime. However, during the fascist era the idea of state sovereignty was misinterpreted and misused in order to pave the way to the unprecedented concentration of powers in the Government that was typical of the age. The use of force, the violations of laws and rights, the abuse and centralisation of power in the hands of the *Duce*, and all other arbitrary use of power for which the totalitarian regime was notorious were ultimately grounded, from a theoretical point of view, in the idea of the sovereign state.[15]

---

[11] The problem had already been put in these terms by Palma, *Corso di diritto costituzionale*, (Firenze, 1883), 149: 'il problema è chi abbia titolo a sovraneggiare nello Stato sovrano'.

[12] That is to say, the period during which the Statuto Albertino was actually in force. For an overview of the historical evolution of the Italian Constitutional institution in English see V Onida, 'Historical Outline of Italian Constitutional Law', forthcoming in Alan (ed.) *International Encyclopedia of Laws*, (Brussels, Kluwer) ch. 1.

[13] Contemporary literature generally agrees that this was exactly the purpose of the doctrine that considered the State as the only sovereign, whereas the king, the parliament, the people and all other institutions were to be characterised as 'arms' of the State body. See for example E Tosato, *Stato—Teoria generale e diritto costituzionale*, in *Enciclopedia del Diritto*, v. XLIII, (Milano, Giuffré, 1990), 778.

[14] Under the influence of Gerber, Laband, Jellinek, and other German authors, in Italy it was VE Orlando who elaborated the idea of the 'State as a legal person', and the connected doctrine that sovereignty was an attribute belonging exclusively to the state. See VE Orlando, *Diritto pubblico generale*, (Milano, Giuffré, 1940).

[15] For a synthesis of the evolution of the doctrines of Sovereignty in Italy during the XIX and XX Century see, in recent literature, TE Frosini, *Sovranità popolare e costituzionalismo*, (Milano, Giuffré, 1997).

For this reason, when the Constitution was enacted, the idea of the *people's sovereignty* sounded like a direct contradiction to the idea of *State sovereignty*, and the question—'who is the Sovereign?'—became even more crucial. There was a tension between the people's sovereignty of article 1 of the Constitution and the traditional idea of state sovereignty, the latter having arrived in a republican age already corrupted by, and associated with, the idea of an unlimited and arbitrary power.[16] At the same time, the new Sovereign—the people—needed the state and its organisation in order to operate as a coherent political entity. This was particularly evident in the external relations of the State; but also for internal politics the People needed to conduct public activities through the State and its institutions. That was the constitutional puzzle of the age: how to reconcile two historical enemies—the People's sovereignty, on which the new order was founded, as stated in article 1 of the Constitution, and the sovereignty of the State—without eliminating either of them.

Whereas some aspects of this debate have lost all interest for the present discussion, others are still pertinent. Some questions surrounding the construction of the provision: 'the sovereignty belongs to the people', that at first glance seem to belong to the past, have, on the contrary, gained new life, as we confront new political circumstances, such as the trends towards supernationalisation and globalisation.

Historically, the key to resolving the quandary was found in the second part of article 1: the people exercise their sovereignty in the manner, and within the limits, laid down by the Constitution. That is to say that sovereignty belongs the people, but the people do not usually carry out directly the powers implied by sovereignty. On the contrary, the Sovereign—the people—usually needs the mediation of the state's institutions in order to exercise all its powers.[17] For that reason the state's organs also share sovereignty, and can be said to *be* sovereign in their own right. By means of the distinction between State *qua* apparatus and State *qua* community,[18] and with the aid of the idea of representative democracy,[19] the result of this debate was the combination of state authority and popular sovereignty, so

---

[16] During the fascist period some studies of sovereignty made the attempt to limit state powers, either by means of the doctrine of the self-limitation of the state or by relying on the corporatist structure of the state. But of course this attempt could not achieve the aim of limiting the arbitrary powers of the fascist regime, because limitations in order to be effective had to come from a subject other than the State. See eg E Crosa, 'Il Principio della Sovranità dello Stato nel diritto italiano' in 1933, *Archivio giuridico Serafini*, 1933, 145 ss, 168 ss.

[17] That was the question implicit in the debate that had developed in the Constituent Assembly about the choice of wording in art. 1: whether the Sovereignty belongs (appartiene) to the people or derives (emana) from the people.

[18] See among many others V Crisafulli, *La sovranità popolare nella Costituzione italiana*, in *Scritti giuridici in memoria di VE Orlando*, vol. I, (Padova, Cedam, 1957) 407 ss., in particular 416–8.

[19] See, among many, V Crisafulli, *La sovranità popolare nella Costituzione italiana*, op. cit.; *Lezioni di diritto costituzionale*, vol. I, (Padova, Cedam, 1970), 80 ss.

that the former was now considered an instrument of the latter. On this reading, the Sovereign is the people, but usually it is up to representative institutions and other public bodies to exercise sovereign powers. Only in exceptional cases does the sovereign directly express itself, such as when it forms a constituent power or through acts of direct democracy.

This argument is still valid today. The problem, today, however, is to discover adequate instruments to guarantee the effective participation of the people—the sovereign—in political and institutional life, in addition to the right to vote in political elections. Representation requires new instruments in order that the political choices of State institutions can actually mirror the preferences of the people, considered as a plural body from which many voices can be heard.[20] During the 1950's, the main problem was giving room to political parties to express popular sovereignty;[21] currently, representation and popular sovereignty demand that we go even further and take into account other subjects and instruments for an effective pluralist discursive democracy.

3. SOVEREIGNTY AND NORMS

In the decades following the 1950's, the attention of legal scholars was drawn to problems that seemed to have nothing in common with the interpretation of popular sovereignty. A new chapter in the book of Sovereignty was opened as a consequence of membership of the European Community and, in particular, by the doctrine of supremacy of the law of the European Community. Here we will focus our attention primarily on the case law of the Constitutional Court.

The story is well known and does not need to be retold in detail.[22] I will simply highlight the main steps in the evolution of the Italian Constitutional Court's position.[23]

---

[20] In recent years the Italian constitutional literature has shown renewed interest in the debate on representative democracy. See for example L Ornaghi, G Ferrara, V Angiolini, A Di Giovine, S Sicardi, P Ardant, in (1998); *Rivista di diritto costituzionale*, L Carlassare (ed), *Democrazia, Rappresentanza, Responsabilità*, (Padova, Cedam, 2001); S Merlini (a cura di) *Rappresentanza politica, gruppi parlamentari, partiti: il contesto europeo*, (Torino, Giappichelli, 2001); N Zanon and F Biondi (eds), *Percorsi e vicende attuali della rappresentanza politica*, (Milano, Giuffré, 2001).

[21] See G Amato, '*La sovranità popolare nell'ordinamento italiano*, in 1962, *Rivista Trimestrale di Diritto Pubblico*, 98 ss., in particular 101 ss.

[22] I have summarised the steps of the evolution in the case law of the Italian Constitutional Court on this point in M Cartabia and JHH Weiler, *L'Italia in Europa—profili istituzionali e costituzionali*, (Bologna, Il Mulino, 2000) 129 ss.

[23] It is impossible to cite the books and articles on this theme without omitting many important studies. Just to mention some basic references in legal literature, which deal with the subject from a comparative perspective, see *Diritto comunitario europeo e diritto nazionale*, edited by the Italian Constitutional Court, (Milano, Giuffré, 1997); AM Slaughter, A Stone Sweet, JHH Weiler (eds.), *The European Court & National Courts*, (Oxford, Hart Publishing, 1998).

From the outset, the Court identified the constitutional ground for the accession of Italy to the European Community in article 11 and its 'limitation of sovereignty' clause. But initially, article 11 was invoked only for the purpose of providing a constitutional basis for the ratification of the Treaties of Paris and Rome by means of an ordinary procedure, which in Italy consists of an ordinary law of Parliament, followed by a formal act of the President of the Republic (articles 80 and 87 Constitution). As regards the Treaties of the European Communities, a constitutional basis was necessary because the new European legal system affected the constitutional powers of the Italian institutions. Since the Parliament had decided to ratify the Treaties by means of an ordinary law, ie without any constitutional amendment, it was all the more imperative to root the law of ratification in a constitutional provision.

At the same time, a dispute arose between the Italian constitutional court and the Court of Justice of the European Communities concerning the problem of supremacy and the direct effect of community norms. It is well known that the war between these courts lasted from 1964 until 1984, when, with the *Granital* decision the Italian Court acceded to the claims of the European Court of Justice,[24] albeit through a completely different legal reasoning: the monist approach of the European Court has always been refused by the Italian Court, which, in contradistinction to the European Court, has construed a theory of supremacy and direct effect within a dualist context.

What is interesting for our purposes is that the hidden reason behind the 20 years' war between the two Courts involved the problem of sovereignty. Under the influence of Kelsen, the Italian Court implicitly followed the idea that sovereignty belongs to that order whose norms are at the top of the *Stufenbau*. According to this conception, recognition of the supremacy of Community norms implied giving up all state sovereignty, because national norms of every level and kind were to be subject to community norms. In this intellectual scheme there is no room for the question: 'who is, or who are the Sovereigns?' There are no actors, institutions, or subjects, but only normative provisions, and sovereignty is a matter of legal norms. If this idea of normative hierarchy is then coupled with a monist perspective, as it is in Kelsen's own work, there is no way out. If sovereignty is an attribute of norms, the higher law must be sovereign.

---

[24] Decision n 170 of 1984. The age of the conflicts between the Italian Constitutional Court and the European Court of Justice which had begun with *Costa v ENEL* (Decision n 14 of 1964) thus came to an end when the Italian Constitutional Court accepted that EC law must prevail over national law. Moreover—and that was the point—when the European legal norms have direct effect, every national judge—not only superior courts, but all lower judges too— must apply the European rules and if necessary disregard all conflicting national norms. The *Granital* decision is still the leading case on the relationship between the European legal system and the Italian one, although the Italian Court has partially corrected its position for cases involving regional laws. On this point see decision n 94 of 1995.

Hence the Italian Constitutional Court has always rejected the monist perspective and interpreted the supremacy of Community law within a dualist context. From this perspective, the supremacy of Community law is not a matter of situating European law at a higher level than national law. Supremacy is understood rather in terms of a distinction between different fields of competence. There is no doubt that European law prevails over national law; however, the reason for its supremacy is not that it is 'higher' than national law. Instead, European law enjoys supremacy because when it operates national law must 'withdraw' (the word used by the Italian Constitutional court) from the fields of competence occupied by the European Community and give the floor to European law. For this reason, it might be said that the Italian court, through its dualist construction, tries to disguise the loss of Italian normative sovereignty.

However, doubts arise from this normative perspective. Following the Italian Court's dualist approach, although the problem of sovereignty appears to be a problem of the supremacy of norms, it is actually treated as a problem of the division of competences or as a matter of jurisdiction. The Constitutional Court makes a great effort to avoid recognising the loss of normative sovereignty suffered by the Member States as a result of membership of the European Community, but it succeeds only in shifting the problem. In the Italian Court's approach, the problem of sovereignty turns out to be a problem of competences, so that the key to solving the riddle of Sovereignty is 'who decides the division of competence?' 'Who has the power of *kompetenz-kompetenz*?' But the Court does not answer these questions; it leaves them open. However, even if we leave aside these questions[25] for the moment, other objections to the normative perspective arise.

Does the loss of normative sovereignty involved in the principle of supremacy of European law genuinely entail the loss of state sovereignty? Can we really say that because it has accepted the supremacy of European norms Italy is no longer a sovereign state? Such an extreme position is unconvincing, because the perspective which looks only to normative hierarchy is but a partial one, quite inadequate to explain the complex relationship between the States and the European Union. It does not take into account the fact that Italy, as well as all other Member States, takes part in the decision- making processes of the European Community, so that every Member State is co-author of European norms.[26] Italy, and every other

---

[25] Regarding sovereignty as a matter of competences see below Section 5.

[26] It was particularly true under the regime of the Luxemburg compromise, when all decisions were taken with the unanimity rule. Nowadays that constitutional balance is partially lost because of the development of majority voting, as has been pointed out by JHH Weiler ('L'Unione e gli Stati membri: competenze e sovranità' in (2000) *Quaderni costituzionali*, 5 ss). However, even though the Member States have lost the veto power on many subjects, arguably European membership does not weaken states in any overall reckoning, as it still endows them with new capacities in many fields of action. See below Section 5.

member State, loses its autonomous power to enact its own norms in some fields of action, because these powers are conferred to European institutions; however, at the same time every Member State gains other powers within the context of the European Community. When we speak of norms, we should not forget that behind them there are institutions vested with normative powers. And sometimes if we look inside these institutions, consider who are their members, and pay attention to the procedural rules for their action, we notice that the losers are in certain respects also the winners.

4. SOVEREIGNTY AND CONSTITUTIONAL VALUES

In order to temper the loss of normative sovereignty caused by the supremacy of Community norms, the Constitutional Court developed the 'Counter-limits' doctrine, which in turn gave rise to the theory of the sovereignty of values. In this respect we could say that Italy has adopted the doctrine of supremacy of European law on the condition of the respect of core constitutional values. So that in Italy European law enjoys *une primauté sous réserve*.

According to the counter-limits doctrine, while Community measures prevail over every kind of national norm, they are not allowed to infringe fundamental values protected by the Constitution, including constitutional fundamental rights. This special protection of fundamental rights and values is concerned with the defence of the last bulwark of national sovereignty. While membership of the European Union requires some limits to national sovereignty (article 11 of the Constitution), there should be some counter-limits, otherwise the *limitation* would turn into the *extinction* of national sovereignty. This is the reason why in the Constitutions of many of the Member States a provision can be found—eg article 11 of the Italian Constitution, article 23 of the German Constitution, article 88 of the French Constitution, article 28 of the Greek Constitution; article 10, para. 5 of the Swedish constitution,—that establishes some 'conditions' for European membership; in most cases these conditions consist in the respect for some basic values, including fundamental rights. As the Italian Constitutional Court stated in decision n 232 of 1989—the most relevant decision on this subject—the fundamental rights and other basic values of the Constitutional system can neither be modified, nor amended, nor even derogated from in a single case because they are vested with a crucial importance for the polity as a whole. They are considered as 'sacred', so that even when the Constitution is amended following the special procedure laid down in article 138 of the Constitution, the amendments are not allowed to affect one of these fundamental rights or principles. This is why the Italian Constitutional court cannot sacrifice the power to submit to judicial review any measures—including the Community acts—that prima facie affect these rights and values.

The Constitutional Court does not specifically identify these definitive, mandatory and intangible Constitutional values. They are generically identified as those values which constitute a logical or historical pre-condition for democracy, such as freedom of speech, freedom of assembly, the principle of equality, free elections and, in general, all the 'fundamental rights'. These rights and principles are supposed to be rooted in article 2, containing the general clause for the protection of fundamental rights, and article 139 of the Constitution, stating that the republican form of the State cannot be amended. As absolute values, they cannot be questioned or affected, either by European norms, or by national powers, including the power of constitutional amendment. Similarly, relations with the Catholic Church, which might entail derogation of constitutional provisions, must conform to these fundamental values, or 'counter-limits'.[27]

One more aspect of the question needs to be stressed in order to mark the distinction in the Counter-limits doctrine between the sovereignty of norms, and the Sovereignty of values. The Counter-limits doctrine does not imply that some constitutional provisions are untouchable. On the contrary, it is based on a distinction between normative provisions and values, ie, a distinction between the *essential contents*[28] of fundamental constitutional values—those that cannot be the object of constitutional amendment and must therefore be considered as inviolable—and the ways of expressing those values, which are subject to evolution (sometimes necessarily) in order to preserve the fundamental values. Sovereignty must refer to this hard core of values, rather than to some parts of the text of the Constitution. And the state retains its sovereignty in so far as it is able to claim that even Community law conforms to these essential values.

---

[27] See, in particular, the Constitutional Court decision n 1146 of 1988. I have discussed the case law of the Italian Constitutional Court on this point in *Principi inviolabili e integrazione europea* (Milano, Giuffré 1995) 141 ss. A similar position was upheld by the German *Bundesverfassungsgericht* in some of its decisions on this matter, but recently it seems to have overruled the previous principles, starting with decision of 7 June 2000, concerning the *Bananenmarkt*. Actually, the German *Bundeverfassungsgericht* seemed to have already abandoned the counter-limits doctrine a long time ago, with the *Solange II* decision of 22 October 1986. However, considering the obscure language used in the subsequent *Maastricht Urteil*, of 12 October 1993 on this point, it is a common view that until the *Bananenmarkt* decision of 2000 the German Constitutional Court maintained a sort of 'sleeping' jurisdiction in relation to all measures that apply European law in violation of the hard core of fundamental rights protected by the German Constitution.
[28] The idea of the essential content of the fundamental values is clearly derived from the German constitutional tradition. The influence of German thought on the protection of fundamental rights in Italy on this point has been analysed by A Baldassarre, *Diritti della persona e valori costituzionali*, (Torino, Giappichelli, 1997), 91 ss. and by P Ridola, 'Libertà e diritti nello sviluppo storico del costituzionalismo', in P Ridola and R Nania (eds), *I diritti costituzionali*, (Torino, Giappichelli, 2001) vol. I, 47 ss.

The idea implicit in the Counter-limits doctrine is that fundamental rights and fundamental constitutional values reflect, to an extent, the identity, political culture and self-understanding of each society. Preserving these values, from this perspective, means preserving the identity of the polity, an identity rooted in the history and culture of the people and expressed in the foundation of the political and legal order within the Constitution. In Habermas's striking phrase, it is a new form of 'constitutional patriotism'[29] that breathes through the protection of the fundamental rights and the basic constitutional values. As with other types of patriotism, constitutional patriotism also has a dark side, and it always risks becoming nothing more than a rhetorical device.[30] Nevertheless, it is precisely because fundamental rights are to some extent perceived as protecting the identity of the *demos* that—generally speaking—the counter-limits doctrine has received a sympathetic hearing. Contemporary polities need a *demos*, and a *demos* needs a common identity, able to assemble the people and build a community. Fundamental constitutional rights constitute an acceptable basis for the collective identity of a *demos* founded on a community of values, replacing the old fashioned *demos* based on nationality, race, blood, or other factors.[31]

The idea of the sovereignty of values has found great favour among many scholars.[32] Sovereignty belongs to those values shared by all of society, they argue. As a consequence, the Sovereign is no longer a person, or a single institution, or any other subject vested with political power. Sovereignty is not the characteristic of a subject, but it is rather the quality of some objective principles. This means that all public powers are tempered by fundamental values; none is absolute. In this context Sovereignty does not represent the untamed strength of political power, but rather it becomes one of its constraints. The theory of sovereignty of values has a clear 'moralising' purpose; and in this purpose lies its appeal.

But although appealing, the putative success of the doctrine is threatened by many shortcomings. The first concerns its vagueness: what are these values? What is their content? Are they rooted in national constitutional provisions or are they universal values shared at the international level? This theory originates, as we have already seen, from the idea of preserving

---

[29] See eg, J Habermas, in *Morale, diritto e politica*, (Torino, 1992) 105 ss.; *L'inclusione dell'altro*, (Milano, Feltrinelli, 1998) 318 ss.

[30] This idea has been recently criticised for its potential fetishisation of the nation state by JHH Weiler, 'Diritti umani, costituzionalismo e integrazione: iconografie e feticismo' (2002) *Quaderni costituzionali* n 3.

[31] For this idea of *demos*, specifically applied to the European Union, see J Habermas, 'Perché l'Europa ha bisogno di una Costituzione' in G Bonacchi (ed.), *Una Costituzione senza Stato*, (Bologna, 2001) 156; *L'Inclusione dell'altro*, (Milano, Feltrinelli, 1998) 167 ss., 218 ss.

[32] See, for example, G Silvestri, 'La parabola della sovranità. Ascesa, declino e trasfigurazione di un concetto' in *Rivista di diritto costituzionale*, 1996, 3 ss., 55 ss.; L Ferrajoli, *La sovranità nel mondo moderno*, (Bari, 1997).

those values that constitute the national identity of a demos. This is the position of the constitutional case law on 'counter-limits', and the position that the doctrine takes as its point of departure. However, for some authors the background changes from the single country to a cosmopolitan context in which the values vested with sovereignty are universal rather than national.[33]

From the case law of the Constitutional Court, there appears to be no doubt that the fundamental values are to be found within the national constitutional order and that they are an expression of the culture of a people.[34] The judicial version of the doctrine is that, through the activity of the state's institutions, and in particular the Constitutional Court, fundamental values express the voice of the state, or rather, the voice of a single demos.[35] In the theoretical version of the doctrine of the sovereignty of values, however, it is putatively universal values that are at stake. Distrust of the state leads to a more generic defence of certain universal values,[36] although it is almost impossible to identify what these are.

A few more words must be added in mitigation of the criticism of this doctrine. The overlap between universal and national expressions of fundamental rights is at least partly due to the very nature of fundamental values and fundamental rights. Fundamental rights are the expression of a culture, but they are also part of a universal heritage that belongs to each man and woman the world over and in all times. In fact, this universal dimension of the protection of fundamental rights is evident in all the international treaties, pacts and other instruments on human rights, which have multiplied since the Second World War, especially under the auspices of the United Nations.[37] Nobody doubts that the universal core of fundamental rights must be recognised in every man and woman, whereas a large band of fundamental rights beyond this core mirrors the identity of each polity. In other words, fundamental rights are in some way at a crossroads between universality and diversity, because they give expression to both natural demands and cultural choices. The latter occurs in particular when

---

[33] See, for example, G Silvestri, 'La parabola della sovranità. Ascesa, declino e trasfigurazione di un concetto' in (1996) *Rivista di diritto costituzionale*, 62 ss.

[34] For this idea of the link between the Constitution and the national culture see P Haeberle, *Verfassungslehre als Kulturwissenshaft* (Berlin, de Gruyter1996) ch. 4.

[35] It should be noticed, however, that up to now it is a silent voice. The Counter-limits doctrine is a sort of nuclear weapon, which is good to have, and better not to use. Even the Constitutional Court deems that it is unlikely that an actual conflict between national and European fundamental rights will arise. See V Onida, 'Armonia tra diversi' e problemi aperti' Quaderui Costituzionali (2002) 549 ss.

[36] The foundational power of universal values and rights in the global system is also stressed by A Baldassarre, *Globalizzazione contro democrazia*, (Roma-Bari, Laterza) 2002, 50 ss.

[37] For an overview of the subject see A Cassese, *I diritti umani nel mondo contemporaneo* (Roma-Bari, 2000).

fundamental rights need to be balanced with other competing social values—such as authority and liberty, freedom of expression and protection of privacy, women's health and right to life of the unborn, and so on and so forth. The way of balancing these competing values depends on the basic choices of each society, and in this respect it reflects the culture of each society.

Yet the doctrine of the sovereignty of values can also be criticised from other perspectives. In particular, it is arguably an exercise in mystification to disconnect sovereignty from the exercise of power. How can values be sovereign by themselves? Do they exist on their own, or do they rather require the interpretation and application of political and judicial institutions, and, in the end, of society as a whole? Values live within the practice and activity of a subject, or rather, of a community of subjects.

A goal of the Counter-limits doctrine of the Constitutional Court is evidently to preserve a role for the Court itself within the process of European integration. At the heart of that doctrine is a question of jurisdiction. The Constitutional Court wants to be the ultimate '*Huter der Verfassung*', even in the context of European integration.

But in the academic version of the theory of the sovereignty of (universal) values, who are the guardians of these values? The answer offered by scholars is unsatisfactorily vague on this point, in so far as they affirm that the Sovereign is in turn each subject, inside or outside the legal order, private or public, national or international, that better ensures the full respect for these universal values.

5. SOVEREIGNTY AND COMPETENCES

Although it is a classical topic of federalism,[38] in the broad sense of the word, the relationship between Sovereignty and the division of competences is not treated as a main concern for the Italian legal order. For instance, inside the national legal system the recent amendment to the Constitution[39] concerning the Regions' powers may have turned upside-down the criteria for the division of competence between the State and the Regions, yet no one in the legal debate has even mentioned the matter of Sovereignty.

From the perspective of European integration, too, few scholars have taken this matter into consideration. For example, the question of *kompetenz-kompetenz* has never been discussed in Italy to the degree that it has in

---

[38] See *The Federalist Papers* nos 42 and 45.
[39] Constitutional Law n 3 of 2001.

Germany.[40] Of course, everybody recognises that European institutions arrogate to themselves some of the powers that belong to national institutions. It is common knowledge that the European Court of Justice has supported this expansion and that revisions of the Treaties—Single European Act, Maastricht, Amsterdam—have considerably increased the powers of European institutions at the expense of national ones. However, common opinion on this point is that article 11 of the Constitution, concerning the limitation of sovereignty, implicitly foresees, and gives general consent to, the transfer of powers to the European Union. The self-evident meaning of the 'limitation of powers' is the sacrifice of the competences of national institutions in favour of supranational or international ones. Indeed, this is precisely the *raison d'être* of article 11 of the Constitution.

However, whereas in other European states—France, for example—a distinction has been made between *limitations* of Sovereignty and the complete *loss* of sovereignty, in Italy nobody has ever seriously held that in order not to violate the boundaries of the concept of the 'limitations of Sovereignty' some bars should exist to the transfer of powers to the European institutions. Nobody has argued that some kinds of power—in matters such as citizenship, immigration, defence, monetary policy, and criminal law, for instance—cannot be exercised at the supranational level in the name of State sovereignty. Nor has anybody put the problem in terms of the quantity of European competences. The Italian Constitutional Court has not yet been called to answer this kind of question; but the situation may occur, and in theory a conflict with the European Court of Justice cannot be excluded[41] unless a definitive solution regarding the division of competences, the justiciability of the principle of subsidiarity and the question of *kompetenz-kompetenz* is found by the Laeken Convention on the Future of Europe, and accepted by the Member States in the future constitutional Treaties for Europe.

In the Italian context, only a few traces of the debate concerning the link between sovereignty and competences can be found, and these traces have been left by the principle of subsidiarity which was introduced by the Maastricht Treaty. For many reasons, eg its flexibility; the potential extension of EU competences that it might provoke; its capacity to bring all matters of social life (even the most nationally sensitive ones such as defence, criminal law, health, education, and so on), into the process of

---

[40] The few notable exceptions in the Italian legal leterature include, GU Rescigno, 'Il tribunale costituzionale federale tedesco e i nodi costituzionali del processo di unificazione europea', in (1994) *Giurisprudenza costituzionale*, 3115 ss., and E Cannizzaro, 'Democrazia e sovranità nei rapporti tra Stati membri e Unione europea' (2000) in *Diritto dell'Unione Europea*, 241 ss.

[41] See V Onida, 'Armonia tra diversi" e problemi aperti' above n 35.

European integration, and to do so in the name of a single open-ended test—the principle of subsidiarity was surrounded by a general climate of mistrust and suspicion at the time of the Maastricht Treaty. Indeed, it is worth remarking that at the very moment the principle of subsidiarity was introduced, even some strands of Italian opinion were moved to declare that state sovereignty demands a limit to the transfer of powers to supranational institutions, that it cannot permit new powers to be handed over to Europe without the state's consent, and, above all, that the competences of the national and the supranational level of government be clearly distinguished.[42] Yet although many scholars predicted an age of confusion and uncertainty, nobody was seriously worried about the survival of the sovereign state. At present a more sympathetic attitude surrounds the principle of subsidiarity and nobody seriously questions its importance.

It is arguable that the reason that the transfer of powers to European institutions is not perceived as a loss of Sovereignty is that the assignment of competences and powers to the European Community is perceived merely as a different way of exercising state powers, not as a way of giving them up.[43] Because of the intergovernmental nature of the Council of the European Union, the political leaders of the Member States still control the European decision-making process, so that they do not feel that they have been excluded from the exercise of powers accorded to European institutions. On the contrary, some actions could never be exercised as such by each single state acting on its own, whereas they can be within the European Union. So the problem turns out to concern a rather different question, namely, the question of the structure, voting system and legitimation of European institutions, and not the question of the allocation of powers.

This line of reasoning is clearly expressed in the theory of Shared Sovereignty:[44] the basic idea is that within a supranational organisation sovereignty is not split into different parts, as has sometimes been claimed under the label of 'Divided Sovereignty' in relation to the federal States; rather, sovereignty is shared, because certain powers are exercised in common, by each state acting together with other states. In fact, the idea of shared sovereignty diverts attention from the question of the division of competences by stressing instead the problem of preserving a role for the

---

[42] P Caretti, 'Il principio di sussidiarietà e i suoi riflessi sul piano dell'ordinamento comunitario e dell'ordinamento nazionale', in (1993), *Quaderni costituzionali* 7 ss.; G Strozzi, 'Alcuni interrogativi a proposito della delimitazione delle competenze dell'Unione europea' in (1994) *Rivista di diritto internazionale*, 136 ss.

[43] This is the thesis upheld by A Carrino, *Sovranità e costituzione nella crisi dello Stato moderno*, (Torino, Giappichelli, 1998).

[44] See E Cannizzaro, 'Esercizio di competenze e sovranità nell'esperienza giuridica dell'integrazione europea', in (1996) *Rivista di diritto costituzionale* 75 ss., who speaks of 'sovranità solidale'; see also A Carrino, *Sovranità e costituzione nella crisi dello Stato moderno*, above n 43, 188, who speaks of 'sovranità condivisa'.

various states within the structure of European institutions (and, we could add, within other international organisations). As we shall see in the next section, this is very similar to the result towards which we are led by the *Antisovereign* theory and by all other theories that stress the problem of the legitimation of supranational and international powers in a world of increasingly diffuse political authority.

The theory of shared sovereignty seems to rely on the regime of the veto power of each Member State inside the Council of the European Union. Recently, however, the unanimity principle has been incrementally set aside, and its place taken by majority voting in more and more fields of action within the European Community. Moreover, in view of the enlargement of the Union, the trend towards majority voting is expected to accelerate. In this new context, where the position of a single Member State is more and more likely to be sacrificed to the will of the majority, can we still speak of Shared Sovereignty? Or is it necessary to adapt this doctrine, or some of its features?

6. SOVEREIGNTY AND GLOBALISATION

In recent years, globalisation—consisting in new and impressionistic processes that are undermining the basic concepts of our state-centred legal, political and social culture—has revitalised the debate about sovereignty. Indeed, this debate is not 'made in Italy', nor is it 'made in Europe' but it affects all countries under the dominant influence of American legal and political thought. Nonetheless, the Italian legal literature also offers some examples of this new trend of study, focused on the effects of globalisation on the remainder of Sovereignty, and they deserve to be discussed.

At the forefront of this new wave of studies in Italy is the 'antisovereign' doctrine.[45] This original and insightful analysis of the processes of globalisation is based on the image of the antisovereign, which explicitly recalls the idea of the 'antipope', or the 'antichrist': a subject which purports to be the veritable antagonist of the Sovereign, that denies his authority, desires to take his place and role, and to this end operates following principles and methods in conflict with and in opposition to those of his enemy.

On this view the globalisation of markets and the economy is the main cause of the nation state's crisis at the present time, a crisis due mainly to the fact that nation states and national constitutions are no longer able to manage and govern the economy because of the trend towards internationalisation and globalisation of commerce. The economy evades the reach or

---

[45] M Luciani, 'L'antisovrano e la crisi delle costituzioni' in (1996) *Rivista di diritto costituzionale*, 124 ss.

scope of national action and this proves profoundly challenging to the legit-imacy and efficacy of the state.

'Antisovereign' are all those entities that control the economic decision-making processes; they contrast with the sovereign state in many respects. Whereas the Sovereign is a subject, the antisovereign is instead a diffuse power. The antisovereign's decisions purport to be a necessary consequence of economic rules, based on neutral, scientific and objective reasons, whereas the sovereign's decisions purport to be the fruits of political and discretionary power. The antisovereign's legitimation relies on the technical nature of its action and goal, namely, to ensure economic prosperity by means of the application of economic rules; it does not seek to be the expression of a people's will nor does it consider itself bound by the rules of the democratic process.[46] The antisovereign provokes the crisis of the nation state, because it takes over a great deal of the states' powers, directly or indirectly. Even those competences that remain in the states' hands are profoundly conditioned by the antisovereign. However, this doctrine argues, the state sovereign has not yet resigned, and the loss of power can and must be stemmed.[47]

Before we turn our attention to the 'pars construens' of the 'Antisovrano' doctrine, where some proposals for preserving power in the hands of the national states are sketched out, a few more general remarks on the doctrine are in order. First, it is easy to observe that in the antisovereign analysis, economic relations are the main feature of the globalising process. The global market, the G7 or G8, the WTO, the IMF, the multinational companies, and so on, are the group of subjects of which the antisovereign consists. In fact the dichotomy Sovereign/antisovereign disguises a tension between economy and politics. And the problem at stake is how to preserve, or how to restore, the power of control over the economy to political institutions.

The same analytical perspective is taken by the doctrine of 'web' or 'network sovereignty'—*la sovranità reticolare*.[48] Although this doctrine reaches different conclusions from those of the Antisovrano—and indeed is openly critical of the latter[49]—the approach is similar. The starting point of the analysis is the 'decalage' between *global* markets and the *national* focus of the political process. Globalisation is seen mainly as a process involving economic activities, and the central issue is how to find new mechanisms for submitting global markets to some kind of deliberative political institutions.

---

[46] M Luciani, *ibid* 160 ss.
[47] M Luciani, *ibid* 171.
[48] C Pinelli, 'Cittadini, responsabilità politica, mercati globali' in *Studi in onore di L Elia*, vol. II, (Milano, Giuffré, 1999) 1257 ss.
[49] C Pinelli, *ibid* 1287 ss.

A more comprehensive vision of the globalising process is taken by Baldassarre in his recent book, *Globalisation versus democracy*.[50] The main causes of globalisation are identified as the Internet, the cybernetic system of communication and the new network information technologies more generally. At present, the main effects of this revolution in communications are evident in economic relations. However, the underlying idea of this book is that, since all human activities, whatever their objects and aims, can also be regarded as acts of communication,[51] globalisation is dramatically upsetting our social and personal life, understood in all its aspects, including the political. The reason is that internet communication renders all human activities indifferent to space and time. When and where an action is taken does not matter, so that the actors in cybernetic communication are 'intangible' or 'virtual subjects' (*soggetti disincarnati*). This indifference to the human dimensions of life—this disembedding of social relations from fixed points of space and time—is also the reason for the crisis of the nation state. The *nomos* of the new global order is irreconcilable with the *nomos* of the international society that preceded it. The latter was based on the idea of national sovereign states acting in the international context as equals. However, globalisation has destroyed state sovereignty, because sovereignty needs a demos and a territory, whereas in the global context there is no demos, and territory, and boundaries, are irrelevant.[52]

Even if these doctrines offer different analyses of the globalising process, they nevertheless raise a common question : what is the future of democracy in the global world? The explicit concern for the destiny of state sovereignty in the global context, as well as the attempt at preserving the supremacy of politics over the economy, both converge in a sole and ultimate commitment—the search for a new form of democracy in the global world.

As far as the 'antisovereign' doctrine is concerned, in order to preserve a central place for politics and for democracy, the proposal is to take international law—understood as a law *inter gentes*, rather than a *jus gentium*—as a point of departure. This means that the states would continue to play a major role in the international arena. The only way to preserve a primary role for politics and democracy is to recognise the states as necessary agents. The idea is that at the supranational, international and global level democracy can only be realised by states, which are to be considered as equals on the international stage, and which must therefore considerably strengthen democratic and parliamentary control of their foreign policy. This path to global democracy necessarily entails remedying the democratic deficit of international organisations such as the UN, IMF, WTO, G8, etc.[53]

---

[50] A Baldassarre, *Globalizzazione contro democrazia*, (Bari-Roma, Laterza, 2002).
[51] A Baldassarre, *ibid* 6 ss.
[52] A Baldassarre, *ibid* 50 ss.
[53] above n 45 M Luciani, *L'antisovrano e la crisi delle costituzioni*, 182 ss.

The idea of increasing the democratic legitimation of international organisations as a way of preserving the basic principles of liberal democracy in the new world is also discussed by the other doctrines, but is considered inappropriate or simply unworkable. 'Network sovereignty' works from the idea that political institutions should play a role of co-ordination between actors in global society, keeping in mind that political accountability is at present directed to subjects that are in turn consumers, workers, members of cultural associations, users of public services, and so on. The activity of political institutions is not addressed to a 'generic' citizen or to an electoral body, but to subjects possessing different qualities and different statuses that need to be satisfied.[54]

A more precise proposal comes from Baldassarre's book. He works from a critique both of the idea of democratic global government, which is simply impossible to conceive because there is no global demos, and of the revival of the role of sovereign states within international organisations. Too many obstacles hinder the revision of traditional organisations, such as the UN, and the transformation of their structures and procedures into genuine democratic ones. His proposal, on the contrary, is based on the idea that the subjects of the global world should be the 'regions of the world,'[55] vast areas gathering all the countries belonging to a homogeneous cultural tradition: occidental, Muslim, oriental, and so on. These regions of the world, corresponding to each area of civilisation, are charged with a double task. First, to reach the highest possible level of integration internally, so that they can build up political institutions that are able to represent the whole regional area. The model could be European integration, or other forms of economic and political integration that developed in the second half of the 20th century. The second task is to take part in a type of indirect global governance, where the countries and the *demoi* of the world are represented through 'regional institutions'.

7. SUMMARY

It is noticeable that in some way all the new doctrines of sovereignty in the 'global' world draw a clear ideational link between the original, historical problem of popular sovereignty and the present challenges of supranational integration, international relationships and the global network. Sovereignty has been awarded to the demos and this is not up for discussion; the only subject vested with sovereign powers is and must remain the demos. In this respect, the discussion of sovereignty in the twenty-first century does not

---

[54] Above n 48 C Pinelli, *Cittadini, responsabilità politica, mercati globali,* 1301 ss.
[55] Above n 50 A Baldassarre, *Globalizzazione contro democrazia,* 360 ss.

disregard the results of the debate from the early twentieth century regarding popular sovereignty.

However, whereas at the origin of the Republic the main question was how to reconcile democracy with the sovereignty of the state, and the solution was found in the distinction between direct and representative democracy, classical representative democracy is currently undergoing a deep crisis: it requires new institutions and procedures to be built in order to preserve democratic principles and the democratic Sovereign in the international, supranational and global arenas. One can agree or disagree with the aforementioned proposals, but surely it must be recognised that they all put the problem of sovereignty in a perspective that respects its minimum meaning and still seeks to connect it to discernible geopolitical trends. That is why I think that there is no way out: either we consider the problem of sovereignty in connection with the role of representative institutions, the idea of the *demos*, and the problem of the democratic legitimation of power; or sovereignty becomes meaningless and should be eradicated from the vocabulary of contemporary political and constitutional life.

14

United Kingdom—Divided on Sovereignty?

KENNETH A ARMSTRONG*

1. INTRODUCTION

FEW COUNTRIES FLAUNT their claims to unitary sovereignty so obviously as the 'United Kingdom' (UK). And yet at the same time there is a clear division of views on what it means to talk of sovereignty in the UK. Notwithstanding the ease with which the UK courts have, by and large, adapted to the UK's membership of the European Community/Union (EC/EU), the interpretations offered of how—constitutionally—this has been achieved, and, whether there has been a constitutional revolution in terms of our understanding of sovereignty, differ markedly between authors. The aim of this chapter is to provide an overview of these debates in the UK. It draws out four perspectives that shape our understanding of sovereignty in the UK—the orthodox view, the common law approach, pluralist approaches and sceptical approaches. While the principal focus of the chapter lies in analysing UK membership of the EU,[1] in the course of discussion the impact of the Human Rights Act 1998 (HRA), the constitutional basis for judicial review of administrative action, and devolution within the UK are also discussed.

---

* School and Department of Law, Queen Mary, University of London.
[1] On which, see also, P Birkinshaw, 'British Report' in J Shwarze (ed.) *The Birth of a European Constitutional Order* (Baden-Baden, Nomos Verlagsgesellschaft, 2001); AW Bradley, 'The Sovereignty of Parliament—Form or Substance?' in J Jowell and D Oliver (eds.) *The Changing Constitution* (4ᵗʰ ed.) (Oxford, Oxford University Press, 2000); P Craig, 'Britain in the European Union' also in Jowell and Oliver (eds.); P Craig, 'Report on the United Kingdom' in A-M Slaughter, A Stone Sweet & JHH Weiler (eds.) *The European Courts and National Courts—Doctrine and Jurisprudence* (Oxford, Hart Publishing, 1998).

2. ALTERNATIVE VISIONS OF THE CONSTITUTION

A. The Orthodox View

At the centre of British orthodox constitutionalism lies the sovereignty of Parliament. It is a unitary concept of sovereignty: unitary legal authority premised upon centralised political authority expressed through the will of Parliament. It is understood as having the following consequences:

> *Validity*—laws enacted by Parliament are to be considered to be legally valid and enforceable;
> *Priority*—it is the duty of the courts to apply the latest will of Parliament over and above any other inconsistent rule of law, including common law rules;
> *Continuity*—sovereignty is continuous and cannot be legally limited.[2]

Parliament cannot, therefore, be the subject of legally binding rules that would limits its legislative powers or permit courts to invalidate Acts of Parliament. As Goldsworthy has noted, it is often contended that this conception of unlimited sovereignty conflicts with ideas of the rule of law.[3] Accordingly, why Parliamentary sovereignty constitutes constitutional orthodoxy rather than constitutional heresy requires some explanation.

One explanation is to consider why it is that laws enacted by Parliament are to be treated as valid and having priority over other legal norms. For Goldsworthy, following Hart's conceptualisation of law into both primary and secondary rules, the effect attributed to primary rules enacted by Parliament is a consequence of the operation of secondary rules of recognition.[4] Legal authority, while manifesting itself in the sovereignty of Parliament, is nonetheless, rooted in fundamental legal rules. These legal rules, in the British constitution are procedural rather than substantive.

If there is no substantive limitation on Parliament's sovereignty, what is to prevent the lawful authority of Parliament being used towards ends which conflict with the rights of the individual or community values? For Goldsworthy, the rule of law is 'first and foremost a political principle, an ideal or aspiration that may or may not be guaranteed by law'.[5] It forms part of a constitutional political morality. According to Loughlin, it is the ethical self-restraint of a ruling class that underpinned the conception of the rule of law inherent in Dicey's approach to Parliamentary sovereignty.[6] It is also because Parliament could be seen, in Goldsworthy's terms, 'as the voice

---

[2] On whether Parliament can bind itself as to the form and manner of future legislative enactment, see Bradley, *ibid.*

[3] J Goldsworthy, 'Legislative Sovereignty and the Rule of Law' in T Campbell, KD Ewing & A Tomkins (eds.), *Sceptical Essays on Human Rights* (Oxford, Oxford UP, 2001).

[4] J Goldsworthy, *The Sovereignty of Parliament* (Oxford, Clarendon Press, 1999).

[5] Above, n 3, p. 61.

[6] M Loughlin, *Public Law and Political Theory* (Oxford, Clarendon Press, 1992), pp. 148–53.

of the community',[7] that it was the duty of the courts to uphold the will of Parliament. Parliament itself represented different constituencies of interests in its component parts—Commons, Lords, Monarch. With the democratisation of the Commons from the Reform Act 1832 onwards, while legislative sovereignty is not the subject of legal limitation, nonetheless, even in Dicey's terms, the legal sovereignty of Parliament was by the 19th century, rooted in a political authority that Paul Craig has described as 'self-correcting majoritarian democracy'.[8] As Harlow argues, '. . . Dicey's doctrine of legal sovereignty is actually premised on the legitimacy of the political order'.[9]

A final element that helps explain constitutional orthodoxy is a belief in the separation of powers. As Loughlin puts it,

> 'The idea here is that Parliament will set the framework of general rules for society, the executive will govern within those rules and an independent judiciary will resolve disputes over the meaning of those rules and will, in particular, keep the executive within the boundaries of the law.'[10]

In consequence, as Lord Bingham notes,

> 'The judicial department did not pretend to stand on a level with Parliament; its functions might be modified at any time by an Act of Parliament, and such a statute would be no violation of the law.'[11]

Nor is the relationship between Parliament and courts one which the courts themselves could unilaterally alter without calling into question the whole basis of unitary legal authority premised upon the political authority of Parliament.

If the orthodox vision has relied upon the perception of Parliament as sovereign law-maker and the courts as its interpretative servant, the growth and diffusion of government has brought the tensions within the model to the fore. The orthodox view has been challenged in the area of judicial review of administrative action. We consider this aspect of sovereignty in transition when considering the 'common law approach' to constitutionalism. For the moment, attention turns to how well orthodoxy has coped with other changes to governance within the UK, namely, membership of the EU and the Human Rights Act 1998.

---

[7] Above, n 4, p. 231.
[8] P Craig, *Public Law and Democracy in the United Kingdom and the United States of America* (Oxford, Clarendon Press, 1990), p. 15.
[9] C Harlow, 'Disposing of Dicey: from Legal Autonomy to Constitutional Discourse?' (2000) 48 *Political Studies* 356, p. 359. See also Loughlin, above, n 6, p. 148.
[10] Above n 6, p. 145.
[11] Lord Bingham of Cornhill, 'Dicey Revisited' (2002) *Public Law* 44.

(i) Membership of the EU

An orthodox constitutional vision seeks to conceptualise UK membership of the EU from the perspective of the domestic constitutional order and the centrality of the sovereignty of Parliament within that order. This suggests, first, that in order for any Treaty obligations to have legal effect within the UK, Parliament must so provide by way of legal enactment, and, secondly, that Parliament retains sovereignty to repeal or amend such an enactment or otherwise legislate in a manner inconsistent with Treaty obligations. Thus, the European Communities Act 1972 (ECA) constitutes the necessary mechanism for giving effect to EU law, which it does in section 2(1) by providing that:

> 'All such rights, powers, liabilities, obligations and restrictions from time to time created or arising by or under the Treaties, and all such remedies and procedures from time to time provided for by or under the Treaties, as in accordance with the Treaties are without further enactment to be given legal effect or used in the United Kingdom shall be recognised and available in law, and be enforced, allowed and followed accordingly; . . .'

If section 2(1) ECA is understood as the necessary constitutional turn of the tap to permit the flow of substantive EU law into the domestic order, an orthodox approach must necessarily reject the view that EU membership can alter the domestic constitutional rules on validity of, or the priority to be given to, the legislative enactments of a continually sovereign Parliament, and to that extent would also, reject any suggestion that the legal effects of EU law within the UK can be determined by EU constitutional law whether contained in the Treaties or in consequence of judgments of the ECJ. Not only does this place orthodoxy in conflict with what we know of the jurisprudence of the ECJ, it is hard to reconcile with section 3(1) ECA which states that:

> 'For the purposes of all legal proceedings any question as to the meaning or effect of any of the Treaties, or as to the validity, meaning or effect of any Community instrument, shall be treated as a question of law (and, if not referred to the European Court, *be for determination as such in accordance with the principles laid down by and any relevant decision of the European Court or any court attached thereto*).' (emphasis added)

This identifies that issues of the meaning and effect of EU law are to be determined by reference to the principles and decisions of the European courts which would include its decisions on the direct effect and supremacy of EC/EU law within the Member States; doctrines that were well established in the ECJ's case-law by the time of UK membership.

Given that an orthodox approach requires full application of the continuity of sovereignty, this means that the ECA would itself be open to both express and implied repeal. However, section 2(4) ECA provides that

'Any enactment passed or to be passed . . . shall be construed and have effect subject to the foregoing provisions of this section'.

From an orthodox perspective this provision cannot be read as in any way entrenching the ECA against any express repeal of the ECA itself, or, indeed, any express derogation from EU obligations. Nonetheless, a modified version of the orthodox approach might accept that section 2(4) prevented any implied repudiation of EU obligations. One might go even further and suggest that it provides a basis for the use of 'strong' interpretative techniques to avoid conflicts.

The orthodox vision of Parliamentary sovereignty finds support in the academic writings of Sir William Wade.[12] But, Wade struggled to reconcile the need to give priority to the law of the Treaty with the orthodox view of the continuity of sovereign legislative power possessed by Parliament. Wade's initial suggestion, therefore, was that whereas Parliament could not for all time make provision for priority to be given to Community law, and whereas it would be 'unreasonable' to ask the courts to perform 'some spontaneous constitutional volte-face of their own', Parliament could instead continually reiterate the primacy of EU law, either through an annual Act of Parliament, or preferably, through each Act of Parliament asserting its compliance with Community law.[13] However, by the conclusion of the *Factortame* litigation[14] in which the House of Lords accepted the obligation to suspend the operation of the Merchant Shipping Act which conflicted with Treaty rules on the right of establishment, Wade was forced to accept that constitutional orthodoxy did not hold true and that 'in the context of Community law Parliament's will is no longer sovereign.'[15] Wade also resisted the temptation to seek to reconcile sovereignty with the priority of EU law through the technique of interpretation. Lord Bridge in *Factortame* had suggested that the effect of section 2(4) ECA was to require courts to interpret statutes as if they contained a provision stating that the Act was without prejudice to directly enforceable Community rights. This would have achieved by interpretation precisely the same result as Wade had earlier suggested, namely the express inclusion of such a provision in future Acts of Parliament. However, Wade dismissed the interpretative route as 'camouflaging' the revolutionary change which he thought had occurred.[16]

---

[12] Eg HWR Wade, 'The Legal Basis of Sovereignty' (1955) *Cambridge Law Journal* 172.

[13] HWR Wade, 'Sovereignty and the European Communities' (1972) 88 *Law Quarterly Review* 1.

[14] *R v Secretary of State for Transport ex parte Factortame (No. 2)* [1991] 1 AC 603.

[15] HWR Wade, 'What has Happened to the Sovereignty of Parliament?' (1991) 107 *Law Quarterly Review* 1.

[16] HWR Wade, 'Sovereignty—Revolution or Evolution?' (1996) 112 *Law Quarterly Review* 568. In reality, the British courts have, with few exceptions, been willing to avoid potential conflicts through interpretative techniques, including acceptance of interpretative techniques derived from EU law itself—see P Craig, 'Britain in the European Union' above n 1, p. 71.

What is crucial to understand is that for Wade, Parliamentary sovereignty is preserved through the operation of a separation of powers in which Parliament legislates and the courts interpret Parliament's will, while both are subject to constitutional rules which neither can unilaterally alter. As Bamforth suggests,[17] for Wade the idea that courts would abandon their traditional adherence to the will of Parliament is revolutionary because the courts themselves would have altered the fundamental rules of the constitutional order, and with it the institutional balance that underpinned the Diceyan model of the constitution. In doing so, this would expose the fragile nature of the institutional constraints binding together the Diceyan constitutional balance with the consequence that Parliament might further limit its own sovereignty or the courts might contemplate new forms of judicial activism including placing substantive limitations on Parliament's legislative powers.

Orthodoxy struggles in the face of UK membership not because the need to give supremacy to EU law paralysed the British courts, unable to find a constitutional compass to guide them out of their difficulties, but precisely because of the ease with which the courts were able to adjust to the new constitutional reality. As Allan argues, if one way of looking at sovereignty is to see it as rooted in the empiricism of Hart with its emphasis upon the actual behaviour of officials, then the actual behaviour of judges indicates that the fundamental rules of the constitutional order are open to change.[18] On this view, Wade attributes too great an inflexibility to the constitutional order. Nonetheless, if we move to a position in which the courts have an ability to alter the fundamental constitutional rules, the authority of the courts must itself be explained. We return to this issue in discussing the common law approach.

(ii) The Human Rights Act

The HRA appears to pose much less of an obvious problem for an orthodox approach to Parliamentary sovereignty than the ECA.[19] The function of the HRA is not to turn the tap to allow the provisions of the European Convention on Human Rights (ECHR) to flow directly into the domestic legal order. Rather, the HRA itself domesticates the ECHR by substantive

---

[17] N Bamforth, 'Ultra Vires and Institutional Interdependence' in C Forsyth (ed.), *Judicial Review and the Constitution* (Oxford, Hart Publishing, 2000).

[18] TRS Allan, 'Parliamentary Sovereignty: Law, Politics and Revolution' (1997) 113 *Law Quarterly Review* 443.

[19] See D Feldman, 'The Human Rights Act 1998 and Constitutional Principles' (1999) 19(2) *Legal Studies* 165, and D Feldman, 'Convention Rights and Substantive Ultra Vires' in C Forsyth (ed.) above, n 17.

incorporation of only certain of its provisions through Schedule 1 of the Act. Moreover, section 2(1) HRA requires UK courts to take account of the jurisprudence of the Strasbourg institutions when adjudicating rather than making judgments of the European Court of Human Rights automatically binding. Compared to the 'incorporation' of European Union law in which the priority to be given to EU law flows from the need to protect the Community character of the law,[20] the HRA is itself a domestic statute seeking to place European human rights norms within a domestic constitutional context.[21] As Feldman puts it, 'The Convention Rights have the potential to be a distinctively British code'.[22] The reconciliation of orthodoxy and the HRA finds its most apparent expression in the inability of the courts—unlike the post-*Factortame* situation applicable to EU law—to disapply an Act of Parliament even if it is declared to be incompatible with Convention rights under section 4 HRA.[23] Instead it falls to Parliament to remedy the conflict. Not surprisingly, the judicial view has been that the HRA is wholly consistent with the sovereignty of Parliament.[24]

Where a potential parallel between the ECA and the HRA is more obvious lies in section 3(1) HRA. It provides that

'as far as it is possible to do so legislation and subordinate legislation must be read and given effect in a way which is compatible with Convention rights'.

In one sense this could be treated as little more than the specific expression of the general norm that statutes are to be interpreted having regard to the presumption that Parliament intends to abide by its international obligations and thus, where there is ambiguity, an interpretation which avoids conflict is to be followed. However, it can also be read as a more specific instruction to courts to adopt an interpretation which avoids conflict even in the absence of ambiguity.[25] This returns us to the same sorts of problems as arise in respect of section 2(4) ECA—at what point do normal canons of construction give way to interpretative exercises that 'camouflage' significant judicial activism? There is, however, a difference in the two contexts.

---

[20] Case 6/64 *Costa v ENEL* [1964] ECR 585.

[21] A normative argument for locating fundamental norms within 'fundamental boundaries' (including that of the domestic constitutional context) can be found in JHH Weiler, 'Fundamental Rights and Fundamental Boundaries: on the Conflict of Standards and Values in the Protection of Human Rights in the European Legal Space' in Weiler, *The Constitution of Europe* (Cambridge, Cambridge UP, 1999).

[22] Above, n 19, p. 192.

[23] Under Section 29(1) Scotland Act 1998 an Act of the Scottish Parliament is not law if it is outside the legislative competence of the Parliament. Adopting legislation in conflict with Convention rights is, in terms of section 29(2)(d) outside legislative competence and the Judicial Committee of the Privy Council has jurisdiction to strike down such legislation.

[24] See eg the judgment of Lord Hoffmann in *R v Secretary of State for the Home Department ex parte Simms* [1999] QB 349.

[25] See G Marshall, 'Two kinds of compatibility: more about section 3 of the Human Rights Act 1988', (1999) *Public Law* 377.

Within the context of EU law, if interpretation cannot resolve the conflict the courts must—contrary to orthodoxy—suspend the operation of Acts of Parliament and give effect to EU law. Within the context of the HRA, where interpretation cannot resolve a conflict, then Parliamentary sovereignty is to be preserved through resort to the declaration of incompatibility. This might suggest a boundary to the use of interpretative techniques as well as a clear return to orthodoxy where interpretation reaches its boundary. Rather than resorting to the camouflage of interpretation to avoid blatant conflicts, orthodoxy would demand that the courts default to the declaration of incompatibility.

However, it is apparent that the HRA's influence may rest more in interpretative techniques of conflict avoidance than in declarations of incompatibility. Even prior to the HRA's introduction, the general presumption that Parliament does not intend to legislate to violate rights, created an interpretative space for the judicial development of fundamental rights protection. The section 3 HRA requirements have given added weight to the creative use of interpretation to resolve conflicts. And, as Campbell has suggested, 'incorporation through interpretation' may take the courts beyond the role assigned to them by the orthodox approach, and lead them to new frontiers of judicial activism.[26]

But if Campbell's fear is of activism under the guise of interpretation, Elliot's view is that this is the lesser of two evils when compared with the potential reach of section 6 HRA.[27] Under section 6(1) HRA, public authorities must act in conformity with Convention rights. For Elliot, there is a danger that this provision is understood as empowering the courts through judicial review to subject public authorities to a form of 'rules-based' review in which—independent of the intent of Parliament in conferring powers upon such bodies—the courts will directly apply fundamental rights norms to constrain such bodies. The point is less whether the role of the courts is referable to an intent of Parliament (after all this issue arises precisely because Parliament has willed the enactment of the HRA) and more that one Parliament would be seen as having bound its predecessors and its successors by entrenching human rights norms as a standard against which to test the exercise of public power. For Elliot, it is constitutionally more appropriate to construct the human rights obligations of public authorities as interpretative constructs implied within their specific legislative grants of authority. The problem for Elliot, however, is that he is forced to rely upon the same sorts of arguments based on implied Parliamentary intent as apply more generally to an ultra vires model of judicial review and which are open

---

[26] T Campbell, 'Incorporation through Interpretation' in T Campbell, KD Ewing & A Tomkins (eds.), above, n 3.
[27] M Elliott, 'Fundamental Rights as Interpretative Constructs: the Constitutional Logic of the Human Rights Act 1998' in C Forsyth (ed.) above n 17.

to the same sort of critique. In particular, we end up with a prioritisation of the conceptual continuity of Parliamentary sovereignty in a way which paradoxically appears to restrict the powers of Parliament to do anything which might smack of entrenchment either of the priority of EU law or protection of human rights. This leaves no room for constitutional development and treats the sovereignty of Parliament not unlike an embalmed Lenin.

According to statistics, only four declarations of incompatibility were issued between 2 October 2000 and 28 February 2002, out of eighty-two cases in which HRA claims were upheld.[28] The remaining seventy-eight cases found their basis in the application of section 6 HRA (fifty-nine cases) and section 3 HRA (nineteen cases). This indicates that from an orthodox perspective, Elliot may be right to fear section 6, while otherwise, it is the section 3 interpretative obligation that is doing more work than the section 4 declaration of incompatibility. If Wade is right to caution against the camouflage of interpretation, the evidence of the HRA indicates that orthodoxy is struggling not only with membership of the EU, but with the HRA itself.

B. The Common Law Approach

A different approach to the question of legal authority can be seen in what will be termed here the 'common law' approach. In short, the common law approach has sought to develop a perspective in which the common law is itself a source of legal authority. The battle between the orthodox approach and the common law approach has been fought on the field of judicial review of administrative action.[29] The crux of the issue is whether the authority of the courts is to be considered as derived from a Parliamentary delegation of authority, or whether it has an original and independent authority rooted in the common law itself.[30] The orthodox response has sought to understand the legal authority of the courts in undertaking judicial review as derived from the will of Parliament. Thus, if decision-makers are delegated governmental tasks through statutory enactment, so too are the courts delegated the task of ensuring that decision-makers act within the limits of the authority granted by Parliament (the *ultra vires* model of judicial review). Any unconstrained exercise of governmental power would challenge the sovereign authority of Parliament itself, and therefore, the courts role is necessarily one of ensuring Parliament's monopoly on

---

[28] Source: HRA Research Project, 2002 (http://www.doughtystreet.co.uk).
[29] See the collection of essays in C Forsyth (ed), above n 17.
[30] P Craig, 'Ultra Vires and the Foundations of Judicial Review' in C Forsyth (ed.) above, n 17.

sovereignty.

Those opposing this view argue that orthodoxy cannot be reconciled with the reality of a modern administrative law the content of which is founded upon judicial decisions.[31] Moreover, far from orthodoxy providing a constitutional constraint on the judiciary, adherence to orthodoxy runs the risk of camouflaging judicial activism behind the 'fig-leaf'[32] of Parliamentary intent, contrary to the very intention of the orthodox approach. In the light of the empirical and analytical attack, proponents of orthodoxy, nonetheless, contend that orthodoxy requires to be adhered to because, 'for reasons of principle and pragmatism, it is not for judges acting on their own motion, to abolish ultra vires.'[33] The resonance with Wade's defence of orthodoxy in the face of the *Factortame* 'revolution' is palpable.

But if orthodoxy has difficulty in sustaining a constitutional theory premised on the unitary authority of Parliament, what then has been the response of the common law approach? Sedley has referred to a:

> 'bi-polar sovereignty of the Crown in Parliament and the Crown in its courts, to each of which the Crown's ministers are answerable—politically to Parliament, legally to the courts.'[34]

By contrast with orthodoxy that demands a unitary legal authority premised on Parliamentary sovereignty as its constitutional metanarrative, if one takes Sedley at his word, then there is the appearance of a plurality of legal authority founded both on the sovereignty of Parliament and that of the courts. However, there is a tendency amongst common law theorists to engage in a counter-factual argument, as Goldsworthy has noted, which contends that as Parliamentary sovereignty is not within the control of Parliament itself, then it must be within the keeping of the courts as a principle of the common law.[35] If one follows this logic we seem to end up with a return to unitary legal authority as the constitutional metanarrative but this time in the guise of the authority of the common law. How then is this to be reconciled with the sovereignty of Parliament? Defenders of the common law approach have never denied that in the face of an express Parliamentary intent to override common law rights, it would be the duty of the courts to uphold the will of Parliament.[36] However, we need to be clear that as far as the common law perspective is concerned, the *rules on*

---

[31] See eg D Oliver, 'Is the Ultra Vires Rule the Basis of Judicial Review'? (1987) *Public Law* 543; P Craig, 'Competing Models of Judicial Review' (1999) *Public Law* 428.

[32] Sir John Laws, 'Illegality—the Problem of Jurisdiction' in M Supperstone and J Goudie, *Judicial Review* (2nd ed.) (London, Butterworths, 1997).

[33] C Forsyth, 'Of Fig Leaves and Fairy Tales: the Ultra Vires Doctrine, the Sovereignty of Parliament and Judicial Review' in C Forsyth above, n 17, p. 45.

[34] Sir Stephen Sedley, 'Human Rights: a Twenty First Century Agenda' (1995) *Public Law* 386.

[35] Goldsworthy, above, n 4, p. 240.

[36] See Craig, above, n 31, p. 446.

priority which govern the relationship between authoritative sources of legal norms (normally statute law and common law) are, nonetheless, in the keeping of the common law and the courts. It, therefore, follows that the courts can change the rules on priority and, thereby, create a set of contingent legal relations and hierarchies between different sources of law.

What then provides the legitimating force for the authority of the common law? The answer that is normally offered is 'the rule of law'. The relationship between the common law and the rule of law is open to very different interpretations. The rule of law might be considered as primarily procedural and aimed merely at ensuring that courts treat as valid and enforceable only those sources of law promulgated in the terms required by constitutional rules of recognition. However, the rule of law might also be considered as supporting the use of the common law in two respects: first, to defend substantive values and substantive rights (the negative aspect), and, second, to instil democratic requirements of openness and participation in decision-making (the positive aspect).[37]

Given that both orthodoxy and the common law approach share an interest in the role of the common law and its protection of the rule of law, it is important to understand the difference in their conceptualisation of the authority of the common law. For Dicey, it was an essentially private law model of the common law which provided the basis for the protection of the rule of law in a world in which all were equally subject to the ordinary law in the ordinary courts. As Craig argues, in the field of private law, the authority of the common law tends to rest on the content of common law rules.[38] Its rationality lies in its inductive problem-solving approach. The developing common law approach, while claiming to be founded upon an age-old tradition of the common law,[39] nonetheless, must be understood as conceptualising a very different common law rooted in a public law model of the common law which is more akin to a European constitutionalisation and codification and whose authority is founded upon its deductive and principled rationality rather than its pragmatism.

Moreover, from the perspective of this 'new' common law constitutionalism, the content of the rule of law is not merely procedural but substantive, including the protection of fundamental rights. Thus, in the context of

---

[37] For a discussion of formal and substantive approaches to the rule of law see D Dyzenhaus, 'Form and Substance in the Rule of Law: A Democratic Justification for Judicial Review', in C Forsyth (ed.) above, n 17.

[38] Craig contrasts a public law model in which the traditional ultra vires approach locates the authority of the courts in the will of Parliament while finding the content of public law norms in the common law, with a private law model in which the authority of the courts and the content of private law are both located within the common law itself: Craig, above, n 30, p. 68.

[39] Craig, above, n 30.

judicial review of administrative action, it provides a basis for substantive review, and in particular, close scrutiny of decisions of the Executive encroaching on fundamental rights.[40] It also provides a basis for interpreting statutes in a way that does not infringe upon constitutional rights protected by the common law. Thus, while stopping short of challenging the validity of legislation itself, the courts have sought to construe legislation in such a way as to minimise any interference with fundamental rights.

It is evident that the adoption of a common law approach in the way described results in the courts developing a strong role in the protection of individual rights when reviewing the actions of the Executive and when interpreting the powers granted to government by Parliament. The issue is much discussed in the context of judicial review. Here our attention focuses upon its implications for UK membership of the EU and for the HRA.

(i) Membership of the EU

Trevor Allan's explanation for the House of Lords' suspension of the Merchant Shipping Act in *Factortame* rests upon the 'existence of good legal reasons'. Allan considers that good legal reasons invoke 'settled doctrine or principle' and a constitutional revolution only occurs 'when a new source of authority is acknowledged, or fundamental rule adopted, which is *not* justified by the existing order, from which the courts have, for whatever reason withdrawn their allegiance'.[41] Thus, for Allan, the non-revolutionary nature of UK membership of the EU is explicable only because of the existence of good legal reasons *justified by the existing constitutional order* and supporting acceptance of EU law within the UK.

Similarly, in his analysis of the *Factortame* decision, Paul Craig offers an explanation 'based on normative arguments of legal principle the content of which can and will vary across time'.[42] Thus, for Craig, 'there is no *a priori* inexorable reason why Parliament, merely because of its very existence, must be regarded as legally omnicompetent'.[43] Accordingly, what the British judges have been doing in giving effect to the primacy of EU law within the UK is simply 'the principled consequence of the UK's membership of the EC'.[44] Furthermore, the role of the courts in placing constraints on the exercise of sovereign power by Parliament in the context of EU law is part of a

---

[40] *Bugdaycay v Secretary of State for the Home Department* [1987] 1 All ER 940; *R v Secretary of State for the Home Department ex parte Brind* [1991] 1 AC 696.
[41] Allan, above, n 18, p. 444.
[42] Craig 'Britain in the EU', above n 1, p. 79.
[43] *Ibid*
[44] *Ibid*

broader trend as also exemplified by the courts' approach to judicial review in the context of the review of legislation or discretion which is said to restrict fundamental rights.[45] In other words, if the common law has developed rules of priority as between different sources of law, then there is little difference between the courts' use of such rules in respect of purely domestic sources (the relationship between Acts of Parliament and common law rules) and the courts' use of these rules as between domestic and European sources of legal norms.

Thus the constitutional explanation offered by the common law approach is one in which the common law has accepted the validity of EU law within the UK and has also altered the rules of priority to give primacy to EU law unless and until Parliament expressly indicates its intention, in whole or in part, to derogate from EU law. If the effect of EU law in the UK is in the keeping of the common law, and if the priority to be given to EU law rests on good legal reasons to be found in the UK constitutional order, then it also follows that UK courts might find good reasons not to accept the authority of EU law either in whole or in part and, thereby refuse to give priority to a provision of EU law over that of national law. If one takes Allan seriously then it is no more revolutionary for the courts to decline to give priority to EU law than it is to accept the priority of EU law, provided, of course, that the reasons are good enough.

With the foregoing in mind, we can, perhaps make sense of the judgment of the Divisional Court in what has become known as the 'Metric Martyrs' case.[46] The judgment arose out of four prosecutions of market traders for *inter alia* the display of produce for sale using only imperial rather than metric weights and measures. The EU Metrication Directive 80/181/EEC as amended in 1989 had been implemented in the UK by way of Regulations adopted in 1994 amending the Weights and Measures Act 1985. The effect was to prevent the use of pounds and ounces as a primary indicator of weight from 1 January 2000. The legal challenge was to the *vires* of the Regulations amending the 1985 Act. The 1994 Regulations were promulgated as provided for in section 2(2) ECA which allows for the implementation of EU obligations by way of Order in Council (including its use to amend Acts of Parliament—a so-called Henry VIII clause). However, the 1985 Act itself also provided a mechanism for its revision and thus, one of the central contentions was that this later Act impliedly repealed the operation of section 2(2) of the ECA insofar as delegated legislation adopted under that provision related to matters within the substantive scope of the

---

[45] Craig, 'Report on the United Kingdom', above n 1, p. 215.

[46] *Thorburn v Sunderland City Council*; *Hunt v London Borough of Hackney*; *Harman and Dove v Cornwall County Council*; and, *Collins v London Borough of Sutton* [2002] EW4 C195 (Admin); [2002] 3WLR 247. In July 2002, the 'Metric Martyrs' were denied leave to appeal to the House of Lords, the highest court of appeal in the UK thereby declining an early opportunity to comment on Sir John Laws' innovative approach.

1985 Act. Hence any attempt to use section 2(2) to adopt the 1994 Regulations would be said to be *ultra vires*. As against this would be the argument that section 2(4) ECA guards against any such implied repeal and that the very function of section 2(2) ECA is to provide the government with a means of adopting delegated legislation to give effect to EU obligations whereas the function of the mechanism within the 1985 Act itself could be said to concern amendments to the Act in purely domestic (non-EU) matters.

Lord Justice Laws found that there was no inconsistency between the provisions of the 1985 Act and the ECA and, therefore, there was no implied repeal of section 2(2). The 1994 Regulations were valid. However, in an *obiter* discussion of the constitutional relationship between the UK and the EU, Lord Justice Laws offered a vision of that relationship rooted solely in the domestic constitutional order. While he accepted that membership of the EU entailed the reception of the substantive law of the EU, he rejected any suggestion that the principle of Parliamentary sovereignty had been in any way altered by the constitutional jurisprudence of the ECJ. The reasons for this, he proposed, was that Parliament had no authority to 'abandon its own sovereignty'; the jurisprudence of the ECJ could not give EU law a status within English law 'to which it could not aspire by any route of English law itself'; and, any modification to the doctrine of sovereignty could not be achieved by incorporation of external texts.

Like the orthodox approach, this approach denies any possibility for *Parliament* to bind its successors through mechanisms such as section 2(4) ECA. But unlike the orthodox approach, Parliament cannot seek to prevent implied repeal because it is a doctrine of the common law within the control of the courts; the same courts 'to which the scope and nature of Parliamentary sovereignty are ultimately confided'. Moreover, for Laws, it is the common law which confers on certain statutes such as the ECA their status as 'constitutional statutes' to which the doctrine of implied repeal need not apply. Accordingly, it is the courts which ensure that the normal domestic rule of priority does not result in substantive provisions of EU law being rendered ineffective by the adoption of post-1972 Acts of Parliament. Thus, for Lord Justice Laws, the common law has recognised a hierarchy of Acts of Parliament and has changed the rules on priority to exclude the application of the doctrine of implied repeal to statutes deemed by the courts to be 'constitutional' in nature.

Not being content to hold that substantive provisions of EU law take effect in priority to post-1972 Acts of Parliament by virtue of the common law, Laws also decided to throw open the possibility of English courts refusing to give effect to EU law where it conflicted with domestic constitutional norms. He suggests that:

'In the event, which no doubt would never happen in the real world, that a

European measure was seen to be repugnant to a fundamental or constitutional right guaranteed by the law of England, a question would arise whether the general words of the 1972 Act were sufficient to incorporate the measure and give it overriding effect in domestic law.'

This flatly contradicts the view of the European Court of Justice in *International Handelsgesellscahft* that:[48]

'. . . the validity of a community measure or its effect within a member state cannot be affected by allegations that it runs counter to either fundamental rights as formulated by the constitution of that state or the principles of a national constitutional structure.'

So what are we to make of this, given that the UK has armed itself not only with a common law protection of fundamental rights, but also the effects of the HRA? It seems evident that for Laws, the courts can further alter the rules on priority so as not to give effect to provisions of EU law within the domestic order where they conflict with fundamental or constitutional rights. Only an express intention to the contrary by Parliament could permit such an EU measure to take effect, and the general wording of the ECA is not such as to constitute a generalisable express intention. In this way, the ECA is treated in the same way as all other statutes in the sense of not permitting violations of fundamental rights except with clear statutory language.

It is apparent that there is potential for conflict between EU norms and the domestic protection of human rights. In the domestic sphere, the HRA mediates tensions between Acts of Parliament and Convention rights through resort to interpretative techniques and declarations of incompatibility. It is obvious that courts would seek to resolve conflicts with EU law through interpretation, but it is unclear what would happen if this is not possible. If UK courts could of their own motion disapply EU law for violation of fundamental rights protected within the domestic order, then this necessarily places EU law below UK law in the hierarchy of norms insofar as domestic courts, in circumstances governed by the HRA, could only issue a declaration of incompatibility in the event that a conflict between UK Law and Convention Rights could not be cured by interpretation. This leads to the curious situation in which in the ordinary course of events, EU law takes primacy over Acts of Parliament in the event of conflicts (EU law acts as a superior norm), yet as between an Act of Parliament and an EU measure both of which were considered to be in conflict with the same fundamental right protected by the UK courts, the UK courts could disapply the EU measure but could only issue a declaration of incompatibility in respect of the Act of Parliament (the EU measure is treated as a species of delegated legislation). Where the conflict is more likely to occur is where a public authority purports to exercise a power under EU law but which the domes-

---

[47] Case 11/70 *International Handeslgesellshaft* [1970] ECR 1125.

tic court considers to be a violation of Convention rights. Can the court apply section 6 HRA in a situation where the authority acts within the scope of EU law? What this evidences is the growing need not only to make sense of UK membership of the EU and the introduction of the HRA separately, but also to think about the consequences of their interrelationship. As Walker notes the debate between rights-sceptics and rights-advocates which events such as the enactment of the HRA provoke must also recognise the impact that EU law (and with it the developing human rights agenda of the EU) has upon those debates.[48]

To conclude, if the approach taken by Laws is to be consistent with Allan's point of departure, then the rules on priority that govern the contingent relations between legal sources can only be open to change because of good legal reasons and not mere judicial diktat. Nonetheless, to succeed as an approach this necessarily must move beyond the domestic realm to consider the arguments of the ECJ itself, not least because the ECJ contests the very basis upon which the UK court would be seeking to develop its rules on priority. This implies a more pluralistic approach to legal discourse and legal reasoning than has been discussed thus far and one that recognises the extent to which this is a topic which has already been the subject of legal discourse between the ECJ and other Member States' jurisdictions, not least the German courts.

(ii) The Human Rights Act

In a sense, much of what can be said here has been dealt with in the discussion of orthodoxy and the HRA. However, it is important to note that for those supporting common law constitutionalism, the very introduction of the HRA can be interpreted as highlighting the failure of the orthodox model to set in place appropriate checks and balances to structure the exercise of governmental power. In suggesting that the UK's largely procedural constitution provided limited mechanisms of control and accountability, Feldman argues,[49]

> 'This was not too serious a problem when politics was dominated by a consensual, high Tory willingness to restrain individualism in order to further communal goods, coupled with a hierarchical model of society in which the élite understood that their position carried obligations with it: the belief that *noblesse oblige*'.

For Feldman and others, the Thatcher era of government indicated how easily a government could free itself from such 19th century ethical restraints and use the power of the state towards its desired ends largely free from

---

[48] N Walker, Human Rights in a Postnational Order: Reconciling Political and Constitutional Pluralism' in T Campbell, KD Ewing & A Tomkins (eds.), above, n 3.
[49] Feldman, above, n 19, p. 166.

legal restraint and subject only to the discipline of 'self-correcting democracy'. The turn to the protection of fundamental rights and the rise of what Loughlin terms 'liberal normativism' succeeded in attracting support not only from the liberal left but also the liberal right.[50]

Not only was this movement towards identifying and protecting fundamental rights conducted at the political level in terms of debates about Bills of Rights and incorporating the Convention, but it can also be detected pre-HRA within the case-law of the courts, utilising the common law as a source of such rights. Using principles of construction, the courts would not interpret statutes as conflicting with fundamental rights unless that intention was clearly expressed by Parliament. Understood in these terms, this approach is consistent with orthodoxy insofar as the *role* of the courts is seen to derive from an implied Parliamentary intent, even if the content of the rights is developed by the courts. But given that the common law approach also accepts its obligations to give effect to the will of Parliament, the very enactment of the HRA is not itself a problem for the common law approach and indeed could even be viewed as a formalisation of the authority of the courts in protecting fundamental rights. The powers which courts have to require public authorities to exercise their powers in accordance with fundamental rights norms under section 6 HRA seems to confirm the common law trends in this area.

The introduction of the HRA can be seen as part of a continuity in the development of a rights culture within the common law. But if Lord Hoffmann is right that,

'. . . the courts of the United Kingdom, though acknowledging the sovereignty of Parliament, apply principles of constitutionality little different from those which exist in countries where the power of the legislature is expressly limited by a constitutional document'[51]

this is surely an indication that a profound change has occurred in the underlying constitutional order in the name of the rule of law. It is obvious that the sort of rule of law being invoked as an underpinning for the development of the common law model is not one rooted in the tradition of the Diceyan constitution, the political morality of a ruling class, or the separation of powers, but instead an attempt to build a rational, principled, legal code fashioned out of the common law and domesticated Convention rights.

C. PLURALIST APPROACHES

There might be thought to be something parochial about the constitutional

---

[50] Loughlin, above, n 6, Chap 9.
[51] *Simms* above, n 24.

discourse thus far discussed insofar as it seems unwilling or unable to contemplate a normativity and authority of law located outside the domestic constitutional order itself. This seems all the more surprising given that the HRA incorporates rights derived from an international law Convention, and given that the European Court of Justice considers that its core doctrines of direct effect and supremacy flow from a 'new legal order'. In this section, we consider pluralist approaches and what they tell us about the nature of sovereignty in general and what is happening to sovereignty in the UK in particular. Because of the potential range of the former, necessarily the emphasis is placed on the latter.

(i) Pluralism and Hierarchy

JDB Mitchell's interpretation of UK membership of the EU saw no constitutional difficulty attached to UK membership. For Mitchell, this arose because of a change in the underlying political and legal facts upon which the orthodox view of sovereignty was based, and the UK, like the other Member States, entered a new constitutional hierarchy in which the new legal order of the EU was supreme.[52] Mitchell was not merely positing an alternative legal authority, but rather a superior legal authority in the form of the EC constitutional order. Indeed, he suggested that the ECA may not have been legally necessary at all, and to the extent that cognisance of it is taken, its provisions are at best declaratory, and derivative, of the legal rights and obligations flowing from the 'new legal order' of Community law. Mitchell simply takes the constitutional template of the nation state and recreates it at a higher level, by giving to the EC itself the features of a constitution. Mitchell's view, while necessarily seeking to make sense of the Community as a distinct legal order, nonetheless, goes too far in the suggestion that the UK constitutional order has simply been subsumed into a constitutional order operating at a higher level.

An alternative conceptualisation, and one which better captures both the enduring nature of domestic constitutional orders and the 'internal perspective' of such orders can instead be found in MacCormick's work.[53] In contrast to both the rigid Hartian interpretation of Wade and the Dworkinian inspired interpretation of Allan, MacCormick offers an account of the *Factortame* judgment which is not strictly Hartian but allows for the same sort of constitutional change as Hart himself envisaged by positing not only secondary rules of recognition but also rules of change.

---

[52] JDB Mitchell, 'The Sovereignty of Parliament and Community Law: The Stumbling Block That Isn't There', (1978) 53 *International Affairs* 33.
[53] Much of Neil MacCormick's work on sovereignty is contained in N MacCormick, *Questioning Sovereignty* (Oxford, Oxford University Press, 1999).

For MacCormick, Parliament, through the ECA effected a constitutional change in the rules of recognition by conferring validity on laws produced at the EU level. As well as conferring validity, it required priority to be given to provisions of EU law over national law. To that extent, Parliament has not limited its right in the future to repeal the ECA itself. All that has happened is that insofar as the ECA remains in force, only an express repeal of the ECA itself will be sufficient to alter again the rules of recognition. In outcome, MacCormick and Allan arrive at the same conclusion—there has been no constitutional revolution. But while Allan conceives this as an achievement of the courts whose authority is rooted in legal principle, for MacCormick, the implication is that it has been Parliament that has brought about this change through an alteration of rules of recognition the fact of which has been accepted by the courts.

The significance of MacCormick's contribution is also his recognition that EU law itself constitutes a distinct legal order with its own internal perspective upon the validity of EU law and its legal effects within national legal orders. There is, therefore, a constitutionalism beyond the nation state. As he highlights, this creates a plurality of legal orders each of which must seek to accommodate the other but utilising its own criteria of recognition and validity. But whereas for Mitchell, the national legal order nests within the EU in a hierarchical way, for MacCormick, there is a non-hierarchical relationship between the EU and the national legal orders. Within this relationship, national legal orders have altered their domestic constitutional norms to provide for the validity and priority to be given to EU law rather than 'any kind of all-purpose subordination of member-state law to Community law'.[54] In other words there is a plurality of legal orders whose relationship one to the other is determined by a set of contingent rules relating to validity, priority and continuity. However, MacCormick rejects the radicial pluralist thesis, suggesting that while national and Community legal orders are non-hierarchical *inter se*, in accordance with a Kelsenian position both orders are in turn subordinated under international law. This offers him a way-out of the conclusion that in the event of incommensurable conflicts between EU and national constitutional law, the solution is necessarily political. Instead, international law offers other legal resources.[55] In this way, MacCormick's pluralism is both limited to the recognition of three levels (national, EU, and international) and constrained ('pluralism under international law'). An alternative approach lies in radical pluralism.

(ii) Radical Pluralism

Neil Walker's work on sovereignty has emphasised the importance of recog-

---

[54] *Ibid*, p. 117.
[55] *Ibid*, p. 120.

nising the development of alternative sites of 'metaconstitutional' discourse beyond the frontiers of the sovereign state.[56] Like MacCormick, he seeks to move 'beyond the sovereign state',[57] but he does not seek to leave behind sovereignty itself. Instead, the concept of sovereignty is refashioned in the form of autonomous, plausible claims to authority and what emerges is a radical pluralism of multiple and competing sites of legal authority. In the context of the UK's membership of the EU, there is a recognition of the EU as constituting an institutional site which not only makes its own claims of sovereignty, but which also offers a rival source of constitutional discourse within the Member States themselves. The discourse of the ECJ provided a legal basis for giving priority to EU norms, or at the least, the UK courts were forced to develop a domestic constitutional discourse which could accommodate EU membership, precisely because of a rival claim to authority emanating from the jurisprudence of the ECJ. But unlike MacCormick, Walker suggests a greater plurality in sites of legal discourse than those of national, EU and international law. Moreover, it is heterarchical rather than hierarchical pluralism.

The multidimensionality which Walker introduces is indeed a necessary corrective to a tendency to bring the language of constitutionalism to a halt at the frontiers of the nation state. Particularly in the context of the European Union, a space is opened up for constitutional discourses operating within and between different levels and, while potentially conflictual and incommensurable, the very process of contestation may be vital to the constitutional health of a multilevel constitutionalism.[58] Consider, for example, the contribution of the legal discourse between the ECJ and the *Bundesverfassungsgericht* in terms of the sensitivity of the ECJ to questions of competence and questions of human rights protection.

In terms of the domestic constitutional order of the UK itself, for Walker, the unitary concept of legal authority based upon the doctrine of Parliamentary sovereignty is 'formal rather than substantive' and 'does not presuppose any particular set of reasons why Parliament should be said to

---

[56] N Walker, 'Beyond the Unitary Conception of the United Kingdom Constitution?' (2000) *Public Law* 384; N Walker, 'Sovereignty and Differentiated Integration in the European Union' (1998) 4(4) *European Law Journal* 355; N Walker, 'Flexibility within a Metaconstitutional Frame: reflections on the future of legal authority in Europe' in G de Búrca and J Scott, *Constitutional Change in the EU: From Uniformity to Flexibility* (Oxford, Hart Publishing, 2000).

[57] MacCormick's conceptualisation of legal pluralism leads him to the conclusion that beyond the sovereign state we occupy a post-sovereign form of constitutional order: see N MacCormick, 'Beyond the Sovereign State' (1993) 56(1) *Modern Law Review* 1.

[58] See Z Bankowski and E Christodoulidis, 'The European Union as an Essentially Contested Project' (1998) 4(4) *European Law Journal* 341; J Shaw, 'Process and Constitutional Discourse in the European Union' (2000) 27(1) *Journal of Law and Society* 4.

[59] 'Beyond the Unitary Conception of the United Kingdom Constitution?', above n 56 p. 393.

be sovereign'.[59] As such, plural forms of government including devolution of powers within the UK, as well as different political philosophies can be reconciled with this unitary concept. And, given the idea of a broader multi-dimensionality in which other sites of legal authority beyond the borders of the existing constitutional order (eg EU and ECHR) provide a basis for constitutional discourse within the UK, for Walker, the unitary concept of the state is not only flexible, but also less central to constitutional thought.[60]

However, perhaps Walker underestimates the extent to which the concept of unitary legal sovereignty is itself challenged within the UK. For if we take Walker's approach and adopt a view of sovereignty which is both less than absolutist, but beyond the minimum threshold that we would expect of a claim to legal authority,[61] then it is apparent that the common law approach described in the previous section offers itself as an alternative source of legal authority rooted in a very different conception of the rule of law than that underpinning the orthodox Diceyan model. Under certain conditions that authority will give way to Parliamentary authority, but absent such conditions, the common law claims its own validity and application.

Moreover, although Walker views the relationship between the legal authority implied by a unitary legal sovereignty and issues of political authority as very flexible, the belief that Parliamentary sovereignty is not grounded in any particular set of reasons does not seem quite right. After all, the dominance of Diceyan orthodoxy about the legal sovereignty of the Westminster Parliament cannot be divorced from a belief in the centralisation of political authority in that institution. Dicey himself was implacably opposed to Irish 'Home Rule' and would probably have opposed devolution of powers within the UK[62] even if the Parliaments or Assemblies created were not sovereign in the absolute sense of having legal priority. The very fact that the UK Parliament exercised its sovereign powers to provide for devolution itself indicated an unease with the matrix of unitary political and legal authority centralised in Westminster.

In any event, even if unitary legal sovereignty can accommodate plural sites of political power, nonetheless, the very language of legal sovereignty in the devolution context may have the effect of shielding us from the very system of government we are trying to explain. Devolution creates its own matrix of legal and political authority. This may be contested from within and from outwith. It is precisely here that Walker's broader discussion of the developing multidimensionality is of importance in that alternative sites of legal and political authority that are non-state and not sovereign in the absolute sense are developing. As our discussion of EU law also shows,

---

[60] *Ibid*
[61] In 'Sovereignty and Differentiated Integration in the European Union', above, n 56, p. 358, Walker adopts a definition of sovereignty as a 'threshold concept'.
[62] See Lord Bingham, above n 11.

these compete with and trouble the prevailing constitutional systems, including the orthodoxy of a centralised legal and political authority in the form of the Westminster Parliament.

D. SCEPTICAL APPROACHES

A somewhat different traditional of public law thought has been concerned to look more directly behind the façade of legal sovereignty, to consider the underlying patterns of political authority and political power. Thus, for Harold Laski, the concept of sovereignty was inextricably linked to the ideal of the state as a unified power embodying the common social purpose of the community. However, this political concept of sovereignty expressed in the unity of the state became transformed into an idea of 'a right of law within the state'.[63] But for Laski, as between the right of law, and the unity of the state, 'In any conflict, the state is *a priori* bound to triumph because the aspect of man that it expresses is common to us all'.[64] However, Laski recognised that empirically, it was government that lay at the heart of the state and government did not necessarily protect the interests of the community as a whole. In this way, the Hegelian ideal of the state as the highest expression of social purpose gave way to the particularistic goals of whoever held the levers of power. Moreover this meant that,

> '. . . the legal theory of sovereignty can never offer a basis for a working philoso-phy of the state. For a legal theory of sovereignty takes its stand upon the beati-fication of order; and it does not inquire—and it is not its business to inquire—into the purposes of the order maintained'.[65]

It was through the centralisation of power in the institution of Parliament—with the consequential constitutionalisation of its legislative supremacy—that a ruling class, educated and trained within a particular political morality, could effectively govern. What for Dicey is the virtue of the unified matrix of legal and political authority was, for Laski, the vice of the continuity of a particular form of social order under the British constitution.

As a corrective to the concentration of power in the hands of an elite, Laski advocated the decentralisation of power, not just in the administra-tion of government, but also the allocation of discrete functional tasks to governmental bodies. He preferred institutional experimentation in govern-ment over the settled form of power implied by what he termed the 'monis-tic conception of the state'. Laski, unlike Dicey, would have felt at home

---

[63] HJ Laski, *The Foundations of Sovereignty* (London, Allen and Unwin, 1921).
[64] *Ibid*, p. 26.
[65] *Ibid*, p. 29.

with contemporary experiments in devolution.

A more contemporary sceptical view which again seeks to shift attention towards issues of political authority and the role of government can be found in John Griffith's discussion of the 'working constitution'.[66] In attacking Sedley's image of a bi-polar sovereignty resting in Parliament and the courts, Griffith contends that Parliament is itself not sovereign in the sense of having the last word, for it is controlled by a highly autonomous Executive. And, whereas common lawyers see this autonomy as a fault in the system to be corrected by the development of an alternative sovereignty in the courts, for Griffith, the UK constitution is premised upon the very centrality of government. Constitutional continuity does not take the form of a continuity of legal authority (whether of Parliament or the common law) but instead there is a continuity of political authority vested in government.

Thus, Griffith denies that any one institution possesses sovereignty. Rather, there is a functional differentiation between the tasks of Parliament, government, and courts; in this relationship it is government that dominates. Griffith is particularly keen to ensure that courts remain within a limited constitutional role of upholding the laws that government enacts through Parliament and of carrying out judicial review but without substantive review of policy decisions.

Of course, if what sovereignty really means is that the courts are to give effect to the laws that *governments* enact through Parliament, this itself creates a problem for Griffith in that government can use that power in ways which alter the balance of power in his 'working constitution' such as the Human Rights Act which he criticises. Only if certain political limitations on government exist can his constitution work. But in the absence of a 21st century political consensus or political morality, it is far from clear how government is itself to be stopped from exercising the very power which Griffith is so keen for it to have.

Where Griffith's insight is a useful corrective lies in respect of EU membership as it is evident that it is the Executive which dominates the negotiation and ratification of Treaties; something which neither Parliament nor the courts can control. It is also clear that in the UK, the successful enactment of legal provisions providing for initial EU membership as well as subsequent changes in light of Treaty revisions is not dependent upon processes of constitutional adjudication or referendum as in some other EU states, but instead is dependent upon the government of the day possessing the requisite majority to enable the appropriate legislation to be passed. In more day to day terms, membership of the EU also enhances domestic Executive autonomy, notwithstanding the creation of

---

[66] JAG Griffith, 'The Common Law and the Political Constitution' (2001) 117 *Law Quarterly Review* 42.

Parliamentary scrutiny mechanisms.

Conversely, however, one of the effects of EU membership has been the empowerment of the domestic courts to utilise EU law to constrain substantively the policy choices of national governments. Griffith's concept of the 'political constitution' fails to keep pace with the very changes that government can bring about to that constitution, not least of which is the effects of the substantive and constitutional law of the EU within the UK.

3. CONCLUSIONS

This chapter has explored the themes of continuity and change through four different approaches to sovereignty in the UK. Orthodoxy struggles to reconcile the changing context of governance with a continuity of political and legal authority centralised in Parliament and supported by a separation of powers between Parliament and Courts. Common law constitutionalists happily accommodate change within a narrative of the continuity of authority of the common law. And yet it is clear that the concept of the common law has itself evolved from an anti-rationalist, inductive and pragmatic idea of the constitution into one that claims its rationality in terms of its deductive and principled order not unlike the entrenched constitutions of other states. Pluralism seeks to accommodate the development of new sites of legal and political authority beyond the state with the claims to authority of states once considered sovereign. Scepticism identifies legal sovereignty as itself a historical achievement within the UK, but one that conceals or distorts the very political order upon which legal authority rests. However, insofar as it seeks to refocus our attention on government, it sometimes seems blinded to the role played by government itself in changing the balance of the constitution.

Not least at the level of ideas, sovereignty is, and always has been in transition in the (dis)United Kingdom.

15

Do Not Mention the Word: Sovereignty in Two Europhile Countries: Belgium and The Netherlands

BRUNO DE WITTE[1]

1. INTRODUCTION

AT A MOMENT in time when there is much attention towards, and some evidence of, convergence between the public law rules and principles of European countries,[2] the concept of sovereignty offers a striking example of continuing divergence in constitutional thought among European countries (more so, admittedly, than in their actual constitutional practice). Belgium and the Netherlands are probably situated at one end of this spectrum, the end at which sovereignty is barely recognised to exist and is not allowed to put obstacles in the way of European integration or international cooperation. However, there are also major differences *between* Belgium and the Netherlands in this respect, so that one cannot lump them together into a generic 'Benelux' position. Both countries may well be politically pro-European, but sovereignty occupies a more prominent place in Belgian constitutional law than in Dutch law. Indeed, one might say that the legal-philosophical picture is the opposite from the political: Belgian political elites are, generally speaking, more ardent promoters of European federalism than their Dutch counterparts, but the Belgian Constitution, and the Belgian constitutional tradition, is less favourable to international cooperation and European integration than the

[1] I am grateful to Leonard Besselink and Jean-Victor Louis for their comments on an earlier version.
[2] See, for a variety of perspectives, P Beaumont, C Lyons and N Walker (eds), *Convergence and Divergence in European Public Law* (Oxford, Hart Publishing, 2002).

Constitution of the Netherlands. One must, however, add immediately that this distinction is more visible at the overall level of constitutional theory than at the level of day-to-day practice of the application and enforcement of international and European law. Both Belgian and Dutch courts comply rather well with their concrete duties under Community law, they actively refer preliminary questions to the ECJ and have never so far refused, or even threatened to refuse, to recognise the supremacy of EC law over domestic law.[3]

I will deal with the two countries in separate sections. In both cases, I will pay attention first to the *internal* constitutional status of the principle of sovereignty and then to the *external* role of sovereignty, particularly in relation to the European integration process. I will conclude with a few words on the potential relevance of the 'Benelux' attitude to sovereignty for the rest of Europe.

2. BELGIUM

(a) 'Tous les pouvoirs émanent de la Nation'

Belgium might, at first sight, appear to be a promising case of 'plural sovereignties'. The unitary state was gradually transformed, from 1970 onwards, into a federal state with extensive legislative and even treaty-making powers for the sub-national authorities (three Communities and three Regions). The country is also known to be deeply divided along cultural-linguistic lines. Curiously however, these major constitutional and political upheavals have not radically altered the established concept of sovereignty. Many of the provisions of the 1831 Constitution (which served as a liberal model-constitution during the whole 19th century) are still in place, and among them is Article 33 (formerly numbered as Article 25) which solemnly states: 'All powers stem from the Nation'.[4] This phrase deliberately echoes a provision of the French Declaration of Rights of 1789; it is fully within the ideological tradition of the French revolution and proclaims the sovereignty of

---

[3] See the evidence assembled in the national reports for the FIDE Congress of 2000: JW de Zwaan, 'The Netherlands (judiciary and authorities) and Article 10 of the EC-Treaty', (2000) 48 *Sociaal-economische wetgeving* 132; A Verhoeven, 'The Application in Belgium of the Duties of Loyalty and Co-operation', (2000) 48 *Sociaal-economische wetgeving* 328.

[4] In the French version of the Constitution: '*Tous les pouvoirs émanent de la nation*'. The article continues as follows: '*Ils sont exercés de la manière établie par la constitution*'.

what was, in 1831, called the 'Nation' and would now, if the article had to be rewritten, be called the 'people'.[5]

In constitutional terms, therefore, there is no Flemish nation or Walloon nation, but only a Belgian nation. In the political and constitutional literature, federalism is obviously a central issue, and the constitutional future of the country is the object of speculation and proposals, but there is no role, in all this, for a theoretical debate on sovereignty, nor is sovereignty used as a political rallying cry by one side or the other (as it is, for example, in Québec). Unlike in other plurinational states, the member states of the Belgian federation (essentially, Flanders and Wallonia) do not correspond to historically constituted nations that could claim original rights that were never surrendered to the state.[6] Flanders and Wallonia never before existed as independent or autonomous units; the city-states and principalities of the *Ancien Régime* had different names and different territories.

Whatever the historical or ideological reasons, the fact is that the several recent rounds of constitutional reform that put in place the federal system have not so far touched the sovereignty principle of Article 33. This does not mean that Article 33, by its own force, could be an effective obstacle to further federalisation or even to a hypothetical dissolution of the country, if the political *rapport de force* work to in that direction. Article 33 would then be modified, or disappear together with the country.

(b) 'Militante européenne de toujours'[7]

The second phrase of Article 33 (ex-Article 25) of the Belgian Constitution states that the powers, stemming from the Nation, must be exercised in the way mandated by the Constitution.[8] This clause, whose original and primary function is to entrench the internal separation of powers between parliament and government (and, in 1831, the King), subsequently assumed the secondary function of prohibiting the delegation of state powers to other states or international bodies. This 'external' implication of Article 33 became prob-

---

[5] The Nation was composed of all the citizens with full political rights, at that time only a small minority of the adult citizens. Now that the franchise has been extended to all adult citizens (the right to vote being extended to women only after the Second World War), the 'Nation' effectively coincides with the 'people'. Therefore, Article 33 is now, in my view, essentially similar to the clauses of 20th century European constitutions, such as those of France, Germany, Italy and Ireland, that vest sovereignty in the people. For a different view, that continues to contrast sovereignty of the *nation* with sovereignty of the *people*, see M Uyttendaele, *Regards sur un système institutionnel paradoxal. Précis de droit public belge* (Bruxelles, Bruylant, 1997), at 42–3.

[6] On the historiographic dimension of the sovereignty debate in other plurinational states, see Michael Keating's chapter in the present volume.

[7] Words borrowed from a commentary in *Le Monde* 5 July 2001, p. 4: '*Militante européenne de toujours, la Belgique ne peut être suspectée de vouloir retarder le processus de l'intégration, au contraire*'.

[8] See n 4 above.

lematic in the immediate post-war period, when Belgium actively helped to create international organisations with powers to take binding decisions applying to and within their member states. Unlike France, Italy and Germany, Belgium ratified the ECSC Treaty and, a few years later, the EEC Treaty without having enacted an express constitutional provision allowing for the transfer of powers to international organisations. In a joint legal opinion for the government, written in 1953, professors from each of the (then) four Belgian law schools expressed the view that actual membership of the ECSC and the envisaged membership of a European Defence Community and a European Political Community were contrary to the Constitution as it stood (in particular its Article 25), and that a new article should be inserted in the Constitution, expressly allowing for a transfer of powers to international organisations.[9] A debate developed on this issue, both in Parliament and in the constitutional law community, but it took sixteen years until, in 1970, a new Article 25bis was inserted in the Constitution to plug the gap. This article, since renumbered as Article 34, allows for the transfer of powers to international organisations. In the twenty years preceding this constitutional reform, Belgian membership of the European Communities may well have been unconstitutional, but in the absence of a constitutional review mechanism, there was no judicial authority to confirm this!

Article 34 reads as follows (in French): '*L'exercice de pouvoirs déterminés peut être attribué par un traité ou par une loi à des institutions de droit international public*'. This short provision is at the same time very open-ended in its scope and rather traditional in its spirit and terms.[10] Its open-ended scope is shown by the fact that the transfer of powers is not made subject to the respect of certain substantive principles (unlike, for instance, in Article 23 of the German Constitution), and that the approval of treaties transferring powers to international organisations is not made subject to any special form of parliamentary assent; such treaties can be approved by a simple majority in both houses of the federal Parliament and/or the various regional parliaments.[11]

---

[9] *Avis donné au Gouvernement par MM. Georges Dor, WJ Ganshof van der Meersch, Paul de Visscher et AJ Mast au sujet des dispositions constitutionnelles qu'il y aurait lieu de réviser en vue de permettre l'adhésion de la Belgique à une communauté politique supranationale*, 17 April 1953, reprinted in P-F Smets, *Les traités internationaux devant le Parlement (1945–55)* (Bruxelles, Bruylant, 1978) at 528–49. Note that one of the authors of the report, Ganshof van der Meersch, later became *procureur-général* of the Court of Cassation and was, in that capacity, the chief inspirer of the *Le Ski* judgment of 1971 mentioned in the text, below.

[10] For an analysis of the text of this article, in the context of the preceding discussions, see JV Louis, 'L'article 25 bis de la Constitution belge', (1970) *Revue du marché commun* 410.

[11] The role of regional parliaments in the approval of treaties is, obviously, of more recent origin. In the present federal system, treaty-making competence is divided in parallel with the internal division of competences between the central State, the Regions and the Communities. Thus, the Treaty of Amsterdam, which is a powers-transferring treaty in the sense of Article 34, is a mixed agreement in Belgian constitutional terms and required the approval of the various assemblies of the central State, the Communities and the Regions.

The traditional nature of Article 34 is apparent, first, from the fact that it refers to 'international institutions', and does not make specific mention of the European Communities, although these are obviously included. The second, and conceptually more important, traditional feature of the new rule is that it was inserted in the Constitution immediately after Article 33 (ex Article 25). Thus, a close connection was established between the traditional principle of national sovereignty and the new attribution of powers clause. In the parliamentary debates on the reform, this connection was emphasised again and again. The intention of the constitutional legislator was to make clear that the allocation of powers to international organisations does not amount to a partial abandonment of sovereignty. Only the *exercise* of powers may be transferred, which implies that these powers will return to the institutions of the state upon termination of the treaty or some other event in the future.

Therefore, the cautious language of Article 34 is the language of *the common exercise of sovereignty* rather than that of the *division of sovereignty*. On the other hand, there is a strong current of scholarly opinion that contests this approach. Belgian professors of European law have been among the most prominent defenders of the concept of *divided sovereignty* as an intellectual tool for understanding the relation between the European Union and its member states.[12] There seems to be a contrast, here, between the federalist views of many Belgian legal scholars and politicians and the rather more traditional intergovernmentalist language of the Constitution.

The 1970 reform did not address the question of the *relation between international law and national law*, on which the Constitution remained entirely silent. However, only one year after the enactment of the new Article 25bis, the Court of Cassation gave a resounding judgment on that question in the case *Franco-Suisse Le Ski*. The well-known *Le Ski* judgment affirmed the primacy of directly effective provisions of international treaties over domestic law.[13] This primacy was based on the very nature of international law. After asserting the supremacy of international treaties in general, the Court went on:

---

[12] JV Louis, *The Community Legal Order*, 2nd ed (Luxembourg, Office for Official Publications of the EC, 1990) at 11 *ff*; P Pescatore, 'L'apport du droit communautaire au droit international public', 6 (1970) *Cahiers de droit européen* 501, at 502–11. Louis is professor of European law at the University of Brussels; Pescatore is a citizen of Luxembourg (and was a member of the ECJ on behalf of his country) but was also, for many years, professor of European and international law at the University of Liège.

[13] See the thorough analysis of *Le Ski*, put in the context of the evolution of the case-law of the Belgian courts before and after 1971, by H Bribosia, 'Applicabilité directe et primauté des traités internationaux et du droit communautaire. Réflexions générales sur le point de vue de l'ordre juridique belge', 29 (1996) *Revue belge de droit international* 33, at 58 *ff*; more briefly, by the same author: 'Report on Belgium', in AM Slaughter, A Stone Sweet and JHH Weiler (eds), *The European Court and National Courts—Doctrine and Jurisprudence. Legal Change in Its Social Context* (Oxford, Hart Publishing, 1998) 1, at 10 *ff*.

'this is a fortiori the case when a conflict exists, as in the present case, between a norm of municipal law and a norm of Community law;

the reason is that the treaties which have created Community law have instituted a new legal system in whose favour the member-states have restricted the exercise of their sovereign powers in the areas determined by those treaties'.[14]

It has often been noted that this wording is close to that used by the ECJ in *Costa v ENEL*,[15] and that *Le Ski* is the national supreme court judgment that probably comes closest to what, in the ECJ's view, is the ideal attitude for a domestic court to adopt. In one respect, though, the *Le Ski* paragraph cited above differs from *Costa v ENEL*, namely where it refers to a restriction of the *exercise* of sovereign powers.[16] This wording, in fact, echoes the then recently enacted Article 34 of the Belgian Constitution, and seems to relate recognition of EC law supremacy to the constitutional authorisation of limitations of sovereignty. However, this comes merely as an afterthought in a judgment that deals with international treaties in general and finds a basis for their privileged position in the domestic legal order in the *pacta sunt servanda* principle of international law, rather than in the limitations of sovereignty clause of the Constitution.

The *Le Ski* judgment did not openly address the question of a conflict between an international treaty and the national *constitution*. A debate on this emerged only after the creation, in the 1980's, of a specialised constitutional court, the Court of Arbitration. Although the jurisdiction of this Court is essentially limited to *federal* matters (conflicts of powers and of norms between the federal and sub-national levels of government), it has assumed the power to decide whether parliamentary acts of assent to an international treaty are compatible with the Constitution. This power, which is exercised *a posteriori*, ie, once parliamentary approval has been given and the treaty has (presumably) been ratified, logically implies that the Constitution is considered to prevail over contrasting provisions of international treaties. That conflict rule has been applied by the Court of Arbitration only to 'ordinary' international treaties so far, but there is no theoretical reason why it could not also exercise this power with regard to the EC and EU Treaties, and to secondary law based on these treaties. So, contrary to what is sometimes thought by observers abroad (who are seduced by the sweeping language of *Le Ski*), the primacy of EC law over national constitutional law is not clearly established in Belgium. A prominent constitutional law professor wondered how a Belgian court could ever give precedence to an international treaty over the Constitution which is the

---

[14] English translation borrowed from H Bribosia, 'Report on Belgium', above n 13, at 17.
[15] On which, see the chapter by Gráinne de Búrca in this volume.
[16] As noted by H Bribosia, 'Report on Belgium', above n 13, at 17.

source of the court's own judicial powers.[17] This position has some logical force, and corresponds to the views of most constitutional lawyers and courts in most European countries.

However, in Belgium itself, this is a contested view. The attitude of the *Cour d'Arbitrage* is at odds with the spirit (though not the letter[18]) of *Le Ski*, and it was strongly criticised by *Avocat-Général* Velu of the *Cour de Cassation* in an official speech,[19] as well as by several legal scholars.[20] In 1996, the Council of State (acting in its capacity of administrative court) joined the ranks of this opposition by strongly affirming the primacy of EC law over national constitutional law.[21] Interestingly enough, the basis for this conflict rule was found by the *Conseil d'Etat* to reside, not in the very nature of international or European law (as in *Le Ski*), but in Article 34 of the Constitution: the transfer of judicial powers to the ECJ, made in accordance with that article of the Constitution, implies that the ECJ's interpretation of the Treaties must be followed, and hence also its case-law affirming the primacy of EC law over national constitutional law.[22] The Council of State judgment is somewhat paradoxical. While ranking the Constitution below international law (at least, below EC law), it affirms that this ranking results from a constitutional rule—which seems to imply that it could also be undone by a constitutional reform of Article 34. It thereby reaffirms, in another manner, the ultimate authority of the Belgian Constitution.

Whatever the views taken on this matter by the Council of State (or by the Court of Cassation), it is the Court of Arbitration that may claim to have final judicial authority in constitutional matters. Therefore, this Court could strike down a transfer of powers to the European Union that went beyond the limits traced by Article 34 of the Constitution, for example, on

---

[17] F Delpérée, 'La Belgique et l'Europe', (1992) 12 *Revue française de droit constitutionnel* 643, at 650: 'A quel titre, [le juge] donnerait-il prééminence à un traité international sur la Constitution qui est le siège de sa propre compétence?'

[18] The conflict, in *Le Ski*, was between EC law and *ordinary* legislation, so that the Court did not have to address the question of a conflict between EC law and the Constitution.

[19] J Velu, 'Contrôle de constitutionnalité et contrôle de compatibilité avec les traités', address to the official reassembly of the Cour de Cassation on 1 September 1992, (1992) 111 *Journal des Tribunaux* 729 and 749.

[20] Strong criticism was expressed by JV Louis, 'La primauté, une valeur relative?', (1995) 31 *Cahiers de droit européen* 23. For an account of the debate, see C Naômé, 'Les relations entre le droit international et le droit interne belge après l'arrêt de la Cour d'arbitrage du 16 octobre 1991', (1994) 71 *Revue de droit international et de droit comparé* 24, and H Bribosia, 'Report on Belgium', n 13 above, at 22–8.

[21] Council of State, judgment of 5 November 1996, nr. 62.922, *Orfinger*, published with note by R Ergec, 'La consécration jurisprudentielle de la primauté du droit supranational sur la Constitution', in (1997) 116 *Journal des Tribunaux* 256.

[22] This, at least, seems to be the reasoning of the Council of State in the following laconic sentence of *Orfinger*: 'que, du point de vue constitutionnel belge, l'autorité de l'interprétation donnée au Traité de Rome par la Cour de justice repose sur l'article 34 de la Constitution, quand bien même cette interprétation aboutirait à arrêter les effets d'une partie des articles 8 et 10 de la Constitution.'

the occasion of the Treaty reforms that may result from the 2004 Intergovernmental Conference. It would be wrong, though, to consider the Court of Arbitration as being a particularly Eurosceptic court. It is one of the very few constitutional courts that has decided to refer preliminary questions to the ECJ when the interpretation of EC law seems relevant to the solution of an internal constitutional dispute.[23] It is also quite clear that, in present circumstances, it would do its utmost to avoid finding a conflict between EU law and the Constitution, and that its legal doctrinal views would bow to political expediency. This is a general characteristic of Belgian legal culture, and it would certainly apply to questions of European integration, because of the overwhelming support for the integration process among the political elite of the country. It is quite obvious, in any event, that the word *sovereignty* itself is not the object of any special reverence in Belgium. It is hardly ever used in the legal and political discourse about European integration.

3. THE NETHERLANDS

The Dutch Constitution distinguishes itself by its utter lack of pretension.[24] This is particularly noticeable in matters of ultimate authority. There is no constitutional provision stating (as in Belgium) that all powers proceed from the people (or the nation) and sovereignty does not appear at all in the text of the Constitution, either literally or in a paraphrase. As regards relations with the outside world, the constitutional reform of 1953, which has subsequently been modified only marginally, is marked by total dedication to the values and needs of international cooperation. International treaties that are duly approved by the Dutch Parliament become the highest law of the land and no judge may refuse to apply self-executing provisions of these treaties, or directly effective 'decisions' taken by an international organisation. This privileged status of international law was naturally extended to European Community law, and sovereignty does not act as a limit to all of this.

(a) A 'Lack of Pretension'

The chapter of the Dutch Constitution dealing with the organisation of state power is partly quaint and partly very matter-of-fact. It is quaint in

---

[23] See references and comment in A Verhoeven, n 3 above, at 338; see also X Delgrange and P van Ypersele, 'La révolution discrète', (1997) 116 *Journal des Tribunaux* 431.
[24] LFM Besselink, 'Constitutionele klimatologie', (1998) 73 *Nederlands Juristenblad* 212, at 212.

designating the Parliament with the *ancien régime* term 'Estates-General' (*Staten-Generaal*) and in devoting no less than eighteen articles to a description of the rights, privileges and duties of the King (Queen) and royal family. Its pragmatic nature is shown by the fact that it describes in turn the role of the Queen, of the government (defined as the Queen-and-her-cabinet), of the parliament and of the courts, but that there is no introductory statement explaining how these institutions relate to each other. Article 50 does state that the Parliament 'represents the entire people',[25] but there is no indication that the Queen, or the government, are also indirectly legitimated by the people, nor is there any more general clause relating all these institutions to some ultimate authority. The principle of sovereignty is thus absent from the Dutch Constitution, which is an anomaly in the context of European constitutionalism. According to one Dutch author, the Netherlands forms, together with Denmark and the United Kingdom, the small band of European countries whose constitution snubs the concept of popular sovereignty.[26]

Why is sovereignty absent? This peculiarity of Dutch constitutional law has historical roots.[27] The absence of sovereignty is, at first sight, surprising, given the fact that ideas of popular sovereignty were very prominent during the Dutch Revolt of the late 16th century and helped to shape the constitutional theory and practice of the newly independent Dutch Republic, though they were quite different from the later doctrines of the French revolution.[28] However, the particular constitutional construction of the new Republic left it unclear for the next two centuries whether the ultimate locus of sovereignty was the separate provinces, or rather the Republic as a whole. Moreover, there was a clear break in historical continuity with the replacement of the Confederation by a unitary state (in the final years of the 18th century) and the establishment of a monarchy in this unitary state (in 1815). The semi-absolutist monarchy only very gradually developed into a liberal democratic regime, through a series of piecemeal reforms, none of

---

[25] 'The Estates-General represent the entire Dutch people'. ('*De Staten-Generaal vertegenwoordigen het gehele Nederlandse volk*').

[26] FH van der Burg, *Europees Gemeenschapsrecht in de Nederlandse rechtsorde* (Deventer, Tjeenk Willink, 1998) at 4. Whether the UK should be included in this list is questionable. The British Lord Chancellor recently expressed the view that 'the doctrine of parliamentary supremacy, seen from a modern perspective, is properly to be viewed as an expression of the political sovereignty of the people' (Lord Irvine of Lairg, 'Sovereignty in Comparative Perspective: Constitutionalism in Britain and America', (2001) 76 *New York University Law Review*, 1 at 14). On sovereignty in the United Kingdom, see Kenneth Armstrong's chapter in this volume.

[27] I have borrowed elements of the following historical excursus from LFM Besselink, 'An Open Constitution and European Integration: The Kingdom of the Netherlands', (1996) 44 *Sociaal-economische wetgeving* 192, at 193–5.

[28] EH Kossmann, 'Popular Sovereignty at the Beginning of the Dutch Ancien Régime', (1981) *The Low Countries Historical Yearbook* 1; see also M van Gelderen, *The Political Thought of the Dutch Revolt 1555–90* (Cambridge University Press, 1992), esp. at 265.

which was the kind of complete constitutional overhaul that could have led to the affirmation of a coherent conception of the sovereignty of the people.

The effect of this non-democratic pedigree of the Dutch Constitution was further reinforced by the revival of radical calvinist thinking in the second half of the nineteenth century. It fought the ideological legacy of the French revolution (as was made clear by the name chosen for the radical calvinist political party: the 'Anti-Revolutionary Party'), and particularly the idea that all power flows from the people. For them, true sovereignty was with God. Whilst they gradually came to terms with the liberal democratic state, the radical protestants elaborated the more modest concept of *sovereignty in one's own sphere* ('*soevereiniteit in eigen kring*'). This was the title of a famous speech held by their political leader Abraham Kuyper at the opening of the new (protestant) Free University of Amsterdam, in 1880. Later, H Dooyeweerd, a professor at the same university, developed this political-theological concept in the language of constitutional theory.[29] 'Sovereignty in one's own sphere' can be considered to be the calvinist equivalent of the catholic notion of subsidiarity; this doctrine held that the state, the church, the family, the school and other social institutions all had their own defined territory of action, and that the state should not unduly interfere with the partial sovereignties of the other social institutions, which were all expressions of the ultimate sovereignty of God. The influential political position of the protestant political parties (who participated in government for most of the 20th century) may have helped to inhibit any attempts to insert popular sovereignty in the Constitution. Finally, by the time of the general constitutional revision of 1953, the monarchy may have lost its political power and the traditional ideological 'pillars' of Dutch society may have crumbled, but the new context of European integration and international cooperation would have made the idea of making reference to sovereignty seem old-fashioned and unappealing.

These historical factors, together with the very pragmatic legal culture of the country, may help to explain the lack of interest among Dutch constitutional lawyers in the notion of sovereignty. The pre-modern attitude towards sovereignty, that continued to hold sway in the Netherlands much longer than in other European countries, may have paved the way for its present post-modern attitude of disdain for the concept of sovereignty. The word sovereignty does not appear in the index of the most detailed

---

[29] See, among many other of his publications on the subject: H Dooyeweerd, *De strijd om het souvereiniteitsbegrip in de moderne rechts- en staatsleer* (1950).

commentary of the Constitution.[30] It is simply not part of the Dutch constitutional alphabet.[31]

(b) An Extraordinary Openness

In the title of a report for the FIDE Conference 1996 dealing with the relationship between the Dutch Constitution and European Community law, Besselink called the former 'an open constitution'.[32] This is an understatement. The constitutional reform of 1953 introduced innovative foreign relations provisions which were greeted at the time by a southern neighbour as the most audacious solution ever proposed to the question of the relation between international and domestic law.[33] This qualification is as appropriate today as it was fifty years ago (the other countries' constitutions have not changed that much on this point!). This openness of the Dutch Constitution to international and European law consists essentially of four features:[34]

1) Article 92 of the Constitution allows for legislative, executive and judicial powers to be conferred on international organisations. There is no indication of limits as to the scope or extent of these powers, nor is it specified that such conferral of powers is temporary or subject to respect for some basic constitutional

---

[30] AK Koekkoek (ed), *De Grondwet. Een systematisch en artikelsgewijs commentaar*, 3rd ed (Deventer, Tjeenk Willink, 2000). The only elaborate contribution on the subject that I came across is an article by Van der Tang in a collective volume called 'General Concepts of Constitutional Law': GFM van der Tang, 'Soevereiniteit', in T Holterman *et al* (eds), *Algemene begrippen staatsrecht*, 3rd ed (Zwolle, Tjeenk Willink, 1991) 5. Yet, even this article is more of an essay on the general history of political ideas than a doctrinal study of Dutch constitutional law.

[31] This remark, it should be emphasised, is limited to Dutch *constitutional law* scholarship. Some Dutch *European and international lawyers* write about the evolution of the principle of sovereignty in European law and international law, but these writings do not specifically consider the evolution of Dutch constitutional law. See, for example: R Barents, *De communautaire rechtsorde* (Deventer, Kluwer, 2000), ch. 3 ('Gemeenschapsrecht en soevereiniteit'); N Schrijver, 'The Changing Nature of State Sovereignty', (1999) 70 *British Yearbook of International Law* 65.

[32] Besselink, above n 27.

[33] P de Visscher, 'Les tendances internationales des constitutions modernes', 80 (1952-II) *Recueil des Cours of the Hague Academy* 511, at 569. For a contemporary commentary on the new constitutional provisions, see HF van Panhuys, 'The Netherlands Constitution and International Law', (1953) 47 *American Journal of International Law* 537.

[34] For more details on the following, see Besselink, above n 27; see also M Claes and B de Witte, 'Report on the Netherlands', in AM Slaughter, A Stone Sweet and JHH Weiler (eds), *The European Court and National Courts—Doctrine and Jurisprudence. Legal Change in Its Social Context* (Oxford, Hart Publishing, 1998) 171; and B de Witte, 'Les implications constitutionnelles, pour un Etat, de la participation à un processus d'intégration régionale', in EH Hondius (ed.), *Netherlands Reports to the Fifteenth International Congress of Comparative Law—Rapports néerlandais pour le quinzième congrès international de droit comparé— Bristol 1998* (Antwerpen, Intersentia, 1998) 379.

values. Any international treaty setting up an international organisation, and any of the revisions of the EC and EU Treaty, is therefore covered by this clause.

2) Article 94 of the Constitution states that provisions of international treaties and of decisions adopted by international organisations shall have precedence over conflicting national law, on the sole condition that they are 'binding on anyone' (that is, self-executing). The express grant of primacy not only to treaties but also to decisions of international organisations (including, obviously, secondary EU law) is quite unique.

3) There is a mechanism for the control of the constitutionality of new treaties, but this control is exercised by the Parliament, not by the courts, and it takes place exclusively at the time a treaty is submitted for approval. If the Parliament considers that a treaty contains provisions that deviate from the Constitution, that treaty may only be approved by a two-thirds majority in both houses (this corresponds to the majority required for constitutional revisions).[35] Once a treaty has been approved, either by the ordinary procedure or by the constitution-override procedure, and has entered into force, it is immune from constitutional review by the courts.[36] Therefore, international law effectively has a higher rank within the Dutch legal order than the Constitution itself.

4) The three preceding points apply to international treaties and international decisions in general, but the 1953 reform was enacted with a particular view to the new supranational features of the European Coal and Steel Community. Therefore, the constitutional clauses obviously apply to the European Treaties, and to EC/EU secondary law. However, despite the fact that these constitutional clauses form a perfect 'reception structure' for European law, a majority among Dutch legal scholars go even further and consider that Euopean Community law applies in the Dutch legal order *on its own authority* and *not* because of the operation of Articles 93 and 94 of the Constitution. A leading constitutional commentary disposes of this question in twelve words: 'EC law has primacy over national law quite apart from Article 94'.[37] The same point is made in Kapteyn and VerLoren van Themaat, the leading textbook on European law.[38] This is, in fact, the dominant view among both European and constitutional law scholars, and, indeed, it is only a few constitutionalists who insist that the conditions for the application of EC law must be found in the Constitution. It does not make a prac-

---

[35] Article 91, para. 3, of the Constitution. This special approval procedure was only applied twice in the fifties, and not once to the European (revision) treaties. There was some controversy on whether the approval of the Treaty of Maastricht required recourse to this stringent procedure, but the Parliament decided that it did not. See Besselink, above n 27, at 200–2.

[36] Aricle 120 of the Constitution: 'The constitutionality of acts of parliament and treaties shall not be reviewed by the courts'.

[37] Only ten words in Dutch: 'EG-recht heeft los van art. 94 voorrang boven nationaal recht', accompanied by a footnote referring to the *Costa/ENEL* judgment of the ECJ (FM Vlemminx and MG Boekhorst, 'Artikel 94', in Koekkoek (ed), *De Grondwet*, above n 30, 465, at 477).

[38] In its most recent English edition: 'a Dutch judge, in the event of a conflict with rules of Community law, would refuse to apply the relevant national provisions not on account of incompatibility with Article 94 of the Dutch Constitution but on account of their incompatibility with Community law'. (PJG Kapteyn and P VerLoren van Themaat, *Introduction to the Law of the European Communities*, 3rd ed by LW Gormley (London, Kluwer Law International, 1998) at 552.

tical difference at all which position one adopts, but the majority attitude is symptomatic and quite unique in Europe.

In view of all this, it should come as no surprise that Dutch legal authors have little use for the concept of *sovereignty* when describing the position of the Netherlands within the European legal order. A commentator on the 1953 reform congratulated the government and parliament for not having used 'sovereignty . . . this mystic and therefore dangerous word'.[39] A more recent report by two constitutional lawyers, devoted to the significance of the Dutch Constitution within the framework of the European legal order, does not mention the word sovereignty at all.[40] European law textbooks written by Dutch authors do not mention it either, except for one whose concluding chapter is entitled 'The semi-sovereign state Netherlands'.[41] In the text of that chapter, no further explanation is given of the meaning of the term 'semi-sovereign state'. The chapter offers a concise description of the constitutional changes brought about by European integration with respect to the role of the legislator, the government and the courts, and it evokes the limits of national policy autonomy caused, above all, by the internal market and EMU. Sovereignty is thus used here as most political scientists would use it, as short-hand for a government's capacity to act, but not at all in the formal meaning which it has in other European legal systems, namely as the ultimate legal authority in a polity.

Further evidence of this relaxed attitude to sovereignty can be found in articles by two influential authors who have moved between academia and legal practice and who have thus contributed to shape the views and actions of the Dutch legal community. In an article about the Dutch state in the European Community, published in 1980, Koopmans argued that the concept of sovereignty could still play a useful role in understanding public international law, but no longer in relation to the EC. He justified this eclectic attitude by pointing out that sovereignty was just a construction of the mind; if it did not have explanatory force in a particular context, such as that of the EC, one could discard it without further ado.[42] In a short article written in 1997, Hirsch Ballin expressed the view that European integration had led to a *patchwork of sovereignty*, with part of it transferred to the EU,

---

[39] HF van Panhuys, above n 33, at 552.

[40] IC van der Vlies and RJGM Widdershoven, *De betekenissen van de Nederlandse grondwet binnen de Europese rechtsorde*, Preadviezen van de vereniging voor de vergelijkende studie van het recht van België Nederland (Deventer, Tjeenk Willink, 1998).

[41] R Barents and LJ Brinkhorst, *Grondlijnen van Europees recht*, 10th ed, (Deventer, Tjeenk Willink, 2001) chapter 16.

[42] T Koopmans, 'De Europese Gemeenschappen en het Nederlandse staatsbestel', (1980) *Rechtsgeleerd Magazijn Themis* 276, at 287. Koopmans was consecutively (and among other things) a professor of Constitutional law at the University of Leiden, a judge at the European Court of Justice and an Advocate-General at the *Hoge Raad* (the supreme court in civil and criminal matters).

part of it kept by the member states, and a third part transferred to the EU under strict control by the states (the second and third pillars, essentially).[43] Here again, the meaning of the word sovereignty bears only a dim resemblance to its meaning in contemporary German, French or Italian constitutional doctrine.

The question arises, at this point, whether the rejection of sovereignty also implies that there are no outer constitutional limits to the degree of integration of the Netherlands in the European Union. An opponent of the proposed 1953 reform of the Dutch Constitution wrote that 'it would be recklessly short-sighted to create a constitutional possibility for the Netherlands to commit harakiri as an independent country'.[44] In the almost fifty years since the reforms were made, the Netherlands may not quite have committed harakiri, but one wonders whether they could legally do so under the present constitutional rules. Article 92 does not put any limits to the nature or scope of the powers that may be devolved to international organisations, and treaties that are contrary to the Constitution can nevertheless be approved, provided that there is a two-thirds majority in Parliament. The only limit implied by the text of Article 92 is that powers must be conferred on an *international organisation*, so that a treaty transforming the EU into something altogether different from an international organisation (say, a federal state) would not be covered by the wording of Article 92. In that case, approval of the treaty should be preceded by a revision of Article 92, or by the enactment of a special constitutional provision on European integration. Yet again, if the Dutch Parliament decided to join a fully federal European Union without such a prior revision of the Constitution, there would be no judicial authority to stop this from happening.

4. CONCLUSION: THE BENELUX AS A LABORATORY FOR POST-SOVEREIGNTY?

There are clear differences between the sovereignty traditions of Belgium and the Netherlands. Belgium fits in the continental European tradition in which sovereignty is a central explanatory concept as well as a principle of positive constitutional law. However, the Belgian political consensus in favour of European integration has led to an almost complete neutralisation

---

[43] EMH Hirsch Ballin, 'Soevereiniteit in de Europese Unie', (1997) 72 *Nederlands Juristenblad* 2005, at 2010. Hirsch Ballin was, at various points in time, professor of Constitutional law at the University of Tilburg, the Minister of Justice of the Netherlands, a member of the Senate, and is now a member of the Council of State, which (in the French way) is both the legal advisor of the government and the highest administrative court.

[44] '*Het zou van roekeloze kortzichtigheid getuigen, in de Grondwet de mogelijkheid te openen, dat Nederland als zelfstandig land harakiri pleegt*'. (CHF Polak, 'Grondwet en internationale overeenkomsten', (1952) 27 *Nederlands Juristenblad* 172, at 177).

of the restraining role that sovereignty might have played in this context. The Netherlands have a very idiosyncratic constitutional tradition, in which the concept of sovereignty never came to full fruition in the first place, and is now ignored or rejected for being antiquated and formalistic. If one combines this with the generous openness to international cooperation inaugurated by the constitutional reforms in 1953, and constantly confirmed since, then the Netherlands is undoubtedly situated at one end of the European spectrum of opinion about the relation between 'sovereignty' and 'European integration'.

Both countries, and particularly the Netherlands, could thus be taken as examples of how the philosophical vision of 'post-sovereignty'[45] can correspond to current constitutional reality. It would be tempting to say that in Belgium and the Netherlands, sovereignty is no longer 'in transition' (as in the title of this book), but has already disappeared into the mists of time. In Dutch constitutional law and constitutional thinking, the concept is treated with embarassment (when not entirely shunned), whereas in Belgium, it has become a relic which is still honoured in the text of the Constitution but almost ignored in constitutional practice. The 'body-politics' of these two countries do not seem to need the 'Artificiall Soul' of sovereignty.[46] This state of affairs seems to equip these two countries particularly well to face further developments in European integration and global interdependence. Questions of allocation of power between regional, national, European and international levels of government, and questions of democratic legitimation of the political authorities operating at all these levels, can be addressed in their own terms, without the distorting conceptual filter of sovereignty.

However, the possible model function of the Benelux countries is marred by the fact that they take their constitution less seriously than most other countries, and by the lack of sustained reflection on alternative constitutional theories that could replace sovereignty. Indeed, the pragmatic attitude to national sovereignty displayed by Belgian and Dutch politicians, judges and academics is refreshing but also problematic, because it is combined with a relative lack of interest in building new post-sovereign theories explaining the interaction between the EU and its member states, and beween European law and national law. To be sure, there are legal theorists in the low countries who actively explore general transformations in the concept of sovereignty,[47] but mainstream constitutional or European

---

[45] N MacCormick, *Questioning Sovereignty* (Oxford, Oxford University Press, 1999), chapter 8 ('On Sovereignty and Post-Sovereignty').

[46] The reference is to T Hobbes, *Leviathan, or the Matter, Forme & Power of a Commonwealth Ecclesiasticall and Civil* (1651), at 1.

[47] See, in particular, the chapter by Hans Lindahl in this volume, as well as his 'European Integration: Popular Sovereignty and a Politics of Boundaries', (2000) 6 *European Law Journal* 239.

Union scholarship is giving little help to the project of developing an alternative account of legal pluralism in Western Europe that rejects anachronistic conceptions of sovereignty, but tries to preserve its role as an 'organising frame for the constitution and regulation of old and new political communities' and as 'as a necessary precondition for the continuation of the virtues associated with political community'.[48] In matters of sovereignty, legal scholars in the Benelux countries have become happily agnostic, and are not looking for a new religion or philosophy.

[48] See Neil Walker's introduction to the present volume.

16

State Sovereignty and European Integration: Public International Law, EU Law and Constitutional Law in the Polish Context

CEZARY MIK

1. INTRODUCTION

European integration is perceived as a serious challenge to state sovereignty. It poses fundamental questions as to whether the Member States retain their sovereignty through the integration process and whether sovereignty can be attributed to the European Union. The matter is of enormous importance for public international law, EU law and national law alike. Until recently, sovereignty, closely linked to the concept of the state, constituted the central notion of the concept of 'international community'. In principle, it assumed that inter-State relations are governed by public international law. Every change in the meaning or the role of sovereignty will modify fundamental concepts of international law. For EU law, state sovereignty is also problematic. It encourages us to reflect upon the nature of EU law, and in particular upon the role of the European Union in its relations with the Member States and their national laws. Contemporary states are still very attached to the idea of sovereignty. They treat it as a basis of their legal existence, and claim it as the cornerstone of domestic law.

These dilemmas will be discussed from three perspectives: public international law, EU law and Polish constitutional law. Neither the philosophical nor the political context will be considered here. Sovereignty will be examined from an external point of view: so-called national (or popular) sovereignty will be excluded, except insofar as it relates to State sovereignty. The starting point will be the perception of state sovereignty in public international law. This is because state sovereignty is not the product of European integration, but has been shaped over centuries. The purpose of this part of the inquiry is to establish the legal substance of sovereignty in the light of international texts and jurisprudence (section 2). The EU law perspective will then be examined. Here considerations will focus on whether sovereignty is a basis or a barrier to European integration and whether it is a useful tool to explain the mechanisms of integration (section 3). In the context of Polish accession to the EU, the point of view of Polish constitutional law is of additional interest. The main questions here are what is the meaning of sovereignty in Polish law and how will the Constitution perceive Poland's sovereignty after EU accession? (Section 4).

2. SOVEREIGNTY IN PUBLIC INTERNATIONAL LAW

A. In search of the substance of sovereignty

(i) General historical and theoretical remarks—the main axes of debate

Sovereignty is certainly a venerable concept in international law. However, many problems remain unresolved. Its *origins* are controversial. We know neither when sovereignty was born nor where to search for its origins (whether in Europe or outside). It is unclear whether it is sufficient to identify sovereignty as merely a socio-political phenomenon or whether it is necessary to prove the existence of clear concepts using the notion of sovereignty itself. If we reject an 'ahistorical' approach to the idea and the substance of sovereignty (its contemporary perception) and if we define it as a legal and political phenomenon, we find sovereignty even in Antiquity.[1] Opinions can also be found that sovereignty appeared as late as the Middle Ages (12th – 14th centuries) as a consequence of the victory of European monarchies in the struggle for independence from the Popes and German Emperors.[2] Finally, a very popular point of view is that sovereignty appeared in the Modern Age (around the 17th century), and more particu-

---

[1] DJ Bederman, *International Law in Antiquity*, (Cambridge University Press, Cambridge 2001), chapter 2. Bederman suggests that 'Ancient States had a self-perception of sovereignty. Indeed, ancient States may have had too-robust sense of self: ethnic, linguistic, religious, and cultural particularism defined ancient States. These factors of separation— of 'differentness' — impelled the creation, expansion, and death of ancient polities. The great Near Eastern empires, the Greek poleis, and Western Mediterranean States all embraced these particularistic features. And they all were capable, by virtue of political centralisation, economic wealth, and military might, of concentrating power to manage relations with other polities. If sovereignty is simply the power and willingness to exclude others from a national territory, ancient States were, most certainly, sovereign' (at 274).

[2] I Popiuk-Rysińska, *Suwerenność w rozwoju stosunków międzynarodowych*, (DWH 'ELIPSA', Warszawa 1993), at 15–35. She views the problem of sovereignty's origins from the perspective of rivalry between the universalism of emperors and popes and the independence of European kings and princes.

larly after the Westphalian treaties in Münster and Osnabrük[3] were concluded (in 1648). If we treat sovereignty first and foremost as a conceptualised idea of law—where the express notion of sovereignty appears—we would have to accept that it has existed since the 13th century or at least since J Bodin's famous book on the State: *De Republica Libri Six* (1576).[4] Sovereignty was introduced into the realm of international law by the classic writers of the 16th and 17th centuries, such as Vitoria, Suarez, Gentili, Grotius, and de Vattel.[5]

The *substance* of sovereignty is also highly disputed. Traditionally, in the doctrine of international law, sovereignty is closely connected with power. The so-called absolute theory of sovereignty, shaped under the influence of the 19th century German school of thought (Hegel, Lasson, etc.,), describes it as the unlimited authority of the state. Sovereignty in this understanding is absolute and indivisible, temporally and territorially unlimited, and is not a transferable power, but rather an inherent attribute of the State. It consists in absolute independence and freedom, leaving no place for international law. Jellinek presented a more cautious version of the concept. He believed that the State can undertake obligations and limit its freedom without losing sovereignty. For him, sovereignty was 'the ability of exclusive self-determination and thus self-limitation'. This option is very popular in theory today. Its contemporary intellectual successor is the German theory of *Kompetenz-Kompetenz*. The State is sovereign when it has the competence to determine the limits of its own specific competencies, when it has the power to have the last word.[6] A modified absolute theory of sovereignty is also accepted in the Polish literature on international law. Polish doctrine drew a distinction between sovereignty and its exercise. Sovereignty itself

---

[3] R Müllerson, *Ordering Anarchy. International Law in International Society*, (Martinus Nijhoff Publishers, The Hague/Boston/London 2000), at 90. In his opinion the Westphalian Peace was anti-hegemonic. For an opposite point of view see A Osiander, 'Sovereignty, International Relations, and the Westphalian Myth', (2001), 55 *International Organisation* No. 2, passim, in particular at 262, 266–8, 270–3, 284. The author suggests that the idea of sovereignty being born in Westphalia is wrong. It results from the propaganda organised by King Gustaf Adolf against the 'universal monarchy' and 'absolute dominion' of the Habsburgs (at 263).

[4] See FX Perrez, *Cooperative Sovereignty. From Independece to Interdependence in the Structure of International Environmental Law*, (The Hague/London/Boston Kluwer Law International, 2000), chapter 1. The Author mentions (at 18 and footnote 44), quoting eg Jan Bartelson's book on the genealogy of sovereignty, that the term was used for the first time by Beaumanoir in the 13th century. At that time sovereignty was considered as a tool to postulate the independence of the Emperor and Pope (sic!). Initially, it was a political concept describing the independence of the prince and then slowly transformed into a legal term.

[5] Ch-A Morand, 'La souverenaité, un concept dépassé à l'heure de la mondialisation?' In L Boission de Chazournes, V Gowlland-Debbas (eds)., *The International Legal System in Quest of Equity and Universality. Liber Amicorum Georges Abi-Saab*, (The Hague/London/Boston, Martinus Nijhoff Publishers 2001), at 155–7.

[6] FX Perrez, op. cit, at 39–45, together with critics of the absolute theory of sovereignty.

was understood as a supreme and unlimited authority. Only its exercise could be restricted.[7] The newer doctrine, however, accentuates the idea that sovereignty is freedom, but not arbitrariness to act. It is subordinated to the authority of international law.[8] An opposing concept of sovereignty perceived as power is found in the theory of relative (divisible, dispersed) sovereignty.[9] Based on different social phenomena (globalisation, transnational activities, democratisation, international integration), it demonstrates that sovereignty is a changing concept rather than a fixed parameter.[10]

When sovereignty is perceived as power, its different aspects remain distinct. One writes about internal sovereignty as opposed to external sovereignty.[11] From another perspective three planes of sovereignty are identified: personal sovereignty (supremacy), territorial sovereignty (supremacy) and organisational sovereignty.[12]

Taking into account the different functions of sovereignty, we can distinguish between negative and positive theories. The most frequent way of presenting sovereignty consists in accentuating its negative side. Sovereignty is freedom, autonomy, State independence from any other centres of power.[13] An interesting aspect of this theory is that State sovereignty here means independence from other States and not from international organisations, or from international integration.[14] Some authors argue, however, that contemporary sovereignty also has a positive side. The starting point of their reasoning, formulated in the context of environmental law, is that sovereignty cannot mean the same in the world of sailing boats as in the world of satellites. Sovereignty is a dynamic, variable idea which

---

[7] L Ehrlich, *Prawo międzynarodowe*, (Wydawnictwo Prawnicze, Warszawa 1958), at 123–5; C. Berezowski, *Prawo międzynarodowe publiczne*, (cz. 1, PWN, Warszawa 1966), at 90–1.

[8] L Antonowicz, *Państwa i terytoria. Studium prawnomiędzynarodowe*, (PWN, Warszawa 1988), at 32; W Czapliński, A Wyrozumska, *Prawo międzynarodowe publiczne. Zagadnienia systemowe*, (Warszawa, C. H. Beck 1999), at 114–5; J Barcz, 'Suwerenność w procesach integracyjnych' in W Czapliński, I Lipowicz, T Skoczny, M Wyrzykowski (eds.), *Suwerenność i integracja europejska*, (Warszawa, Centrum Europejskie Uniwersytetu Warszawskiego, 1999), at 31–2.

[9] Generally see R Müllerson, above n 3, at 127–134.

[10] On this theory see B Kingsbury, 'Sovereignty and Inequality', (1998), 9 *European Journal of International Law* at 610–8. Very similar in effects is the theory of the dualisation of sovereignty. See J-D Mouton, 'L'Etat selon le droit international: diversité et unité' in *L'Etat souverain à l'aube du XXIᵉ siècle*. (Paris, Colloque de Nancy, Editions A Pédone, 1994), at 88–93 (together with its critics).

[11] See, eg, A Bleckmann, commentary to art. 2 (1), in B Simma (ed.), *The Charter of the United Nations. A Commentary*, (Oxford, Oxford University Press 1995), at 79–80.

[12] See, eg, B Kingsbury, above n 10, at 615.

[13] See J Touscoz, *Droit international*, (Paris, PUF 1993), at 67–8; J Kranz, 'Suwerenność państwowa' in WJ Wotpiuk (ed.), *Spór o suwerenność*, (Warszawa, Wydawnictwo Sejmowe 2001), at 105–6.

[14] A Wasilkowski, 'Uczestnictwo w strukturach europejskich a suwerenność państwowa', (1996), *Państwo i Prawo* no. 4–5, at 20.

'has to be examined in relation to its historical context, political practice, related theoretical terms and the needs and requirements of its time'.

Changing circumstances over centuries have not led to its demise. On the contrary, sovereignty has adapted itself perfectly to new conditions. Today, sovereignty means, above all, the authority to be a member of the international community. Resulting from the social nature of sovereignty, it involves responsibility understood as 'a generalised charge or duty to fulfil an obligation' to co-operate. Sovereignty as responsibility to co-operate 'requires all sovereign states to co-operate and to contribute in good faith to the best solution of the common problems'. It

'creates a common, but differentiated responsibility to co-operate. Thereby, the new approach to sovereignty addresses possible fears of the weaker, poorer and less developed states of being subject to a new hidden and more sophisticated colonialism or imperialism of developed states'.[15]

An analytical approach to sovereignty encourages us to consider its *legal nature*. Unfortunately, there is no clear consensus in the field of international law either. First, for some authors sovereignty is a social fact (or can be described as such), whereas for others it is a concept created by law. In the former case sovereignty is pre-legal.[16] In the latter it can be a legal notion, a principle, or a legal rule. When sovereignty is presented as a legal notion it is identified as a virtue of the State, a specific quality of its power. As such it helps to distinguish the State from other subjects of international law.[17] Sovereignty perceived as a principle, or, and in particular, as a legal rule, can be equated with a sum of powers. As a legal term sovereignty is only partially linked to social reality. It belongs to *Sollen* rather than to *Sein*.[18]

(ii) Different manifestations of sovereignty in contemporary international law

In international instruments and jurisprudence of the 20th and 21st centuries, sovereignty is expressly present in different forms. The following, at least, can be identified: sovereignty *per se*, sovereign equality, territorial sovereignty, sovereign rights and permanent sovereignty over natural resources. An analysis will help us to understand what sovereignty really is in public

---

[15]   FX Perrez, op. cit, at 245–246 and at 331ff.
[16]   In this regard see A Klafkowski, *Prawo międzynarodowe publiczne*, (Warszawa, PWN 1979), at 140.
[17]   J Barcz, above n 8, at 31–2; J Kranz, above n 13, at 105–7.
[18]   J Verhoven observes that sovereignty as a socio-political fact can not be found at all. J Verhoven, 'Suwerenność i integracja: kilka konkretnych zagadnień' in E Poptawska (ed.), *Konstytucja dla rozszerzającej się Europy*, (Warszawa, Instytut Spraw Publicznych 2000), at 62.

international law. Moreover, it is necessary to consider how sovereignty as a general concept relates to such notions as (political) independence, jurisdiction and national sovereignty. Finally, it is necessary to tackle the problem of the so-called limitation of sovereignty (or sovereign rights).

(iii) Sovereignty per se

It seems that sovereignty as a notion first appeared in scholars' texts. We do not know exactly when it was introduced into positive international law (jurisprudence, resolutions and, especially, treaties). In the period before and immediately after the First World War it was not as popular as it is today. In fact, sovereignty was not clearly recognised as a principle in the *Covenant of the League of Nations* (sovereign equality even less so). However, it can be found in article 22 in the context of 'colonies and territories which [. . .] have ceased to be under the sovereignty of the States which formerly governed them [. . .]'. In that sense, Max Huber, the arbiter, in the Case of Palmas Islands (1928) decided that

> 'Sovereignty in the relations between States signifies independence. Independence in regard to a portion of the globe is the right to exercise therein, to the exclusion of any other State, the functions of a State'.[19]

Today, the term 'sovereignty' appears very often in treaties and resolutions of international organisations. Sovereignty is present, for instance, in the *Convention on International Civil Aviation* of 1944. Article 1 of the Convention states: 'The Contracting States recognise that every State has complete and exclusive sovereignty over airspace above its territory'.[20] According to the *Treaty on Principles Governing the Activities of States in the Exploration and Use of Outer Space, including the Moon and Other Celestial Bodies* of 1967, outer space cannot be subject to national appropriation by claims of sovereignty by any means (article II).[21] Article 6 (1) of

---

[19] Arbitral Award of 4.4.1928, *passus* quoted in: O Casanovas, *Unity and Pluralism in Public International Law*, (Martinus Nijhoff Publishers, The Hague/New York/London 2001), at 176. See also the individual opinion of Judge Anzillotti in the Case concerning Customs Regime Between Germany and Austria, Advisory Opinion of 19.3.1931, PCIJ Publ., Series B, No. 41, at 24, where he wrote: 'Independence as such understood is really no more than the normal condition of States according to international law; it may also be described as *sovereignty (suprema potestas)*, or external sovereignty, by which is meant that the State has over it no other authority than that of international law'. For the contemporary exposition of that thought (sovereignty implies suprema potestas and summa potestas) see the dissenting opinion of Judge Kreća in the judgment of 11.7.1996, *Case concerning Application of the Convention on the Prevention and Punishment of the Crime of Genocide* (Preliminary Objections), para. 13 (see also para. 4), ICJ Rep., at 4.

[20] Text: H. von Mangoldt and VT. Rittberger (eds.), *The United Nations System and its Predecessors*, vol. I, *The United Nations System*, (Oxford, Oxford University Press 1997), at 1265.

[21] *Ibid.*, at 595.

the *UNESCO Convention for the Protection of World Cultural and Natural Heritage* of 1972 declares that cultural and natural heritage situated on the territory of the Contracting States is recognised as a world heritage, while fully respecting the sovereignty of the states in question.[22] Important statements on sovereignty are included in the *UN Convention on the Law of the Sea* (UNCLOS) of 1982.[23] In particular, article 89 declares that 'No State may validly purport to subject any part of the high sea to its sovereignty'. Furthermore, in article 137 (1) the Convention provides that 'No State shall claim or exercise sovereignty or sovereign rights over any part of the area or its resources [. . .]. No such claim or exercise of sovereignty or sovereign rights [. . .] shall be recognised'.

The term 'sovereignty' is more generously used in treaties constituting regional organisations with general competence.[24] Thus, sovereignty is mentioned in the preamble of the *OAS Charter* (1945). The Member States declare that the

> 'essential value lies in the desire of the American peoples to live in peace and, through their mutual understanding and respect for the sovereignty of each other, to provide the betterment of all, in independence, in equality and under law'.

The states of the Americas have established the OAS in order, eg, to 'defend their sovereignty, their territorial integrity, and their independence' (article 1 (1)). In article 3 they reaffirm, eg, the principle that 'International order consists essentially of respect for the personality, sovereignty, and independence of States [. . .]'. Sovereignty is also present in the *OAU Charter* (1963), designed 'to safeguard and consolidate the hard-won independence as well as the sovereignty and territorial integrity of our states' (preamble). The purpose of the Organisation is, *inter alia*, 'to defend their sovereigns'. One of the fundamental principles is to respect the sovereignty of each state together with the territorial integrity and the right to independent existence (article III (3)). Article IV states that the members of the Organisation can each be an 'independent sovereign African State'. The term sovereignty also appears in the *Charter of the League of Arab States* (1945). The Member States have pledged 'to safeguard their independence and sovereignty' (article II). In article V concerning peaceful settlement of disputes, sovereignty co-exists with and complements state independence and territorial integrity.

Sovereignty can be found in different resolutions. For instance, in the *Declaration on Territorial Asylum* of 1967 sovereignty is a basis for the right to grant asylum. The situation of persons acquiring asylum is, without prejudice to the sovereignty of States, of concern to the international

---

[22] *Ibid.*, at 1122.
[23] 21 *International Legal Materials* 1261 (1982).
[24] All texts quoted in the paper are available on the web-site of the regional organisations.

community (article I (1) and II (1)).[25] In 1978 the General Assembly adopted a resolution on disarmament and arms limitation. This reads:

> 'The arms race impedes the realisation of purposes, and is incompatible with the principles, of the Charter of the United Nations, especially respect for sovereignty, refraining from the threat or use of force against the territorial integrity or political independence of any State [. . .]'.[26]

The UN Security Council often refers to the respect or restoration of (full) sovereignty, independence and territorial integrity, eg in its resolutions concerning sanctions against Iraq or the establishment of peace in Iraq or in Bosnia-Herzegovina.[27] The *Declaration of the UN Conference on the Human Environment* of 1972, approved by the General Assembly, obliges States-Parties of the future multilateral or bilateral arrangements or other appropriate means in the field of environment to take into due account the sovereignty and interests of all States' (principle 24).[28]

Sovereignty also appears in contemporary international jurisprudence. In particular, the ICJ in the *Case concerning Military and Paramilitary Activities in and against Nicaragua* found 'the principle of respect for State sovereignty'. It considered sovereignty as a 'basic legal concept' which has its foundations in customary international law. Sovereignty extends to the internal waters and territorial sea of every state and to the air space of its territory. Its manifestations include sovereign equality and territorial sovereignty.[29]

The above analysis of the idea of sovereignty leads to the following preliminary conclusions: 1) sovereignty is associated exclusively with states. It is a feature of each state. Nonetheless, it is not defined; 2) sovereignty is different from the independence and personality of states; 3) it has the status of a fundamental principle or purpose of the international system; 4) sovereignty is a basis for state rights and claims. However, if they are contrary to other fundamental principles of international law, claims based upon sovereignty will not succeed; 5) sovereignty is associated with the territory of the state; 6) the principle of State sovereignty has a customary-law character; 7) its particular normative manifestations include sovereign equality and territorial sovereignty.

(iv) Sovereign equality

The notion of 'sovereign equality' was first officially incorporated in the *UN Charter* of 1945. At the outset it acquired the status of a legal princi-

---

[25]   H. von Mangoldt and V. Rittberger (eds.), above n 20, at 462.
[26]   *Ibid.*, at 221.
[27]   *Ibid.*, at 655, 658, 664, 667, 713–4.
[28]   *Ibid.*, at 353.
[29]   Judgment of 27.6.1986, para. 212, ICJ Rep., at 111.

ple, the first among the principles mentioned there (article 2 point 1; see also article 78). Sovereign equality as such was, and still is, largely accepted and it has been repeated in many resolutions of UN bodies, especially the General Assembly. The *Declaration on Principles of International Law* of 1970 is a good example (although sovereign equality does not occupy first place there).[30] A newer instance is the *UN Millennium Declaration* adopted on 8th September 2000. The UN Members declared their will 'to support all efforts to uphold the sovereign equality of all States, respect for their territorial integrity and political independence [. . .]'.[31] 'Sovereign equality' was used by the Security Council, a good example being the *Declaration on ensuring an effective role for the Security Council in the maintenance of international peace and security, particularly in Africa* adopted by the Security Council meeting of Heads of States and Governments in the course of the Millennium Summit on 7th September 2000. It contains the following promises:

'Pledges to uphold the Purposes and Principles of the Charter of the United Nations, reaffirms its commitment to principles of sovereign equality, national sovereignty, territorial integrity and political independence of all States'.[32]

Sovereign equality is also confirmed at the regional level. Particular examples can be found in the *OAU Charter* where the sovereign equality of all Member States hand-in-hand with sovereignty per se, constitutes the fundamental principle of the Organisation (article III point 1). Sovereign equality is also present in the *Final Act of the CSCE* of 1975 (Declaration on Principles, principle I).[33] However, sovereign equality is absent in the *OAS Charter* and in the *Charter of the League of Arab States*. In those treaties, sovereignty and equality were separated (see article 3 (b) and 10 of the *OAS Charter*; article 2 and 3 of the *Charter of the LAS*).

'Sovereign equality' is not defined in international treaties or other international instruments. In fact, the expression itself is rather unfortunate. Some authors rightly observe that the term is wrongly formulated. It is not that equality is sovereign, but that the sovereignty of every State is equal.[34] What is the essence of sovereign equality? Article 2 (1) of the *UN Charter*

---

[30] Resolution 2625 (XXV), annex. See also the Charter of Economic Rights and Duties of States — GA Resolution 3281 (XXIX), art. 2 (2c), 17. Texts: H. von Mangoldt and V. Rittberger (eds.), above n 20, at 155–63, 266–78. For further discussion, see Bardo Fassbinder's chapter in the present volume.

[31] A/RES/55/2. The UN web-site.

[32] S/RES/1318 (2000), annex; text of the Declaration: 40 *International Legal Materials* 252 (2000), at 252–4.

[33] Text: A Bloed (ed.), *From Helsinki to Vienna: Basic Documents of the Helsinki Process*, (Dordrecht/Boston/London, Martinus Nijhoff Publishers 1990), at 43–100.

[34] The critics of the principle from travaux préparatoires and a dogmatic perspective, see K Mbaye in the commentary to the Art. 2 (1) of the Charter in JP Cot, A Pellet (eds.), *La Charte des Nations Unies. Commentaire article par article*, (Paris, ECONOMICA 1991), at 84–90.

states shortly: 'The Organisation is based on the principle of the sovereign equality of all its Members'. It does not explain the problem. In this context the *Declaration on Principles of International Law* (1970) is important as an authoritative interpretation of the *UN Charter*. We read here:

'All States enjoy sovereign equality. They have equal rights and duties and are equal members of the international community, notwithstanding differences of an economic, social, political or other nature.
In particular, sovereign equality includes the following elements:
States are juridically equal;
Each State enjoys the rights inherent in full sovereignty;
Each State has the duty to respect the personality of other States;
The territorial integrity and political independence of the State are inviolable;
Each State has the right freely to choose and develop its political, social, economic and cultural systems;
Each State has the duty to comply fully and in good faith with its international obligations and to live in peace with other States'.

Again this explanative formula has been subtly criticised. It is argued that sovereign equality is so general and so capacious as to encompass all principles of international law.[35] Nonetheless, it is clear that the 1970 Declaration elucidates the essence of sovereign equality to some extent. First, it shows that the sovereignty of all states is legally equal ('States are juridically equal'). Secondly, states' rights result from sovereignty. Rights are inherent in full sovereignty.[36] It means that they are not limited and that there is not a 'numerus clausus' of rights. They are presumed in each state ('Each State enjoys the rights inherent in full sovereignty'). As far as sovereign equality is concerned this is, in my opinion, the principal message of the Declaration. Moreover, the Declaration points out that every state has the duty to respect the personality of other states, the duty to comply fully and in good faith with its international obligations and to live in peace with other states. It also mentions the fundamental right stemming from sovereignty: the right of the state freely to choose and develop its political, social, economic and cultural systems.

Sovereign equality appears not only in Cold War documents, but also subsequent ones. It belongs to normative reality both at the universal and—in principle—at the regional level. Sovereign equality is always perceived as fundamental for international relations between states—almost all states of the contemporary world, including members of the European Union. Two ideas: sovereignty and equality are intrinsically connected in the term 'sovereign equality'. Both of them are linked with states. State sovereignty

---

[35] W Czapliński and A Wyrozumska, above n 8, at 118.
[36] A Bleckmann, above n 11, wrote: 'the principle of sovereignty provides a justification for comprehensive powers of the states, eg their 'general freedom of action', at 82.

(as distinct from independence and national sovereignty) is the source of rights of states. Equality plays the role of a universal standard for how the states are treated. In this light Müllerson is correct in writing that sovereign equality is an ordering principle in international society.[37]

(v) Territorial sovereignty

Sovereignty is generally associated with state territory. At the same time it is distinguished from the principle of territorial integrity. Territorial sovereignty is a conceptual expression of the link between sovereignty and territory. This concept was shaped in international jurisprudence. The importance of a territorial basis for sovereignty and the links between territory and the rights resulting from it were highlighted by the International Arbitration Tribunal in the *Case of the Government of the State of Eritrea v. the Government of Republic of Yemen*. It noted that 'According to this modern international law, the legal concept of "territorial sovereignty" became a cornerstone for most of the State powers [. . .]'.[38] According to the ruling of The Arbitration Tribunal in the *Case concerning the utilisation of waters of the Lac Lannoux*, territorial sovereignty profits from this presumption. It may be rebutted only through international obligations.[39]

In the *Case concerning Military and Paramilitary Activities in and against Nicaragua* the ICJ approved the opinion that sovereignty extends to land, sea and air territory, and added that every state has the duty to respect the territorial sovereignty of others. Sovereignty is a basis for state powers. The Court stated: 'It is also by virtue of its sovereignty that the coastal State may regulate access to its ports'.[40] Thus, both courts deemed state powers to be founded on sovereignty having a territorial basis. As far as legal status is concerned, there is no difference between the territorial sovereignty of states.

However, the meaning of territorial sovereignty is not entirely clear. At first glance territorial sovereignty means that sovereignty always has a territorial basis. It is exercised over a certain territory. Nonetheless, a problem may arise when part of a State's territory is transferred to another State. It is questionable whether sovereignty is transferred together with the territory in question. The PCIJ in the *Case concerning Certain German Interests in Polish Upper Silesia prima facie* answered this question positively. It mentions 'the transfer of sovereignty over the portion of Upper Silesia allot-

---

[37] R Müllerson, above n 3, at 122–3.
[38] Award of 9.10.1998, para. 131, 40 *International Legal Material* 900 (2001), at 921. The Tribunal added: 'the concept of territorial sovereignty was entirely strange to an entity such as medieval Yemen'. *Ibid.*, at 923.
[39] Award of 16.11.1957, (1958), 62 *Revue Générale de Droit International Public* at 99.
[40] See footnote no.22, at 111.

ted to Poland'. The Court also noticed that the Treaty of Versailles 'merely contemplates the possible renunciation of sovereignty over the territories in question' and later it considered a 'change of sovereignty'.[41] Similarly the ICJ in the *Case concerning maritime delimitation and territorial questions between Qatar and Bahrain* speaks of acquisition of sovereignty over a territory.[42]

An analogous problem might arise from the derogation from territorial sovereignty in the context of extradition and asylum. However, the reasoning of the ICJ is slightly more rigorous. In the *Asylum Case* the Court observed that in the case of territorial asylum the extradition decision 'implies only the normal exercise of territorial sovereignty'. There is no question of derogation from state sovereignty. On the other hand, in the case of diplomatic asylum such a decision

> 'involves a derogation from the sovereignty of that State. It withdraws the offender from the jurisdiction of the territorial State and constitutes an intervention in matters which are exclusively within the competence of that State. Such a derogation from territorial sovereignty cannot be recognised unless its legal basis is established in each particular case'.[43]

The 'prima facie' impression from these Courts' decisions is that sovereignty is transferable or derogable. But this impression is false. In fact, with the cession of a part of a state's territory only the scope of the territorial basis of sovereignty changes, not sovereignty itself. In the case of diplomatic asylum, the reasoning of the Court is imprecise. It confuses sovereignty and jurisdiction. The acceptance of diplomatic asylum means that a state recognises the limitation of its personal and territorial jurisdiction. Of course, even such a limitation ought to have a clear legal basis and be freely agreed by that State. In this context, one may conclude that sovereignty is inalienable.

(vi) Sovereignty, independence and jurisdiction

The relationship between *sovereignty* and *independence* is considerably confused. In the *Covenant of the League of Nations*, political independence rather than sovereignty was considered as a principle (see article 10). In this context, in the *Case concerning S.S. 'Lotus'* the PCIJ stated that 'International law governs relations between independent States. [. . .] Restrictions upon the independence of States cannot be presumed'.[44] Similarly, in the advisory opinion on *Autonomy of Eastern Carelia* the same

---

[41] Judgment of 25.5.1926, PCIJ Publ., Series A, No. 7, at 29–31.
[42] Judgment of 16.3.2001, para. 206, 40 *International Legal Materials* 847 (2001), at 889.
[43] Judgment of 20.11.1950, ICJ Rep., at 274–275.
[44] Judgment of 7.9.1927, PCIJ Publ., Series A, No. 10, at 18–9.

Court found that article 17 of the Covenant (settlement of disputes) 'only accepts and applies a principle which is a fundamental principle of the independence of States'.[45]

At present, (political) independence appears in many international instruments simultaneously with sovereignty. They accompany each other, eg, in treaties establishing contemporary regional organisations, like the OAS, the OAU or the LAS, as well as in many UN resolutions.[46] Therefore independence can neither be deemed identical to sovereignty nor be perceived as its legal or political extension. Although the adjective 'political' is sometimes joined to independence, it is a legal notion with an autonomous meaning. However, both independence and sovereignty describe the status of states in international law. Independence refers to the position of a state, especially towards other states. It describes not only its separateness and distinctness,[47] but also its non-subordination to any other subject of international law. As such it is a basis of a state's freedom from any coercion or interference and for the freedom to act.[48] Sovereignty is concerned with the formal condition (or legal capacity) for territorial entities to call themselves states and constitutes a basis for all possible rights.

The relationship between *sovereignty* and *jurisdiction* is not very clear either. Nevertheless, in the *Case concerning S.S. 'Lotus'* quoted above, the PCIJ stated that criminal jurisdiction has a territorial character: 'it cannot be exercised by a State outside its territory except by virtue of a permissive rule derived from international custom or from a convention'. International law does not, however, prohibit a state from 'exercising jurisdiction in its own territory, in respect of any case which relates to acts which have taken place abroad, and in which it cannot rely on some permissive rule of international law'. At the same time the Court declared that the right of a state to 'exercise jurisdiction rests in its sovereignty'. Thus, jurisdiction rests on, and *eo ipso* is exercised within, state territory.[49]

---

[45] The Advisory Opinion of 23.7.1923, PCIJ Publ., Series B, No. 5, at 27.

[46] For instance: the UN General Assembly declarations concerning the inadmissibility of intervention and interference in the internal affairs of States of 1965 (res. 2131(XX)) and of 1981 (A/RES/36/103), the resolution of 1974 dealing with the definition of aggression (res. 3314(XXIX)), the declaration on the enhancement of co-operation between the UN and regional organisations in the maintenance of international peace and security (A/RES/49/59). All texts available on the UN web-site.

[47] L Henkin, *International Law: Politics and Values*, (Dordrecht/Boston/London, Martinus Nijhoff Publishers 1995), at 10.

[48] See the GA Declaration on the Granting of Independence to Colonial Countries and Peoples of 1960, 1514(XV), text: ibid.; Advisory Opinion of the ICJ on the Legality of the Threat or Use of Nuclear Weapons of 8.7.1996, para. 22, ICJ Rep. 1996, at 226.

[49] Stern interprets the judgment in the Lotus Case in the sense that 'jurisdiction to enforce is strictly territorial and can never, therefore, be extraterritorial'. At he same time, the jurisdiction to prescribe and the jurisdiction to adjudicate 'can both be extraterritorial, as long as the prescribing or adjudicating State respects the limitations placed on such exercises of jurisdiction by international law'. B Stern, 'How to Regulate Globalisation?' in M Byres (ed.), *The Role of Law in International Politics*, (Oxford, Oxford University Press 2000), at 256–7.

However, in contrast to sovereignty, which has a strictly territorial nature, jurisdiction can, in some circumstances, also be exercised outside state territory. It therefore has a functional character. As a result, the State is responsible for any acts executed within its jurisdiction, even if outside its territory. Jurisdiction means effective power. International human rights law constitutes a good example to explain the difference between jurisdiction and sovereignty. In this domain the principle of state responsibility is jurisdiction, not sovereignty. Thus every state is responsible vis-à-vis individuals for any violations independently of where they take place.[50] The same situation applies to the area of the law of the sea where the state has jurisdiction over its own ships or over certain areas within its competence.

(vii) State Sovereignty and national or popular sovereignty

National (or popular) sovereignty rarely appears in international law. International law focuses on the sovereignty of States. Until recently, the sovereignty of nations was in principle external to the realm of international law. The idea of permanent sovereignty over natural resources and the concept of the self-determination of peoples represent two of the few attempts at introducing it into international law. The first one was promoted by the UN General Assembly, which in 1962 adopted a resolution on the *Permanent Sovereignty of States over Natural Resources.*[51] In the context of decolonisation it considered peoples and nations as the subjects of the right to permanent sovereignty (although States were also recognised as subjects of that right). The second concept, formulated in the category of subjective rights, was included in both International Covenants on Human Rights of 1966 (article 1).

Recently, the problem has found a novel expression as a result of the international protection of human and peoples' rights (see article 19–24 of the *African Charter on Human and Peoples' Rights* of 1981) and, in particular, the idea of democratic governance.[52] It assumes that all states should be democratic and based on the rule of law as well as on respect for human rights and fundamental freedoms as pre-conditions for lasting peace. In other words, it presumes that the nation (or people) is sovereign and as such becomes the source of state authority. Thus, the concept of democratic governance reinforces national sovereignty.

---

[50] See the judgment of the European Court of Human Rights of 26.6.1992, *Drozd and Janousek v. France and Spain*, A/240, para. 91. See also T Zwart, *The Admissibility of Human Rights Petitions*, (Dordrecht/Boston/London, Martinus Nijhoff Publishers 1994), at 95–9.
[51] Resolution 1803(XVII). Text: the UN web-site. FX Perrez, above n 4, at 69–109. According to the Author, resolution 1803 became a restatement of customary international law (at 92).
[52] See also Art. 28 of the Universal Declaration of Human Rights (1948). A Cassese, *International Law*, (Oxford, Oxford University Press, 2001), at 371.

Nevertheless, in international law the sovereignty of states is not the same as the sovereignty of nations. They operate at different levels and play distinct roles. State sovereignty not only legitimates the State in its international legal relations, but is also a source of all state rights. Today, national sovereignty retains its importance at inter-state level. It expresses the idea that the nation is the highest authority of the State. As such it enables us to describe the State régime as democratic and allows us to legitimise, ex ante or ex post, certain decisions of the executive. In fact, the sovereignty of nations (or peoples) raises problems for international law only in so far as it regulates the domestic relations in this field.

(viii) Sovereignty and sovereign rights. Permanent sovereignty over natural resources

Sovereignty in international law is a basis for state rights. In this regard, the PCIJ stated in the *Case of S.S. 'Wimbledon'* that 'the right of entering into international engagements is an attribute of State sovereignty'.[53] According to the *Fisheries Jurisdiction Case* decided by the ICJ, the acceptance of its compulsory jurisdiction 'is a unilateral act of State sovereignty'.[54] The CSCE Helsinki Final Act stipulates that the participating states will respect

> 'all the rights inherent in and encompassed by its sovereignty, including in particular the right of every State to juridical equality, to territorial integrity, and to freedom and political independence. They will also respect each other's right freely to choose and develop its political, social, economic and cultural systems as well as its right to determine its laws and regulations. [. . .] They also have the right to belong or not to belong to international organisations, to be or not to be a party to bilateral or multilateral treaties including the right to be or not to be a party to treaties of alliance; they also have the right to neutrality' (principle I).

Such rights may be described as sovereign.[55] However, international law also recognises the concept of sovereign rights *tout court*. The UNCLOS makes this apparent. The Convention clearly distinguishes four legal titles:

> 1) sovereignty of the coastal State which, according to article 2, 'extends, beyond its land territory and internal waters and, in the case of an archipelagic state, its archipelagic waters, to an adjacent belt of sea, described as the territorial sea' (see also article 49);
> 2) sovereign rights within the exclusive economic zone which, according to article 56 (1a), 77 and 78, concerns exploration and exploitation, conservation and management of natural resources of waters superjacent to the sea-bed and of the sea-bed and its subsoil as well as with regard to other activities for the economic

---

[53] Judgment of 17.8.1923, PCIJ Publ., Series A, No. 1, at 25.
[54] Judgment of 4.12.1998 (Jurisdiction), para. 46, website of the ICJ.
[55] A Cassese, above n 52, at 89–90.

exploitation and exploration of the zone; or sovereign rights over the continental shelf pertaining to exploration and exploitation of natural resources;

3) jurisdiction which can be exercised over foreign ships or with regard to the establishment and use of artificial islands, installations and structures, marine scientific research and the protection and preservation of the marine environment in the EEZ or on the continental shelf (article 27, 28, 56 (1b), 94);

4) control within the contiguous zone (article 33).

Thus, according to the UNCLOS sovereign rights constitute a kind of legal title weaker than sovereignty. They differ from sovereignty because although they apply to certain territories they are exercised outside State territory and are restricted substantially and territorially. In fact they have a functional nature. In that regard, in the *Case concerning maritime delimitation and territorial questions between Qatar and Bahrain* the ICJ indicated: 'Delimitation of territorial seas does not present comparable problems [to the delimitation of the continental shelf or superjacent water column— C.M.], since the rights of the coastal state in the area concerned are not functional but territorial, and entail sovereignty over the sea-bed and the superjacent waters and air column'.[56] At the same time sovereign rights produce the same effects as rights consequent upon sovereignty and exercised within state territory: they exclude others from activities reserved to the state and from profiting from such sovereign rights. Sovereign rights also differ from jurisdiction and control as far as they do not presuppose effective supremacy over the object of rights (see article 77 (3) of the UNCLOS).

(ix) Limitations on sovereignty

The key to understanding the concept of sovereignty is the problem of its possible limitations (or derogations). As the PCIJ stated in the *Case of S.S. 'Wimbledon'*:

> 'The Court declines to find in the conclusion of any Treaty by which a State undertakes to perform or refrain from performing a particular act an abandonment of its sovereignty'.

And later:

> 'No doubt any convention creating an obligation of this kind [article 380 of the Versailles Treaty—right of passage through the Canal of Kiel—C.M.] places a restriction upon the exercise of sovereign rights of the State, in the sense that it requires them to be exercised in a certain way'.[57]

---

[56] The ICJ stated: 'maritime rights derive from the coastal State's sovereignty over the land, a principle which can be summarised as 'the land dominates the sea' [. . .]'. It added: 'islands, regardless of their size, in this respect enjoy the same status, and therefore generate the same maritime rights, as other land territory.' Judgment of 16.3.2001, para. 185, 40 *International Legal Metarials* 847 (2001), at 883–4 and 886.

[57] Judgment of 17.8.1923, PCIJ Publ., Series A, No. 1, at 25.

Thus the Court perceives the conclusion of an agreement as a restriction of the exercise of sovereign rights, not as a transfer or abandonment of sovereignty. It leads only to a situation where the State has to exercise its sovereign rights in a certain way.

The ICJ appears more radical. In the *Case concerning military and paramilitary activities in and against Nicaragua* (1986) it stated:

> 'A State, which is free to decide upon the principle and methods of popular consultation within its domestic order, is sovereign for the purpose of accepting a limitation of its sovereignty in this field. This is a conceivable situation for a State which is bound by institutional links to a confederation of States, or indeed to an international organisation'.[58]

In fact, a limitation of sovereignty should not be understood as its renunciation. It means rather that the freedom to decide upon the principle and methods of popular consultation must be exercised in a way freely agreed. A limitation of sovereignty should be understood exactly in the same way as is a restriction on the exercise of sovereign rights in the reasoning of the PCIJ.

B. Conclusions—sovereignty as legal capacity

The very short inquiry carried out above leads to some general conclusions:

1) Although appearing in different manifestations and not clearly defined, state sovereignty in international law is characterised by convergent understandings. Formally, *sovereignty is an abstract normative concept established and determined by international law* rather than a sociological reality of the contemporary international community. As a notion internal to international law, it makes sense only within this framework.[59] Rather than being a legal rule, sovereignty establishes and describes the legal position of states as a certain category of subjects of international law. It presupposes that all states, notwithstanding the differences between them, enjoy the same sovereignty. It is in that sense that sovereignty may be considered as a principle of international law.

2) In substantive terms, *sovereignty, as a concept strictly associated with states, may be recognised as an inherent, inalienable, primary, general, equal, territorial, exclusive legal capacity to act*. Sovereignty is inherent in the state because it is attributed to it from its origin. There is no state without sovereignty and no sovereignty without the state. As an inherent feature of the state it is inalienable. Rights resulting from sovereignty are equally inalienable. Sovereignty is a capacity to act of a primary nature meaning it is attributed to states directly by international law. Sovereignty is a general characteristic. It is a basis for all the rights (or powers) of the state. The sovereignty of states is formally equal. No sovereignty is better,

---

[58] Judgment of 27.6.1986, para. 259, ICJ Rep., at 131.
[59] O Casanovas, op. cit, writes outright that sovereignty 'is not defined by its content but from a relational dimension between the State and International Law'. States are directly and immediately subjects of public international law (at 115).

larger, stronger or more powerful than another sovereignty. Potentially, the same rights result from the sovereignty of every state. Sovereignty is always territorially based. It exists only over state territory. This is one of the reasons why it cannot be attributed to international organisations, which are of a functional nature. Sovereignty is also an exclusive capacity because it excludes other subjects from acting on State territory unless based on international law. Sovereignty is legal capacity. At the same time it is neither authority nor independence. State sovereignty belongs to the same formal category of normative concepts as human dignity and human rights or as the so-called rules of organisation for the personality and rights of international organisations (although this is of a secondary nature).

3) International law recognises the *concept of the limitation of sovereignty or sovereign rights*. However, such a limitation means only that states freely agree to exercise sovereignty (or the rights resulting from it) in a certain way or agree partially not to exercise it. Limitations can be decided in relation to other states and/or international organisations/the international community. Such a limitation cannot be interpreted as a deprivation of sovereignty. An involuntary deprivation of sovereignty, on the other hand, necessarily entails the demise of a state.

3. SOVEREIGNTY IN EUROPEAN UNION/COMMUNITY LAW

A. General remarks on international regional integration

The notion of international regional integration belongs to economics or politics rather than to law, although international law uses it as well. However, its meaning is ambiguous. Integration is very often contrasted with classical forms of inter-state co-operation. However, if we agree that international integration is a product of the actions of states, we have to accept that it is a qualified form of co-operation. The intensity of internal links and the dynamics of integration depend on the will of integrating states. In fact, they vary widely. Regional integration can mean various things. Currently, integration processes are mostly of an economic character and take place within the framework of international organisations.

According to the literature on international law at least two models of integration may be distinguished: the European model and the American model.[60] The European Union, and in particular the European Communities, constitutes the paradigm of European integration. It expresses the idea of progressive integration, the final result of which, however, is not clearly known. In the European model the structure of the organisation is very well developed. The European Communities have legal personality within the meaning of international law. There is a well-

---

[60] J-Y Morin, 'Rapport introductif' in *Perspectives convergentes et divergentes sur l'intégration économique*. (Paris, Colloque du Québec, Editions A Pédone 1993), at 32–4.

structured system for the internal acts of its institutions. They have supranational characteristics. The scope of their powers increases incrementally. Internal disputes are resolved through European courts (ie a judicial method is used), and individuals have access to European courts when acts of the institutions are challenged. The European model of integration is followed by certain African communities (in particular the AEC, ECOWAS, COMESA, and in part the SADC).[61] NAFTA represents an opposite model of integration. It is based on the idea of free trade.[62] There, the institutional structure is much weaker. Formally, NAFTA does not enjoy international personality and its internal legal system is very modest. Internal disputes are settled through non-judicial bodies. Although these two models are so different, the material scope of NAFTA becomes closer and closer to the European model (it encompasses not only free movement of goods and competition rules, but also, eg, agriculture, energy, investments, services, freedom of establishment, labour and environment). In this context one can observe some tendency towards the convergence of these organisations. Between these two models of integration there are also mixed ones such as the Mercosur.[63]

Sovereignty is perceived differently in these organisations. Generally, it is not expressly mentioned in the treaties establishing regional organisations. One of the very few exceptions is the SADC. Its Member States are conscious of their 'duty to promote interdependence and integration' (preamble), but they declare that the principle of action of the SADC and its members is the 'sovereign equality of all member States' (article 4 (a) of the SADC Treaty). However, the remaining African communities are an interesting case (AEC, ECOWAS, COMESA). In all the treaties constituting them it can be read that the principle of sovereign equality is superseded by the principle of equality and inter-dependence of member States (article 3 (a) of the AEC Treaty; article 4 (a) of the ECOWAS Treaty; article 6 (a) of the COMESA Treaty). Moreover, in the preamble of the ECOWAS Treaty the Member States declare that their integration efforts

'may demand the partial and gradual pooling of national sovereignties to the Community within the context of a collective political will'. While in the preamble of the COMESA Treaty we read that member States have regard 'to the principles of international law governing relations between sovereign States. . . .'

---

[61] Treaties constituting those economic communities: 30 *International Legal Metarials* 1991, at 1245 (AEC); 35 *International Legal Metarials* 1996, at 663 (ECOWAS); 33 *International Legal Metarials* 1994, at 1072 (COMESA), 32 *International Legal Metarials* 1992, at 116 (SADC).
[62] Treaties establishing the NAFTA: 32 *International Legal Metarials* 1993, at 296, 613, 1480, and 1545.
[63] The Mercosur treaties: 30 *International Legal Metarials* 1991, at 1043; 36 *International Legal Metarials* 1997, at 693; 34 *International Legal Metarials* 1995, at 1244.

The replacement of the principle of sovereign equality may suggest that sovereignty does not represent any value to organisations based on regional integration and is contrary to the principle of equality and inter-dependence. In my opinion such a conclusion would be incorrect. Sovereignty as a legal capacity to act should not be seen in opposition to inter-dependence. Rather, sovereignty is a basis for integration and allows states to develop integration. It is rather state *independence* (vis-à-vis other states) that loses its sense for members of an economic community This loss, however, is only qualified, for in all such communities a withdrawal procedure is provided for or is retained by the states themselves.

B. Manifestations of sovereignty in EU/EC law

(i) General remarks

The European Union is founded on the European Communities, supplemented by the policies and forms of co-operation established by the Treaty on European Union (article 1(3)(1) TEU). There is no doubt that it is an 'integration-type' organisation. The Treaty on European Union is 'a new stage in the process of European integration undertaken with the establishment of the European Communities' (preamble). Although expressly not endowed with international personality (see, however, article 24 and 38 TEU), the EU has as its mission to organise, in a manner demonstrating consistency and solidarity, the relations between the Member States and their peoples (article 1(3)(2)). The integrative nature of the Union is well demonstrated in its objectives enumerated in article 2.

Nevertheless, the level of integration within the Union is divergent. The differences result from the scope and intensity of the powers conferred upon the Union by the Member States. The largest conferment of powers refers to the so-called first pillar (the European Communities), which is sometimes referred to as 'supranational'. It is closely linked with the quality and scope of objectives as well as tasks of the Communities (see in particular article 2–4 of the EC Treaty).[64] More 'intergovernmental' is the Common Foreign and Security Policy (second pillar) where conferment is practically absent. Member States act together, especially through the European Council and the Council of the European Union. The third pillar, police and judicial co-operation in criminal matters, is of an intermediary nature—the European Parliament and the Commission are more engaged here than in the second

---

[64] On the specific nature of the first pillar see G Isaac, 'Le 'pilier' communautaire de l'Union européenne, un 'pilier' pas comme les autres', (2001), *Cahiers de Droit Européen* No. 1–2, at 45–89.

pillar, and the ECJ plays a certain role—but it is still closer to intergovernmentalism. Thus, real problems in dealing with sovereignty arise mainly in the first pillar.

(ii) Limited powers of the Community

In 1957 in Rome several European States decided to establish the European Economic Community. It is beyond doubt that when the Treaty of Rome was concluded they were sovereign and independent in the meaning of international law. However, on the basis of the Treaty they agreed that the Community would have autonomous legal personality and its own institutions empowered within the framework of the Treaty to legislate or to undertake other activities. Regulatory powers permit the European Community to create its own legal order. During the dynamic development of the integration process the powers of the Community widened. Besides express and complementary powers (article 235; now article 308), implied powers appeared. The ECJ, interpreting the Treaty, differentiated Community powers into exclusive powers and, generally speaking, non-exclusive powers.[65]

In 1992 in Maastricht together with a change of name from the EEC to the European Community, and a further widening, and indeed differentiation of its powers, Member States decided to include a clear principle of conferred powers in the EC Treaty. According to article 3 b (current article 5) (1), 'The Community shall act within the limits of the powers conferred upon it by this Treaty and of the objectives assigned to it therein'. Thus, the principle expressly states that powers of the Community are specific and limited, not general. They cannot be presumed and therefore any legal act of the Community should have a clear legal basis.[66] The principle of conferred powers indicates that the restricted capacity of the Community to act is a consequence of the conferment of powers by EU Member States. The precise nature of this restriction is not, however, clear.

---

[65] See eg J Rideau, *Droit institutionnel de l'Union et des Communautés européennes*, (Paris, LGDJ 1994), at 376–9.

[66] V Constantinesco, comments on Art. 3 b, in: V Constantinesco, R Kovar, D Simon (eds.), *Traité sur l'Union européenne. Commentaire article par article*, (Paris, ECONOMICA 1995), at 108–9; A Dashwood, 'The Limits of European Community Powers, (1996), 21 *European Law Review* No.2, passim. Some authors suggest that the principle of conferred powers 'adds nothing to existing law'. PJG Kapteyn, P VerLoren van Themaat, *Introduction to the Law of the European Communities*, 3rd ed, (London/The Hague/Boston, Kluwer Law International, 1998), at 137–8. Formally it's true. Yet, Art. 5 may be interpreted as a barrier against the uncontrolled expansion of powers and, read together with the subsidiarity principle, a symptom of new trends in the philosophy of integration. Besides, it has an explanatory force. See S Weatherill, *Law and Integration in the European Union*, (Oxford, Clarendon Press, 1995), at 38–9.

(iii) The nature of Community powers in the light of the jurisprudence of the ECJ and its doctrinal interpretations

The Treaty is silent as to the nature of conferred powers (whether or not they are sovereign) and as to the character of conferment. Does it prejudice the sovereignty of the Member States for the benefit of the European Community? Is it definitive or not? In fact, the words 'sovereignty' and 'sovereign powers (or rights)' are nowhere present in the Treaty. Neither the European Community, nor the European Union is classified as sovereign. Despite some arguments,[67] it is generally accepted that neither the European Union nor the European Community is a state.[68] From where has the discussion about sovereignty in the European Community arisen?

The problem has its source in some statements of the European Court of Justice from the early 1960s on. The Court first expressed its opinion in the case *Van Gend en Loos* (1963). It stated:

'The Community constitutes a new legal order of international law for the benefit of which *the States have limited their sovereign powers*, albeit within limited fields'.[69]

One year later, in the case *Costa v. ENEL* it continued by saying:

'By creating a Community of unlimited duration, having its own institutions, its own personality, its own legal capacity and capacity of representation on the international plane and, more particularly, *real powers stemming from a limitation of sovereignty or a transfer of powers from States to the Community, the Member States have limited their sovereign rights*, albeit within limited fields' [. . .] (emphasis added).

The ECJ added that:

'The transfer by the States from their domestic legal systems to the Community legal system of the rights and obligations arising under the Treaty carries with it *a permanent limitation of their sovereign rights, against which a subsequent unilateral act incompatible with the concept of Community cannot prevail.*[70]

It completed this statement in the cases *Commission v Italy* and *Commission v France* where it decided that the limitation of the sovereign rights of Member States is of a definitive nature meaning that a State's powers cannot return to the State if not based on an explicit treaty provision. The effect of this limitation is that no provisions of national law may

---

[67] See eg A von Bogdandy, 'The European Union as a Supranational Federation: A Conceptual Attempt in the Light of the Amsterdam Treaty', (2000), 6 *Columbia Journal of European Law* at 27–54; L C Backer, 'The Extra-National State: American Confederate Federalism and the European Union', (2001), 7 *Columbia Journal of European Law* at 173–240.
[68] See eg S Griller, DP Droutas, G Falkner, K Forgó and M Nentwich, *The Treaty of Amsterdam. Facts, Analysis, Prospects*, (Wien/New York, Springer Verlag 2000), at 66–86.
[69] Judgment of 5.2.1963, Case 26/62, [1963] ECR 1.
[70] Judgment of 15.7.1964, Case 6/64, [1964] ECR 592.

be invoked to override it.[71] In 1991, once again, the ECJ repeated its thesis that 'Community treaties established a new legal order for the benefit of which the States have limited their sovereign powers', this time however, 'in ever wider fields [. . .]'.[72]

Part of Community law doctrine derives from the far-reaching conclusions of the ECJ. Some authors argue that Member States share their sovereignty with the Community. This may be understood in two ways: 1) that EU Member States exercise sovereignty together at the EU level; or 2) that they gave up some of their sovereign rights in favor of the EU. For followers of the first approach, sovereignty is a set of powers. States can transfer some of them to integration-type organisations. However, this transfer is not complete. Only some specific powers are transferred, to be exercised collectively within the framework of the organisation.[73]

According to the second approach, the Member States lost part of their sovereignty in favour of the Community. Thus, the European Community may be called sovereign (instead of the States or together with them, depending on the field in question) or at least a 'non-sovereign commonwealth of post-sovereign States'.[74] This approach presupposes at least the beginning of the end of state sovereignty and sovereignty of the nation-state.[75]

There is also a theory of 'soft sovereignty' in the European Community which assumes that limitations of state sovereignty may result from the practice laid down in the founding treaties as constitutional treaties. In the case of the EC, the practice concerning implied powers and article 308 ECT (or complementary powers) is influential. It is claimed that they have caused the erosion of the principle of conferred powers even before Maastricht through the de facto additional transfers of sovereignty.[76]

In my opinion all these theories are either wrong or premature.

---

[71] Judgments of 14.12.1971, Case 7/71, para. 20, [1971] ECR 1003, and of 13.7.1972, Case 48/71, para. 9, [1972] ECR 527.
[72] Opinion 1/91 of 14.12.1991, para. 21, [1991] ECR I–6079.
[73] D Obradovic, 'The Doctrine of Divisible Sovereignty in the Community Legal Order', (1996), 1 *Studia Prawno-Europejskie* at 31–6; JV Louis, *L'ordre juridique communautaire*, (Bruxelles/Luxembourg, Office des Publications Officielles des Communautés européennes), 1993), at 15, 17; R Müllerson, above n 3, at 132.
[74] N MacCormick, 'Democracy, Subsidiarity, and Citizenship in the "European Commonwealth" in N MacCormick (ed.), *Constructing Legal Systems. "European Union" in Legal Theory*, (Dordrecht/Boston/London, Kluwer Academic Publishers 1997), at 338–9.
[75] E No'l, 'L'Erosion de l'Etat-Nation dans un système d'intégration économique: le cas de la Communauté européenne' in Ch Philip, P Soldatos, *Au delà et en deçà de l'Etat-Nation*, (Bruxelles, Bruylant 1996), at 95–109.
[76] MM Martin Martinez, *National Sovereignty and International Organisations*, (The Hague/Boston/London, Kluwer Law International 1996), at 97, 105–148.

C. Critical appraisal

(i) General remarks on EU/Member State sovereignty

Considering the ECJ's position, it has never said that the EC is sovereign,[77] or that Member States have lost their sovereignty. The Court decided only that Member States have limited their sovereign powers in some areas. Only in *Costa v ENEL* did it find that the limitation of sovereign powers resulted from 'a limitation of sovereignty or a transfer of powers from the Member States to the Community'. Nevertheless, even in this case sovereignty is not lost. Moreover, the Court is unclear whether the limitation of sovereign powers is a consequence of a limitation of sovereignty or of a transfer of powers. Although Community law doctrine frequently quotes the *Costa v ENEL* formula, at least as far as sovereignty is concerned, it has never been repeated in later jurisprudence. The Court and its Advocate Generals have several times invoked the more reasonable formula from the judgment in *Van Gend en Loos*.[78]

In fact, in the European Community, fully in conformity with the EC Treaty, the ultimate competence to decide (ie sovereignty) still belongs to the Member States. All decisions as to the scope and the dynamics of integration are adopted or approved by the European Council—in other words by the Heads of States or Governments of the Member States (article 4 TEU). Any modification of the founding treaties requires ratification by all the Member States (article 17, 42, 48 and 49 TEU). Although, formally, reservations to the founding treaties are not acceptable, the practice of so-called 'opt-outs' and 'declarations' demonstrates that Member States need not accept all of the newly negotiated obligations (eg article 69 EC, additional protocols concerning the UK, Ireland and Denmark). In some areas, EU Member States have explicitly restricted the Community's powers (eg article 34, 45, 64, 135 EC). Meanwhile, the Community is unable to determine its own powers. Even when it can legislate based on its complementary powers, ie when the Community has neither explicit nor implied powers (article 308 ECT), it has to accept some limits to its operations. In a famous opinion in 1996, the ECJ stated that article 235 (current article

---

[77] The only example found is the opinion of Advocate General La Pergola, 30.9.1997, *NIFPO and NIFF* v. *Department of Agriculture for Northern Ireland*, C–4/96, footnote 7, [1996] ECR I–681. La Pergola stated that the Community, 'acting as a single sovereign entity' had concluded fisheries agreements with non-member States.

[78] See judgment of 3.4.1968, *Firma Molkerei-Zentrale Westfalen/Lippe GmbH v. Hauptzollamt Padeborn*, Case 28–67, *impicite*, [1968] ECR 143; opinion 1/91 of the ECJ on the *Draft of the EEA Agreement*, para. 21, [1991] ECR I–6079; opinion of Advocate General Van Gerven, 27.10.1993, *H.J. Banks and amat Co. Ltd v British Coal Corporation*, Case C–128/92, para. 25, [1994] ECR I–1209; opinion of Advocate General Cosmas, 19.1.1999, *Andersson and Wakkeras-Andersson v Swedish State*, Case C–321/97, para. 48, [1999] ECR I–3551.

308) 'cannot serve as a basis for widening the scope of Community powers beyond the general framework created by the provisions of the Treaty as a whole and, in particular, by those that define the tasks and the activities of the Community'.[79]

The States' power to have the final word is confirmed by general treaty law. According to the *Vienna Convention on the Law of Treaties* of 1969 (this Convention applies to treaties establishing international organisations—article 5), States may dissolve the European Union. This possibility can be exercised by decision (on the basis of common agreement of its Members—article 54) and in the case of *rebus sic stantibus* (article 62). A withdrawal from the European Union of any individual State is also legally possible on the basis of a common agreement of the Member States (article 54; only unilateral withdrawal is inadmissible). The lack of an appropriate basis for withdrawal in the EU Treaty itself is not any barrier in this respect.

There is also an external argument to support the thesis that despite any limitations, EU Member States retain their sovereignty. In many treaties to which the European Community is (or can be) a party there can be found clauses typical of a regional economic integration-based organisation. According to these treaties, such an organisation is composed of *sovereign* states of a given region which have transferred competence in respect of matters covered by the concluded treaty.[80] Thus, states remain sovereign despite a transfer of powers to the organisation, even where such powers are differentiated in their scope and nature. The concept of sovereign states is accepted in most such clauses. Only occasionally do they relate simply to states or directly to the European Community.[81]

---

[79] Opinion 2/94 of 28.3.1996 concerning *the EC accession to the European Convention on Human Rights*, paras. 29 and 30, [1996] ECR 1759. In the context of the Laeken Declaration on the Future of the European Union one of questions to be answered is if it is necessary to introduce into the Treaty a clause to safeguard the States' powers if they are not attributed to the Community. Annex I to the Conclusion of the Laeken European Council, 14–15.12.2001, at 22, SN 300/1/01 REV 1.

[80] See: Convention on the conservation of Antarctic marine living resources (1980), Art. XXIX, OJ L 252 of 5.9.1981, at 27; Convention on the conservation of migratory species of wild animals (1979), OJ L 210 of 19.7.1982, at 11; International Convention on the harmonisation of frontier controls of goods (1982), art. 16 (2), OJ L 126 of 12.5.1984, at 3; Vienna Convention for the protection of the ozone layer (1985), art. 1 (6), OJ 1988, L 297 of 31.10.1988, at 10; Convention on biological diversity (1992), art. 2, OJ L 309 of 13.12.1993, at 3; The Energy Charter Treaty (1994), art. 1 (3), OJ L 380 of 31.12.1994, at 24; Convention on the protection and use of transboundary watercourses and international lakes (1992), art. 23, OJ L 186 of 5.8.1995, at 44; UN Convention to combat desertification in countries experiencing serious drought and/or desertification particularly in Africa (1994), art. 1 (j), OJ L 83 of 19.3.1998, at 3; Convention on the Transboundary Effects of Industrial Accidents (1992), art. 27, OJ L 326 of 3.12.1998, at 6. See also the UN Convention against Transnational Organised Crime (2000), art. 2 (j), annexed to the resolution of the UN General Assembly (A/RES/55/25), not yet approved by the EU. It is interesting in the context of the last treaty that it uses the term 'regional **economic** integration organisation' [C.M.], although its subject-matter is not economic and, in the case of the EU, outside the powers of the European Community.

[81] See eg the UNCLOS, Annex IX, art. 1, OJ L 179 of 23.6.1998, at 3.

(iii) Limitation of EU Member State sovereignty

The Luxembourg Court has stated that the conferment of powers leads to a limitation of the sovereign rights of Member States, of a permanent and definitive nature. However, taking into account the meaning of the limitation of sovereign powers in public international law, it can be concluded that Member States have agreed only that within the framework of the European Community some of their sovereign powers will not be exercised or that they will be exercised in a certain way. They have accepted that in specific matters within Community competence, EC institutions have replaced the States, through direct regulatory activities (regulations) or by directing the regulatory activities of the States (directives). As a rule, Community powers are not exclusive, meaning EU Members still have the right to act. Only very few Community powers are exclusive. Even then, they are not entitled sovereign.

Moreover, the ECJ considers that a permanent and definitive limitation of sovereign rights prevents the powers conferred to the Community from returning to the States *without an express treaty provision*, so confirming that the limitation is relative and dependant on the will of the States. As a result, some powers may cease to belong to the Community, a situation that is not purely theoretical. The European Council *Laeken Declaration on the Future of the European Union* (2001), regarding a better division of powers between the EU and its Members reads:

> 'Thus the important thing is to clarify, simplify and adjust the division of competence between the Union and the Member States in the light of the new challenges facing the Union. This can lead both to *restoring tasks to the Member States* and to assigning new missions to the Union, or to the extension of existing powers, while constantly bearing in mind the equality of the Member States and their mutual solidarity'.[82]

D. Conclusions

Neither the EC Treaty nor the jurisprudence of the ECJ undermines the sovereignty of EU Member States. They remain fully sovereign as they preserve their full and exclusive legal capacity. In this context, the concept of a transfer of sovereign powers from the States to the Community (or, indeed, the concept of shared sovereignty) is contrary to international law as well as to the current state of Community law. Moreover, the concept of divisible sovereignty, understood as sovereignty exercised by the Member States together is also unacceptable. It undermines the autonomous person-

---

[82] Annex I to the Conclusion of the Laeken European Council, above n 79, at 21.

ality of the Community and is in conflict with the idea of the conferment of powers which underlies the powers of the European Community.

4. SOVEREIGNTY IN POLISH CONSTITUTIONAL LAW

A. The Sovereignty of Poland in historical perspective

(i) General remarks

If we accept that a State's sovereignty means its legal capacity to take all internal and external actions attributed to it *ex lege internationalis* it is undeniable that in principle Poland was a sovereign state from the moment of its revival after the Second World War. However, the conditions of the exercise of State sovereignty have been changing throughout the years. Until 1989, the status of national sovereignty was lower, although it was also changing during this period. At least three periods can be distinguished: 1944–89 (the victory of Solidarity and the end of communism in Poland), 1989 (first constitutional reforms)—1997 (the adoption of the new Constitution), 1997—present. The last period will be discussed separately.

(ii) Poland's sovereignty 1944–89

The year 1944 brought Poland freedom from Nazi occupation and at the same time introduced it to Soviet occupation. The first stage was the most difficult (1944–56). Then, formally, the sovereignty of Poland was indeed undermined. The new state faced the de facto destruction of a part of its territory, with the rest of the country occupied by Soviet troops, the expanded jurisdiction of Soviet courts over Polish citizens,[83] and infiltration of public authority structures, Polish army and security services. In 1949 the Council for Mutual Economic Assistance was established. It operated for ten years without any legal basis. Finally, in 1959, an agreement was concluded. Within the framework of the CMEA the so-called specialisation of production was introduced. In fact, it meant that the capacity to

---

[83] As a result of the agreement concluded in Moscow in 1944 between the Polish Committee of National Liberation (established under Soviet control!) and the USSR Government. According to the latest, however well-established, case law of Polish courts, Poland partially renounced its judicial jurisdiction over Polish citizens and over Polish territory in favour of a foreign State. Supreme Court, Order of 8.2.1995, I KZP 38/94, *Wokanda* 1995, No. 4, at 17; Supreme Court, Resolution of 21.6.1995, I KZP 5/95, OSNKW 1995, No. 9, at 53; Supreme Court, Order of 8.12.1997, III KRN 168/95, *Prokuratura i Prawo* 1998, No. 4, at 17; Constitutional Court, Order of 15.12.1998, SK 8/98, OTK 1998, No. 7, at 123; Wroclaw Court of Appeal, Judgment of 14.10.1999, II Aka 321/99, OSA 2000, No. 5, at 22.

take economic decisions depended upon Soviet rule-makers and the Soviet economy.

In 1952, together with the Constitution modelled after Stalin's Constitution of 1936 (the draft text was 'improved' by Stalin himself), Poland changed its name and became 'the People's Republic of Poland' (PRP). Article 1 of the Constitution stated: '1. PRP is a State of popular democracy. 2. In the PRP, authority belongs to the working class of the towns and villages'. In article 6 can be read: 'Armed forces of the PRP safeguard the sovereignty and independence of the Polish People [. . .]'. Article 15 (2) stipulated that Sejm (the Parliament) as a representation of the workers fulfils the sovereign rights of the Nation. Thus, the PRP's Constitution accentuated the sovereignty of the working class vis-à-vis the nation and even the people. Sejm had no practical importance even in later periods. The real sovereign was the Communist party supported by the Soviet State—which also became true in a formal sense after the Constitution was amended in 1976. The newly inserted article 3 (1) stated that the Polish Unified Workers' Party was the leading force in society. Poland was constitutionally obliged to maintain friendship with the Soviet Union and other communist countries (article 6 (2)). State sovereignty did not exist.

In 1955 Poland joined the Warsaw Pact. From a legal point of view the basic treaty did not contain any provision undermining the sovereignty of the parties. Its preamble obliges contracting parties to follow the goals and principles of the UN Charter (including sovereign equality). The parties agreed to act in the interest of further tightening and developing friendship, mutual co-operation and aid in accordance with the principle of respecting the independence and sovereignty of Member States. The treaty was directed against external enemies (article 4, *casus foederis*). Unfortunately, practice departed from the letter of the treaty. Soviet troops were located freely over Polish territory, without any legal grounds for doing so. Only personal jurisdiction over Soviet soldiers was regulated (in agreements between Poland and USSR of 1956 and 1957). In an attempt to rectify the situation, Polish international law doctrine invented a new legal concept limiting territorial supremacy—relating to the stay of foreign troops on State territory. But *lege artis*, the stay of foreign military forces was contrary to international law. Soviet forces withdrew in 1993.

The so-called Brezniev doctrine of limited sovereignty formulated in 1968 in order to justify the invasion of Czechoslovakia also strongly influenced the exercise of Poland's sovereignty when the Warsaw Pact was in force. It stipulated that if communism was endangered, the Soviet army and, sometimes, the armies of its allies had the right to intervene in a State which was party to the Pact regardless of the will of the national government in question.[84]

---

[84] D. Carreau, *Droit international*, 7ᵉ édition, (Paris, Editions A Pédone 2001), at 81, 569–570.

(iii) Poland's sovereignty 1989–97

The electoral success of Solidarity in 1989 enabled the first constitutional reforms (in 1989 and 1991). They aimed at eliminating the rules connected with the communist regime and at restoring the sovereignty of the nation and the state (eg the name of the State was changed into the Republic of Poland; article 2 (1) ensures that the Nation holds the supreme power in the RP). All provisions confirming Poland's dependence on the Soviet Union were deleted. A more general amendment took place in 1992 when the so-called Small Constitution was adopted. It was in force until 1997 and mostly regulated matters concerning the organisation of the State. Provisions regarding constitutional principles amended in 1989 were still in force.

During the transitional period Poland became a member of many international organisations reinforcing its democratic, sovereign and independent status, including, in 1991, the Council of Europe. It became a party to numerous conventions concluded within this framework, including, in 1993, the European Convention on Human Rights. In 1991 the CMEA and the Warsaw Pact were dissolved.

B. Sovereignty in the light of the Constitution of 1997

(i) General remarks

The 1997 Constitution does not contain many rules concerning sovereignty in general.[85] Most of them pertain to the sovereignty of the Nation. State sovereignty is not particularly stressed. However, in order to understand the constitutional perception of State sovereignty and its relationship with national sovereignty it is necessary to examine all the provisions concerning sovereignty.

(ii) Sovereignty of the Nation

As far as the nation's sovereignty is concerned, the preamble of the Constitution states that in 1989 the Polish nation recovered 'the possibility of a sovereign and democratic determination of its fate'. And although later article 1 declares that the purpose of the RP 'shall be the common good of all its citizens', article 4 (1) declares that the supreme power shall be vested in the nation. According to the doctrine of constitutional law, supreme power is synonymous with sovereignty. The 'nation' means all the citizens

---

[85] C. M. K.: *Polish Constitutional Law. The Constitution and Selected Statutory Materials*, (Warsaw, Bureau of Research, Chancellery of the Sejm 2000), at 25.

of the Republic (and not an ethnic group). The nation as a holder of power is not, however, defined precisely. This is the perspective from which the principle of national sovereignty is drawn. It means that, eg, only the nation can be sovereign in a state, not a monarch or a political party. Moreover, in conformity with article 4 (2), the nation exercises its supreme power directly or through its representatives, especially Parliament.[86] The representatives of the nation are not only parliamentary deputies, but also each person elected by the people (eg the President, members of local councils). The power of the nation is not exhausted in elections. It is realised through a combination of direct and representative democracy.[87]

Some Polish literature on constitutional law distinguishes between the principle of the sovereignty of the nation and the principle of state sovereignty.[88] The former justifies the origin of authority and determines the way it is exercised. The latter is concerned with the condition of the State as a subject capable of deciding freely and without any interference in all matters pertaining to it.[89]

(iii) Sovereignty of the State

The principle of state sovereignty does not have such a clear constitutional basis as the principle of the sovereignty of the nation. It derives from several stipulations and is joined with the principle of independence.[90] However, only some of these stipulations (article 5 and 26) were included as constitutional principles. Article 5 states that the RP safeguards the independence and integrity of its territory. Article 26 (1) adds that military forces serve the independence and integrity of Poland's territory. Other important elements of the principle were inserted into specific provisions. For example, article 126 (2) provides that the President of the Republic safeguards

---

[86] See in this context the Supreme Court, resolution of 29.11.1995, I KZP, OSNKW 1996, No. 1, at 3. It recognised the Polish legislator as a sovereign in the field of criminalisation of certain acts.

[87] Z Witkowski in Z Witkowski (ed.), J Galster, B Gronowska, A Bien-Kacala, W Szyszkowski, *Prawo konstytyucyjne*, (Toruń, TNOiK 1998), at 58 and 59; L Garlicki, *Polskie prawo konstytucyjne*, (Warszawa, Liber 2000), at 55–7. See, however, the Constitutional Court, judgment of 26.5.1998, K 17/98, OTK 1998, No.4, at 48. The Court recognised that governing bodies as well as other bodies not directly elected by the people but appointed by the Constitution to implement the will of the Nation can be considered an expression of national sovereignty only *sensu largo*.

[88] See B Banaszak, *Prawo konstytucyjne*, (Warszawa, C H Beck 1999), at 204–17; P Sarnecki in P Sarnecki (ed.), *Prawo konstytucyjne RP*, (Warszawa, CH Beck 1999), at 122–6; W Skrzydlo (ed.) *Polskie prawo konstytucyjne*, (Lublin, MORPOL 2000), at 129–31. These authors write only about national sovereignty. However, even then they restrict the meaning of the sovereignty of the Nation to democracy.

[89] Z Witkowski, above n 87, at 61; L Garlicki, above n 87, at 54–9.

[90] Z Witkowski, above n 87, at 61; L Garlicki, above n 87, at 58–9. In both cases sovereignty and independence are clearly distinguished.

the sovereignty and security of the state. Yet, article 104 (2), containing the oath of newly elected deputies, shows that they are obliged to safeguard the sovereignty and interests of the state.

Polish courts sometimes refer to state sovereignty.[91] However, it is not clear whether they consider it as a principle or only as a feature of the state. Thus, the Supreme Court, in the context of diplomatic immunities, formulated the principle that no sovereign and independent state as a subject of international law may be subject to the law of any other state.[92] The same Court, considering the question of the status of judgments by foreign courts, noticed that the concession in the sphere of State sovereignty refers to the enforcement of judgments rather than the recognition of effects thereof.[93] The Constitutional Court has decided an interesting case pertaining to the right of association of soldiers.[94] First it ruled that the sovereign legislator had transferred a part of the trade unions' tasks, in the domain of soldiers' rights, to the state. Later, it concluded that sovereign state authorities are free to decide on the broadening of protection vis-à-vis soldiers beyond international obligations.

5. POLAND'S SOVEREIGNTY AND THE EUROPEAN UNION

In principle, the Polish Constitution is formally adjusted to Poland's accession to the European Union.[95] Although it is silent about the European Union specifically, crucial rules in this field can be found in article 90, which provides:[96]

---

[91] See the pre-constitutional case: Supreme Court, resolution of 21.5.1948, C III 2150/47, OSN 1947, at 60 (it says that after the unconditional surrender, Germany lost its sovereignty and Poland acquired sovereign possession and power over the Regained Territories. From the moment of an effective incorporation of these territories, Poland expanded its jurisdiction. Thus, it excluded the application of German laws).

[92] See eg the Supreme Court, judgment of 18.3.1998, I PKN 26/98, OSNAPiUS 1999, No. 5, at 172.

[93] Order of 27.4.2001, III CZ 4/2001, *Biuletyn SN* 2001, No. 8, at 6.

[94] The judgment of 7.3.2000, K 26/98, OTK 2000, No. 2, at 57.

[95] However, some modifications on the date of accession are not excluded. See C Mik, 'Przekazanie kompetencji przez Rzeczpospolitą Polskę na rzecz Unii Europejskiej i jego następstwa prawne (uwagi na tle art. 90 ust. 1 Konstytucji)' in C Mik (ed.), *Konstytucja Rzeczypospolitej Polskiej z 1997 roku a członkostwo Polski w Unii Europejskiej*, (Toruń, TNOiK 1999), at 156–8; M Kruk, 'Konstytucja narodowa a prawo europejskie: czy Konstytucja Rzeczypospolitej Polskiej wymaga zmiany?' in E Poptawska (ed.), above, at 175–86; P Winczorek, 'Kilka uwag w kwestii dostosowania Konstytucji Rzeczypospolitej Polskiej do wymogów prawa europejskiego' in Ibid., at 187–92.

[96] Art. 90, although of a broader scope of application, was inserted in order to allow for accession. S Biernat, 'Constitutional Aspects of Poland's Future Membership in the European Union', (1998), 36 *Archiv für Völkerrechts* Heft 4, at 400.

'1. The Republic of Poland may, by virtue of international agreements, confer[97] upon an international organisation or international institution the competence of organs of State authority in relation to certain matters.

2. A statute, granting consent for ratification of an international agreement referred to in paragraph 1, shall be passed by the Sejm by a two-thirds majority vote in the presence of at least half of the statutory number of Deputies, and by the Senate by a two-thirds majority vote in the presence of at least half of the statutory number of Senators.

3. The granting of consent for ratification of such agreement may also be by a nation-wide referendum in accordance with the provisions of Article 125.

4. Any resolution in respect of the choice of procedure for granting consent to ratification shall be taken by the Sejm by an absolute majority vote taken in the presence of at least half of the statutory number of Deputies'.

Article 90 contains rules of two types. The first one is included in paragraph 1. It deals with the problem of the conferment of state powers in some areas upon an international organisation or an international institution. In fact, it touches implicitly upon state sovereignty. The second type of rule, regulated in paragraphs 2–4, pertains to the question of indirect acceptance of conferment (by parliament) or direct acceptance of conferment by the Polish people (in a referendum). Thus, these rules may be associated with national sovereignty. As a result, the sovereignty of the state and of the nation are separated in article 90, whilst remaining functionally linked to each other.

As far as state sovereignty is concerned, it is necessary to elucidate *the idea of the conferment of competence of state authority*. An introductory observation indicates that the constitutional provision allows neither for the limitation of state sovereignty nor for the limitation of sovereign rights. It merely provides that Poland is ready to confer the competence of its organs to an international organisation. The omission of the term 'sovereignty' from article 90 was significant. Some authors argue that the reason was not only the problem of the imprecise nature of sovereignty, but also the wish to stress that EU accession neither deprives nor restricts Poland in its sovereignty. In that context the concept of conferment should be understood as an authorisation to an international organisation to act in certain areas and as linked to an objective limitation of the exercise of competence in these areas. Such an authorisation is based on the assumption that it may be revoked.[98] Yet, if we agree that the limitation of sovereignty (or sover-

---

[97] In my opinion the use in *Polish Constitutional Law. The Constitution and Selected Statutory Materials*, above n 85, at 46, of the word 'delegate' as a translation of the Polish word 'przekazac' is wrong. I decided to replace it for the purposes of this paper with the word 'confer'. See also the translation by S Biernat, op. cit, at 400 ('the transfer of competence').

[98] K Dzialocha, comments on art. 90, in L Garlicki (ed.), *Konstytucja Rzeczypospolitej Polskiej. Komentarz*, (Warszawa, Wydawnictwo Sejmowe 1999), at 3. For the opposite point of view see L Garlicki, above n 87, at 58 (accession will mean 'a certain limitation of the international sovereignty of Poland'), and S Biernat, above n 96, at 406–7.

eign rights) means that the state, while remaining sovereign, refrains from exercising some rights or undertakes to exercise them in a certain way, it is possible to accept this idea also in the context of article 90 (1). Of course, as a rule, the limitation of sovereignty is of a consensual character. It can be revoked, but not unilaterally.[99]

Conferment concerns the competence of state authority. The Constitution does not distinguish between different bodies and levels of power. Virtually all state bodies, including the government, may be affected by conferment. In practice, however, conferment refers mainly to legislative powers. In other words, by its accession Poland agrees that all organs involved in legislative activities, national or local, may be restricted in their competence.

The accession agreement authorises the conferment of powers of state authorities *in certain areas* to the European Union. In general terms they correspond with the tasks conferred upon the European Community. Nevertheless, conferment of all or even most of these powers may be regarded as presumptively unconstitutional.[100] Although article 90 does not provide for any formal barriers to it, the concept of substantive (material) limits is applicable according to which at least constitutional principles and norms guaranteeing human and civil rights (Chapters One and Two of the Constitution) must remain untouched by the conferment of powers.[101] Frequently the Constitutional Court's approval for conferment is sought or at least a finding of compatibility in terms of respect for the identity of the Constitution.[102] Real problems may, however, result from the post-accession practice of the Constitutional Court. The recognition of the primacy of Community law over Polish law is a pre-condition of accession. If the Constitutional Court applies primary or secondary Community law on condition that it is in conformity with the Constitution,[103] as is proposed, it will go against the very foundations of the European Community. In my opinion Poland will use other legal procedures to challenge the validity of secondary law (*vide* article 35 TEU; article 230 EC).

The consent to conferment is granted either by the Polish Parliament in a special, qualified majority vote or as the result of a referendum. These procedures allow the justification and legitimisation of the act of conferment. Thus, the Nation as a sovereign has the possibility to express its will

---

[99] C Mik, above n 85, at 149–50.
[100] Compare S Biernat, above n 96, at 405.
[101] C Mik, above n 85, at 154–6; S Biernat, above n 96, at 406.
[102] L Garlicki, 'Pozycja prawa wspólnotowego wobec krajowego porządku prawnego' in *Suwerenność i integracja europejska*, above n 87, at 116, is of the opinion that if consent were granted in the referendum, the jurisdiction of the Constitutional Court would be excluded.
[103] In favour of the general precedence of the Constitution over Community law: M Safjan, 'Konstytucja a członkostwo Polski w Unii Europejskiej', (2001), *Państwo i Prawo* No. 3, at 9–12. The Author is currently the President of the Polish Constitutional Court.

indirectly or directly. If consent is based on a referendum (which is the most likely solution), it should be organised after the authentication of the accession treaty but before its formal ratification by the President. According to article 125 of the Constitution, the result of the referendum is binding, 'if more than half of the number of those having the right to vote have participated in it'. A negative result precludes ratification. The problem may arise that the referendum is not binding because of too low participation (consent is necessary in order to ratify the Accession Treaty). In that case, in my opinion, the referendum vote will be an indicator for Parliament, which should have the final word.

6. CONCLUSION

A very short overview of the issue of state sovereignty in the light of the process of European integration leads us to the conclusion that Member States preserve their sovereignty in the European Union. Such a conclusion stems from both international law and EC law. However, states limit their sovereignty in the sense that they agree in the constitutional treaties not to legislate at all or not to legislate freely in some areas. At the same time the states remain Masters of the Treaties. They determine the fate of European integration, shape and modify their obligations within its framework and may withdraw from them on the basis of the agreement concluded with other Members. Thus, there is no need to render sovereignty relative or to change its contemporary paradigm. Polish constitutional law confirms that. Even after accession, State sovereignty will remain intact, although it may have become more self-limiting.

17

Postmodern Versus Retrospective Sovereignty: Two Different Discourses in the EU and the Candidate Countries?

ANNELI ALBI

1. INTRODUCTION

I N THE CONTEMPORARY world, legal, political and economic treatises are revising the concept of sovereignty or even casting doubt on its explanatory value. They suggest that this historically fluid and socially conditioned concept needs to be adapted to globalisation, a phenomenon which has shifted the task of providing for the common good from the state to transnational communities. Supreme authority has become dispersed between numerous regulatory and judicial entities at international, supranational and national levels. The transformation of sovereignty is particularly obvious in the context of fifty years of European integration—for instance, approximately two thirds of legislation derives from EU institutions; EU law is supreme and directly applicable; national currencies have been replaced by the euro and citizens of the Member States enjoy EU citizenship.

Meanwhile, to those researching the constitutional aspects of EU enlargement it seems that the theory of sovereignty in Eastern Europe inhabits a quite different reality. Autonomous control or even statehood having been (re-)established merely a decade ago, Central and Eastern European countries (CCEEs) operate firmly in the traditional language of sovereignty, independence, the ethnically defined nation-state and national self-determination. In some Candidate Countries, verbatim definitions of the pre-communist period have been used by authoritative constitutional institutions to assess EU membership. Awareness of the constitutional impact of the EU has registered in CCEE literature only in the last couple of years. Nevertheless, post-Maastricht conceptual discourse on revising sovereignty and adapting the locus of democratic legitimacy has been largely absent in Eastern European legal theory, and there are no significant contributions to the search for a post-modern conception of sovereignty.

Compared to EU Member States, the fundamental significance of sovereignty in Eastern Europe is, in fact, strongly entrenched in the constitutional basis of the Candidate Countries. This paper suggests that Eastern European constitutions stand out in terms of their 'souverainist' nature. Nine out of ten constitutions in the Central and Eastern European Candidate Countries set forth complex provisions on sovereignty and independence, while this distinction is rare in Western European constitutions. Until recently, nine constitutions did not contain provisions on the transfer of powers to international organisations. The provisions on sovereignty are subject to numerous safeguards and their amendment is rather difficult, often requiring a broad social consensus in a referendum.

This constitutional framework leaves a strong imprint on the Candidate Countries' theoretical discussions about constitutional amendments with regard to the effect of EU accession on sovereignty. First, the constitutionally entrenched distinction between independence and sovereignty probably explains why the Candidates Countries' legal theory tends to allow a partial delegation of sovereignty to the EU of state competencies or internal sovereignty, whereas independence, meaning statehood or external sovereignty, must be retained. Second, the European Union tends to be addressed in the (draft) constitutional amendments as an international organisation or a confederation of states, which, in the author's view, probably tries to build a psychologically more neutral bridge between, on the one hand and, total constitutional silence with regard to any and all external entities, and on the other hand, prospective membership of a deeply integrated supranational organisation. Third, CCEE legal theory tends to take a traditional ethnocultural approach to popular sovereignty and to restrict the democratic legitimisation of EU policies to national referendums and participation of national parliaments. This contribution suggests that the imminent wave of CCEE constitutional adaptations could provide an opportunity for revising these traditional approaches to the sovereign nation state.

2. THE 'SOUVERAINIST' NATURE OF EASTERN EUROPEAN CONSTITUTIONS

(a) Complex sovereignty provisions: independence and sovereignty

The particular importance of sovereignty in the construction of the state appears first if we compare Eastern European constitutions with their Western counterparts. Among the fourteen written constitutions of the EU Member States, six do not mention sovereignty at all, declaring simply that the people form the source of power.[1] Another four use a one-sentence formula, *à la* 'sovereignty belongs to the people',[2] regarding external and internal sovereignty as a unified phenomenon vested in the people. Only three constitutions draw a distinction between sovereignty and independence: Luxembourg (Articles 1 and 32), Portugal (Preamble, Articles 1, 2, 3.1 and 7.1) and Ireland (Preamble and Article 5).

Meanwhile, Central and Eastern European constitutions set forth complex sovereignty provisions, which are presented in Table 1. Nine of the ten Candidate Countries' constitutions distinguish between *sovereignty* and *independence*. The former implies internal sovereignty, meaning the state's power or competences; the latter signifies external sovereignty, in the sense of independent statehood in international relations. Besides this distinction, CCEE constitutions add numerous safeguards to the provisions on sovereignty, as well as rendering these difficult to amend or even prohibiting their amendment. The Baltic and Romanian constitutions form the most protectionist group, while the new 1997 Polish constitution is open to international cooperation.

The widely entrenched distinction between sovereignty and independence in Central and Eastern Europe has, in the author's view, particular historical roots. While in Western Europe, fifty years of EU integration has rendered this distinction devoid of meaningful content, in Central and Eastern Europe these terms form a precondition for explaining the earlier situation regarding sovereignty. As is well known, Eastern Europe was surrendered by the Potsdam and Yalta agreements to the Soviet sphere of influence after the Second World War. The countries suffered for five decades under a totalitarian communist regime, which had a detrimental impact on their nations, as well as affecting their cultural, economic and social life. In the case of Central and South-Eastern European countries, the USSR controlled de facto their internal sovereignty—the content of lawmaking activity—while they formally retained independent statehood (external sovereignty). The sovereignty/independence distinction also played an important role in the case of the Baltic States and Slovenia, even though, forming a part of the USSR and the Yugoslav Federation respectively, they possessed neither internal nor external sovereignty. In other words, their processes of liberation underwent distinct stages, first achieving sovereignty and then independence. Their liberation movements were initiated with the Declarations of Sovereignty, according to which federal laws were only applicable subject to a prior ratification by local parliaments. This was shortly followed by the Declarations of Independence, which marked the (re-)appearance of independent states in international

---

[1] Germany, Belgium, Sweden, Austria, the Netherlands and Denmark.
[2] Italy, France, Spain and Greece. The Finnish Constitution has two separate sentences in this regard.

relations. The matter of sovereignty remains sensitive due to the continuing fragility of the geopolitical situation of Central and Eastern European countries on the border or in the neighbourhood of unpredictable Russian power.

Table 1: Provisions on sovereignty and independence and their safeguards.

Estonia	Preamble: established on the inalienable right of the people of Estonia to *national self-determination.* . . 1. Estonia is an *independent* and *sovereign* democratic republic, wherein the *supreme power of the state is vested in the people.* 1.2. The *independence* and *sovereignty* of Estonia are *timeless and inalienable.* 54. An Estonian citizen has a duty . . . to defend the *independence* of Estonia.
Latvia	1. Latvia shall be an *independent* democratic Republic. 2. The *sovereign power* of the Latvian State shall belong to the *People of Latvia.*
Lithuania	Preamble: having for centuries defended its freedom and *independence* . . .; embodying the innate right of each person and the People to live and create freely in . . . the *independent State* of Lithuania. 1. The State of Lithuania shall be an *independent* and democratic republic. 2. *Sovereignty* shall be *vested in the People.* 3.1. No one may limit or restrict the *sovereignty of the People* or make claims to the *sovereign powers of the People.* 3.2. The People and each citizen shall have the right to oppose anyone who encroaches on the *independence* . . . of Lithuania by force. 135.1. In conducting foreign policy, the Republic of Lithuania . . . shall strive to *safeguard* . . . *independence* . . . 136. The Republic of Lithuania shall participate in international organizations provided that they do not contradict the interests and *independence* of the State.
Romania	1.1. Romania is a *sovereign, independent, unitary, and indivisible Nation State.* 2.1. *National sovereignty* resides with the Romanian people . . . 2.2. No group or person may exercise *sovereignty* in their own name. 8.2. Political parties . . . contribute to the definition and expression of the political will of the citizens, while observing *national sovereignty* . . . 37.2. Any political parties or organizations which, by their aims or activity, militate against . . . the *sovereignty, integrity,* or *independence* of Romania shall be unconstitutional. 80.1(1) The President . . . is the safeguard of *national independence* . . . 82.2. President's oath: 'I solemnly swear . . . to defend . . . Romania's *sovereignty, independence* . . .' 117.1. The Armed Forces shall . . . guarantee the *sovereignty, independence* . . . of the State. 148.1. prohibits amendment of the provisions on the *national, independent character of the state.*

Hungary	2.1 The Republic of Hungary shall be an **independent**, democratic constitutional state. 2.2 In the Republic of Hungary all **power is vested in the people**, who exercise their **sovereignty** through elected representatives and directly. 5. The State of the Republic of Hungary shall defend . . . the **sovereignty of the people**, the **independence** . . . of the country. 6.1 The Republic of Hungary . . . shall refrain from the use of force and the threat thereof against the **independence** . . . of other states 19.2. Exercising its rights based on the **sovereignty of the people**, the Parliament shall ensure the constitutional order of society . . . 51.1. The General Prosecutor and the Office of the Public Prosecutor . . . shall prosecute to the full extent of the law any act which violates or endangers the . . . **independence** of the country. 68.1. The national and ethnic minorities living in the Republic of Hungary participate in the **sovereign power of the people**.
Czech R.	Preamble: at the time of the renewal of an **independent** Czech state . . . 1. The Czech Republic is a **sovereign**, unified, and democratic law-observing state . . . 2.1. All **state power** derives from the people . . . 9.2. Any change of fundamental attributes of the democratic law-observing state is inadmissible.
Slovakia	Preamble: proceeding from the natural right of nations to **self-determination** . . . 1. The Slovak Republic is a **sovereign**, democratic, and law-governed state. 2.1. **State power** is derived from the citizens . . . 34.3. The enactment of the rights of citizens belonging to national minorities and ethnic groups . . . must not be conducive to jeopardizing the **sovereignty** . . . of the Slovak Republic . . . 106. The National Council of the Slovak Republic can recall the president from his post if the president is engaged in activity directed against the **sovereignty** . . . of the Slovak Republic.
Bulgaria	Preamble: in awareness of our irrevocable duty to guard the **national and state integrity** of Bulgaria. 1.2. The entire **power of the state** shall derive from the people. 1.3. No part of the people, no political party nor any other organization, state institution, or individual shall usurp the expression of **popular sovereignty**. 9. The armed forces shall guarantee the **sovereignty**, security, and **independence** of the county . . . 44.2. No organization shall act to the detriment of the country's **sovereignty** and **national integrity**, or the **unity of the nation** . . . 18.2 and 3. The state shall exercise **sovereign rights** . . . 24.2 The foreign policy of . . . Bulgaria shall have as its uppermost objective the . . . **independence** of the country . . .

Slovenia	Preamble: Whereas it is in keeping with the Basic Constitutional Charter on *Independence* and *Sovereignty* of the Republic of Slovenia . . . Acknowledging that we Slovenians created our own national identity and attained our nationhood based on . . . the fundamental and permanent right of the Slovenian people to *self-determination* . . . 3.1. Slovenia is a state of all its citizens and is based on the *permanent* and *inalienable* right of the Slovenian people to *self-determination*. 3.2 [Title '*Sovereignty*'] . . . the supreme power is vested in the people.
Poland	Preamble: . . . Homeland, Which recovered, in 1989, the possibility of a *sovereign* and democratic determination of its fate . . . 5. The Republic of Poland shall safeguard the *independence* and integrity of its territory . . . 4.1. *Supreme power* in the Republic of Poland shall be vested in the Nation. 104.2 Deputie's oath: 'I do solemnly swear to . . ., to safeguard the *sovereignty* . . . of the State . . .' 126.2. The President of the Republic shall . . . safeguard the *sovereignty* . . . of the State . . .

On a descending scale of 'souverainism', we start from the Baltic constitutions. Prompted by oppressive history and (re-)adopted at the beginning of the 1990s when Soviet troops were still in occupation in the countries, they reflect the primary quest to assert the republics' independence from Russia. The constitutions start with the CCEE-characteristic distinction between independence and sovereignty, adding several safeguard clauses. The Estonian constitution declares that sovereignty and independence are timeless and inalienable and it also mentions the inalienable right of the Estonian people to self-determination. The Lithuanian constitution prohibits the usurpation of or claims to the sovereign powers of the people. According to both constitutions, the people have the duty to protect the countries' independence.

The Romanian constitution declares that Romania is a sovereign, independent, unitary and indivisible nation state, in which national sovereignty resides with the Romanian people. Sovereignty may not be exercised in the name of any group or person. Political organisations have to respect, and the president and the army to safeguard, the sovereignty and independence of the state. Amendment of the constitution with regard to the national and independent character of the state is prohibited.

Independence and sovereignty also feature in the constitutions of Hungary, the Czech Republic, Bulgaria and Slovenia. In addition, they have the following safeguards. In Hungary, the goal of the state is to protect sovereignty and independence. The Prosecutor's Office is responsible for prosecuting acts against Hungary's independence. Sovereignty is further mentioned in connection with Parliament's exercise of rights and the participation of national minorities in the sovereign power of the people. Independence is addressed in connection with Hungary's pledge to refrain from the use of force against the independence of other countries. The Bulgarian constitution emphasises the national character of the Bulgarian state, prohibits the usurpation of popular sovereignty and recalls the irrevocable duty to guard national and state integrity. Bulgaria's foreign policy and its army have to protect, and all organisations have to respect, the country's sovereignty, independence and national integrity. The Czech constitution prohibits the amendment of provisions on 'the fundamental attributes of the democratic law-observing state'. The Slovenian constitution recalls sovereignty and independence in the Preamble and, being a new state, it also underlines the permanence and inalienability of the right of self-determination.

The term 'independence' is absent only in the Slovak constitution, which nevertheless seems to distinguish conceptually between external and internal sovereignty, speaking in separate provisions about the 'sovereign state' and 'state power'. In addition, the President is to be recalled for activities against sovereignty, and national minorities may not jeopardise Slovakia's sovereignty.

Poland stands at the liberal end of CCEE constitutions and, since adopting the new constitution in 1997, it is prepared for imminent EU accession. Furthermore, instead of statehood provisions, it begins with the principle of the rule of law and with a declaration that the objective of the state is to provide for the common good. However, the independence and sovereignty formula remain: Poland has to safeguard its independence, while the Deputies and the President have to safeguard the sovereignty of the state.

(b) Absence of provisions on the transfer of powers to international organisations

The literature on CCEE constitutions usually acknowledges their openness to international law. In many cases providing expressly for direct applicability and the supremacy of the treaties, they stand out, in a comparative European context, for their 'international law-friendly' nature.[3] However, it has rarely been noticed that while all the constitutions of EU Member States have a clause on delegating powers to international organisations and six of them to the European Union specifically, CEE constitutions are closed with respect to the delegation of powers to international organisations.

---

[3] K Korkelia, 'New Trends Regarding the Relationship between International and National Law (with a special view towards the states of Eastern Europe)', (1997) *Review of Central and East European Law*, 227.

Initially, nine constitutions out of ten in the Eastern European Candidate Countries did not contain any provisions on the transfer of powers to international organisations. Only the Lithuanian constitution allowed for Lithuania's participation in international organisations, 'provided that they do not contradict the interests and *independence* of the State' (art 136). The Lithuanian 'Founding Fathers' have reconciled the quest for Western cooperation and potential danger from the East by explicitly prohibiting Lithuania's participation in organisations based on the former USSR (art 150). The Estonian constitution authorises Parliament to ratify treaties on joining international organisations (art 120), but does not speak about a transfer of powers. The Slovak constitution authorises membership of a 'state alliance' (art 7), which was, according to most authors, aimed at a closer relationship with the Czech Republic.[4]

However, with a view to imminent EU accession, the Czech and Slovak constitutions have recently been amended with regard to international and EU cooperation and Poland has provided for the delegation of powers to international organisations since the adoption of its new constitution in 1997. The other countries are currently preparing amendments, which are discussed in more detail in Section Three.

(c) Safeguards for amending sovereignty provisions

Besides the safeguards already mentioned, many Central and Eastern European constitutions subject the amendment of sovereignty provisions to a mandatory or optional referendum with a lengthy procedure, requiring a high social consensus.[5] The constitutions of Romania and the Baltic States share the most restrictive constitutional amendment procedures, while the Slovakian, Czech and Hungarian amendment procedures are relatively liberal. In comparison, referendums generally have an unimportant role in the constitutional amendment procedures of EU Member States and six of them do not use referendums at all.[6]

First, some CCEE constitutions, as already mentioned, simply prohibit the amendment of fundamental constitutional provisions (Romania and Czech Republic) or declare some principles timeless and inalienable (Estonia and Slovenia). Secondly, the amendment of sovereignty provisions requires a referendum in four constitutions and is optional in two. The

---

[4] See for a summary of the Slovakian literature M Hoskova, 'Legal Aspects of the Integration of the Czech Republic and Slovakia into European Security and Economic Structures', (1994) 37 *German Yearbook of International Law*, 91.
[5] Title VI and Art 90 of the Romanian Constitution; Chapter 15 of the Estonian Constitution; Chapter 14 of the Lithuanian Constitution; Arts 76–80 of the Latvian Constitution; Chapter XII and Art 125 of the Polish Constitution; Part 9 and Art 90 of the Slovenian Constitution.
[6] Germany, Luxembourg, Belgium, Spain, Greece and the Netherlands.

Romanian constitution requires a referendum for any constitutional amendment, the constitutions of Estonia, Latvia and Lithuania for amending the fundamental provisions proclaimed in the first chapters. Poland provides for an optional referendum specially for amending the state-fundamental provisions of Chapter I and for joining international organisations. The Slovenian constitution provides for a referendum for any constitutional amendment, if required by 30 Deputies. In Bulgaria, constitutional amendments may not be submitted to a referendum, but the Grand National Assembly has to be specially elected in order to amend matters concerning, *inter alia*, changes related to the form of state or the form of government, direct applicability of the constitution, supremacy of international law and ratification of any international instruments envisaging such changes. Finally, referendums require a wide popular consensus. The usual requirement is majority approval with a 50% turnout, while most extreme is the case of Lithuania, where three quarters of all citizens who have voting rights must consent to amend Article 1 (its status as an independent and democratic republic).

3. THEORETICAL PERSPECTIVES IN THE CANDIDATE COUNTRIES CONCERNING THE EU'S IMPACT ON SOVEREIGNTY

(a) The European Union: an international organisation?

The above-described 'souverainist' nature of Candidate Countries' constitutions predetermines to a large extent the framework of the theoretical discussions on amending the constitutions for EU accession. This section discusses the 'international organisation' approach to the European Union taken in CCEE legal theory and expressed in some (draft) constitutional amendments, which probably forms a psychologically important bridge with regard to moving from constitutional silence on international cooperation to membership of a deeply integrated supranational organisation.

In the Member States of the EU, the standard political, judicial and academic language describes the EU as a supranational organisation. In addition, three major conceptual approaches to the EU can be distinguished, although they are often overlapping and intertwined. First, the 'federalist' approach suggests that the EU already functions under the principle of federalism, or forms a novel type of federalism, such as integrative federalism[7] or a supranational federation.[8] Second, the 'post-Maastricht

---

[7] K Lenaerts 'Federalism: Essential Concepts in Evolution—the Case of the European Union', (1998) 21 *Fordham International Law Journal*, 746ff.
[8] A Van Bogdany, 'The European Union as a Supranational Federation: A Conceptual Attempt in the Light of the Amsterdam Treaty', (2000) 6 *Columbia Journal of European Law*, 27ff.

revisionist discourse', mainly representing European legal academics, is in search of an alternative, non-statist approach to the EU federation-confederation dispute. Due to the Union's multifaceted legal nature, the new theories propose that the EU should be qualified in novel terms, such as multilevel constitutionalism,[9] European Commonwealth[10] or—a standard approach in political science—a system of multilevel governance. This revisionism is based mainly on the following effects of European Union membership: upon the states as a sovereign nation state

> *Government*—approximately two thirds of a Member State's legislation derives in varying degrees from EU institutions.
> *State's tasks*—the EU has competence also in core fields of state sovereignty such as monetary and defence policy, internal security and foreign policy.
> *Legal order*—EC law is supreme and directly applicable with regard to national legal orders, including national constitutions.
> *State's veto*—is increasingly limited by the extensive use of qualified majority voting.
> *National currencies*—have been replaced by the Euro in twelve Member States.
> *People*—Member States' citizens have EU citizenship.
> *Constitution*—the Treaties go much further than the traditional international treaties, so that the ECJ and many academics call the body of the functionally constitutional texts 'the constitutional charter'. In addition, the Charter on Fundamental Rights has been adopted.
> *Popular sovereignty*—the European Parliament is directly elected and has important powers due to the co-decision procedure. Democratic legitimacy thus derives from both the national and the European level.
> *Legal personality*—belongs to the Communities, but the EU also has treaty-making powers within the Third Pillar, which leaves the state's international capacity to act rather limited.
> *Secession*—according to the predominant view, it is not possible to withdraw from the Union.
> *Territory*—is becoming blurred due to the free movement of EU citizens and the regime of free movement of goods, services, labour and capital. In addition, the boundaries of territorial competence are being replaced by the boundaries of functional competence by international organisations.

Finally, there is the 'traditional' or 'nation-statist' approach, which regards the EU as an association of states that does not significantly undermine state sovereignty. Advocated mainly by the Member States' constitutional courts and constitutional lawyers, it found its major expression in the German and Danish *Maastricht* decisions. However, this approach is

---

[9] I Pernice, 'Multilevel Constitutionalism and the Treaty of Amsterdam: European Constitution-Making Revisited', (1999) 36 *Common Market Law Review*, 703.
[10] N MacCormick, *Questioning Sovereignty: Law, State, and Nation in the European Commonwealth* (NY, OUP, 1999); R Bellamy, D Castiglione, 'Building the Union', (1997) 16 *Law and Philosophy*, 421ff.

declining into political rhetoric, as the post-Maastricht critique has powerfully demonstrated the shortfall of this concept in corresponding effectively
to the EU's far-reaching effects on the traditional sovereign nation state.
The current preparation of fundamental reforms by the Convention on the
Future of Europe set up at Laeken in December 2001, such as adopting a
constitution for the EU, is further diminishing the role of the 'traditional'
approach.

However, the last approach remains predominant in the legal theory of
Eastern European Candidate Countries. Awareness of the constitutional
impact of the EU has appeared in CEE literature only in the last couple of
years.[11] Still, Eastern European academia tends to devote only minimal
space to analysing the legal nature of the EU and to view the Union therefore as a mere international organisation or a confederation of states, which
does not significantly affect national sovereignty. The post-Maastricht
conceptual discourse on the EU's novel legal nature tends to be absent in
CEE literature, as is a significant engagement in the Debate on the Future
of the Union. The international organisation approach in academia has
found official incorporation in the constitutional amendments of several
Candidate Countries, drafted or already adopted with a view to joining the
European Union:

—The new Polish constitution, adopted in 1997, permits 'delegation to an international organisation or international institution of the competences of the
organs of State authority in relation to certain matters' (art 90). The 'international
organisation' approach had also been taken in four earlier draft constitutions.[12]
—The Czech constitutional amendments, adopted on 18 October 2001, permit
the transfer of 'some powers of the organs of the Czech Republic . . . to an international organisation or institution' (new Section 10a).[13]
—In Hungary, the international organisation approach is taken in the new draft
constitution of 1997,[14] prepared by a special Parliamentary Committee on the
basis of Parliament's guidelines adopted in the document 'Conception of the new
Hungarian Constitution'.[15] The new draft article 3 offers two versions, both
allowing the 'transfer of legislative, executive or judicial powers defined by the
Constitution' to 'international organisations or institutions'.

---

[11] Reported with regard to Hungary by A Harmathy, 'Constitutional Questions of the
Preparation of Hungary to Accession to the European Union', in A Kellermann, J W De
Zwaan, J Czuczai (eds.), *EU Enlargement. The Constitutional Impact at EU and National
Level* (The Hague, Asser Press, 2001), 123; on the Czech and Slovak Republics by Hoskova,
above note 4, 91 and 87 and on Slovenia by P Vehar, 'Constitutional Problems in the Period
of Pre-Accession in the Republic of Slovenia', in Kellermann et al., above note 11, 370. The
same is true of the Estonian literature.
[12] These are presented in A Wasilkowski, 'The Future Polish Constitution from the Perspective
of Poland's Membership of the European Union', (1993) *Droit Polonais Contemporain*, 14–15.
[13] Constitutional Act No 395/2001, entering into force on 1 June 2002.
[14] 'Constitution of the Republic of Hungary (Draft)', (1997) 38 *Acta Juridica Hungarica—
Hungarian Journal of Legal Studies*, No 3–4, 168–234.
[15] Parliament Resolution No 119/1996 on 21 December, 1996.

—In Lithuania, the Working Group, established under the Chancellery of the Lithuanian Parliament, proposed in September 1998 a clause on delegating competences to the organs of international organisations (Article 136).[16] However, following conference discussions with a number of foreign experts on the conceptual and technical problems of this approach,[17] the new draft amendments of October 2000 propose special provisions on the transfer of competences to the European Union.[18]

—In Latvia, the initial draft amendments, composed under the auspices of the PHARE and Latvia's European Integration Bureau in 1999, recommended a provision authorising the conclusion of treaties on membership of international organisations (Article 68).[19] However, in March 2001, a special Working Group proposed official draft amendments, which subject EU accession to a referendum with a reduced turnout requirement (Articles 68 and 79),[20] but remained merely procedural in terms and did not mention the delegation of powers.

—The initial draft constitutional amendments of Slovakia, submitted by a group of Parliament Members in June 2000, proposed an amendment on the transfer of sovereign rights to international organisations. However, the final amendments, adopted by the National Council in 23 February 2001,[21] are addressed explicitly to the European Union (Article 7).[22]

—In Slovenia, the draft amendments of July 2001 enable Slovenia to 'join international organisations of a supranational nature' (Article 3).[23]

—In Estonia, the draft amendments, composed by the Constitutional Experts' Commission in 1998, are addressed directly to the European Union (Articles 1.3 and 123[1]).[24] However, the amendments define the EU as 'an association of states' and subject its future integration to the condition 'that it does not undermine the basic principles and tasks of Estonian statehood, as provided in the Preamble'. According to the Commission, these provisions permit participation only in a

---

[16] 'Republic of Lithuania Constitutional Law on the Amendment of Articles 136 and 138 of the Constitution of the Republic of Lithuania. Draft.' Working Group established under the Seimas Chancellery, in *Stojimas I Europos Sajunga Ir Konstitucija. Seminaro Medziaga 29–30.06.1999* (Vilnius, Eugrimas, 2000), 136.

[17] Available in English in the collection *Stojimas I Europos Sajunga . . .*, above note 16.

[18] V Vadapalas, 'Lithuania: The Constitutional Impact of Enlargement at the National Level', in Kellermann et al, above note 11, 366–368.

[19] 'Constitutional and Administrative Facilitation of Effective Law Approximation and European Union Membership', European Integration Bureau, PHARE Technical Assistance to the Approximation of the Latvian Legislation to that of the European Communities, December 1999.

[20] 'The Theoretical Foundation of the Amendments to Satversme proposed by the Working Group', (Riga, Ministry of Justice, November 2001).

[21] Constitutional Act No 90/2001, in effect since 1 July 2001.

[22] V Kunova, 'Constitutional Aspects of the Accession of the Slovak Republic to the European Union', in Kellermann et al., above note 11, 335.

[23] 'Predlog za začetek postopka za spremembe ustave Republike Slovenije (26.7.2001)' [Proposal to initiate the Procedure of Changes to the Constitution of the Republic of Slovenia], in Poročevalec—Drzavnega zbora Republike Slovenije, 6 August 2001, 4 [unofficial translation].

[24] 'Võimalik liitumine Euroopa Liiduga ja selle õiguslik tähendus Eesti riigiõiguse seisukohalt' [Potential EU accession and its legal consequences to Estonian constitutional law.], 1998, www.just.ee/juridica2.html

confederative Union and not in a federation, which would emerge if an EU constitution or a bicameral European Parliament were introduced.

Even though the EU's supranational nature is occasionally mentioned, the expressions 'supranational' and 'international organisation' tend to be used more or less interchangeably. For instance, in Poland, legal theory does not distinguish between international organisations and supranational organisations.[25] In Lithuania, the Working Group explains that the EU forms an international organisation and, constitutionally, participation in the EU does not differ from participation in the United Nations or the Council of Europe.[26] A couple of years later, its Rapporteur explained that 'membership of the European Union is membership of an international organisation, even a supranational one'.[27] In Slovakia, Professor Vlasta Kunova mentions the need to determine 'the scope of supranational rights, that will be transferred to the international organisation'[28] and Daniela Novi**kova from the Comenius University recommends 'a constitutional regulation of exclusive rights transferred to the supranational authority' by a clause on 'international organisations or institutions'.[29] In the Czech Republic, Professor Jiri Malenovski has proposed draft constitutional amendments for international organisations, which would also be meant for supranational organisations.[30] In Hungary the only alternative draft by 1999, offered by Professor Jozsef Nemeth, was addressed to 'international intergovernmental organisations'.[31]

In fact, this approach finds support from the comparative situation within the Member States, since six constitutions are silent on the EU, accommodating EU membership under provisions on international organisations. Clauses on EU membership are only found in the German, French, Austrian, Irish, Portuguese and Swedish constitutions; the Finnish and Belgian constitutions regulate some specific issues related to EU integration.

---

[25] Informal comment by Cesary Mik on his draft contribution to the present volume, presented at the EUI workshop, Florence, 21–22 September 2001.
[26] 'Republic of Lithuania Constitutional Law . . .', above note 16, 142.
[27] Vadapalas, above note 18, 354.
[28] Kunova, above note 22, 333.
[29] D Novačkova, 'Contractual Obliations between the Slovak Republic and the European Community and its Member States with a focus on the Approximation of Laws', (1999) 13 *Medzinarodne Otazky* No 1, 159.
[30] J Malenovsky, 'Résumé: Projet commenté des articles de la Constitution de la République tchèqèe régissant ses rapports au droit international' (1999) *Pravnik No 5*, 403–04.
[31] J Nemeth, 'Az Europai Integracio es a Magyar Alkotmany', in A. Bragyova (ed.), *Nemzetközi Jog az Uj Alkotmanyban—Tanulmanyok* (Budapest, Közgazdasagi es Jogi Könyvkiado, 1997) at 110–12, cited in G Lissauer, 'The Potential Impact of European Union Membership on Hungary's Constitution', LL.M Thesis of the University of Kent at Canterbury, 1999, 55, who does not subscribe to this view and offers alternative EU-amendments.

However, before transposing Western models to the East, they should them-selves first be critically examined:[32]

> 'For the West the need to consider carefully how best to advise and assist the process of constitutional reconstruction in the East imposes an obligation to examine closely the West's own institutions. How are they functioning? Do they meet contemporary demands? On what values do they rest and how effectively do they sustain them? This kind of critical approach to democratic constitutionalism in the West must surely be an integral part of any consideration of the models which it may be practicable and desirable to recommend to the East.'

In fact, the silence in several Member State constitutions with regard to EU membership has been criticised for suffering from a 'European deficit', for failing effectively to reflect the distribution and exercise of powers in contemporary EU Member States.[33] Further, in the author's view, constitu-tional silence does not express the doctrinal approach to the EU, but has rather been a contingency of difficult constitutional amendment procedures or a relict of particular historical developments. As to the former, most EU constitutions which lack a provision on transferring powers, require for amendment of the constitution or its sovereignty provisions the approval of two houses of parliament or the dissolution of parliament (Belgium, Luxembourg, Spain, Greece, the Netherlands and Finland); in Spain and Denmark, a referendum is provided. Regarding particular historic develop-ments, the Benelux countries adopted provisions on international organisa-tions in the 1950s especially with a view to EC membership, and their subsequent amendment has not been on the agenda since these countries have traditionally been European integration friendly and no constitutional conflicts have arisen. Luxemburg's clause on the 'temporary' transfer of sovereignty has been explained by the small size of its population and the resulting lack of legal discussion. Italy has been preparing a major consti-tutional revision for several years, which includes EU provisions, but the whole plan collapsed in 1998 for political reasons.[34]

The CEE countries, however, should seize the moment of the forthcom-ing constitutional adaptations, which are anyway on the agenda for immi-nent EU accession. It would be advisable to incorporate into the conceptual basis of the amendments the EU standard approach of 'supranational organisation', in order to meet the rationale of the constitutions of deter-mining the distribution of powers, particularly in the light of fundamental

---

[32] J Hesse, 'Introduction. Constitutional Policy and Change in Europe: the Nature and Extent of the Challenges', in J Hesse and N Johnson (eds.), *Constitutional Policy and Change in Europe* (Oxford Nuffield European Studies, OUP, 1995), 4.
[33] B De Witte, 'Constitutional Aspects of European Union Membership in the Original Six Member States: Model Solution for the Applicant Countries?' in Kellerman et al, above note 11, 73.
[34] See for the six original Member States De Witte, above note 33.

reforms currently being prepared by the EU Convention. In addition, the author is of the view that the expression 'supranational organisation' should not be regarded as a transitional concept before the EU's eventual development into a federation, but would remain appropriate even in the case of introducing an EU constitution or a bicameral European Parliament, considering the novel multidimensional structure of the Union. Further, a direct reference to the EU in CCEE constitutional amendments would, compared to the 'international organisation' approach, leave a wider room for interpretation when ratifying post-enlargement treaties, as the difficult constitutional amendment and referendum procedures of the future CEE Member States, briefly described in Section Two, may threaten paralysis of the treaty-making mechanisms in a Union of 25–27 Members.[35] However, several CEE constitutional projections also call for a clause on international organisations, as sovereignty may also be restricted by participation in the WTO, Council of Europe, NATO and the UN.

(b) Delegating sovereignty while preserving independence?

In Western Europe, legal, political and economic treatises are revising the concept of sovereignty, or even casting doubt on its explanatory value. Revisionist concepts usually proceed from the following considerations: (a) most fields of contemporary life have become internationalised, shifting the task of providing for the *common good* from the national to the transnational level; (b) *supreme authority* has become dispersed between numerous regulatory and judicial entities on international, supranational and national levels; (c) sovereignty has been *fluid and socially conditioned* during successive historical eras; and (d) *boundaries of territorial competence* have been overlaid with boundaries of functional competence of international organisations. In the context of the European Union, the most far-reaching effects of integration on the traditional sovereign nation state were listed in the previous section. The EU standard approach operates with divided, shared or commonly exercised sovereignty. The post-Maastricht conceptual discourse has put forward alternative concepts such as post-sovereignty or

---

[35] The argument on the impact of CEE constitutional amendment and referendum procedures on the EU treaty amendment mechanisms is developed in Albi A. 'Referendums in the CEE Candidate Countries: Implications for the EU Treaty Amendment Procedure' in Hillon C. *EU Enlargement: A 'Legal' Approach.* (Oxford, Hart, forthcoming 2004), and Albi A. 'Referendums in Eastern Europe: The Effects on Reforming the EU Treaties and on the Candidate Countries' Positions in the Convention.' European University Institute, *Robert Schuman Centre Working Paper*, No 2002/65.

governance beyond the state,[36] late sovereignty,[37] open statehood[38] and sovereignty belonging to the Member States jointly through the Intergovernmental Conference.[39]

Meanwhile, in the Eastern side of the continent, legal theory tends to operate in the traditional language of sovereignty, independence, the ethnically defined nation state and national self-determination. In some cases, as already noted, verbatim definitions of the pre-Soviet period are used in authoritative constitutional institutions to assess EU membership. The post-Maastricht discourse on revising sovereignty is rarely considered and there are no Eastern European contributions to theories of post-modern sovereignty. Among very few studies pointing out the need to revise the constitutional discourse in this part of the world, Professor Miroslaw Wyrzykowski notes that

> '. . . European integration requires a relinquishing of the traditional notion of sovereignty, ie of the value most appreciated today in Eastern Europe as one of the greatest successes achieved due to the collapse of communism.'[40]

In the context of drafting constitutional amendments for EU accession, discussions on sovereignty tend to follow the constitutionally predetermined distinction between sovereignty and independence: certain powers, competences or sovereign rights (internal sovereignty) may be delegated, whereas independence and statehood must be retained. This also helps to account for the international organisation or confederation approach described above, as membership in these clearly preserves independence. The Estonian Expert Commission has applied the definition of sovereignty provided by A. -T. Kliimann, who was a constitutional lawyer of the First Republic (1918-1940). On the basis of this, the Expert Commission stated that Estonia may delegate sovereignty (power or competences of the state) to the EU, whereas independence has to be retained

---

[36] MacCormick, above note 10.

[37] See Neil Walker's contribution to the present volume.

[38] S Hobe, 'The German State in Europe After the Maastricht Decision of the German Constitutional Court', (1994) 37 *German Yearbook of International Law* at 113; also K Meessen, 'Hedging European Integration: the Maastricht Judgement of the Federal Constitutional Court of Germany' (1994) 17 *Fordham International Law Journal* at 524ff; M Zuleeg, 'The European Constitution under Constitutional Constraints. The German Scenario' (1997) *European Law Review*, 22.

[39] B De Witte, 'Sovereignty and European Integration: the Weight of Legal Tradition', in A M Slaughter, A Stone Sweet, J Weiler (eds.), *The European Court and National Courts—Doctrine and Jurisprudence: Legal Change in Its Social Context*. (Oxford, Hart, Publishing, 1998), 304; also W Van Gerven, 'Toward a Coherent Constitutional System within the European Union' (1996) 2 *European Public Law* 86.

[40] M Wyrzykowski, 'The Constitutions of Eastern European Countries in the Structure of European Constitutionalism', in R Bieber and P Widmer (eds.), *L'Espace Constitutionnel Européen*. (Zürich, Schulthess Polygraphischer Verlag, 1995), 161.

[41] A T Kliimann, 'Eesti iseseisvuse areng' [Development of Estonia's independence] (1935) Õigus No 2, 49–50, cited in 'Võimalik liitumine Euroopa Liiduga . . .', above note 24.

so that Estonia may not become part of a federal Europe. Reflecting a recurrent theme in its report, the Lithuanian Working Group states on many occasions that

'[a]ccession to the European Union does not mean loss of independence or its limitation; it means delegation of a part of one's State competence to EU bodies along with the consent to delegate one's sovereign rights in certain areas defined in the treaties establishing the European Union.'

Independence is retained as '[i]t has been universally recognised and is beyond doubt that Member States of the European Union are fully-fledged members in international relations and organisations.'[42] The Latvian Working Group also concludes that EU accession involves a delegation of state competences (internal sovereignty), but does not undermine Latvia's independence.[43] However, applying a modern interpretation of 'open state-hood' to the concept of independence, on the recommendation of the present author,[44] it is the first official case in the Baltic countries of conceding the need to revise fundamentally the concept of sovereignty of the First Republic and adapt it to the needs of 21st century. The concept of open statehood, often used in German legal literature, has been most eloquently developed by S. Hobe. In the contemporary world, he writes,

'[. . .]most of the tasks, aims and purposes of the State, like *eg* security, safety, defence and welfare are characterised by a specific international element; one can even go so far as to describe the openness of the State to international coopera-tion as a central aim of statehood'.[45]

However, the concept of sovereignty used in Latvian legal theory and university education has been based mainly on definitions of sovereignty and independence of constitutional lawyers of the First Republic, especially of Professor Karl Dishlers.[46] The same is true in the other Baltic countries.

In Poland a conceptually similar approach is taken, using a somewhat different vocabulary. Internal sovereignty is addressed in the language of 'power competences', which may be delegated, whereas 'sovereignty' takes

---

[42] 'Republic of Lithuania Constitutional Law . . .', above note 16, 141 and Vadapalas, above note 18, 353.

[43] 'The Theoretical Foundation of the Amendments to Satversme . . ., above note 20, 6ff.

[44] According to the Legal Secretary of the Working Group, Arnis Buka from Latvia's Ministry of Justice, the Working Group used in its work the author's earlier paper A Albi, 'Estonia's Sovereignty in Perspective of EU Accession: Rethinking traditional constitutional concepts', Tartu University, Bachelor Thesis, 1999 (in English), which pointed out the need to modernise the sovereignty approach and recommended the 'open statehood' concept at p 23.

[45] S Hobe, 'Statehood at the End of the 20th Century—The Model of the 'Open State': A German Perspective', (1997) *Austrian Journal of International and European Law*, at 150 and Hobe (1994) and other authors referred above note 38.

[46] Author's interview with Solvita Golbene, Saeima's Chancellery, Riga, 20 April 2000, based on her Master's thesis on the impact of EU integration on Latvia's sovereignty, and Arnis Buka, Ministry of Justice.

the meaning of external sovereignty, which must be preserved. Professor Cesary Mik explains that according to Polish constitutional theory, the omission of the notion of sovereignty in Art 90 of the Polish constitution of 1997 is intended to express that 'accession to the European Union does neither deprive nor restrict Poland of its sovereignty'. Instead, 'it is possible to delegate ... to the European Union the powers of State authorities in certain areas.'[47] Professor Wladyslaw Czaplinski comments that the state can be either sovereign or not, since the notion of limited sovereignty does not exist in international law, whereas competences, apart from '*compétences étatiques*', may be transferred.[48]

The traditional 'nation-statist' views also appear from the tendency of CCEE literature to concentrate on the conservatory elements of sovereign statehood, while legal theory within EU countries usually focuses on the broad range of transformations caused to the sovereign state as a result of the EU. For instance, the Estonian and Latvian expert commissions explain that independence is retained due to the right of secession from the EU; the Estonian Commission alludes to the absence of an EU constitution or a European Parliament equivalent in powers to national parliaments. Wladyslaw Czaplinski refuses to see (external) sovereignty undermined, since the '*competences étatiques*' have been retained, the most important decisions are made by unanimity and the EU protects national identity. Extensive argument on the conservatory elements of independent statehood has been put forward by the Rapporteur of the Lithuanian Working Group, who argues against any fundamental changes to the traditional criteria of independent statehood.[49] The tendency not to regard the EU as a substantial threat to sovereignty also appears from the fact that many CCEE reporters in a recent conference on Eastern European constitutional adaptations did not mention sovereignty at all when discussing the constitutional impact of EU accession.[50]

Since there is no common agreement about new concepts of sovereignty on the horizon, CEE countries, when preparing their constitutional amendments, could proceed from the EU standard concept of transferring sovereign powers for their common exercise. The distinction between independence and sovereignty is losing its substantial meaning in the context of European integration, considering the EU's multifaceted effects on traditional sovereign statehood. However, if the constitutionally embedded distinction between sovereignty and independence is to be retained, it

---

[47] Mik, present volume.
[48] W Czaplinski, 'L'intégration européenne dans la constitution polonaise de 1997', (2000) *Revue du marché commun et de l'union europeen* No 436, 171.
[49] Vadapalas, above note 18, 353–6.
[50] See the reports by Balas, Ciobanu-Dordea, Vehar, Harmathy, and Nikodem in the collection of the conference proceedings by Kellermann et al, above note 11.

would be possible to apply the standard EU approach, mentioned above, of 'transferring sovereign powers for their common exercise' to the internal aspect of sovereignty, whereas independence could be interpreted in light of the 'open statehood' concept. This concept would help to avoid discussions concerning the stage of development of EU integrations that would put an end to independent statehood, such as adopting a constitution, and it has already proved its feasibility by being adopted by the Latvian Expert Commission.

(c) Popular sovereignty: national democratic legitimisation of EU policies?

Finally, the traditional 'nation-statist' approach also underpins Eastern European discussion concerning popular sovereignty. In the European Union, post-*Maastricht* academic discourse on democracy is untying democratic legitimacy from the nation-state and opening it up to the European level. It builds mainly on the work of Joseph Weiler[51] and Jürgen Habermas,[52] according to whom the European *demos* should be based on common transcending cultural and political values or universal constitutional principles, instead of organic ethno-cultural values, in order to legitimise democratic representation through the European Parliament.

Meanwhile, Eastern European academic discourse as well as citizenship and language legislation tend to approach the nation through the ethnocultural concept of the homogeneous nation state.[53] The nation is viewed as a community of fate sharing the same language, history and culture. In the EU context, CEE writings associate legitimisation with the intergovernmental and national democratic mechanisms, in line with the argument of the German *Maastricht* decision.[54] Legitimacy is attributed to the participation of national parliaments in EU affairs, the responsibility of governments

---

[51] J Weiler, 'Does Europe Need a Constitution? Demos, Telos and the German Maastricht Decision', (1995) 1 *European Law Journal* at 219ff; and J Weiler, *The Constitution of Europe: Do the New Clothes Have an Emperor? and Other Essays on European Integration* (Cambridge, CUP, 1999).

[52] J Habermas, 'The European Nation State. Its Achievements and Its Limitations. On the Past and Future of Sovereignty and Citizenship', (1996) 9 *Ratio Juris*; J Habermas, 'The European Nation-State and the Pressures of Globalization' (1999) *New Left Review* No 235, 44ff.

[53] Also suggested by Wyrzykowski, above note 40, 161; U Preuss 'Patterns of Constitutional Evolution and Change in Eastern Europe', in Hesse and Johnson, above note 32, 113ff, and W Sokolewicz, 'The Relevance of Western Models for Constitution-Building in Poland', in Hesse and Johnson, above note 32, 256.

[54] See eg Hoskova, above note 4, 88; B Berke 'Community Law and National Legal Order', in P C Müller-Graff (ed.), *East Central Europe and the European Union: From Europe Agreements to a Member Status* (Baden-Baden, Nomos, 1997) 61ff and the three Baltic reports, discussed in A Albi, 'The Central and Eastern European Constitutional Amendment Process in light of the Post-Maastricht Conceptual Discourse: Estonia and Baltic States' (2001) *European Public Law* 433–54.

towards national parliaments, and to referendums. There seems to be very little awareness of the EU democratic deficit, the legitimising capacity of the European Parliament and of a nascent European identity as its basis. Most conservatively, the Estonian Expert Commission contends that under the principles of popular sovereignty and national self-determination, power belongs to the Estonian people, whereas a European Parliament equivalent to national parliaments would mean a federal Union, in which Estonia may not participate. The Lithuanian Working Group reiterates on several occasions that the EU does not harm, but strengthens democracy and the rule of law.[55] The President of the Lithuanian Working Group had earlier written that democracy, both philosophically and pragmatically, cannot be realised without sovereignty.[56] With regard to Poland, Prof. Sokolewicz has pointed out:

> 'As with other European states, Poland will face the unprecedented phenomenon recently termed constitutional pluralism, which stands in sharp contrast to what is popular in our part of the continent [CEEC]: the tendency to think mainly in terms of national sovereignty, self-definition, and often even the homogeneity of a national state.'[57]

The author suggests that imminent constitutional amendments in CEE countries would offer an occasion for officially recognising in their constitutions the exercise of popular sovereignty on dual levels, by introducing a provision on the European Parliament and its elections, besides the traditional amendments on the right of information of national parliaments on EU affairs. Although this proposal does not find support in comparative perspective, it could be argued that Member States' constitutions suffer from a 'European Parliament deficit', except in Austria and Portugal, whose constitutions address European Parliament elections. In other words, the idea of popular sovereignty—that power is vested in the people—forms an underlying principle of the constitution, and it is time to recognise its exercise on dual levels—through national parliaments as well as the European Parliament. This is particularly the case with the constitutions of Latvia and Romania, which explicitly declare that power belongs to '*the People of Latvia*' and the '*Romanian people*' respectively.

4. CONCLUSION

This chapter suggests that the drafting of constitutional amendments for imminent EU accession in CEE Candidate Countries reveals that while in

---

[55] 'Republic of Lithuania Constitutional Law . . .', above note 16, 141ff.
[56] S Staciokas, 'Democracy and Sovereignty (The Lithuanian experience)', in *Philosophy and Democracy* (*Vilnius*, 1996), 99.
[57] Sokolewicz, above note 53, 256, with reference to Preuss, above note 53.

Western Europe, fifty years of EU integration have lead to a revision of the concept of sovereignty, Eastern European countries, having only recently re-established their sovereignty, tend to operate with traditional concepts. This is partly predetermined by CCEE constitutions, which, in complex provisions, differentiate between sovereignty and independence, subject them to various safeguards and to a difficult amendment procedure, and do not contain provisions on delegating powers to international organisations. Following this constitutional framework, CCEE (draft) constitutional amendments tend to address EU integration under 'international organisation' provisions and constitutional theory allows the delegation of sovereignty (ie those powers and competences which form part of internal sovereignty) to the EU, whereas independence (ie external sovereignty and statehood) has to be retained. This chapter suggests that the forthcoming wave of CCEE constitutional reforms provides an opportunity for re-examining these traditional concepts in more radical terms and incorporating more far-reaching changes into the conceptual structure of the amendments.

18

The Debate About Sovereignty in the United States: A Historical and Comparative Perspective

JEFFREY GOLDSWORTHY

1. INTRODUCTION

IT IS WIDELY believed 'that there is something new, or, as is often said, *sui generis*, in the constitutional structure of the European Union.'[1] But is this novelty or uniqueness due to the way that structure divides, diminishes, or demolishes sovereignty? Those familiar with the long history of debates concerning sovereignty within federal systems will be inclined to deny that it is. The upshot of those debates was to discredit the traditional theory that in every polity some person or body necessarily possesses sovereign (that is, supreme and unlimited) law-making authority.[2] In standard federal systems, sovereignty has been divided and distributed among so many different institutions that it no longer makes much sense to talk about sovereignty at all. The question, then, is whether the European Union poses some further, new challenge to the traditional theory of sovereignty. If not, the novelty or uniqueness of its constitutional structure requires some other explanation.

The vexed question of sovereignty within federal systems was first raised in the United States, and there are many similarities between the development of its constitutional structure and that of the European Union's. The former

---

[1] R Bellamy and D Castiglione, 'Building the Union: The Nature of Sovereignty in the Political Architecture of Europe', (1997) 16 *Law and Philosophy* 421 at 441.

[2] I am concerned with legal rather than political sovereignty, in the 'internal' rather than 'external' sense of the term: see N MacCormick, *Questioning Sovereignty* (Oxford, Oxford UP, 1999), 126–30. Legal sovereignty is law-making authority within a polity that is legally both supreme and unlimited—which means, unlimited by any norms, concerning the substance of legislation, that are either judicially enforceable or prescribed by a formally enacted legal instrument: see J Goldsworthy, *The Sovereignty of Parliament, History and Philosophy* (Oxford, Clarendon Press, 1999), 9–16.

was also described—by one of its main architects, James Madison—as 'emphatically *sui generis*': 'so unexampled in its origin, so complex in its structure, and so peculiar of its features' that it did not fit within traditional political vocabulary.[3] This was a common assessment. In *Hunter v Martin* (1815), '[i]t was justly observed, in the argument, that our system of government is *sui generis*, unlike any other that now exists, or that has ever existed'.[4]

The American structure was regarded as unique in several respects. The very idea of a written constitution, adopted by 'the people' in order to demarcate and limit the powers of their governmental organs, was novel. The institution of judicial review, whereby courts presumed to invalidate legislation deemed inconsistent with that constitution, was unprecedented. But for Madison, the new Constitution confounded political orthodoxy by creating a compound republic, 'neither wholly national nor wholly federal', in which sovereignty was divided between the nation and the states.[5]

Most of Madison's contemporaries did not agree that the Constitution divided sovereignty. It was widely believed that 'the people', who had supposedly enacted it, retained ultimate sovereignty and superintending authority over all organs of government. But were they the people of the nation as a whole, or the peoples of the states as separate entities? The essential nature of the American union was for many decades the subject of passionate disagreement, even more so than that of the European Union is now. Indeed, that disagreement persists in a muted form even today. Was the Constitution a basic law enacted by the sovereign people of a single nation, or a compact between the sovereign peoples of independent states? Or was Madison right in believing that 'the people' had succeeded in doing what most political thinkers denied that any sovereign could do, by permanently surrendering a portion of their sovereign power?

These rival theories had very practical, as well as theoretical, implications. They determined how the Constitution should be interpreted, and especially the respective powers of the nation and the states. They determined who had ultimate authority to interpret it: for example, whether national courts could over-ride state courts, and whether the states could 'interpose' their authority to nullify national measures they deemed unconstitutional. Above all, these theories determined whether the states retained authority to secede from the Union. That question was only finally settled by a terrible civil war, in which over six hundred thousand men perished. There is, perhaps, some lesson to be learned from that.

---

[3] James Madison, quoted in DR McCoy, *The Last of the Fathers; James Madison and the Republican Legacy* (Cambridge, Cambridge UP, 1989), 149–50.
[4] *Hunter v Martin, devisees of Fairfax* (1815) 18 Va 1; 4 Munf 1, p4 para4. See also Calhoun, text to n 78, below.
[5] James Madison, *Works*, IV, 420–1, quoted in C E Merriam, *A History of the Theory of Sovereignty Since Rousseau* (New York, Columbia UP, 1900), 164; see also *ibid*, 166.

2. SOVEREIGNTY IN REVOLUTIONARY AMERICA

The location of sovereignty in the United States perplexed political thinkers at the time of its founding, and has continued to do so ever since. This is not surprising, given that disputes about sovereignty helped cause both the war by which the Americans won their independence from Britain, and nearly a century later, the civil war that narrowly averted the dismemberment of their nation.

The War of Independence was provoked mainly by the British Parliament's attempt to enforce its claim to sovereignty over the American colonies.[6] Although the American rebels rejected that claim, most of them accepted the then popular thesis that there is necessarily a sovereign in every polity. Gordon Wood describes that thesis as a 'powerfully persuasive assumption' that 'pervaded the arguments of the whole Revolutionary generation'.[7]

At an early stage of their disagreements with Britain, some Americans attempted to show that Parliament had supreme legislative authority over 'external' matters such as trade, which were of common concern to Britain and its colonies, but no authority over matters 'internal' to each colony, which were the exclusive concern of local legislatures. They argued, in effect, that sovereignty was divided between the imperial and the local legislatures, both being supreme and uncontrollable within their respective domains.[8] In doing so, they were challenging one of the most fixed dogmas of the day: the indivisibility of sovereignty.[9] But their attempt was eventually regarded as a failure: by the early 1770s, most Americans felt compelled to accept the dogma.[10] Because they agreed that sovereignty was 'all or nothing' – unlimited or nonexistent—they concluded that the British Parliament had no legitimate authority over them.[11] Instead, sovereignty in the colonies necessarily belonged exclusively to their colonial legislatures. James Madison later wrote that at the time of the revolution, '[t]he legislative power was maintained to be as complete in each American Parliament, as in the British Parliament'.[12]

According to Wood,

'[t]he problem of sovereignty was not solved by the Declaration of Independence. It continued to be the most important theoretical question of politics throughout

---

[6] B Bailyn, *The Ideological Origins of the American Revolution* (enlarged ed., Cambridge Mass., Belknap Press, 1992), 198.
[7] GS Wood, *The Creation of the American Republic 1776–1787* (Chapel Hill, University of North Carolina Press, 1969), 345.
[8] Bailyn, above n 6, 216.
[9] *Ibid*, 198 and 202.
[10] *Ibid*, 224–5; Wood, above n 7, 350 and 353.
[11] *Ibid*, 350–4.
[12] G Hunt (ed.), *The Writings of James Madison*, vol. VI, 373, quoted by RL Schuyler, *Parliament and the British Empire* (Hampden Conn., Archon Books, 1963), 196.

the following decade, the ultimate abstract principle to which nearly all arguments were sooner or later reduced.'[13]

The Articles of Confederation were essentially a compact among the states, which preserved their separate sovereignties.[14] The second Article declared:

'Each state retains its sovereignty, freedom and independence, and every power, jurisdiction, and right, which is not by this confederation expressly delegated to the United States, in Congress assembled.'[15]

Limited powers were conferred on the Continental Congress, and '[c]ommercial regulation and taxing power, indeed all final governmental, lawmaking power remained with the states.'[16] Between the creation of the Confederation and that of the federal Constitution, the main challenge to the sovereignty of state legislatures came, not from the vesting of powers in the Congress, but from the emerging idea that true sovereignty belonged to the people.[17]

During the war with Britain, many Americans began to distrust their local legislatures. The extraordinary demands of war-time mobilisation led to the enactment of legislation curtailing rights, especially to property, that would never have been countenanced in peacetime.[18] The resulting grievances inspired a novel idea: that popular conventions, invested with an authority superior to that of ordinary legislatures, should establish written constitutions limiting the powers of all other organs of government.[19] Previously, there had been no lawful, institutional means for 'the people' to express its collective will, other than by electing legislators; and therefore the legislature was generally taken to be the voice of the people. Although previous colonial constitutions had often been described as fundamental laws that only the people could alter, since elected legislatures, and they

---

[13] Wood, above n 7, 354.
[14] *Ibid*, 354–61; AR Amar, 'Sovereignty and Federalism', (1987) 96 *Yale Law Journal* 1425, 1446–8; M Diamond, 'What the Framers Meant By Federalism', in RA Goldwin, ed., *A Nation of States, Essays on the American Federal System* 2nd ed.,(Chicago, Rand McNally, 1974) 25, 29–31; JR Stromberg, in D Gordon, (ed)., *Secession, State & Liberty* (New Brunswick and London, Transaction Publishers, 1998), 115 and 118n 81; C H Van Tyne, 'Sovereignty in the American Revolution', (1906–7)12 *American Historical Review* 529; A C McLaughlin, *A Constitutional History of the United States* (New York, Appleton-Century, 1935), 135; SH Beer, *To Make A Nation: The Rediscovery of American Federalism* (Cambridge Mass., Harvard UP, 1993), 194; J Story, *Commentaries on the Constitution of the United States* (reprint, New York, Da Capo Press, 1970), 320.
[15] Quoted in Wood, above n 7, 358.
[16] *Ibid*, 356.
[17] *Ibid*, 362–3.
[18] See J Rakove, 'Parchment Barriers and the Politics of Rights', in MJ Lacey and K Haakonssen, (eds)., *A Culture of Rights: The Bill of Rights in Philosophy, Politics and Law, 1791–1991* (Cambridge, Cambridge UP, 1991), 122–4.
[19] Wood, above n 7, 306–7, 328–9, 342–3, 364–5 & 383.

alone, represented the people, it was difficult to deny that they could alter those constitutions on the people's behalf.[20] But the new idea of popular conventions, specially convened to create or amend constitutions, offered a method by which the people could control their legislatures. This gave concrete, practical form to what had previously been an abstract, theoretical idea: that the power of an elected legislature really belonged to the people it represented—and therefore that the people, rather than the legislature, were truly sovereign.[21]

This emerging conception of popular sovereignty was greatly complicated by the agreement of the thirteen states, in 1788, to adopt a new federal Constitution. How that development affected the location of sovereignty has been a subject of disagreement ever since. Did it amount to the creation of a nation in which sovereignty was vested in the people of the nation as a whole? Or was sovereignty retained by the peoples of each of the individual states? Or was it divided between the people of the nation and the peoples of the states? These questions were not clearly resolved at the time of the founding, and perhaps could not have been, given the conflicting opinions strongly held on the subject. But soon after the new Constitution was adopted it became necessary to answer them, in order to resolve disputes concerning the proper interpretation of the powers it conferred. For one thing, it was not clear who had ultimate authority to settle such disputes: the Supreme Court, other branches of the national government, state legislatures, or conventions representing the people of each state.

The Anti-Federalists vehemently opposed the proposed Constitution on the ground that it would create a national juggernaut, which would inevitably subordinate the states and curtail individual liberty. Their objection was based largely on the received wisdom, which they constantly reiterated, that sovereignty was unlimited and indivisible. It followed that either the state legislatures or the national Congress would eventually predominate, and they were convinced that it would be the latter.[22] This was 'the most powerful obstacle to the acceptance of the new Constitution the opponents could have erected.'[23]

Most Americans probably continued to accept the dogma that sovereignty was indivisible.[24] They included Federalists such as Alexander Hamilton.[25] At the Philadelphia Convention, he warned that '[t]wo sovereignties cannot coexist within the same limits', and that either the national

[20] *Ibid*, 273–6.
[21] Amar, above n 14, 1432–39.
[22] Wood, above n 7, 527–8.
[23] *Ibid*, 528–9.
[24] Amar, above n 14, 1435 n 40.
[25] JH Read, *Power versus Liberty; Madison, Hamilton, Wilson and Jefferson* (Charlottesville, University Press of Virginia, 2000), 58 and 72.

or the state governments would eventually subordinate the other.[26] He attempted to ensure that the new Constitution would confer sufficiently ample powers on the national government to guarantee its supremacy. But his attempt failed, and consequently, he believed that a contest for supremacy was inevitable. Later, as a member of the national government, he strove to aggrandise its powers to ensure that it would prevail.[27]

During the debates over the ratification of the Constitution, the Federalists realised that the most effective response to the objection that sovereignty was indivisible was to concede the point. They argued that the Constitution did not attempt to divide ultimate sovereignty, which was, and would remain, vested in the people; it merely divided ordinary governmental powers between the national and state governments. This theory, propounded most eloquently and forcefully by James Wilson, eventually became 'the basis of all Federalist thinking.'[28] For example, it was used to justify the novel idea of judicial review of the constitutional validity of legislation. As Hamilton argued, this did not presume a superiority of the judicial to the legislative power, '[i]t only supposes that the power of the people is superior to both'.[29] As another Federalist put it, the power of the people was 'paramount to every constitution, inalienable in its nature, and indefinite in its extent'.[30] It has consequently been claimed that '[s]overeignty in the United States therefore proved to be as transcendent and absolute, as despotic and uncontrollable, as in the United Kingdom; the final irony of the American Revolution was that Sir William Blackstone's analysis prevailed in the end'.[31]

3. SOVEREIGNTY VESTED IN THE PEOPLE OF THE NATION

According to its Preamble, the Constitution was ordained and established by 'We the People of the United States'. James Wilson held that 'the people', who had thereby delegated powers to both the national and state governments, remained superior to their delegates, and retained ultimate sovereignty.

---

[26] Read, above n 25, 72.
[27] *Ibid*, 72–3.
[28] Wood, above n 7, 530–2.
[29] C Rossiter, (ed)., *The Federalist Papers* (New York, New American Library, 1961), no. 78, 467–8.
[30] Quoted in E S Morgan, *Inventing the People: The Rise of Popular Sovereignty in England and America* (New York, Norton, 1988), 281.
[31] JCD Clark, *The Language of Liberty 1660–1832* (Cambridge, Cambridge UP, 1994), 140; see also Wood, above n 7, 599. Sir William Blackstone had enunciated the doctrine of parliamentary sovereignty in his *Commentaries on the Laws of England* (Oxford, 1865), which were very influential in the United States as well as Britain.

'There necessarily exists in every government a power, from which there is no appeal; and which, for that reason, may be termed supreme, absolute, and uncontrollable. Where does this power reside? ... [I]n our governments . . . . [it] remains in the people. As our constitutions are superior to our legislatures; so the people are superior to our constitutions. The consequence is, that the people may change the constitutions, whenever and however they please.'[32]

Wilson differed from some of the other founders in holding that the Constitution was established by a single, national, people, rather than by the separate peoples of the thirteen states.[33] There were two versions of this theory. According to the first version, advanced by Wilson himself, this national people pre-existed and had created the thirteen states, rather than *vice versa*.[34] This version was later adopted by prominent opponents of state sovereignty and secession, such as Joseph Story, Daniel Webster, and Abraham Lincoln.[35] On this view, the people formed themselves into a nation long before they ratified the federal Constitution: they did so by adopting the Declaration of Independence, and establishing the Continental Congress. The thirteen colonies drafted new state constitutions only after receiving that Congress's permission to do so.[36] As Lincoln put it, 'The Union is older than any of the States; and in fact created them as States.'[37] The federal Constitution, as its Preamble was said to declare, merely made 'more perfect' a national union that preceded it. According to the second version of the theory, the peoples of the states only became a single national people when they ratified the federal Constitution. Sovereignty belonged to the peoples of the states before that transformation, but to the people of the nation thereafter. That seems to have been Chief Justice John Marshall's opinion.[38] Both versions of the theory are still defended today.[39]

But this theory is vulnerable to two damaging objections: the first challenges the existence of a national people at the relevant time, and the second, their possession of sovereignty. The first objection is that the Constitution was not established by, and did not itself establish, a single, national, people. As we have seen, under the preceding Confederation, the states were sovereign.[40] The federal Constitution was required to be ratified, not by a majority of the people nation-wide, but by popularly elected

---

[32] Quoted in Read, above n 25, 99.
[33] *Ibid*, 89–90.
[34] *Ibid*, 43 and 110.
[35] See Mark E Brandon, *Free in the World, American Slavery and Constitutional Failure* (Princeton, Princeton U.P., 1998), 174–5.
[36] See, eg, J Rakove, *Original Meanings, Politics and Ideas in the Making of the Constitution* (New York, Knopf, 1996), 164.
[37] Quoted in Brandon, above n 35, 190.
[38] Amar, above n 14, 1461.
[39] The first version is defended by Beer, above n 14, and Rakove, above n 36, 163–8; the second is defended by Amar, above n 14, 1460–61.
[40] Text to nn 14–16, above.

conventions in at least nine of the thirteen states, and could not bind any state in which it was not so ratified. It is therefore more plausible to regard it as having been ratified by the separate peoples of the states, rather than the united people of an already existing nation. That disposes of the first version of the theory. But the second version is also dubious, if Kenneth Stampp is right to argue that in its early decades

> '[t]he Union was valued less for its own sake than as a means to certain desirable ends ... [T]here were few signs of the kind of American national identity from which might grow a concept of a perpetual union as an essential end in itself.'[41]

National identity only developed gradually, during the first half of the nineteenth century.[42]

The second objection to the theory is even more formidable. Even after the adoption of the Constitution, it seems impossible to attribute continuing legal sovereignty to the people of the nation as a whole. They have never possessed a sovereign legal power to amend the Constitution, or indeed, any direct, unmediated law-making power.[43] As Henry Monaghan points out, 'in our over 200 years under the Constitution, that Constitution has never seen a national 'We the People' vote on anything. For constitutional purposes, voting on every issue, from presidential elections down, has always been state by state.'[44]

Article V of the Constitution requires that any amendment first be proposed by a two-thirds majority of either both Houses of Congress, or the state legislatures, and then passed by three-quarters of either the state legislatures or special state conventions (the choice between these alternatives being made by Congress). The people of the nation can neither propose, nor directly ratify, amendments. A minority of the people, scattered across the less populous states, can effectively veto constitutional amendments endorsed by a nation-wide majority.[45] Conversely, such a minority, if distributed across a sufficient number of states, could conceivably pass a constitutional amendment opposed by a majority.[46] Article V was adopted specifically to prevent a nation-wide majority of the people being able to over-ride the sectional interests of particular states, especially the less populous ones. 'No one believed that a simple majority of people

---

[41] K Stampp, 'The Concept of a Perpetual Union', (1978–9) 65 *Journal of American History* 2, 20.

[42] *Ibid*, 28.

[43] H P Monaghan, 'We the People[s], Original Understanding, and Constitutional Amendment', (1996) 96 *Columbia Law Review* 121 at 121–2.

[44] *Ibid*, 168.

[45] A R Amar 'Philadelphia Revisited: Amending the Constitution Outside Article V', (1988) 55 *University of Chicago Law Review* 1043 at 1060.

[46] Elai Katz, 'On Amending Constitutions: The Legality and Legitimacy of Constitutional Entrenchment', (1996) 29 *Columbia Journal of Law and Social Problems* 251, text to n 28.

(however defined) in population-rich states could amend the national Constitution.'[47] At the Philadelphia Convention, where Article V was first proposed, '[t]he idea of a single national body politic whose people were the source of supreme power, and therefore of the supreme law, was not even a debatable position'.[48] Those founders who initially advocated a strongly nationalist constitution, under which the states would be clearly subordinate bodies, were forced to compromise. Thereafter, in order to defuse opposition to the new Constitution, they assured the public that state rights would be fully protected by various constitutional mechanisms that included Article V.[49]

Akhil Reed Amar has recently responded to this objection by arguing that the people of the nation can lawfully exercise their sovereign power to change the Constitution by majoritarian action outside the process prescribed by Article V.[50] He argues that the people have the right 'to alter or abolish their government . . . (by convention) on any occasion at the pleasure of the People', regardless of Article V, which binds only the organs of government, and not the people.[51] 'Congress would be obliged to call a convention to propose amendments if a majority of American voters so petition; and . . . an amendment could be lawfully ratified by a simple majority of the American electorate.'[52]

Amar's arguments have met with detailed and devastating criticisms.[53] As one critic concludes, Amar

'disregards the language of the text, the apparent intention of the framers, the core of what we believe today, the benign policies underlying the text [the protection of both individual and state rights from pure majoritarianism], and, most fundamentally, the structure of sovereignty.'[54]

---

[47] Monaghan, above n 43, 139.

[48] T Anderson, *Creating the Constitution: The Convention of 1787 and the First Congress* (Pennsylvania, Pennsylvania U.P., 1993), 160.

[49] Monaghan, above n 43, 149-153.

[50] A R Amar, 'The Consent of the Governed: Constitutional Amendment Outside Article V', (1994) 94 *Columbia Law Review* 457; 'Philadelphia Revisited: Amending the Constitution Outside Article V, (1988) 55 *University of Chicago Law Review* 1043. See also B Ackerman, *We the People 2: Transformations* (Cambridge Mass., Harvard U.P., 1998), 69–95.

[51] Amar, 'Philadelphia Revisited', above n 50, 1435.

[52] A R Amar, 'Popular Sovereignty and Constitutional Amendment', in S Levinson, (ed), *Responding to Imperfection, The Theory and Practice of Constitutional Amendment* (Princeton, Princeton U.P., 1995) 89, 89 n 1.

[53] See, eg, Monaghan, above n 43; DR Dow, 'When Words Mean What We Believe They Say: The Case of Article V', (1990) 76 *Iowa Law Review* 1; JR Vile, 'Legally Amending the United States Constitution: The Exclusivity of Article V's Mechanisms', (1991) 21 *Cumberland Law Review* 271; BW King, 'Wild Political Dreaming: Historical Context, Popular Sovereignty, and Supermajority Rules',(2000) 2 *University of Pennsylvania Journal of Constitutional Law* 609.

[54] David R Dow, 'The Plain Meaning of Article V', in Levinson, above n 52, 138 n 91; see also *ibid*, 141.

Amar relies heavily on statements of the founders affirming the inalienable right of the people to alter their form of government. But they were invoking Locke's theory that, as a last resort remedy for extraordinary oppression, the people have a right to dissolve their constitution and replace it with a new one. This was a right of revolution, not of constitutional amendment; it was available only when tyranny could not be remedied by other means; and it was a right of natural law, not positive law.[55]

Samuel Beer argues that the American founders attributed two kinds of sovereignty to the American people: one to overthrow and reconstitute governments, which was unlimited by human law, and the other to exercise governmental powers according to the laws conferring and controlling them.[56] If so, then the two powers the founders had in mind would seem to be, first, an extra-legal, revolutionary power to dissolve governments and establish new ones in their place, which does not qualify as *legal* sovereignty, and secondly, a political power to control governments that is far too divided, diffuse, and indirect to be called legal *sovereignty*. The people of the nation can sensibly be described as sovereign only in a vague, political sense.[57]

The failure of the theory that the people of the nation are legally sovereign leaves three other theories in contention, to which I now turn.

4. SOVEREIGNTY VESTED IN THE SEPARATE PEOPLES OF THE STATES

Most Federalists agreed that 'the people' who had established the Constitution retained sovereign power. Proponents of state rather than national sovereignty argued that 'the people' were the peoples of the states considered separately. They interpreted the words 'We the People of the United States' as shorthand for 'We the People of Connecticut, Delaware, Georgia, New York . . . [etc]'.[58] After all, the Constitution was drafted by a convention of delegates appointed by state legislatures, was required to be ratified by popularly elected conventions in at least nine of the thirteen states, and could not bind any state in which it was not so ratified. No less an authority than James Madison acknowledged in *The Federalist* that

---

[55] Goldsworthy, above n 2, 151–3. Amar's reply, that the American founders transformed this extra-legal and extraordinary right of revolution into a legal and routine right of constitutional amendment, is unpersuasive: see King, above n 53, Parts IV and V.
[56] Beer, above n 14, 336.
[57] L B Orfield, 'Sovereignty and the Amending Power Part II', (1929) 15 *Iowa Law Reveiw* 504, 504–9.
[58] The abbreviated form was necessary due to uncertainty about which states would ratify the Constitution: Stampp, above n 41, 11. For further discussion, see Beer, above n 14, 253–4 and 323; Brandon, above n 35, 192; Stromberg, above n 14, 118; Ostrowski, above n 14, 177.

'[t]he Constitution is to be founded on the assent and ratification of the people of America . . . not as individuals composing one entire nation, but as composing the distinct and independent States to which they respectively belong . . . Each state, in ratifying the Constitution, is considered as a sovereign body independent of all the others, and only to be bound by its own voluntary act.'[59]

For many people—although not Madison himself—it followed that the United States was constituted by a voluntary compact between the peoples of independent states, who necessarily retained sovereign authority within their respective territories, and therefore the right to withdraw from the compact.[60]

The very concept of 'ratification' of the Constitution by equal and independent 'states', borrowed from the field of international relations, tended to imply ideas such as state sovereignty and secession.[61] Indeed, political theorists since the sixteenth century, who analysed both the internal and external relations of states in terms of sovereignty, had tended to obliterate intermediate forms of statehood between the unified state and mere alliances of states. Federal states such as Switzerland were depicted as voluntary leagues between sovereign states.[62] By the late eighteenth century, this conception of federalism was so pervasive that the Anti-Federalists, who advocated state sovereignty, could plausibly complain that the Federalists were distorting the true meaning of federalism.[63] This way of thinking was very influential for many decades:

'By the end of the 1820s . . . the idea of secession as a constitutional right of the sovereign states was fully developed, [but] the secessionist argument still lacked a comprehensive and effective rebuttal. More than that, the language of state sovereignty had become deeply embedded in the American vocabulary. Almost everyone spoke of the Union as 'our confederacy', of the Constitution as a 'compact'. The term 'sovereign' was associated with the states far more than with the federal government . . . Meanwhile, formulations of the idea of a perpetual union remained rare, brief, and incomplete.'[64]

Thomas Jefferson was the most influential proponent of the theory of state sovereignty.[65] He virtually equated 'the people' with 'the states'.[66] In

---

[59] C Rossiter, (ed), *The Federalist Papers*, above n 29, no.39, 243–4.
[60] See, eg, 'Amphitycon', in G Gunther, (ed), *John Marshall's Defence of McCulloch v Maryland* (Stanford, Stanford U. P., 1969), 56, and Spencer Roane, in id., 140–3.
[61] P Riley, 'The Origins of Federal Theory in International Relations Ideas', (1973) 6 *Polity* 87 at 89.
[62] *ibid*, 93–100, 105–6.
[63] *ibid*, 118. See also M Diamond, 'The Federalist's View of Federalism', in G Benson, (ed), *Essays in Federalism* (Institute for Studies in Federalism, 1961) 21, esp. 23–33 and 39–41.
[64] Stampp, above n 41, 28.
[65] Read, above n 25, 121.
[66] *ibid*, 146–8; see also WD Moore, 'Reconceiving Interpretive Autonomy: Insights From the Virginia and Kentucky Resolutions', (1994) 11 *Constitutional Commentary* 315 at 319.

the late 1790s, to protest the enactment by Congress of the draconian Alien and Sedition Acts, he helped secure the Kentucky legislature's passage of Resolutions asserting the right of the states to be the final judges of the constitutionality of their own and the national government's acts.[67] At about the same time, James Madison helped write the Virginia Resolutions, which also condemned the Alien and Sedition Acts. Although Madison's approach was more restrained than Jefferson's,[68] there were many similarities between the two sets of resolutions. Both denied that any branch of the national government, including the federal judiciary, could be the exclusive or final judge of the powers delegated to that government, because otherwise it could expand those powers at will.[69] Both also asserted that the final judge of the extent of the powers delegated by the constitutional compact had to be the parties to it: the states. Both also claimed that the states could 'interpose' their authority in order to preserve the Constitution and their rights under it.[70] The Kentucky Resolutions went further and suggested that the states could 'nullify', within their territories, acts of the national government that they deemed unconstitutional.[71]

These Resolutions were very influential; in later years, several other state legislatures issued similar ones.[72] In the 1830s, the Kentucky and Virginia Resolutions were cited to support extreme theories of state interposition, nullification, and secession. Federal tariff legislation enacted in 1828 was attacked as unconstitutional by southern agricultural states. Vice-President John C. Calhoun of South Carolina argued that each state, as a party to the original compact, retained ultimate sovereignty within its own territory, and could interpose its authority between the national government and the people, by declaring federal legislation null and void and preventing its enforcement.[73]

Madison strenuously denied that these extreme theories were supported by his and Jefferson's stated opinions of 1798–1800. If individual states could nullify national laws, he objected, the Constitution would succumb to the same disorders that had plagued the earlier Confederation.[74] He explained his earlier position as being that the states could proclaim their opinion that national laws were unconstitutional, and call for their repeal, but not assume

---

[67] Read, above n 25, 141.
[68] L. Banning, *The Sacred Fire of Liberty: James Madison and the Founding of the Federal Republic* (Ithaca, Cornell U.P., 1995), 388–9. Read, above n 25, 46–7. McCoy, above n 3, 135.
[69] Moore, above n 66, 320.
[70] The Virginia Resolutions are quoted in Banning, above n 68, 389. See also Madison's 'Report on the Virginia Resolutions', a reply to critics of the original Resolutions, quoted in *ibid*, 390, and Moore, above n 66, 333–41.
[71] The Kentucky legislature passed two sets of Resolutions, in 1798 and 1799: see Moore, above n 66, 331–2. See also Banning, above n 68, 387 and Read, above n 25, 145–6.
[72] McLaughlin, above n 14, 338–47.
[73] McCoy, above n 3, 131–2. See also Spencer Roane, in Gunther, above n 60, 148–9.
[74] McCoy, above n 3, 135.

the judicial function of invalidating them, or actively resist their execution.[75] However, he had more difficulty dissociating Jefferson from the ideas of the nullifiers. Jefferson had used the word 'nullification', apparently referring to the right of individual states to 'take measures' to ensure that unconstitutional federal laws 'shall [not] be exercised within their respective territories'.[76] Moreover, he subsequently endorsed the right of a state to secede from the union: 'to sever ourselves from that union we so much value rather than give up the rights of self-government which we have reserved'.[77]

Calhoun agreed with Madison that the constitutional structure of the American federation was 'new, peculiar and unprecedented'.[78] But he denied that this was due to its having divided sovereignty, on the ground that this was impossible. 'I maintain that sovereignty is in its nature indivisible. It is the supreme power in a State, and we might just as well speak of half a square, or half a triangle, as of half a sovereignty.'[79] In his opinion, sovereignty remained with the states (meaning the peoples of the states[80]), which had delegated some of their powers to the national government for limited purposes. If the national government exceeded its powers, any state could nullify its acts within its borders, acting, for this purpose, through a specially convened convention of its people.[81]

Calhoun and his followers also denied that the United States Supreme Court possessed an authority to interpret the Constitution superior to that of state Supreme Courts. This view had previously been vigorously asserted by the Supreme Court of Appeals of Virginia, which included Judge Spencer Roane. Jefferson had intended, on becoming President, to appoint Roane to the Chief Justiceship of the United States Supreme Court, but was frustrated by John Adams's last-minute appointment of John Marshall.[82] Jefferson warmly commended Roane's outspoken criticisms of Marshall's nationalist jurisprudence, which aggrandised the authority of the federal judiciary.[83]

In *Hunter v Martin*, the Virginian court had held that the federal and state judiciaries possessed equal authority, within their respective jurisdictions, and denied that the former could over-rule decisions of the latter.[84] As

---

[75] McCoy, above n 3, 141–2.

[76] Ibid. 143–7; Moore, above n 66, 320–1.

[77] Quoted in Banning, above n 68, 389–90; see also D W Livingston, 'The Secession Tradition in America', in Gordon, above n 14, 15.

[78] Quoted by A O Spain, *The Political Theory of John C Calhoun* (New York, Bookman Associates, 1951), 173. For Madison, see the text to n 3 above.

[79] Spain, above n 78, 173.

[80] *Ibid*, 176.

[81] *Ibid*, 201–2.

[82] See Kerr, 'If Spencer Roane Had Been Appointed Chief Justice Instead of John Marshall' (1934) 20 *American Bar Association Journal* 167, and 'Judge Spencer Roane of Virginia: Champion of States' Rights—Foe of John Marshall' (1953) 66 *Harvard Law Review* 1242.

[83] Roane's essays are collected in Gunther, above n 60; for Jefferson's approval, see 'Judge Spencer Roane of Virginia', above n 82, 1253 n 96 and 1256 n 114.

[84] 18 Va 1; 4 Munf 1 (Va 1815).

Judge Cabell explained, the national and state governments were separate and independent, could act only through their own organs, and could neither command nor enforce the obedience of the other.

'[T]he federal government was a league, or treaty, made by the individual states, as one party, and all the states, as another; [and] when two nations differ, about the construction of a league, or treaty, existing between them, neither has the exclusive right to decide it; and [therefore] if one of the states should differ with the United States, as to the extent of the grant made to them, there is no common umpire between them, but the people, by an amendment of the constitution.'[85]

The federal Constitution and national laws validly made under it were indisputably binding on state judges, but in cases arising within state jurisdiction state courts were entitled to decide for themselves what the Constitution and national laws required.[86] The Virginia court was not alone in adopting this attitude: a total of seven state courts at various times did the same.[87] Calhoun and his followers agreed with them. Although the United States Supreme Court over-ruled the Virginian court in *Martin v Hunter's Lessee*,[88] exercising a statutory power of appellate review that the state court had declared unconstitutional, Calhoun refused to concede the point, citing other examples in which state independence had been successfully maintained.[89]

Calhoun became the leading theorist of state sovereignty, and his writings influenced many other southern statesmen.[90] The theory was put into practice most dramatically when the southern states purported to secede from the Union and establish a new confederacy. The idea that each state had voluntarily joined the Union, and therefore could choose to withdraw from it, was by no means implausible. James Wilson himself had said that the Preamble to the Constitution necessarily implied that '[t]hose who ordain and establish have the power, if they think proper, to repeal and annul'.[91] If so, and if the peoples of the states had established the Constitution, then they must have retained the right to repeal and annul it within their borders. This idea was not confined to the south. From 1803 to1821, secession was seriously proposed on at least five occasions in various north-eastern states,

---

[85] *Ibid*, p.23 sect. 29, per Judge Roane, quoting the Pennsylvania Supreme Court in *Commonwealth v Cobbett* 3 Dall (Pa) 342.

[86] *Ibid*, p.5 sect. 6; p.11 sect.12.

[87] Warren, 'Legislative and Judicial Attacks on the Supreme Court of the United States—A History of the Twenty-fifth Section of the Judiciary Act', (1913) 47 *American Law Review* 1, 161.

[88] (1816) 1 *Wheaton* 304.

[89] Spain, above n 78, 200.

[90] *Ibid*, 190.

[91] Quoted by Amar, above n 52, 105.

due to disaffection with national policies.[92] Radical northern abolitionists (of slavery) persistently advocated secession, in order to escape anticipated domination of the Union by southern slaveholders.[93]

'At times in the country's history the movement for secession was every bit as strongly and conscientiously pursued in New England as it was in the South.'[94]

Only in 1869 did the Supreme Court hold, for the first time, that the Constitution had established an indestructible union.[95] But general acceptance of this conclusion was the result of force rather than reasoned argument.[96]

'Because . . . the logic behind it was far from perfect, because the Constitution and the debates over ratification were fraught with ambiguity, the pessimistic premonition of John Quincy Adams, expressed in a letter of 1831, was tragically fulfilled. 'It is the odious nature of the question', he wrote, 'that it can be settled only at the cannon's mouth.'[97]

5. SOVEREIGNTY VESTED IN THE COLLECTIVE PEOPLES OF THE STATES

An obvious claimant for sovereignty under any Constitution is the person or body with the power to amend it. The English legal positivist, John Austin, who insisted that there is a sovereign in every polity, concluded that in the United States

'the sovereignty of each of the states, and also of the larger state arising from the federal union, resides in the states' governments as forming one aggregate body; meaning by a state's government, not its ordinary legislature, but the body of its citizens which appoints its ordinary legislature, and which, the union apart, is properly sovereign therein.'[98]

This conclusion was an inference from Article V of the Constitution, the amending provision.[99] Austin's analysis attracted some supporters,

---

[92] Brandon, above n 35, 183; Thomas J DiLorenzo, 'Yankee Confederates: New England Secession Movements Prior to the War Between the States', in Gordon, above n 14, 147–50; McLaughlin, above n 14, ch.XXV.
[93] Brandon, above n 35, 183–4; Livingston, above n 77, 11.
[94] Brandon, above n 35, 198.
[95] *Texas v White* (1869) 74 U.S. (7 Wall.) 700.
[96] Riley, above n 61, 93 and 107.
[97] Quoted in Stampp, above n 41, 33.
[98] J Austin, *The Province of Jurisprudence Determined* (H L A Hart, (ed), London, Weidenfeld and Nicholson, 1954), 251.
[99] *Ibid*, 251 n 22.

including the eminent British constitutional lawyer, A.V. Dicey.[100] Dicey agreed that

> 'The legal sovereignty of the United States resides in the States' governments as forming one aggregate body represented by three-fourths of the several States at any time belonging to the Union.'[101]

But there are a number of flaws in this analysis. First, Article V does not vest sovereignty in the states alone, whether acting through legislatures or conventions, because no amendment can be passed without the co-opera-tion of the national Congress. If the amending power amounts to sover-eignty, it is vested in a variety of institutions, national and state, which can combine in any one of four alternative ways.[102] Secondly, as James Bradley Thayer pointed out, it is doubtful that all these institutions, meeting at different times over a period of months or even years, constitute a single body that can aptly be described as a sovereign.[103] It is true that a sovereign can consist of several persons or bodies meeting at different times and places; the British Parliament, for example, consists of a monarch and two Houses.[104] But as the number and variety of bodies that share a power increases, and as the size of the majorities required to exercise the power increases, the ability effectively to exercise it decreases. An impaired ability to act may be due to internal as well as external constraints; just like a natu-ral person, a body or combination of bodies may be handicapped by its own character or anatomy. It is a question of degree, but at some point a body or combination of bodies may, by virtue of its internal constitution, be so disabled from effective action that it cannot be regarded as possessing truly sovereign agency.[105] In the United States, the consent of three quarters of fifty state legislatures or conventions is extremely difficult to obtain. As Dicey conceded, the putative American sovereign is

> 'a despot hard to rouse. He is not, like the English Parliament, an ever-wakeful legislator, but a monarch who slumbers and sleeps. The sovereign of the United States has been roused to serious action but once during the course of more than a century . . .[and] a monarch who slumbers for years is like a monarch who does not exist.'[106]

---

[100] A V Dicey, *Lectures Introductory to the Study of the Law of the Constitution* 2nd ed., (London, MacMillan, 1886), 135. See also Richman, 'From John Austin to John C Hurd', 14 *Harvard Law Review* 353.

[101] Dicey, above n 100, 136–7.

[102] Orfield, above n 57, 513 and 517.

[103] 'Dicey's Law of the English Constitution', reprinted in J B Thayer, *Legal Essays* (Boston, Boston Book Co, 1908), 191, 202.

[104] M Radin, 'The Intermittent Sovereign', (1940) 39 *Yale Law Journal* 514, 523–4. See also Orfield, above n 57, 516–17.

[105] Goldsworthy, above n 2, 14.

[106] Dicey, above n 100, 137.

Thirdly, the amending power is not unlimited. It has been argued that it could not be used to repeal the Constitution in its entirety, or to make amendments that would change its fundamental character, such as by replacing the Republic with a hereditary monarchy.[107] Whether the power is subject to unexpressed, implicit limits cannot be settled here.[108] But Article V expressly provided that the importation of slaves could not be prohibited before 1808, and still provides that no state can be deprived of its equal representation in the Senate without its consent. As there are currently fifty states, this is a significant restriction. The amending power is in this regard powerless, and therefore does not qualify as full sovereignty. To further complicate the definition of the putative sovereign, by adding that for this purpose it includes whichever state's consent is required, is surely implausible.[109] That would merely strengthen the objection that Article V divides the amending power among so many different bodies, which can combine in so many different ways, that it cannot sensibly be regarded as vested in a single sovereign.

For all these reasons, as Lester Orfield concluded in 1931,

> '[t]he nature of the federal amending power demonstrates the futility of the concept of sovereignty [in the United States] . . . The involved explanations made necessary and the metaphysical difficulties encountered in ascribing sovereignty to the amending power show the barren aridity of the term . . . The amending power is an artificial sovereign.'[110]

6. SOVEREIGNTY DIVIDED BETWEEN THE NATION AND THE STATES

As we have seen, American theorists before the revolution initially tried to prove that sovereignty in the colonies was divided between the Imperial Parliament and local legislatures, but eventually abandoned the attempt.[111] However, their efforts influenced political thought during the subsequent founding of the Constitution. They had suggested that it was possible, and might be salutary, to divide sovereignty among different levels of government.

> 'Later analysts, starting where the colonists had left off before Independence and habituated to think in terms of 'qualified sovereignty', 'lesser sovereignties', 'the divisibility of sovereignty,' would continue the effort to make federalism a logical as well as a practical system of government.'[112]

---

[107] Thayer, above n 103, and Radin, above n 104, 525.
[108] See JR Vile, 'The Case Against Implicit Limits on the Constitutional Amending Process', in Levinson, above n 52, 191.
[109] *Contra*, Orfield, above n 57, 519–20.
[110] *Ibid*, 521–2.
[111] See text to nn 8–11, above.
[112] Bailyn, above n 6, 228.

Alexander Hamilton agreed that the people were the ultimate source of the Constitution's legitimacy, but denied that they were sovereign in a practical, operational sense. 'The people' were incapable of actively guiding government, or of preventing it from exceeding its powers. The people took direct action only in extraordinary situations of revolution. For almost all practical purposes, sovereignty was vested in government; indeed, sovereignty was government, and a political society without sovereignty would be a people without government.[113] Hamilton was reluctant to agree that sovereignty could be divided, and strove to ensure that the national government would possess it de facto.[114] Nevertheless, to defuse opposition to the proposed Constitution, he publicly argued that it would divide sovereignty between the national and state governments:

'the State governments would clearly retain all the rights of sovereignty which they before had, and which were not ... *exclusively* delegated to the United States'; 'a concurrent jurisdiction in certain cases results from the division of the sovereign power.'[115]

James Madison was the principal proponent of the theory that the Constitution successfully divided sovereignty.[116] He conceded that it was a compact entered into by the sovereign peoples of the several states.[117] But he also maintained that they had thereby agreed to form a single, national people for certain purposes.[118] Americans were for those purposes a single people, represented in the House of Representatives, and for other purposes many peoples, represented on an equal basis in the Senate.[119] As Monaghan puts it, 'the American Constitution rested on *two* pillars: namely, 'We the People' (nationally understood) *and* the several states (ie, 'We the People' thereof) as independent political communities.'[120] Madison held that sovereignty was divided accordingly.[121]

'[T]he supreme power, that is, the sovereignty of the people of the States, was in its nature divisible, and was in fact divided ... as the States, in their highest sovereign character, were competent to surrender the whole sovereignty and form

---

[113] Read, above n 25, 57–8, 75 and 85–6.
[114] See text to nn 25–7, above.
[115] C Rossiter, (ed.), *The Federalist Papers*, above n 59, no 32, 198 and 201. See also M Forsyth, *Unions of States, The Theory and Practice of Confederation* (New York, Leicester U.P., 1981), 108.
[116] Spain, above n 79, 168–9. For others see *ibid*, 170.
[117] See Read, above n 25, 43–4, comparing *The Federalist* nos. 39 and 46, and Banning, above n 68, 443 n 30. See also *ibid*, 139, 386, and 393.
[118] McCoy, above n 3, 135.
[119] Read, above n 25, 44–5; Monaghan, above n 43, 138; McCoy, above n 3, 149.
[120] Monaghan, above n 43, 129, and see also *ibid*, 138–9.
[121] McCoy, above n 3, 149–50.

themselves into a consolidated State, so they might surrender a part and retain, as they have done, the other part.'[122]

This they had done, with 'the portions surrendered by the States composing the Federal sovereignty over specified subjects', and 'the portions retained forming the sovereignty of each over the residuary subjects within its sphere.'[123]

Amar maintains that at this time, Madison was the only significant theorist to adopt this theory: '[a]lmost every other major figure thought that ultimate sovereignty was indivisible and therefore had to reside solely in either a state or a continental people.'[124] But if that is the case, so much the worse for them! As Madison insisted, '[i]t is difficult to argue intelligibly concerning the compound system of government in the United States without admitting the divisibility of sovereignty.'[125] If sovereignty is indivisible, then 'the political system of the United States is a chimera, mocking the vain pretensions of human wisdom.'[126] The Supreme Court, and a number of political theorists including de Tocqueville, later agreed that the Constitution divided sovereignty between the nation and the states.[127]

Madison conceded that the Constitution was a compact between the sovereign peoples of the several states. The only way to avoid the conclusion that these peoples retained their sovereignty, including power to withdraw from the compact, was to hold that a sovereign could irrevocably bind itself or surrender part of its power. This contravened a popular dogma in the political thought of the day, which was a major plank in Calhoun's theory of state sovereignty.[128] But it was plausibly argued that not all compacts were revocable, especially compacts by which constitutions and governments were established. Most Americans conceived of constitutions in Lockean terms, as being founded ultimately on consent. According to Locke, that consent could be revoked, but only as a remedy of last resort for quite extraordinary oppression, and then only by the extra-legal means of revolution, which dissolved the constitution. The revocation of consent was not a lawful power within the framework of the constitution.[129]

Opponents of state nullification and secession took the same view of the compact that established the federal Constitution. It was an agreement to

---

[122] Madison, *Letters and Other Writings* (1865 ed.) vol. IV, 390–1, quoted by McLaughlin, above n 14, 438 n 25.
[123] Madison, quoted by McCoy, above n 3, 149–50.
[124] Amar, above n 14, 1452–53 n 113.
[125] Madison, *Works*, IV 420–1, quoted in C Merriam, above n 5, 164.
[126] Madison, *Works*, IV, 61, quoted in Merriam, above n 5.
[127] *Chisholm v Georgia* (1792) 2 *Dallas* 419, especially 435 per Iredell J.; *McCulloch v Maryland* (1819) 4 *Wheaton* 316, at 410 per Marshall CJ. See Merriam, above n 5, 165 for the political theorists.
[128] Spain, above n 79, 191 and 196.
[129] See Goldsworthy, above n 2, 151–2.

establish a system of government and law that necessarily bound the parties to it, who retained the extra-legal right of revolution, but no legal right to withdraw from it. Otherwise submission to law would be a matter of individual discretion, and there would be no permanence or security in government. In this respect, there was no difference between constitutions and governments at the national, and at the state, levels.[130] Towns and counties had no more right than individuals to nullify state laws, or secede from their states, and the states themselves were in the same position with respect to the Union. The Constitution was enforceable law—in its own words, 'the supreme law of the land'—not a mere treaty whose efficacy depended on voluntary compliance.[131] As Joseph Story explained,

> 'A government may originate in the voluntary compact or assent of the people of several states, or of a people never before united, and yet when adopted and ratified by them, be no longer a matter resting in compact; but become an executed government or constitution, a fundamental law, and not a mere league.'[132]

During the ratification debates, the critical distinction between a constitution, and a league or treaty, had often been adverted to.[133] Story pointed out that Anti-Federalists had opposed the Constitution precisely because it was intended to establish a more effective and permanent form of government than the Confederation.[134] The arguments of Calhoun and his followers, if they prevailed, would frustrate that intention.[135]

Crucial to this argument is the premise that the sovereign parties to the original compact assumed legally binding obligations that limited their sovereignty thereafter. As Story explained, a constitution 'is a permanent form of government, where the powers, once given, are irrevocable, and cannot be resumed or withdrawn at pleasure.'[136] To enjoy the benefits of a constitution, a people must abide by its terms.[137] Consequently, although a state might, in an extreme case, attempt secession, this was 'not a right derived from the constitution', and as an extra-legal right, 'it must be at the

---

[130] McLaughlin, above n 14, 446, 448.
[131] Story, above n 14, 295–6, 302–9, and 320–2.
[132] Story, above n 14, 335. See President Andrew Jackson's statement quoted in McLaughlin, above n 14, 450.
[133] See, eg, *The Federalist* no.33, quoted in Amar, above n 14, at 1461, and other material quoted in *ibid*, 1463 n 162.
[134] Story, above n 14, vol. I, 325 (ch.III, para. 357).
[135] *Ibid*, 289 (para.321).
[136] *Ibid*, 319.
[137] Vile, above n 53, 296.

risk of all the penalties attached to an unsuccessful resistance to established authority.'[138]

Amar has recently attempted to revive the old idea that sovereignty is illimitable and indivisible, arguing that 'the People of 1787 were incapable of binding a future convention of the People, even if they had tried'; '[t]o contest this is to deny the sovereign right of the People to alter their government at any time for any reason, and to attempt to bind the *source* of all law—the sovereign People—with a law of its own creation'.[139] But that is precisely what the peoples of the states did. As John Vile points out,

> '[t]hinkers as diverse as Daniel Webster and John C. Calhoun agreed that popular sovereignty was not an invitation to 'tumultuous assemblies' to write new constitutions as they pleased. Rather, it was for the people to proceed according to the forms by which they had previously bound themselves.'[140]

To protect the fundamental rights of individuals and of states against ordinary majorities, 'the people' imposed controls not only on the ordinary power of legislation, but also on their own extra-ordinary power of constitutional amendment. By doing so, they limited their own sovereignty.[141]

7. SOME COMPARISONS WITH EUROPE

Many of the disagreements about the nature of the European Union—and in particular, the location of ultimate sovereignty and supreme judicial authority within it—are analogues of similar disagreements that strained the American Union during the first seventy-five years of its constitutional development.

In the United States, the theory that the people of the nation are legally sovereign, has always been the weakest of the contending theories. The opposite theory, which held that the peoples of the several states were sovereign, was more plausible before the civil war, but could not be maintained thereafter. The most plausible theory denies that there is any single locus of sovereignty in the United States, because it is permanently divided among a variety of institutions at both national and state levels.

[138] Senator Edward Livingston, during the Senate debate over nullification (1830), quoted in Stampp, above n 41, 29. The legality of secession was a crucial issue: Abraham Lincoln complained that the secessionists 'sugar-coated' their 'rebellion' by the 'ingenuous sophism . . . that any State of the Union may, *consistently* with the national Constitution, and therefore *lawfully* and *peacefully*, withdraw from the Union': *Message to Congress*, July 4, 1861, quoted in H Jaffa, 'Partly Federal, Partly National': on the Political Theory of the Civil War', in RA Goldwin, (ed.), *A Nation of States, Essays on the American Federal System* 2nd ed., (Chicago, Rand McNally, 1974) 109, 110.
[139] Amar, above n 14, 1465 n 167.
[140] John C Vile, above n 14, 279.
[141] Dow, above n 54, 136; Orfield, above n 57, 508–9.

In the European Union, it cannot be plausibly maintained that sovereignty resides either in the institutions of the Union, or in the people of all the member states considered as an aggregate. There, too, it is more plausible to hold that the member states or their peoples possess ultimate sovereignty. Indeed, that theory is more credible in Europe today than it was in the United States before the civil war. The European Union is plainly the creature of treaties between member states—and between their governments, rather than their peoples. It is much more like a compact between sovereign states than the United States ever was: there is no basis for the claim that it is the creature of a supranational 'We the People'. The right to secede is, at least in the domestic constitutional law of some member states such as Britain, universally admitted even by Europhiles. Those domestic laws are therefore committed to something like the state sovereignty theory propounded by Calhoun in the United States. An open question is whether they should also recognise a right of member states to nullify central laws or directives. Calhoun himself said: 'There are many who acknowledge the right of a State to secede, but deny its right to nullify; and yet, it seems impossible to admit the one without admitting the other.'[142] If the greater power of secession is conceded, how can the lesser power of nullification be denied?

No right of member states to secede is recognised by the law of the European Union itself, because international law governing the right of withdrawal from international organisations has changed since the early nineteenth century.[143] If the European Union had been created then, the right of member states to secede could not have been doubted. By denying that member states have a right to secede, the law of the European Union is committed to something like Madison's theory, that the sovereign states which created the Union thereby irrevocably surrendered part of their own sovereignty.

What distinguishes the European Union from the United States today is not the absence of any single locus of sovereignty—that is common to both systems—but rather, the different reasons for that absence. Europe lacks a single, unified legal system within which sovereignty is divided. There is no European equivalent of the United States Constitution—no fundamental law that underpins both central and member state legal systems, combines them into a harmonious whole, and provides (in principle) a single answer to all disputed questions. In Europe, there are many legal systems—that of the centre, and those of the member states—whose fundamental laws provide different answers to the analogous constitutional questions arising there. The reason that sovereignty is divided is that these fundamental laws

---

[142] John C Calhoun, *Works*, VI, 170, quoted in McLaughlin, above n 14, 445.
[143] J Weiler, 'Alternatives to Withdrawal From An International Organization: the Case of the European Economic Community', (1985) 20 *Israel Law Review* 282.

either themselves involve a division of sovereignty, or recognise different sovereigns. For example, the constitutional law of the United Kingdom still recognises its own Parliament as sovereign, whereas the law of the European Union assumes a permanent division of sovereignty. The constitutional structure of the United States was widely believed to be *sui generis* because it divided sovereignty. If that of the European Union is now *sui generis*, this is not because it divides sovereignty. It is because it is not governed by a single, unified legal system, but rather by many legal systems that are systematically inter-connected but not entirely harmonious.

It might be better if federal and quasi-federal systems such as those of the American and European unions were no longer analysed in terms of 'sovereignty'. The American experience vindicates Patrick Riley's claim that the oddness of much federal theory—its tendency to paradox and contradiction—stems from its failure to acknowledge that indivisible sovereignty is simply incompatible with federalism. Federalism attempts to reconcile regional autonomy, which is incompatible with national sovereignty, with effective national decision-making in a stable union of regions, which is incompatible with regional sovereignty.[144] All genuinely federal theories, by opposing the concentration of ultimate authority at either the national or regional levels, 'are doctrines of anti-sovereignty . . . Federalism ought to have been a pure theory of anti-sovereignty.'[145]

Unfortunately, attempts to fit the square peg of sovereignty within the round hole of federalism have had worse consequences than theoretical paradox and contradiction. They have inflamed political disputes and contributed to the outbreak of violence. In North America, controversies about sovereignty helped spark war between Britain and its colonies, and almost a century later, the civil war. Of course, theoretical disagreement was not the primary cause of either war. But rival theories of sovereignty were enlisted on both sides of disputes about central versus regional authority, and made compromise more difficult. As Riley has argued,

> 'as (or if) the world gradually moves away from the idea of strict sovereignty, by assuming either that it is no longer necessary . . . or that it was never necessary . . . federalism can be reconceived—along lines of rational negotiation, discussion, and mutual concession.'[146]

The question of secession from the European Union will not be resolved by a theoretical or legal analysis of sovereignty. If it becomes a genuinely practical question, Riley's prescription of negotiation, discussion, and mutual compromise will be crucial. As Donald Livingston has warned:

---

[144] Riley, above n 61, 87–8.
[145] *Ibid*, 107.
[146] *Ibid*, 120.

'The debate over the European Union today resembles the debate of 1787–89 between the Federalists and Antifederalists, the latter of which feared that the Constitution would end in a consolidated nationalism, and the former who assured them that such could never happen. One hopes that this will not degenerate into something like the shouting match between southerners who claimed that the Constitution was not a consolidated regime and northern unionists who declared that it was and always had been. But it could. One already hears from the left the claim that the European Union is an instrument for achieving human rights and that the powers surrendered to the Union cannot be recalled. This was exactly Lincoln's doctrine. Unless the right of secession is thought through and faced squarely, one can imagine Europe re-enacting the melancholy history of the United States.'[147]

---

[147] Livingston, above n 77, 22–3, italics added.

Part C

Constitutional Perspectives II: The View from Europe

19

Sovereignty and the Supremacy Doctrine of the European Court of Justice

GRÁINNE DE BÚRCA

1. INTRODUCTION

THIS SHORT CONTRIBUTION was prompted by a question which arose during a seminar on the subject of the supremacy of EC law, concerning whether the terms 'supremacy of EC law' and 'sovereignty of the EC' refer to the same concept. There was some confusion on the matter, and the purpose of this brief contribution is to examine the relationship between these two terms. As this book demonstrates, sovereignty is a fundamental but complex notion which has been defined in many different ways and in many different contexts. This chapter focuses primarily on the conceptual definition of ultimate, self-defining legal authority but also draws occasionally on the political sense of actual authority and control.

The supremacy doctrine of the European Court of Justice—the power and originality of which is almost dulled now by the familiarity of the famous judicial passages—will be examined with two questions in mind. The first is whether the supremacy doctrine necessarily entails or presupposes a claim to sovereignty on behalf of the EC (and more problematically, but less likely, of the EU[1]), and the second is whether it necessarily presupposes a claim of

---

[1] It is unclear whether the legal claim to sovereignty which, according to this chapter, underlies the reasoning in the *Van Gend en Loos* and *Costa v Enel* cases, nn 8 and 10 below, applies only to the EC or whether it applies also to the EU. However, given that little of non-Community EU law (ie the law of the second and third pillars) can have direct effect, the possible meaning of its 'supremacy' over national law also remains unclear. If there are no agreed juridical mechanisms for settling the question of the primacy of second and third pillar law over national law, the claim to automatic primacy over national law may be difficult to make. However, the fact that the doctrine of supremacy may not apply to all EU law does not necessarily mean that a claim of EU sovereignty cannot be made.

abandonment or loss of sovereignty on the part of the Member States. The plausibility of those claims will be considered primarily by reference to a legal-conceptual understanding of the notion of sovereignty, and to a lesser extent in the light of a more political or practical understanding of the notion.

2. SUPREMACY OF EUROPEAN LAW AND THE SOVEREIGNTY OF THE EC/EU

The EC and EU Treaties, despite the fact that they confer legal personality and capacity in international relations on the European Community and an increasing degree of external authority on the European Union—which announces its intention in Article 2 TEU to 'assert its identity on the international scene'—do not themselves make a clear claim to sovereignty on behalf of the European polity.[2] It has been the Court of Justice which, over time, has purported to clarify the legal nature and, increasingly, the constitutional nature of the new order established by the series of European treaties. Further, the authority of the Court's rulings in this regard have never been seriously undermined nor politically challenged despite the opportunity for the Member States, at every Intergovernmental Conference, to overturn or amend them.[3] Despite the enormous changes in the European polity over the decades since the early 1960s, and most notably its evolution from Community to Union, the twin principles of supremacy and direct effect remain fairly central to the legal conception of the polity.[4] Does this assertion by the Court of Justice of the supremacy of EC law necessarily entail a claim that the EC is a sovereign polity, or does the supremacy doctrine in fact make a rather more limited claim?

---

[2] The 'external' dimension of EC and EU sovereignty is a crucial issue but not one which is addressed in this short chapter. For some discussions see T Tiilikainen 'To Be or Not to Be? An Analysis of the Legal and Political Elements of Statehood in the EU's External Identity' (2001) 6 *European Forign Affairs Review* 223, JW de Zwaan 'Legal personality of the European Communities and the European Union' (1999) 30 *Netherlands Yearbook of International Law* 75, K Lenaerts and E de Smijter 'The European Union as an Actor under International Law' (1999/2000) 19 *Year Book of European Law* 95 and the editorial comment 'The European Union: A New International Actor' (2001) 38 *Common Market Law Review* 825

[3] Some, on the contrary, see the protocol on subsidiarity and proportionality, which was attached by the Amsterdam Treaty to the EC Treaty and therefore has Treaty status itself, as the first affirmation by the Member States through the IGC of the doctrines of supremacy and direct effect. See, more dramatically now, Art. I-10[(1)] of the draft European constitutional treaty published on 12 June 2003 following the convention on the future of Europe.

[4] For an account of the way in which the supremacy doctrine of the Court gradually embedded itself in domestic legal orders, see K Alter, *Establishing the Supremacy of European Law* (Oxford, OUP, 2001).

(a) hypothesis 1: supremacy of EC law does not entail sovereignty

On one analysis, the doctrine of supremacy can be conceived of and understood in a reasonably limited way, as involving little more than a pragmatic rule of priority for dealing with the situation where there is a conflict or inconsistency between a particular EC measure and a national law measure. In this sense it can be seen simply as a requirement of non-application in a specific context of a particular rule of national law when there is a provision of EC law which conflicts directly with it. To use Bruno de Witte's terms, it can be seen as 'a duty to disapply a provision of national law' in certain circumstances. Following in the vein of this argument, sovereignty on the other hand, unlike supremacy, is an absolute rather than a relative concept[5] in the sense that it entails a claim to autonomy which, although it tends to be asserted both 'internally' and 'externally'[6] does not necessarily depend on the existence of nor define itself crucially by reference to any other competing power or authority.[7] Furthermore, the concept of sovereignty, at least in its legal sense tends, unlike supremacy, to be institutionally located. Thus sovereignty is said to reside—in a context such as that of the UK, for example—in the institution of Parliament, or in other political contexts it may be said to reside in the constitution. Supremacy on the other hand can be understood not necessarily as an inherent 'property' of EC law, but as a pragmatically-inspired direction to national judicial and other authorities as to what should occur when a given provision of EC law appears to be inconsistent with a provision of national law.

(b) hypothesis 2: supremacy of EC law is founded on a claim to sovereignty

On a different analysis, however, the supremacy doctrine can be understood as a more fundamentally grounded claim to normative authority and self-

---

[5] As against this, Steve Weatherill argues that the supremacy of EC law is an absolute notion: his use of the term absolute in this context, however, is intended to refer to the fact that the doctrine applies to the priority of any provision of directly effective EC law, however minor and technical, over any provision of national law, however weighty and fundamental, rather than an argument that the doctrine can be understood independently of any relationship with conflicting national law. S Weatherill, *Law and Integration in the European Union* (Oxford, OUP, 1995) 106, and see for discussion B de Witte, 'Direct Effect, Supremacy and the Nature of the Legal Order' in P Craig and G de Búrca (eds) *The Evolution of EU law* (Oxford, OUP, 1999).

[6] See the chapters of Bardo Fassbender and Michael Keating in the present volume.

[7] Sovereignty and autonomy are related but not identical in meaning: there can be degrees of loss of autonomy consistent with the retention of sovereignty, whereas a loss of sovereignty implies something more fundamental. A cumulative loss of autonomy may lead to a point where it can no longer plausibly be maintained that a particular entity retains ultimate or final authority.

government, as a fundamental claim to 'sovereignty' in the legal sense of ultimate authority. Hans Lindahl in his chapter in this volume argues that the reasoning of the *Costa v Enel* judgment[8] in which the supremacy doctrine was first fully articulated can be construed as an assertion of sovereignty. He argues that by claiming that the EC legal order is a new and independent legal order, the European Court of Justice denies any external reference point in terms of the lawmaking capacity of the new order, and that this 'constitutionalisation of the Treaties' implies that the EC is a sovereign polity.[9]

If the familiar chain of reasoning in the articulation of the supremacy doctrine is scrutinised anew, these two hypotheses—(a) that supremacy entails a limited functional rule for allocating priority in a practical situation of conflict or (b) that supremacy entails a fundamental claim to sovereignty'—can be tested. In *Costa*, it is true, the ECJ certainly emphasised the practical importance of a principle of primacy of EC law over conflicting national law, in the sense of declaring that this was necessary in the interests of uniform application of common market rules and the effectiveness of the common market, but it also went on to emphasise the independence and autonomy of European law in a way which suggests a less functional and more strongly normative claim:

> 'the law stemming from the treaty, *an independent source of law*, could not, because of its special and *original nature*, be overridden by domestic legal provisions, however framed, without being deprived of its character as community law and without *the legal basis of the Community* itself being called into question' (emphasis added)

It seems clear that the words of this paragraph, which emphasise the independence and original nature of EC law, were intended to assert an autonomous and non-derivative legal authority, as Hans Lindahl also points out in his contribution.

In a separate claim, the Court declares that the states in transferring powers to the Community legal system have brought about 'a permanent limitation of their sovereign rights', but a crucial corollary of this is that the powers of the Community are henceforth to be autonomous and original, not subject to any limitations or derogations on the part of the Member States other than those defined by the Community itself. Thus the claim to supremacy over conflicting national law, even if it amounts in practical terms to a rule of priority for determining outcomes in specific cases of

---

[8] Case 6/64, *Flaminio Costa* v. *ENEL* [1964] ECR 585

[9] Various commentators have argued, however, that the lack of an agreed competence-competence, or the capacity to define the scope of its own competence, is the strongest indicator that the EC/EU lacks sovereignty. However, both the interpretative role of the ECJ, and indeed the potential encroachment on the autonomy of the Intergovernmental Conference process by the recent constitutional Convention, point in a different direction, even if weakly as yet.

inconsistency, is also a consequence which flows from the more fundamental prior claim made in the judgment: that the EC legal order and its authority are independent, autonomous and non-derivative.

The foundations or basis for the supremacy claim are even more pronounced in the earlier *Van Gend en Loos* judgment,[10] which established the doctrine of direct effect of EC law. In this case, the importance of the substantive objectives of European integration (which, at the time, consisted mainly of the establishment of a common market) was emphasised as part of the rationale for the conclusion that EC laws should directly bind individuals and should be directly enforced by national courts. Four features were listed in the *Van Gend* case as building blocks towards the conclusion that 'the Community constitutes a new legal order' for the benefit of which 'Member States have limited their sovereign rights'.

The *first* of these was the substantive objective of establishing the common market, and the *second* was the setting up of 'institutions endowed with sovereign rights', or in other words, the lawmaking institutions of the Community. The *third* consisted of the rather weak democratic elements existing at that time, ie

'that the nationals of the states brought together in the Community are called upon to cooperate in the functioning of this Community through the intermediary of the European Parliament and the Economic and Social Committee',

And the *fourth* was the existence of the preliminary reference mechanism of ex-Article 177 which 'confirms that the states have acknowledged that community law has an authority which can be invoked by their nationals before [national] courts and tribunals'. These four elements—the substantive objective of creating a common market, the deliberate setting up of new institutions with 'sovereign rights' (this being a clear assertion by the ECJ of the sovereignty of the EC institutions) and with law and policy-making powers to that end, a number of democratic elements in the institutional structure, and finally state recognition of the authority of EC law in the establishment of a mechanism indicating that national courts should be applying EC law—supply the rationale and justification for the Court's primary claim ('the conclusion to be drawn from this is':) that the EC is a new, independent and sovereign legal order and, as a secondary claim, that its laws can directly confer rights on individuals.

The *Van Gend en Loos* case thus established the legal doctrine of direct effect rather than supremacy, but like the *Costa* case which subsequently introduced the supremacy doctrine, the direct effect doctrine followed as one of the consequences of the Court's prior assertion, based on the four factors outlined above, of the autonomy and independence of the EC legal

---

[10] Case 26/62, *NV. Algemene Transporten Expeditie Onderneming van Gend en Loos v Nederlandse Administratie der Belastingen* [1963] ECR 1

order. While it is not the aim of this chapter to engage in a normative assessment of the ECJ's sovereignty claim, it can nonetheless clearly be seen that the various factors listed by the Court were intended not only to assert but also to provide a basis for legitimating its claim to sovereignty and supremacy. Conceptually, therefore, it can be said that while the doctrines of supremacy and direct effect articulated by the European Court of Justice do not in themselves *entail* or include a prior judicial assertion of the independence, original nature and autonomy of the EC legal order, these legal doctrines nonetheless follow as consequences from that assertion. In other words, they follow from the ultimate self-defining authority of that legal order. Supremacy of EC law is thus a consequence of the sovereignty of the EC rather than vice versa.

It is also noteworthy that the four factors outlined above which underpinned the supremacy and sovereignty claims of the ECJ in 1962 are somewhat changed today, although the doctrine is unchanged and has embedded itself firmly within the legal culture of the EC. First, the substantive objectives of the polity have broadened considerably beyond a common market, as is evident not only from the preamble to the EU and the EC Treaties but also from the range of policy fields which have been expressly added; secondly its institutions, although not greatly changed, have been strengthened in various ways; thirdly, the 'weakly democratic' elements are stronger since the European Parliament became directly elected and acquired decision-making powers; and fourthly the preliminary reference mechanism has developed into an effective and constant channel of communication between the EU and the individual legal systems of Member States, as a result of which most national courts and tribunals routinely treat EU law as authoritative and effective within their systems. Thus the original foundations for the legal claim to sovereignty of the European legal order have not grown weaker over the years since the early rulings of the Court of Justice, even if their legitimacy—in particular in terms of popular sovereignty and democracy—remains vigorously contested.

A related aspect of the question whether the ECJ's claim to supremacy entails a claim of sovereignty, however, concerns the *plausibility* of the sovereignty claim, which engages a more political meaning of the term. In other words, do the constituent Member States and their constitutionally authoritative organs accept the ECJ's claim in theory and in practice? Much has been written on this subject, by individual constitutional law scholars from almost all of the Member States, and in a number of collaborative research projects.[11] The general picture is one of broad acceptance in practice of the primacy of the EU legal order, but with a range of different conceptual and constitutional perspectives on how and why European law

---

[11] See eg A Slaughter, A Stone Sweet and J Weiler (eds) *The European Court and National Courts: Doctrine and Jurisprudence* (Oxford, Hart Publishing, 1998); K Alter n. 2 above.

takes precedence. Very few of these perspectives expressly include recognition of the EC or the EU as a fully sovereign polity and many involve the assertion of a residual but ultimate national constitutional control over the recognition of the authority of the EU legal order.[12] Nonetheless, both from the point of view of the EU and of the Member States, the European polity appears to hold all of the pragmatic cards, with its expansive, well-established and functional legal doctrines such as *effet utile* and direct effect, to promote the authority and primacy of EC law in practice. The occasional 'shots over the bows' fired by the German, Danish and other constitutional courts and their reassertions of the sovereignty of the domestic legal orders do not necessarily undermine either the ECJ's claim to sovereignty on behalf of the European polity, nor, for the most part, Member State recognition of that claim. The residual and even dormant nature of such ultimate national constitutional control can itself be seen as evidence of the fact that some of the more traditional understandings of sovereignty are changing.[13]

3. SUPREMACY OF EUROPEAN LAW AND THE SOVEREIGNTY OF THE MEMBER STATES

The second dimension of the question under consideration concerns the implications of the supremacy doctrine for the legal sovereignty of the Member States. Does the ECJ's claim to supremacy of EC law necessarily entail a claim that the Member States have transferred or have thereby lost their sovereignty—their ultimate legal authority—to the EU?

Beginning with the perspective articulated by the Court of Justice in its case law, it is notable that since *Costa* and *Van Gend*, there have been very few judgments in which reference has been made to the term sovereignty, either in relation to the Member States or in relation to the EU itself. Virtually all of the cases which do invoke the term, since the early 1970s, concern sovereignty over fishing waters, or so-called 'fiscal sovereignty' in tax cases. One interesting exception was in a ruling given on the Euratom Treaty in 1978 concerning the compatibility with the Treaty of a draft nuclear Convention, where the Court's reasoning stressed not only the independence and autonomy of the Community in the exercise of the powers

---

[12] For a further account, see P Craig and G de Búrca, *EU Law* 3rd edn (Oxford, OUP, 2002), Chap 7.

[13] Even in the UK, in the colourful 'metric martyrs' case in 2002, in which four traders were convicted for failing to display metric rather than imperial measurements in accordance with EC law, the High Court declared that while the fundamental basis of the UK's relationship with the EU rested in domestic and not EU law, the European Communities Act 1972 which gave effect to EC law in Britain was a special 'constitutional statute' and therefore not subject to implied repeal: *Thoburn v Sunderland County Council, Hunt v London Borough of Hackney; Harman and Dove v Cornwall County Council;* and, *Collins v London Borough of Sutton* QBD, 18 February 2002.

originally transferred to it by the Member States, but asserted also a corresponding loss of sovereign power on the part of the states:

> 'To the extent to which jurisdiction and powers have been conferred on the Community under the EAEC treaty it must be in a position to exercise them with unfettered freedom. The Member States, whether acting individually or collectively, are no longer able to impose on the Community obligations which impose conditions on the exercise of prerogatives which thenceforth belong to the Community and *which therefore no longer fall within the field of national sovereignty*'.[14] (emphasis added).

(a) transfer of 'sovereign rights' or transfer of sovereignty?

Nonetheless, as has been noted by Bruno de Witte,[15] in his examination of the language used by the ECJ in many of its rulings on the subject, as well as the language used in several of the constitutions of the Member States, it is true that references to a strong notion such as a transfer of sovereignty are rare or non-existent. He draws a distinction between a transfer of sovereign rights or limitation of sovereignty on the one hand, and a *transfer of sovereignty* on the other hand. The former is acknowledged to be possible under a number of national constitutional provisions, and it is also reflected in the judgments of the Court of Justice. Thus in *Van Gend* and *Costa* alike, the ECJ declared that the states have 'limited their sovereign rights' and in *Costa* that a 'limitation of sovereignty or a transfer of powers from the states to the Community' had taken place.

What assistance can be drawn from this distinction between the notion of 'transfer of sovereign rights' which seems to be conceptually and constitutionally acceptable to many states, and the notion of a transfer of sovereignty, which does not? The implication appears to be that few if any Member States, through their constitutional organs, are prepared to acknowledge or assert that their membership of the EU has amounted to a transfer of ultimate legal authority. The argument instead is that although the states have delegated their authority, or have transferred some of their powers, or have even transferred 'sovereign' rights, they have not transferred or alienated their very sovereignty itself. What could it mean to speak of transferring sovereign rights without transferring sovereignty? Does it signify that the 'rights' transferred could be unilaterally withdrawn, and that although while they are legitimately exercised by the EC it is the EC which has ultimate authority in defining their scope, a state may nonethe-

---

[14] Ruling 1/78 [1978] ECR 2151
[15] See B de Witte 'Sovereignty and European Integration: the Weight of Legal Tradition' in A Slaughter *et al*, n. 9 above, and 'Direct Effect, Supremacy and the Nature of the Legal Order', in *The Evolution of EU Law*, n. 3 above.

less decide to retract those powers and that authority to itself again? This, however, seems increasingly implausible as a claim, certainly as a matter of political reality, but even also as a matter of constitutional law in many Member States, in which there is no obvious provision for unilateral retraction of powers transferred as a result of membership of the EU. Even the possibility of and the process for withdrawal from membership of the EU remains an uncertain and unresolved subject in EU law and in national constitutional laws.

(b) 'shared' or 'divided' sovereignty?

Might the distinction drawn instead suggest that only certain circumscribed powers are definitively transferred to the EU whereas others are clearly not, so that sovereignty is retained in certain spheres while it is transferred in others? This might also suggest one possible meaning of the difficult notion of 'shared' or 'divided' sovereignty, in other words that ultimate authority is split between different jurisdictions or entities in accordance with subject matter areas, rather than that authority is shared across a number of polities and jointly held and exercised in a more complex way. This brings us back also to an initial qualification of the ECJ's claim in the *Van Gend* and *Costa* cases that Member States had transferred their sovereign rights to the EC: in other words, the Court's assertion that this limitation of national sovereignty had taken place only 'within limited fields'. On this reasoning, the Member States retained sovereignty and remained sovereign within those fields of policy which were not transferred to the Community, and correspondingly, the Community gained sovereign authority only within the transferred field.

There are a number of reasons, however, why this particular conceptual depiction of 'divided sovereignty' or 'shared sovereignty' within the EU is unconvincing.[16] In the first place, the powers and spheres of legitimate policy action have grown vastly since the judgment in *Van Gend* was given—and a juridical reflection of this can perhaps be seen in the fact that in a later ECJ ruling, Opinion 1/91 on the European Economic Area agreement, the claim that the Member States have limited their sovereignty and transferred sovereign rights is repeated, but the qualification 'albeit within limited fields' is omitted.[17] In the second place, and related to this point, it

---

[16] In more philosophical and less pragmatic terms, De Witte suggests that 'shared sovereignty' be seen as something which lies with the 'peoples of the European Union taken together, rather than with each of those peoples separately'; 'Sovereignty and European Integration: the Weight of Legal Tradition' n 15 above.
[17] Opinion 1/91 [1991] ECR I–6079. Contrast the case of 28/67, *Firma Molkerei-Zentrale Westfalen/Lippe GmbH v Hauptzollamt Paderborn* [1968] ECR 143, which was decided only six years after *Van Gend* and which included the formula 'albeit within limited fields'.

is increasingly difficult to identify clearly policy areas 'which fall within the field of national sovereignty', to borrow the ECJ's phrase in the *Euratom* case,[18] in the sense of areas in which the authority of the state is self-defining and ultimate. Even the term fiscal sovereignty seems strained in the European context where many aspects of EC law and policy affect the tax freedom of Member States. There are now so many widely acknowledged and accepted 'transverse' European Union legal obligations and principles that it can reasonably be argued that there is no sphere of national policy which is fully autonomous and which is not capable of being significantly circumscribed by a rule or principle of EU law. Tax policy, health policy, cultural and educational policy are all areas which remain supposedly within the primary and ultimate legal authority and control of the Member States. And yet these areas of national policy have been substantially affected in very direct ways by the norms, principles and practices of EU law which cut across sectoral and subject-matter areas of this kind. Nor is this circumscription purely a matter of legal principle: the primacy of EC law is asserted regardless of the nature of the national law or policy which is in conflict,[19] and it has been rare for there to be outright national refusal to acknowledge the authority of the European provision,[20] however reluctant, partial or problematic compliance may be in some situations. If the notion of 'national sovereignty' is to retain meaning in the context of such significant, potentially all-embracing and cross-cutting constraints, our understanding of the term sovereignty must itself necessarily be changed and diluted.

Similarly, just as the claim that Member States remain sovereign 'within limited fields' requires a rethinking of the notion of sovereignty, the parallel claim that the EU possesses limited 'functional sovereignty' must also be questioned further. The claim that its powers and rights are granted and exercised 'within limited fields' and only 'within the scope of its objectives' suggests that the EU's sphere of sovereign authority has sectoral and functional limits. However, just as the fields of national policy in which ultimate authority is readily apparent are increasingly few, the supposedly functional 'limits' to the EU's sovereign authority are equally difficult to identify. In other words, the notion of 'functionally limited sovereignty' in the context of the EU seems, if not oxymoronic, somewhat meaningless.

Once the delineation of competences and the lines of actual political authority and control have become so blurred that powers over most policy

---

[18] N 12, above.
[19] Case 11/70, *Internationale Handelsgesellschaft mbH v Einfuhr-und Vorratsstelle für Getreide und Futtermittel* [1970] ECR 1125.
[20] See for an unsuccessful challenge to the supremacy principle on the basis that it should not apply to merely individual administrative EC acts: C–224/97, *Ciola v Land Vorarlberg* [1999] ECR I–2517, para 24.

spheres are complexly shared by both the EU and Member States, the notion of functionally limited sovereignty becomes more difficult to comprehend. The EU is empowered to act in the field of the internal market, to legislate to ensure the free movement of goods and services between states. It is only very weakly empowered to legislate in the field of culture and the Member States retain a strong area of legislative autonomy in the field of cultural policy, yet *Bosman* and its progeny showed the difficulty of delineating national and regional autonomy in the area of sport.[21] The organisation and financing of education and health, and the core of education and health policy are clearly left to the Member States, with only weak subsidiary powers granted at EU level.[22] But the recent series of cases concerning the funding of medical treatment supplied in different parts of the EU, and the response to these from various Member States, demonstrates the way domestic autonomy and actual authority can be constrained and affected both in law and in practice.[23] Can it plausibly be said that the EU exercises sovereign powers in the internal market field and the Member States sovereign authority in the field of health? Or is it the case that neither the EU nor the Member States assert and exercise ultimate authority within either field? It might be said that these are simply difficult boundary disputes which indicate that, as in any federal system, the margins of the spheres in which the EU and the Member States respectively are sovereign will be contested at times. Yet in the context of the EU in which such contested questions of authority and control arise on a daily basis, this explanation lacks conviction, and the notion of functionally limited sovereignty seems therefore difficult to sustain.

4. CONCLUSION

On a re-examination of the foundational case law of the Court of Justice on the doctrine of supremacy, it appears that this doctrine is based by the Court on a claim to the original and independent authority of EC law. In other words, while the supremacy doctrine is not synonymous with the sovereignty of the EC, the former is based, according to the Court, on the

---

[21] See eg cases C–415/93, *Union Royale Belge des Sociétés de Football Association and others v Bosman* [1995] ECR I–4921, C–176/96, *Jyri Lehtonen, Castors Canada Dry Namur-Braine ASBL v FRBSB* [2000] ECR I–2681 and C–51/96 & C–191/97 *Deliege v Ligue Francophone de Judi et Disciplines Associées ASBL* [2000] ECR I–2549
[22] See however C–184/99, *Rudy Grzelczyk v Centre Public D'Aide Sociale d'Ottignes-Louvain-la-Neuve (CPAS)* [2001] ECR I–6193
[23] Cases C–120/95 *Decker* [1998] ECR I–1831, C–158/96 *Kohll v Union des Caisses de Maladie* [1998] ECR I–1931, C–368/98 *Vanbraekel v ANMC* [2001] ECR I–5363 and C–157/99 *Geraets-Smits v Stichting Ziekenfonds, Peerbooms v Stichting CZ Groep Zorgverzekeringen* [2001] ECR I–5473.

latter. The same is true of the notion of direct effect, which is closely linked in doctrinal terms with the principle of supremacy. Both of these legal concepts are derived by the ECJ from a set of premises which appear as a justification for its claim to sovereignty on behalf of the EC. The factual bases for these premises, which include the objectives of the EC, the powers and rights of its institutions, the democratic elements in its structures, and the preliminary reference procedure, have if anything strengthened over the years, and the supremacy doctrine has embedded itself as a central element of the *aquis communautaire*. It is less clear, however, whether the supremacy doctrine necessarily entails a claim that the Member States have lost or transferred their sovereignty. While a 'transfer of sovereignty' is incompatible with the constitutional provisions of certain Member States, the alternative notions of a limited 'transfer of sovereign rights', of divided or shared sovereignty, or of a transfer of 'functionally limited sovereignty', ultimately do not seem to provide a satisfactory account, in conceptual or in practical terms, for the reality of today's EU.

20

Sovereignty at the Boundaries of the Polity

'Theoretically, sovereignty is nowhere more absolute than in matters of emigration, naturalisation, nationality and expulsion.'[2]

1. INTRODUCTION

IN THIS CHAPTER I use the case of European Union electoral rights to examine points of contestation around concepts of sovereignty and power in the EU context. The wider context of the chapter is the enquiry into the significance of sovereignty at the boundaries of the polity. Sovereignty is the subject of contestation in the EU context, not only amongst academics but also between politicians and opinion-formers in the Member States and those in the EU institutions. The key questions seem to be: 'what is the European Union?'; 'what might it become?'; and 'how does it impact upon the Member States and national sovereignty?'. The chapter identifies and elaborates three important sets of contestations over electoral rights involving both EU migrants and third country nationals resident in the Member States which in turn illluminate the broader issues about sovereignty and indeed citizenship.[3] The presentation highlights the role of

[1] Professor of European Law and Jean Monnet Chair at the University of Manchester. This paper draws upon research conducted jointly with Dr Stephen Day, at the University of Leeds, on 'The Boundaries of Suffrage'. It forms part of the ESRC One Europe or Several Research Programme project entitled *Strategies of Civic Inclusion in Pan-European Society* (L213 25 2022). The financial support of the ESRC is gratefully acknowledged. Many thanks, for comments, to Neil Duxbury and Neil Walker, and to the participants in Workshop No. 14 on *The Political Participation of Immigrants and their Descendants in Post-War Western Europe*, ECPR Joint Sessions of Workshops, Turin, Italy, March 2002.

[2] H Arendt, *The Origins of Totalitarianism* (New York, Harcourt Brace, 1973) at 278.

[3] As Linda Bosniak points out, citizenship is a classic example of an essentially contested concept in the WB Gallie/William Connolly sense of the term: L Bosniak, 'Denationalizing Citizenship' in T A Aleinikoff and D Klusmeyer (eds.), *Citizenship Today: Global Perspectives and Practices* (Washington, DC, Carnegie Endowment for International Peace, 2001).

debates on sovereignty and related concepts of competence, powers and even subsidiarity in the construction of a vital element of the EU polity: the boundaries of its suffrage.

A paradox faces all polities: so long as the criterion for allocating political rights of participation has been overwhelmingly the formal one of nationality and so long as the gateways to nationality have been restricted by states exercising national sovereignty, many who live and perhaps indeed are born within the boundaries of any given polity have been unable to participate politically, fully or even partially. Many factors have given rise to this scenario, including the globalisation and interpenetration of economies coupled with the uneven distribution of economic well-being, the existence of repressive state regimes which deny political and personal freedoms and give rise to refugee populations, the fact that state boundaries sometimes change whether by consent or force, and the existence of entities such as the EU which positively encourage migration. All of these factors generate mobility. The proportion of non-national residents in the Member States of the European Union continues to rise,[4] even when official governmental discourse has been set against immigration.[5] In 1994, the average of non-EEA nationals (ie third country nationals)[6] as a proportion of the population of the fifteen Member States was 2.7 per cent, with Germany riding high at 6.3 per cent, no doubt in part because of its restrictive naturalisation policies. Since then, net immigration into the EU has continued steadily, but with little overall population growth because of declining birth rates. Yet in Germany by 2000 the proportion was 8.9 per cent of residents, or 7.3 million foreigners.[7] Furthermore, migration has changed in recent years—or at least scholars of migration have now constructed a more complete picture of the nature of migration. As Allan Williams comments,[8] it is wrong to assume that all migration is temporary, legal and for work purposes. In fact, more diffuse patterns are evolving, a point reinforced by the fact that, as he notes, 'across Europe, the pattern of national provision has produced a bricolage of territories with differentiated rights for different migrant groups', the EU remains 'a highly fragmented migration space', borders have 'varying degrees of permeability and closure', and overall the

---

[4] Helpful summary statistics on migration are compiled and published by the University of Konstanz Center for International and European Law on Immigration and Asylum: http://www.uni-konstanz.de/FuF/ueberfak/fzaa/english/index.htm.

[5] For a review of different policies, see J Apap, *Shaping Europe's Migration Policy. New Regimes for the Employment of third country Nationals: A Comparison of Strategies in Germany, Sweden, the Netherlands and the UK*, CEPS Working Document No. 179, December 2001.

[6] For statistical purposes in relation to migration, the EEA states of Iceland, Liechtenstein and Norway are generally assimilated to the EU–15.

[7] *Migration News*, Vol. 9, No. 3, March 2002 (http://migration.ucdavis.edu/).

[8] A M Williams, 'New Forms of International Migration: In Search of Which Europe?' in H Wallace (ed.), *Interlocking Dimensions of European Integration* (London, Palgrave, 2001), at 103–4.

EU can be described as a 'mosaic of migration spaces'. Similarly, the legal circumstances of different groups of migrants will vary dramatically.

This state of affairs raises normative as well as policy challenges for any host polity. Citizenship theories often present two competing claims: citizenship as a universal status and good, and citizenship as marking out the boundaries of each polity from all other polities. Any normative claim to moral purchase made on behalf of a particular version of citizenship as the membership badge for a bounded community needs to be evaluated by reference to the standards according to which the boundaries themselves have been set. Justice is not, *contra* the common interpretation given to Michael Walzer's approach, either solely an internal matter or even one which necessarily involves applying principles distinguishing sharply between the internal and external spheres.[9] On the contrary, a polity's claim to be 'a liberal constitutionalist democracy' (a claim made on behalf of all of the existing EU Member States and indeed any future Member States by a combination of Articles 6 and 49 TEU), and to offer 'universal citizenship', must be tested not only by reference to what happens within the polity (majoritarian practices, rule of law, protection of minorities, fundamental rights, etc.), but also by reference to the boundaries that it sets with the rest of the world, the extent to which those boundaries are treated as permeable, fuzzy or negotiable, and the manner in which 'strangers' are treated at the boundary as well as internally.

Along with justice, of course, the concept of sovereignty is profoundly implicated in the task of determining the boundaries of the suffrage. Most migration scholars agree that sovereignty continues to play a role in relation to the evolution of immigration politics and the legal regulation of migration, but deep fault lines appear in migration scholarship regarding the extent and impact of factors such as globalisation and regional integration projects including the EU upon migration regimes and politics. There is controversy over the putative emergence of a form of 'postnational membership', supplanting or at least complementing national citizenships.[10]

---

[9] M Walzer, *Spheres of Justice. A Defense of Pluralism and Equality* (New York, Basic Books, 1983); discussed in L Bosniak, 'Membership, Equality and the Difference that Alienage Makes', (1994) 69 *New York University Law Review* 1149 and L Bosniak, 'Universal Citizenship and the Problem of Alienage', (2000) 94 *Northwestern University Law Review* 963.

[10] See, for the debate: C Joppke, *Immigration and the Nation State: The United States, Germany, and Great Britain* (Oxford, Oxford University Press, 1999); C Joppke, 'The Legal-Domestic Sources of Immigrant Rights. The United States, Germany, and the European Union', (2001) 34 *Comparative Political Studies* 339; R Hansen, 'Migration, citizenship and race in Europe: Between incorporation and exclusion', (1999) 35 *European Journal of Political Research* 415; S Sassen, 'The *de facto* Transnationalizing of Immigration Policy' in C Joppke (ed.), *Challenges to the nation-state: Immigration in Western Europe and the United States* (Oxford, Oxford University Press, 1998); Y Soysal, *Limits of Citizenship: Migrants and Postnational Membership in Europe* (Chicago, University of Chicago Press, 1994). See also, in the EU immigration policy context, D Kostakopoulou, 'Floating Sovereignty: A Pathology or a Necessary Means of State Evolution?', (2002) 22 *Oxford Journal of Legal* Studies 135.

The two points about justice and sovereignty can be linked by examining the contestations which take place over issues such as electoral rights for non-nationals. Rather than focusing directly on sovereignty itself, the chapter looks instead to the sites of contestation around issues of sovereignty in relation to the electoral rights questions, and to the analysis of the outcomes of those contestations in terms of arguments about the nature of the EU-polity and about appropriate policy responses to societal challenges of immigration and non-national residents for the EU and its current and future Member States. The analysis attempts to highlight links, wherever possible, between what is decided, how it is decided, and where it is decided.

Beginning with a rehearsal working through some of the diverse relationships between sovereignty and the determination of the boundaries of the suffrage, the chapter examines the difficulties attaching to the definition of the polity—and hence its boundaries—where there are the forces of Europeanisation, globalisation and regionalisation in play. While the argument and the picture presented coincidentally cohere neatly with more general claims about the transformation of sovereignty as an organisational focus for political and legal power,[11] that transformation is not directly examined. The sites of contestation selected for closer examination concern case studies in EU policy-making (the debate over the electoral rights directives and the debate over electoral rights for third country nationals) and the national politics of immigration and electoral rights in Austria, Belgium, Germany, UK and—as an example of an accession state—Estonia.

The examination of sites of contestation will show how increasingly complex constellations of power, authority and institutions encompassing both the EU *and* its Member States, as well as other international organisations and the regional and local levels of government within the Member States, pose considerable challenges in terms of the pursuit of the goal of promoting 'good' governance which is appropriate to a liberal polity. Each of the Member States under consideration can safely be classed as a liberal state, even though they each have very different nationhood traditions as well as contrasting immigration histories and practices. Estonia, likewise, aspires to liberal nation-statehood, as a litmus test of its political suitability for accession to the EU. The presentation of differing national political positions on immigration and electoral rights will illustrate how common remain invocations of nation, citizenship and territorial sovereignty, as well as how strong remain some of the conventions of political expediency such as the preservation of governing coalitions within the politics of electoral rights. Appeals to cosmopolitan values of justice and fair treatment, in contrast, carry less resonance. So far as this chapter examines law and

---

[11] These are points made amply elsewhere in this volume.

policy-making in relation to electoral rights within the EU, its Member States and—to a more limited extent—accession states, it highlights the complex interrelationships between the procedural question of 'who decides?' and the substantive question 'about what?'. This interrelationship is particularly intense wherever competence (the EU jargon for legislative power) is divided or shared between more than one site of authority.

The chapter also reviews in its conclusion the extent to which the invocation of the normative principle of alien suffrage influences 'polity-ideas' about how the EU and its Member States *ought* to treat third country nationals, at least so far as regards political and electoral rights. In this 'polity idea', the concept of sovereignty is more a shadow at the table than a clearly articulated presence. Moreover, the paradox of the 'bounded polity' and equally bounded conception of citizenship which is tied to the polity has become even more politically salient since the events of 11 September 2001 from which sovereignty has arguably re-emerged as a factor crucial to understanding the developing world order.[12] The aftermath of the terrorist attacks on that day has made a significant contribution to bringing the sovereignty debate and the debate about the fair treatment of non-nationals to centre stage.[13] The contestations which continue to exist between these competing visions of the boundaries of the polity represent, ironically, the best hope for a less-bounded and more fluid concept of membership, in a world where states and non-state polities must seek peaceful co-existence.[14]

2. SOVEREIGNTY, BELONGING AND THE STATE

'electorate: noun (treated as sing. or pl.) all the people in a country or area who are entitled to vote in any election.'[15]

'Everyone has the right to take part in the government of his country, directly or through freely chosen representatives.'[16]

The *New Oxford Dictionary of English* definition of the 'electorate' is an example of the circular nature of so many arguments about the boundaries of the suffrage and hence of the polity. *Who* are those 'entitled to vote'? In a democracy aspiring to apply the principle of popular sovereignty and to

---

[12] On international migration and security in relation to 11 September 2001 see T Faist, ' 'Extension du domaine de la lutte': International Migration and Security before and after 11 September 2001', (2002) *International Migration Review* forthcoming (Spring).
[13] For an appeal to justice and fairness in relation to US policies, see R Dworkin, 'The Threat to Patriotism', *The New York Review of Books*, 28 February 2002.
[14] I am grateful to Neil Walker for bringing out this point.
[15] *The New Oxford Dictionary of English* (Oxford, Clarendon Press, 1998).
[16] Article 21(1) of the Universal Declaration of Human Rights.

translate this into a practice of more or less universal suffrage,[17] this should surely be the 'people' in the sense of the 'demos'. Who, then, are the 'people'? The 'members' of the given country or area, that is, those who *belong*, would seem to be the obvious answer. It remains, then, to determine who decides who belongs, on what authority and how. The act of determining the group of people entitled to vote (the electorate) certainly seems logically prior to the holding of an election, but the fact of determination seems equally to presuppose some pre-political authority which claims to determine the boundaries of the polity. The conclusion must be, however, that the definition itself has taken us no closer to understanding who the 'electorate' actually is. On the contrary, we need a pre-existing theory of the polity and in particular of the boundaries of the polity to lend meaning to the concept of 'electorate'.

In an era of sovereign non-overlapping polities (ie states), the position is rather easy to determine. Membership is ascribed in large measure internally by nationality law, by reference to a range of factors such as place of birth, affiliation, marriage or longterm residence. States, as sovereign entities, have the power to make determinations of nationality.[18] They are largely free to choose whether to allow dual nationality and to determine the conditions under which naturalisation or registration as a citizen for first or second generation migrants is permitted. Rainer Bauböck terms this order of formal membership a case of territorial sovereignty; and its distinctive feature is that it claims to be complete and discrete:[19]

> 'Completeness means that everybody is at any point in time subject to the territorial sovereignty of a state; discreteness implies that nobody is subject to more than one state simultaneously.'

Unsurprisingly, formal membership is a necessary precursor, in this system, to the acquisition of voting rights.

Public international law, especially—in the modern era—human rights law, can step in to deal with failures in the system such as the withdrawal of nationality, expulsion from the national territory and any other denial of rights, to regulate or prevent conditions such as statelessness, and to protect groups such as refugees; private international law deals with certain types of conflicts of law (or perhaps better dissonances) which can occur between

---

[17] Wider struggles over the extension of the suffrage fall outside the scope of this research. The symbolic and practical importance of the scope of the suffrage is reflected in measures as diverse as Article 21(1) of the Universal Declaration of Human Rights, the Declaration of Independence (1776) or the Declaration of the Rights of Man and Citizen (1789), especially in so far as the latter focus upon popular sovereignty.

[18] *Nottebohm Case (Liechtenstein v. Guatemala)* 1995 ICJ 4 (judgment of 6 April 1955).

[19] R Bauböck, 'Changing the Boundaries of Citizenship. The inclusion of immigrants in democratic polities' in R Bauböck (ed.), *From Aliens to Citizens. Redefining the Status of Immigrants in Europe* (Avebury/European Centre Vienna, Aldershot, etc., 1994) at p207.

different national legal orders in relation to the differing conditions of recognition of, for example, the acquisition of nationality on marriage or affiliation conditions relating to children or grandchildren. Historically, international law tended to set its face against dual nationality as an unnecessary source of confusion, and so states could feel justified in disallowing it or seeking to reduce instances of its occurrence. More recent developments, such as the 1997 European Convention on Nationality acknowedge its utility, in particular as a means of allowing women to pass on their citizenship more easily and of facilitating the integration of immigrants without forcing them arbitrarily to renounce their former citizenship. Some authors contend that there is an increasing convergence towards a European 'norm' in nationality law, with greater tolerance of dual nationality.[20]

3. GLOBAL, EUROPEAN AND REGIONAL CHALLENGES

'Are we, as some contend, on the verge of developing new notions of citizenship and community, ones that successfully weave together our multiple allegiances from the local to the universal? Should the notion of individual membership in a single nation state be replaced by an emphasis on group representation, cultural rights, and membership in multiple countries? Or would such new notions of transnational and multicultural citizenship threaten basic principles of [national] democracy? Will the shared civic identity that makes both self-governance and the protection of rights possible suffer if these changes come to pass?'[21]

Even though globalisation, Europeanisation and regionalisation are all contested terms which in turn designate highly contested phenomena, they certainly contribute heavily to the argument that the picture painted in the previous paragraph no longer approximates to the reality of world affairs—if, indeed, it ever did. For example, Bauböck himself presents—in relation to states—two additional scenarios of 'orders of membership' involving increasing areas of overlap between territories, namely nominal citizenship and societal membership.[22] The former scenario complements rather than undermines the pattern of territorial sovereignty, bringing in a more

---

[20] R Hansen and P Weil (eds.), *Towards a European Nationality. Citizenship, Immigration and Nationality Law in the EU* (London, Palgrave, 2001); PJ Spiro, 'Dual Nationality and the Meaning of Citizenship', (1997) 46 *Emory Law Journal* 1411; R Koslowski, 'Demographic Boundary Maintenance in World Politics: Of International Norms on Dual Nationality' in M Albert, D Jacobson and Y Lapid (eds.), *Identities, Borders, Orders: Rethinking International Relations Theory* (Minneapolis/London, University of Minnesota Press, 2001).

[21] N M J Pickus (ed.), *Becoming American. America Becoming*, Final Report, Duke University Workshop on Citizenship and Immigration, 1997: (www.pubpol.duke.edu/people/faculty/pickus/immigration).

[22] Bauböck, above n. 19.

complex political and legal map in which the possibilities of changes of nationality through naturalisation for mobile populations are regarded as crucial to the preservation of democracy and stability via a principle of formal inclusiveness; the latter scenario, however, begins to separate out the civic, civil and social dimensions of citizenship, by focusing upon the areas of participation and entitlement ascribed to non-national migrants *without* the necessity for formal membership, such as participation in welfare state institutions, and access to public goods such as education and health care. Neither case, however, necessarily detaches political participation from the acquisition of formal membership, although the latter scenario highlights the contestability of political exclusion. These scenarios together highlight how states are able to deliver the paradox of internal inclusiveness founded on external exclusiveness, or what Christian Joppke calls the post-Marshallian dimension of citizenship.[23] They do not begin, however, to address the complexities of the challenge to patterns of belonging which emerge in a multi-level polity such as the EU, viewed in conjunction with both its Member States (some federal, some unitary in nature) and an emerging trans-European legal domain constructed by the Council of Europe and the OSCE. In this context, there are at least three sets of pressures pertinent to the boundaries of the suffrage which the snapshot of sovereign or even semi-sovereign overlapping states offered thus far fails adequately to capture.

Since the coming into force of the Treaty of Maastricht (1993), European Union law has guaranteed a supranational concept of 'citizenship of the Union', anchored in judicially enforceable guarantees of the free movement of persons and non-discrimination on grounds of (Member State) nationality.[24] The citizens of the Union are the nationals of the Member States (Article 17(2) EC). Citizenship of the Union builds upon an extensive heritage of free movement law, dating back to the 1950s, initially covering only economically active persons and their dependent families, but gradually extended by the Court of Justice to cover a variety of more 'marginal' categories such as students and tourists. Subsequent legislative developments also covered students, retired persons and those of independent means. Together these developments were themselves often said to form a putative form of non-Treaty-based European citizenship, to which the actual Treaty rights have added little save an additional legal veneer.[25]

---

[23] C Joppke, *Immigration and the Nation States. The United States, Germany, and Great Britain* (Oxford, Oxford University Press, 1999), at 6.

[24] Articles 17 and 18 EC, as interpreted by the Court of Justice in Case C–85/96 *Martínez Sala* [1998] ECR I–2691 and Case C–184/99 *Grzelczyk* v. *Centre public d'aide sociale d'Ottignies-Louvain-la-Neuve*, judgment of 20 September 2001.

[25] See generally J Shaw, 'The Interpretation of European Union Citizenship', (1998) 61 *Modern Law Review* 317.

Although the exercise of the free movement rights has often disappointed optimistic supranational policy makers, at least in terms of the numbers taking advantage of the rights if not in terms of the capacity of such rights to generate a limited form of proto 'European' identity, the numbers of EU nationals resident in other Member States, whose rights are therefore substantially regulated by EU law rather than national immigration law, are not trivial. Citizenship, in other words, can be said to contribute to a polity-building scenario in relation to the EU and thus to a theory of the EU as a polity, although most discussions of this question tend to be heavily coloured by underlying attitudes as to whether this is seen as a good thing or not. What cannot be doubted are the pressures at the national level unleashed by these developments.

Second, the supranational context has developed within a wider frame of globalisation. The European Union and its Member States are by no means immune to the pressures of globalisation, including global population movements. The latter are often precipitated by the search for greater economic prosperity, by the volatility of capital investment and commodity markets, as well as by attempts to escape repressive or ineffective government regimes. All of these trends often give rise to clandestine and therefore illegal immigration. There are larger populations of third country nationals in each of the Member States than there are of nationals of other Member States (second country nationals).

The third country national was never a complete stranger to EU law, at least so far as s/he was a member of a family of an EU national taking advantage of free movement rights or was a national of a state with which the EU had contractual relations such as an Association Agreement (eg Turkey or Morocco, and more recently the countries of Central and Eastern Europe), but the years just before and since the millenium have witnessed a noticeable shift in both rhetoric and regulatory framework. The Treaty of Maastricht created the Justice and Home Affairs Third Pillar, seen largely as an ineffective regulatory framework. Partly to correct these failures, the Treaty of Amsterdam established the creation of an Area of Freedom, Security and Justice as an objective for the EU, and offered new policy instruments for achieving this objective. The legal framework for regulating the external and internal borders and the movement of third country nationals was reshaped around a new title within the EC Treaty and the third pillar limited to a focus on police and judicial cooperation. The Treaty of Amsterdam also brought about the incorporation of the Schengen agreement on borders into the EU legal framework. At Tampere in October 1999, the European Council approved a programme of measures to implement the Treaty provisions, a programme under which the Commission acquired a greater policy initiation role, although it continues to share this role with the Member States. The 'flavour' of the emerging new policies has always remained a little uncertain, as it has paired a rhetoric of enhancing fair treatment for third country nationals, which is most obvious in a number of Commission proposals, with a securitisation agenda driven in particular by a number of Member States worried about the effects of immigration and willing to elide the differences between illegal immigration, international crime and terrorism across borders.

Finally, pressures from the regions should not be ignored. The narratives and practices of intra-state federalism within the European Union have undergone significant development in the last twenty years, both in terms of the creation and disintegration of states which may broadly be described as federal. One existing federation, Austria, has acceded to the EU in the last ten years, joining Germany which was an original member of the European Communities. Belgium, Italy, Spain and—latterly—the United Kingdom have each gone down *sui generis* routes towards devolution and regional autonomy involving the decentralisation of 'national' power, in response to internal pressures for species of federalisation or even full-blown independence. New sites of electoral power and distinctively 'regional' politics have been created often to diffuse claims to national autonomy. Emerging new constituencies within the EU are also evident. The regions within the EU where assemblies or parliaments have legislative powers have sought to form a more unified power bloc,[26] disillusioned at the ineffectiveness of the Committee of the Regions and concerned that the debates about the future of the EU in the supposedly representative Convention on the future of the union established in February 2002 might exclude their interests.[27] The enlargement dimension of the EU has also been affected. Three former federal states (Czechoslovakia, the USSR and Yugoslavia) have collapsed or disintegrated, with huge bloodshed in the latter case. In all three cases their disappearance as states has altered the geopolitical configuration of candidate states seeking EU membership.

In sum, overlapping polities, complex constellations of power and authority linked with a variety of international, supranational, national and regional institutions, and substantial populations of non-national residents, characterise the EU and its Member States, a phenomenon set to spread with the enlargements of the next few years to include many states with historically rather fuzzy notions of statehood and citizenship. How has each of these sets of pressures and changes impacted upon the political participation rights of non-nationals and the reconstruction of the boundaries of the suffrage? To what extent is the scope of nationality still the exclusive test of belonging for the purposes of determining who can vote,

---

[26] Second Presidential Conference of the Regions with Legislative Power, Resolution: Towards The Reinforced Role Of The Regions With Legislative Power Within The European Union, Liège, 15 November 2001.

[27] Germany chose a 'regional' politician as one of its two parliamentary representatives, the Prime Minister of Baden-Württemburg, Erwin Teufel, who is also a member of the *Bundesrat*.

and—wherever this remains the case—how much longer could it continue to fulfil this function given the potentially disruptive effects of large numbers of resident non-nationals? Will nationality, in practice, cede ground as a test of affiliation for the purposes of electoral rights to the increasingly open-textured concept of citizenship, where gradations of entitlement linked to varying intensities of belonging to a particular polity are quite common? Indeed, most polities increasingly accord a range of citizenship-type entitlements, especially welfare state benefits and access to public goods such as health and education, to resident non-nationals, even though in some states this practice remains politically contested and raises demands for strict divisions to be drawn between *legal* and *illegal* immigrants. Some states, especially those in Eastern Europe which see themselves as 'kin-states', have also enacted laws purporting to give preferential treatment to co-ethnics abroad.[28] Both of these developments challenge the ideal type of the territorial state, and the assumption that the regulation of personal status will be overwhelmingly bounded by concepts of territory *and* citizenship bonded together, or at least that states will predominantly be concerned with the regulation of those who reside on their territory.

In the domain of electoral rights, to what extent have the EU and its Member States already adopted what might be termed the liberal and cosmopolitan principle of alien suffrage? Do they accept the normative claim that states ought, on grounds of the protection of human rights and/or the furtherance of inclusive democracy, to include within at least some dimensions of the franchise (eg for local elections) those longterm resident non-nationals who have formed substantial connections with their new place of residence as a result of the duration or type of residence? So far as they have done, have we indeed moved to a scenario of postnational membership? Has the immigration sovereignty of liberal states substantially dissolved?

In the EU, 'European citizenship' rights have since 1993 included the right for EU citizens resident in a Member State other than the one of which they have nationality to stand and vote in local elections and European parliamentary elections. They represent much of the limited added value of Maastricht's citizenship provisions. Peter Oliver calls them 'a valuable step

---

[28] The most controversial example of a law enacted by a kin-state according preferential treatment to co-ethnics abroad is the Hungarian status law. Such laws can be seen as an attempt to exercise or 'develop' sovereignty externally, even if they are presented and justified in 'postmodern' terms of fuzzy statehood and fuzzy citizenship. The Status law is the mirror image scenario of the 'fair treatment' of resident non-nationals, namely the question of the treatment of co-ethnics abroad and whether the 'home' state can legitimately claim jurisdiction to accord them rights *other* than directly in respect of their membership link (ie expatriate voting rights). See B Fowler, 'Fuzzy citizenship, nationalising political space: A framework for interpreting the Hungarian 'status law' as a new form of kin-state policy in Central and Eastern Europe', *One Europe or Several* Working Paper 40/02 (www.one-europe.ac.uk).

towards (the) fuller integration' of Community migrants in the host state.[29] Although there had previously been initiatives from the Commission for widening the suffrage in relation to local elections and from the European Parliament in relation to the scope of its own electorate, no measures were introduced until the Treaty of Maastricht. Two Council Directives were adopted in the mid-1990s to instrumentalise the Treaty rights contained in Article 19 EC and the Commission has been tasked with monitoring implementation and—if necessary—taking action before the Court of Justice on the basis of Article 226 EC in respect of national failures to implement the rules.[30] It did this with Belgium, and has threatened it also in respect of a number of German *Länder*. As part of the *acquis communautaire*, these electoral rights must be adopted also by the accession states, and this dimension of compliance is again policed, in the first instance, by the Commission in its role as negotiator and reporter to the Member States, which ultimately agree accession.[31] Since 2000, the electoral rights have also featured in the EU's own Charter of Fundamental Rights (Articles 39 and 40).[32] Whatever the novelty of the electoral rights, take up rates have been extremely low,[33] both in terms of voting and standing, and there is little evidence at the national level of political parties adjusting many aspects of their political programmes to tailor them to the particular types of issues which residence as an EU citizen in another Member State might be expected to raise. Formally, the new electoral rights could therefore be said to be a failure. The boundaries of EU suffrage remain state-centred, as EU citizenship is premised upon Article 17(2) EC and upon the EU citizen already having the nationality of one of the Member States. Even so, they represent one case of partial alien suffrage, restricted to certain forms of elections and certain categories of beneficiaries, and adopted not because

[29] P Oliver, 'Electoral Rights under Article 8B of the Treaty of Rome', (1996) 33 *Common Market Law Review* 473.
[30] Until recently the Commission has not reported extensively on the Local Elections Directive: see Second Commission Report on Citizenship of the Union, COM (97) 230 (available at http://europa.eu.int/comm/internal_market/en/update/report/citen.pdf). In 2002 it issued a Report: Com (2002) 260 of 30 May 2002. Not all Member States responded to the questionnaire sent out by the Commission. Reports have been produced on the implementation of the European Parliamentary voting rights: COM(97) 731 (January 1998) and COM(2000) 843 (December 2000).
[31] Reference to progress on the implementation of the electoral rights as part of the *acquis* can be found in the Commission's regular reports on progress towards accession for each of the states in question. See for 2000: http://europa.eu.int/comm/enlargement/report_11_00/ index.htm
[32] The Charter of Fundamental Rights of the European Union, solemnly proclaimed by the Presidents of the Council of Ministers, the European Commission and the European Parliament, at the European Council Meeting in Nice, December 2000, OJ 2000 C364/1.
[33] See M Méndez Lago, 'The Political Rights of Immigrants: The Case of EU Nationals in the 1999 Spanish Local Elections', Paper presented at the ECPR Joint Sessions, Workshop No. 14, *Political participation of immigrants and their descendants in Post-War Western Europe*, Turin, 22–7 March 2002; J Shaw and S Day, 'Implementing Union Citizenship: The Case of Alien Suffrage and the European Union', EURCIT Workshop on 'The Constitution of European Democracy', Institute for Advanced Studies, Vienna, September 29–October 1 2000.

there have been moves at national level to improve the treatment given to migrants, but because of supranational legal *fiat* put in place by the consent of the Member States to treaty amendments and to the extension of the purview of the EU.

Meanwhile, the political participation of resident third country nationals remains a matter for national law within the EU Member States, although a number of Member States have joined other European states in signing up to the Council of Europe's Convention on the Political Participation of Foreigners in Local Life.[34] Concluded in 1992, the Convention entered into force in 1997. Of the Member States, Denmark, Finland (most recently), Italy (partially), the Netherlands and Sweden have ratified. The United Kingdom has signed, but not ratified. It offers a template of incremental steps towards enhancing the political participation rights of non-nationals, up to and including the right to vote in local elections; signatories commit themselves to implementing these, but there are—as with most international instruments—no sanctions for non-compliance. The case made for the Convention is strongly 'liberal democratic', as direct references in the Explanatory Report to the values of the Council of Europe including 'individual freedom, political liberty and the rule of law, which form the basis of all genuine democracy, and its attachment to the universal and indivisible nature of human rights and fundamental freedoms' make clear. These inspirations are reflected in the Preamble. The incremental template set up by the Convention envisages a staged introduction of three levels of political participation rights by signatory states, although the states may 'opt out' of the second and third stages.[35] The first stage, which in essence just complements the European Convention on Human Rights and Fundamental Freedoms, protects the basic civil liberties of foreigners by according them freedom of expression and freedom of assembly and association, on the same basis as nationals.[36] The second level involves consultative bodies to represent foreign residents at local level; and the third and final level involves the right to vote in local authority elections.

The political institutions of the Council of Europe have returned to the theme of political participation of foreigners in local elections in more recent times, with the Parliamentary Assembly adopting a Recommen-

---

[34] Signed on November 5 1992; European Treaty Series, no. 144; www.conventions.coe.int/.

[35] Italy's partial ratification includes a declaration opting out of the third stage.

[36] The provisions of the ECHR do not provide clear cut protection for the political rights of aliens. In *Piermont v France* (27 April 1995, 314 ECHR (series A), the Court of Human Rights adopted its first decision on Article 16, which provides that 'Nothing in Articles 10, 11 and 14 shall be regarded as preventing the High Contracting Parties from imposing restrictions on the political activity of aliens.' It held that in certain circumstances it does not apply to citizens of the European Union when on the territory of other Member States—but this does not protect third country nationals: J Kokott and B Rudolf, 'Commentary on *Piermont v France*', (1996) 90 *American Journal of International Law* 456. See also Article 3 of Protocol No. 1 which requires the holding of free and fair elections in the contracting states.

dation in January 2001 urging contracting states to introduce further rights for migrants, including the right to vote and stand in local elections for those established for a minimum of three years.[37] D'Oliveira suggests that the Convention, which refers simply to 'every foreign resident', is part of a framework of international law (he is not specific about the other instruments upon which he relies for his argument) which casts doubt on whether it is permissible for a distinction to be drawn between nationals of the Member States and others when granting voting rights.[38] On the other hand, others have argued that while the relevant provisions are not entirely consistent, the right to vote is one of the few rights in international law which may validly be limited to citizens.[39] Even so, it is important to cite other sources of international law which may buttress the approach taken in the Convention, including the Lund Recommendations on national minorities adopted within the context of the Organisation of Security and Cooperation in Europe (OSCE) and the approach taken by the Commissioner of the Council of the Baltic Sea States (CBSS) on Democratic Development. The former measures are aimed at 'national' minorities who can be expected to have national citizenship and so have limited relevance to the immigration scenario.[40] The CBSS Commissioner has reported on the situation with regard to voting rights and the right to stand for public office in the Member States of the Council, and recommended that these states adhere to the Council of Europe Convention and institute voting and standing rights for non-nationals.[41] Also relevant is the mirror image scenario, namely the permissible means of providing fair treatment for co-ethnics abroad, bearing in mind that this constitutes an interference in state sover-

---

[37] Recommendation 1500 (2001), 26 January 2001.

[38] H U J d'Oliveira, 'European Citizenship: Its Meaning, Its Potential' in R Dehousse (ed.), *Europe after Maastricht: An Ever Closer Union?*, (Munich, Law Books in Europe, 1994) at 142–3.

[39] J P Gardner (ed.), *Citizenship: The White Paper* (London, Institute for Citizenship Studies/The British Institute of International and Comparative Law, 1997), Hallmark 3: Right to Vote at 42.

[40] OSCE High Commissioner on National Minorities, Lund Recommendations: Effective Participation of National Minorities in Public Life (September 1999) (http://www.osce.org/hcnm/documents/recommendations/index.php3).

'Effective participation of national minorities in public life is an essential component of a peaceful and democratic society . . . (1) These Recommendations aim to facilitate the inclusion of minorities within the State and enable minorities to maintain their own identity and characteristics, thereby promoting the good governance and integrity of the State. (2) These Recommendations build upon fundamental principles and rules of international law, such as respect for human dignity, equal rights, and non-discrimination, as they affect the rights of national minorities to participate in public life and to enjoy other political rights. (3) States shall guarantee the right of persons belonging to national minorities to take part in the conduct of public affairs, including the rights to vote and stand for office without discrimination.'

[41] See CBSS Commissioner, *Rights of Non-citizens residing legally in the Member States of the CBSS. Voting Rights and the Right to Stand for Public Office*, Survey Part I, February 1996 and CBSS Commissioner, *Annual Report 2001–2002*, presented March 2002 (www.cbss-commissioner.org).

eignty. The Council of Europe's European Commission for Democracy through Law (the Venice Commission) accepted a report in late October 2001 which represents the first step towards the development of international norms governing kin-state policy towards co-ethnics abroad.[42]

Inevitably, there are considerable differences of approach amongst the Member States on this matter, ranging from a relatively inclusive approach (eg in Ireland, the Netherlands and the Nordic states), to complete—constitutionally based—exclusion of non-nationals from all aspects of an avowedly national *demos* (notably in Germany). Some Member States adopt a policy of partial inclusion (the UK gives electoral rights to Commonwealth and Irish citizens, but for *all* elections) or inclusion based on reciprocity (eg Spain). In some Member States, such as Belgium, France and Italy, there is ongoing contestation within the legislature about third country national voting rights. Overall, adoption of the principle of alien suffrage is still rather patchy, although a bare majority of eight out of fifteen Member States in 2003 conferred at least some rights. Calls at the national level, especially from left of centre parties and migrants' organisations, to narrow down or even eliminate those gaps in entitlements between different categories of migrants which are based on the incident of EU citizenship have resonated in the European Parliament. It adopted resolutions calling for the extension of the local franchise in the Member States to third country nationals.[43] However, when the Commission proposed a draft Directive on the rights of longterm resident third country nationals, it expressed the opinion that there was no EU competence to require the Member States to enact electoral rights under the legal basis which it used for the proposal (Article 63 EC),[44] and the European Parliament accepted this supposition regarding competence in its amendments to the initiative. This competence argument (developed further in section five[45]) echoes an earlier, pre-Maastricht, competence argument in relation to voting rights for EU citizens themselves (see section four).

At the regional level, new political structures seem to call for the determination of electorates without reference to the test offered by an exclusive legal form of belonging (ie nationality) which by definition can only attach to the *national* state. To recognise the 'nationality' of a region would seem, on the contrary, in effect to recognise its independence, which is precisely what the regional structures are generally intended to avoid. In the case of the UK, internal 'federalisation' determined by legislation adopted by the

---

[42] See generally Fowler, above n.28. Council of Europe, *Report on the Preferential Treatment of National Minorities by their Kin-State*, adopted by the Venice Commission at its 48th Plenary Meeting, Venice, October 19–20 2001 (Document CDL–INF (2001) 19).

[43] See below at nn 114 and 115.

[44] Proposal for a Council Directive concerning the status of third-country nationals who are long-term residents, COM(2001) 127, 13 March 2001.

[45] See further below at n 116 *et seq.*

national Westminster parliament takes the form of the denial rather than the partial recognition of a continuing claim by some political forces to national sovereignty (Scotland, Wales).[46] This denial is linked to an attempt to diffuse that radical claim into a more muted form of regional autonomy or 'devolution' of varying degrees of intensity. This may be one reason why the elections to the devolved political institutions in Scotland and Wales have been assimilated to local elections under UK electoral law, rather than to national elections. The same position applied to the election of a new Mayor in London.[47] Consequently, resident EU nationals entitled to vote in municipal elections under Article 19 and Directive 94/80 do form part of the nationally-defined franchise for these elections (and indeed in the regional referendums which preceded each of these elections to ascertain whether the regional 'people' wanted new forms of representation or political authority[48]). The UK has thus diffused the EU electoral rights down to the regional level, and tied this cosmopolitan development in an interesting way to the internal federalisation of the UK. This scenario is not reflected in other Member States such as Germany and Austria where *Länder* elections are assimilated to national elections.

The points outlined here set the stage for the remaining task of this chapter, that of illuminating the contestations which surround the determination of the boundaries of the suffrage. The next three sections focus, in turn, on contestations within the EU institutions and between the institutions and the Member States; on the contestability of electoral rights in national political discourse; and on the development of the EU's wider and indeed deeper role in relation to third country migrants. To be sure, these sections also highlight the need—at a conceptual level—to reconsider the continuing relevance of *traditional* state-centred concepts of sovereignty, and the need for theories which explain both the persistence as well as the transformation of recognisable forms of sovereignty, whether by reference to legal pluralism or concepts of multi-level governance. That task is beyond the scope of this chapter. What is noticeable, however, is the frequency with which deeper ideological arguments about the ethical claims of third country nationals, for example, are refracted in EU discourse into that much more banal level

---

[46] The case of devolution and Northern Ireland is different. The Northern Ireland Act does recognise the possibility of eventual secession, by accepting that the future of Northern Ireland is to be decided by its own people and that secession and joining into a united Ireland could be envisaged if decided upon by a majority of the people of Northern Ireland (s. 1(1) of the Northern Ireland Act 1998).

[47] S. 3(1) of the Local Government Elections Regulations 1995 (SI 1995, no. 1948) provides the basic amendments to the local electorate to incorporate the requirements of EU law; see also s. 17 of the Great London Authority Act 1999; s. 11 of the Scotland Act; s. 10 of Schedule 1, Government of Wales Act 1998; s. 2(2) of the Northern Ireland (Elections) Act 1998, which extends electoral rights to EU nationals, even though it is a rather different case of devolution.

[48] Eg ss. 1(2) and 2(2) of the Referendums (Scotland and Wales) Act 1997.

and form of internal sovereignty debate, namely the dispersal of competences and powers amongst a plurality of public authorities within a multi-
level governance system, especially one as unstable and unfinished as the
European Union. This concerns the debate about who (ie the Member
States or the EC/EU or a combination of both through the medium of
shared competence) *ought* to regulate questions such as immigration policy
governing the conditions of entry of nationals of third states and the status
of third country nationals already resident within the Member States
(including their political rights).

4. ELECTORAL RIGHTS AND THE EU INSTITUTIONS: CONCEPTION, COMPETENCE, COMPROMISE AND COMPLIANCE

'Every citizen of the Union has the right to vote and to stand as a candidate at
elections to the European Parliament in the Member State in which he or she
resides, under the same conditions as nationals of that State.'

'Every citizen of the Union has the right to vote and to stand as a candidate at
municipal elections in the Member State in which he or she resides under the
same conditions as nationals of that State.'[49]

The institution of a limited range of EU electoral rights in 1993 as part of
the Maastricht citizenship package represented for the EU institutions, especially the Commission and the European Parliament, the culmination of a
longstanding debate. Debates about the scope of the EU suffrage dated back
to the early 1960s when they were first raised in the European Parliament
in the context of discussions on direct elections.[50] There are a number of
historical roots to the present day discussions. D'Oliveira highlighted the
twin roots of the current electoral rights as 'the emergence of a Community
or Union collectivity' and the 'principles of democracy'.[51] Thus on the one
hand, the debates about electoral rights grew out of the development of free
movement rights under the Treaty and through the case law of the Court of
Justice; in legal literature dating back to the 1970s there were calls for such

---

[49] Articles 39(1) and 40 of the *Charter of Fundamental Rights of the European Union*, OJ
2000 C364/1.
[50] A Connolly, 'Alien suffrage in the European Union and direct elections to the European
Parliament 1951–1980', CIVIC Working Paper 2/2001. It is important to acknowledge my
considerable debt to the PhD research conducted by Dr Anthea Connolly on Alien Suffrage in
the EU (1999–2002), which has examined in detail the parliamentary and other institutional
debates about electoral rights and citizenship in the EU: *The Theory and Practice of Alien
Suffrage in the European Union*, unpublished PhD thesis, University of Manchester, 2003.
[51] H U J d'Oliveira, above n 38 at 142.

'free movers' to be conceived as 'Community citizens'.[52] Electoral rights on this view are rights ancillary to the practice of migration by EU citizens, rights to be established by the EU acting as a protective polity in order to foster a deeper sense of involvement on the part of the EU migrant with the host state and with certain aspects of its political culture, and to limit the prejudice in terms of the loss of political rights which the migrant may suffer as a result of moving away from her home state.

This in turn connects to the second root of EU electoral rights, namely the impulse towards greater formal democratisation of the institutions of European integration through popular participation, especially moves coming from within the European Parliament. Members of the original 'Assembly' discussed the issue of allocating certain voting rights on the basis of residence rather than nationality when debating the introduction of direct elections, from the 1960s onwards. It seemed illogical to many participants in the debate to suggest direct elections *without* safeguarding the completeness of the democratic principle by extending voting rights also to those who had taken advantage of the free movement rights guaranteed by the Treaty. A link to a putative 'citizenship' for the emergent 'Euro-polity' was again then swiftly made, especially by the European Commission, which later made concrete suggestions for local election voting rights, only finally adopted in the Treaty of Maastricht.[53]

Jeffrey Lewis has researched the negotiation of the terms of the local elections directive in a case study of the work of the Committee of Permanent Representatives (Coreper) as a crucial cog in the EU's decision-making structures.[54] His interview data suggests that the Treaty of Maastricht was decisive in giving the European Community competence to adopt the local elections directive. Although the issue had had plenty of political salience when it was a proposal from the Commission, and not inconsiderable

---

[52] See W Böhning, *The Migration of Workers in the United Kingdom and the European Community* (London, OUP, 1972) cited in B Wilkinson, 'Towards European Citizenship? Nationality, Discrimination and Free Movement of Workers in the European Union', (1995) 1 *European Public Law* 417 at 418; R Plender, 'An Incipient Form of European Citizenship', in F Jacobs (ed.), *European Law and the Individual* (Dordrecht, North Holland, 1976); A Evans, 'European Citizenship: A Novel Concept in EEC Law', (1984) *American Journal of Comparative Law* 679. G Ress, 'Free Movement of persons, services and capital' in Commission of the European Communities (ed.), *Thirty years of Community law* (Luxembourg, OOPEC, 1981), at 302 has a section entitled 'Are we on the way towards creating European citizenship?'.

[53] See Commission Report to the European Parliament on *Voting Rights in local elections for Community nationals*, COM(86) 487, also published as Bull-EC Supp. 7/86; Commission proposal for a Council Directive on Voting Rights for Community Nationals in Local Elections in their Member State of Resident, COM(88) 371; amended proposal COM (89) 524.

[54] J Lewis, 'Is the 'Hard Bargaining' Image of the Council Misleading? The Committee of Permanent Representatives and the Local Elections Directive', (1998) 36 *Journal of Common Market Studies* 479. For recent coverage of this institution, which is still regarded as rather mysterious, see F Guerrera and D Dombey, 'Overlooked powers behind Europe's throne', *Financial Times*, 31 March 2002.

support from some quarters, Lewis' interviewees at Coreper doubted whether the EC Treaty before Maastricht conferred the necessary competence to act on the European Community. Yet the Member States have often been willing in policy domains as sensitive as sex equality law, environmental policy and consumer protection to use the residual legal basis of what was then Article 235 EEC (now, post-Amsterdam, Article 308 EC) to adopt legislation by means of a unanimous vote in order to further the Community's objectives when there was no other specific legal basis in the Treaty, and it could arguably have done so again with electoral rights. The 'lack of competence' argument was more likely to have been more about stressing that it was simply too early for the then European Community—until citizenship had been constitutionalised by the Treaty of Maastricht—to engage so deeply with the local electoral sovereignty of the Member States. In particular, only with the 'constitutionalisation' of citizenship, could those Member States which needed national constitutional amendments in order to implement the electoral rights be expected to act.[55] Lewis acknowledges this point by referring to the effects of the 'grand bargain' and package deal of Maastricht.

When it came to implementing the Maastricht provisions, it was the local elections directive which proved to be the more controversial and difficult to negotiate through the EU political process. The European Parliamentary elections directive, which did not in the same way impugn the electoral sovereignty of the Member States as it was not seen as engaging in a direct way with how they govern themselves, passed through relatively unproblematically. The Commission and the European Parliament had some early skirmishes over the issue of qualifying residence periods in the local elections directive,[56] and both the European Parliament and ECOSOC felt that they were substantially disenfranchised within the political process because of the restrictive nature of the legislative procedure laid down in Article 18 EC.[57] However, these skirmishes were overshadowed by the crucial negotiation phases within Coreper.

---

[55] This can also be discerned from a Council Press release of 1990 cited by Lewis, above n 54 at 494: when the foreign ministers discussed this dossier in June 1990 they noted 'political, constitutional and legal problems in connection with this proposal which prevent certain Member States from taking up a final position'.

[56] Report of the Committee on Legal Affairs and Citizens' Rights and the opinions of the Committee on Institutional Affairs and the Committee on Regional Policy A4–0011/1994. Proposal for a Council Directive laying down detailed arrangements for the exercise of the right to vote and to stand as a candidate in municipal elections by citizens of the Union residing in a Member State of which they are not nationals (COM(94) 38; OJ 1994 C105/8).

[57] Own initiative opinion of the Economic and Social Committee on the proposal for a Council Directive laying down detailed arrangements for the exercise of the right to vote and to stand as a candidate in municipal elections for citizens of the Union residing in a Member State of which they are not nationals. (94/C 393/29) OJ 1994 C 393/186.

The Commission's draft directive was presented to Council in April 1994 but was referred to Coreper soon thereafter. It only came back to the General Affairs Council in December 1994, where it was effectively rubber stamped by the ministers on the basis of the political compromise reached in Coreper.[58] Coreper was given the file to deal with not because it was a narrow technical issue—the traditional image of what Coreper is there to deal with in the EU institutional system—but precisely because it was too political. Had the debate been politicised, through Council discussions, a decision might never have been reached—and certainly not as quickly as it was. Lewis argues that the socialisation processes of Coreper have created an ideal decision-making environment for this and other challenging dossiers, creating, in the case of the local elections directive, the frame for cross-national understanding of crucial domestic political difficulties of some Member States, whilst also achieving what might be regarded as a surprisingly high level of 'equal treatment' for resident non-national EU voters. Hence generalised residency requirements were removed from the original Commission draft, but the capacity to reserve leadership roles such as the position of mayor for nationals preserved national sensitivities over sovereignty. Special arrangements for EU voters must be made at the national level, so that states such as Denmark are not allowed to deem compliance with the Treaty and the Directive simply by applying their existing alien suffrage arrangements which subject non-nationals to a three year residency requirement. This reinforced the process of distinguishing between second and third country nationals. Likewise French attempts to institute a partial quota system for EU representatives in municipalities with over 20 per cent non-national EU citizens in the electorate was received sympathetically, but ultimately fell victim to pressure to enact a measure within the spirit of the Maastricht citizenship provisions. Even so, a special derogation was effectively enacted for Luxembourg. It covered Member States where the proportion of EU voters in the whole state on January 1 1996 was more than 20 per cent of the electorate; such Member States are entitled to restrict the right to vote to those satisfying a qualifying residence period of no more than the term of office of the municipal council, and the right to stand to those satisfying a qualifying residence period of no more than twice the term of office of the municipal council (Article 12(1)). Only Luxembourg falls into this category.[59]

Particular attention was paid in Coreper to the case of Belgium where it was evident that application of the directive could alter delicately balanced linguistic majorities/minorities within municipalities (involving French speakers, Dutch speakers and German speakers). Since its original 'commu-

---

[58] Lewis, above n 54 at 493.
[59] In a 1999 Report, the Commission concluded that the derogation could still validly apply: COM(1999) 597.

nautaire' enthusiasm for local electoral rights as a nation state 'at the heart of Europe', Belgium had had to face up to a very different political problem in the context of its own very delicately balanced federal arrangements for the various linguistic communities. It was evident that it was quite out of the question for the Belgian government to achieve the necessary constitutional change which required the consent of all communities without a derogation. Lewis maintains that the members of Coreper were able to be sympathetic to and react to the Belgian Ambassador's need for a derogation, based on these domestic political constraints. These domestic political constraints were better understood by the Ambassadors, socialised in the world of Coreper and living in Brussels, than they would have been by the Ministers themselves, who might have been tempted to make political capital. Unlike some of the other arguments put forward by national delegations the Belgian argument was seen to be a 'good' argument, one which could be accepted in the national capitals provided it was carefully presented by the Ambassadors to their political masters and mistresses. Overall, Coreper operated as a functional decision-making forum in which national arguments for special treatment could be heard, evaluated and either accepted or rejected, without posturing or threats of vetos, or quid pro quo concessions which might have led to a 'race to the bottom' in terms of the content of decisions adopted.

Detailed scrutiny of the implementation and application of the directive at national level and of the lack of impact at the domestic level in terms of visibility and take-up of the electoral rights is not included in this chapter.[60] In some respects, compliance at national level has been a field of contestation. In any event, the high level of variation in arrangements for local government at the national level combined with the absence of a provision in the directive requiring Member States to report comprehensively on implementation have made this a difficult *dossier* for the Commission to pursue.[61]

The most obvious case of non-compliance with the local elections directive was that of Belgium; despite its special derogations, Belgium still failed to implement the directive, until after it had been the subject of an enforcement action in the Court of Justice brought by the Commission.[62] It was almost a formality for the Court to declare that Belgium had failed to comply with its treaty obligations. Thereafter, Belgium did comply, and by

---

[60] For details of many of the national implementing measures, see the information provided on the Commission's Justice and Home Affairs Website: http://europa.eu.int/comm/justice_home/unit/elections/elections_menu_en.htm.
[61] This has not been assisted by the fact that the *dossier* moved around 2000 from the internal market Directorate General to the DG for Justice and Home Affairs, although materials on voting rights can be found still on the websites of both DGs.
[62] Case C–323/97 *Commission v. Belgium* [1998] ECR I–4281.

the deadline for registration, some 17.3 per cent of the eligible 496,000 EU nationals had registered to vote in the October 2000 local elections, which were the first set of municipal elections which they could vote in, and this despite the compulsory nature of voting in Belgium.[63] This was, however, a considerable increase on the 7.71 per cent of eligible EU citizens who registered to vote in the 1999 European Parliamentary elections.

At the national level, despite generalised apathy, some EU citizens have found themselves dissatisfied with the scope of the provisions and have sought redress. For example, an Italian citizen resident in Vienna began an action in the Austrian courts, contesting his exclusion from the electoral roll in relation to the Vienna city elections. Vienna is both a city and a *Land* and elections to the latter are not included in the EU provisions; for the purposes of the local elections directive, it is the *Bezirke* (municipalities), not the city itself which represents the relevant local governmental authorities where EU citizens can vote. It was held by the Austrian Constitutional Court that because the City Council has the power to make laws it is quite proper that both the Council Directive on local elections and also the implementing Austrian legislation should provide that an EU citizen does not have the right to vote in the City Council elections, but only in elections at the level of *Bezirke*. Consequently, the exclusion of EU nationals was in conformity with Austrian law and EU law.[64] The Court also refused to refer the case to the Court of Justice under Article 234 EC, and sidestepped an attempted challenge by the complainant to the legality of the local elections directive itself, on the grounds that it infringed the principle of non-discrimination between EU nationals.

5. OPENING THE NATIONAL PANDORA'S BOXES: ELECTORAL RIGHTS IN NATIONAL POLITICAL DISCOURSE

'Today there is simply not the political will to address the issue of voting rights at the national level'.[65]

'Je n'ai pas changé politiquement. J'étais et je reste favourable à l'octroi du droit de vote aux étrangers. Mais je sais aussi que, dans le meilleur des cas, même si l'on devait voter le 12 mars, tout cela n'adviendrait pas avant 2006, année durant laquelle se déroulera le prochain scrutin communal. Dès lors et dans ces

---

[63] On non-national participation in the October 2000 elections (including the participation of nationals of non-Belgian origin), see D Jacobs, M Martiniello and A Rea, 'Changing patterns of political participation of immigrants in the Brussels Capital Region. The October 2000 elections', Paper presented to the Sixth International Metropolis Conference, Workshop No. 14 on the Political Participation of Migrants, Rotterdam, 27 November 2001.
[64] Decision of the Austrian Constitutional Court of 12 December 1997, B3113/96, B3760/96.
[65] Interview with a representative of the Austrian Social Democratic Party, Vienna, June 2000.

conditions, il serait pour le moins inélégant de mettre en difficulté un partenaire du gouvernement.[66]

This section focuses upon the contestability of electoral rights for non-nationals within national political discourse, above and beyond the more specialised question of EU electoral rights. EU electoral rights are, after all, a species of migrants' rights,[67] and so they intersect with fundamental questions which must be answered in order to determine the boundaries of *any* polity, especially questions about immigration and ethnic relations policies and politics, nationality law, the culture of national politics, and the scope and nature of the *demos* at *national* as well as at the *Union* level. Even so, a 'national politics' of ethnic relations or immigration is a complex phenomenon. Correlations might be expected, for example, between party attitudes towards immigration and the degree of penetration of non-national electoral rights into the national political cultures. The invocation, by national politicians, of a sense of belonging, membership and identity associated with the territorial state is, as we shall see, quite common in discourse on electoral rights.

Proponents of alien suffrage must address the conundrum of how to combine a sense of cosmopolitanism as a defence against tribalism with a sense of bounded communities as a defence against rootlessness. The case *for* alien suffrage is typically supported by versions of liberalism/liberal democracy, with a splash of cosmopolitanism (eg a putative international 'right to democracy'), and a desire to bring voting rights into a continuum of inclusion rather than confining them to the dichotomy of membership (ie yes/no and in/out).[68] Consequently, it downplays the significance of (formal legal) national citizenship, and concentrates upon issues of 'societal membership' highlighted above.[69] This is a concept which combines both empirical observation of the extent of migrant incorporation in host societies, and a normative element contending that host polities *ought* in principle to seek to include migrants within societal frameworks including political institutions. Societal membership presupposes a relatively high degree of non-exclusivity in the affinity of the migrant, and assumes substantial overlap as a result between different polities.

---

[66] Belgian Deputy Prime Minister and Foreign Minister Louis Michel on why he intervened to prevent a vote in the Belgian Senate to institute local electoral rights for third country nationals expected to take place on 12 March 2002, quoted in Le Soir en Ligne, 20 February 2002 (http://users.skynet.be/suffrage-universel/bevo0202.htm).

[67] See generally S Day and J Shaw, 'European Union Electoral Rights and the Political Participation of Migrants in Host Polities', (2002) 8 *International Journal of Population Geography* 183.

[68] See the types of arguments put forward by activist groups such as the *Alliance for Residency-Based European Citizenship* and the campaign for *Universal Franchise*: http://ourworld.compuserve.com/homepages/Paul_Oriol/ and http://users.skynet.be/suffrage-universel/

[69] Bauböck, above n.19.

Meanwhile, the case *against* alien suffrage is generally premised upon versions of communitarianism combined with a formalist notion of boundaries and membership. Assumptions are sometimes made about the capacity of the non-national to play the role of the active citizen in a 'thick' republican conception of citizenship, because of doubts about shared commitments or loyalties. The strength—in practice—of the case against is well evidenced by the fact that the majority of EU Member States (and especially the most populous states) grant no or only very restricted alien suffrage to third country nationals above and beyond the requirements of EU law. Pessimistically, Lardy suggests that the fact

> 'that such proposals have rarely been discussed seriously in modern times is, however, more likely a reflection of the preoccupation with territorial sovereignty which characterises the modern State than an objection to the franchise extension based on principles rooted in political theory . . . In many States the issue appears never to have arisen; the restriction of voting rights to legal citizens is regarded as a reasonable and administratively convenient device for delimiting the electorate, and one which requires no justification.'[70]

Where voting rights have been extended, the reasons for the extension have varied considerably. In the Scandinavian countries, for example, pressure often originated in Social Democratic political parties. The initial drive by the Swedish Social Democrats in the 1970s to extend the franchise stemmed from their belief, according to Zig Layton-Henry, that

> 'to exclude long-term residents from voting not only violated principles of representative democracy, but would foster divisions between natives and immigrants and would encourage the neglect of immigrants' grievances, thus fostering alienation and bitterness.'[71]

In other words, it was associated with a policy of integration. Voting rights extensions have not invariably been associated with liberal states. One of the few recent examples of the extension of the right to vote to non-nationals involved the case of foreign workers, or *VertragsarbeiterInnen* in the German Democratic Republic. Right at the death of the GDR, in 1990, a new law was promulgated that enabled this group of 100–200,000 persons to vote at all levels after six months of residency. Ironically, few of them remained much longer in the united Germany, just as the law itself did not survive reunification. Many foreigners were sent home with one way tickets just before German reunification in 1990.[72]

---

[70] H Lardy, 'Citizenship and the Right to Vote', (1997) 17 *Oxford Journal of Legal Studies* 75 at pp 98–9. See also H Lardy, 'The Political rights of Union Citizenship', (1997) 2 *European Public Law* 611.

[71] Z Layton-Henry, 'Citizenship and Migrant Workers in Western Europe' in U Vogel and M Moran (eds.), *The Frontiers of Citizenship* (London, Macmillan, 1991) at 120.

[72] On the reality for foreigners in the GDR, see S Geyer, 'Ausländer in der DDR. Frischfleisch für den Sozialismus', *Der Spiegel*, 5 May 2001.

In the United Kingdom, the extension of the franchise to Commonwealth and Irish citizens appears to be widely seen across political parties as an historical accident.[73] In a recent debate in the House of Commons, Conservative MP Douglas Hogg suggested that

'If we were starting from scratch, we probably would not extend the franchise to citizens of the Commonwealth or Ireland. Their right to vote has happened for historical reasons, but it is quite difficult, if one sets about defining why people should have the vote, to say with any great confidence that citizens of Ireland or the Commonwealth should have it.'[74]

His views were quite closely echoed in the views of the Labour Government minister, George Howarth MP:

'Whatever the historical reasons for their existence, the arrangements with the Commonwealth should not necessarily be taken as a precedent for arrangements with other countries that currently do not apply.'[75]

The same debate on a Bill to extend the franchise to excluded categories of nationals framed a wider discussion on the possible extension of the franchise to all non-nationals. Labour MP Harry Barnes proposed an amendment to this effect. He argued for residence-based 'citizenship' on the grounds that those who are resident in a given polity are affected by decisions made by political representatives, and should therefore have the right to participate in their election. Finding himself largely alone in the House of Commons in making the argument for alien suffrage and residence-based voting, Barnes appealed to cosmopolitanism:

'We now have a cosmopolitan world in which people move in and out of different areas. It is not always clear to people what their nation is. However, it is clear where they are, and the Government and administration responsible for making decisions that immediately affect their lives at that time can be clearly identified. We should develop electoral registration that is based on those circumstances, while recognising that there is sense in terms of citizenship.'[76]

Opposition to the amendment, which was eventually withdrawn without vote, centred on maintaining the reciprocal link between the citizen and the state. According to Liberal Democrat MP Robert MacLennan:

---

[73] See Home Affairs Selection Committee, Fourth Report, Session 1997–1998, Electoral Law and Administration, para. 117 *et seq.*
[74] Debate on the Representation of the People Act 2000 extending the franchise to certain categories of previously excluded persons such as the homeless, those remanded in custody and not yet convicted, and patients resident in mental hospitals who are not detained offenders, Hansard, House of Commons, 15 December 1999, Douglas Hogg MP, Col 296. See H Lardy, 'Democracy by Default: The Representation of the People Act 2000', (2001) 62 *Modern Law Review* 63.
[75] George Howarth, MP, Column 301.
[76] See Hansard, House of Commons, 15 December 1999, Cols 293–305 for the debate. Harry Barnes, MP at Columns 303–4.

'the state has the duty to look after its citizens, and the citizen must exercise his or her duty to be interested in how that service is provided. The notion of citizenship would be under challenge, perhaps even under threat, if that very considerable right were partly diminished by being no longer a characteristic of citizenship, but simply the happenstance of residence.'[77]

His views were echoed by Douglas Hogg

'the right of voting—the duty to vote—runs with citizenship. It is part of that relationship with society that involves affinity and allegiance; it is part of being a member of a society . . . I certainly do not think that (the right to vote) should arise simply from the fact that a person is affected by the consequences of legislation.'[78]

Looking at the varying success and failure stories of campaigns to widen the franchise, commentators regularly conclude that the primary determinant of extensions of the franchise remains the possibility of coalitions between major national political parties.[79] Interestingly, in fact, as Dirk Jacobs has shown by comparing the cases of the Netherlands and Belgium, arguments about the nature of the national polity can be used—in different settings—both to support (the Netherlands) and to contest (Belgium) the enfranchisement of resident aliens. In the Netherlands, the decision after ten years of parliamentary debate to extend municipal voting rights to non-nationals who had been resident in the Netherlands for at least five years was taken in the context of what he terms a 'discourse coalition' based on a temporary hybrid of different inclusionary and mildly exclusionary discourses coming from different positions on the political spectrum. The step was taken so that the government appeared to be doing something at a key point in time about certain acute inter-ethnic tensions, but this 'something' was in fact based on a secret agreement amongst the principal political actors not to promote open discussion in order to restrict the capacity of the extreme political right to find a platform for its segregationist exclusionary discourse. In Belgium, where the issue has remained under constant political scrutiny and an amendment to Article 8 of the Constitution on citizenship was put in place in 1998 to allow the adoption of a law granting electoral rights to third country nationals to be adopted no earlier than January 1 2001, no such opportunity for a decisive discourse coalition has yet arisen. On the contrary, as the quotation from Louis Michel, Belgian Foreign Minister, at the head of this section tellingly highlights, the issue fell

---

[77] Robert MacLennan MP, Column 295.
[78] Douglas Hogg MP, Column 296.
[79] D Jacobs, 'Discourse, politics and policy: the Dutch parliamentary debate about voting rights for foreign residents', (1998) 32 *International Migration Review* 350; D Jacobs, 'The debate over enfranchisement of foreign residents in Belgium', (1999) 25 *Journal of Ethnic and Migration Studies* 649; J Rath, 'Voting Rights' in Z Layton-Henry (ed.), *The Political Rights of Migrant Workers in Western Europe* (Sage, London, 1990).

victim in early 2002 to the complexities of the Belgium coalition government system. A proposal for the necessary legislative measure had been placed before the Senate and was due to be voted on in March 2002, but faced opposition from Flemish participants in the current Belgian coalition government—themselves under electoral and political pressure from the extreme rightwing and nationalist Vlaamse Blok. In contrast, there is near unanimity across political forces within the Brussels-Capital region and Wallonia about the desirability of extending voting rights to third country nationals. By demonstrating his unwillingness to see a measure adopted at the present, Michel effectively undermined the proposals before Senate. His reasoning was that he did not wish to embarrass a coalition member over an issue which would not become a reality until 2006, when the next local elections will be held. Immigrants' rights were sacrificed to a greater political good, although Michel expressed his intention to see that the issue was made part of the political programme of the next national government, which he has every intention of heading up.[80] On 12 March 2002, a proposal on third country national voting rights was rejected in the Internal Affairs Committee of the Belgian Senate[81] and this was followed on 28 March 2002 by a close vote in plenary (36 votes to 33) against the measure. The expendability of the measure as far as the centre-right Flemish Liberal party was concerned was well illustrated by a comment by its leader, Karel de Grucht: 'It's not something that if you don't give it, it breaches a fundamental right.'[82]

A closer look at the immigration politics and histories of Germany and Austria illuminates the nature of political contestations within polities with an historically 'ethnic' conception of the *demos*, but with current political debates over immigration and integration.

Germany has no active political debate about alien suffrage for third country nationals at the present time. An emerging constitutional debate driven largely at the regional level by the efforts of two *Länder*—Schleswig-Holstein and Hamburg—to extend the right to vote and run for office at local level to non-nationals was brought to a rather abrupt conclusion by rulings on the part of the Federal Constitutional Court determining that alien suffrage (beyond the precepts of EU law) is currently not constitutionally possible in Germany.[83] These judgments were based upon the 'popular sovereignty' principle enshrined in the German constitution which attaches in turn to the principles upon which German nationality law was

---

[80] See n 66 above. Further press commentary is collected online at http://users.skynet.be/suffrage-universel/bevo0202.htm.

[81] M Vandemeulebroucke, 'Le vote des étrangers est mis au frigo. La commission de l'Intérieur du Sénat rejette le projet par neuf voix contre six', *Le Soir en Ligne*, March 12 2002.

[82] Quoted in 'No Belgium votes for non-EU residents', BBC World, 28 March 2002 (news.bbc.co.uk).

[83] Judgments of the Court of 31 October 1990, BVerfGE 83, 37 II.

at that time based, namely *ius sanguinis*.[84] It is possible that the issue could be reviewed again, in the future, following the successful—if contested— revision of the citizenship law brought about in the wake of unification and the election of the Red-Green coalition in 1998.[85] Indeed, the 1998 Coalition Agreement between the Social Democratic Party (SPD) and the Greens when they entered government together declared that 'to promote integration, those foreigners living here who do not possess the citizenship of an EU Member State *shall also receive the right to vote in district and local elections.*'[86] However, the principle cannot be instituted without a constitutional amendment. In this instance, Germany's principle of the federal dispersal of power cedes ground to the principle of constitutional supremacy.

In the meantime, the issue will not be pushed by either the SPD or the Greens. According to a spokesperson, 'Politicians are agreed that the topic was simply not one in which the party of the far left, Party of Democratic Journalism could engage even with its own members let alone society at large'.[87] There do exist some local campaigns to support at least the exist- ing electoral rights, such as that in Hessen, where the SPD actively sought the support of EU nationals, organised meetings with other social-demo- cratic sister organisations, such as PASOK (Greece) and translated leaflets. However, these are localised positions: 'There is no national policy, though, it differs from town to town'.[88] According to the Greens, the constitutional barrier means there is no current chance of change: 'The fact that a two- thirds majority would be needed to amend the constitution without CDU support means it was simply pointless attempting to pursue this issue. There are no victories if you struggle too hard.'[89] The changes to the citizenship law were, in the view of the Greens, already a significant change. They welcomed changes such as a more standardised procedure lessening discre- tion given to public officials in each of the *Länder*, and in particular the

---

[84] See the summary and analyses in R Rubio-Marín, *Immigration as a Democratic Challenge: Citizenship and Inclusion in Germany and the United States* (Cambridge, Cambridge University Press, 2000) Ch. 8. See also G L Neuman, ' 'We are the People': Alien Suffrage in German and American Perspective', (1992) 13 *Michigan Journal of International Law* 259 and O Béaud, 'Le droit de vote des étrangers: l'apport de la jurisprudence constitutionnelle alle- mande à une théorie du droit de suffrage', (1992) *Revue française de Droit administratif* 409.
[85] *Gesetz zur Reform des Staatsangehörigkeitsrechts* (StARG) of 15 July 1999 (BGBl. I, p1618). On this see generally S Green, 'Beyond Ethnoculturalism? German Citizenship in the New Millenium', (2000) 9 *German Politics* 105 and S Green, 'Citizenship Policy in Germany: The Case of Ethnicity over Residence' in Hansen and Weil, above n 20.
[86] SPD-Green Coalition Agreement, Chapter IX(7), available from the SPD homepage (www.spd.de) (italics added).
[87] Interview with Martin Hantke, advisor to Dr Sylvia-Yvonne Kaufmann, MEP, Berlin, May 2000.
[88] Interview with Peter Hamon (Sozialdemokratische Gemeinschaft für Kommunalpolitik in der Bundesrepublik), Berlin, May 2000.
[89] Interview with Malti Tanja, Office of Claudia Roth, MdB, Berlin, May 2000.

weakening of *ius sanguinis*: 'The principle of *jus soli* was the most important element of the new law.'[90] Concerns surround the requirement to opt at the age of 23 for German or another citizenship:

'All agree especially the first generation that they don't want to lose their Turkish passport. It's like a picture of your family in the bedroom. They feel that the new citizenship is like forcing them to hand over this picture.'[91]

The conservative CDU continues to refer back to the symbols and 'perks' of citizenship: 'citizenship rights are a privilege for those who belong', and 'if such rights are proliferated for the many then they are no longer special for the few.'[92] The rhetoric sometimes comes rather close to a form of narrow ethnocentrism: 'A child's connection to his or her parents is the most important issue, not the political community and this is something that needs to be cherished. While a child of Turkish parents can join the political community via the *jus soli*, his or her language and culture are Turkish.'[93] The CDU has also managed to campaign quite successfully to prevent the proliferation of dual nationality by presenting what was proposed by the SPD/Green coalition as amounting to the granting of a special right particularly benefiting the Turkish population.

From mid 2001 onwards the debate was dominated by proposals brought forward by the governing coalition for a new immigration law to foster the immigration of skilled and highly qualified foreigners into Germany, in particular in order to address skills shortages in the German labour market. Part of the political controversy which the draft law has attracted is the contrast which it provides with a soaring domestic unemployment rate of over 10 per cent in January 2002. Conservative Chancellor candidate Edmund Stoiber epitomised the debate when he declared that 'with 4.3 million unemployed, we can't have more foreign workers coming to Germany . . . who is going to pay for integrating these workers. I've not heard the chancellor saying he'll give the billions it will cost to pay for this. Will industry pay?'[94] The draft law originated in a report from an independent Commission appointed by the Interior Minister Schily, which was published in July 2001. The Commission was chaired by a member of the CDU, Rita Süssmuth, and the report (*Arranging immigration, promoting integration*)[95] made the case for planned and targeted

---

[90] Interview with Cem Ozdemir, MdB, Berlin, May 2000.

[91] Interview with Cem Ozdemir, MdB, Berlin, May 2000.

[92] Interview with CDU representative, May 2000. See also the example of the Junge Union, Main-Kinzig, a conservative youth organisation, which explicitly argues against local election voting rights for third country nationals: 'the right to vote is the foremost (vornehmste) right of the citizen' (www.ju-main-kinzig.de/Programm/Auslander/auslander.html).

[93] Interview with CDU representative, Berlin, May 2000.

[94] *Migration News*, Vol. 9, No. 2, February 2002 (http://migration.ucdavis.edu/).

[95] Williamson, 'Schröder welcomes radical reform of immigration', *Financial Times*, 5 July 2001.

immigration. This moves away from the rather more haphazard admission of some 200,000—300,000 newcomers per year which occurs at present on the basis of family unification, asylum seekers and ethnic Germans.

By March 2002, the draft law was in serious trouble in the German parliament, particularly in the Upper House, the *Bundesrat*, where the respresentatives of the *Länder* sit. In view of the impending national elections in September 2002 to the *Bundestag*, the SPD/Green coalition was unwilling to see the draft immigration law—which would be Germany's first ever—mired in a joint commission of the two houses, as that would be likely to prevent its adoption. After its approval in the *Bundestag* by 320 votes to 225, the law was passed in the *Bundesrat* on 22 March 2002 by the narrowest of margins (35 votes to 34). The representatives of the state of Brandenburg, ruled by a coalition of the SPD and CDU were split on the issue, but ultimately the vote went with the SPD Prime Minister who voted in favour, bringing with him Brandenburg's four votes. Normally, in those circumstances, as *Land* votes must be cast as a block, the state would abstain.[96] The move provoked a constitutional crisis, with the opposition members of the *Bundesrat* walking out and insisting—backed up by a threat of legal action—that the Federal President Johannes Rau should not pass the draft into law.[97] As a Social Democrat himself, Rau did eventually approve the law, although he did not act hastily. However, in early 2003 the Federal Constitutional Court struck down the law on procedural grounds.

The political furore in March 2002 re-emphasised that immigration *policy* is largely a smokescreen for the real debate which continues to divide the parties in Germany, the question of the *integration* of foreigners and what this means in terms of national culture and even sovereignty. For immigration itself will continue—regardless of whether the law is enacted. Consequently, the argument made by a CDU leader that the 'law would completely change German society within a few years' seems apocalyptic.[98] On the other hand, it may well represent a substantial strand of public opinion, since some polls do suggest that between nine and 25 per cent of German voters would support an anti-immigrant party in the 2002 elections. Further fuel was added to the debate when former Chancellor Helmut Schmidt published a new book in which he claimed that Germany had admitted too many foreigners, whom it could not properly assimilate, and that Germans were really xenophobes at heart.[99]

Political opposition to immigration has also re-entered the Austrian political mainstream in recent years, since the formation in early 2000 of the controversial coalition government involving the People's Party (ÖVP) and

[96] *Migration News*, Vol. 9, No. 3, April 2002 (http://migration.ucdavis.edu/).
[97] D Kommers, 'Constitutional Politics in Germany', (2002) 3 *German Law Journal* no. 4 (www.germanlawjournal.com).
[98] *Migration News*, Vol. 9, No. 1, January 2002 (http://migration.ucdavis.edu/)
[99] 'Germans are 'xenophobes' says Schmidt', BBC World, 29 March 2002 (news.bbc.co.uk).

the Freedom Party (FPÖ) then led by Jörg Haider. This event also precipitated similarly controversial 'sanctions' against Austria by the other fourteen Member States of the EU. The FPÖ achieved its success which delivered it political power in the federal elections of October 1999 on the back of a political programme incorporating opposition to the cosy system of *Proporz*, a form of political patronage, presided over by the Social Democrats (SPÖ) and the ÖVP for 40 years, allowing them to carve up all major positions in government and the public sector, plus a policy opposing further immigration into Austria. Its 1999 election manifesto referred to Austria being 'swamped by foreigners', and it made use of the discredited Nazi term *Überfremdung* in the context of Vienna. Somewhat moderated since then, its rhetoric is still determinedly anti-multiculturalism:

> 'I don't see why we must be multi-cultural. You see what kind of difficulties it makes in most countries. Our country has more [immigrants] [in proportion to size] than other countries. They should become more Austrian those who want to stay here—learn German, enter into our culture—but we don't want to have more of them.'[100]

However, the Austrian Government's official position shows how it has taken pains to reaffirm its position within the European political mainstream, declaring its future to be at the 'heart of Europe'.[101] 'Modern' Austria is, of course, a relatively young state, and some of its postwar self-image has been constructed on the basis of a sense of Austria more as victim than as perpertrator of Nazi atrocities. However, the Government Declaration likewise commits Austria to a self-critical scrutiny of its National Socialist past.

Postwar reconstruction also involved the development of Austria into a federal republic in which the nine *Länder* administer nationality law.[102] There are also strong discretionary elements in the naturalisation process, and the most recent amendments in 1998 were concerned with tidying up weaknesses in the current laws resulting from anomalies, such as whether a language test was required, in the application by the *Länder*, and were not an attempt to liberalise the laws. Austria's nationality laws remain substantially based on *ius sanguinis*, with little space for dual nationality, a point actively supported by the current government:

> 'People with double citizenship can only be loyal with reservation. Double citizenship discriminated against Austrians, because they only had one citizenship, which will increase the danger of political conflict. Those who apply for Austrian

---

[100] John Gudenus, FPÖ Deputy, quoted in 'Head to Head: Is Haider a threat?', *BBC News*, February 29 1990.

[101] See Declaration by the Austrian Government, *Responsibility for Austria—A Future in the Heart of Europe*, Vienna, 3 February 2000 (www.undp.org/missions/austria/r040200a.htm).

[102] R Bauböck and Dilek Çinar, 'Nationality Law and Naturalisation in Austria' in Hansen and Weil, above n 20 at 258.

citizenship should want to be integrated fully and not attach more importance to another land and there is no possibility of deportation for convicts. In my opinion two identities are impossible.'[103]

The point is further illuminated by the FPÖ/ÖVP coalition agreement. While declaring their commitment to democracy and human rights, the two parties grouped 'Internal security and the integration of immigrants' under the same heading in the following terms:

> '3.9 The granting of Austrian citizenship marks the completion of successful integration. The criteria for acquiring citizenship must be observed. The path to citizenship should be laid out as a process of ever closer integration. The ultimate granting of citizenship should not be a purely administrative formality but should be given a proper form (by holding naturalisation ceremonies in a festive style).
>
> 3.10 One of the requirements should be verifiable proof of German language skills and of basic knowledge about Austria and the European Union. This proof can be furnished by submitting a certificate of the successful attendance of a certified adult education course or by passing a test.'

Austria remains an exception to any putative European trend towards 'the harmonisation and liberalisation of citizenship acquisition by immigrants and their descendants'.[104] Bauböck and Çinar maintain however that it is not a conception of the nation as an ethnic community which drives such restrictive policies, but rather an attempt to close the Austrian welfare state off from 'strangers' as much as possible.

Electoral rights for non-nationals, beyond the confines of EU law, are simply not an issue at the present time in Austria. According to the SPÖ 'Today there is simply not the political will to address the issue of voting rights at the national level'.[105] Nominally, the SPÖ might be expected to be in favour of widening the suffrage. Indeed, they admit that 'Our theoretical goal is close to the Greens, but in practice in the world of politics it is necessary to make compromises'.[106] As the same interviewee indicated, the fear of losing political capital has motivated debate: 'Between 1989 and 1993, with over 120,000 immigrants in Vienna, no one within the SPÖ continued to

---

[103] Interview with Dr Peter Mak, *Ministerialrat*, Austrian Ministry of the Interior, Vienna, June 2000.

[104] Bauböck and ,inar, above n.102 at 267.

[105] Interview with Robert Leingruber, International Secretary of the Austrian Social Democratic Party, Vienna, June 2000.

[106] Franz Jerabek, Office of the Fund for Integration and assistant to SPÖ City Councillor and Member of the City Government, Renate Brauner, Vienna, June 2000. Renate Brauner, who continues to push the issue of electoral rights, was very much in a minority in Viennese politics, but in late 2002 a so-called "Demokratiepaket" was enacted by the Vienna *Landtag*, which had an SPÖ/Green majority, *inter alia* to extend electoral rights in Municipal Councils (*Gemeinderat*) to non-EU nationals with five years' prior residence. The ÖVP and the FPÖ have brought a constitutional challenge to the new law, and the FPÖ conducted an expensive billboard publicity campaign against the new law in Spring 2003.

talk about voting rights for third country nationals'. However, the SPÖ in Vienna was responsible for a more limited project for third country national rights, by establishing the Integration Fund. This latter body has proposed a model for the city whereby immigrants can vote for a representative body which is then able to *consult* with the municipal council. The Steering Committee for the Fund is the *Kuratorium*, established by the City. It issues guidelines for the Integration Fund and determines its tasks and goals. The *Kuratorium* is a body with 18 seats, of which three are reserved for migrants and NGOs. The Greens and the Liberals wanted this to be seven.

Outside the EU, in the candidate countries, the issue arises in a slightly different way. Accession to the EU will eventually require the adoption of laws, such as those on electoral rights and non-discriminatory access to membership and formation of political parties, and these laws may run counter to polity-ideas which are still evolving. For example, one of Estonia's major challenges since its independence from the Soviet Union in the August coup of 1991 has been that of defining the polity, and hence of defining the suffrage. Although the reasons for excluding Russians from the citizenry and hence from the suffrage were understandable in the early years of Estonian independence, the exclusionary arguments in favour have become increasingly hard to sustain both in the face of external political pressure from the OSCE and from the EU, and in the light of greater internal political maturity and experience with democratic practices and the rule of law.[107] Internally, Estonia wished to avoid a 'one country, two societies' scenario. Externally, it found itself more pressurised by international norms and organisational pressure than longer established liberal states would do both in the form of OSCE recommendations and in terms of the pressure to conform both with the *acquis communautaire* and the 'EU mainstream' prior to accession being contemplated. In this sense, there may be a positive synergy between steps taken internally entirely with a view to settling the status of the substantial Russian minority, and steps taken in view of accession which are concerned only with the status of those who will become Estonia's 'second country nationals', *ie* the other members of the EU at the time when enlargement eventually occurs.

Although Estonia is clearly a very different case to the Member States discussed in this Section, there is a baseline similarity between the types of arguments used by political elites and other opinion-formers, involving the construction of the boundaries of the suffrage around notions of state sovereignty, the *demos*, and—less frequently—access to limited public goods. In that context, both 'national cosmopolitanism' (eg in the form of multiculturalism or the admission of the rights of resident minorities) and 'transnational cosmopolitanism' (eg in the form of some form of putative

---

[107] S Day and J. Shaw, 'The boundaries of suffrage and external conditionality: Estoria as an applicant member of the EU', (2003) 9 *European Public Law* (forthcoming).

European identity) can represent a threat, and there may be strong resistance within the polity to redefining its boundaries in an inclusive way. This section has sought to elaborate upon the generally slow pace of development of electoral rights for non-nationals, above and beyond what EU law demands of Member States. Even political parties which would—consistently with other aspects of their political programmes—be expected to support electoral rights for non-nationals, whether in the name of democracy, human rights or better race relations or integration of foreigners find themselves politically unable in certain types of circumstances to support what risks being a politically unpopular proposition. Electoral rights are an area of contestation within domestic politics, but more often that contestation is not directly over the question itself, but is diffused into the domestic politics of immigration and citizenship more generally, or the politics of domestic coalition-building and maintenance.

The point in this section has not been to discern unilinear trends in policy-making, or to predict outcomes of political debates at the national level, but to interrogate more closely some of the contestations themselves. The intensity of some of the debates presented here, with rhetorics shifting between defence of the nation and sovereignty and the need to maintain the privileges of citizenship certainly does not reveal that the effect of EU electoral rights has been to render the debate about electoral rights and political participation of non-nationals more generally into a banal and non-contentious issue at national level.[108] On the contrary, in this context the assertion of immigration sovereignty—whether as symbol of autonomy or demonstration of policy independence—seems alive and well. Through the politics of electoral rights, political actors can, however, project their vision of the 'polity idea' appropriate to the nation state.

6. THE AREA OF FREEDOM, SECURITY AND JUSTICE: DEVELOPING THE EU'S WIDER ROLE IN RELATION TO MIGRANTS

'The European Union must ensure fair treatment of third country nationals who reside legally on the territory of its Member States. A more vigorous integration policy should aim at granting them rights and obligations comparable to those of EU citizens. It should also enhance non-discrimination in economic, social and cultural life and develop measures against racism and xenophobia. . . . The legal status of third country nationals should be approximated to that of Member States' nationals.'[109]

---

[108] C Wihtol de Wenden, 'Les élections locales d'étrangers dans les pays européens', in B Delemotte and J Chevallier (eds.), *Étranger et Citoyen. Les immigrés et la démocratie locale* (Licorne/L'Harmattan, Amiens/Paris, 1996) at 30.
[109] European Council Conclusions, Tampere, 19/20 October 1999, points 18 and 21.

'Although the importance of voting rights and access to nationality for the integration of third-country nationals who are long-term residents is now generally acknowledged, the EC Treaty provides no specific legal basis for it.'[110]

The contestations raised at national level have resonated within the EU's own law and policy-making *vis-à-vis* third country nationals. In the EU, debates on electoral rights for third country nationals have often reflected the wider debate on immigration policy. Here the national mix of political debate on what *ought* to be done both in terms of planning and regulating immigration of all kinds, as well as determining the appropriate treatment of residents, is supplemented by the crucial question 'By whom?'. In addition, the parallelism of the status of migrants whether EU citizens or third country nationals represents a continuous challenge to policy-makers, given the currently exclusive nature of EU citizenship. For example, in the discussions regarding the elaboration of the Fundamental Rights Charter in 2000, a document from the Praesidium asked whether, 'where rights are reserved for citizens alone, should there be a general clause to the effect that such rights may be extended to third-country nationals?'[111] In the event, a negative answer was given, as it was also in relation to pressure at the 1996 IGC[112] to use the Treaty of Amsterdam to widen the scope of EU citizenship.[113]

At the present time there are no proposals currently on the table for measures to be adopted at the EU level to *require* Member States to confer local electoral rights on long-term third country nationals. The furthest which any institution has gone thus far is the European Parliament, which

---

[110] Proposal for a Council Directive concerning the status of third-country nationals who are long-term residents, COM(2001) 127, para. 5.5 of the Explanatory Memorandum; OJ 2001 C 240E/79.

[111] Charte 4170/00, 'Proposed articles on the rights of citizens (Article A to J)', 20 March 2000.

[112] See European Union Migrants' Forum, *Proposals for the Revision of the Treaty on European Union at the Intergovernmental Conference of 1996* and Churches' Commission for Migrants in Europe, *Third Country Nationals in the European Union: The Case for Equal Treatment*, available at http://europarl.eu.int/hearings/igc1/doc20_en.htm and http://europarl.eu.int/hearings/igc1/doc7_10_en.htm respectively.

[113] For the arguments on the extension of Union citizenship to third country nationals see, for example, D Kostakopoulou, *Citizenship, Identity and Immigration in the European Union: Between Past and Future* (Manchester, Manchester University Press, 2001) and A Føllesdal, 'Third Country Nationals as European Citizens: the case defended' in D Smith and S Wright (eds.), *Whose Europe? The Turn Towards Democracy* (Oxford, Blackwells, 1999). Føllesdal's argument, unlike Kostakopoulou's, necessitates national policies of allowing easy access to naturalisation by third country nationals. See also H Staples, *The Legal Status of Third Country Nationals Resident in the European Union* (The Hague/London, Kluwer, 1999) at pp 335–5. Some writers suggest the imposition of criteria in additon to stable residence, such as employment or other economic activity, language proficiency, 'attachment to the Union' and even the consent of the third country itself, upon whose nationals EU citizenship would be conferred: D O'Keeffe, 'Union Citizenship' in D O'Keeffe and P Twomey (eds.), *Legal Issues of the Maastricht Treaty* (Chichester, Wiley, 1994).

has suggested an amendment to a Commission proposal on long-term resident third country nationals which would encourage the Member States *themselves* to adopt such measures. This builds upon more 'abstract' statements of policy, such as advocating the extension of electoral rights to third country nationals in its resolution on the 1996 IGC[114] and in a recent resolution on the 'Barcelona Euro-med' process.[115]

The Commission's proposal for a Directive governing the status of long-term resident third country nationals has been one of the flagship measures of the evolving Area of Freedom, Security and Justice. The original proposal excluded electoral rights from the scope of the rights for third country nationals, on the grounds that there is no explicit competence within the Treaty to enact such rights.[116] This suggests a relatively narrow interpretation of Article 63(3) and (4) EC, which provide for the adoption of measures regarding conditions of residence of third country nationals, and is at odds with Norbert Reich's suggestion to use Article 63 as the basis for developing a 'quasi-citizenship' for third country nationals by thickening out the concept of 'legal residence' in the Member States.[117]

The measure passed to the European Parliament for consultation. The competence argument advanced by the Commission was accepted in the Report on the proposed Directive for the European Parliament's Committee on Citizens' Freedoms and rights, Justice and Home Affairs, prepared by Sarah Ludford, a British Liberal Democrat MEP.[118] Adopted by a majority of only 19 to 11, the Report proposed for adoption by the European Parliament plenary session a substantial number of amendments to the Commission's proposal, quite a number of which were clearly motivated by the heightened securitisation agenda following the events of 11 September 2001. Even though the report was prepared with the aid of key migration policy NGOs,[119] in certain respects, the proposed amendments appeared less generous in terms of rights for resident third country nationals, proposing only that their rights should be 'similar' to those of EU citizens, rather than 'as near as possible' (Article 1). The Committee noted in its justification that

---

[114] European Parliament Resolution on the convening of the Intergovernmental Conference and evaluation of the work of the Reflection Group, 13 March 1996, para. 4.16.
[115] European Parliament Resolution on the Commission Communication to prepare the fourth meeting of Euro-Mediterranean foreign ministers 'reinvigorating the Barcelona Process', 1 February 2001, para. 49. It was voted in at plenary by a narrow majority (235 votes to 222, with 56 abstentions), on a proposal from the far-left GEU/NGL group.
[116] Proposal for a Council Directive concerning the status of third-country nationals who are long-term residents, COM(2001) 127, 13 March 2001.
[117] N Reich, 'Union Citizenship—Metaphor or Source of Rights?', (2001) 7 *European Law Journal* 4 at pp 18–19.
[118] Report on the proposal for a Council Directive concerning the status of third-country nationals who are long-term residents, A5–0436/2001, 30 November 2001.
[119] The Migration Policy Group, the Welfare Council for Immigrants, the European Network Against Racism and the Immigration Law Practitioners Association.

'Although the Tampere conclusions provide for an approximation of the legal status of third-country nationals to that of Member State nationals (paragraph 21), harmonisation in the form of equal status would do away with any incentive to seek citizenship of the host Member State, a step which third-country nationals should be encouraged to take with a view to fostering integration.'

In similar vein, several amendments refer to skills in the host nation language(s) needing to be acquired by the resident non-national in order to foster integration, although these came not from the Rapporteur, but from the Conservative/Christian Democrat grouping on the Committee. In other key respects, the amendments proposed by the Committee extended the draft Directive, and electoral rights were a crucial heading under which extensions were proposed, albeit through the medium of national law. Before adoption of the Report and a legislative resolution, at plenary on 5 February 2002 the amendments went through a further process of revision. Eventually the Parliament adopted by a large majority, but with the UK Conservative group voting against, a text adding to the list of areas under which third country nationals were to be guaranteed equal treatment by the host Member State a new heading of 'participation in community life at local level' (new Article 12(1)(ib) of the draft directive). This presumably refers to institutions of civil society rather than political participation rights, for in the very next paragraph, voting (but not standing) rights are added as a specific example of an area in which Member States may *choose* to accord equal treatment:

'Member States may extend the benefit of equal treatment to matters not referred to in paragraph 1, *such as active participation in political life, including voting rights at local and European level.*' (Article 12(2); italics indicate amendment proposed).

The statement of justification in the Report refers to the competence argument, in the following terms:

'Whilst there is no competence under the Treaties to provide for voting or other political rights in a Member State this should not preclude Member State governments using their prerogative to provide such within their national legislation.'

The Rapporteur's Explanatory Statement elaborates a little further:

'The proposal does not grant voting rights as the Commission considers this is not covered by the legal base. The rapporteur understands that this is a politically sensitive issue for some Member States, although she considers that the grant of voting rights at least at local and European level ought to be encouraged as a factor of responsible integration. She therefore recommends a reference to an option for Member States to grant long term resident third country nationals the right to vote in municipal, national and European elections.'

Voluntarism on the part of the Member States and the recognition of national competence seem to be the order of the day. Even the proponents of the extension of electoral rights to third country nationals themselves appeared to regard this as a merely symbolic statement, one which is unlikely to find its way into the final legislative text and therefore of minimal practical impact.[120] Even so, there seems a distinct contradiction between a statement which explicitly limits the extent to which third country nationals 'deserve' equal rights to EU citizens, on the grounds that they should be encouraged to naturalise, and another statement encouraging the Member States to accord local electoral rights on the grounds that this is a successful method of integration of the same group of immigrants. The type of 'consensus' approach to policy-making which is fostered by the European Parliament's role within the EU policy process, and reinforced by its strong Committee system, also has what might be perceived as the disadvantage of allowing the adoption of proposed amendments to the Commission's draft which are not quite internally consistent. This has the definite effect of blurring the underlying concept of the 'polity' which the European Parliament is deploying in its policy-making endeavours. Interestingly, though, the resonances between these debates and those much earlier debates about the internal dimensions of the polity and the demos engaged in the context of direct elections seem weak. The Parliament has moved away from the twin roots of EU electoral rights in grand ideas of democracy and citizenship based on free movement to focus on concerns on balancing the internal and external dimensions of 'fair treatment' or justice, and on the appropriate level of assimilation and integration of immigrants. Similarly, the debates on competence, sovereignty and—potentially— subsidiarity have come to the fore.

7. CONCLUSION: DEMOS CONSTRUCTION AND 'POLITY IDEAS'

This chapter has not focused directly upon the issue of sovereignty, the precise nature of citizenship in the EU context or the normative challenge which alien suffrage raises both for the EU as an emerging polity, and for the Member States and candidate states. The premises on which it has proceeded are, however, clear. The language of sovereignty under conditions of Europeanisation, globalisation and regionalisation is a contested discourse, and that is one important reason why there remains no clear answer to the question 'what is the EU?' or indeed 'what should it do?'. As the chapter has shown, much of this uncertainty at the EU level—in the

---

[120] Interview with Julia Bateman, European Parliamentary research assistant to Baroness Sarah Ludford, MEP, 21 February 2002. I am very grateful to Anthea Connolly for sharing this interview data with me.

specific context of electoral rights for third country nationals—has been diffused into a debate about competence. At the national level, debates about third country nationals—such as the debates on electoral rights in Belgium and on immigration policy in Germany—so often become mired in the internal politics of coalition-building or preservation, and the balance between different bodies within a legislative assembly.

Ultimately, however, it is impossible to avoid the normative and ethical dimensions of determining the boundaries of the suffrage, however banal much political discourse appears to render it. The link demands to be made between the process of *demos* construction for a legitimate European Union comprising multiple sites of political authority and the wider normative question of the 'polity idea' which the EU needs for self-sustenance, namely the 'normative ideas about a legitimate political order'.[121]

For a complex multi-level polity with constitutional pretensions such as the EU problems may arise if just two clear cut ethical ideas dominate the debate. That is, if the position of resident non-nationals is presented as a straight contest between the logic of citizenship grounded in nation state incorporation, where naturalisation is the legal formalist key to access, and the logic of universal personhood, which is global and is not connected to the specific European context. Self-evidently, with the concept of Union citizenship including electoral rights the EU has gone beyond a form of narrow national incorporation. However, equally obviously, the gaps in its policies on third country nationals hitherto and the apparent willingness to defer to national sovereignty over questions such as electoral rights make it clear that the project is not one of cosmopolitan inclusion. On the contrary, it is one which incorporates a degree of exclusion, and still based on the formal badge of nation state membership. But nation state membership within the Euro-polity is not a thick enough conception of membership in the long term either to sustain an evolutionary concept of citizenship of the Union grounded in the EU's own constitutional edifice nor an ethically sustainable basis for EU 'fair' treatment of third country nationals, given the sharp variations between different national laws and policies on issues such as access to citizenhip and dual nationality. It does not recognise that Union citizenship effectively undermines the binary divide of national and international and raises the question of what type of polity-idea underscores the Euro-polity itself.

In the introduction to this chapter, a link was drawn between the types of questions triggered by the task of determining the boundaries of the suffrage and the highly topical issue of the treatment of non-nationals after

---

[121] See the use and definition of this term by M Jachtenfuchs, T Diez and S Jung, 'Which Europe? Conflicting Models of a Legitimate European Political Order', (1998) 4 *European Journal of International Relations* 409 at 409.

11 September 2001. Clearly, here is not the place to extemporise in full about these highly contested questions. It suffices to note how quickly things can change. Earlier in 2001, the challenge appeared to have been expressed quite clearly by Rogers Smith:

> '. . . normatively, I too would like to see a complexly federated world of 'weak' political peoples in which individuals could freely choose to belong to many roughly equal and only 'semi-sovereign' communities at once. [But] . . . the political dynamics of people-building make the achievement of such arrangements on an enduring basis precarious. Those of us with normative reservations about absolutist senses of allegiance thus face major challenges in considering how we can forge stable forms of political membership that eschew them'.[122]

Such words seemed quickly outdated as the state as site of authority has experienced a powerful resurgence. Yet the evidence from the contestation of electoral rights suggests that matters should perhaps never have been seen in such terms in the first place. The message of this chapter, on the contrary, concerns the need to track carefully the ongoing contestation of polity ideas, including ideas about sovereignty, legitimacy and power, in relation to the boundaries of the suffrage, without presuming either the eventual disappearance of the sovereign nation state, or the inevitable failure of the supranational project and the cosmopolitan ideals which, in part, it embodies.

---

[122] R Smith, 'Citizenship and the Politics of People-Building', (2001) 5 *Citizenship Studies* 73 at 74.

21

Contrapunctual Law: Europe's Constitutional Pluralism in Action

MIGUEL POIARES MADURO*

1. INTRODUCTION

WHAT IS peculiar about the nature and legitimacy of the European legal order and its relationship with national legal orders? And what consequences follow from that both for our understanding of the law and sovereignty in general and in making constitutional proposals for the future of the European Union? These are the questions to be addressed in this chapter. It has now become usual to highlight how the different national and European perspectives on the notion of ultimate authority in Europe require a constitutional pluralist conception of the relationship between European and national constitutionalism. However, it is rare to draw from that any consequences as to the overall interpretation and application of EU law[1] and as to the way we should address its constitutional questions. The focus tends to be on the issue of kompetenz-kompetenz and the possibility of a conflict between EU law and national constitutions. The explanation for this lies in the fact that such ultimate conflicts of authority are seen as representing the issue of sovereignty: what is the ultimate source of power in the political and legal organisation of society? In strict legal terms, it corresponds to establishing the validating norm of all other rules and exercises of normative power in a given legal system.

Still, the question of ultimate authority is not simply a question of last resort in case conflicts ever arise between the two legal orders. In reality, it will hopefully become clear throughout the chapter that the issue of ulti-

---

* Faculdade de Direito da Universidade Nova de Lisboa
[1] EU Law refers to the law of the different Treaties of the European Union, including the law of the European Community. In many instances it would still be more appropriate to refer to EC law than to EU law. However, for the sake of simplicity, I generally use the expression EU law throughout the text.

mate authority is of importance with regard to other meanings of sovereignty. One could talk of at least two such other meanings of sovereignty (both of which could be included under the label of political sovereignty): first, the autonomy of a political community in determining its policies (self-government): its power to exercise independently the traditional functions of governance; second, the autonomy of a political community in defining participation and representation in that political community: its power to structure autonomously the representation and participation of different members and groups in the framing of its policies. The question of ultimate authority is mainly presented as a question about legal sovereignty. However, it also impacts on these aspects of political sovereignty. The way the question of ultimate authority is addressed in European law impacts on the epistemology of EU law (what the EU legal order is and how we can know it), on its legitimacy (how can EU law legitimise itself), and on the forms of policy-making and representation and participation linked to the notion of political sovereignty.

I will start by presenting the two different narratives on the question of ultimate authority developed by the European Court of Justice and national constitutional courts. Following that, I will review in more detail the traditional rhetoric on the construction of a European legal order and its relationship with national legal orders. I will reconstruct this process, contrasting the top-down character of that traditional rhetoric with the bottom-up legitimacy that supported and, in fact, moulded the European legal order. This will hopefully help to demonstrate how the plurality of claims of authority made by EU law and national constitutions actually impacts on the content of EU law and its relationship with the political sovereignty of the States. Next, I will move into a more theoretical analysis in highlighting the pluralist nature of European constitutionalism and how this require us to assume a different understanding of the law. I will refer to this understanding as contrapunctual law. I will also put forward the framework principles that I believe must be safeguarded in order to protect and develop Europe's constitutional pluralism. I will conclude by addressing the impact of this conception upon some of the constitutional questions currently faced by the Union.

2. THE QUESTION OF ULTIMATE AUTHORITY:
TWO NARRATIVES

If an alien were to land on earth and (let us assume the impossible . . .) were to be interested on the relationship between European law and national law, his perception of reality would vary considerably depending on whether he would land on the European Court of Justice or some national constitutional courts. One thing would not change however: he or she (in case aliens have gender differences) would not question the source of ultimate authority. If one reads exclusively the European Court's of Justice narrative of the relationship between European law and national law one is presented with the absolute supremacy of European law. As the Court stated in *Internationale Handelsgesellschaft*:

> 'The law stemming from the Treaty, an independent source of law, cannot because of its very nature be overriden by rules of national law, however framed, without being deprived of its character as Community Law and without the legal basis of the Community itself being called into question. Therefore the validity of a Community measure or irs effect within a Member State cannot be affected by allegations that it runs counter to either fundamental rights as formulated by the Constitution of that state or the principles of a national constitutional structure'.[2]

If our alien were a dedicated researcher he could reinforce this perspective of supremacy by reading in many EU law textbooks a similar account of how EU law has been received by national legal orders: EU law states that it is supreme over national law and is generally applied as such by national courts. Exceptions are rare and presented as pathological instances in an otherwise steady and increased flow of national judicial compliance with the supremacy of EU law. It follows that EU law prevails over national legal orders and occupies the primary position in the relationship of hierarchy between national and EU legal orders, being the higher law of the land, the holder of the ultimate authority. What defines the authority between EU law and national law is the 'normal state of the affairs' and that corresponds to the supremacy of Community law. As stated, national deviations from that rule are only conceived as pathological instances and not as elements demonstrating that the legitimacy of Community law is still dependent upon national law.

However, it would be possible to explain the supremacy and uniform application of EU law without challenging the traditional conception of sovereignty and its *locus* in the state. In fact, as Bruno de Witte has powerfully explained, even the principles of supremacy and direct effect, usually identified as the cornerstones of the constitutionalisation of Community law, could be developed and generally applied without changing, in a substantial manner, the character of the Treaties and Community norms as international law.[3] There are other instances where international norms

---

[2] Case 11–70, *Internationale Handelsgesellschaft mbH v Einfuhr- und Vorratsstelle für Getreide und Futtermittel*, [1970] ECR 1125, para. 3. Other language versions are even clearer in stating that Community norms would be supreme with regard to all national norms independently of their hierarchy in national legal systems (the French version, for example, says that Community norms cannot see their validity questioned by national norms 'quelles qu'elles soient'.

[3] B De Witte, 'Direct Effect, Supremacy and the Nature of the Legal Order', in Craig and de Burca (Eds.), *The Evolution of EU Law* (Oxford, Oxford University Press, 1999), mainly pp. 181 and 209.

enjoy direct effect and supremacy without that implying any challenge to the ultimate authority of national constitutions. On the contrary, it is often those constitutions that confer that power upon international rules. Even the claim of authority that is made by international rules under international monist theories of international law supremacy is not conceived as challenging the fundamentals of national constitutional sovereignty since that supremacy is linked to a previous self-binding commitment of the States supported by *pacta sunt servanda*. In this case, these international instances of shared, pooled or even limited state sovereignty do not really challenge state sovereignty since those exercises of international sovereignty are delegated by the States and limited by the strict mandates of that delegation. Why cannot EU law supremacy and direct effect be traced back to such an understanding of international law and its relation with national constitutional law? Or why cannot the supremacy and direct effect of EU law be seen as secured by the recognition of its authority by national constitutions in all Member States? Such understandings safeguard the uniform application of EU law without challenging the ultimate authority of national constitutions and its connection with the source of the *pouvoir constituant* at national level. However, this vision is not the one embraced by the Court of Justice and, moreover, it does not fit with the nature and extent of the claim of authority made by EU law and the European political community. The Court of Justice grounded the direct effect and supremacy of Community law in a direct relation between Community norms and the peoples of Europe. The founding decision of the Court of Justice in *Van Gend en Loos* is, in effect, the declaration of independence of EU law with regard to the authority of the Member States. The treaty is presented as much more than an agreement between States; it is an agreement between the peoples of Europe that established a direct relationship between EC law and those peoples.[4] That source of direct legitimacy established a political link authorising a claim of independent normative authority. Legal authority was therefore to be derived from an autonomous conception of the European legal order. This corresponded, in fact, to a claim of independent political and legal authority that meant that the European Communities were, in the words of the Court, endowed with sovereign rights.[5] But this claim of sovereignty is not easily compatible with simultaneously respecting state sovereignty and maintaining the traditional conception of sovereignty itself. That traditional conception is based on an indivisible notion of sovereignty, that can be limited in scope but not challenge in its notion of an ultimate authority or single origin of power

---

[4] Case 26–62, NV *Algemene Transport- en Expeditie Onderneming van Gend & Loos v Netherlands Inland Revenue Administration*, [1963] ECR 3.
[5] *Ibid.*

(traditionally the State). In this light, it is natural that some have argued against the autonomy of European law. The EU could limit State sovereignty in light of the State's delegation of authority but could not claim its own independent sovereignty in opposition to that of the State. But the reality is that such claim of independent political and legal authority has been made by the European legal order[6] and was followed by an affirmation of EU powers well beyond what could be traced back to a delegation by the States. This is, therefore, a competing claim with that of the States and requires a notion of sovereignty that moves even beyond the ideas of shared, pooled or limited sovereignty. It requires us to embrace a notion of competing sovereignties.

Let us assume now that our alien were to land on the rooftop of some national constitutional courts. He/she would still be convinced that there is no question as to the final holder of authority but, in this case, the holder of such authority would be national constitutions. On this perspective, the application of national law by national courts under a principle of supremacy with regard to most national law is owed to the authority granted to it by national constitutions or other national legal acts of similar authority. At the same time, EU law may even see its supremacy recognised *vis-à-vis* particular national constitutional norms but that would be the case only if conditions imposed by national constitutional law are satisfied. And it is for national constitutional courts to assess whether that is the case and when EU law must defer to national constitutions. National constitutional courts become the last judicial authority in deciding conflicts of jurisdiction between the EU and national legal orders. National constitutions are interpreted so as to guarantee the supremacy of EU law with regard to the general body of national norms but they are also seen as conditioning that supremacy upon certain national constitutional requirements and on retaining for themselves the ultimate power of authority. In this context, as an author puts it,

> 'the idea that EC law can claim its primacy within national legal orders on the basis of its own authority seems as implausible as Baron von Munchhausen's claim that he had lifted himself from the quicksands by pulling on his bootstraps'.[7]

In this case, it is the power of deciding upon the exception on the part of national constitutions that, following Carl Schmitt, would determine the State as the holder of the final authority. For many national constitutional lawyers, there is not even a conflict of constitutional authority since EU law cannot be conceived as holding such constitutional power. It may have acquired constitutional forms of governance but it does not have constitu-

---

[6] See also the contributions to the this volume by Grainne de Burca and Hans Lindahl.
[7] de Witte, 'Direct Effect, Supremacy and the Nature of the Legal Order', above n 3, at 199.

tional authority to set against national constitutional authority. This would be so because there has not been an exercise of original constitutional power (*pouvoir constituant*) at the EU level. For some, European constitutionalism may not even have the necessary preconditions (a demos for example) to promote such an exercise of *pouvoir constituant* at the EU level.[8] Moreover, it is contentious that there could be a competitive exercise of *pouvoir constituants* between the European Union and the nation states. Such competitive exercise would again challenge the idea of ultimate authority and source of validity that is inherent in the traditional conception of sovereignty.

The reaction of national constitutionalism to the claim of ultimate authority made by European constitutionalism has been the object of several previous studies.[9] It is possible to identify two different types of national constitutional challenges to that claim.

A. National Constitutional Ratification

This is effectively required by all national legal orders with regard to Treaty changes. In national systems that allow ex-ante control of international treaties, any ratification of an EU treaty may be subject to constitutional judicial control to monitor its compatibility with the national constitution. In national systems that do not envisage this type of judicial review it nevertheless is common to subject the process of ratification of the EU treaties either to a political debate addressing the question of their compatibility with the national constitution or, as it happened in the case of UK accession to the European Communities, to the adoption of a particular national legal act of special value that can be said to serve as an instrument of constitutional validation and incorporation. This also reflects the way in which national transfers of sovereignty to the EU are conceived at the national level: to be acceptable they must be construed as a limited transfer of sovereignty compatible with the procedural and substantive values of the national constitution. Such compatibility can either be expressly regulated in the constitutional text or be a simple consequence of the need for

---

[8] See the discussion in the final section below.
[9] Notably (and referring only to studies that have a general and/or comparative approach): A M Slaughter, A Stone and J H H Weiler, *The European Courts and National Courts—Doctrine and Jurisprudence* (Oxford, Hart Publishing, 1998); Mary Volcansek, *Judicial Politics in Europe* (New York, Peter Lang, 1986); Bruno de Witte, 'Direct Effect, Supremacy and the Nature of the Legal Order', above n 3; Constance Grewe and Hélène Ruiz Fabri, *Droits constitutionnels européens* (Paris, PUF, 1995) *Establishing the Supremacy of European Law: The Making of an International Rule of Law in Europe* (Oxford, Oxford University Press, 2001). See also the collection of cases in A Oppenheimer (ed.), *The Relationship Between European Community Law and National Law: the Cases* (Cambridge, CUP, 1994).

national constitutional ratification of any 'constitutional amendment' of the EU (through Treaty revision).[10] Even where there are specific constitutional provisions authorising the transfer of sovereign powers, this is not understood as authorising a constitutional derogation from the other national constitutional provisions. Except where the national constitution itself attributes supra-constitutional value to EU rules,[11] the transfer of sovereignty must take place in accordance with specific procedural and substantive conditions regarding the content and manner of the transfer[12] and with other constitutional values and rules.[13]

The perspective of national constitutionalism, derived from what we have described as the requirement of national constitutional ratification, is that the authority of EU law can be accepted but only in so far as it is compatible with national constitutional identity. Any new claims of authority from EU law must therefore be accepted by national constitutions even if the latter will not exercise permanent jurisdiction over EU acts. This requirement of national constitutional ratification can be said to express the view that the authority of EU law ultimately depends on the national constitutions.[14] This claim of ultimate authority from national constitutions can, however, be compatible with a system that would otherwise recognise EU law's supremacy and even supra-constitutional value but only in so far as EU law derives from a Treaty which has passed the test of national constitutional ratification. Therefore, even the recognition of EU law as having supra-constitutional value would not constitute an abandonment of an ultimate claim of authority on the part of national constitutions so long as at

---

[10] See, for examples, of national constitutional norms on the subject: Italy (Art. 11 and how it was interpreted by the Italian Constitutional Court in *Frontini*, Decision n 183 of 27 December 1973); Spain (Art. 93 ff.); Belgium (Art. 34); Germany (Art. 23); Denmark (Art. 20); Portugal (Art. 7); Netherlands (Art. 92.).

[11] This is the case in the Netherlands. See for an in-depth analysis and some potential problems, Claes and de Witte, Report on the Netherlands in, Slaughter, Stone and Weiler, op. cit. See further De Witte's contribution to the present volume

[12] In some cases, for example, the transfer must be clearly limited and determinable. See, for example: Denmark (Art. 20); Sweden (Art.5); Austria (Art. 92); Belgium (Art. 25).

[13] See the French, German and Spanish Maastricht Decisions: Decision of 2 September 1992 of the *Conseil Constitutionnel*; Decision of 12 October 1993 of the *Bundesverfassungsgericht*; Decision n 1236 of 1 July 1992 of the *Tribunal Constitucional*.

[14] It can however be asked if, de facto, it is really EU law that depends on national constitutional amendments, or if it is more the case that national constitutions must amend themselves in order to fit with EU law? See Francisco Lucas Pires, ' "Competência das Competências": Competente mas sem competências?', *Revista de Legislação e Jurisprudência*, (1998) n°3885, at 356.

the national level that supra-constitutional value remained dependent on constitutional ratification of EU law.[15]

There are, however, national constitutional claims that go much further in challenging the ultimate authority of EU law. That is the case of national constitutions that are interpreted so as to allow for the judicial review of EU acts.

B. National Constitutional Review of EU law

Here, a first distinction is between States that have mechanisms of constitutional judicial review and those that do not have them. For the latter, the possibility of conflict between national constitutions (whether formal or material constitutions) and European constitutionalism takes place only at the moment of ratifying the Treaties. The political and legal processes of national ratification of the Treaties are the only mechanisms of constitutional control available in this case and the possibilities of actual conflict are strongly reduced. The situation is more complex in the case of States that have in place mechanisms of constitutional judicial review but, again, there is no single template. In some cases, the possibility of conflict may be eliminated by granting supra-constitutional status to EU norms.[16] In other cases the probability of conflict is higher or lower depending on the variety and type of legal actions (ex-ante, ex-post, concentrated, diffuse) available to challenge the constitutionality of any legal norm (including EU rules). Where there is no possibility of ex-post constitutional judicial review, the

---

[15] That is notably the case of the Netherlands which gives EU rules (and in general, any self executing international rules) supra-constitutional value. Moreover, it expressly authorises constitutional transfers of authority to the EU. But even in such a case, the fact that such supra-constitutional value or constitutional transfers of authorities are dependent upon certain conditions and processes established in the Dutch constitution demonstrates that the ultimate constitutional authority still belongs to the Dutch constitution and the latter may even change the 'rules of the game' in its relationship with European law. In other words, the supra-constitutional value given to EU law ultimately depends on the national constitution itself.

[16] This the case of the Netherlands (Articles. 60 to 67), and, with some doubts after the Irish Supreme Court decision in the Grogan case (*Society for the Protection of the Unborn Child v Grogan [1997] IESC 4; [1989] IR 753 (6th March, 1997)*, also of Ireland (Art. 29 n.3 and the European Communities Act of 1972). It also appears to be, de facto, the case in United Kingdom with regard to its material constitution. For long, it has been common to reconcile the supremacy of European norms with Parliament sovereignty through a fiction whereby all acts of Parliament were to be read in a manner compatible with EU law by virtue of a previous decision of the Parliament itself. However, this fiction is each day more difficult. *The Factortame case (R v Secretary of State for Transport, ex parte Factortame Ltd, [1991] 1 AC 603)* may have represented the most clear assumption by the British judicial system of the supremacy of EU law even with regard to principles of the British material constitution. However, the possibility is still admitted that the UK parliament can breach expressly EU law and that in such a case the Parliament act would prevail. This would again reinstate its final authority. For recent developments, see Kenneth Armstrong's contribution to the present volume.

possibility of conflict between EU acts (other than Treaties) and national constitutions is, to a large extent, eliminated.[17]

Where there are more developed systems of constitutional judicial review, the willingness of national constitutional courts to review the constitutional validity of EU acts is the key question. In spite of some 'constitutional threats' such willingness appears to be quite limited. One of the most original and active constitutional courts in this respect has been the German constitutional court. This court has developed a theory that allows some form of constitutional control while preventing specific conflicts since it, in general, does not review specific EU acts. It is a theory of constitutional review of EU acts that, at the same time, adapts to the claim of authority made by EU law. This is in my view the originality of the 'so long as . . .' doctrine. This was originally developed by the German constitutional court to address potential conflicts between Community rules and German fundamental rights. In its first decision on such a potential conflict the German constitutional court stated that, in light of the absence of a catalogue and system of fundamental rights protection in the European Communities, it would review the validity of Community acts with regard to the fundamental rights of the German Basic Law.[18] However, once the European Court of Justice considered that fundamental rights constituted part of the general principles of Community law according to which it would review the validity of Community acts, the German Constitutional Court changed its position and presented the famous 'so long as . . .' doctrine. It stated that for as long as the European Court of Justice guarantees a sufficient level of protection of fundamental rights *vis-à-vis* Communtiy acts, the German Constitutional Court will no longer *exercise* its jurisdiction in reviewing those acts.[19] The key notion here is exercise. The German Constitutional Court maintains its jurisdiction over EU law but, at the same time, prevents specific collisions by restraining itself from exercising its jurisdiction so long as EU law continues to satisfy the basic principles of the German Constitution. The *Maastricht* decision of the German court raised fears that it would reinstate its jurisdiction over EU acts, although recent decisions appear to reinstate the 'so long as . . .' doctrine as the dominant theory guiding the German Constitutional Court in its relationship with EU law.[20]

---

[17] But it may still happen if, as in France, EU legislative proposals must first be submitted by the national government to the national parliament, thereby triggering the posibility of constitutional review. See Jens Plotner, Report on France, in Slaughter, Stone and Weiler, above n 9, at 53.

[18] Judgment of 29 May 1974, Solange I, 37 BVerfGE 271.

[19] Judgment of 22 October 1986, Solange II, 73 BVerfGE 339.

[20] For the *Maastricht* decision, see Judgment of 12 October 1993 of the *Bundesverfassungsgericht*, English version available in 33 International Legal Materials 388 (1994); for a more recent decision more comfortably in accord with Solange II, see the *Banana* Decision of June 7, 2000 – 2 BvL 1/97. See further Miriam Aziz's contribution to the present volume.

Such a doctrine envisages national constitutional control over the constitutional tenets of the legal system of the European Union and not a case by case review of the validity of its acts. So long as those tenets remain compatible with those of the national constitution, no review of EU acts will take place and conflicts are avoided between the two legal systems. In this way, instead of being a threat to the uniform application of EU law such a doctrine can be interpreted as protecting the uniform application of EU law while preserving national constitutional control over such law.[21] But what would happen if a national constitutional court came to the conclusion that the EU legal order no longer satisfied the basic canons of its national constitution? Two possible approaches could be taken: the national constitutional court could start reviewing the validity of specific EU acts with the national constitution (it would reinstate the exercise of the jurisdiction that it claims in abstract); but the national constitutional court could also simply affirm the threat to national constitutional identity and from that require either a revision of the Constitution or withdrawal of the State from the European Union in light of the systemic constitutional conflict detected. The positions taken in this regard will depend much upon the specific national constitutional provisions regulating these matters. Below we discuss this question in more detail but, for the moment, it is only important to note that the position of the German Constitutional Court appears to be the former: if a systemic constitutional conflict is detected it will reinstate the exercise of what it claims to be its jurisdiction to review the validity of specific EU acts in light of the German Constitution.

Some national constitutional courts have, however, embraced a more aggressive doctrine.[22] They still admit the possibility of reviewing the validity of EU acts on a case by case basis. It is the traditional case of the Italian Constitutional Court[23] and, more recently, the Belgian *Cour d'arbitrage*.[24] Nevertheless, even in these cases, the national courts are respectful of EU law and accept, in part, its claim of authority with regard to national constitutional law. They will only review EU acts if they conflict with fundamental principles of the Constitution and not any national constitutional norm. This respect is confirmed by the fact that an EU act has never been struck down under this doctrine. The position of these national courts appears to

---

[21] The British doctrine that still envisages the possibility of the Parliament adopting express acts contracting EU law could be made compatible with a similar reading if it were considered that the Parliament would only do so if needed to protect UK constitutional identity.

[22] Others still simply ignore the question of national constitutional review of EU acts.

[23] Decision no. 170, Granital, of 8 June 1984, followed by other decisions. In particular. see Decision 232/89, Spa Fragd v. Amministrazione delle Finanze, of 21 April 1989. See also Marta Cartabia's contribution to the present volume.

[24] Judgment no. 12/94, Ecoles Europeenes, of 3 February 1994 (Moniteur Belge 1994) para B.4–5. See also, but in a more limited way, the Danish Supreme Court decision regarding the Maastricht Treaty (Judgment of 6 April 1998 in Case I 361/1997, available in English in (1999) 3 *CMLR* pp. 854–62.

be similar to the one of the German Constitutional Court in that their aim is to safeguard the core of the national constitution rather than to review the validity of EU acts *vis-à-vis* the Constitution in general.

In this light, the possibility of national constitutional review of EU law under these doctrines is mainly a development of the idea inherent in the requirement of national constitutional ratification: protecting national constitutional identity rather than reviewing the compatibility of specific EU acts with specific national constitutional provisions. As stated, I will come back to this question below when discussing how to make compatible the different claims of ultimate authority made by EU and national constitutionalism. The next section is devoted, instead, to an analysis of how the veto power over EU law[25] that is still maintained by national law operates in practice and what this implies about the nature of the European legal order. In other words, how does European constitutional pluralism operates in practice, and how does it affect the special character of EU constitutional law?

3. THE IMPACT OF CONSTITUTIONAL PLURALISM ON THE NATURE OF THE EUROPEAN LEGAL ORDER

'Tucked away in the fairyland Duchy of Luxemburg and blessed, until recently, with benign neglect by the powers that be and the mass media, the Court of Justice of the European Communities has fashioned a constitutional framework for a federal-type structure in Europe'[26].

So reads one of the most famous sentences in European legal literature, describing how the European Court of Justice transformed Community law into a *legal order of its own*[27] placed in the highest degree of a new legal hierarchy vis a vis national legal orders. Eric Stein's wonderful description of the role undertaken by the Court of Justice has much truth in it but, at the same time, it may mislead us in really understanding how the emergence of a new supreme legal order was possible and took place in Europe. Though the European Court of Justice really did benefit from being tucked away in Luxemburg and neglected by the powers that be and the mass media, the sentence may also lead us to think that the Court of Justice developed this new legal order in isolation, *on its own*. That was not the case. In fact, the creation of the European legal order was a cooperative

---

[25] See Chalmers, D, 'Judicial Preferences and the Community Legal Order', (1997) 60 *Modern Law Review*, 164, at 180.
[26] E Stein, 'Lawyers, Judges and the Making of a Transnational Constitution' (1981) 75 *American Journal of International Law* 1.
[27] See Case 6/64, Judgement of 15/07/1964, *Costa v Enel*, [1964] ECR 585. See also Case 26/62, *Van Gend en Loos*, [1963] ECR 1 and Case 14/68, *Walt Wilhelm*, [1969]1.

process involving a larger group of actors that can be described as forming a European legal community. It was this community of legal actors that empowered the Court of Justice and legitimised the creation of this new supranational or federal legal order. But it was also this legal community that influenced the content of that legal order and partially controlled and limited its supremacy.

The traditional rhetoric on the emergence of the European legal order describes the creation of an autonomous legal order vested with supremacy and direct effect *vis-à-vis* national legal orders. The stress is on the consti-tutionalisation of this legal order (its self-sufficient nature integrated by concepts of constitutional law) and its federal architecture with regard to national legal orders. This is related to the creation of an entire legal frame-work composed of well-known principles such as supremacy, direct effect, fundamental rights, a system of jurisdictional guarantees and a framework of horizontal and vertical separation of powers[28]. As we have seen the European Court of Justice itself emphasised this top-down conception of EU law and its relationship to national legal orders. In great part, this followed the need for the Court to establish its authority and that of EU law in accordance with traditional visions of law. Law has always been conceived as hierarchicaly organised. There was always something—a 'grundnorm', 'a rule of recognition', or positivised natural law, conceived as the 'higher law' of the legal system: the criterion of validity for all other legal norms. The internal conception of the EU legal order was also made to fit this model by the European Court of Justice. EU primary law will be the 'higher law' of the Union,[29] the criterion of validity of secondary rules and decisions as well as that of all national legal rules and decisions within its scope. Moreover, the Court of Justice is the highest court of this legal system and therefore enjoys the monopoly of interpretation of the rules.

But the success of this process of creation of a European legal order was only possible because the Court looked for and found the cooperation of different national legal actors. For this, it also had to 'negotiate' with those actors, in particular, but not only, with national courts. This was funda-mental both in promoting the developments of the European legal order and securing its legitimacy. The Court developed doctrines promoting the

---

[28] For a more detailed analysis see, for example, K Lenaerts, 'Constitutionalism and the Many Faces of Federalism', *American Journal of Comparative Law*, vol 38, n 2, 1990, pp. 205–63; G F Mancini, 'The making of a constitution for Europe', *Common Market Law Review*, 26, 1989, pp. 595–614; Stein, Eric, 'Giuristi, Giudici e la creazione di una Constituzione Transnazionale', in *Un nuovo diritto per l'Europa*, (Milano, Giuffre, 1991) or, 'Lawyers, Judges and the Making of a Transnational Constitution,' (1981) *American Journal of International Law*, p. 1.

[29] One might even rank some rules higher than others, raised to the status of material limits on the revision of the Treaty on European Union; but that is a discussion I will not enter into in here.

participation of a variety of national actors. Notably, it promoted the 'subjectivation' of the Treaties. The Treaties are not simply to be interpreted as an agreement between States, but as having been created for the 'peoples of Europe': Community rules are directed towards individuals and can be invoked by them. EC law is seen as a new source of rights to which litigants can appeal. One could say, along with Burley and Mattli, that 'the Court created a pro-Community constituency of private individuals by giving them a direct stake in promulgation and implementation of Community Law'.[30]

The Court was also quite open to the questions posed by national courts and often relied on them to come up with original interpretations of Community rules. At the same time, the role played by national courts in requesting rulings from the ECJ and in applying these rulings[31] provided ECJ decisions with the same authority as national judicial decisions. This created a dynamic that Volcansek has characterised as 'a pattern of positive reinforcement for national courts seeking preliminary rulings'[32]. This dynamic promoted cooperation and discourse with national courts and helped establishing the autonomy and authority of Community law. National courts are responsible for the effective incorporation of EU Law into national legal orders. But the other side of that is the dependence of EU law on national courts and litigants. Awareness of this power gives to these legal actors a powerful input into EU law itself. The relationship established between national courts and individuals on the one hand and the European Court of Justice on the other thus becomes one of dialogue rather than dictation. Legal discourse concerns the two-way relationship that is established between a court on the one side, and other actors with independent jurisdictions and similar or competing interpretations of the law on the other. Sometimes, this legal discourse may be subject to a final authority but, as we will see, it is arguable that in the European legal order there is no such hierarchy in legal discourse.

I would like to stress that this discursive element is important not only to explain how the creation of a European legal order was possible and legitimised. In addition, the *ongoing* role played by a larger legal community

---

[30] Burley, Anne-Marie and Mattli, Walter, 'Europe Before the Court: A Political Theory of Legal Integration', (1993) 47 *International Organization*, p. 41, at p. 521.

[31] Why national courts were willing and available to do so is another question. See, Weiler, J H H, 'Journey to an Unknown Destination: A retrospective and Prospective of the European Court of Justice in the Arena of Political Integration, (1993) 31 *Journal of Common Market Studies*, 417, at pp. 423 ff; Burley and Mattli, Europe Before the Court, op. cit., at p. 60. In the same sense, Weiler, J H H, 'A Quiet Revolution, above n 9, at pp. 62 ff; and the chapters by Karen Alter, Mattli and Slaughter, and Alec Stone in Slaughter, Stone and Weiler, above n 9.

[32] In her words: 'the Court of Justice accepted all conceivable requests from national courts and invited wide participation', Volcansek, Mary L, *Judicial Politics in Europe*, (New York, Lang, 1986.) at p. 265.

means that legal outcomes and interpretations are a continuing function of this larger legal community and not simply the ECJ. In part, this is a general consequence of the nature of legal discourse. The language of courts in defining what the law is does not become their exclusive property. It is taken over and used by a broader legal community with meanings that may be different from those originally intended. The decisions of courts signal their policy and priorities for judicial activity with regard to the overall demand for judicial intervention. But if court decisions transmit to the legal community judicial willingness or lack of it to intervene in certain areas of the law, courts may sometimes end up saying more than they wanted to say or being interpreted more broadly than they wanted to be interpreted. Judicial decisions are not the property of courts but of the legal community and this includes other legal actors whose preferences for judicial activity may vary from those of courts. The final allocation of judicial and legal resources is determined like everything else in a market: by the demand for judicial intervention brought to courts by legal actors and by the supply of that judicial activity by courts.[33] The currency for transactions in this market of judicial activity is legal reasoning but the motives behind the transactions may vary greatly. Judicial criteria are not simply a result of judicial drafting but of a complex process of supply and demand of law in which the broader legal community participates; judicial decisions do not single-handedly command the use of law but are subject to 'appropriation' and transformation by other legal actors. What the law becomes, of course, is invariably a consequence of a multilogue between these different legal actors (including different courts and litigants). This discursive character assumes however a particular relevance in the context of EU law inasmuch as many of its key developments are not in practice subject to the final 'silencing' authority of the ECJ. The unusual open-texture of EU law is due to the circumstances that we have identified and upon which EU law has based its legitimacy and effectiveness. They explain why the discursive character of EU law often assumes the peculiar character of a discourse among equals.

A good example of how EU law can only be properly understood as a product of a larger community of legal actors is the Sunday Trading Saga and the references made to the Court of Justice on this issue by a variety of British courts. They asked for a preliminary ruling of the European Court of Justice on the compatibility of the British rules prohibiting trade on Sunday with Articles 28 and 30 (at the time 30 and 36) of the EC Treaty. In these cases, national economic actors used the free movement of goods provision of the EC Treaty to challenge national rules that inhibited their economic freedom by prohibiting trade on Sundays. The possibility of this

---

[33] Neil Komesar, *Law's Limits—The Rule of Law and the Supply and Demand of Rights*, (Cambridge and New York, CUP, 2001).

challenge arose from the traditionally very broad interpretation given by the Court of Justice to the concept of a measure having an equivalent effect to a quantitative restriction. It was sufficient that a national regulation could affect trade for it to be considered such a measure, without any requirement of a de iure or de facto discriminatory impact on imported products. Once established that it could affect trade, the national measure would only be acceptable if necessary and proportional to the satisfaction of certain public interests.[34] Under this criterion, measures restricting the free movement of goods needed to be both necessary to the pursuit of a EU recognised public interest and proportional to the goal to be achieved. In other words, the costs arising from the restriction imposed on the free movement of goods should not exceed the benefits derived from the public interest pursued by the measure. What happened was that economic operators used the broad scope granted by the Court to the concept of restriction on the free movement of goods to subject any national regulation of the market to that judgment of necessity and proportionality. This allowed them to promote re-deliberation on different national policies at the European level even where a real concern with the freedom of trade between States did not exist. In the case of Sunday trading, the Court of Justice initially left that judgement of necessity and proportionality to national courts. This led to opposing decisions on the validity of the prohibition of trade on Sunday by these national courts due to the different assessments made on the necessity and proportionality of that prohibition. A wider analysis of the Court of Justice case law on the free movement of goods[35] (including its subsequent decision in *Keck and Mithouard*)[36] makes clear that the broad scope traditionally given to Article 28 by the Court of Justice was not intended to promote the review of all market regulation. The aim was not the judicial construction of Article 28 as an economic due process clause controlling the degree of public intervention in the market.[37] However, economic operators 'appropriated' the broad scope granted to the free movement of goods to, in effect, challenge virtually any regulation of the market. The participation of a plurality of actors in the definition of

---

[34] See Maduro, Miguel Poiares, *We The Court, The European Court of Justice and The European Economic Constitution*, (Oxford, Hart Publishing, 1998).

[35] *Ibid.*, chapter 3.

[36] Joined Cases C–267/92 and C–268/91, *Keck and Mithouard*, [1993] ECR I–6097. In this decision the Court restricted the scope of application of Article 30 in order to discourage 'the increasing tendency of traders to invoke Article 30 of the Treaty as a means of challenging any rules whose effect is to limit their commercial freedom even when such rules are not aimed at products from other Member States.' (para. 14). But even this decision has not prevented economic operators to continue to develop new interpretations that allow them to challenge national regulations limiting their economic freedom even where those measures do not discriminated against out-of-state trade.

[37] See Maduro, above n 34, ch.3.

what the law is and the allocation of judicial resources is particularly clear in this instance.

The Sunday trading cases are also a particular good example of the discourse taking place between the European Court of Justice and national courts. As stated, the Court of Justice initially allocated to national courts the judgment on the necessity and proportionality of the national prohibition to trade on Sunday. But the consequence of this approach was that conflicting national decisions were adopted by the British lower courts on the basis of their different assessments of that necessity and proportionality. Eventually, the issue arrived at the House of Lords (by then there had also been further decisions of the ECJ regarding the Sunday trading rules in cases raised by courts of other Member States). The House of Lords was not prepared itself to harmonise the different lower courts decisions by making a final judgment on the proportionality of the Sunday trading rules. That would be the normal course of action to follow in accordance with the broad powers given by the Court of Justice to the national judiciary in this case. Instead, the House of Lords decided to refer the case back to the European Court of Justice.[38] This was clearly a message to the Court of Justice—a refusal of the role that the latter had offered to British courts. The drafting of the questions by the House of Lords clearly expressed its dissatisfaction with what it saw as a very under-determined and unclear rule regarding the tests of necessity and proportionality. The fact that the application of such a test, had been placed by the Court of Justice in the hands of national courts was perhaps understood by the House of Lords as an attempt by the Court to distance itself from the political sensitivity of a case that was largely a consequence of its own broad interpretation of the free movement of goods. The consequence, however, had been growing litigation and contrasting decisions on the subject of Sunday trading in a British judicial system that found itself mired in a matter that the House of Lords probably considered as not suitable for courts.[39] Therefore, the House of Lords passed the baton back to the ECJ, requesting from it much more detailed and specific criteria on how to measure the necessity and proportionality of regulatory measures. In its reply the European Court preferred simply to recognise the admissibility of the prohibition to trade on Sunday,[40] changing the approach followed in its initial decision on Sunday trading. Yet the 'protest' by the House of Lords may also have a played a role in the Court's subsequent decision in *Keck and Mithouard*.[41] In that decision, the

---

[38] *Council of the City of Stoke-on-Trent and Norwich City Council v B & Q*, House of Lords, Order of 20/05/91.
[39] See Rawlings, Richard, 'The Eurolaw Game: Deductions from a Saga', (1993) 20 *Journal of Law and Society*, 309, at p. 318.
[40] Case C–169/91, *Stoke-on-Trent*, [1992] ECR I–6635.
[41] Joined Cases C–267/92 and C–268/91, *Keck and Mithouard*, [1993] ECR I–6097.

ECJ restricted the scope of application of the free movement of goods. It may have been that, faced with the increased litigation under the free movement of goods, the Court was attempting, with its first Sunday Trading decision, to develop a strategy that would allow it to maintain its traditional interpretation of those rules by promoting a higher involvement of national courts on the application of the criteria of necessity and proportionality. But, as that approach did not get a favourable reaction from some of those national courts (in particular the House of Lords), as a consequence, the Court now sought an alternative solution to the problem—one which involved a refinement of its traditional interpretation of Article 28.

The Sunday trading cases are, therefore, a particular good example of the discursive nature of EU law and its profound dependence on a constituency of social and legal actors that must be taken into account in order to fully understand what EU law is and how it operates. Their extended role in developing EU law and securing its legitimacy has, in turn, a profound impact in explaining EU law, knowing what it is and addressing its normative questions. These circumstances, to a large extent, make those social and legal actors equal partners to the European Court of Justice in the development of EU law.

4. SIX IMPLICATIONS OF EUROPE'S CONSTITUTIONAL PLURALISM

Europe's constitutional pluralism has profound practical consequences in different aspects of the European legal order and its impact on the political and legal sovereignty of the States. In order to take seriously Europe's constitutional pluralism one must take into account at least six consequences that result from the nature of EU law, its legitimacy, and its relationship with national law and the national political process.

A. The legitimacy of EU law

The legitimacy of EC law is to be found in its bottom-up construction. The reason for this lies not only in the 'veto power' of national courts with regard to the implementation and effectiveness of Community law[42] but also in the way that national courts and other legal actors shape the interpretation and application of that law. To neglect this in future developments of the EU legal order is to undermine the basis of its legitimacy and social acceptance. It was the support of a broad constituency of legal actors

---

[42] See See Chalmers, D, 'Judicial Preferences and the Community Legal Order', (1997) 60 *Modern Law Review*, 164, at 180.

(mainly national courts and litigants) that 'authorised' the European Court of Justice to 'free' EU law from indirect legitimacy through the State and make a claim of independent legal and political authority.

B. The question of democracy in the pluralist legitimacy of EU law

The founding of the legitimacy of EU law on a constituency of actors that forms the European legal community raises the question of participation in that community. The judicialisation of European integration imposes a particular burden on the legitimacy of EU law and the role played by the courts. Similarly, the pursuit of that legitimacy through the mechanisms of participation and representation given by the judicial process to individual litigants requires those mechanisms to be the subject of democratic analysis and review. Participation and representation must be enhanced and democratised in the processes of interpretation and application of EU law. This must not continue to be the domain of a restricted set of social actors or of particular national courts. We must focus on the composition and construction of the European legal community when reforming the EU legal order. This issue requires the question of democracy in Europe to be extended to the question of how to democratise EU legal and judicial discourses.

C. The epistemology of EU law

The study of the role of national courts and other national legal actors is crucial to an understanding of the legitimacy and effectiveness of Community law and the way in which the latter is developed by the Court of Justice. But is also particularly important in epistemological terms for a true knowledge of the Community legal order. This is a product not only of the construction of European law by the Court of Justice but also of the broader national legal communities' appropriation of that body of law. Therein lies a third implication of constitutional pluralism: not only is EU law the product of a broader legal community but, as a consequence, it can only be really known in that light. We need to pay more attention to the national European courts[43] and the way in which they interpret and apply European law. Otherwise we may be mistaking the tree for the forest. Good examples of this are the cases where national courts have gone further that the ECJ in extending the protection granted by EU law in

---

[43] For example, Joseph Weiler, Anne-Marie Slaughter and Alec Stone Sweet in above n 9, talk of the European *Courts* of Justice to emphasise this characteristic of EU law.

cases of horizontal direct effect and discrimination against a State's own nationals.[44]

D. Coherence and integrity in EU law

The fourth consequence is that if EU law is the product of a broader legal community composed of actors from different national legal orders, then the coherence and integrity of the European legal order can only be effectively secured if the dialogue also occurs between different national courts or, more broadly, between the different national legal communities. A coherent EU legal order will require both vertical discourse (between the ECJ and national courts) and horizontal discourse (between national courts).

E. The scope of EU law

Another consequence is that the scope of EU law is as much a function of national problems as it is of European issues. For national actors, EU law is simply a new source of arguments to be used in the context of whatever conflicts affect their interests. As we saw with regard to the Sunday trading cases, it was possible for domestic economic actors to challenge national regulatory policies through EU law and subject them to an alternative process of decision-making. As Rawlings comments, Community law became 'the European defence of domestic actors against national policies'.[45] These instrumental 'appropriations' of law by the different legal actors lead to a transplantation of legal rules into different communities of discourse. Two important questions arise: what are the consequences of importing EU law arguments into national legal debates, and vice-versa? And, is the influencing of national legal and political debates in purely domestic issues a legitimate role for European law?

---

[44] Examples of the first have been referred to by national judges in the context of a project on the application of EU labour law by national courts (later published as a book: S Sciarra (ed.) *Labour Law in the Courts—National Judges and the ECJ*, (Oxford, Hart Publishing, 2000). For examples of the second (where national courts applied EU law in cases that the European Court of Justice had excluded from the scope of application of European law because it had considered them as purely internal to the State): Cour de cassation, chambre criminelle, Comité national de défense contre l'alcoolisme C Rossi de Montalera et autres, 16 juin 1983, reported in RTDE, 19, 1983: 468; Tribunal d'instance de Bressuire (greffe de Thouars), Commissaire de police de Thouars C M Cognet, Centre Leclerc, 10 avril 1987, reported in RTDE, 23, 1987: 553.

[45] Rawlings, above n 9, at p. 313.

F. The nature of the challenge to sovereignty

The relevance of national dynamics to the application of EU law demonstrates that the challenge to national sovereignty does not really lie in a transfer of competences from the States to the Union. The Europeanisation of national political and legal disputes often corresponds to an attempt by certain national actors to shift the balance of participation and representation in the resolution of those disputes at national level. Frequently, what changes is the balance of representation and participation between different national actors in the definition of a certain policy and not so much the European or national character of the policies. It is a strategic Europeanisation, not an ontological one. Strategic Europeanisation alters the national actors that dominate certain policies and in this way represents a different challenge to sovereignty. It challenges the form of political sovereignty of the State that I have identified with its autonomy in defining the scope and patterns of representation and participation in the framing of domestic policies.

5. THE NATURE OF THE EUROPEAN LEGAL ORDER: FROM PRACTICE TO THEORY

We have seen how EU law is the product of discourse among the actors of a broad European legal community in which the voice of some of those actors may even oppose the will of the Court of Justice. But can this discursive understanding be taken even further, to the point where it becomes the foundation of the legitimacy of the European legal order and of its distinctive identity? In other words, is that discourse related to a form of legal pluralism upon which the European legal order must be found? Or, is that legal order also ideally to be subject to a hierarchical organisation that grants to either the European Court of Justice or national constitutional courts the role of final authority in deciding conflicts within the European legal community? This is the question of legal sovereignty in Europe.

We have seen how the rhetoric of European law appears to assume that the final authority between EU law and national law belongs to the former. We have also seen how that is related to the need of fitting EU law with the classical hierarchical organisation of legal systems. But European integration 'attacks' this hierarchical understanding of the law. In reality, both national and European constitutional law assume in the internal logic of their respective legal systems the role of higher law. According to the internal conception of the EU legal order developed by the European Court of Justice, Community primary law will be the 'higher law' of the Union, the criterion of validity of secondary rules and decisions as well as that of all national legal rules and decisions within its scope. Moreover, the Court of

Justice is the higher court of this legal system. However, a different perspective is taken by national legal orders and national constitutions. Here, Community Law owes its supremacy to its reception by a higher national law (normally constitutions). The higher law remains, in the national legal orders, the national constitution and the ultimate power of legal adjudication belongs to national constitutional courts. In this way, the question of who decides who decides has different answers in the European and the national legal orders[46] and when viewed from a perspective outside both national and Community legal orders requires a conception of the law which is no longer dependent upon a hierarchical construction and a conception of sovereignty as single and indivisible. Such a conception of sovereignty has been under challenge by notions such as shared or pooled sovereignty but what the relationship between the EU and national legal orders invites is an even more challenging notion: that of competitive sovereignty.

Such a form of legal pluralism has been convincingly argued for by Neil MacCormick[47] and more recently by Neil Walker.[48] However, the Maastricht Decision of the German Constitutional Court and the possibility of this Court striking down a Community legal act on its decision on the Bananas regulation,[49] have again raised fears of actual conflicts between national courts and the ECJ disrupting the European Union legal order and ultimately the process of European integration. The general tendency may be for national courts to comply with the 'European Constitution' but, as the first part of this chapter shows, there is still on the part of several national high courts a resistance to the absolute supremacy of EU law. This is visible both in the authoritative self-description of national constitutionalism and in the dependence of EU law effectiveness upon national law and national courts. In the striking formulation of Damian Chalmers: 'national law still holds a veto power over national law.'[50] The shadow of this veto is important even when it is not exercised. The European legal order is characterised both by the 'norm' (national courts compliance with supremacy

---

[46] Rossa Phelan has made a detailed analysis of the different viewpoints on the relationship between national and the European legal order depending on whether it is observed from the perspective of EC law, national constitutional law or even public international law. See *Revolt or Revolution: The Constitutional Boundaries of the European Community*, (Dublin, Sweet & Maxwell, 1997).

[47] MacCormick, R Neil, 'Beyond the Sovereign State', (1993) 56 *Modern Law Review*, 1.

[48] Walker, N, 'The Idea of Constitutional Pluralism', (2002) 65 *Modern Law Review*, no. 3, 317. See also his contribution to the present volume.

[49] See, for example, M Kumm, 'Who Is the Final Arbiter of Constitutionality in Europe?', Harvard Jean Monnet Chair Working Papers 10/98, www.law.harvard.edu/Programs/JeanMonnet/papers/98/98–10-.html. See also: Armin Von Bogdandy, 'The legal case for unity: The European Union as a single organization with a single legal system', (1999) 36 *Common Market Law Review* 887.

[50] See Chalmers, D, 'Judicial Preferences and the Community Legal Order', (1997) 60 *Modern Law Review* 164, at 180.

and direct effect) and, as Schmitt would argue, by the power of exception still affirmed, but never exercised, by national constitutional courts. In fact, the possibility of the latter ends up also determining how the normal application and interpretation of EU law takes place.

There are, therefore, powerful pragmatic and normative reasons not to adopt a hierarchical alternative imposing a monist authority of European law and its judicial institutions over national law. That solution would be difficult to impose in practical terms and could undermine the legitimacy basis on which European law has developed.[51] Though the grammar used by EU lawyers in describing the process of constitutionalisation may assume a top-down approach, the reality, as we have seen, is that the legitimacy of European constitutionalism has developed in close co-operation with national courts and national legal communities. That, in turn, has had an increasingly bottom-up effect on the nature of the European legal order.[52] We have also seen that, in spite of their claims to ultimate authority and legal sovereignty, both the EU and national legal orders make more or less explicit concessions towards the claim of authority of the other legal order. They make the necessary adjustments to their respective claims in order to prevent an actual collision. EU law has introduced substantive constitutional changes such as fundamental rights in order to accommodate the claims made by national constitutions. National constitutions have been interpreted in a manner that tends to prevent the review of specific EU acts.

There is another reason to adopt a pluralist conception of the European legal order. It is related to a broader conception of the legitimacy of the process of European integration—one that grounds the legitimacy of European integration in its role of correcting the constitutional limits of national political communities and reshaping the notion of constitutionalism associated with those national political communities. This notion traditionally relates constitutionalism to a single political community and, at the same time, tends to concentrate power in a final authority through its hierarchical organisation. However, arguably, this partly contradicts constitutionalism itself since it eliminates one of its mechanisms for limiting power. In fact, the openness of the question of 'who decides who decides' and the lack of a ultimate authority can be linked to the values of constitutionalism as one of its guarantees of limited power. In a multi-level or federal system it is the vertical or federal conception of constitutionalism (as a form of limited government at the State and federal level) that requires the issue of 'who decides who decides' to be left unresolved. Of course, all constitu-

---

[51] In the words of Chalmers, 'the regime is able to develop provided it does not significantly disrupt the egalitarian relations enjoyed between national courts and the Court of Justice', ibidem.

[52] Kamiel Mortelmans, 'Community Law: More than a Functional Area of Law, Less than a Legal System', (1996) *Legal Issues of European Integration*, 23, at 42–3.

tional systems have historically developed forms of allocating the final authority as a way of preventing conflicts and guaranteeing that constitutional resolutions are accepted by all. But what if what makes the European legal order unique is that the open question should remain open? And what if it is the foundation of European integration in different political communities and the democratic added value arising from that together with their capacity for mutual correction of each other's constitutional malfunctions that requires legal pluralism to be maintained? On the one hand, European constitutionalism promotes inclusiveness in national constitutionalism both from an external and internal perspective: from an external perspective, it requires national constitutionalism to take into account out-of-state interests that may be affected by the deliberations of national political communities and limits the possible abuses that could derive from the concentration of power in national communities inherent in the traditional conceptions of constitutionalism and sovereignty;[53] from an internal perspective, the challenges brought by European constitutionalism to the sovereignty of national deliberations under national constitutionalism also allows a new form of voice to national disempowered groups and often re-introduces true deliberation in areas of the national political process that have become prisoner of a certain composition of interests or of certain unchallengeable definitions of the public good. On the other hand, national constitutionalism also serves as a guarantee against the possible concentrations and abuses of power from European constitutionalism and, at the same time, requires the latter to constantly improve its constitutional standards in light of the challenges and requirements imposed on it by national constitutions. As long as the possible conflicts of authority do not lead to a disintegration of the European legal order, the pluralist character of European constitutionalism in its relationship with national constitutionalism should be met as a welcome discovery and not as a problem in need of a solution.

To develop this line of thought, we have to start reasoning in the realm of what could be called contrapunctual law. Counterpoint is the musical method of harmonising different melodies that are not in a hierarchical relationship *inter se*. The discovery that different melodies could be heard at the same time in an harmonic manner was one of the greatest developments in musical history and greatly enhanced the pleasure and art of music. In law we too have to learn how to manage the non-hierarchical relationship between different legal orders and institutions and to discover how to gain from the diversity and choices thereby offered us without

---

[53] Weiler refers to this function of European law as the principle of constitutional tolerance. See Weiler, J H H, 'The Principle of Constitutional Tolerance', in Snyder (ed.), *The Europeanisation of Law: The Legal Effects of European Integration*, (Oxford, Hart Publishing, 2000)

generating conflicts that ultimately will destroy those legal orders and the values they sustain. There is much to be gained from a pluralist conception of the EU legal order. But, to take full advantage of this legal pluralism we need to discover forms of reducing or managing the potential conflicts between legal orders while promoting communication between them and requiring courts to conceive of their decisions and the conflicts of interests at hand in the light of a broader European legal order—one which arises from the discourse between EU and national legal orders.

The European legal order should be conceived of as integrating the claims of validity of both national and EU constitutional law. But for such a European legal order to be viable and fulfil the aims we ascribe to it, it must comply with a set of requirements to be highlighted next. These are the requirements that make harmony possible within a context of different melodies.

6. THE PRINCIPLES OF CONTRAPUNCTUAL LAW

These are the principles to which all actors of the European legal community must commit themselves and according to which the EU legal order must be structured as a system of law. This commitment is voluntary but it may still be presented as a limit to pluralism. It can nevertheless be argued that this is the limit to pluralism necessary to allows the largest extent of pluralism possible. In a sense, for pluralism to be viable in a context of a coherent legal order there must be a common basis for discourse. Such a basis is a set of principles shared by all the participants that, while respecting their competing claims of authority, guarantees the coherence and integrity of the European legal order. These are understood as framework principles that characterise the form of European legal pluralism and regulate the relation among the different national legal orders and between these and the EU legal order. It is these different legal orders that make what we could define as the broader European legal order. These principles guarantee that the European legal order will both fulfil the aims involved in its pluralist conception and guarantee the harmony between the diversity of legal discourses and forms of European power that such a pluralist conception entails. Some of these principles are requirements of any legal order but, as I will argue, they assume a particular character in their application to the European legal order.

These principles are such that they make it possible for the processes of justification of national and European decisions to be based on different arguments while their actual application leads to compatible decisions. In many respects they simply enhance and refine the mechanisms of mutual recognition, discourse and compatibility already present in the current relation between some national constitutional courts and the European Court of Justice. They are aimed at promoting what could be described as 'incompletely theorised agreements':[54] the possibility of agreeing on particular legal outcomes without an agreement on the fundamental values that may justify those outcomes. In the case of the supremacy and direct effect of EU Law it is perhaps more appropriate to talk about the mutual recognition of different justifications conducive to the same legal outcome. A coherent and integrated European legal order will be possible, even in the context of competing claims to final legal authority, to the extent that those claims may be reconciled. For this to be the case, it is not necessary for the hermeneutics of the different legal orders to be based on the same criteria of recognition of the applicable legal norms. For contrapunctual law to be viable, it is however necessary to create a set of rules that is shared by the different legal systems in putting forward and applying their different claims of authority. This set of principles allows the different legal orders to adjust to the claims of the others and so prevents conflict between these claims. Borrowing the language of systems theory, we may say that the problem of compatibility between different legal systems or sub-systems is presented as a problem of coordination whose only answer can be found in each system adapting its own set of perspectives to the possible contacts and collisions with other systems.[55]

There are three requirements that guarantee mutual adaptation and the development of a coherent legal order in a context of constitutional pluralism: 1) the theories of deliberation and justification on which the national and European courts base their decisions must be universalisable to all the participants; 2) each theory must be constructed so as to adjust and adapt to the competing theories; 3) they must be conducive to an agreement on specific outcomes. The fulfilment of these requirements is what guarantees both the pluralism of the European legal order and its coherence and integrity in a context of equal participation between all the judicial actors involved. They assure that the competing claims of authority do not to lead to the erosion of the European legal order. The principles which follow attempt to provide the framework necessary to the fulfilment of those requirements. They can be called the harmonic principles of contrapunctual law.

---

[54] The expression belongs to Cass Sunstein, *Legal Reasoning and Political Conflict*, (New York, Oxford University Press, 1996). The use of the expression does not entail an adoption of the theory of judicial action and legal reasoning defended by Sunstein in that book.

[55] K Gunther, 'The Idea of Impartiality and the Functional Determinacy of the Law', (1998/89) *Northwestern University Law Review*, 151, at p. 155. In a similar sense: Catherine Richmond, 'Preserving the Identity Crisis: Autonomy, System and Sovereignty in European Law', (1998) 16 *Law and Philosophy*, 377, at 417, discussed in more detail in the text below.

A. Pluralism

This principle assumes two dimensions: a foundational and a participative dimension. The first, is the requirement, already discussed, that any legal order (national or European) must respect the identity of the other legal orders; its identity must not be affirmed in a manner that either challenges the identity of the other legal orders or the pluralist conception of the European legal order itself. In this respect, Catherine Richmond has proposed an attractive framework for the 'legal indeterminacy' entailed in the non-hierarchical relationship between national and European legal orders. She argues that each legal order has its own viewpoint on the same set of norms[56] and that each is bound to take into account the changes in that set of norms arising from the other legal orders:

> 'each time a norm is created or amended in one particular legal order, the cognitive arrangement of norms must, from any one particular viewpoint, be shuffled around in order to accommodate the change'.[57]

However, no legal order should be forced to abandon its own viewpoint (or, if you prefer, its own cognitive framework). In her own words:

> 'A state of legal indeterminacy is only stable, however, as long as no *normative* challenge is made to it which challenges the *political* basis of the cognitive model adopted . . . Therefore it is in all parties' interest to preserve the indeterminacy in the Community, enabling each to latch on to the model of legal authority that is politically most comfortable'.[58]

Identity is lost if it is not self-determined. On the other hand, such self-determination should not dispute the self-determined identity of the other legal orders. One of the consequences must be that each time a legal order changes the set of norms shared with the broader European legal order it ought to do it in a manner that can be accommodated by the other legal orders. Therefore pluralism entails the recognition and adjustment of each legal order to the plurality of equally legitimate claims of authority made by other legal orders. This has profound consequences for the way that national constitutional law has to adjust and incorporate EU law. But it also requires EU law to respect the claims of national constitutional. This may take different forms: continuing to require national constitutional ratification of European constitutional reforms; express recognition of a right to constitutional exit; continued attention to the claims of national constitutions in reforming certain aspects of EU law. Some of these aspects will be

---

[56] In the suggestive expression of Jo Shaw: 'each national constitution creates a different "gateway" for the EU legal order'. 'Postnational Constitutionalism in the European Union', (1999) 6 *Journal of European Public Policy* 579 at 595.
[57] above n 55 at 417.
[58] *Ibid.*

taken up again below when we will discuss how to deal with possible constitutional conflicts.

The other dimension of pluralism requires such a discourse to take place in such a way as to promote the broadest participation possible. So far, one of the legitimacy deficits faced by the European legal order lies in the fact that it tends to be mainly the domain of an elite of repeat litigants. The transaction and information costs involved in EU law litigation tend to promote the participation of a particular group of litigants in the construction of EU law. These litigants often coincide with multi-national companies and are supported by cross-national legal strategies while, for example, national court involvement in this litigation does not benefit from the same cross-national perspective or coordination. Also the dialogue between national courts and the European Court of Justice tends to develop along separate national lines, raising the prospects of comparisons and competitions between those different European dialogues. Do all national courts participate in an equal manner and do they all have equal bargaining power? Does the European Court of Justice develops privileged partners for dialogue? The uneven form of dialogue would correspond, to use a *cliché*, to a democratic deficit in European legal discourse. Instead, a true European legal order and a true European legal discourse can only be based on equal participation of the different actors composing the emerging European legal community.

B. Consistency and Vertical and Horizontal Coherence

How do we guarantee that Europe's constitutional pluralism will not erode the uniform and coherent application of EU law? A pluralist conception may be very attractive as an abstract form of legitimacy for EU law but many fear its application will be impossible and ultimately destroy the European legal order. The concept of coherence which underlies this perspective is one of coherence as unity of the legal system: making sure that each new legal decision is coherent with the previous legal decisions. It is this coherence of the legal system that appears to be challenged by the 'authorisation' to have competing determinations of the law. But this is often due to the fact that such systemic coherence is associated with theoretical coherence (that all decisions are based on a unifying legal theory). However, coherence of the legal system does not require a single and generalised theory of the law. It is possible to have a coherent legal order in a context of competing determinations of the law so long as all the participants share the same commitment to a coherent legal order and adjust their competing claims in accordance with a minimal set of discourse principles. One such principle must be precisely to engage in a coherent construction of a common legal order. This requires their decisions to be deliberated and justified so as to fit with the previous decisions of the other participants and, in that way, safeguard the coherence of the legal order.

When national courts apply EU law they must do so in such a manner as to make those decisions fit the decisions taken by the European Court of Justice but also by other national courts. This is particularly important in light of the fact that a vertically imposed uniform interpretation and application of EU law by the Court of Justice will not be sufficient. One consequence in the growth of EU law related litigation is that an increased amount of the burden of interpreting and applying EU law will fall de facto even if not de iure upon national courts. As is well known, the EC Treaty establishes that national courts have the faculty or the obligation (in decisions from which there is no possibility to appeal) to refer to the ECJ any questions on the interpretation of any Community rule that may be the subject of disputed interpretations.[59] However, the growth in litigation and the increased burden thereby imposed on the resources of the European Court of Justice and on the time-frame of national judicial processes means that de facto an increased number of issues will be decided by national courts. The European Court of Justice itself is leaving the interpretation of many under-determined EU legal concepts to national courts. It is sufficient to recall the example of the Sunday Trading cases and the increased tendency of the ECJ to allocate to national courts the burden of deciding on the proportionality and necessity of national measures that affect the free movement of goods. There are other areas where that delegation of powers to national courts also fulfils the purpose of allowing EU law to fit closer to national constitutional law. That can be said to be the case in the area of fundamental rights where the Court has often recognised a EU fundamental right but left to the national court a large degree of discretion in the determination of the content of that right.[60] In other areas of EU law, the Court allocates to national law itself the detailed task of implementing or protecting a certain European right but subjects such delegation to control by reference to certain EU legal principles.[61] The role of 'adapting' national law to those European legal principles belongs to national courts. In all these cases, the allocation of such broad powers to national courts in defining EU law may be justified by the need both to promote a better allocation of judicial resources at European level and to allow the particular national context to be taken into account (including national constitutional values). However, the increased role played by national courts in the interpretation of EU law and in the development of its legal principles also means that the

---

[59] See Article 234 EC Treaty and Case 283/81, *Cilfit*, [1982] ECR 3415.
[60] See, for example: C–260/89, *ERT*, [1991] ECR I–2925; Case C–368/95, *Familiapress v Heirich Bauer Verlag*, [1997] ECR I–3689.
[61] For example, in the case of State liability for violations of Community law, or in the case of the indirect effect of Directives.

coherence of the European legal order and its uniform application must be promoted at a horizontal level. Any national court must take into account the interpretations of the same European rules and legal principles made by other national courts. This requires them to fit any 'national interpretation' of EU law with the interpretations given by other national courts and the European Court of Justice. It is this that will guarantee both vertical and horizontal coherence of the European legal order.

Coherence requires that European legal discourse take place not only between national courts and the ECJ but also among national courts. Yet the direct coordination and exchange of information which sometimes already takes place between lawyers and litigants in different Member States does not appear to be shared by courts in different Member States. In effect, the different national courts appear to understand their dialogue with the Court of Justice as isolated from the dialogues of the courts of other Member States. It also appears to be rare for national courts to take into account the decisions taken by other national courts.[62] This highlights a systemic gap in the understanding of the European legal order by the different national courts. There is one European legal order as internally conceived by the European Court of Justice while there are different and isolated European legal orders as applied by the different national legal communities. Though national courts may feel that they have a role to play in shaping the European legal order they understand that legal order as a product of the European Court of Justice and not of a broader legal community including other national courts. This reinforces some of the risks involved in the current forms of European legal discourse and the development of this horizontal form of discourse and coherence should be a priority in the reform of the EU judicial system.

There is another principle that serves the purpose of promoting a coherent and integrated legal order. It is the principle of universalisability. Since it can also understood in autonomous terms it will be analysed as a further framework principle of contrapunctual law.

C. Universalisability

The European legal order should be conceived as integrating the decisions of national and European courts. In this context, any judicial body (national or European) should be obliged to reason and justify its decisions

---

[62] Though some examples can be found and are referred to in Slaughter, Stone and Weiler, above n 9, at xiii (see also the national reports by H Bribosia and P Craig). These examples appear, however, to relate to the founding issue of recognising the supremacy and direct effect of Community law. To my knowledge there is no study or evidence of any extended horizontal discourse between national courts on the interpretation and application of the substantive corpus of EU norms.

in the context of a coherent and integrated European legal order. However, for this to be possible and in order to satisfy the requirement of equality in the competing determinations of EU law, any national decisions on EU law should be argued in 'universal' terms. The idea is to require the universalisability of national decisions on EU law. A national court (and, in particular, a national constitutional court) must justify their decisions in a manner that could be universalisable. Such decisions must be grounded in a doctrine that could be applied by any other national court in similar situations. If national courts become aware that the decisions they take will become part of European law as interpreted by the 'community' of European and national courts, they will internalise in their decisions the consequences for future cases in other national courts and the system as a whole. This will prevent national courts from using the autonomy of their legal system as a form of evasion and free-riding and will engage the different national courts and the ECJ in a true discourse and coherent construction of the EU pluralist legal order. This form of discourse will promote a virtuous cycle in the application and construction of EU law, with national courts feeling 'bound' by the decisions of their counterparts in other Member States.[63] Finally, such a principle of universalisability will require national courts to internalise the effects of their decisions on other national legal orders.

D. Institutional Choice

In a context of competing authorities in determining what the law is, institutional choice becomes ever more crucial. A pluralist legal order multiplies the forums for conflict resolution and the arguments and institutions to which one can appeal to promote a redefinition of a certain composition of interests. As we saw, material definitions of the scope of the different legal systems will not work in a context of a plural legal community. The only way to define the borders of the different legal systems and promote an appropriate allocation of legal resources (judicial and otherwise) among them is by reinforcing the mutual understanding of their respective virtues and malfunctions and their awareness that they are only one among a variety of institutional alternatives. This means that each legal order and its respective institutions must be fully aware of the institutional choices involved in any request for action in a pluralist legal community. However, as the work of Neil Komesar has demonstrated, institutional choices are often the product of poor institutional analysis.[64] The importance of insti-

---

[63] See Joseph Weiler, 'A Quiet Revolution: The European Court of Justice and Its Interlocutors', (1994) *Comparative Political Studies*, 510, at 522.
[64] See *Imperfect Alternatives—Choosing Institutions in Law, Economics and Public Policy*, (Chicago and London, Chicago University Press, 1994).

tutional choices in a context of legal pluralism only serves to reinforce the need to do adequate comparative institutional analysis to guide courts and other actors in making those choices. In this way, contrapunctual law also requires the adoption by legal actors of a new legal methodology along the lines of the comparative institutional analysis developed by Komesar.[65]

7. THE FUTURE OF EUROPEAN CONSTITUTIONAL PLURALISM: FROM THEORY TO PRACTICE

I would like to conclude by reviewing some of Europe's constitutional issues in light of the model of European constitutional pluralism argued for in this chapter. The aim is to highlight the normative power of this model of constitutional pluralism in addressing some of the most pressing issues in the current European constitutional debate. The issues selected are the risk of constitutional conflicts, the adoption of a European constitution and the delimitation of competences and the scope of EU law. Of course, these issues have been lent a sharp topicality by the publication by the Convention on the Future of Europe of a draft Constitutional Treaty in June 2003. In what follows, I do not consider the particular proposals put forward in the draft Treaty, both because it is not at all clear whether or to what extent these proposals will survive the Intergovernmental Conference of 2003-4, and because in any case the very idea of constitutional pluralism renders problematic the particular conception of a written constitution adopted in accordance with methods familiar from the national constitutional context that lies at the heart of the Convention's endeavours.

A. Preventing Constitutional Conflicts

Once one accepts a model of constitutional pluralism for the European legal order one is bound to be confronted with question of possible conflicts between EU law and national constitutions. This question has been answered in different ways by some of the most prominent authors arguing in favour of constitutional pluralism in Europe. Neil MacCormick has assumed this potential for conflict but has considered it as contingent and to be dealt with outside EU law. In the event that conflicts do arise they should be dealt with in the context of international law.[66] Joseph Weiler, in

---

[65] Unfortunately, we do not have the space to develop this analysis in here. For an in depth analysis see: Komesar, *Law's Limits*, above n 33, and *Imperfect Alternatives*, above n 64. See also: Maduro, *We The Court*, above n 34.

[66] Neil MacCormick, 'Risking Constitutional Collision in Europe?', (1998) 18 *Oxford Journal of Legal Studies*, 517.

his turn, has argued in favour of a new Constitutional Council composed of EU and national constitutional judges that would decide possible conflicts of competences between the EU and national legal orders.[67] A third solution would be to promote a form of radical pluralism where even the conflicts would be understood and dealt with in different ways by the European and national legal orders. National constitutional authorities could still derogate from EU law, although that would not itself be recognised by EU law. Further any conflict and any derogation should be pursued in accordance with a set of principles which should be justified in a universal manner, even if subject to different national applications. This appears to be the position advanced by Mattias Kumm under a theory that he has labelled as liberal legal pluralism.[68] There are substantial differences between these different solutions. MacCormick and Weiler argue that the best way to prevent conflicts in such a pluralist legal order would be to subject them to a *primus inter pares* (either public international law or a special Constitutional Court). Mattias Kumm attempts to preserve as much as possible the pluralist conception and therefore does not really solve the possibility of conflict. Instead, he 'authorises' national constitutional courts to review the constitutional validity of EU acts so long as they do so in accordance with a set of principles he includes under the heading of liberal legal pluralism, with the result restricted to national constitutional law.[69]

These theories present two sets of problems. The first is that again they focus mainly on how to deal with the question of ultimate authority in the context of a possible collision between a EU act and a national constitution. They ignore the impact that constitutional pluralism has on the overall application of EU law in the different national legal communities. Therefore, they are devised for the exceptional (the possibility of an ultimate conflict between the ECJ and a national constitutional court) and not to guide the ordinary state of affairs (the regulation of the relationship between the ECJ and national courts in the overall application and inter-

---

[67] J H H Weiler, 'The European Union Belongs to Its Citizens: Three Immodest Proposals', (1997) 22 *European Law Review* 150.

[68] Kumm, Who Is the Final Arbiter, above n 9 He indicates three principles that should guide national constitutional courts in the review of Community legislation: the principle of constitutional fit; the principle of expanding the rule of law; and the principle of democratic legitimacy. According to him: 'the best set of doctrines within a particular constitutional context at a particular time is the one that realises these principles to the highest degree possible, all things considered' (at 25). I must note that in a previous article I criticised Mattias Kumm's theory for not taking into account the need of universalisability and coherence in the judgments by national constitutional courts affecting EU law (see Maduro, Miguel Poiares, 'The Heteronomys of European Law', (1999) 3 *European Law Journal*). However that critique was based on an early text of Kumm's article. In the final version of his paper he appears to take more seriously the need for coherence and universalisability at the national level (see, for example, at 28). Depending on the extent to which he incorporates those values into his theory our positions may be much closer than I assumed in that article and, to some extent, still do in this chapter.

[69] Kumm, *Ibid.*

pretation of the European legal order by a broad community of European and national judicial actors). A more complete theory must embrace these two aspects since both are affected by the competing claims of authority of European and national constitutionalism. The second set of problems concerns the solution of the 'collision hypothesis' and varies between the different theories. MacCormick's theory really comes down to subjecting such conflicts to the inter-governmental politics of the European Union since it is not clear how international law could give an appropriate and satisfactory legal solution to a potential conflict between the European Union and a Member State. Joseph Weiler proposal aims at 'europeanising' such conflicts. By subjecting those conflicts to a new institution of the EU, one would be granting to the EU the final authority. The only difference would be that this authority would be vested in an institution with a higher participation of national constitutional courts. Such a solution can only with difficulty continue to be called one of constitutional pluralism. And it is not at all clear that national constitutional courts would be prepared to give up their claim to final authority in exchange for participation in a new EU institution that they could not really control. Kumm adopts a more radical pluralist approach: the fact that the deviations would take place under national law and not EU law means that the integrity and uniformity of EU law would be safeguarded. But this will only be so from a purely formal perspective. Further, the fact that the deviations would be legitimised on national constitutional grounds[70] and 'not affect' EU law may promote the use and abuse of those national constitutional exceptions. Ultimately, it could lead to a 'race to the bottom' between national courts in creating national constitutional derogations from EU law. Moreover, it is a theory that does not stimulate the horizontal dialogue between national courts that I believe to be of utmost importance in a promoting a truly coherent but plural European legal order.

My view is different. In the first place, as stated above I believe that any judicial body (national or European) would be obliged to reason and justify its decisions in the context of a coherent and integrated EU legal order.[71] Secondly, both European and national legal orders must create the necessary mechanisms to adjust to the claims of authority of the other legal orders. For example, the increased discretion left to national courts by the European Court of Justice will be of particular importance if applied in areas of possible conflict with national constitutional law. In fact, that already appears to be the case in the area of fundamental rights.[72] On the one hand, EU law adapts itself to the national constitutional claims by giving national courts a higher discretion in those areas. One the other

[70] As said above, Kumm's theory may actually be more nuanced than I am assuming in here, in which case it will be closer to that argued for in here.
[71] I already advanced this thesis in 'The Heteronyms of European Law', above n 68.
[72] See the cases cited in n 60.

hand, the claim for uniform application of EU law is safeguarded by the national constitutional courts' explicit or implicit recognition that they will not review the validity of specific EU legal acts in light of national constitutional law.[73] In fact, I would argue that their claim of ultimate authority should only be exercised in the event of a systemic conflict arising between the integrity of the European legal order and the integrity of the national constitution. In that case, national constitutional courts could still affirm their ultimate authority either at a moment of constitutional ratification or by creating a situation of constitutional exit. In the latter case, the constitutional conflict could be established by a national constitutional court in a specific case but would have to be of such importance as to affect the entire constitutional relationship between the European Union and the Member State and, therefore, to raise the issue of exit. Only such an understanding of national constitutional authority by national constitutional courts is capable of respecting the principles of contrapunctual law highlighted. In exchange for this adjustment of the national constitutional claims of authority to the claim of authority of EU law, the European Court of Justice ought to recognise an enhanced role for national courts and national constitutionalism in the interpretation and application of EU law. Pluralism further requires that if any part does not fulfil its obligations towards the other, the latter be discharged from its reciprocal obligations. Mutual adjustment and recognition are crucial for constitutional pluralism to function.

Uniformity would be further safeguarded, even in light of higher discretionary powers being granted to national courts, by the obligation imposed on national courts to frame their decisions in universal terms and to secure the consistency between any such national decision and the European legal order as a whole. In other words, national decisions on EU law should not be seen as separate national interpretations and applications of EU law but as decisions to be integrated in a system of law requiring compatibility and coherence. At first sight, a proposal to continue to recognise a measure of independent normative authority of national legal orders while integrating them in a broader pluralist European legal order may appear to promote and multiply national deviations from the European rule of law. However, this assumption must be confronted with the dynamics of law and legal reasoning. The integrity and coherence of the pluralist legal order will stem from the obligation of any national legal order to construct their 'independent' conception of EU law in a manner that is compatible with the other conceptions and with a coherent European legal order. Again, I prefer to rely on the framework principles of contrapunctual law highlighted and on 'simply' requiring any national and European legal actors to adhere to them and the conception of the European legal order they entail.

[73] See above section 2B.

B. The Constitutional Question

The conception of the European legal order argued for is also not easily compatible with the notion of a European constitution modelled after national constitutions. As indicated by the draft Constitutional Treaty recently promulgated by the Convention on the Future of Europe, the idea of such a constitution for Europe is gaining strength. The aim is to replace or complement the Treaties by a formal constitution establishing Europe's constitutional principles, fundamental rights and political organisation, all legitimated by a form of constitutional adoption similar to that of national constitutions (eg a referendum). Several arguments are put forward in defence of such a thesis. Some are linked to the need to address pressing European constitutional issues such as fundamental rights, a clear allocation of competences and a 'truly' democratic institutional system for the Union. However, though these issues must be debated in light of theories of constitutionalism and democracy and though a constitutional process may be the best way to conduct such debates, there is no requirement that they be settled in the form familiar from national constitutions. The same reforms can be introduced by legal instruments not having the character of a formal constitution and the constitutional process may take place without the 'shadow' of a formal constitution. But there are other more powerful arguments put forward in favour of a formal constitution.[74] First, this Constitution is expected to clarify the present constitutional system and the relationships of authority between national constitutions and the European constitution. Second, the process of drafting a formal constitution will be itself a polity building process and would finally grant to the European citizens ultimate control over constitution-making in Europe. The European demos will be a product of this exercise of *pouvoir constituant* at the European level. It is with respect to these two arguments that the notion of European constitutional pluralism becomes particularly relevant. Should we really aim at clarifying the present relationship between the European and national constitutions? Is it not a particular trademark of European constitutionalism that it was built in co-operation with national constitutions?[75] Does that not reflect the nature of the relationship between the European and national constitutions as non-hierarchical and based on discourse and mutual adaptation? And, finally, does this, in turn, not reflect

---

[74] For a critical summary of the arguments in favour of a European formal constitution, see also Joseph Weiler, 'Federalism and Constitutionalism: Europe's Sonderweg', Jean Monnet Chair Working Papers, No. 10/00, available at www.jeanmonnetprogram.org/papers/index.html

[75] See: D Chalmers, 'Judicial Preferences and the Community Legal Order', (1997) 60 *Modern Law Review*, 164, particularly at 180; K Mortelmans, 'Community Law: More than a Functional Area of Law, Less than a Legal System', (1996) 1 *Legal Issues of European Integration*, 23, at 42–43.

the nature of European constitutionalism as found on the competing claims of the European and national political communities? If we answer positively to these questions, then our answer to Europe's constitutional question should be found on a constitutional model that protects the peculiar nature of its constitutional pluralism.

What we are discussing is not simply a question of words. The problem with the adoption by Europe of the constitutional model of the nation state is that it brings with it the conceptions of political authority and sovereignty inherent in that model. It reflects a particular model of constitutionalism, that of national constitutionalism, which is associated with a State and an ultimate sovereign authority. It reflects a form of constitutionalism that is not and ought not to be that of European constitutionalism. Europe's constitutionalism should express its claim of independent political authority through a constitutional model different from that of the State (in its form and mechanisms of adoption).[76] This will still allow a constitutional process to take place in Europe as part of a process of polity building. It may actually prove to be a better way to involve all European citizens in the process of European integration and the establishment of its political identity since it will save much 'constitutional energy' that would otherwise be lost on the stark question of whether or not to adopt a formal constitution.

C. The Scope of EU Law and the Question of Competences

The discursive nature of European law and its dependence on a broader legal community has called our attention to an often-overlooked aspect of the dialogue between national courts and the ECJ. The scope of EU law may be more, or at least as much, a function of national problems demanding judicial intervention, than of EU law priorities for intervention in the national sphere. In other words, the impact of EU law may be stronger in areas where national courts or other national social actors make use of it to address what they foresee as national problems that cannot be corrected through national rules or the national political process. This is a simple consequence of the fact that the impact of European law is as much a function of the preferences of the other actors of the European legal community (such as national courts) as it is of the ECJ. It is therefore not surprising that national courts have, on occasions, given horizontal direct effect to Directives or applied EU rules in purely internal situations that the Court of Justice has consistently considered as outside the scope of application of EU

---

[76] It ought, for example, to continue to depend on what we have defined as national constitutional ratification. That will be one of the ways in which European constitutionalism is influenced to its claim to independent political authority to that of national constitutionalism.

law.[77] The overarching paradox is that European law may have greater impact in areas where the European dimension is weaker than in areas where the European dimension suggests stronger penetration of European rules in national legal systems but the European rules do not fit the preferences for judicial activity of national courts or other national actors.

This highlights a consequence of constitutional pluralism that has already been referred to: the borders of political and legal action disappear and with them so does the autonomy of the different political communities in defining the balance of representation and participation in their traditional domestic policies. National social actors will simply make use of the variety of national and supranational *fora* available to try to pursue their interests. The emergence of such a European political community as a space for political and legal action with regard to open and undetermined social goals is incompatible with its subjection to an express and limited catalogue of competences. If, indeed, it were still be possible to create such a limited and clear catalogue of express competences, this would imply that the European Union possessed such a closed and limited remit that there would be no need to constitutionalise or democratise it. Legitimacy would instead be derived from the States' limited delegation of powers and restricted to that set of expressly delegated competences. Once we move beyond that, the subjection of the definition and implementation of competences to a political discourse of democratic and constitutional character means that any dividing line will be a product of that discourse itself and legitimated by it. Any attempts at a clear and definitive allocation of competences is bound to fail in light of the dynamics of political action that are inherent in a context of competing political communities. The issue of competences should instead concentrate on the framing of the institutions that exercise them and on the transparency necessary for political accountability, so that citizens know who exercises which competences on their behalf and with whose consultation and participation.

---

[77] See Chalmers above n 75.

Index

Please note that references to footnotes are denoted by page number, followed by 'n' and number of note.

absolute theory of sovereignty, 369–70
absolutism, 256, 257
abstention, rules of, 118, 137
abuse of power, 146, 161, 181
accountability, 206
acquis communautaire, 53, 472
Adams, John, 435
AEC (African Economic Community) Treaty (1994), 385
Afghanistan,
  Soviet military intervention (1979), 302
African Charter on Human and People's Rights (1981), 380
Agamben, Georgio, 88
Albania, 302
Albi, Anneli, 401–21
Alexander the Great, 242
Alien and Sedition Acts (United States), 434
alien suffrage principle, 471–87
Allan, Trevor, 338, 342, 345
Althusius, Johannes, 256
Amar, Akhil Reed, 431, 441
Amsterdam, Treaty of (1997), 158, 275, 469, 495
analogia entis (analogy of being), 245
Ancient Near East, 230, 238, 240
Anti-Federalists (United States), 427, 433, 442
Antisovereign theory, 322–4
Aquinas, Thomas, 245
Area of Freedom, Security and Justice, 469, 494–500
Arendt, Hannah, 62, 66, 71, 80, 111
aristocracy,
  as government form, 68
Aristotle, 63, 68, 244
Armstrong, Kenneth A, 327–50
Aron, R, 218
Articles of Confederation (1777), 121–2, 426
asebeia (impiety), 241
Association Agreements, 469
associationalism, 182
auctoritas (personal authority), 240, 241, 242, 243
audi alterem partem (listen to the other side), 183, 184
Austin, John, 76, 172, 437
Austria,
  accession to Union, 470
  electoral rights, 490–3
Austrian Freedom Party (FPÖ), 491

authority,
  of courts, Parliamentary intention, 343
  imposition of, unification of state, 211, 212
  nature, 66–7
  and rule of law, 215
  of state, unlimited, 369
  traditional, 242
autonomy,
  constitutional, 128–31
  as diachronic process, 20
  late sovereignty, 23
  personal, 147
  xenonomous, 112–14
Axial Age/differentiation, 245, 247, 250, 251, 252, 256
Aziz, Miriam, 279–304

balance of power doctrine, 181, 182–3, 349
Baldassarre, A, 324, 325
Baltic States, 403
Bananas litigation, 25, 291, 293, 521
Barnes, Harry, 485
Basic Law,
  German Federal Constitutional Court, 151, 285, 287, 291, 292, 509
Basque society, 208
Bauböck, Rainer, 466, 467
Beer, Samuel, 432
behavioural revolution (1960s), 192
behaviourism, 55
Belgium, 351, 352–8
  Constitution,
    Art 33, 352–4, 355
    Art 34, 354, 355, 356, 357–8
  Coreper, 480–1
  Court of Arbitration, 356, 357
  deliberative democracy, 206
  European Treaties, ratification, 354
  Franco-Suisse Le Ski judgment, 355, 356, 357
  Internal Affairs Committee of Belgian Senate, 487
  'militante européenne de toujours', 353–8
  nationalism in, 202, 208
  Netherlands contrasted, 364–5
    see also Netherlands
  sovereignty, common exercise of, 355
  'tout les pouvoirs émanent de la nation', 352–3
  Vlaamse Blok, 487
  voting rights, 486
Bellamy, Richard, 167–89

Bellarminus, Cardinal, 246, 247
Benelux countries,
   international organisations, adoption of
      provisions, 414
   as laboratory for post-sovereignty, 364–6
   see also Belgium; Netherlands
Bentham, Jeremy, 9
Berlin Wall, fall of (1989), 146
Berman, Harold J, 247
Bodin, Jean,
   mixed power, 180
   origins of sovereignty, 88, 116
   political relationship, 60
   popular sovereignty, 37
   public power, 64–5, 67
   'Six Books of the Republic', 263, 369
   theology, 231, 236, 247, 252, 256
'Bodin's Evil', 261
Bonn Conventions (1952), 283
Boom, S J, 106–7
boundary maintenance,
   late sovereignty (EU), 25
Bratman, M, 43n22, 46, 51, 53
Brezhnev, Leonid Ilyich/*Brezhnev* doctrine, 280,
      298, 302, 394
Brierly, J L, 141
Buijs, G J, 229–57
Bulgaria,
   amendment of sovereignty provisions, 409
   independence/sovereignty, 406, 407
Bundesverfassungsgericht jurisprudence,
   EU integration, 290–3
Burley, Anne-Marie, 513

Cadiz, constitution of, 205
Caesar Augustus, 240
Calhoun, John C, 284, 434, 435, 442
Calvin, John, 233
Campbell, T, 334
Canada,
   nationalism in, 208
   see also Quebec
capitalist state, 298
Capitant, René, 267
Carré de Malberg, Raymond, 267
Cartabia, Marta, 305–26
*Case concerning Certain German Interests in
      Polish Upper Silesia* (PCIJ), 377
*Case concerning maritime delimitation and
      territorial questions between Qatar and
      Bahrain,* International Court of Justice
      (ICJ), 378, 382
*Case concerning Military and Paramilitary
      Activities in and against Nicaragua* (ICJ),
      374, 377, 383
*Case of the Government of the State of Eritrea v
      the Government of Republic of Yemen,*
      International Arbitration Tribunal, 377

Case of S S Wimbledon (PCIJ), 381, 382
Castañeda, H-N, 43n22, 45n27
Catalonia, 203, 204
CBSS (Commissioner of the Council of the
      Baltic Sea States), 474
Central and Eastern European countries
      (CCEEs), 401
   EU impact on sovereignty, 409–20
   delegation of sovereignty, 415–19
   Union as international organisation,
      409–15
   independence/sovereignty, 402–7
   Declarations, 403
   preservation of independence, 415–19
   nation-statist views, 418, 419
   post-Maastricht revisionist discourse, 401–2,
      409–10, 411, 415–16, 419
   'souverainist' nature of constitutions, 402–9
   amendment of provisions, safeguards,
      408–9
   independence/sovereignty, 402–7
   transfer of powers, absence of provisions,
      407–8
   Western counterparts contrasted, 402–3
Centre for Transboundary Legal Development
      (Tilburg University), 33
CFSP (common foreign and security policy),
      152, 154, 386
Chalmers, Damian, 521
charisma, 241, 242, 246
Charter of Economic Rights and Duties of States
      (1974), 134
Charter of Fundamental Rights (2000),
      European Union (EU), 151–2, 165, 472
Charter of the LAS, 375
Charter of the League of Arab States (1945),
      373, 375
Chevallier, Jean-Jacques, 262, 265–6
Chicago Walgreen Lectures, 257
Christianity, 246, 247, 254, 256
Cicero, Marcus Tullius, 80
citizenship,
   German law, 300
   meaning, 285
   residence-based, UK, 485
   sovereignty of citizens, 147, 163, 165, 299
      see also human rights; sovereign equality;
      sovereign rights
   theories of, 463
   of the Union, 468, 471
Citizenship Law (1913), 285
civil condition, 63
coexistence, international law of *see* inter-
      national law of coexistence
Cohen, Joshua, 92, 93, 94
Coleman, Jules, 38n12
COMESA (Common Market for Eastern and
      Southern Africa) Treaty (1995), 385

comitology, rise of, 90
Comitology committee structure, 29–30
Committee of Permanent Representatives
  (Coreper), 478, 480–1
Committee of the Regions (CR), 188
common commercial policy, 156
common fisheries conservation, 156
common foreign and security policy (CFSP),
  152, 154, 386
common transport policy, 156
Commons, and Parliament, 329
communism, 298
competences,
  Bangladesh Case, 157
  EU sovereignty claim, 23
  exclusive, foreign policy area, 156
  Italian sovereignty, 319–22
  as official/institutional matter, 69
  shared exercise of, France, 273–5
  as 'sovereign rights', 155, 156
  see also Kompetenz-Kompetenz (competence
    of its competence)
concept of sovereignty, 6–9, 115
  as closure concept, 255–7
  elusive, 191–3
  failure of, 34–5
  justice, 463, 464
  as new tradition, 169–70, 232–3
  political science, 191
  scepticism, 5
  secularised theological, 232–5
  theological background, 229–57
Connolly, William, 221, 223–4
Conservative Party (British), 200–1
Constant, Benjamin, 307
constitutional democracies,
  convergence with international law, 145–7
constitutional law,
  defined, 9
constitutional pluralism, 517–20
  and actor-pluralism, 52
  and constitutional unitarianism, 54
  democracy, 518
  dimensions, 4
  EU law,
    coherence, 519
    epistemology, 31, 518–19
    integrity, 519
    legitimacy, 517–18
    scope, 519, 536–7
  future, 531–7
    competences question, 536–7
    conflict prevention, 531–4
    constitutional question, 535–6
  impact on nature of European legal order,
    511–17
  and sovereignty, 3–5, 520
constitutional unitarianism,

constitutional pluralism as, 54
constitutional values,
  and sovereignty (Italy), 315–19
constitutionalism, international law,
  115–43
  equality of states, 120–4
  international law of coexistence *see* inter-
    national law of coexistence
  multilevel, 13, 14
  sovereign equality *see* sovereign equality
  sovereign rights *see* sovereign rights
    (international community)
continuity,
  late sovereignty, 19–21
contrapunctual law, 501–37
  constitutional pluralism *see* constitutional
    pluralism
  European legal order, nature, 520–4
  higher-order normative unity, amounting to,
    105n25
  principles, 524–31
    coherence (vertical/horizontal), 527–9
    consistency, 527–9
    institutional choice, 530–1
    pluralism, 526–7
    universalisability, 529–30
  ultimate authority, 502–11
    national constitutional ratification,
      506–8
    national constitutional review, 508–17
Convention on International Civil Aviation
  (1944), 372
Convention on the Law of the Sea (1982),
  373
Convention on the Political Participation of
  Foreigners in Local Life (1992), 473
Convention for the Protection of World
  Cultural and Natural Heritage
  (UNESCO) 1972), 373
Convention on the Rights of the Child (1989),
  146
cooperation,
  international law of *see* international law of
    cooperation
Coreper (Committee of Permanent
  Representatives), 478, 480–1
corpus reipublicae mysticum/ corpus mysticum,
  246, 253
cosmopolitan democracy, 146–7, 152
Cotonou Agreement, 161
Council of Europe,
  Commission for Democracy through Law,
    475
  Convention on the Political Participation of
    Foreigners in Local
    Life (1992), 473
  human rights, respect for, 148
  Polish membership, 395

Council for Mutual Economic Assistance
(Poland), 393
Counter-limits doctrine (Italy), 315–19
counterpoint, 523
CR (Committee of the Regions), 188
Craig, Paul, 329, 337, 338
creatio ex nihilo (pure commencement in
politics), 111
Creveld, Van, 232
crimen laesae maiestatis (highness), 241
Croce, Benedetto, 67, 69
Czech Republic,
amendment of sovereignty provisions, 408
EU cooperation, 408
independence/sovereignty, 406
Czechoslovakia,
Soviet military intervention (1968), 302

Dahrendorf, Ralph, 207
das Volk (the People), 287
de Beze, Theodor, 256
de Búrca, Gráinne, 12, 53, 449–60
de facto sovereignty, 172, 195, 284, 304
De Gaulle, Charles, 267, 270
de Grucht, Karel, 487
de Jouvenel, Bertrand, 57
de jure sovereignty, 172, 195, 284, 304
de Malberg, Carré de, 273
de Miñón, Miguel Herrero, 204
de Witte, Bruno, 351-66, 456, 503
death penalty, 275
Declaration on Principles of International Law
(1970), 375, 376
Declaration on Territorial Asylum (1967), 373
Declaration of the UN Conference on the
Human Environment (1972), 374
democracy,
cosmopolitan, 146–7, 152
deliberative, 161, 206
economic/legal processes damaging,
177–8
as ethos, 223–4
as form of rule, 223–4
global, new forms of, 201
as government form, 68
participatory model (polyarchism), 55, 92,
93, 161
pluralism, 518
and pre-sovereignty system, 181
and self-determination, 196
state form of, 286
see also plurinational democracy
demos, the,
constitutional values, 317
exclusion of non-nationals, 475
mixed sovereignty, 184, 187
'people', defined, 466
political/legal sovereignty, 174

Denmark,
deliberative democracy, 206
electoral rights, 480
Derrida, J, 100
D'Estaing, Valéry Giscard, 16n36
devolution of power,
effects, 178
and Northern Ireland, 476n46
United Kingdom, 347–8
Dicey, A V, 328, 329, 337, 347, 348, 349
on United States, 438
diffusion problem,
late sovereignty, 26–7
direct effect doctrine, 344, 453, 454, 455, 504
disaggregated sovereignty, 15, 18
Dishlers, Karl, 417
distinctiveness,
late sovereignty, 19, 21–2
divided sovereignty concept,
and Belgium, 355
federalism, 423
Shared Sovereignty Theory, 321
United States, 424, 439–43, 445
D'Oliveira, H U J, 474, 477
domestic politics,
international politics, split with, 215–17
domestic sovereignty, 7, 8
dominium (power of mastery), 60, 62
dominus/dominus et deus, 233, 240, 241
Dooyeweerd, Herman, 256, 257, 360
'double hermeneutic', 16
Draft Declaration on Rights and Duties of States
(UN International Law Commission),
127
dual federalism, promotion, 164–5
dualism, 11n23, 118
Dupré, Louis, 248
Durand, Bernard, 58–9
Dutch constitution,
absence of sovereignty, 359
calvinist thinking, 360
and monism, 11n23
open nature of, 361–4
pretension, lack of, 358–61

Eastern European constitutions *see* Central and
Eastern European
countries (CCEEs)
EC *see* European Community
EC Treaty *see* Treaty of Rome (1957)
ECHR *see* European Convention on Human
Rights (ECHR)
ECJ (European Court of Justice) *see* European
Court of Justice (ECJ)
Economic and Social Committee (ESC),
188
ECOSOC (Economic and Social Committee),
479

ECOWAS (Economic Community of West African States) Treaty (1993), 385
ECSC (European Coal and Steel Community) Treaty, 354
effet utile doctrine, 455
Egypt,
  Hyksos occupation of, 230
Eisenstadt, S N, 245
Elazar, Daniel J, 204
electoral rights, 482–94
  EU institutions, 477–82
    competence, 478–9
    compliance and non-compliance, 481–2
    compromise, 480–1
    conception, 477–8
  Germany, 487–90
electorate, defined, 465–6
Elliot, M, 334
empire,
  as concept, 85–6
  as representation of cosmic order, 238
Enlightenment,
  equality of states, 121, 122
equality of states principle, 120–4
  'procedural equality', 123
equidistance, 254
ERTA principle,
  competences, 156
ESC (Economic and Social Committee), 188
Estonia,
  amendment of sovereignty provisions, 408, 409
  Constitutional Experts' Commission, 416, 418, 420
  electoral rights, 493
'eternity clause',
  German Basic Law, 292
EU (European Union) *see* European Union (EU)
EU Treaty *see* Treaty of European Union (TEU) (1992)
Euratom Treaty (1978), 455
'Euro' zone,
  diffusion problem, 26
Europaoffenheit (European ideal), 288
European Commission,
  and comitology, rise of, 90
  White Paper on European Governance, 91
European Community,
  ECJ jurisprudence, 388–9
  limited powers, 387
  local elections directive, 478
  and national legal orders, 345
  as new legal order, 107
  relations with other international organisations, 156
  'soft sovereignty', 389

sovereignty of, supremacy of European law, 450–5
European Convention on Human Rights (ECHR),
  and Convention on the Political Participation of Foreigners, 473
  Human Rights Act (1998), 332
  human rights obligations, 148
  infringement of, 177
  Polish membership, 395
European Convention on Nationality (1997), 467
European Council, 469
European Court of Human Rights, 177, 333
European Court of Justice (ECJ), 449–60
  authority of, 450
  case law,
    Commission v Italy/France, 388
    Costa v ENEL, 107, 109, 110, 112–13, 356, 388, 390, 452, 455, 456, 457
    Van Gend & Loos case law, 106, 107, 112, 388, 390, 453, 456, 457
  Community treaties, constitutionalisation, 89–90, 105–6, 109, 110
  on European Union, 81, 187
  on foreign relations policy, 153
  human rights, respect for, 148
  Italian Constitutional Court, dispute with, 313
  jurisprudence, 388–9
  political moments, 214
  and popular sovereignty, 52
  role, 511
  'shared'/'divided' sovereignty, 457–9
  sovereignty of EC/EU,
    supremacy founded on claim to sovereignty, 451–5
    supremacy not entailing sovereignty, 451
  sovereignty of member states, 455–9
  supremacy doctrine, 12, 21, 449–60
    founded on claim to sovereignty, 451–5
    not entailing sovereignty, 451
    sovereignty of EC/EU, 450–5
    sovereignty of member states, 455–9
    transfer of 'sovereign rights'/ 'sovereignty', 457–9
  see also International Court of Justice (ICJ)
European integration,
  challenge to sovereignty posed by, 289–96
European Parliament,
  and accountability, 206
  direct elections to, 274
  limited powers, 149
European Union (EU),
  Charter of Fundamental Rights (2000), 151–2, 165, 472
  and citizen rights, procedural, 147
  claim to sovereignty, competences, 23

European Union (EU) (*cont.*):
  common foreign and security policy (CFSP),
    152, 154, 386
  constitutional pluralism *see* constitutional
    pluralism
  customs union rules, 154–5
  Debate on Future, 411
  delegation of sovereignty, preservation of
    independence, 415–19
  direct effect doctrine, 344, 453, 454, 455, 504
  empowerment of EU citizens, 154–5
  federalism, 409, 470
  foreign policy,
    CFSP (common foreign and security
      policy), 152, 154, 386
    concurrent powers, 156–7
    constitution, ineffective, 152, 153–4
    national powers, 158
    progressive extension of powers, 157
  foundation, 386
  human rights,
    respect for, 148
    Union as international democracy based
      on, 150–2
    see also European Convention on Human
      Rights
  as international organisation, 409–15
  international regional integration,
    384–6
  international relations law,
    as catalyst for change (international
      organisations), 160–1
    multi-level constitutionalism, need for
      strengthening, 161–5
    re-allocation of sovereign rights, 155–7
  late sovereignty *see* late sovereignty (EU)
  law,
    coherence, 519
    democracy, 518
    as 'discursive' product, 52
    epistemology, 31, 518–19
    integrity, 519
    legitimacy, 517–18
    national constitutional review, 508–17
    scope, 519, 536–7
    sovereignty in, 384–9
    substantive fundamental rights, 150
    supremacy of, 450–5
  member state sovereignty, 390–2, 455–9
    limitations, 392
    'shared'/'divided' sovereignty, 457–9
    transfer of sovereign rights/sovereignty,
      456–7
  and mixed sovereignty systems, 186–7
  multi-level constitutionalism, need for
    strengthening, 161–5
  national foreign policy actions, outside EU
    framework, 158–9

  national foreign relations powers, joint
    exercise, 158
  Netherlands, integration of, 364
  non-EEA nationals in, 462
  participation, 159–60
    different forms, other international
      organisations, 159–60
  policies, national democratic legitimisation,
    419–20
  and Polish sovereignty, 397–400
  post-sovereignty, shift to, 178–9
  purpose, 81
  re-allocation of sovereign rights, limited
    delegation, 155–7
  reconceptualising sovereignty in, 10–18
  representation of sovereignty in, 24, 87–114
    unity representation, 101–12
  sovereignty in law,
    Community, limited powers, 387
    ECJ jurisprudence, 388–9
    general, 386–7
    international regional integration, 384–6
    manifestations of sovereignty, 386–9
    nature of Community powers, 388–9
  and state sovereignty, 170, 367
  supranationalism, 13, 294, 386, 413, 414
  UK membership, 327, 344
    common law approach, 338–42
    ECA 1972, 330–1, 344, 345
    Factortame litigation, 331, 336, 338, 344
    Henry VIII clause, 339
    'Metric Martyrs' case, 339
    orthodox view, 330–2
  xenonomous autonomy, 112–14
  see also European Commission; European
    Community;
  European Convention on Human Rights
    (ECHR);
  European Council; European Court of Justice
    (ECJ); European Parliament
ex lege internationalis, 393
exclusivity,
  late sovereignty, 23
external/internal sovereignty *see* internal/exter-
  nal sovereignty

Fassbender, Bardo, 115–43
Favoreu, Louis, 276
FCC *see* German Federal Constitutional Court
federalism,
  and Belgium, 356
  and decision-making, 182
  division of sovereignty, 423
  dual, 164–5
  and EU, 409, 470
  see also United States
Federalists (United States), 427–8, 433
Feldman, D, 333, 342

feudal state, 298
Final Act of the CSCE (1975), 375
Foucault, Michel, 19, 35, 38
Four Powers, 280, 282, 284
FPÖ (Austrian Freedom Party), 491
France, 261–77
  Third Republic, 267, 268, 269, 273
  Fourth Republic, 269
  Fifth Republic, 267
  competencies, shared exercise, 273–5
  Constitution of 1958, 270
    Article 55, 274
    Article 89, 271, 272
  Constitutional Council, 262, 267, 270, 271
  as Fatherland of Human Rights, 269
  history, 268–9
  lego-centrism, end of, 270–3
  limits, 270–3
  nationalism in, 202, 206
  New Caledonia, decision on, 268, 269, 276
  pointsman, theory of, 270
  souveranisme in, 87
  sovereignty,
    establishment, 58–9
    external dimension, 268–70
    limits, 270–3
    national v people's, 264–8
    roots, 262–4
    shared, 276–7
    transfers, 273–5
  see also French Declaration of Rights (1789);
    French Revolution (1789)
Frankfurt, H, 238
freedom,
  meaning, 248
Fremde (foreigners), 286
French Declaration of Rights (1789), 352
French Revolution (1789), 262, 263, 264
FRG (Federal Republic of Germany),
  post-1945, 279–81, 282–5
Friedmann, Wolfgang, 117, 118, 130, 139
Friendly Relations Declaration, UN General
  Assembly (1970), 126, 129, 131,
  136
fundamental rights, 73, 150, 318

GATT (General Agreement on Tariffs and
  Trade), 153, 154–5
GDR (German Democratic Republic),
  citizenship law, 300
  constitution, 303
  'destalination' reforms, 299
  founding of, 298
  and sovereignty, 282, 297–303
    state concept, 298
  Soviet Union and, 299, 302, 303
Gelasius, Pope, 246
Gellner, Ernest, 196

General Affairs Council, 480
General Agreement on Tariffs and Trade
  (GATT), 153, 154–5
geordnetes Handlungsgefüge, 296
German Federal Constitutional Court,
  Banana case, 25, 291, 293, 521
  Brunner decision, political character of
    sovereignty, 82
  Euro decision, 293
  and European integration, 290–3
  foreigners' voting rights decision, 286–7
  Maastricht judgment, 291, 293
  'post-étatist' view, 294
  Solange decisions, 51–2, 290, 291, 292
German Fundamental Law (1949),
  eternity clause, 271
Germany, 279–304
  accession to Union, 470
  Bundesrat, 490
  Bundesverfassungsgericht jurisprudence, EU
    integration, 290–3
  East German nationhood, socialism, 299–301
  electoral rights, 487–90
  European integration, challenge to sover-
    eignty posed by, 289–96
  Federal Republic of,
    Basic Law, 151, 285, 287, 291, 292, 509
    post-1945, 279–81, 282–5
  Kompetenz-Kompetenz (competence of its
    competence), 22, 24n58, 26,
    67–8, 163, 165
  Länder, 280, 287, 295, 472, 488, 491
  limited sovereignty, 280, 301–3, 304
  nationalism in, 206
  popular sovereignty/nationhood, 285–9
  Red-Green coalition (1998), 488
  reunification (1990), 280, 281, 284, 304
  Social Democratic Party (SPD), 488
  sovereignty, 'claw back' process, 281
  state theory, influence, 293–6
  see also GDR (German Democratic Republic);
    German Federal Constitutional
    Court
Gerstenberg, Oliver, 92–3
Gicquel, Jean, 276
Giddens, Anthony, 16
global regimes,
  growth, 178
globalisation,
  and challenges to sovereignty, 198, 199
  and cosmopolitan democracy, 146–7,
    152
  Italian sovereignty, 311, 322–5
  and phases of sovereignty, 10
  sovereign equality, 139–41
  and supranational context, 469
GLOBUS seminar (Tilburg University), 33
Gnosticism, ancient, 244

God,
  as Creator of cosmos, 244
  inscrutability of, 247–52
  as lawmaker, 247
  particularisation of, 252–5
  and representative, 256
Goldsworthy, Jeffrey, 328, 336, 423–46
Gorbachev, Mikhail Sergeyevich, 298
Great Powers, 122–3
Grégoire, Abbé, 122
Grewe, Wilhelm, 122
Griffith, John A G, 349, 350
Grimm, Dieter, 95, 96, 106, 107, 109
Grundnorm, 170, 174, 184, 187, 512
Guéhenno, Jean-Marie, 199
'gunman theory' of law (Hart), 36

Habermas, Jürgen, 89, 94, 95, 207, 419
Haider, Jörg, 491
Haiti, intervention in, 148
Hamilton, Alexander, 427, 428, 440
Hardt, Michael, 84–6
Harlow, C, 329
Harrington, James, 181, 182
Hart, Herbert Lionel Adolphus, 36, 328, 344
Hatshepsut (Egyptian Queen), 230, 238, 247
Hegel, G W F, 288–9
Held, David, 194, 199–200, 201
Heller, Herman, 124–5, 282, 295, 296
Helsinki Final Act, 381
Hinsley, F H, 129
Hobbes, Thomas,
  'actor'/'author' terminology, 47
  equality of states, 121
  and mixed power, 180
  political sovereignty, 172
  sovereignty theories, 37
  tenets of sovereignty, 60, 62–3, 65, 68, 69, 72
  and theology, 239, 247, 252
Hobe, S, 417
Hogg, Douglas, 485, 486
Holy Roman Empire, 57, 58, 194
Howarth, George, 485
Huber, Max, 118, 372
human dignity, 147, 163
  'eternity clause', 292
human rights,
  Council of Europe, 148
  and democratic self-government, 147
  EU as international democracy based on,
    150–2
  France as Fatherland of, 269
  HRA *see* United Kingdom: Human Rights Act
  International Covenants (1966), 380
  multi-level constitutionalism, 161–3
  popular sovereignty, 145
  sovereignty, in international law/constitu-
    tional democracies, 145, 146

year of (1789), 263
  see also European Convention on Human
    Rights (ECHR)
Human Rights Act (UK), 329
  common law approach, 341, 342–3
  judicial activism, 334
  orthodox view, 332–5
Hungary,
  independence/sovereignty, 406–7
  and international organisations, 413
  Soviet military intervention (1956), 302
Huysmans, Jef, 209–27

ICJ (International Court of Justice) *see*
    International Court of Justice (ICJ)
Identity Thesis (ID),
  popular sovereignty, 42, 43, 45
immigration,
  Austria, 490–3
  Germany, 487–90
imperator,
  meaning, 240
imperator in regno suo, 253
imperium, 263
in regno suo,
  theology, 252
Incoherence argument (I), 8, 33, 38–41, 51
independence,
  sovereignty contrasted, 403
Indian Ocean,
  French rule, 268, 269
individual sovereignty,
  enlargement, 154
  human rights recognition, 146
  reconciliation with other types of sovereignty,
    147–52
Integration Fund (SPÖ), 493
integration law,
  international laws distinguished, 149
Inter-Allied Control Council, 282
interdependence sovereignty, 7–8
intergovernmental organisations,
  growth, 178
internal/external sovereignty,
  France, external dimension, 268–70
  Incoherence argument (sovereignty
    problems), 40–1
  international law of coexistence, 117,
    145
  Italian Constitutional Court, 307
  Poland, 417–18
  Soviet control, 403
  and Westphalian paradigm, 194–5
International Arbitration Tribunal,
  *Case of the Government of the State of Eritrea v
    the Government of Republic of Yemen*,
    377
international community concept, 367

International Court of Justice (ICJ),
  Case concerning maritime delimitation and territorial questions between Qater and Bahrain, 378, 382
  Case concerning Military and Paramilitary Activities in and against Nicaragua, 374, 377, 383
  Fisheries Jurisdiction Case, 381
  and human rights, 148
  see also European Court of Justice (ECJ); Permanent Court of
  International Justice (PCIJ)
International Covenants on Human Rights (1966), 380
International Criminal Court, establishment (1999), 275
international law,
  constitutional democracies, convergence with, 145–7
  constitutionalism in *see* constitutionalism, international law
  defined, 9
  EU compliance, 159, 163
  manifestations of sovereignty, 371–2
  and popular sovereignty, 380
international law of coexistence, 141–2
  evolution, 145
  integration law distinguished, 149
  sovereignty in, 116–20
international law of cooperation (UN), 117, 148
  integration law distinguished, 149
international legal sovereignty, 7, 8
international organisations,
  EU as, 409–15
  EU participation, different forms in, 159–60
  law of, EU international relations law as catalyst for change, 160–1
international politics,
  national politics, split with, 215–17
International Relations, 218
INT_L, 45–6, 47, 48
Ireland,
  deliberative democracy, 206
irreversibility,
  late sovereignty, 19, 24–5
Italian Constitution,
  case law, 306, 307–8, 312–25
  Sovereignty of the People, 305–6, 311
Italy, 305–26
  constitutional revision, collapse of, 414
  Republic, foundation of (1948), 305
  sovereignty,
    and competences, 319–22
    constitutional values, 315–19
    evolving nature, 305–9
    and globalisation, 311, 322–5
    and King, 310
    and norms, 312–15, 316

  and the people, 310–12
  'polysemic' nature, 307, 308–9
Ius Commune, 284
ius sanguinis principle, 285–6, 299, 304, 488, 491

Jacobs, Dirk, 486
James, Alan, 197
James I of England/James VI of Scotland, 231–2, 255
Jaspers, Karl, 245
Jáuregui, Gurutz, 196, 201
Jefferson, Thomas, 433–4
Jewish people, 285
Joppke, Christian, 468
judicial review,
  ultra vires model, 334, 335
Julius Caesar, 242
jurisdiction,
  substance of sovereignty, 379–80
  US Constitution, 436
jus ad bellum (right to go to war), 117, 129
jus cogens rule, 137
jus gentium, 324
jus soli principle, 489
justice,
  concept of sovereignty, 463, 464

Kant, Immanuel, 9
Kantorowicz, Ernst H, 38n10, 253
Keating, Michael, 191–208
Kelsen, H, 9, 11n23, 142
  on concept of sovereignty, 243, 246
  and Italian Court, 313
  positivism, 76–7
  and radical pluralism, 345
  sovereign equality, 128–9, 131
Kentucky Resolutions (1830s), 434
Kliimann, A-T, 416
Komesar, Neil, 530
Kompetenz-Kompetenz (competence of its competence),
  and cooperation, 163, 165
  and Italian Constitutional Court, 314, 319–20
  late sovereignty, 22, 24n58, 26
  and public power, 67–8
  and substance of sovereignty, 369
Koopmans, T, 363
Kosovo debate (1999-2000), 35n2
Krasner, S D, 7, 8, 17, 22n52
Krushchev, Nikita Sergeyevich, 298
Kumm, M, 533
Kunova, Vlasta, 413
Kupyer, Abraham, 360

Ladeur, K-H, 294
Laeken Convention on the Future of Europe (2001), 16n36, 320, 392, 411

Länder (Germany), 280, 287, 295, 472, 488, 491
Langlois, Simon, 202
language, sovereignty, 10, 11n23, 15, 17
Lardy, H, 484
Laski, Harold, 348, 349
late sovereignty (EU), 19–31
    autonomy, 23
    boundary maintenance, 25–6
    continuity, 19–21
    and deferred sovereignty, 53
    diffusion problem, 26–7
    distinctiveness, 19, 21–2
    exclusivity, 23
    irreversibility, 19, 24–5
    language, 19
    and political science, 191
    pouvoir constituant/constitué, 19–20
    precariousness of, 25–31
    reflexivity question, 27
    transformative potential, 19, 25
Latvia,
    amendment of sovereignty provisions, 409
    expert commission, 418
    sovereignty concept, legal theory, 417
    Working Group, 417
law, the (and sovereignty), 213–15
Law of the Sea Tribunal, 151
Lawson, George, 70
Layton-Henry, Zig, 484
Le Bel, Philippe, 263
League of Nations,
    Assembly, 123–4
    Covenant (1919), 123, 372, 378
    foundation, 130
    and international law, 119
Lecourt, Robert, 269
Lefort, Claude, 97–8
legal capacity,
    sovereignty as, 383–4
legal order, 213–15
legal positivism, 74–80
legal sovereignty, 171–5, 432
legality,
    legitimacy distinguished, 214
legibus solutus, 38, 248
legitimacy,
    EU law/policies, 419–20, 517–18
    legality distinguished, 214
lego-centrism (France), 270–3
Lewis, Jeffrey, 478–9
LEX scheme,
    popular sovereignty, 34, 51–4
liberal normativism, 343
Lincoln, Abraham, 429
Lindahl, Hans, 34, 76n99, 87–114, 214, 225, 452
Lithuania,
    amendment of sovereignty provisions, 409
    Founding Fathers, 408

independence/sovereignty, 406
    Working Group, 413, 417, 418, 420
Livingston, Donald, 445–6
Locke, John, 61, 239
Lords, and Parliament, 329
lordship,
    office distinguished, 63
Lotus Case,
    Permanent Court of International Justice,
        117, 378, 379
Loughlin, Martin, 55–86, 328, 329, 343
Loyseau, Charles, 60, 63
Luxembourg,
    electoral rights, 480
    'temporary' transfer of sovereignty clause,
        414

Maastricht Treaty *see* Treaty of European Union
    (TEU)
MacCormick, Neil, 15, 75–6, 78, 187, 344, 345,
    521, 531, 533
MacLennan, Robert, 485–6
Madison, James, 424, 425, 432, 433, 435, 440,
    441
Maduro, Miguel Poiares, 22n53, 52, 501–37
Magna Carta, 205
maiestas, 241, 242, 243
Manila Declaration on the Peaceful Settlement
    of Disputes (1982), 137
Mann, Golo, 141
Marduk, 238
Maritain, Jacques, 256–7
Marshall, John, 429, 435
Marxism/Leninism, 298, 303
matrix of sovereignty,
    definition, 209
    domestic/international politics, divide
        between, 216–17
    law (and sovereignty), 213
    political, defining, 212
    radical antagonism, 222
    spectre of sovereignty, 210–11
    and unity, 211, 226
Mattli, Walter, 513
Mendras, Henri, 261
meta-language, 10, 11n23, 16, 17, 18
Michel, Louis, 486
Middle Ages, 57–9, 368
Mik, Cezary, 367–400
Mill, John Stewart, 196
Millennium Declaration (2000), 375
Mitchell, J D B, 344, 345
mixed sovereignty,
    shift from pre-sovereignty, 170, 180–8
Modern Age, 368
modern state,
    emergence of, sovereignty concept, 56
    sovereignty as facet of, 57–9

Monaghan, Henry, 430, 440
Monarch, and Parliament, 329
monarchy,
  as government form, 68
monetary policy,
  sovereign rights, 156
monism, 11n23
  pluralism and, 92
  rejection by Italian Court, 314
Monnet, Jean, 269
monotheism, 240–3
  unqualified, 244
Montesquieu, Charles-Louis de Secondat, 72–3,
    79n111, 80, 265
  and balance of power, 182
Moscow Declaration on General Security
    (1943), 125
multi-level constitutionalism (EU), 161–5
  case law, 163
  cooperation and dialogues, national/inter-
    national courts, 163–4
  dual federalism, promotion, 164–5
  human rights, approach based on, 161–2
  'multi-level', meaning, 90
  national/international law, human rights
    protection, 162–3
  and *ultra vires* acts, 164
  and United Kingdom, 346
multilevel governance, 200, 201, 208
multiple-self syndrome, 44
Münchhausen-trilemma, 35
Münster Treaty (1648), 194, 369

Napoleon Bonaparte, 268
nation-state, 195–7
  plurinational democracy, 195–7
  and political science, 191–2
  and Redundancy Argument, 34
national sovereignty *see* popular sovereignty
nationalism, 202–5
  dark side of, 206
  and Soviet Union, 302
nationality,
  defined, 196–7
  ius sanguinis, based on, 285–6
NATO (North Atlantic Treaty Organisation),
  Yugoslavia, action against, 35n2
natural law, doctrine of, 119
natural rights, 72
Nazis, 285, 393
Negri, Antonio, 84–6
Nemeth, Jozsef, 413
neo-liberalism, 198, 200
Netherlands, 358–64
  Belgium contrasted, 364–5
  voting rights, 486
  see also Belgium; Dutch Constitution
network sovereignty, 323, 325

New Caledonia,
  French decision, 268, 269, 276
Nice Treaty, 157
nominalism, 248–52
nomos,
  global order, 324
non-intervention principle, 7, 8
  and rules of abstention, 118
norms,
  and sovereignty (Italy), 312–15, 316
North Atlantic Treaty Organisation *see*
    NATO (North Atlantic Treaty
    Organisation)
Northern Ireland, 208
  devolution of power, 476n46
Noumea Agreements (1998), 276, 277

Oakeshott, Michael, 59, 62, 63
OAS Charter (1945), 373, 375
OAU Charter (1963), 373, 375
Oberdorff, Henri, 276
Oberman, Heiko, 249
object-language, 10, 11n23, 17, 18
Occupation Authorities, 283
Occupation Regime, 283
office concept (*officium*), 63–5
Ohmae, Kenichi, 199
oikos,
  polis distinguished, 60
Oliver, Peter, 471–2
OMC (Open Method of Co-ordination), 30
open statehood concept, 417
Opinion 1/76 principle,
  competences, 156
Oppenheim, L, 123
orbis terrarum (unified world), 241
Orfield, Lester, 439
OSCE (Organisation of Security and
    Co-operation in Europe), 468, 474
Osnabrück Treaty (1648), 194, 369
ÖVP (Austrian People's Party), 490–1
Ozment, Steven, 250

pacta sunt servanda, 504
Papal Revolution, 247
par in parem imperium non habet, 283–4
Paris Agreements (1954), 283n22
Parliamentary sovereignty doctrine (UK),
    common law approach, 336
  orthodox constitutionalism, 328
    EU membership, 330, 331, 332
    Human Rights Act (1998), 335
  pluralism, 346
patria, 254
pax sovietica, 302
PCIJ (Permanent Court of International Justice)
    see Permanent Court of International
    Justice (PCIJ)

Peace of Westphalia (1648), 9, 121, 145, 193–4
people's sovereignty,
    and national sovereignty (France), 264–8
Perestroika, 298
Permanent Court of International Justice
        (PCIJ),
    Autonomy of Eastern Carelia, 378–9
    Case concerning Certain German Interests in
        Polish Upper Silesia, 377
    Case concerning S.S. Lotus, 117, 378, 379
    Case of S S Wimbledon, 381, 382
Pernice, Ingolf, 13, 14n31
Petersmann, Ernst-Ulrich, 145–65
Peterson, Erik, 243–4, 246, 247
phases of sovereignty, 9–10
Philadelphia Convention, 427–8, 431
Philo, 244
Plaid Cymru (Welsh nationalist party), 203
Plato, 229
plenitudo potestatis (supreme power), 58, 253
Plotke, David, 98
pluralism,
    constitutional *see* constitutional pluralism
    hierarchy and (UK), 344–5
    mixed constitution, 186
    and monism, 92
    radical (UK), 345–8
    United Kingdom, 342, 343–8, 350
plurinational democracy, 205–8
Poiares, Miguel, 111
pointsman, theory of, 270
Poland,
    Constitution of 1997, 395–7
        adoption, 395
        general sovereignty, 395
        sovereignty of nation, 395–6
        sovereignty of State, 396–7
    constitutional law, sovereignty in, 393–7
        historical perspective, 393–7
    and European Union, 397–400
    historical phases,
        1944-89, 393–4
        1989-97, 395
        1997 onwards, 395–7
    Republic of, 395
    sovereignty,
        constitutional law, 393–7
        and exercise of, 369–70
        and independence, 407
        internal/external, 417–18
        of nation, 395–6
        of State, 396–7
    and Soviet Union, 302, 395
polis, oikos distinguished, 60
political relationship,
    not deriving from property relationship,
        59–61
    public power as product, 65–7

political representation, logic, 95–101
    citizen participation, as political representa-
        tion, 99
    elections, 100
    implications, 99–101
    interest representation/representation of
        common good, 100
    presence and absence, 96–9
    Treaty of Rome, 104
political science,
    challenges to sovereignty, 198–201
    and concept of sovereignty, 191–3
    and modernity, 192
    nation-state, 191–2, 195–7
    and plurinational democracy, 205–8
    stateless nations, shared sovereignty, 201–5
    Westphalian paradigm, 193–5
political sovereignty, 171–5
polity,
    and regime, 173–5, 185
polity, boundaries of, 112, 461–500
    Area of Freedom, Security and Justice, 469,
        494–500
    belonging, and state, 465–7
    challenges (global, European and regional),
        467–77
    demos construction, and 'polity ideas',
        498–500
    electoral rights, 482–94
        Austria, 490–3
        Estonia, 493
        EU institutions, 477–82
        Germany, 487–90
    electorate, defined, 465–6
Pollard, A F, 65
polyarchism, 55, 92, 93
Polynesia,
    French colonisation, 269
pontifex maximus, 242
'pooled' sovereignty, 281
pooling of sovereignty, 14
popular sovereignty,
    characteristics, 264–5, 266–7
    definition, French constitutional law, 266
    development, 765
    discourse principle (Habermas), 94
    and EU, 170, 419–20
    Germany,
        alien suffrage, 487
        nationhood (German), 285–9
        socialism (East German nationhood),
            299–301
    human rights, 145
    Identity Thesis (ID), 42, 43, 45
    and international law, 380
    invention of concept, 263
    LEX scheme, 34, 51–4
    nationhood, German, 285–9

and people's sovereignty (France), 264–8
and pro-sovereignty view, 168
quasi-indicators, 43, 49
Reflexive Polity Thesis, 45
Reflexivity Thesis (RF), 42–5
representations, 45–50
  actor and author, 47–50
  first person plural, 46
  intention, 46, 47
  Rousseau on, 41–2, 47n32, 265
self-determination, 145
and state sovereignty, 168, 380–1
  see also state sovereignty
United States, 427
voting rights, 465–6
Portugal,
  deliberative democracy, 206
positivism, 55
and public law, 74–80
post-sovereignty,
  Benelux as laboratory for, 364–6
  and pro-sovereignty, 167–8, 169
  on rights, threats to, 168
  shift to, 175–80
  terminology, 205
postmodern/retrospective sovereignty, 401–21
  Central and Eastern European countries
    (CCEEs), 'souverainist' nature, 402–9
  EU, impact on sovereignty, 409–20
potentia absoluta/potentia ordinata, 248–9, 250,
  251, 255
potestas (actual legal powers), 240
potestas in populo principle, 62
Potsdam agreement, 403
pouvoir constituant/ constitué,
  contrapunctual law, 506, 535
  late sovereignty, 19–20
  and theory of the pointsman, 270
  unity representation, 89–90, 91, 93, 105–10
power,
  and jurisdiction, 380
  and sovereignty, 7, 369
  supreme, 41
  see also private power; public power
pre-sovereignty,
  shift to mixed sovereignty, 170, 180–8
princeps/princeps legibus solutus, 67, 240, 241
Principate, period of, 240
private power,
  public power differentiated, 61–3
privatisation, 178
privileging, structural, 14
pro-sovereignty, 176
  and post-sovereignty, 167–8, 169
property relationships,
  political relationships not deriving from,
    59–61
PRP (People's Republic of Poland), 394

public international law, sovereignty in, 368–84
public law,
  and positive law, 74–80
public law system,
  as expression of sovereignty, 73–4
public power,
  official (not personal), 63–5
  private power differentiated, 61–3
  as product of political relationship, 65–7
  sovereignty as expression of, 67–8

QUANGOS, 178
quasi-indicators,
  popular sovereignty, 43, 49
Quebec, 202, 203–4
quia voluntas est voluntas, 251
quod principi placuit legis habet vigorem, 59, 67,
  241

radical antagonism,
  matrix of sovereignty, 222
Rechtsstaat, 175
reductionism, functional, 199
Redundancy argument (R), 8, 33, 34, 35–8, 51
Reflexive Polity Thesis (RP),
  popular sovereignty, 45
Reflexivity Thesis (RF),
  popular sovereignty, 42–5
regime,
  and polity, 173–5, 185
Reich, Norbert, 496
relational sovereignty, 68–71, 74
relative sovereignty, 370
religion,
  nationalisation of, 194
republicanism, 170, 181, 183
res publica, 60
resources, natural,
  permanent sovereignty over, 381–2
rex est imperator, 237–9, 240
Richmond, Catherine, 526
rights,
  product of expression of sovereignty, 71–3
Riley, Patrick, 445
Rokkan, Stein, 204
Romania,
  amendment of sovereignty provisions, 408
  independence/sovereignty, 406
Rome Treaty *see* Treaty of Rome
Rousseau, Jean-Jacques,
  popular sovereignty, 41–2, 47n32, 265
  symbolism, 239
RP (Republic of Poland), 395, 396
Ruiz, Lester, 66
rule of law,
  and authority, 215
  and common law, 337
  and democratic ethos, 224

rule of law (*cont.*):
  economic/legal processes damaging, 177
  Incoherence argument, 39
  and parliamentary sovereignty, 328
  and pre-sovereignty, 181
  Redundancy argument, 37
  rule of persons, 170
  spectre of sovereignty,
    authority to command, 213
    international/national politics, split
      between, 215, 216
    unity, 212
rules of recognition, 174
Russian Freedom Treaty (proposed), 303

Sabel, Charles, 92, 93, 94
SADC Treaty (Africa), 385
St Paul, 254
San Francisco Conference,
  on sovereign equality, 125, 127, 128, 129,
    131, 134, 136
Scandinavian countries,
  voting rights, 484
scepticism,
  concept of sovereignty, 5
  United Kingdom, 348–50
Schengen Agreements (1991), 158, 275
Schmitt, Carl,
  contrapunctual law, 505
  definition of sovereignty, 215, 295
  and Heller, debate with, 296
  homogeneity of people of a State, 286
  on 'sociology of law', 234
  sovereignty tenets, 77, 78, 79n112
  theological concept,
    sovereignty as, 232–5
    symbolism, 239
  and transnational politics, 222
Schuman, Robert, 269
Schütz, Alfred, 94
Scottish Declaration of Arbroath (1320), 205
Scottish National Party, 203
Scotus, Duns, 248
Sedley, Sir Stephen, 336, 349
self-determination,
  and democracy, 196
  popular sovereignty, 145
  unity representation, 107
separation of powers doctrine, 181–2, 329,
    332
  Belgium, 353
Settlement Convention (1952), 282–3
shared sovereignty,
  and divided sovereignty, 321, 457–9
  France, 276–7
  stateless nations, 201–5
  supremacy doctrine, 457–9
Shaw, Jo, 112, 461–500

si veut le roi, si veut la loi; car tel est notre plaisir,
    59
Sieyès, Emmanuel Joseph, 70, 71, 263, 264
slave state, 298
Slovakia,
  supranational rights, 413
Slovenia,
  independence/sovereignty, 403, 406
social contract theory, 39–40, 41–2, 265
Social Democrats (SPÖ), 491, 492, 493
Socialist Unity Party (SED), 297
societas, 62
société des nations, 121
Socrates, 37n9
Sokolewicz, W, 420
Solidarity Party (Poland), 395
Sørenson, Georg, 171, 173–4
sovereign equality,
  consistency requirement, 146
  as constitutional autonomy, 128–31
  in globalisation age, 139–41
  international law of coexistence, 145
  mutual relations of states, 136–8
  as new concept, 127–8
  post-1945 sovereignty, 124–31
  public international law, 374–7
  and supranationalism, 138
  in United Nations (UN), 134–6
    Charter (1945), 125–7, 129–30, 134, 135,
      136, 374, 376
  see also equality of states principle
sovereign rights,
  common commercial policy, 156
  common fisheries conservation, 156
  common transport policy, 156
  concurrent foreign policy powers, 156–7
  EU competencies as, 155, 156
  international community constitution, 131–8
    participation rights, 133–4
    protecting constitutional autonomy, 132
  limited delegation to EU, 155–7
  monetary policy, 156
  permanent sovereignty, 381–2
  transfer, ECJ supremacy, 456–7
'sovereign state',
  as standard member of international
    community, 115, 138
sovereignty,
  acts of, 307
  archaeology of, 237
  challenges to, 198–201, 289–96, 467–77,
    520–4
  concept *see* concept of sovereignty
  de facto, 172, 195, 284, 304
  de jure, 172, 195, 284, 304
  deferred, 53
  defined, 6, 118, 128–9, 307, 374
    see also concept of sovereignty

ECJ, supremacy doctrine, 449–60
elusive concept, 191–3
in EU *see* European Union (EU)
external/internal *see* internal/external
    sovereignty
in France *see under* France
in Germany *see under* Germany
in one's own sphere (Dutch Constitution), 360
independence contrasted, 403
in Italy *see under* Italy
late *see* late sovereignty (EU)
legal, 171–5, 432
as legal capacity, 383–4
legal nature, 371
limitations, 382–3
matrix of *see* matrix of sovereignty
as modern state, facet of, 57–9
negative/positive theories, 370–1
as new doctrine, 169–70, 232–3
normative implications, 31–2
norms, 312–15, 316
origins, 368
of Parliament *see* Parliamentary sovereignty
    doctrine (UK)
phases, 9–10
in Poland *see under* Poland
popular *see* popular sovereignty
postmodern, 401–21
and power, 7, 41
problems, 34–41, 87, 244
public law system, expression of, 73–4
public power *see* public power
reconceptualising (EU), 10–18
relational nature of, 68–71, 74
retrospective, 401–21
rights as product of expression of, 71–3
shared *see* shared sovereignty
spectre *see* spectre of sovereignty
'speech acts', 6, 7
standard picture, 90–5, 112
substance of *see* substance of sovereignty
tenets, 55–86
territorial, 377–8
transition, in, 80–6
untamed side, 142
in USA *see under* United States
of values, 315–19
Sovereignty of the People, 305
Soviet Union (former),
    Constitution (1977), 302
    GDR, relationship with, 299, 302, 303
    interventionism, 301–2
    Polish dependence, 395
    and state concept, 298
sovrainetez (the top), 233
Spain,
    deliberative democracy, 206–7
    nationalism in, 202, 204, 205

spectre of sovereignty,
    international and domestic politics, split
        between, 215–17
    law (and sovereignty), 213–15
    and political, 210–17
        law (and sovereignty), 213–15
        unity (and sovereignty), 211–12
    and transnational politics, 221–6
    unity (and sovereignty), 211–12
SPÖ (Social Democrats), 491, 492, 493
Staatsbürger, 287
Staatsbürgerschaftsgesetz, 299
Staatsvolk (people), 288, 294
Stalin, Joseph, 394
state sovereignty,
    demos, defining, 168
    and EU, 170, 367
    EU Treaty, silence on, 151
    and Poland, 397
    and popular sovereignty, 168
    popular sovereignty, 168, 380–1
        see also popular sovereignty
    as principle of public international law,
        145–6
    and UN practice, 148
    Westphalian paradigm, problems,
        193–5
state-centrism, 90
stateless nations,
    as deliberative communities, 207
    shared sovereignty, 201–5
Stein, Eric, 511
Stoiber, Edmund, 489
Story, Joseph, 429, 442
subjective rights, 72
subsidiarity principle, 320, 321
substance of sovereignty, 368–83
    disputes, 369–70
    historical issues, 368–9
    independence, 378–9
    jurisdiction, 379–80
    limitations on sovereignty, 382–3
    manifestations, in contemporary international
        law, 371–2
    sovereign equality, 374–7
    sovereignty per se, 372–4
    state sovereignty/popular sovereignty,
        380–1
    territorial sovereignty, 377–8
substantive fundamental rights, 150
sufficient reason principle (Leibniz), 88–9
Sumerian King List, 230, 238, 253
Sunday Trading Saga, 514–16
supranationalism,
    cooperation, 120
    European Union, 13, 294, 386, 413, 414
    and globalisation, 469
    and sovereign equality, 138

supremacy doctrine (ECJ), 12, 21, 449–60
  Costa v ENEL decision, 107, 109, 110,
    112–13, 452, 455, 456, 457
  'divided' sovereignty, 457–9
  EC/EU sovereignty, 450–5
    member states, 455–9
    supremacy founded on claim to sover-
      eignty, 451–5
    supremacy not entailing sovereignty, 451
  'shared' sovereignty, 457–9
  'sovereign rights', transfer, 456–7
  transfer of sovereign rights/sovereignty,
    456–7
  Van Gend & Loos case law, 106, 107, 112, 388,
    390, 453, 456, 457
Supreme Court,
  United States, 427
Süssmuth, Rita, 489

territorial sovereignty,
  substance of sovereignty, 377–8
TEU (Treaty on European Union) *see* Treaty on
  European Union (TEU) (1992)
Thatcher, Margaret, 342
Thayer, James Bradley, 438
theology, 229–57
  Creator-God, 244
  in regno suo, 252
  inscrutability of god, 247–52
  layers of meaning,
    elements, 236–7
    inscrutability of god, 247–52
    monotheism, 240–3, 244
    particularisation of god, 252–5
    rex est imperator, 237–9, 240
  monotheism, 240–3, 244
  nominalism, 248–52
  political, 229
  sovereignty as secularised theological concept,
    232–5
  transcendence, 244, 245, 247, 249, 254
Thirty Years War (1648), 194
Three Powers, 283
Tilburg University,
  GLOBUS seminar at, 33
Tocqueville, Alexis de, 202
Tomoschat, Christian, 131
transcendence, 244, 245, 247, 249, 254
transformative potential,
  late sovereignty (EU), 19, 25
transnational flows, 217–20
transnational politics,
  flows, transnational, 217–20
  and spectre of sovereignty, 221–6
    see also spectre of sovereignty
  transnationalism, understanding of, 210
  see also matrix of sovereignty
Trasymachus, 37n9

Treaty of Amsterdam (1997), 158, 275, 469, 495
Treaty on European Union (TEU) (1992),
  background, 387
  citizenship of Union, 468
  EU foreign policy powers, extension, 157
  and France, 271–2
  and integration, 386
  international law, EU compliance, 159
  Justice and Home Affairs Third Pillar, 469
  and local elections, 478
  post-Maastricht revisionist discourse, 401–2,
    409–10, 411, 415–16, 419
  reconceptualising sovereignty, 14
  referendum authorising ratification, 275
  secession provision, 176
  subsidiarity principle, 320, 321
  Treaty of Rome, challenge by German court,
    107
Treaty on the Final Settlement (1990), 284
Treaty of Münster (1648), 194, 369
Treaty of Nice, 157
Treaty of Osnabrück (1648), 194, 369
Treaty of Paris (1951), 120
Treaty on Principles Governing the Activities of
  States in the Exploration and Use of
  Outer Space (1967), 372
Treaty of Rome (1957),
  background, 387
  constitutionalisation, 106–7, 110
  on EC external relations powers, 155
  International Criminal Court, establishment,
    275
  international law, EU compliance, 159
  political representation, logic, 102, 103, 104
  Preamble, 102, 103
Treaty of Versailles (1919), 282
Triepel, Heinrich, 118
Tully, Jim, 177
Two-Plus-Four Treaty (1990), 284

UK (United Kingdom) *see* United Kingdom
Ulpian (lawyer), 241, 248
ultimate authority,
  contrapunctual law, 502–11
UN (United Nations) *see* United Nations (UN)
UNCCPR (UN Covenant on Civil and Political
  Rights), 150
UNCESCR (UN Covenant on Economic, Social
  and Cultural Rights), 150
UNCLOS (UN Convention on the Law of the
  Sea) (1982), 373, 381, 382
UNESCO Convention for the Protection of
  World Cultural and Natural Heritage
  (1972), 373
union state,
  defined, 204
Unitarianism, 18
United Kingdom, 327–50

common law approach, 329, 335–43, 350
  EU membership, 338–42
  Henry VIII clause, 339
  Human Rights Act, 341, 342–3
  'Metric Martyrs' case, 339
  priority rules, 336–7, 339, 342
Conservative Party, 200–1
Constitution, alternative visions, 328–50
  common law approach, 329, 335–43, 350
  orthodox view, 328–35, 350
  pluralist approach, 343–8
  sceptical approach, 348–50
deliberative democracy, 206–7
devolution of powers, 347–8
EU membership, 327, 344
  common law approach, 338–42
  ECA 1972, 330–1, 344, 345
  Factorame litigation, 331, 336, 338, 344
  Henry VIII clause, 339
  'Metric Martyrs' case, 339
  orthodox view, 330–2
Factorame litigation, 331, 336, 338, 344
Human Rights Act, 329
  common law approach, 341, 342–3
  judicial activism, 334
  orthodox view, 332–5
nationalism in, 202
orthodox constitutionalism, 328–35, 350
  EU membership, 330–2
  Human Rights Act, 332–5
pluralism, 342, 343–8, 350
  hierarchy and, 344–5
  radical, 345–8
sceptical approach, 348–50
voting rights, extension of, 485
see also Parliamentary sovereignty doctrine
  (UK)
United Nations (UN),
  Charter (1945),
    Declaration on Principles of International
     Law, 376
    sovereign equality in, 125–7, 129–30, 134,
     135, 374
    Warsaw Pact, 394
  Convention on the Law of the Sea (1982),
    373
  Convention on the Rights of the Child (1989),
    146
  Declaration on the Human Environment
    (1972), 374
  diffusion problem, 26
  founding of, 124
  Friendly Relations Declaration (1970), 126,
    129, 131, 136
  human rights covenant (1966), 146
  International Law Commission, Draft
    Declaration on Rights and Duties of
    States (1949), 127

international law of cooperation *see*
  international law of cooperation (UN)
Millennium Declaration (2000), 375
sovereign equality in, 134–6
  Charter (1945), 125–7, 129–30, 134, 135,
    136, 374, 376
  see also UNCCPR (UN Covenant on Civil and
    Political Rights); UNCESCR (UN
    Covenant on Economic, Social and
    Cultural Rights)
United States, 423–46
  Alien and Sedition Acts, 434
  American structure, unique nature, 424
  Anti-Federalists, 427, 433, 442
  Articles of Confederation (1777), 121–2, 426
  case law, 435, 436
  collective peoples of states, sovereignty vested
    in, 424, 437–9
  Constitution,
    Art V, 430–1, 437, 439
    adoption (1788), 427, 430
    divided sovereignty, 424, 439–43, 445
    established by a single people, 429
    jurisdiction, 436
    Preamble, 436
    ratification, 429–30, 433
  Continental Congress, 426, 429
  Declaration of Independence, 429
  equality of states principle, 121–2
  European comparisons, 443–6
  Federalists, 427–8, 433
  Kentucky Resolutions, 434
  'later-in-time legislation', 145
  nation and states, sovereignty divided
    between, 439–43
  people of the nation, sovereignty vested in,
    424, 428–32
  Philadelphia Convention, 427–8, 431
  and political science, 193
  and popular sovereignty, 427
  revolutionary America, sovereignty in, 425–8
  Senate, as 'graveyard of treaties', 145
  separate peoples of states, sovereignty vested
    in, 424, 432–7
  sovereignty,
    divided, 424, 439–43
    nation and states, divided between, 439–43
    in revolutionary America, 425–8
    vested in collective peoples of states, 424,
     437–9
    vested in people of nation, 424, 428–32
    vested in separate peoples of states, 424,
     432–7
  Supreme Court, 427
  Virginia Bill of Rights (1776), 121
  Virginia Resolutions, 434
  War of Independence, 425
  see also San Francisco Conference

unity,
  German thought, 295–6
  and limits, 225
  and matrix of sovereignty, 211, 226
  and radical plurality, 222
  role, self-reference, 45
  and sovereignty, 211–12
unity representation, 101–12
  initiative, seizing, 111–12
  'pouvoir constituant', 'pouvoir constitué'
    (dialectic between), 89–90, 91, 93,
    105–10
  unity problem, 101–5
Universal Declaration of Human Rights, 256
Untertanen Verband, 287
Urwin, Derek, 204
USA *see* United States

values, sovereignty of, 315–19
van Roermund, Bert, 28, 33–54, 94
Varro, M Terentius (Roman author), 229
Vattel, Emer de, 121, 122
Venice Commission, 475
Versailles Treaty (1919), 282
VG (administrative court), 292
Vienna Congress (1814-15), 122
Vienna Convention on the Law of Treaties
    (1969), 137, 391
Vile, John, 443
violence, legitimate, 37
Virginia Bill of Rights (1776), 121
Virginia Resolutions (1830s), 434
Voegelin, Eric, 253
Volcansek, Mary, 513
Volk, 286
Völkergeister, 289
Völkerschaften (people), 299
Volksdemokratie (people's democracy), 298

Wade, Sir William, 331–2, 336, 344
Waldenfels, B, 47, 108

Walker Neil, 3–32, 52, 213, 342, 345, 347, 348,
    521
Walker, RBJ, 221
Walzer, Michael, 463
War of Independence (US), 425
Warsaw Pact, 302, 303, 394
  dissolution, 395
We, 47, 48, 49, 50
web (network) sovereignty, 323, 325
Weber, Max, 39, 241, 242
Webster, Daniel, 429
Weiler, Joseph, 419, 531–2, 533
Weimar Constitution (WRV), 287, 295
West Indies,
  French colonies in, 268
Westphalia, Peace treaties of (1648), 9, 121,
    145, 193–4
Westphalian paradigm, 193–5
  plurinational democracy, 193–5
Westphalian phase, 9, 10
Westphalian sovereignty, 7, 8
William of Ockham, 248
Williams, Allan, 462
Wilson, James, 428, 429, 436
Wood, Gordon, 425–6
working constitution (UK), 349
workplace democracy, 182
World Trade Organisation (WTO),
  diffusion problem, 26
  dispute settlement bodies, 151, 153, 154, 155,
    165
WRV (Weimar Constitution), 287, 295
Wyrzykowski, Miroslaw, 416

Yalta agreement, 403
Yugoslav Federation, 403
Yuguslavia, former, 159, 302

Ziller, Jacques, 261–77